Readings in Urban Theory

Readings in Urban Theory

Edited by Susan S. Fainstein and Scott Campbell

Editorial arrangement and Introduction Copyright © Susan Fainstein and Scott Campbell 1996

First published 1996
2 4 6 8 10 9 7 5 3 1

Blackwell Publishers Inc.
238 Main Street
Cambridge, Massachusetts 02142, USA

Blackwell Publishers Ltd
108 Cowley Road
Oxford OX4 1JF
UK

Library of Congress Cataloging-in-Publication Data

Readings in urban theory / edited by Susan S. Fainstein and Scott Campbell.
    p.   cm.
  Includes bibliographical references and index.
  ISBN 1–55786–608–2. — ISBN 1–55786–609–0 (pbk.)
    1. Cities and towns. 2. Urban economics. I. Fainstein, Susan S.
  II. Campbell, Scott (Scott D.), 1958–
  HT151.R35   1996
  307.76—dc20   95–35754
                                                             CIP

British Library Cataloguing in Publication Data

A CIP catalogue record for this book is available from the British Library.

Printed in Great Britain by T.J. Press, Padstow, Cornwall

This book is printed on acid-free paper

Contents

20.52

Acknowledgments

We wish to thank our editor, Simon Prosser, for his support and suggestions, and Hooshang Amirahmadi for making resources of the Department of Urban Planning and Policy Development at Rutgers University available for this project. We also thank Yi-Ling Chen, Antonia Casellas, Soraya Goga, and John Ottomanelli for their assistance.

Titles of articles reprinted here are the same as in all the originals. For book excerpts, we have generally used the original book title, the chapter title, or a combination thereof. The texts are, whenever possible, reprinted in full. We have deleted short sections of the original text only when a book chapter excerpt refers to another chapter of the book not included in this reader.

We are grateful to the publishers for their permission to reprint from the following material:

Fishman, Robert. 1987. *Bourgeois Utopias: The Rise and Fall of Suburbia*. Copyright © 1987 by Basic Books, Inc. Reprinted by permission of Basic Books, and division of HarperCollins Publishers, Inc. (excerpt: "Bourgeois Utopias: Visions of Suburbia," pp. 3–17, 103–33).

Sassen, Saskia. 1991. *The Global City*. Copyright © 1991 by Princeton University Press. Reprinted by permission of Princeton University Press. Original pp. 3–13.

Castells, Manuel. 1989. *The Informational City*. Oxford: Blackwell, pp. 7–32 (excerpt: "The Informational Mode of Development and the Restructuring of Capitalism").

Markusen, Ann. 1987. *Regions*. Copyright © 1987 by Ann Markusen. Reprinted by permission of Rowman and Littlefield Publishers (excerpt: "The Economics of Postwar Regional Disparity").

Markusen, Ann, Peter Hall, Scott Campbell and Sabina Deitrick. 1991. *The Rise of the Gunbelt: The Military Remapping of Industrial America*. New York and Oxford: Oxford University Press, pp. 26–49 (excerpt: "Reading the Map: A Theory of Military–Industrial Places").

Fainstein, Susan S. 1990. "The Changing World Economy and Urban Restructuring," in Dennis Judd and Michael Parkinson (eds), *Leadership and Urban Regeneration*. Copyright © 1990 by Sage Publications. Reprinted by permission of Sage Publications, Inc. Original pp. 31–47.

Wilson, William Julius. 1987. *The Truly Disadvantaged*. Chicago: University of Chicago Press, pp. 140–64 (excerpt: "The Truly Disadvantaged: The Hidden Agenda").

Fainstein, Norman. 1993. "Race, Class, and Segregation: Discourses about African Americans," *International Journal of Urban and Regional Research* 17(Fall), pp. 384–403.

Keating, W. Dennis. *The Suburban Racial Dilemma: Housing and Neighborhoods*. Philadelphia: Temple University Press, pp. 237–54 (excerpt: "Toward Greater Racial Diversity in the Suburbs").

Squires, Gregory D. 1991. "Partnership and the Pursuit of the Private City," in Mark Goettdiener and Chris Pickvance (eds), *Urban Life in Transition*. Newbury Park: Sage, pp. 123–40.

Logan, John and Harvey Molotch. 1987. *Urban Fortunes*. Berkeley: University of California Press, pp. 50–98 (excerpt: "The City as a Growth Machine").

Smith, Neil. 1986. "Gentrification, the Frontier, and the Restructuring of Urban Space," in Neil Smith and Peter Williams (eds), *Gentrification of the City*. Boston: Allen and Unwin, pp. 15–34.

Beauregard, Robert. 1993. *Voices of Decline: The Postwar Fate of US Cities*. Oxford: Blackwell, pp. 3–33 (excerpt: "Voices of Decline").

Sorkin, Michael. 1992. "See you in Disneyland," in Michael Sorkin (ed.), *Variations on a Theme Park: The New American City and the End of Public Space*. New York: Hill and Wang, pp. 205–32.

Harvey, David. 1992. "Social Justice, Postmodernism, and the City," *International Journal of Urban and Regional Research* 16, pp. 588–601.

Introduction: Theories of Urban Development and their Implications for Policy and Planning

Susan S. Fainstein
and Scott Campbell

This book presents a set of readings that analyze the economic, social, geographic, and political context of urban policy within the United States and the United Kingdom. It is a companion volume to a book of readings on planning theory, but it is intended for any reader whose concern is urban and regional development. Thus, it addresses two audiences: first, policy-makers, who must understand the context in which they work in order to behave intelligently; and second, people who wish to achieve general insights into urban and regional processes.[1] As discussed in greater detail at the end of this chapter, we selected the readings to address a set of questions concerning the interaction of economy, culture, politics, policy and space. In this introduction we discuss the major themes of the readings and present our viewpoint concerning the determinants and effects of urban form.

Urban Policy and the Urban Condition

At the end of the twentieth century urban areas are vastly different from the metropolises of a hundred years earlier. The old central cities that still lend their names to metropolitan areas contain a shrinking proportion of regional wealth and population. Although some cities are the command centers of the global economy or nests of technological innovation, others have lost economic function even while they still encompass large populations. Environmental pollution, traffic congestion, racial and ethnic discrimination, and financial crises afflict many urban cores. At the same time gentrified neighborhoods adjacent to low-income areas display the emblems of affluence, and suburban enclaves of privilege, increasingly set off by walls and gates, sharpen the distinctions between the haves and have-nots. More and more people live in metropolitan areas, but even the most economically successful of these regions manifest sharply uneven development.

The economic, social, and environmental circumstances of urban areas have stimulated calls for reform ever since the Industrial Revolution brought large masses of people to live within cities. The circumstances in which efforts at change are made are not fixed, and reformers can pursue strategies that push the edges of the possible, thereby remaking the circumstances in which they operate. But the situation in which they find themselves at any historical moment limits their range of feasible actions. Existing economic, political, and spatial relations create a web in which those seeking to improve the urban condition must function. Therefore, in addition to requiring a set of techniques, mastery of pertinent information, and entrepreneurship, good policy-making demands a deep understanding of what can be done. Numerous blueprints for change have been offered, ranging from the utopian solutions proposed by advocates of the garden city to the computer simulations of more recent analysts to the redistributive schemes of equity planners. These efforts, however, have run up against forces that resist the implementation of the reformers' visions. In order to understand the potential for consciously designed urban change, it is necessary to analyze the elements of the urban context and calculate their malleability.

Context circumscribes policy in three ways. First, it defines priorities. The historical situation in which policy-makers find themselves causes certain issues to become salient to the public and therefore to be at the top of the agenda. For example, rural depopulation and rapid economic growth in the nineteenth century combined with labor exploitation to generate overcrowding and disease within the industrial city. These conditions in turn stimulated demands for sanitary regulation, housing codes, and parks development and made these the object of governmental action. After World War Two, the release of pent-up consumer demand combined in the United States with political support for home ownership to produce rapid suburbanization and hence the need to develop transportation, education, sanitation, and other services for new suburban residents. Most recently, restructuring of the world economy, industrial flight, and increased unemployment have transformed metropolitan areas in the United States and United Kingdom once again, forcing local policy-makers to place economic development at the top of their agenda. While policy-makers can affect the massive social processes that call for policy responses – and indeed the character of these processes consists partly of policy components – policy is largely reactive rather than formative.

Second, broad cultural and ideological currents constrain the alternatives that policy-makers can consider. The expansion of public programs takes place when general public opinion calls for governmental solutions to social problems and opposition of the propertied class to such intervention has declined. Thus, the greatest expansion of planning and the welfare state in the United States occurred during the Great Depression. At that time social movements of the unemployed, a widespread sense of emergency, and a loss in legitimacy by those whom President Roosevelt called "malefactors of great wealth" changed attitudes toward governmental activism. Working within this permissive framework, the government became the employer of last resort, hiring millions of workers to carry out public works schemes. Similarly, in Great Britain in the immediate aftermath of World War Two the great majority sensed that the country had to be rebuilt for everyone; at the same time the war had broken down class barriers and weakened conservative opposition to an activist state. Within the context of these broader feelings of responsibility for all members of the national community, Parliament established the National Health Service, and local councils engaged in massive social housing construction programs. In both the US and the UK the threat posed by the Soviet Union and the fear that socialism would spread if government did not improve the general standard of living further bolstered support for governmental social welfare activities during the postwar period.

Within both these countries the end of the Cold War, tax revolts, conservative electoral triumphs, and the waning of any effective left-wing threat have delegitimized active government. Privatization and restrictions on governmental intervention are currently the order of the day. Although policy analysts often advocate other, more generous ways of dealing with social problems caused by industrial displacement and growing income inequality, the tenor of the times makes adoption of these measures extremely difficult.

Third, short of fundamental restructuring of the whole economic and social system, only certain policy choices are capable of implementation within any territory. It is not the imagination of policy-makers that primarily constrains the range of available solutions to urban and regional problems but rather the social facts that they must confront. Thus, in the nineteenth century utopians proposed ideal cities that gained much popular support but could never achieve successful, stable operation. These idealistic constructs all demanded a level of social equality at odds with the profit-driven market economies in which they had to function. Even the more practical philanthropists who advocated the construction of decent housing for working-class people failed in their aims. They built model tenements to demonstrate the advantages of space, light, and air for the preservation of public health, but their activities did not affect the bulk of the working class. Essentially the economic system in which they operated precluded the raising of large sums of money to invest in housing for those who could not pay an adequate rent. Only later, when legislative bodies accepted the legitimacy of using tax money for redistributive purposes, did subsidies allow the development of affordable housing.

Later periods reveal similar examples. Within the US, postwar metropolitan transportation problems could not be addressed through the expansion of rail systems because the sprawling form of metropolitan development meant that population densities were insufficient to provide enough ridership. In both the US and the UK contemporary economic development planners are unable to stimulate the growth of jobs appropriate for the skills of displaced industrial workers because jobs at this level have been replaced either by machines or by competition from abroad. Even within the same country urban policy-makers face sharply different circumstances depending on whether they are in growing or declining areas. In regions enjoying rapid expansion, planners can seek to extract public benefits from developers desiring to build, while in declining areas they desperately offer concessions to investors. In sum, there are objective preconditions to the adoption of a particular policy approach that simply may not be present.

The Determinants of Urban and Regional Form

Economic, cultural, and political factors have interacted to create contemporary spatial forms. Thus, even though the United States and Great Britain have proceeded through roughly similar stages of economic change producing many similarities of spatial development, analyses of their metropolitan areas reveal important differences as well (see Buck and Fainstein, 1992). The broad forces that, in the century after 1870, created similar outcomes were rooted in a manufacturing economy and a rapidly-growing urban population. During the early part of the period manufacturing developed within industrial districts and required dense agglomerations of workers living nearby to operate the machines; at the same time commercial and retail activities clustered in central business districts (CBDs). Later, both countries witnessed the rise of suburbanization. The desire of residents to escape urban dangers fueled the outward exodus, as discussed by Fishman in this volume. Changes in transportation technology gradually made it possible for workers to live farther from their places of employment and industries to spread out to cheaper, more extensive sites.

The decentralization of jobs and population has produced giant conurbations in both the US and the UK. At the same time the two nations continue to display important differences in urban form and housing configuration. British settlements mostly have sharp boundaries demarcated by greenbelts; the endless strip development characterizing the outskirts of American cities is absent. Housing within Britain is mainly attached, even in suburban areas, and lot size is much smaller. There is less rigid income segregation in housing in Britain than in the US.

Some of the spatial differences between the UK and the US derive from their differing population densities and racial/ethnic compositions. Others, however, stem from the historically different patterns of settlement in the two countries as well as from the attitudes generated by this history. Whereas British cities trace their roots to close-knit medieval towns and villages, American metropolises mostly began in an epoch of commercial capitalism and speculative land development. These differing starting points in part account for differing perceptions of appropriate social and land-development policy. The British public places a higher premium on collectively enjoyed open space than does its American counterpart. British values include the communality resulting from denser settlement, whereas Americans opt strongly for greater privatism and retain the model of the frontier homestead. The much greater availability and dispersion of publicly subsidized housing in Britain result in part from the absence of the racial and ethnic conflicts that reinforce class division in the US. Until recently at least, the British electorate supported a larger role for government in providing basic security for individuals. The consequence of the social and cultural dissimilarities between the two countries is stronger land-use regulation and a historically more beneficent welfare state in the UK, which in turn amplify the differences in urban form. We thus see broadly similar socio-spatial patterns produced by past economic and technological forces and variations within them caused by culture, politics, and policy.

Contemporary Economic Restructuring

Economic restructuring of the last 25 years has transformed the shape of cities and regions once again. Production and population have been decentralizing, while economic control has become increasingly concentrated in multinational firms and financial institutions. The new logic of production, employment, and distribution has engendered changes in land use and social occupation; it has caused a reordering of the urban hierarchy and of the economic and political links between places (see the chapter by Markusen). Common trends within Europe and the US include the displacement of a manufacturing-based by an information-based economy with corresponding declines in industrial and increases in service employment (Castells, this volume). These have been accompanied by the rapid growth of financial and producer services[2] sectors within cities at the top of the urban hierarchy and the flight of industry and population from others. Whereas the growth of manufacturing and suburbanization stimulated different policy responses in the UK and in the US, contemporary economic restructuring has evoked similar strategies of deregulation and the promotion of private-sector property development.

Theorists have attempted to understand this transformation through a variety of lenses. Mainstream economic theory emphasizes market competition as the driving force of economic change. Analysts in this tradition point to the lower costs of labor in less developed countries, the entrepreneurship and weaker regulations of the newly industrializing countries (NICs), and the lowering of transportation costs as the key elements pressing on the manufacturers of the wealthy nations (see, e.g., Porter, 1990). In order to grapple with competition that can produce at lower cost, these manufacturers must cut their own costs of production. They can do so by moving their factories to locations that offer cheap labor, by replacing labor with capital, or by shrinking their wage and benefit bill. Within the framework of this analysis, industrialists have no choice but to compete by getting more from their labor forces.

Theorists on the left have emphasized the power of capitalists in bringing about changes that have increased the profitability of investment while weakening the influence of labor. The dominant explanation (although by no means universally held) among these thinkers concerns a switch in "regimes of accumulation" (see Amin, 1995). According to this theory the major capitalist nations previously were dominated by "Fordist" regimes based on mass production, mass consumption, and the welfare state. During the 1970s, however, profits fell and Fordist approaches no longer served the interests of capitalists. Consequently, the leaders of multinational corporations imposed a new, "post-Fordist" regime that involved very high mobility of capital from sector to sector and place to place ("flexible accumulation"). It was accompanied by flexible production techniques allowing customized manufacturing, just-in-time inventories, and short production runs. A new "mode of regulation" made possible the imposition of this regime. This mode of regulation diminished the welfare state, reduced the power of the unions, and supported social institutions that would enhance competitiveness.

The two interpretations of capital restructuring are not mutually exclusive. Both outlooks recognize the existence of greater competitiveness within industries and among places. The progressive/left analysis, however, goes beyond simply identifying the global forces that prompted capitalists to restructure and attempts to root them in a theory of class conflict. The issue between the two portrayals thus concerns the causes and consequences of a similarly perceived set of processes. According to mainstream theory recent changes have resulted inevitably from the laws of the marketplace. This theory assumes that the benefits of enhanced competitiveness flow to all workers in expanding industries and to all residents of places that achieve economic growth. In contrast, left analysis attributes global restructuring to the exercise of class power by a world capitalist class threatened by working-class absorption of an increasing share of production during the Fordist period. In the post-Fordist era capitalists have regained the upper hand, and it is primarily owners, upper management, and possessors of high informational skills who reap the benefits of economic expansion. Growth and decline occur simultaneously, and the social distribution of the benefits of growth is highly uneven.

Both views identify spatial change. Within the reshaped economic geography of the US and the UK, we can detect a number of different types of cities and regions with characteristic spatial configurations. Those which are discussed in the readings include declining manufacturing centers, global cities, expanding and contracting regions, and military-industrial centers. We look briefly here at each of these types.

Declining industrial centers

The departure of industry has resulted in declining manufacturing centers afflicted with high levels of unemployment. Although some of these cities have maintained active CBDs, they all manifest vast empty tracts of abandoned industrial space.[3] The causes of their plight are manifold (see Bluestone and Harrison, 1982). Competition from other advanced industrial countries, especially Japan, has displaced many of the mature industries of the US and Britain, particularly in the electronics and automobile sectors. Industry has departed to suburban areas and peripheral regions both at home and abroad, so as to take advantage of cheaper land and labor, less burdensome regulation, weaker or nonexistent unions, and government incentives. Whereas until recently less developed countries specialized in the provision of raw materials, under the "new international division of labor" many perform the role of "platform economies" that import capital goods and export finished products at prices lower than manufacturers in the developed world can meet. As markets for goods grow more rapidly outside the old core countries than within them, producers increasingly open factories close to the sources of the new demand. When industry has remained in place but modernized, it has substituted capital for labor, allowing it simultaneously to increase production and reduce its workforce.

The industrial cities of Europe and the United States have all felt the impact of these changes. Especially striking is the suddenness with which they have been affected; many cities lost as many as a hundred thousand or more manufacturing jobs in the decade 1974–1984. They have sought to compensate through nurturing growth in the service sector, but increases in service employment have not compensated for the losses.

Global cities

The term "global city"refers to those cities in which control of the world financial system rests, where cultural production influences the whole world, and where the business service sector sells its products to the globe (see the chapter by Saskia Sassen). Global cities are cosmopolitan, boasting numerous foreign visitors and a panoply of opportunities to consume. New York, London, and Tokyo are the premier global cities; Los Angeles, Paris, and Hong Kong also have some claim to the title. Global cities have attracted scholarly attention because their financial and business service sectors have seemingly resisted the forces of decentralization that have affected most other industries.

Global pre-eminence, however, does not protect a city from unemployment and neighborhood deterioration. Many commentators have remarked on the sharp discrepancies so visible in these cities, where the world's most affluent people live in close proximity to the impoverished homeless, where extraordinarily prosperous districts abut abjectly poor ones (see Fainstein et al., 1992; Mollenkopf and Castells, 1991). Global cities are, however, much more complex than the simple notion of a dual city implies. As well as containing rich and poor, they encompass groups of upwardly mobile immigrants and aspiring artists, masses of unionized government employees, large student populations, and vast numbers of middle-level white collar workers. They have had increasing numbers of both single-parent and multiple-earner housholds. Because individuals with the same income may have strikingly different family situations and future prospects, simple descriptions of class stratification are inadequate (see Mingione, 1991).

Expanding and contracting regions

Because the dynamics of restructuring produce uneven development – i.e., simultaneous growth and decline within a nation, a region, and a metropolitan area – it is to be expected that within the same country some regions are experiencing expansion while others are suffering from disinvestment. Expanding regions are ones that, because of "good business climates" and governmental investment, are benefiting from the shifts of industry described above. Contracting regions suffer from obsolete industrial structures and socio-political systems that businesses regard as inhospitable to their profit-maximizing goals. Throughout the 1980s the fortunes of the American southwest and the British southeast improved relative to the rest of the nation. Recent developments, however, indicate that, in the volatile competition among places, no region can easily sustain its advantage. We are currently seeing greater relative growth in some "rustbelt" areas, while parts of the previously prosperous sunbelt have suffered large employment losses. Moreover, it becomes increasingly clear that the rate of development varies substantially within regions and metropolitan areas. Aggregate figures disguise this unevenness, and terms like sunbelt and frostbelt are too gross to capture the changes that are occurring.

Military–industrial centers

For many areas during the 1970s and 1980s, hope for the future lay in high-tech development. Closer analysis, however, especially in the wake of the end of the Cold War, reveals that high-tech expansion was closely tied to military investment (see the chapter by Markusen et al.). With the dramatic reductions in military expenditures for weapons production, military bases, and research and development ensuing from post-Cold War cuts in defense budgets, the "gunbelt" is facing the reality that its seemingly eternal upward trajectory was not based on a monopoly of the industries of the future. Although the problem is particularly acute in the United States, it also affects those regions of Britain, particularly along the M4 corridor connecting London and Bristol, that were tied to the defense establishment. Thus, in both the US and the UK the ebbing of growth in those areas that did best during the 1980s is largely attributable to changing patterns of national government investment.

The military–industrial centers are therefore the places that can be most directly affected by public policy. If defense conversion programs adequately substitute investment in civilian production for the obsolete defense complexes, then formerly defense-dependent locales can emerge relatively unscathed. Without concerted government action, however, a rapid decline in resources directed at these areas will produce a new wave of deindustrialization and abandonment.

Implications

From one point of view the continual ebb and flow of investment from place to place indicate the potential for laggards to catch up and the equalizing characteristics of a market-based economy. If areas have high labor costs, then business will go elsewhere, the price of labor will drop, and business will come back. Eventually everyone benefits. Such an assessment, however, does not consider the social costs borne disproportionately by particular communities. When jobs leave their original locations, communal ties are destroyed and neighborhoods languish; even if recovery ultimately occurs, those who lose their jobs or are forced to move may never benefit. Moreover, some cities may never bounce back but instead may suffer an irredeemable loss of human capital and of customary relations among producers and consumers (see Fainstein and Markusen, 1993). Nor does a sanguine evaluation of capital mobility address the growing social inequality that has resulted from a system in which business has been able to drive down wages by threatening to move away. In other words the changing spatial forms of the era of restructuring have important consequences. These can be summed up by analyzing the social creation and meanings of urban space.

Social Space

Urban space gains its meaning as a consequence of the activities carried on within it, the characteristics of the people who occupy it, the form given to it by its physical structures, and the perceptions with which people regard it. Consequently such space does not simply exist; it is instead a social creation. Yet, although the product of creative activity, spatial relations once formed take on a seeming fixity, a life of their own. For example, once ethnic and racial ghettos come into being, they perpetuate themselves through the interaction of majority exclusionary practices and minority preferences. Having been identified on the basis of their residents' characteristics, they become a defined territory, comprising a dependable voting bloc for politicians, a perceived area of danger or source of exotica for outsiders, a specialized niche in the real-estate market, and a source of particular types of labor. Similarly, central business districts result from a concentration of investment in office buildings and retail establishments. After they become established, they welcome certain kinds of activities and exclude others, enhance the potential profitability of buildings within their boundaries, and become symbolic of the economic health of the cities in which they are located.

The character of the built environment both determines the profits and losses that derive from investments made within a given territory and reinforces the nature of social relations between races and classes. Thus, governmental responses to economic restructuring that have depended on a strategy of urban redevelopment have provoked intense political conflict, and the investment decisions of private property developers have stimulated both choruses of support and furious antagonisms. The process of economic restructuring described above has reorganized spatial relations. Its consequences are visible in revived central business districts, rapidly growing "edge cities," and increased spatial segregation of class and racial groups. It has produced a fragmented landscape wherein the identities that people formed with place over the generations have been undercut, often to be replaced by synthetic versions of the main streets, villages, and marketplaces of old (see the chapter by Sorkin).

The changes stimulated by economic restructuring have been

mediated by the political process and its policy output. In virtually all cities policy-makers have perceived their economic base as endangered by competition from other places and have striven to devise programs that would attract expanding businesses. Usually they have identified office-based and touristic sectors as offering the most promise for future development. Consequently they have provided various kinds of financial assistance and regulatory relief to developers and occupiers of new office, retail, and entertainment-oriented space. At the same time, "marginal businesses" have suffered from governmental neglect. Workers in declining sectors have therefore found themselves doubly disadvantaged – by the disappearance of employment opportunities and by the biases of the public sector in favor of jobs with entry requirements that they cannot meet.

Role of Politics and Polity: The Case of Urban Redevelopment

In both the United States and Great Britain, there is a typical, though by no means uniform, history of urban redevelopment.[4] Within the United States, business groups, usually in concert with political leaders, promoted their vision of the revitalized city, often forming organizations that provided governments with plans and technical advice (see the contributions by Logan and Molotch; Squires).[5] Urban movements, driven by equity, preservationist, and environmental concerns, frequently opposed subsidized downtown redevelopment and unregulated profit-driven expansion. They also, although less frequently, promoted alternative plans for neighborhood redevelopment. The outcomes of these contests have varied. Regardless, however, of whether the result has been growth or decline, greater or less equity, deal making on a project-by-project basis rather than comprehensive planning has always been the main vehicle for determining the uses of space.

Overall, business interests have dominated the negotiations among government, community, and the private sector on the content of redevelopment (see Stone, 1993). They have been supported by elite and middle-class consumers seeking a more exciting downtown and attractive, centrally located housing. Neighborhood and lower-income groups have received some gains in some places from redevelopment. Generally, however, the urban poor, ethnic communities, and small businesses have suffered increased economic and locational marginalization as a consequence. The emphasis on office-based employment within most large redevelopment schemes has reinforced the decline of manufacturing jobs and contributed to the employment difficulties of unskilled workers. While businesses have received direct subsidies, taxpayers at large have borne the costs and received benefits only as they have trickled down.

And, as Neil Smith's discussion of gentrification shows, increases in property values have forced out residents, raising their living expenses and shattering communities.

In many cities regeneration strategies have been successful in creating a revitalized core (see Judd and Parkinson, 1990; Frieden and Sagalyn, 1989). The numbers of people working in city centers has increased, and tourists and suburbanites have patronized the hotels, stores, and restaurants in the renovated shopping districts. Whereas most cases of government-sponsored redevelopment have displayed the biases described above, in some cities political leaders have followed a more redistributive strategy. Chicago's late mayor, Harold Washington, while not forgoing CBD-development, gave strong support to non-profit neighborhood organizations for housing construction and fostered community economic development schemes (Mier, 1993). Sheffield's Labour-led city council first embarked on a radical program for industrial revival and social housing construction. When that approach failed, due to conflicts with the central government and an inability to attract capital, the city shifted to a more moderate but nevertheless still progressive method of drawing in investment. While depending on a partnership with the private sector and seeking to stimulate tourism, it also focused on improving educational and training opportunities and expanding the supply of affordable housing for both renters and owners (Lawless, 1990).

US/UK redevelopment experiences compared

British and American experiences differed before the 1980s. Redevelopment in Britain was less dependent on private-sector participation. The intimate relationship between local elected officials and real-estate interests that is a hallmark of US local government, wherein developers are the largest contributors to municipal political campaigns, did not (and still does not) exist in Britain. British local authorities restricted private development and built millions of units of council (i.e. public) housing. In contrast, "slum clearance" was a major component of the American urban renewal program, resulting in the demolition but not the replacement of tens of thousands of units of poor people's housing. In additon, land taking for highway building produced an even greater loss of units.

In Britain social housing (i.e. publicly-owned or subsidized housing at below-market rents) was placed throughout metropolitan areas, minimizing gross ethnic and income segregation. American public housing, while much more limited in scope, was available to only the poorest residents and was usually located in low-income areas. Urban renewal efforts, often derisively labeled "Negro removal" programs by their opponents, targeted ghetto areas that were near to business centers or to more affluent residential districts. Their intent was either to extend the more prosperous area or to cordon it off from the threat of lower-class invasion.

Their effect was to displace nonwhite residents into more isolated, homo-geneously minority territories.

As in the United States, British local authorities raised revenues through a tax on business and residential property (known as "rates").[6] Unlike their American equivalents, however, if British local governments were unable to meet the service demands on them through internal sources, they received a compensating central government grant. They therefore did not need to attract business and high-income residents to maintain themselves and could afford to be more attuned to the negative environmental and social impacts of growth.

During the 1980s development policies in the UK and US converged.[7] In general, the dominant objective in both countries was to use public powers to assist the private sector with a minimum of regulatory inter-vention. Earlier emphases in redevelopment programs on the provision of housing, public amenities, and targeted benefits to low-income people were downplayed, as aggregate economic growth – measured by the amount of private investment "leveraged" – became the criterion of program success.

The sponsors of the regeneration programs of the 1980s claimed that they had achieved a remarkable reversal in the trajectory of inner-city decline. Numerous studies, however, have characterized this growth as extremely uneven in its impacts, primarily benefiting highly-skilled professionals and managers and offering very little for workers displaced from manufacturing industries except low-paid service-sector jobs. Moreover, as economic restructuring and contraction of social benefits produced a broadening income gap, growing social inequality expressed itself spatially in the increasing residential segregation of rich and poor, black and white (see the chapters by Norman Fainstein and by Dennis Keating). Rapid development also produced undesirable environmental effects. While the gleaming new projects upgraded the seedy appearance of many old core areas and brought middle-class consumers back to previ-ously abandoned centers, their bulk and density often overwhelmed their surroundings, stifled diversity, and, in the crowded cores of London and New York, overloaded transportation and pedestrian facilities.[8]

Cultural Manifestations of Urban and Regional Development

The reconstructed urban cores now constitute nodes within a multi-centered system of metropolitan urban regions. These regions have changed significantly from the era when the CBD defined their hearts. Although the old CBD may retain its dominance over certain industries like financial services and tourism, other parts of the region have assumed numerous functions including wholesaling, manufacturing, research, retailing, and commercial services. These activities may be concentrated in technology parks, office complexes, and shopping malls, or they may be strung along highway corridors in single-purpose units. Stylish and expensive residential areas may be close to the old CBD, as in New York's upper east side or London's Mayfair, or far on the periphery but nonetheless in convenient commuting distance of the new suburban work complexes. Residential developments, whether within or outside the boundaries of the central city, are set off by barriers or fully enclosed by walls, separating the homogeneous community within from the more diverse population without.

Some interpreters consider that spatial form breeds culture, and that these new spatial forms have created a more divided society, although the extent to which spatial proximity and distance alone influence perceptions and behavior remains a subject of hot debate. Louis Wirth (1938), in his famous essay "Urbanism as a Way of Life," set forth the case for the relation between spatial configuration and culture, arguing that the urban characteristics of size, density, and heterogeneity produced a culture of impersonality and alienation. Later, critics of suburbia argued that its neatly arranged housing on large lots encouraged conformity and competitive consumerism. Most recently, social commentators like Mike Davis and Michael Sorkin, whose essays appear in this volume, have contended that gated communities and "theme-parked" developments produce an intolerant public hostile to diversity and opposed to public programs that would benefit the poor. Their arguments are the obverse side of William Julius Wilson's (1987), who argues that the spatial isolation of low-income African-Americans in inner-city ghettos produces detachment from the labor market, low expectations, and deviant behavior.

Whether or not a less artificial, more diverse environment would, as writers like Richard Sennett contend,[9] produce a better society is a question not easily answered. Proximity of differing groups can breed enmity as well as tolerance. The indifference encouraged by distance, even while it may produce fear and lack of empathy, can also create a buffer that prevents open warfare. Without settling this debate, however, we can agree with the cultural critics of spatial forms that it is possible to "read" the divisions and values of a society in the lineaments of its spatial configurations. And, as Beauregard argues in his essay, the ways in which people perceive their cities and regions in turn shape their development.

The Readings

The readings selected for this volume all investigate issues concerning the interaction of economy, culture, politics, policy, and space. The criterion of selection was their germaneness to addressing the themes briefly sketched out in this introduction: the changing urban and regional system, its social impacts, the effect of publicly sponsored redevelopment programs, and the cultural meanings of spatial relations. These are, we believe, the fundamental underpinnings of urban and regional theory. Although there are important differences among the authors represented, they largely share a common paradigm of political-economic analysis.

The volume is thus intended to address a set of questions rather than to provide a survey of the field. We rejected the approach of being encyclopedic and trying to present at least two viewpoints on every issue. There is considerable merit in such a strategy, but we were unable to find readings that matched up well in this way. Moreover, we were committed to bringing contemporary works to the attention of our readers, and much of the most recent writing on urban and regional theory falls within the political-economy paradigm.[10] We also failed to include classic pieces on urban and regional development, although we had originally wished to do so. This omission resulted primarily from space limitations; moreover, such works are readily available in existing anthologies (see, inter alia, Gutman and Popenoe, 1970; Sennett, 1969).

In sum, then, we have assembled a collection of readings that examines the following questions:

1   What is the spatial, economic, social, and political character of the urban and regional system in the US and UK and how has it changed?
2   What are the causal factors underlying this change?
3   What is the impact of spatial segregation on the economic and social situation of minority groups?
4   What have been the economic and social effects of governmental programs for urban redevelopment?
5   What has been the cultural significance of changes in the urban and regional system?

The outlook on theory incorporated here envisions it as a convincing general explanation of events and processes. Theory in social science may assist in predicting the future, may allow the generation of testable hypotheses, and may define the foundations of a discipline. In our view, however, these functions alone do not define the role of theory. For us, its transcendent purpose is to make sense of the world and to show how particular phenomena form part of a broader scheme.

We have therefore chosen readings that make coherent arguments buttressed with various kinds of evidence but which do not usually rigorously present their findings as falsifiable hypotheses. Rather, their authors make a number of arguments concerning underlying causes, many of which are open to dispute. We believe that they have incisively depicted the new urban and regional environment and have developed important approaches to explaining its causes, meaning, and consequences. Our intention, however, is that readers of this book will use these arguments as starting points for the development of their own theories.

Notes

1 In this introduction we discuss the major themes of the volume and refer to the readings as they bear on these themes. Summaries of the various contributions are given in the four "Introductions to Parts."

2 The term "producer services" refers to businesses like law, accounting, management consulting, and advertising that sell their products to other businesses.

3 Changes in trade patterns and the containerization of bulk cargo for waterborne shipping has had a similar impact on many port-dependent cities, resulting in desolate waterfront areas that formerly were centers of bustling activity and extreme congestion. (See Campbell, 1993.)

4 This discussion is drawn fron Fainstein (1994), pp. 5–9.

5 The prototype organizaton was the Allegheny Conference. Organized in 1943 under the leadership of Richard King Mellon, head of Pittsburgh's leading bank, it drew up the plans for the transformation of Pittsburgh from a manufacturing to a service city. The public sector's role was primarily the reactive one of implementing the Allegheny Conference's strategies. The partnership between private and public sectors was institutionalized within the city's Urban Redevelopment Authority. (See Sbragia, 1990.)

6 British businesses no longer pay taxes to local municipal authorities. Instead all business taxes are collected by the central government and redistributed to localities. Consequently no local authority achieves any revenue advantage through attracting business development.

7 A number of studies are explicitly comparative and reach something of a consensus concerning the similarities in the impact of global economic restructuring on UK and US cities and on the direction of urban policy in the two countries. See, for example, Barnekov, Boyle, and Rich (1989) and Sassen (1991).

8 Among the many studies that reach the conclusions summarized in this paragraph, see especially Parkinson, Foley, and Judd (1988); Squires (1989); Logan and Swanstrom (1990); Ambrose (1986); and Fainstein et al. (1986).

9 See his essay in Campbell and Fainstein, (1996).

10 Because the mainstream, market paradigm is already so well established, social scientists operating within it tend to take it for granted rather than elaborating it theoretically.

References

Amin, Ash, ed. 1995. *Post-Fordism*. Oxford: Blackwell.

Ambrose, Peter. 1986. *Whatever Happened to Planning?* London: Methuen.

Barnekov, Timothy, Robin Boyle, and Daniel Rich. 1989. *Privatism and Urban Policy in Britain and the United States*. Oxford: Oxford University Press.

Bluestone, Barry, and Bennett Harrison. 1982. *The Deindustrialization of America*. New York: Basic.

Buck, Nick, and Norman Fainstein. 1992. "A comparative history," in Susan S. Fainstein et al., *Divided Cities*. Oxford: Blackwell.

Campbell, Scott. 1993. "Increasing trade, declining port cities: port container-ization and the regional diffusion of economic benefits," in Helzi Noponen, Julie Graham and Ann Markusen, eds, *Trading Industries, Trading Regions*. New York: Guilford Press. pp. 212–55.

Campbell, Scott, and Susan S. Fainstein. 1996. *Readings in Planning Theory*. Cambridge, MA: Blackwell.

Fainstein, Susan S. 1994. *The City Builders*. Oxford: Blackwell.

Fainstein, Susan S., Norman Fainstein, Richard Child Hill, Dennis Judd, Michael Peter Smith. 1986. *Restructuring the City*. New York: Longman.

Fainstein, Susan S., Ian Gordon, and Michael Harloe. 1992. *Divided Cities*. Oxford: Blackwell.

Fainstein, Susan, and Ann Markusen. 1993. "The urban policy challenge: inte-grating across social and economic development policy." *North Carolina Law Review*, 71 (June): 1463–86.

Frieden, Bernard J., and Lynne B. Sagalyn. 1989. *Downtown, Inc.* Cambridge: MIT Press.

Gutman, Robert, and David Popenoe, eds. 1970. *Neighborhood, City, and Metropolis*. New York: Random House.

Judd, Dennis, and Michael Parkinson, eds. 1990. *Leadership and Urban Regeneration*. Newbury Park: Sage.

Lawless, Paul. 1990. "Regeneration in Sheffield: from radical intervention to partnership." Pp. 133–51 in Dennis Judd and Michael Parkinson, eds, *Leadership and Urban Regeneration*. Newbury Park: Sage.

Logan, John R., and Todd Swanstrom, eds. 1990. *Beyond the City Limits*. Philadelphia: Temple University Press.

Mier, Robert. 1993. *Social Justice and Local Development Policy*. Newbury Park: Sage.

Mingione, Enzo. 1991. *Fragmented Societies*. Oxford: Blackwell.

Mollenkopf, John, and Manuel Castells, eds. 1991. *Dual City*. New York: Russell Sage.

Parkinson, Michael, Bernard Foley, and Dennis Judd, eds. 1988. *Regenerating the Cities: The UK Crisis and the US Experience*. Manchester: Manchester University Press.

Porter, M. 1990. *The Competitive Advantage of Nations*. New York: Free Press.

Sassen, Saskia. 1991. *The Global City*. Princeton: Princeton University Press.

Sbragia, Alberta. 1990. "Pittsburgh's 'third way': the nonprofit sector as a key to urban regeneration." Pp. 51–68 in Dennis Judd and Michael Parkinson, eds, *Leadership and Urban Regeneration*. Newbury Park: Sage.

Sennett, Richard, ed. 1969. *Classic Essays on the Culture of Cities*. New York: Appleton-Century-Crofts.

Squires, Gregory, ed. 1989. *Unequal Partnerships*. New Brunswick, NJ: Rutgers University Press.

Stone, Clarence. 1993 "Urban regimes and the capacity to govern: a political economy approach." *Journal of Urban Affairs*, 15(1): 1–28.

Wilson, William Julius. 1987. *The Truly Disadvantaged*. Chicago: University of Chicago Press.

Wirth, Lewis. 1938. "Urbanism as a way of life." *American Journal of Sociology*, 44 (July).

Part I

The Changing Urban and Regional System

Introduction to Part I

The readings in Part I examine the changes in spatial relations that have produced the contemporary urban and regional systems of the United States and Great Britain. The elements of this system are: multi-nodal metropolitan areas, a hierarchy of cities connected by a web of telecommunications but differentiated by their economic roles, and regions distinguished by their economic bases and social structures. Some of the factors creating this system trace back to the nineteenth century; others have only recently come into prominence.

Robert Fishman examines the history of the residential suburb, which he regards as the archetypal expression of contemporary Anglo-American civilization. He traces the demand for suburban residence not to changes in transportation modes but to a new form of family life. The demand generated by this family-centered mode of living presented a profitable opportunity for developers. Thus, suburban development spread rapidly as investors bought up inexpensive agricultural land and converted it into far more remunerative buildable lots.

Whereas Fishman recounts the history of peripheral metropolitan growth, Sassen analyzes the renewed importance of "global cities." These are places that occupy the apex of the world's urban hierarchy. It is in these cities that the decisions are made which govern the flows of capital in the world. Their current heightened influence arises from a seemingly paradoxical cause: the simultaneous decentralization of industry and concentration of control in multinational firms. Both of these factors in turn – the disaggregation of production and the enormous capital needs of huge industrial conglomerates – intensify the role of financial institutions and providers of business services in coordinating economic activity. The financial and advanced services sectors cluster in just a few locations. Consequently their increased prominence reinforces the position of the cities in which they locate.

Castells's exploration of the informational city examines the relationship between economic restructuring and technological transformation. While denying technological determinism, he argues that new technologies have allowed the development of a world capitalist system with infomation processing as its core activity. This reconstituted system of production is at the base of contemporary spatial forms.

Ann Markusen examines the economic forces which create regional coherence and differentiation in the US. Like the other authors in this section, she identifies important changes in the geography of production that accumulated during the postwar period and accelerated after the mid-1970s. She relates these to the new international division of labor, the profit cycle in different industrial sectors, and the militarization of the American economy.

In the first selection by Markusen, she only briefly examines the regional impacts of the military economy. In the second essay, she and her co-authors analyze the effects of defense procurement on regional development in more detail. Because defense industry does not operate within a competitive market environment characterized by numerous buyers and sellers, its geographic pattern differs from that of other sectors. The great size of defense expenditures in the US makes the "military-industrial" complex a significant factor causing the demographic and employment shifts of the US since the 1930s.

Susan Fainstein takes up the debate over whether urban change results from deliberate actions or impersonal forces. She contends that both interpretations of urban development are correct and the usefulness of each depends on what one wishes to explain. She offers a number of suggestions for progressive local policies but concludes that without a supportive national movement, major local initiatives will be stymied.

Bourgeois Utopias: Visions of Suburbia

Robert Fishman

> Our suburban architecture . . . reveals the spirit and character of modern civilization, just as the temples of Egypt and Greece, the baths and amphitheaters of Rome, and the cathedrals and castles of the Middle Ages help us to comprehend and penetrate the spirit of previous civilizations.
>
> César Daly, 1864[1]

Every civilization gets the monuments it deserves. The triumph of bourgeois capitalism seems most apparent in the massive constructions of iron and steel that celebrate the union of technology and profit: the railroad terminals, exposition halls, suspension bridges, and skyscrapers. One does not look to suburbia for the modern equivalents of the Baths of Caracalla or Chartres cathedral.

But, if like Daly quoted above, we are seeking the architecture that best reveals "the spirit and character of modern civilization," then suburbia might tell us more about the culture that built the factories and skyscrapers than these edifices themselves can. For suburbia too was an archetypal middle-class invention, perhaps the most radical rethinking of the relation between residence and the city in the history of domestic architecture. It was founded on that primacy of the family and domestic life which was the equivalent of the bourgeois society of the

Reprinted by permission from Robert Fishman, 1987, *Bourgeois Utopias: The Rise and Fall of Suburbia*.

intense civic life celebrated by the public architecture of the ancient city. However modest each suburban house might be, suburbia represents a collective assertion of class wealth and privilege as impressive as any medieval castle. Most importantly, suburbia embodies a new ideal of family life, an ideal so emotionally charged that it made the home more sacred to the bourgeoisie than any place of worship. The hundred years of massive suburban development that have passed since Daly wrote can only confirm his judgment that the true center of any bourgeois sociey is the middle-class house. If you seek the monuments of the bourgeoisie, go to the suburbs and look around.

Suburbia is more than a collection of residential buildings; it expresses values so deeply embedded in bourgeois culture that it might also be called the bourgeois utopia. Yet this "utopia" was always at most a partial paradise, a refuge not only from threatening elements in the city but also from discordant elements in bourgeois society itself. From its origins, the suburban world of leisure, family life, and union with nature was based on the principle of exclusion. Work was excluded from the family residence; middle-class villas were segregated from working-class housing; the greenery of suburbia stood in contrast to a gray, polluted urban environment. Middle-class women were especially affected by the new suburban dichotomy of work and family life. The new environment supposedly exalted their role in the family, but it also segregated them from the world of power and productivity. This self-segregation soon enveloped all aspects of bourgeois culture. Suburbia, therefore, represents more than the bourgeois utopia, the triumphant assertion of middle-class values. It also reflects the alienation of the middle classes from the urban-industrial world they themselves were creating.

I wish to understand the significance of suburbia both for modern culture and for the modern city first by tracing this urban form back to its origins in the late eighteenth century and then by showing the evolution of the suburban tradition of design to the present. I adopt this historical method in part because, like so many great inventions, suburbia has always seemed contemporary. In the United States, people are often surprised to learn that suburbs existed before 1945. Even César Daly was unaware that the mid-Victorian English suburbs he observed were the product of an urban evolution that was already a century old at the time he wrote.

Only by examining the eighteenth-century origins of suburbia can one grasp its radical departure from all previous traditions of urban structure as well as its crucial role in reshaping the modern city. In order to clarify this "suburban revolution" in metropolitan structure I must first define the precise meaning of the "suburb." The word means literally "beyond the city," and thus can refer to any kind of settlement at the periphery of a large city. A former mill town in the process of being swallowed up by an expanding metropolis, or a newly built industrial area on the urban fringes – these, strictly speaking, are as much "suburbs" as the most affluent bedroom community.

I am concerned [here] only with the middle-class suburb of privilege, and I shall use the words "suburb" and "suburbia" to refer only to a residential community beyond the core of a large city. Though physically separated from the urban core, the suburb nevertheless depends on it economically for the jobs that support its residents. It is also culturally dependent on the core for the major institutions of urban life: professional offices, department stores and other specialized shops, hospitals, theaters, and the like. The true suburb, moreover, is more than a collection of dense city streets that have reached the edge of the built-up area. The suburb must be large enough and homogeneous enough to form a distinctive low density environment defined by the primacy of the single family house set in the greenery of an open, parklike setting.

I should emphasize that the suburb, in my definition, is not necessarily a separate political unit. In selecting a site for a nineteenth-century suburb, developers carefully considered such questions as topography or access to the central city, but virtually ignored whether an attractive location was within or outside the political jurisdiction of the central city. Only in the twentieth century did a separate political identity become important in maintaining a separate social or design identity. Even today almost all large cities have suburbs as I define them within their borders.

Suburbia can thus be defined first by what it includes – middle-class residences – and second (perhaps more importantly) by what it excludes: all industry, most commerce except for enterprises that specifically serve a residential area, and all lower-class residents (except for servants). These social and economic characteristics are all expressed in design through a suburban tradition of both residential and landscape architecture. Derived from the English concept of the picturesque, this tradition distinguishes the suburb both from the city and from the countryside and creates that aesthetic "marriage of town and country" which is the mark of the true suburb.

One need only contrast this definition with the realities of the eighteenth-century city to see how radically suburbia contradicted the basic assumptions that organized the premodern city. Such cities were built up on the principle that the core was the only appropriate and honorific setting for the elite, and that the urban peripheries outside the walls were disreputable zones, shantytowns to which the poorest inhabitants and the most noisome manufacturers were relegated.

In London – a typical premodern city in this respect and one with a special relevance to this study – income and social standing declined markedly as one moved from the center to the outskirts. These social distinctions were enshrined in the language itself. From its earliest usage in the fourteenth century until the mid-eighteenth century, a "suburbe"

– that is, a settlement on the urban fringe – meant (in the definition of the *Oxford English Dictionary*) a "place of inferior, debased, and especially licentious habits of life." The canon's yeoman in Chaucer's *Canterbury Tales* says of himself and his master, a crooked alchemist, that they live "in the suburbes of town. We lurk in corners and blind alleys where robbers and thieves instinctively huddle secretly and fearfully together . . ."[2]

In Shakespeare's London so many houses of prostitution had moved to these disreputable outskirts that a whore was called "a suburb sinner," and to call a man a "suburbanite" was a serious insult.[3] One nineteenth-century writer has described the inhabitants of the suburb of Cripplegate in the seventeenth century as

> *a population of tanners and skinners, catgut makers, tallow melters, dealers in old clothes, receivers of stolen goods, charcoal sellers, makers of sham jewelry, coiners, clippers of coin and silver refiners, who kept their melting-pots ready day and night for any silver plate that might come to hand, toilers in noisome trades and dishonest dealers . . . Forgers of seals, of bills, of writs, professional pick-purses, sharpers and other thieves, conjurors, wizards and fortune tellers, beggars and harlots found a refuge here.*[4]

If the modern suburb can be defined as a peripheral zone in which people of means choose to live, then such a district was literally unthinkable in the premodern city, a contradiction in the basic terms that defined urban structure.

Indeed, even the concept of a residential district from which commerce and industry had been excluded was inconceivable for the premodern city. The basic principle of a city like London before 1750 was that work and residence were naturally combined within each house. Almost all middle-class enterprises were extensions of the family, so that it was not only the Spitalfields weaver who lived with his loom or the grocer who lived above his shop. The banker conducted business in his parlor, the merchant stored his goods in his cellar, and both housed and fed their apprentices along with their families.

This intimate connection of work and residence explained the universal attraction of the wealthy bourgeoisie to the urban core. When workplace and residence are combined, the best location for transacting one's business determined the location of one's house. In a mercantile city this location was almost invariably the most crowded district of the urban core.

I should emphasize here that even the relatively wealthy core areas were never upper-class neighborhoods in the modern sense. Just as the idea of a district devoted to a single function – a residential district or a business district – was foreign to the premodern city, so too was a single-class district. John Strype describes the privileged parish of St Giles in the

Fields as possessing "a mixture of rich inhabitants, to wit, of the Nobility, Gentry, and Commonality, but, withal, filled with abundance of poor."[5]

The wealthy might, at best, occupy large townhouses that fronted on the principal streets. But the poor inevitably crowded into the narrow alleyways and courtyards that existed literally in the backyards of the rich. This "medley of neighborhood," as Strype put it, was accepted without question. The poor were often servants in nearby houses, or workers in the multitude of small workshops found throughout the city. As one eighteenth-century writer observed, "Here lives a personage of high distinction; next door a butcher with his stinking shambles! A Tallow-chandler shall be seen from my Lord's nice Venetian window; and two or three brawny naked Curriers in their Pits shall face a fine Lady in her back Closet, and disturb her spiritual Thoughts."[6] Here indeed we find the "mixed uses" frequently romanticized by twentieth-century "post-suburban" planners. These mixed uses often had a functional basis, as when workshops clustered around the homes of merchants who dealt in their products. Sometimes they seem bizarre, as when a notorious "crime district" called Alsatia could be found adjoining the Temple, the center of English law.[7] In any case, the basic principles of the modern suburb had no precedents in the premodern city.

The suburb as we know it, therefore, did not evolve smoothly or inevitably from the premodern city; still less did it evolve from those disreputable outlying districts which originally bore the name of "suburbes." The emergence of suburbia required a total transformation of urban values: not only a reversal in the meanings of core and periphery, but a separation of work and family life and the creation of new forms of urban space that would be both class-segregated and wholly residential.

Who then invented suburbia and why? To ask the question is to formulate a major thesis, which is that suburbia was indeed a cultural creation, a conscious choice based on the economic structure and cultural values of the Anglo-American bourgeoisie. Suburbanization was not the automatic fate of the middle class in the "mature industrial city" or an inevitable response to the Industrial Revolution or the so-called transportation revolution.

Yet, if suburbia was an original creation, it was not the product of an architect of genius who conceived the modern suburb in a single vision, which then gradually inspired the design profession and eventually the middle class. Indeed, in this history of suburban design, professional architects and city planners play a remarkably limited role.

Suburbia, I believe, was the collective creation of the bourgeois elite in late eighteenth-century London. It evolved gradually and anonymously by trial-and-error methods. Wealthy London bankers and merchants experimented with a variety of the traditional housing forms available to them to create an original synthesis that reflected their values. Suburbia was improvised, not designed. Its method of evolution paralleled that of the contemporaneous Industrial Revolution, then taking place in the north of England, which also proceeded by trial-and-error adaptation. In both cases one senses the power of a class with the resources and the self-confidence to reorder the material world to suit its needs.

The motives that inspired the creation of suburbia were complex. Here I would emphasize only one, which seems to me the most crucial. The London bourgeoisie who invented suburbia were also experiencing a new form of family, which Lawrence Stone has called "the closed domesticated nuclear family." Inner-directed, united by strong and exclusive personal ties, characterized in Stone's phrase by "an emphasis on the boundary surrounding the nuclear unit," such families sought to separate themselves from the intrusions of the workplace and the city. This new family type created the emotional force that split middle-class work and residence.[8]

The bourgeois residence was now freed from traditional patterns to be redesigned as a wholly domestic environment – the home of a family that acted primarily as an emotional rather than an economic unit. This home, moreover, need not be restricted to the crowded districts of the urban core, as the logic of business location had formerly dictated. It was free to seek a more appropriate setting beyond the city in the picturesque villages that surrounded London. There, within easy commuting distance to the city by private carriage, these merchants and bankers could construct their "bourgeois utopia" of leisure, neighborliness, prosperity, and family life.

To this strong cultural impetus to suburbanization was soon added an equally strong economic motive. The suburban idea raised the possibility that land far beyond the previous range of metropolitan expansion could be transformed immediately from relatively cheap agricultural land to highly profitable building plots. This possibility provided the great engine that drove suburban expansion forward. Builders in both England and the United States adapted more easily to the needs of suburban development than they did to the more difficult challenge of creating middle-class districts within the city. Suburbia proved to be a good investment as well as a good home.

Middle-class suburbanization thus entered into the structural logic of the expanding Anglo-American city. It formed an integral part of what Frederick Law Olmsted perceived to be "the most prominent characteristic of the present period of civilization . . . the strong tendency of people to flock together in great towns."[9] Suburbia might appear to be a flight from the city but, seen in a larger, regional context, suburbanization was clearly the outer edge in a wider process of metropolitan growth and consolidation that was draining the rural areas and small towns of their population and concentrating people and production within what H. G. Wells called "the whirlpool cities."[10]

In 1800 only 17 percent of the English people lived in settlements larger than 20,000 people.[11] Cities were then places for highly specialized forms of consumption, manufacture, and trade. The real work of the world took place in the villages and in the countryside. By 1890, however, 72 percent of the English population lived in districts classified as "urbanized."[12] In the United States in 1800 less than 4 percent of the population lived in cities of 10,000 or more; by 1890 that figure had reached 28 percent.[13] Behind these statistics lies a fundamental shift in the role of the modern city. Where premodern cities had been parasitic on the larger societies, the new industrial metropolis emerged as the most efficient and productive site for the most characteristic modern industries.[14]

As such "whirlpool cities" as London, Manchester, and New York came to dominate the world economy, their attraction grew ever more powerful. In these centers of exchange and information, crowding seemed to work; in other words, intense congestion led not to chaos and decline but to further expansion. In the nineteenth century the expression "urban crisis" referred to the explosive growth of the great cities, and to horrified critics it seemed that almost the whole population of modern nations would soon be sucked into the already crowded urban centers.[15]

Inevitably, these whirlpool cities had to expand physically, to break the barriers of size that had always constrained urban growth. The only question was if they would grow in the traditional manner, with the wealthy massed at the core and the poor pushed ever farther into the periphery; or if the middle class would use their wealth and resources to seize the unspoiled land at the urban fringe for their suburban "bourgeois utopia," forcing the working class into an intermediate "factory zone" sandwiched between the central business district and the suburbs.

Broadly speaking, continental and Latin American cities opted for the traditional structure, while British and North American cities followed the path of middle-class suburbanization. This distinction, still fundamental in so many of the world's great cities, had nothing to do with the supposed backwardness of continental cities as compared to their Anglo-American counterparts. Paris in the nineteenth century became far more intensively industrialized than London, and the French capital developed a network of omnibuses, streetcars, and railroads that matched the transportation facilities in any English or American city. Yet the Parisian middle class remained loyal to the central city; the transportation system in Paris was used to move Parisian industry and its workers to the suburbs, and every further advance in transportation and industry has meant moving factories and the working class even farther from the city while the Parisian middle class has solidified its hold on the urban core.

However "objective" the "industrial city" might appear in diagrams from the Chicago School of sociology, its form rests ultimately on the values and choices of the powerful groups within the city. The decision of the bourgeoisie in Manchester and the other early industrial cities in the 1840s to suburbanize created the basic structure of the Anglo-American industrial city, while the decision of the comparable group in Paris of the 1850s and 1860s (aided by considerable governmental aid and intervention) to live in apartment houses in the center created the modern continental-style city.

In both cases the key actor was that elite of the middle class, the bourgeoisie. By "bourgeoisie" I mean that part of the middle class which through its capital or its professional standing has attained an income level equal to the landed gentry, but whose daily work in urban offices ties it to middle-class style of life. Their personal resources permit them to create new patterns of living, while the values they share with the rest of the middle class make them the model for eventual emulation by the less prosperous. The history of suburbia must therefore be a cultural and social history of the Anglo-American bourgeoisie. They are the pioneers whose collective style and choices define the nature of suburbia for their era.

For these English and American bourgeois pioneers, the "frontier" was inevitably the urban periphery, with its relatively cheap, undeveloped land. In continental cities massive governmental intervention – the nineteenth-century versions of urban renewal – opened the possibility of reshaping the urban core for bourgeois uses. In England and the United States, laissez-faire urban economics turned the core into a tangle of competing uses. Only the periphery was sufficiently undefined to permit innovation. Indeed, the fate of the periphery was ultimately decisive in defining the whole structure of the Anglo-American city. In this Darwinian struggle for urban space, the bourgeoisie sought not only land for their commercial and industrial enterprises but also land for their dreams: their visions of the ideal middle-class home. These dreams are now deep in the structure of the twentieth-century city.

The history of suburbia is thus a history of a vision – the bourgeois utopia – which has left its mark on thousands of individual suburbs, each with its own distinctive history. But I believe that all these communities can be linked to a single suburban tradition of architectural and social history. In attempting to outline the principal stages in the evolution of this tradition, I have been forced to depart from the usual method of suburban history, which is to examine one community over time. No single suburb adequately represents all the stages of suburban evolution, so I have selected a series of communities that seem best to embody the suburban idea at each crucial point of innovation.

These suburbs are not typical of their time but rather exemplary. Built rapidly in periods of unusual growth and prosperity, they incorporate in their design a creative response to contemporary changes in the structure and economy of modern cities. Unconstrained by previous building, responding to new social and cultural forces, these communities are truly "of their time." Through a series of often uncoordinated decisions by developers, builders, and individuals, a new style arises, which is then copied in hundreds of other suburbs. These exemplary suburbs create the image that, at any particular time, defines the suburban tradition. This image then becomes an active force in urban history, shaping subsequent decisions by speculators and home buyers that transform the urban landscape.

The first models for this process – and consequently the inevitable starting point for this book – were those earliest of modern suburbs which took shape on the outskirts of London in the second half of the eighteenth century. They not only defined the essential suburban image for all subsequent development but, in their strict segregation of class and function, they also implied a new structure for the modern city.

These implications were first worked out in practice not in London itself but in the early nineteenth-century industrial cities of northern England. The suburbs of Manchester, which form the second group of exemplary suburbs, were the necessary catalyst in reshaping the whole structure of the modern industrial city. For the first time one sees a middle class that is wholly suburbanized; and, as necessary correlates, a central business district devoid of residents and a crowded, smoky factory zone between the central business district and suburbia. Frenzied land speculation, bitter class conflict, and the alluring image of the bourgeois utopia combined to restructure the basic components of the city.

By the 1840s Manchester had established a model for middle-class suburbanization that was to endure fundamentally unchanged for a century. In the 1850s and 1860s this suburban model established itself outside the rapidly growing cities of the United States but was decisively rejected in France. There, as we have seen, the bourgeoisie maintained their hold on the urban core. This dichotomy creates an important problem for any history of suburbia: why did this bourgeois utopia take hold only among the "Anglo-Saxon" bourgeoisie, when the equally bourgeois French followed a very different vision?

The answer hinges both on long-term differences between French and Anglo-American images of the city and on the specifics of Eugène-Georges Haussmann's massive rebuilding of Paris. In any case, the great apartment houses along the new boulevards of Paris – as well as their counterparts in Vienna's Ringstrasse – created a powerful counterimage that shaped the continental city into a structure diametrically opposed to that of the English city. At the same time, and for equally strong cultural and economic reasons, the American middle class adopted the English model of bourgeois suburbanization so decisively that ever since Americans have been convinced that it was they who invented suburbia.

Indeed, after 1870 the site of the "exemplary" suburb shifted decisively to the United States. It happened not because of any loss of enthusiasm for the suburban ideal in England. The slowing of the British economy,

first apparent in the late nineteenth century, combined with the explosive growth of the American industrial city, meant that English suburbs
were more constrained by the past, while the United States was forced to
innovate.

The suburbs that arose outside the American industrial cities at the end
of the nineteenth century were the classic embodiments of the whole
history of suburbia. They not only summed up the design tradition now
more than a century old, but they provided the model that all subsequent
suburbs have attempted to imitate. Structurally, these suburbs were at
once separate from the industrial city and yet, through the streetcar and
the steam railroad, easily accessible to it. Socially, they housed a powerful and self-conscious bourgeoisie that combined the old business and
professional elite with the "new middle class" anxious to establish its
separateness from the immigrant cities. In design, the substantial houses
set in open, tree-shaded lots summed up that blend of property, union
with nature, and family life which defines the suburban tradition. I have
chosen the suburbs of Philadelphia to exemplify this era – though the
suburbs of Boston, New York, Baltimore, St Louis, and especially Chicago
would have served just as well.

If there is a single theme that differentiates the history of twentieth-
century suburbia from its nineteenth-century antecedents, it is the
attempt to secure for the whole middle class (and even for the working
class as well) the benefits of suburbia, which in the classic nineteenth-
century suburb has been restricted to the bourgeois elite alone.
Inevitably, this attempt was to change the basic nature both of suburbia
and of the larger city. For how can a form based on the principle of exclusion include everyone?

This paradox is exemplified in the history of Los Angeles, the suburban metropolis of the twentieth century. From its first building boom in
the late nineteenth century, Los Angeles has been shaped by the promise
of a suburban home for all. The automobile and the highway when they
came were no more than new tools to achieve a suburban vision that had
its origins in the streetcar era. But as population spread along the streetcar lines and the highways, the "suburbs" of Los Angeles began to lose
contact with the central city, which so diminished in importance that
even the new highways bypassed it. In the 1920s, a new urban form
evolved in which the industries, specialized shopping, and offices once
concentrated in the urban core spread over the whole region. By the
1930s Los Angeles had become a sprawling metropolitan region, the basic
unit of which was the decentralized suburb.

This creation of a suburban metropolis signaled a fundamental shift in
the relationship of the urban core and its periphery, with implications
extending far beyond Los Angeles. As we have seen, the suburb emerged
during the era of urban concentration, when the limitations of communications and transportation combined to draw people and production

into the crowded core. By the 1920s an interrelated technology of decentralization – of which the automobile was only one element – had begun to operate, which inexorably loosened the ties that once bound the urban functions of society to tightly defined cores. As the most important urban institutions spread out over the landscape, the suburb became part of a complex "outer city," which now included jobs as well as residences.

Increasingly independent of the urban core, the suburb since 1945 has lost its traditional meaning and function as a satellite of the central city. Where peripheral communities had once excluded industry and large-scale commerce, the suburb now becomes the heartland of the most rapidly expanding elements of the late twentieth-century economy. The basic concept of the suburb as a privileged zone between city and country no longer fits the realities of a posturban era in which high-tech research centers sit in the midst of farmland and grass grows on abandoned factory sites in the core. As both core and periphery are swallowed up in seemingly endless multicentered regions, where can one find suburbia?

This problem forms the heart of my concluding chapter in the book from which this essay is drawn, "Beyond Suburbia: The rise of the Technoburb." Kenneth Jackson in his definitive history of American suburbanization, *Crabgrass Frontier*, interprets post-World War II peripheral development as "the suburbanization of the United States," the culmination of the nineteenth-century and early twentieth-century suburban tradition.[16] I see this development as something very different, the end of suburbia in its traditional sense and the creation of a new kind of decentralized city.

Without anyone planning or foreseeing it, the simultaneous movement of housing, industry, and commercial development to the outskirts has created perimeter cities that are functionally independent of the urban core. In complete contrast to the residential or industrial suburbs of the past, these new cities contain along their superhighways all the specialized functions of a great metropolis – industry, shopping malls, hospitals, universities, cultural centers, and parks. With its highways and advanced communications technology, the new perimeter city can generate urban diversity without urban concentration.

To distinguish the new perimeter city from the traditional suburban bedroom community, I propose to identify it by the neologism "technoburb." For the real basis of the new city is the invisible web of advanced technology and telecommunications that has been substituted for the face-to-face contact and physical movement of older cities. Inevitably, the technoburb has become the favored location for those technologically advanced industries which have made the new city possible. If, as Fernand Braudel has said, the city is a transformer, intensifying the pace of change, then the American transformer has moved from the urban core to the perimeter.[17]

If the technoburb has lost its dependence on the older urban cores, it now exists in a multicentered region defined by superhighways, the growth corridors of which could extend more than a hundred miles. These regions, which (if the reader will pardon another neologism) I call techno-cities, mean the end of the whirlpool effect that had drawn people to great cities and their suburbs. Instead, urban functions disperse across a decentralized landscape that is neither urban nor rural nor suburban in the traditional sense. With the rise of the technoburb, the history of suburbia comes to an end.

Urbanity versus Suburbanity

> . . . already, there are to be found [in suburbia] . . . the most attractive, the most refined and the most soundly wholesome forms of domestic life, and the best application of the arts of civilization to which mankind has yet attained.
>
> Frederick Law Olmsted, 1868[18]

In the early 1850s two visitors came separately to England with a particular interest in suburbs. César Daly was already France's best known architectural writer and editor of the *Revue générale de l'architecture*. Once a follower of the utopian socialist Charles Fourier, Daly still retained his interest in designing the perfect dwelling for the modern age. Outside London he unexpectedly discovered a new solution: the suburban villa. He saw at once its origins in middle-class aspirations to domesticity; its aesthetic possibilities as the marriage of urban and rural architecture; its financial possibilities as the residence of choice for an increasingly prosperous and powerful bourgeoisie. Daly was convinced that suburbanization was inevitable for the middle class, not only in England but also in France.[19]

Frederick Law Olmsted, the other visitor, arrived from New York in 1850 in more modest circumstances. Twenty-eight years old, a gentleman farmer on Staten Island with literary aspirations, Olmsted had not yet found the vocation as a landscape architect and planner that would make him famous. While touring England making notes for a book, he saw Birkenhead Park near Liverpool; and, though he could not have realized it at the time, he encountered there the prototypes for his later work both as a park designer and as a suburban planner.[20]

Birkenhead Park was designed by Joseph Paxton, who began his career as a gardener and wound up creating the Crystal Palace for the Great Exposition of 1851. In 1844 Paxton laid out a public park of picturesque design that became a model for New York's Central Park, designed by Olmsted and Calvert Vaux. More importantly for our purposes, Paxton surrounded the park with a picturesque suburb. The curving roads and artful plantings, the substantial villas on separate lots recall not only Manchester's Victoria Park of 1837 but also John Nash's Park Village of twenty years before. The suburb that Olmsted saw in 1850 not only summed up the tradition of English suburban design; it also embodied the principles that Olmsted was to apply so widely and so successfully in the United States.[21]

Olmsted's advocacy of suburbia developed more slowly than Daly's, but both men came to share a common faith that, in Olmsted's words, "no great town can long exist without great suburbs."[22] Indeed, the 1850s and 1860s seemed to be the ideal time to advocate and to profit from the mass suburbanization of the middle class both in France and in the United States. In both countries the middle class still tended to occupy the crowded center of the cities. A Parisian bourgeois family of 1850 lived much as their London counterparts had done a century before: in town-houses that combined work and residence, located in neighborhoods even more crowded than those of the City of London.[23] A New York, Philadelphia, or Boston merchant of the same period occupied premises that resembled those of the Manchester middle class *before* the subur-banization of the 1830s and 1840s: townhouses virtually next door to warehouses, with artisans and casual laborers crammed into alleyways just behind the more substantial residences.[24]

Yet the French and the American middle class had come to share precisely those cultural preferences which, in England, had led to subur-banization. The Victorian emphasis on domesticity was by no means confined to those territories where the Queen herself actually ruled. In French and American publications one can find the same stress on the primacy of the family and the emotional ties that bind it; the necessity of privacy and isolation of the family unit; and the consequent need to sepa-rate the domestic sphere from the world of work. One also finds the same desire for class separation: the growing uneasiness at close contact between classes; the rejection of neighborhoods that make such contacts inevitable; and the search for class-segregated bourgeois residential neighborhoods, which the older city could not provide.

At the time that these cultural preferences took hold, namely, the 1850s and 1860s, French and American cities were beginning to experi-ence that explosive growth which, in England, had made the restructuring of middle-class housing patterns not only necessary but profitable. In France urban growth had lagged behind that of England. Only in the late 1840s, when a national rail network centered on Paris was begun, did the conditions exist for extensive urban redevelopment.[25] American cities had always grown rapidly but from a relatively small base. Lacking the gigantism of an imperial city like London or the accelerating growth of the northern English industrial cities, the American cities retained the form of the eighteenth-century mercantile city well into the nineteenth century.

French and American cities thus reached a stage of rapid change and inevitable transformation precisely when English models were most influential.[26] The Great Exposition of 1851 carried the implicit message that the English had invented the form of the modern age. It seemed only natural that French and American entrepreneurs who were rushing to adopt the technological innovations of the English bourgeoisie would also adopt their invention in the field of housing, the middle-class residential suburb. Both Daly and Olmsted were ardent nationalists, but in championing suburbia they gratefully accepted England's example.

The 1850s and 1860s did see the beginning of the great rehousing of the middle class in France and America, but only in the United States did this transformation take the suburban form that Daly and Olmsted anticipated. Olmsted not only witnessed the emergence of the "great suburbs" he had predicted; he himself participated in planning suburbs of a scale and design that surpassed their English models. In this same period, by contrast, Daly saw his beloved suburban villa relegated to a position of minor and eccentric use among the French middle class, who overwhelmingly preferred the form of housing the English most despised: an apartment in a large building located on a busy boulevard near the center of the city. In Paris it was the well-to-do who maintained their hold on the inner city, while industry and workers were pushed toward peripheral "suburbs" known primarily for their poverty and dreariness.

The history of a city like Paris thus lies outside the history of suburbia as it is defined in this book. This chapter will nevertheless examine the Parisian experience, because only by understanding how and why a modern city rejects suburbia can we fully understand why other cities embrace it. The Parisian middle classes were as bourgeois as their Anglo-American counterparts; they shared many of the same assumptions about family and urban life; they had reached a comparable level of economic development; yet they rejected suburbia. Thus, suburbia proved to be neither a universal middle-class phenomenon, nor a localized English housing type. It was instead an Anglo-American phenomenon, with some influence on northern and central European cities but very little in those European or Latin American cities which took their lead from Paris. A closer look at Paris will help to explain this resistance to suburbia. Similarly, a comparison of Anglo-American cities with Paris will help to explain why middle-class housing choices not only created different kinds of residential areas but ultimately also created different kinds of cities.

Paris in 1850

Its residents called it "the capital of the universe," but anyone who knew its narrow, dark, fetid, and overcrowded streets could well understand why Daly predicted the imminent suburban flight of the middle class.

Although the city walls had ceased to provide any real barrier to urban expansion, the vast majority of the city's 1.054 million people still lived within the boundaries established by the seventeenth-century walls. In the business district of the Right Bank, where most of the city's middle class both lived and worked, population densities were more than double even the most crowded London district of the same period; indeed, they exceeded the densities of New York's Lower East Side in the 1930s.[27]

Under these circumstances, middle-class families rarely had even a complete row house to themselves. The old three- and four-story structures generally had a merchant's shop on the ground floor, a sitting room behind the shop, his family's dining room, kitchen, and bedrooms crowded onto the second and third floors, with any space above rented to poor artisans who were forced to put both their workshops and their families into a single garret room. Frequently these artisans did piecework for the merchant who lived below, so a whole mercantile establishment – owners, workers, and their families – was crowded into a single small house.[28]

Although this system was well adapted to the needs of small-scale luxury trades, which were the heart of the Parisian economy, it took a terrible human toll, as is perhaps best symbolized by the recurrent cholera epidemics. (The most recent, that of 1848–49, claimed more than 19,000 lives.)[29] The impenetrable maze of streets, virtually unrelieved by any open space, not only bred disease in its open sewers and gutters; it also made any kind of direct travel between the different districts of the city impossible. Yet the close physical contact between rich and poor in these isolated "urban villages" did not create any measure of class harmony. On the contrary: it bred the ferocious class hatred of the June Days of the Revolution of 1848, in which more than 3,000 workers died defending their barricades against the rifles and artillery of the army.[30]

Yet less than a mile from this region of overcrowding, disease, and class conflict lay open fields and quiet villages. Beyond the central zone defined by the line of the seventeenth-century fortifications could be found an intermediate zone enclosed by the eighteenth-century customs wall, which marked the legal limits of the city in 1850. A mile beyond the customs wall was a nineteenth-century line of fortifications, which in 1860 became the new boundary of the enlarged city. The outer area between the customs wall and the new fortifications was still virtually rural. Already the Parisian middle class had begun to erect summer villas there, just as their London counterparts had done outside London a century before. Daly, who printed the plans and elevations of many of these villas in his architectural journal, hailed them as the French forerunners of a comparable great movement of Parisian suburbanization.[31]

Nevertheless, by 1850 only a few of the French bourgeoisie had taken the crucial step and converted their summer and weekend villas into full-time residences. The lack of enthusiasm for suburbanization was not due to inadequate transportation between the rural outskirts and the center. On the contrary, Paris had a surprisingly efficient horse drawn omnibus system – the London system was, in fact, established by French entrepreneurs who copied the Parisian model – and there were even steam railroads that made the trip in less than half an hour.[32]

During the 1840s the most prosperous French merchants and bankers – the counterparts of the English group that had established Clapham – did leave the crowded center, but not for suburban villas. Instead, they created a new urban district, called the Chaussée d'Antin after its principal street. Located on the Right Bank at what was then the northwest edge of the city, the Chaussée d'Antin embodied the "suburban" principles of domesticity, privacy, and class segregation, but in an urban setting. The Chaussée d'Antin presented a solid front of luxurious structures that proclaimed their affiliation with the city and not the countryside.[33]

The characteristic building type of the Chaussée was the apartment house, but these grand edifices had nothing in common with the haphazardly divided row houses of the older districts. Their real design affiliation was with the aristocratic *palais*, most notably the eighteenth-century Palais Royal, the archetypal upper-class apartment dwelling that the duke of Orléans had built as a profitable speculation behind his own palace. The apartment houses of the Chaussée were urban palaces for the upper middle class, their imposing five- and six-story façades copied from the classical forms of the Palais Royal or from other eighteenth-century aristocratic urban mansions.[34] Behind these façades lay not a jumble of workspace and family space but elegant suites of rooms, each apartment generally occupying a whole floor.[35]

The new apartments were very much residential space. Offices and salesrooms remained in the urban core, which – like the City of London and the center of Manchester – was changing into a nonresidential business district. They were also class segregated spaces. Although rents decreased as one ascended the stairs, all apartments were designed for the well-to-do, and those garret spaces which remained under the roof were used for servants from the apartments below.[36]

The apartment houses of the Chaussée d'Antin were to be as influential for the French bourgeoisie as the suburban villas of Clapham or Victoria Park had been for the English. They established a model of affluent domesticity toward which the middle class could aspire. In England the Evangelical movement had united defense of the family with a strong antiurbanism. Not only must the family be separated from the world of work; it must leave the corrupting city completely for the natural world of the countryside. The French bourgeoisie also felt strongly the ideal of domesticity, but, lacking the Puritan tradition of the Evangelicals, they saw no contradiction between family life and the pleasures of urban culture. On the contrary, their ideal combined a bourgeois concern for family isolation and privacy with a ready access to the theaters, balls, cafés, and restaurants of Paris that had previously been the privilege of the upper class. The urban apartment house – at once aristocratic in its façade and thoroughly bourgeois in its domestic arrangements – exactly expressed this ideal.[37]

By a curious paradox, the English evangelicals, though extravagantly loyal to the established political order, rejected aristocratic tastes in urban culture as dangerous and dissolute. Their French counterparts, who violently rejected aristocratic political leadership, nonetheless were extravagantly loyal to the aristocratic urban ideal. As Louis Bergeron writes, the fundamental conquest of the Great Revolution in France was "the 'democratization' of an aristocratic style of life which in previous ages had been both a source of envy and a source of oppression."[38] Bergeron's phrase, "the 'democratization' of an aristocratic style of life", describes exactly the dominant impulse behind the great middle-class Parisian innovation in urban housing, the large apartment house.

If the apartment house provided an ideal for middle-class life, we might nevertheless wonder whether this ideal was attainable for anyone but the elite of the bourgeoisie who inhabited the Chaussée d'Antin. In the 1840s the relatively undeveloped Parisian housing industry was poorly equipped to cope with the special demands of large apartment houses. First, locating a suitable site was a major problem; most streets were too narrow for such high buildings, and even property along the principal streets was divided into small parcels jealously guarded by their owners. Capital for undertaking a large building was equally difficult to obtain. The French notaries, who performed the same function of placing mort-gages as the English solicitors, were even less able to provide large lump sums for a major construction project.[39]

In view of these limitations, it seemed unlikely that apartment houses would ever be built in sufficient numbers to satisfy the pent up demand of the middle class in the central districts for a new form of domestic living. A few might be erected in an area of special privilege to serve as a symbol for the elite; but that the majority of the middle class could be housed in such *beaux quartiers* seemed as unlikely as the local draper being invited to dine with the Rothschilds.

In this context Daly's prediction of middle-class suburbanization made sense. The suburban villa might not be the first choice of the French middle class, but it admirably suited both the strengths and the weak-nesses of the French housing trade. No great concentration of capital was needed; villas could be built one by one on whatever cheap land at the outskirts was most readily available. Piece by piece, using only the small, scattered sums that the notaries were able to provide, a suburban belt outside Paris could take shape. As in England, where villas clustered around particularly favored spots, a suburban style would be established that would draw the mass of the French middle class out of the city.

This predictable result never took place. Instead, a massive government intervention into the French housing market totally changed the rules of the game and made possible the construction of apartment houses near the center of Paris on a scale that no one could have foreseen.

Baron Haussmann and the Rebuilding of Paris

This government intervention was Louis Napoleon's and Eugène-Georges Haussmann's reconstruction of Paris. Napoleon III wished to transform Paris into a grand imperial capital, and to this end he gave virtually dictatorial powers to the prefect of Paris, Baron Haussmann. Haussmann's plan was to cut wide, straight boulevards through the maze of narrow streets, buying up and demolishing any buildings that stood in the way. These boulevards were to provide the crucial means of communication that would finally unite Paris into a great city.[40]

But opening new routes of communication was far from Haussmann's only concern. He wished to make the new boulevards truly monumental, which required that they be lined with massive, luxurious buildings. He settled on the new apartment houses of the Chaussée d'Antin as the building type that best suited his needs. These elegantly designed structures, uniform in height and sumptuous in decoration, would provide the glorious architectural borders to complement the width of the boulevards. Socially, the new apartment houses would make the boulevards the center of life and fashion. Politically, these elaborate and prestigious dwellings would reward the bourgeoisie and symbolize their adherence to the Napoleonic regime.[41]

Haussmann therefore set to work to ensure that apartment houses along the boulevards be built quickly, in sufficient numbers, and to his specifications. His goal, he proclaimed, was to make sure that a new boulevard was "completely lined with finished houses the moment it was opened to traffic."[42] The basic financial and administrative techniques were first tried in the frantic efforts to complete the buildings on the extension of the Rue de Rivoli in time for the World's Fair of 1855. By the end of the 1850s these techniques had been perfected.

Haussmann controlled the most valuable prize from his massive demolitions: the prime land that bordered the new boulevards. Suddenly a wealth of prime sites opened in the heart of Paris, and Haussmann reserved this land for builders committed to erecting apartment houses according to his plans. These favored builders often got the land for less than its market value.[43]

Moreover, the government made it possible for developers to escape the limitations of the traditional mortgage market and to receive as much credit as they required from a government sponsored mortgage bank. The Crédit foncier, as it was called, raised money by selling shares to small investors throughout France. It then combined these investments into large sums, which it loaned – at Haussmann's direction – to Parisian apartment house developers. These developers were thus assured of almost unlimited capital with which to erect apartment houses and long-term mortgages when the apartment houses were complete.[44]

Finally, the largest developers formed joint stock companies, which also raised money from small investors. These companies permitted them to operate on an even larger scale; and thus respond to the unprecedented opportunities created by the continuing construction of boulevards throughout the Second Empire. They were, in effect, industrial scale operations employing permanent staffs of architects, engineers, craftsmen, and foremen on projects throughout the city. The most prominent such company was the Société Immobilière de Paris, founded by the Pereire brothers. Needless to say, such companies enjoyed a special relationship with Haussmann and with the Crédit foncier.[45]

Haussmann's reliance on state power and state supported banks and corporations reflects the philosophy derived by Henri de Saint-Simon that the underdeveloped French economy must be organized in order to undertake the large-scale task of modernization. Haussmann mobilized the Parisian building industry to accomplish what private enterprise unaided could never have attempted. With power and profit both committed to the task of middle-class housing, the boulevards were soon lined with the apartment houses of Haussmann's vision.

The governmental initiative suddenly made the middle-class cultural ideal of the luxury apartment house attainable. The massive boom promoted the rapid improvement in apartment house design and standards of construction, an improvement furthered – ironically – by César Daly's publishing the most notable innovations in his journal. These structures presented an elaborate and expensive carved stone façade to the street. A classical ordering of half-columns or pilasters provided the basic discipline, which was relieved by exuberant sculptured detail – lions' heads, maidens' bodies, cornucopia – around windows, over doorways, or wherever it could be fitted. Wrought iron balconies provided the necessary horizontal accent.[46]

Most apartment houses had shops on the ground floor, grouped around a large central entrance where the residents entered and through which carriages could pass to an inner courtyard. The shops not only provided income to the building's owners but also helped to ensure that the boulevard itself would have a lively street life. Nevertheless, to ensure privacy the shops did not connect with the residences. Servants and tradesmen used the back stairs, while only the residents and their guests used the main stairway.[47]

The apartments were usually decorated with parquet floors, elaborate plastering, marble fireplaces topped with gilt framed mirrors, and other luxuries that proclaimed the occupant's (spiritual) kinship with the aristocracy. Even within the apartment the distinction was maintained between the family rooms – living room, dining room, parlor, and bedrooms, usually arranged as a suite of interconnecting rooms facing the street – and the servants' space (including the kitchen) facing the interior courtyard.[48] At night the servants slept in the garrets under the roof. The French thus introduced into the heart of the city the same domestic isolation that the English had achieved by fleeing to suburbia.

Not surprisingly, the Parisian middle class moved en masse to the apartments of the boulevards and the *beaux quartiers*; and their loyalty to the large apartment house has never wavered. The consequences of Haussmannization have further ensured that the suburban ideal would make few converts among the Parisian bourgeoisie. First, Haussmann's financial arrangements choked off the supply of small investments that might have supported gradual suburbanization. The savings of small French investors, which in England and the United States found their way into the hands of small suburban builders, were instead attracted to the shares of the Crédit foncier or the joint stock development companies that financed the apartment houses that Haussmann desired. In England the network of small investors and small builders had guaranteed a constant supply of suburban houses for the market. In France, that supply network never developed, while the government sponsored apartment house network flourished.

At the same time, Haussmann's activities drastically altered the social geography of the city. The poor, who received none of the largess that Haussmann bestowed on the favored bourgeoisie, found their neighborhoods demolished and were forced by government policy to move to the outskirts. Industry too was forced to the periphery, and a working-class industrial belt was formed in precisely those picturesque areas which might have attracted middle-class villas.[49]

The industrialization of Paris in the mid-nineteenth century thus had the opposite effect it had in Manchester. It hastened the movement of the working class to the outskirts, and the growing industrial belt at the periphery confirmed the middle class in their loyalty to central areas. "Suburbanization" in the French sense has thus come to refer almost exclusively to a working-class or lower middle-class movement to the periphery.

Haussmann was forced to resign in 1870 after conservative bankers raised serious questions about his financial procedures, and the regime itself collapsed in the defeat of the Franco-Prussian War later that year. Nevertheless, the Third Republic confirmed the work of the Second Empire, acknowledging that in the twenty years of Haussmannization, Paris had achieved its classic form.[50] And this form exercised a deep fascination on other western European cities, starting with Lyons and Marseilles.[51] In the late 1860s Vienna began its Ringstrasse development, another government sponsored effort to create a zone of privilege in the urban core based on monumental apartment houses whose façades imitated Baroque palaces and whose apartments housed the bourgeoisie. From Vienna the form spread through central and eastern Europe.[52]

The example of Paris proves that middle-class suburbanization was never the inevitable fate of the bourgeoisie. With bourgeois commitment to a distinctly urban culture, the central city could be rebuilt to suit their values. But this rebuilding was impossible without a government willing to intervene massively both in the housing market and in the urban fabric. In the nineteenth century, suburbia represented the path of small-scale enterprise and laissez-faire. The great Parisian boulevards lined with rows of apartment houses expressed the union of middle-class values with authoritarian planning.

Suburbia Comes to the United States

Although, as Mark Twain claimed, good Americans when they die may go to Paris, living Americans have sought a very different kind of city. In the very years that Paris was rejecting the bourgeois residential suburb, American cities made it an integral part of their structure. The roots of this acceptance go deep in the culture and economy of the American middle class, so deep that even the most careful students of American suburbia have assumed that suburbanization was "made in the USA." Nevertheless, the comparison of English and American cities shows not only the priority of English suburban designs but also a surprising loyalty on the part of the American bourgeoisie to the urban row house and mixed neighborhood, long after the English bourgeoisie had opted for the detached or semidetached suburban villa.

Kenneth Jackson's definitive history, *Crabgrass Frontier: The Suburbanization of the United States*, presents the most comprehensive argument for the indigenous origins of American suburbia. He demonstrates effectively that the first half of the nineteenth century saw a significant separation of work and residence in American cities – a vital prerequisite for suburbanization – and also that the middle class tended to move their homes from the core to increasingly prestigious areas of peripheral residence. He even identifies what he calls "the first commuter suburb," Brooklyn Heights, across the harbor from lower Manhattan, in "the early decades of the nineteenth century." (The commuters traveled by ferry.)[53]

A true suburb, however, is more than the edge of a city inhabited largely by the middle class. It must embody in its design a "marriage of town and country," a distinct zone set apart both from the solid rows of city streets and from rural fields. This design is more than a cosmetic feature. It protects and defines the villa community even after it has been surrounded by subsequent growth, and it sets the pattern for low density development. As we have seen, Clapham and other suburbs outside London had attained this true suburban design in the late eighteenth century, well before the first ferry service linked Manhattan and Brooklyn Heights in 1814.

What is notable, not only in Brooklyn Heights but in other "fringe areas" of early nineteenth-century American cities, is that the American bourgeoisie – though tending toward the peripheries – still resolutely favored the urban row house. To be sure, the richest merchants, imitating their London counterparts, had as early as the mid-eighteenth century constructed beautiful villas in the fields beyond the settled areas of New York, Philadelphia, and Boston.[54] But these villas remained summer or retirement homes and never coalesced into genuine communities as in London. Still less was there an American John Nash to turn these tendencies into community design.

In Brooklyn Heights, as Jackson notes, an early developer did propose in 1823 to sell large lots for an "association" of detached villas there. But when development actually came over the next twenty years, it took the form of conventional urban row houses similar to those being constructed in Manhattan.[55] That was the pattern not only in New York and Brooklyn but in the other large cities as well. The march of brick and then brownstone townhouses up Manhattan Island remained the great symbol of urban growth in antebellum America. They advanced as a solid mass, pushed from below by the continuous conversion of houses in lower Manhattan to commercial uses. In turn, this expansion pushed farther to the outskirts a disorderly mass of noisome enterprises and squatters, which continually threatened to engulf the few merchants' villas that stood in the countryside outside the solid streets.

This process was echoed in the stately advance of Philadelphia's elite from Society Hill west toward Rittenhouse Square and in the movement of the Boston bourgeoisie out from Beacon Hill to the most impressive row house development of the nineteenth century, the Back Bay. Begun in the 1840s, the Back Bay reached its peak of townhouse construction only in the 1860s and 1870s.[56]

The absence of a true suburban style in the United States is hardly surprising. American cities lacked the sheer bulk of London, which had more than a million residents in 1800, compared to 60,000 in New York.[57] London's size not only suggested the need to escape but also provided the critical mass of bourgeoisie necessary to define an alternative style. No large American city in the period, moreover, had the industrial importance of Manchester, so their mercantile offices and workshops did not generate either the intense pollution or the intense class conflict of that city. One also senses that the American bourgeois elite did not feel the same pressing need to isolate themselves in walled retreats like Manchester's Victoria Park; neither did they seek out the individual display of a free standing, highly ornamented villa. As one New York

writer put it in the 1880s, "The brownstone front is a democratic institution; it being the most elegant and fashionable style of house, millionaires
have been satisfied to show their splendour rather by interior decoration,
pictures and statuary, than by fine architecture or external magnificence."[58] No doubt "patrician" is a better word than the writer's
"democratic" to describe such houses. They represent a collective self-
confidence in their owners' ability to dominate the urban scene, regardless
of the poverty and commercialism constantly pressing in around them.

What, then, caused the suburban form to supplant the townhouse
among the American bourgeoisie after the mid-nineteenth century? The
answer is clearly related to the loss of that self-confidence which had
sustained residence in a disorderly, democratic city. No doubt the most
familiar reasons are still the most valid: mass immigration, industrialization, and machine politics. Underlying all of them is the great impetus
that operated at Manchester: the desire for class segregation.

For all but the wealthiest, an urban townhouse district represented a
considerable economic and social risk. The wealthy could afford to move
their residences as the dictates of fashion changed, or even to ignore these
dictates as they chose. Many New York dowagers remained loyal to the
posh districts of their youth even when they had been converted to warehouses, vowing like Edith Wharton's mother to be moved "only by the
undertaker."[59] At the other extreme, Andrew Carnegie could build his
mansion at Fifth Avenue and 91st Street in 1889 when the site was
surrounded by squatters' hovels. He was confident that he would
eventually be surrounded by more suitable neighbors. In the interim he
remained Andrew Carnegie.

The less secure members of the middle class had much more to lose if
they were caught in a rapidly changing urban neighborhood engulfed by
commercialism or the poor. As late as the 1860s Philadelphia gentlemen
built alley cottages to rent to poor families behind their new row houses,
which fronted on the main street.[60] Such intentional mingling of rich and
poor, comparable to that which obtained in Manchester thirty years
earlier, no longer was desirable once the ideal of single-class neighborhoods took hold in the United States as it had in England.

Once again, the choice was essentially simple. Either develop some
coordinated political and economic construction program to "reclaim" the
center for the middle class, or turn to the periphery where distance alone
sufficed to isolate the bourgeoisie and enable piecemeal development to
work effectively. In the absence of Napoleon III and the autocratic French
state, there could be no American Haussmann. At most, an exceptionally
fortunate urban row house district like Boston's Back Bay might, through
excellent planning and strictly enforced land use controls, achieve stability and identity in the heart of the city. But, as American cities swelled
with a new immigrant population, the single-class elite residential district
seemed incompatible with the urban core.

At the same time, the example of English suburbia provided a ready-made, pretested model of a stable, peripheral community with which to direct the anarchic forces of land speculation and development. Such a model was especially important because, before 1850, an isolated, detached villa residence beyond the city – however elegant – was at least as great a financial risk as any urban dwelling. In a letter of 1860 Olmsted gives a vivid picture of the financial difficulties to which the owners of detached villas in still rural sections of Manhattan were subjected:

> *Yet where five years ago there was nothing but elegance and fashion, you now see unmistakable signs of the advance guard of squalor, an anxiety to sell out on the part of the owners of the finest villas, no sales except for public houses, and an absolute deterioration in value of property. Look again at the Brooklyn suburbs. Jersey City. See the process repeated at Philadelphia and Boston.*[61]

Olmsted's analysis of the problem was essentially the same as John Nash's in London fifty years earlier. As was the case in northwestern London in the 1810s, villas built haphazardly along the roads leading out of New York City were exceptionally vulnerable to "nuisances" as the city expanded. The isolated villas were soon joined by workshops seeking a convenient location along the highway, and workshops brought workers seeking "cheap tenements and boarding houses." So, Olmsted concludes, "gradually from a quiet and secluded neighborhood, it is growing to be a noisy, dusty, smoking, shouting, rattling, and stinking one."[62]

As Olmsted realized, distance from the city alone could not prevent this suburban decay. If true suburbs were to be built, what was needed was "to offer some assurance to those who wish to build villas that these districts shall not be bye and bye invaded by the desolation which thus far has invariably advanced before the progress of the town."[63] The American suburb could expect none of the implicit deference that had protected Victoria Park, Manchester from decay even during the years of its bankruptcy. Olmsted observes that unsold villas on the edge of Manhattan were soon occupied by the shanties and pigsties of Irish squatters, who kept their goats on the untended lawns and stole the timber.[64]

Like Nash, Olmsted saw the solution in a conscious process of planning and design that would isolate a tract of undeveloped land from all "undesirable" uses and define that land as a suburb suitable only for middle-class dwellings. Suburban design must become a recognized commodity, but it required a relatively wide understanding of the suburban ideal among developers, builders, and home buyers.

This ideal did spread, even more rapidly than Olmsted could have predicted. It did not, I believe, emerge from an indigenous Jeffersonian tradition of domestic architecture and antiurbanism that had somehow lain dormant in the American urban soul. The success of the suburban ideal in mid-nineteenth century America came from a group of publicists who successfully presented – one might say marketed – the English suburban villa as the ideal American dwelling.

The Americanization of Suburban Style

Kenneth Jackson has identified the three authors between 1840 and 1875 who were "the most important voices in shaping new American attitudes toward housing and residential space" as Catharine Beecher, Andrew Jackson Downing, and Calvert Vaux.[65] I would add that the most salient characteristic of all three was their debt to the English sources of the suburban style: Evangelical domestic ideology and the picturesque tradition of design. Indeed, the more often they proclaimed their truly American character, the more deeply they borrowed from English precedents. Nevertheless, they succeeded in Americanizing the English detached villa and in putting forward the suburban style as an attractive alternative to the urban row house, which still dominated bourgeois aspirations. With a truly spiritual fervor they preached the virtues of the detached villa in a picturesque landscaped setting as the ideal environment for American domesticity.

Catharine Beecher, whose *Treatise on Domestic Economy* (1841) became the definitive statement of American domestic ideology, was formed both intellectually and emotionally by the doctrines of the Clapham sect. Her father, Lyman Beecher, was the most influential exponent of Evangelical theology among the American clergy. Her sister, Harriet Beecher Stowe, produced in *Uncle Tom's Cabin* the great antislavery novel that added popular appeal to Wilberforce's doctrines. And Catharine herself was a true daughter of Clapham, convinced of woman's higher religious role and aptitude, intent on establishing a woman's sphere in an unspiritual man's world, and sure that domesticity was the means by which woman's spirituality would play its part in uplifting American life.[66]

Beecher's great success was in embodying these ideas in a manual of domestic economy the clarity, organization, and good sense of which made it the definitive handbook of the American home. Yet throughout her carefully elaborated instructions on, for example, the layout of a kitchen or the feeding of infants, there was implicit the great Evangelical theme that the home was the best source of Christian morality. As such, it must be separated from the profane concerns of the city. Women must see the importance of their role as homemakers and reject the temptations of urban life. Homemakers, she wrote, were "agents in accomplishing the greatest work that was ever committed to human responsibility. It is the building of a glorious temple, whose base shall be coextensive with the bounds of the earth."[67]

Beecher was never a publicist for suburbia as such, but her *Treatise* was crucial in spreading the Evangelical idea of the sanctified home, which, as in England, led directly to suburbia in America. There was nothing in her writing of which Wilberforce or Hannah More could not approve, except for her constant emphasis on the special role to which providence had called the United States. This view led to a vision of the importance of the home that even Ruskin could not equal. The United States, she believed, was the hope of the world, but that hope could only be realized through the beneficent influence of women, to whom "is committed the exalted privilege of extending all over the world those blessed influences, which are to renovate degraded man."[68] But this "renovation" could only take place in the context of a truly spiritualized American home.

Andrew Jackson Downing, whose *Cottage Residences* was published the year after Beecher's *Treatise*, was her necessary counterpart in the field of domestic architecture. If Beecher Americanized the doctrines of Wilberforce, More, and the other Evangelicals, Downing Americanized the designs of John Nash and the picturesque movement. Like Beecher, he believed "above all things under heaven, in the power and influence of the *Individual Home*."[69] His constant concern was to demonstrate that only the picturesque villa or cottage, "whose humble roof, whose shady porch, whose verdant lawn and smiling flowers all breathe forth to us, in true earnest tones, a domestic feeling that at once purifies the heart and binds us closer to our fellow beings" – only the picturesque could truly embody Beecher's vision of a sacred home.[70]

Downing thereby amalgamated the picturesque aesthetic with Evangelical piety to produce the same suburban synthesis of design and moralism that had inspired the English. He began his career as a landscape gardener for the affluent estates that lined the Hudson River, but his real education came from his immersion in the forms of the English picturesque. His influence derived from the success with which he compiled and popularized the dominant styles of English villa architecture for consumption in the United States. He was especially indebted (to put it politely) to J. C. Loudon, the architect and journalist who, as we have seen, was a dominant influence in England.[71]

In view of Downing's sources of inspiration, it is hardly surprising that his ideal American house was "An Irregular Cottage in the Old English Style," a design based on fantasies of medieval England set in a miniaturized version of an eighteenth-century landed estate. This type of cottage would fit very nicely into Nash's Park Village, from which, indeed, it was indirectly derived (via Loudon). Downing had well absorbed Nash's essential lesson: that picturesque architecture is not an authentic revival of the past – true authenticity is irrelevant – but an emotional style, the association of which "strengthens and invigorates our best and holiest affections."[72] What counts are the feelings inspired by architecture, the capacity to make "the place dearest to our hearts a sunny spot where social sympathies take shelter securely under the shadowy eaves, or glow and entwine trustfully with the tall trees or wreathed vines that cluster around, as if striving to shut out whatever bitterness or strife may be found in the open highways of the world."[73] Only the picturesque – preferably the Gothic – could embody the irregular, spontaneous, and irrational quality that made the home an emotional refuge from the marketplace. And only a natural setting could protect the home against the city, that "arid desert of business and dissipation." In 1850 he published a plan for his ideal "country village," in which detached houses on tree-lined streets surround a landscaped public park – an American Birkenhead Park.[74] Through Downing, the design philosophy of English suburbia entered into the mainstream of American domestic architecture.

Calvert Vaux, the third of Kenneth Jackson's important American voices, was born and trained in England. Downing met him in Paris in 1850 and brought him back to the United States. This background is clearly reflected in Vaux's *Villas and Cottages* (1857), though he too emphasizes the uniquely American character of his designs in terms borrowed directly from the English Evangelicals and the European picturesque architects.[75] His most important contributions came, however, as a partner first of Downing and then, after Downing's untimely death in 1852, of Olmsted.

Perhaps the culmination of this phase of English suburbia's assimilation by America came in Llewellyn Park, New Jersey (1857), an elaborately landscaped villa development in the foothills of the Orange Mountains. Named for its principal developer, Llewellyn S. Haskell, and designed by him and the architect Alexander Jackson Davis, Llewellyn Park was conceived as a picturesque assemblage of villas on curving roads surrounding a fifty-acre shared park, the Ramble. Kenneth Jackson calls it "the world's first picturesque suburb"; but, as John Archer has recently demonstrated, Llewellyn Park comes directly out of the half-century-old English tradition of picturesque suburban development, starting of course with Park Village but also including Calverley Park, Tunbridge Wells (Decimus Burton, 1827–28), Prince's Park, Liverpool (Joseph Paxton and James Pennethorp, 1842) and Victoria Park, Manchester.[76]

Yet, if Llewellyn Park borrows heavily from these English precedents, it also embodies a relationship to the landscape that does seem distinctly American. Its dramatic mountainside site, with views extending down to Manhattan some twelve miles away, has little in common with the level, placid settings of English suburbs. There is an intensity in the attempt to retain the natural setting unknown in England. With lots matched carefully to the sloping ground, careful landscaping to accentuate the terrain, a prohibition of fences to divide the property, and the expanse of the Ramble, the large villas of Llewellyn Park seem almost swallowed up in nature.[77]

As Walter Creese has pointed out, Llewellyn Park owes much to the country estates of the Hudson Valley where Davis, Downing, and others attempted to find a style to match the grandeur of the scenery.[78] If the suburb is the meeting place of the city and nature, then the American suburb must attempt to match the greater dimensions of the American landscape. Most suburbs after Llewellyn Park have shirked this challenge, but the design tradition begun there later gave rise, as will be seen, to the houses poised dramatically on the Santa Monica Mountains, the Hollywood Hills, and the Palos Verdes Peninsula overlooking Los Angeles and the Pacific Ocean.

Olmsted and Riverside

As Llewellyn Park shows, the English origin of American suburbia does not mean that American planners and architects were doomed forever to imitate English models. The career of Frederick Law Olmsted is the clearest proof that an American steeped in the English landscape tradition could use this tradition creatively to formulate a suburban vision for the United States.

Even before Olmsted visited England and Birkenhead Park in 1850, he had already studied with great care the major works of English picturesque design. While still a student in his native Hartford, Connecticut, he found and read in the public library the most important works of the English picturesque: Uvedale Price's *An Essay on the Picturesque*, the source for the idea of the "picturesque village"; and William Gilpin's *Picturesque Tours*, which described admiringly the early suburban development around London. At the end of his career, Olmsted was still recommending Price and Gilpin, which he described as "books of the last century, but which I esteem so much more than any published since, as stimulating the exercise of judgment in matters of my art, that I put them into the hands of my pupils as soon as they come into our office, saying, 'You are to read these as seriously, as a student of Law would read Blackstone.'"[79] He also found in the Hartford Public Library the works of Humphrey Repton, Nash's sometime partner and principal practitioner of picturesque landscaping; and the pastoral poet William Shenstone, a contemporary of Cowper and an advocate of the picturesque aesthetic.[80]

Having learned the theory from these works, Olmsted was able to appreciate the practice of the suburban style when he saw it in England in 1850. He was then an unknown writer struggling to make a living as a gentleman farmer on Staten Island. In 1857, while still a part-time farmer and author, he was chosen as superintendent of New York's Central Park, which was then a dreary, undeveloped wasteland. The competition for the design of the park brought him into partnership with Calvert Vaux and gave him his first opportunity to practice his ideas of the picturesque. The winning design established Olmsted, Vaux and

Company as the nation's leading landscape architects and as the heirs of Downing's aesthetic leadership.[81]

Despite – or perhaps because of – Olmsted's intensive urban experience while working on Central Park, he had come by the 1860s to advocate the suburb as the "most attractive, the most refined, the most soundly wholesome" form of domestic life.[82] This attitude was not due to any slavish imitation of English ways; neither could the creator of one of the greatest urban parks be called antiurban. It proceeded from a careful analysis of the problems of the modern city and of nineteenth-century America.

As Olmsted asserted in 1868, "the most prominent characteristic of the present period of civilization has been the strong tendency of people to flock together in great towns."[83] He saw this trend as essentially positive, leading not only to the "unprecedented movement of invention, energy, and skill" in the modern age, but also to the diffusion among the mass of city dwellers of comforts, luxuries, and culture that had once been available only to an elite. Yet this flocking together has its negative aspects in the psychological strains of living in crowded areas, the "peculiarly hard sort of selfishness" which inevitably takes hold in cities where conditions "compel us to walk circumspectly, watchfully, jealously," and to "look closely upon others without sympathy."[84] Such strains could lead to nervous breakdowns among the elite or to vice, crime, and intemperance among the masses.[85]

For Olmsted, as for the Evangelicals, nature was the great remedy against the evils of the city. Only if urban dwellers can experience a daily "change both of scene and air" will their physical, psychological, and moral health be maintained, and the full benefits of the city for civilization preserved. Olmsted promoted the urban park for the same reason he promoted suburbia, as "strongly counteractive to the special enervating conditions of the town."[86] Indeed, he conceived the park as a kind of in-town suburb, accessible to rich and poor. The dominating aim of park design must be "to completely shut out the city from our landscapes."[87]

But Olmsted's confidence in the healing power of urban parks diminished in the 1860s, and he grew especially critical of the urban row house – even one close to a park – as a proper home. The New York brownstone, he wrote, was "really a confession that it is impossible to build a convenient and tasteful residence in New York, adapted to the civilized requirements of a single family, except at a cost which even rich men find prohibitive."[88] At the same time, he came to believe that a villa in a properly planned suburb could, at much less cost, provide both easy access to all the benefits of urban civilization and far better opportunities for contact with nature.

The suburb, he argued, did not betoken an ebbing of the nineteenth-century flood tide of urbanization but "a higher rise of the same flood"; it was "not a sacrifice of urban conveniences but their combination with the special charms and substantial advantages of rural conditions of life."[89] As he put it in a letter to Edward Everett Hale, the suburb meant "elbow room about a house without going into the country, without sacrifice of butchers, bakers, & theaters."[90] Unlike the Clapham Evangelicals, Olmsted did not see suburbanization as a withdrawal from urban culture. He emphasized that not only jobs would be accessible but the whole range of advantages only obtainable in the city. Villa residents, he stated, want and will find "the advantages of society, of compact society, of the use of professional talent in teachers, and artists and physicians . . . They want to be served in a regular, exact, punctual, and timely manner with superior comestibles, and whatever else it is desirable to have supplied to a family, freshly, frequently, or quickly on demand."[91] In thus combining town and country, the suburb was indeed "the best application of the arts of civilization to which mankind has yet obtained."[92]

The suburb was therefore the perfected form of city dwelling, and Olmsted hoped that it would soon be available not only to the rich but to all. "I never lose an opportunity," he wrote to Hale, to urge the

> *ruralizing of* all *our urban population and the urbanizing of our rustic population. For I regard it as doubtful which of two slants toward savage condition is most to be deplored and struggled with, that which we see in the dense poor quarters of our great cities and manufacturing firms or that which is impending over the scattered agricultural population of more especially the sterile parts of the great West.*[93]

These ideals were very much in Olmsted's mind when, at the request of a businessman named E. E. Childs, he undertook in 1868 to plan the suburb of Riverside, Illinois. It was not, however, a suburb for "all." As Olmsted confessed, "the laws of supply and demand compel me to *work* chiefly for the rich and to study rich men's wants, fashions and prejudices."[94] But Olmsted brought to this project not only his deep knowledge of English sources and his own genius for design, but also his ideal of what an American suburb could be. His plan represents both a summation of previous Anglo-American suburban design and a highly personal statement of Olmsted's vision of a community in harmony with nature. If there is a single plan that expresses the idea of the bourgeois utopia, it is Olmsted's Riverside.

Childs had acquired a featureless 1,600-acre tract of Midwest prairie – "low, flat, miry, and forelorn," Olmsted called it[95] – relieved only by the Des Plaines River and by the tracks of the Chicago, Burlington, and Quincy Railroad, which ran to Chicago some nine miles away. As with Central Park, Olmsted had no ready-made picturesque features to work with. Design alone had to create both the landscape and the community.[96]

The plan aimed for the balance of man and nature that had defined suburbia since Clapham – the community of houses in a park. It relied on the same picturesque design language that Nash employed at Park Village: tree-lined roads that contrast with the "ordinary directness" of the city streets through their "gracefully-curved lines, generous spaces, and the absence of sharp corners, the idea being to suggest and imply leisure, contemplativeness, and happy tranquility."[97]

But Olmsted carried through this idea not only on a scale ten times as great as Park Village but with a far greater attention to the crucial interplay of public and private spaces. The developers provided the basic landscape through extensive plantings of trees and shrubs along the curving roads and in the public "greens." The plan called for 7,000 evergreens, 32,000 deciduous trees, and 47,000 shrubs.[98]

In addition, Olmsted prescribed that each house be set back at least thirty feet from the road and that "each householder shall maintain one or two living trees between his house and his highway-line."[99] Here Olmsted was reacting against the English practice seen at Victoria Park of each villa owner surrounding his property with a wall – "high dead-walls," – Olmsted called them, "as of a series of private madhouses."[100] In Riverside, the tree shaded front lawns of the houses continue the effect of parkland in from the roadsides. So the homeowners on their own property were to contribute to and enhance the theme of the "community in the park."

Yet Olmsted did not wish to merge all the individual lots into a single undifferentiated landscape; that, he thought, was the great fault of Llewellyn Park. "In the present shape of civilization people are not in a healthy way who do not want to make the line between their own families and family belongings and others, a rather sharp – at least a well-defined one," he advised.[101] The aim, again, was balance between the family and the community. "The essential qualification of a suburb is domesticity, and to the emphasizing of the idea of habitation, all that favors movement should be subordinated."[102] He desired a setting of "pleasant openings and outlooks, with suggestions of refined domestic life, secluded, but not far removed from the life of the community."[103]

The "life of the community" was provided for in the extensive public spaces: more than 700 of the 1,600 acres were for common use.[104] Olmsted specified that, in addition to the private domestic needs of each family, a suburb must engender "the harmonious association and co-operation of men in a community, and the intimate relationship and constant intercourse, and interdependence between families."[105] To this end he specified an arcadian array of pleasure grounds: village greens, playgrounds, croquet and ball grounds, sheltered resting spots along the roads. The river would be dammed to form a lake for boating and ice skating, and the lake surrounded by public walks and "pretty boat landings, terraces, balconies overhanging the water, and pavilions at points desirable for observing regattas, mainly of rustic character, and to be half overgrown with vines."[106]

Olmsted further recommended that land for a wide, landscaped pleasure drive be purchased to connect Riverside with the outskirts of Chicago. Lined with fashionable villas, this drive would not only provide a pleasant route between suburb and city; its constant traffic of elegant carriages and riders would also make the drive a center of social activity.[107] Olmsted once recalled the great pleasure he derived from being on the Champs Elysées and watching the fashionable crowd that promenaded there. A community, he held, must gratify "the gregarious inclination," the desire to "see congregated human life."[108] Riverside would provide even this archetypically urban delight with an American suburban counterpart to Haussmann's Parisian boulevards.

Yet, in evaluating the pleasures of the Riverside environment, we should not forget one important contrast with similar amenities that Olmsted included in his plans for urban parks. In writing about Central Park Olmsted was particularly proud of the mixture of classes who enjoyed it, the "vast number of persons brought closely together, poor and rich, young and old, Jew and Gentile."[109] Riverside, however, was a paradise for the few. And if, in Catharine Beecher's phrase, the creation of an American community of homes was "the building of a glorious temple," than that temple was built on land speculation.

In fact, the Riverside plan existed only in the context of a speculative enterprise to sell lots, and to sell them at a price sufficiently above the cost of the original agricultural land and of the subsequent improvements that the investors could enjoy a substantial profit. These lots could command such elevated prices only if, as Olmsted realized, they offered "very decided and permanent advantages for suburban residence."[110] "Permanence" in this context meant essentially the long-term capacity to exclude. Lurking in the wonderful elaboration of the plan was Olmsted's memory of the Manhattan villas overrun by the "Dutch boarding houses and groggeries" and occupied by Irish squatters who kept pigs and stole the timber. Olmsted's picturesque aesthetic and his attempt to envision a truly civilized community cannot be disentangled from his equally pressing aim of creating a tightly knit, exclusive society that would enjoy forever the unique benefits of its affluence.

It is somehow fitting that this ultimate bourgeois utopia should be the product not just of land speculation – that was inevitable – but of a particularly egregious form of financial legerdemain. Olmsted admitted that the Riverside Improvement Company was a "regular flyaway speculation," managed "on Gold Exchange and Erie [Railroad] principles [two notorious financial scandals of the period]."[111] When in the early 1870s lots sold more slowly than had been anticipated, one of the promoters who was also City Treasurer of Chicago pilfered more than $500,000 from city accounts to cover cost overruns at Riverside.[112] Even this illegal transfusion of funds did not save the project from the consequences of the Panic of 1873 and the subsequent depression. By 1874 the Company was bankrupt.[113]

The bankruptcy did not destroy Riverside; as with Manchester's Victoria Park and its financial difficulties, the best planned suburbs seem to have both an inherent propensity to bankruptcy and also a remarkable ability to survive it. But financial distress did mean the curtailment of many of the finer features of Olmsted's plan, most notably the grand pleasure drive. The suburb developed slowly over the next thirty years and took on many of the general characteristics of the "railroad suburbs" that flourished at the turn of the century. In his admirable analysis of Riverside, Walter Creese acknowledges that "Olmsted never quite reached the effect he wished," but Creese still calls Riverside "The Greatest American Suburb."[114]

The bankruptcy, however, does emphasize that the whole "green world" of community, family life, and union with nature that Olmsted strove to create in Riverside rested ultimately on a frighteningly unstable economic base. The bourgeois utopia depended for its survival on market forces that even the bourgeoisie could not control.

Notes

1   César Daly, *L'architecture privée au XIXe siècle sous Napoléon III*, 2 vols in 3 (Paris: Morel, 1864), 1:20; my translation.

2   Chaucer, *Canterbury Tales*, Canon's Yeoman's Tale, lines 557–60:

   In the suburbes of a town . . .
   Lurkynge in hernes and in lanes blynde,
   Whereas thise robbours and thise theves by kynde
   Holden hir pryvee fereful residence. . .

3   *Oxford English Dictionary*, s.v. "suburb."

4   Quoted in Pat Rogers, *Grub Street: Studies in a Subculture* (London: Methuen, 1972), 26.

5   John Strype in John Stow, *A Survey of the Cities of London and Westminster and the Borough of Southwark* [orig. ed. 1598], "corrected, improved, and very much enlarged in the year 1720" by John Strype, 6th ed., 2 vols (London: Innys & Richardson, 1754–55), ii, 76.

6   Anonymous article in *Old England* (London), 2 July 1748.

7   *Encyclopaedia Britannica*, 11th ed., s.v. "London."

8   Lawrence J. Stone, *The Family, Sex and Marriage in England, 1500–1800* (New York: Harper & Row, 1977), part 4.

9   Frederick Law Olmsted, "Preliminary Report upon the Proposed Suburban Village at Riverside, near Chicago" (New York, 1868); reprinted in S. B. Sutton, ed., *Civilizing American Cities: A Selection of Frederick Law Olmsted's Writings on City Landscapes* (Cambridge, Mass.: MIT Press, 1971), 293.

10   H. G. Wells, "The Probable Diffusion of Great Cities" (1900), in *Anticipations and Other Papers*, vol. 4 of *The Works of H. G. Wells* (New York: Scribner's, 1924), 39. Wells himself attributes the phrase to George Gissing.

11 Adna F. Weber, *The Growth of Cities in the Nineteenth Century*, rev. ed. (Ithaca, N.Y.: Cornell University Press, 1963; orig. ed. 1899), 47.

12 Ibid.

13 Ibid., 39.

14 For the best scholarly analysis of the city's changing role over time, see Paul M. Hohenberg and Lynn H. Lees, The *Making of Urban Europe, 1000–1950* (Cambridge, Mass.: Harvard University Press, 1985).

15 Andrew Lees, *Cities Perceived: Urban Society in European and American Thought, 1820–1940* (New York: Columbia University Press, 1985), 136–88. As Lees emphasizes, these negative views were balanced by more positive evaluations of the impact of urbanization.

16 Kenneth T. Jackson, *Crabgrass Frontier: The Suburbanization of the United States* (New York: Oxford University Press, 1985).

17 Fernand Braudel, *Capitalism and Material Life, 1400–1800*, trans. Miriam Kochan (New York: Harper & Row, 1975), 373, for the concept of the city as "transformer."

18 Olmsted, Vaux and Co.,"Preliminary Report upon the Proposed Suburban Village of Riverside, near Chicago" (New York, 1868), reprinted in S. B. Sutton, ed., *Civilizing American Cities: A Selection of Frederick Law Olmsted's Writings on City Landscapes* (Cambridge, Mass.: MIT Press, 1971), 295. This report will be referred to subsequently as "Riverside."

19 Daly describes his trip to London in "Maisons d'habitation de Londres," *Revue générale de l'architecture* 13 (1855), 57–63. His definitive statement on suburbs can be found in "Des Villas," in his *L'Architecture privée au XIXᵉ siècle sous Napoléon III*, 2 vols in 3 (Paris: Morel, 1864), 18–27. See also Hélène Lipstadt, "Housing the Bourgeoisie: César Daly and the Ideal Home," *Oppositions* 8 (Spring 1977): 35–47; and Donald J. Olsen, *The City as a Work of Art: London. Paris. Vienna* (New Haven: Yale University Press, 1986), 165–71.

20 Laura Wood Roper, *FLO: A Biography of Frederick Law Olmsted* (Baltimore: Johns Hopkins University Press, 1973), chap. 6.

21 Ibid.

22 Olmsted, Vaux, "Riverside," 295.

23 David Pinkney, *Napoleon III and the Rebuilding of Paris* (Princeton: Princeton University Press, 1958), 8–11.

24 The periphery of an antebellum American city is perhaps best described in Henry C. Binford, *The First Suburbs: Residential Communities on the Boston Periphery 1815–1860* (Chicago: University of Chicago Press, 1985); pre-suburban Philadelphia is vividly evoked in Roger Miller and Joseph Sirey, "The Emerging Suburb: West Philadelphia, 1850–1880," *Pennsylvania History* 47 (1980): 102–4. See also Edward K. Spann, *The New Metropolis: New York City, 1840–1857* (New York: Columbia University Press, 1981), chap. 8; and Betsy Blackmar, "Re-walking the 'Walking City': Housing and Property Relations in New York City, 1780–1840," *Radical History Review* 21 (Fall 1979): 131–150.

25 Olsen, *City as a Work of Art*, chap. 4.

26 For an illuminating comparison of mid-nineteenth century London and Paris, see Lynn Lees, "Metropolitan Types: London and Paris Compared,"

in H. J. Dyos and Michael Wolff, *The Victorian City: Images and Realities* (London: Routledge and Kegan Paul, 1973), 1: 413–28.

27   Pinkney, *Napoleon III*, 7.

28   Adeline Daumard, *Maisons de Paris et propriétaires parisiens au XIXe siècle* (Paris: Éditions Cujas, 1965), 96.

29   Pinkney, *Napoleon III*, 23.

30   William L. Langer, *Political and Social Upheaval, 1832–1852* (New York: Harper & Row, 1969), 346–50.

31   César Daly, "Maisons d'été des environs de Paris," *Revue générale de l'architecture* 17 (1859): 269–70.

32   Norma Evenson, *Paris: A Century of Change, 1878–1978* (New Haven: Yale University Press, 1979), 76–79; Pinkney, *Napoleon III*, 167–70.

33   Xavier Aubryet, "La Chaussée d'Antin," in *Paris Guide* (Paris: Librairie internationale, 1867), 2: 1338–48.

34   Michel Gallet, *Stately Mansions: Eighteenth Century Paris Architecture* (New York: Praeger, 1972).

35   Olsen, *City as a Work of Art*, 42–44.

36   Daumard, *Maisons de Paris*, 90–91.

37   Olsen, *City as a Work of Art*, 94–96 and 114–25; Evenson, *Paris*, 200–201; and Daumard, *Maisons de Paris*, 99–100.

38   Louis Bergeron, *France Under Napoleon* (Princeton: Princeton University Press, 1968), 204.

39   Daumard, *Maisons de Paris*, 80–88.

40   See especially Pinkney, *Napoleon III*, chaps 2–6. The cultural meaning of Haussmann's plans is brilliantly described in Marshall Berman, *All That Is Solid Melts into Air: The Experience of Modernity* (New York: Simon and Schuster, 1982), chap. 3, "Baudelaire, Modernism in the Streets."

41   Jeanne Gaillard, *Paris, la ville, 1852–1870* (Paris, Champion, 1970), 70–82.

42   Ibid., 77.

43   Bailleux de Marisy, "Des Sociétés foncières et leur rôle dans le travaux publics," *Revue des deux mondes* 34 (1863): 193–216.

44   Ibid., especially 194–200; also Pinkney, *Napoleon III*, 193–206.

45   Bailleux de Marisy, "La Ville de Paris, ses finances et ses travaux publics," *Revue des deux mondes* 47 (1863): 775–836.

46   Daly, *L'Architecture privée*. See also William H. White, "On Middle Class Houses in Paris and Central London," *Transactions of the Royal Institute of British Architects*, Sessional Papers (1878): 21–55.

47   Ibid. 16–20; Olsen, *City as a Work of Art*, 124.

48   Daly, *L'Architecture privée*, 18–19.

49   Pinkney, *Napoleon III*, 165–66.

50   Evenson, *Paris*, 15–24; and Anthony Sutcliffe, *The Autumn of Central Paris* (London: Edward Arnold, 1970).

51   See, for example, the recent study by Michel Lacave, "Stratégies d'expropriation et haussmannisation: l'exemple de Montpellier," *Annales: économies. sociétés. civilisations* 35 (September–October 1980): 1011–25.

52   Carl E. Schorske, *Fin-de-siècle Vienna* (New York: Knopf, 1979), chap. 2; Olsen, *City as a Work of Art*, chap. 5.

53   Kenneth T. Jackson, *Crabgrass Frontier: The Suburbanization of the United States* (New York: Oxford University Press, 1985), 20–33.

54   See especially the Philadelphia villas now preserved in Fairmont Park.

55   Jackson, *Crabgrass Frontier*, 32.

56   Bainbridge Bunting, *Houses of Boston's Back Bay* (Cambridge, Mass.: Harvard University Press, 1967), 5–6.

57   For New York population, Jackson, *Crabgrass Frontier*, 27; for London, B. R. Mitchell, *European Historical Statistics* (New York: Columbia University Press, 1978), 13.

58   *Distinctive Private Houses* (1881), quoted in M. Christine Boyer and Jessica Sheer, "The Development and Boundary of Luxury Neighborhoods in New York, 1625–1890," paper presented to the "Culture of Cities" seminar, New York University, 1980, p. 100.

59   Ibid., 83. The best account of wealthy townhouse development in Manhattan, which emphasizes the commitment of the New York elite to the city, is M. Christine Boyer, *Manhattan Manners: Architecture and Style, 1850–1900* (New York: Rizzoli, 1985).

60   Miller and Sircy, "The Emerging Suburb," 103.

61   Frederick Law Olmsted to Henry H. Elliot, 27 August 1860, in *The Papers of Frederick Law Olmsted*, Charles Capen McLaughlin, ed. (Baltimore: Johns Hopkins University Press, 1980), vol. 3; *Creating Central Park*, Charles E. Beveridge and David Schuyler, eds (1983), 262.

62   Ibid., 265. Olmsted's view of suburbia in the context of his larger urban vision has been thoughtfully analyzed in David Schuyler's important book, *The New Urban Landscape: The Redefinition of City Form in Nineteenth-Century America* (Baltimore: Johns Hopkins University Press, 1986), esp. chap. 8, "Urban Decentralization and the Domestic Landscape."

63   Ibid., 263.

64   Ibid., 260–61.

65   Jackson, *Crabgrass Frontier*, 61–67.

66   Kathryn Kish Sklar, *Catharine Beecher: A Study in American Domesticity* (New Haven: Yale University Press, 1973).

67   Ibid., 160. See also the important discussion of Beecher in Delores Hayden, *The Grand Domestic Revolution: A History of Feminist Designs for American Homes, Neighborhoods, and Cities* (Cambridge, Mass.: MIT Press, 1981).

68   Sklar, *Catharine Beecher*, 159.

69   Andrew Jackson Downing, *Rural Essays*, ed. George William Curtis (New York: G. P. Putnam, 1853), xxviii. For this account of Downing I am much indebted to Phillida Bunkle, who allowed me to see her work on Downing in manuscript. Downing's significance for American domestic architecture is best assessed in Vincent J. Scully, Jr, *The Shingle Style and the Stick Style*, rev. ed. (New Haven: Yale University Press, 1971); and his significance for urban design in Schuyler, *The New Urban Landscape*.

70   Downing, *Cottage Residences* (orig. ed. 1842; reprinted from the 1873 ed. under the title *Victorian Cottage Residences*, New York: Dover Publications, 1981), ix. For discussions of American domestic ideology in this period, see especially Gwendolyn Wright, *Building the Dream: A Social History of Housing in America* (New York: Pantheon Books, 1981), chaps 5–6; David Handlin, *The American Home: Architecture and Society, 1815–1915* (Boston: Little, Brown, 1979), chaps 2–4; and Clifford Edward Clark Jr, *The American Family Home, 1800–1960* (Chapel Hill: University of North Carolina Press), chaps 1–3.

71 For Downing's debts to Loudon, see Scully, *The Shingle Style*, xxviii; and John Archer, "Country and City in the American Romantic Suburb," *Journal of the Society of Architectural Historians* 42 (May 1983): 143.

72 Downing, *Cottage Residences*, ix.

73 Ibid.

74 Downing, *Rural Essays*, discussed in Schuyler, *The New Urban Landscape*, 153–156. Schuyler traces Downing's plan to his reaction against a developer's conventional grid plan for Dearman (now Irvington), New York.

75 Calvert Vaux, *Villas and Cottages* (New York: Harper, 1857).

76 Jackson, *Crabgrass Frontier*, 76–79; John Archer, "Country and City," 139–56.

77 Christopher Tunnard, *The City of Man*, 2nd ed. (New York: Scribner's, 1970), 181–86; Schuyler, *The New Urban Landscape*, 157–60.

78 Walter L. Creese, *The Crowning of the American Landscape* (Princeton: Princeton University Press, 1985), 85.

79 Olmsted to Elizabeth Baldwin Whitney, 16 December 1890, *Papers of Frederick Law Olmsted*, 3: 366.

80 Olmsted to Hartford, Conn. Board of Park Commissioners, draft ca. 1895, *Papers of Frederick Law Olmsted*, 3: 41.

81 Roper, *FLO*, chaps 12–13. See also the important insights on Olmsted in Thomas Bender, *Toward an Urban Vision: Ideas and Institutions in Nineteenth Century America* (Lexington: University of Kentucky Press, 1975).

82 Olmsted, Vaux, "Riverside," 295.

83 Ibid., 293.

84 Frederick Law Olmsted, "Public Parks and the Enlargement of Towns," *American Social Science Association* (Cambridge, Mass.,1870), reprinted in Sutton, ed., *Civilizing American Cities*, 66, 80.

85 Ibid., 93.

86 Ibid., 73.

87 Ibid., 80.

88 Quoted in Jackson, *Crabgrass Frontier*, 75.

89 Ibid., 294.

90 Olmsted to Edward Everett Hale, 21 October 1869, Olmsted Papers, Library of Congress, no. 01916. I am indebted to Charles E. Beveridge of the Olmsted Papers project for supplying me with the transcript of this letter.

91 Olmsted to Elliot, *Papers of Frederick Law Olmsted*, 264.

92 Olmsted, Vaux, "Riverside," 295.

93 Olmsted to Hale, Library of Congress, no. 01916.

94 Ibid.

95 Olmsted, Vaux, "Riverside," 292.

96 For Riverside, see especially Creese, *Crowning*, 219–40, "Riverside: The Greatest American Suburb"; and Schuyler, *The New Urban Landscape*, 162–66.

97 Olmsted, Vaux, "Riverside," 300.

98 Creese, *Crowning*, 227.

99 Olmsted, Vaux, "Riverside," 302.

100 Ibid., 301.

101 Olmsted to Hale, Library of Congress, no. 01916.

102   Olmsted, Vaux, "Riverside," 303.
103   Ibid., 299.
104   Creese, *Crowning*, 228.
105   Olmsted, Vaux, "Riverside," 303.
106   Ibid., 304.
107   Ibid., 296–98.
108   Olmsted, "Public Parks and the Enlargement of Towns," 74–75.
109   Ibid., 75.
110   Olmsted, Vaux, "Riverside," 292.
111   Olmsted to Hale, Library of Congress, no. 01916.
112   Creese, *Crowning*, 223.
113   Ibid., 224.
114   Ibid., 228.

3

The Global City

Saskia Sassen

For centuries, the world economy has shaped the life of cities. This chapter is about that relationship today. Beginning in the 1960s, the organization of economic activity entered a period of pronounced transformation. The changes were expressed in the altered structure of the world economy, and also assumed forms specific to particular places. Certain of these changes are by now familiar: the dismantling of once-powerful industrial centers in the United States, the United Kingdom, and more recently in Japan; the accelerated industrialization of several Third World countries; the rapid internationalization of the financial industry into a worldwide network of transactions. Each of these changes altered the relation of cities to the international economy.

In the decades after World War II, there was an international regime based on United States dominance in the world economy and the rules for global trade contained in the 1945 Bretton Woods agreement. By the early 1970s, the conditions supporting that regime were disintegrating. The breakdown created a void into which stepped, perhaps in a last burst of national dominance, the large US transnational industrial firms and banks. In this period of transition, the management of the international economic order was to an inordinate extent run form the headquarters of these firms. By the early 1980s, however, the large US transnational banks faced the massive Third World debt crisis, and US industrial firms experienced sharp market share losses from foreign competition. Yet the international economy did not simply break into fragments. The geography and composition of the global economy changed so as to produce a complex duality: a spatially dispersed, yet globally integrated organization of economic activity.

Reprinted by permission from Saskia Sassen, 1991, *The Global City*.

The point of departure for the present study is that the combination of spatial dispersal and global integration has created a new strategic role for major cities. Beyond their long history as centers for international trade and banking, these cities now function in four new ways: first, as highly concentrated command points in the organization of the world economy; second, as key locations for finance and for specialized service firms, which have replaced manufacturing as the leading economic sectors; third, as sites of production, including the production of innovations, in these leading industries; and fourth, as markets for the products and innovations produced. These changes in the functioning of cities have had a massive impact upon both international economic activity and urban form: cities concentrate control over vast resources, while finance and specialized service industries have restructured the urban social and economic order. Thus a new type of city has appeared. It is the global city. Leading examples now are New York, London, and Tokyo. These three cities are the focus of this research.

As I shall show, these three cities have undergone massive and *parallel* changes in their economic base, spatial organization, and social structure. But this parallel development is a puzzle. How could cities with as diverse a history, culture, politics, and economy as New York, London and Tokyo experience similar transformations concentrated in so brief a period of time? Not examined at length in my study, but important to its theoretical framework, is how transformations in cities ranging from Paris to Frankfurt to Hong Kong and São Paulo have responded to the same dynamic. To understand the puzzle of parallel change in diverse cities requires not simply a point-by-point comparison of New York, London, and Tokyo, but a situating of these cities in a set of global processes. In order to understand why major cities with different histories and cultures have undergone parallel economic and social changes, we need to examine transformations in the world economy. Yet the term *global city* may be reductive and misleading if it suggests that cities are mere outcomes of a global economic machine. They are specific places whose spaces, internal dynamics, and social structure matter; indeed, we may be able to understand the global order only by analyzing why key structures of the world economy are *necessarily* situated in cities.

How does the position of these cities in the world economy today differ from that which they have historically held as centers of banking and trade? When Max Weber analyzed the medieval cities woven together in the Hanseatic League, he conceived their trade as the exchange of surplus production; it was his view that a medieval city could withdraw from external trade and continue to support itself, albeit on a reduced scale. The modern molecule of global cities is nothing like the trade among self-sufficient places in the Hanseatic League, as Weber understood it. The first thesis advanced in this book is that the territorial dispersal of current economic activity creates a need for expanded central control and management. In other words, while in principle the territorial decentralization of economic activity in recent years could have been accompanied by a corresponding decentralization in ownership and hence in the appropriation of profits, there has been little movement in that direction. Though large firms have increased their subcontracting to smaller firms, and many national firms in the newly industrializing countries have grown rapidly, this form of growth is ultimately part of a chain. Even industrial homeworkers in remote rural areas are now part of that chain. The transnational corporations continue to control much of the end product and to reap the profits associated with selling in the world market. The internationalization and expansion of the financial industry has brought growth to a large number of smaller financial markets, a growth which has fed the expansion of the global industry. But top-level control and management of the industry has become concentrated in a few leading financial centers, notably New York, London, and Tokyo. These account for a disproportionate share of all financial transactions and one that has grown rapidly since the early 1980s. The fundamental dynamic posited here is that the more globalized the economy becomes, the higher the agglomeration of central functions in a relatively few sites, that is, the global cities.

The extremely high densities evident in the business districts of these cities are one spatial expression of this logic. The widely accepted notion that density and agglomeration will become obsolete because global telecommunications advances allow for maximum population and resource dispersal is poorly conceived. It is, I argue, precisely because of the territorial dispersal facilitated by telecommunication that agglomeration of certain centralizing activities has sharply increased. This is not a mere continuation of old patterns of agglomeration; there is a new logic for concentration. In Weberian terms, there is a new system of "coordination," one which focuses on the development of specific geographic control sites in the international economic order.

A second major theme of this chapter concerns the impact of this type of economic growth on the economic order within these cities. It is necessary to go beyond the Weberian notion of coordination and Bell's (1973) notion of the postindustrial society to understand this new urban order. Bell, like Weber, assumes that the further society evolves from nineteenth-century industrial capitalism, the more the apex of the social order is involved in pure managerial process, with the content of what is to be managed becoming of secondary importance. Global cities are, however, not only nodal points for the coordination of processes (Friedmann 1986); they are also particular sites of production. They are sites for (1) the production of specialized services needed by complex organizations for running a spatially dispersed network of factories, offices, and service outlets; and (2) the production of financial innovations and the making of markets, both central to the internationalization and expansion of the financial industry. To understand the structure of a global city, we have to understand it as a place where certain kinds of work can get done, which is to say that we have to get beyond the dichotomy between manufacturing and services. The "things" a global city makes are services and financial goods.

It is true that high-level business services, from accounting to economic consulting, are not usually analyzed as a production process. Such services are usually seen as a type of output derived from high-level technical knowledge. I shall challenge this view. Moreover, using new scholarship on producer services, I shall examine the extent to which a key trait of global cities is that they are the most *advanced* production sites for creating these services.

A second way this analysis goes beyond the existing literature on cities concerns the financial industry. I shall explore how the character of a global city is shaped by the emerging organization of the financial industry. The accelerated production of innovations and the new importance of a large number of relatively small financial institutions led to a renewed or expanded role for the marketplace in the financial industry in the decade of the 1980s. The marketplace has assumed new strategic and routine economic functions, in comparison to the prior phase, when the large transnational banks dominated the national and international financial market. Insofar as financial "products" can be used internationally, the market has reappeared in a new form in the global economy. New York, London, and Tokyo play roles as production sites for financial innovations and centralized marketplaces for these "products."

A key dynamic running through these various activities and organizing my analysis of the place of global cities in the world economy is their capability for producing global control. By focusing on the production of services and financial innovations, I am seeking to displace the focus of attention from the familiar issues of the power of large corporations over governments and economies, or supercorporate concentration of power through interlocking directorates or organizations, such as the IMF. I want to focus on an aspect that has received less attention, which could be referred to as the "practice" of global control: the work of producing and reproducing the organization and management of a global production system and a global marketplace for finance. My focus is not on power, but on production: the production of those inputs that constitute the capability for global control and the infrastructure of jobs involved in this production.

The power of large corporations is insufficient to explain the capability for global control. Obviously, governments also face an increasingly complex environment in which highly sophisticated machineries of centralized management and control are necessary. Moreover, the high level of specialization and the growing demand for these specialized inputs have created the conditions for a freestanding industry. Now small firms can buy components of global capability, such as management consulting or international legal advice. And so can firms and governments anywhere in the world. While the large corporation is undoubtedly a key agent inducing the development of this capability and is a prime beneficiary, it is not the sole user.

Equally misleading would be an exclusive focus on transnational banks. Up to the end of the 1982 Third World debt crisis, the large transnational banks dominated the financial markets in terms of both volume and the nature of firm transactions. After 1982, this dominance was increasingly challenged by other financial institutions and the innovations they produced. This led to a transformation in the leading components of the financial industry, a proliferation of financial institutions, and the rapid internationalization of financial markets rather than just a few banks. The incorporation of a multiplicity of markets all over the world into a global system fed the growth of the industry after the 1982 debt crisis, while also creating new forms of concentration in a few leading financial centers. Hence, in the case of the financial industry, a focus on the large transnational banks would exclude precisely those sectors of the industry where much of the new growth and production of innovations has occurred; it would leave out an examination of the wide range of activities, firms, and markets that constitute the financial industry in the 1980s.

Thus, there are a number of reasons to focus a study on marketplaces and production sites rather than on the large corporations and banks. Most scholarship on the internationalization of the economy has already focused on the large corporations and transnational banks. To continue to focus on the corporations and banks would mean to limit attention to their formal power, rather than examining the wide array of economic activities, many outside the corporation, needed to produce and reproduce that power. And, in the case of finance, a focus on the large transnational banks would leave out precisely that institutional sector of the industry where the key components of the new growth have been invented and put into circulation. Finally, exclusive focus on corporations and banks leaves out a number of issues about the social, economic, and spatial impact of these activites on the cities that contain them, a major concern in this chapter and one I return to below.

A third major theme explored in this chapter concerns the consequences of these developments for the national urban system in each of these countries and for the relationship of the global city to its nation-state. While a few major cities are the sites of production for the new global control capability, a large number of other major cities have lost their role as leading export centers for industrial manufacturing, as a result of the decentralization of this form of production. Cities such as Detroit, Liverpool, Manchester, and now increasingly Nagoya and Osaka have been affected by the decentralization of their key industries at the domestic and international levels. According to the first hypothesis presented above, this same process has contributed to the growth of service industries that produce the specialized inputs to run global production processes and global markets for inputs and outputs. These industries – international legal and accounting services, management consulting, financial services – are heavily concentrated in cities such as New York, London, and Tokyo. We need to know how this growth alters the relations between the global cities and what were once the leading industrial centers in their nations. Does globalization bring about a triangulation so that New York, for example, now plays a role in the fortunes of Detroit that it did not play when that city was home to one of the leading industries, auto manufacturing? Or, in the case of Japan, we need to ask, for example, if there is a connection between the increasing shift of production out of Toyota City (Nagoya) to offshore locations (Thailand, South Korea, and the United States) and the development for the first time of a new headquarters for Toyota in Tokyo.

Similarly, there is a question about the relation between such major cities as Chicago, Osaka, and Manchester, once leading industrial centers in the world, and global markets generally. Both Chicago and Osaka were and continue to be important financial centers on the basis of their manufacturing industries. We would want to know if they have lost ground relatively, in these functions as a result of their decline in the global industrial market, or instead have undergone parallel transformation toward strengthening of service functions. Chicago, for example, was at the heart of a massive agroindustrial complex, a vast regional economy. How has the decline of that regional economic system affected Chicago?

In all these questions it is a matter of understanding what growth embedded in the international system of producer services and finance has entailed for different levels in the national urban hierarchy. The broader trends – decentralization of plants, offices, and service outlets, along with the expansion of central functions as a consequence of the need to manage such decentralized organization of firms – may well have created conditions contributing to the growth of regional subcenters, minor versions of what New York, London, and Tokyo do on a global and national scale. The extent to which the developments posited for New York, London, and Tokyo are also replicated, perhaps in less accentuated form, in smaller cities, at lower levels of the urban hierarchy, is an open, but important, question.

The new international forms of economic activity raise a problem about the relationship between nation-states and global cities. The relation between city and nation is a theme that keeps returning throughout this book; it is the political dimension of the economic changes I explore. I posit the possibility of a systematic discontinuity between what used to be though of as national growth and the forms of growth evident in global cities in the 1980s. These cities constitute a system rather than merely competing with each other. What contributes to growth in the network of global cities may well not contribute to growth in nations. For instance, is there a systemic relation between, on the one hand, the growth in global cities and, on the other hand, the deficits of national governments and the decline of major industrial centers in each of these countries?

The fourth and final theme in this chapter concerns the impact of these new forms of and conditions for growth on the social order of the global city. There is a vast body of literature on the impact of a dynamic, high-growth manufacturing sector in the highly developed countries, which shows that it raised wages, reduced inequality, and contributed to the formation of a middle class. Much less is known about the sociology of a service economy. Daniel Bell's (1973) *The Coming of Post-Industrial Society* posits that such an economy will result in growth in the number of highly educated workers and a more rational relation of workers to issues of social equity. One could argue that any city representing a post-industrial economy would surely be like the leading sectors of New York, London, and increasingly Tokyo.

I will examine to what extent the new structure of economic activity has brought about changes in the organization of work, reflected in a shift in the job supply and polarization in the income distribution and occupational distribution of workers. Major growth industries show a greater incidence of jobs in the high- and low-paying ends of the scale than do the older industries now in decline. Almost half the jobs in the producer services are lower-income jobs, and half are in the two highest earnings classes. In contrast, a large share of manufacturing workers were in the middle-earning jobs during the postwar period of high growth in these industries in the United States and United Kingdom.

Two other developments in global cities have also contributed to economic polarization. One is the vast supply of low-wage jobs required by high-income gentrification in both its residential and commercial settings. The increase in the numbers of expensive restaurants, luxury housing, luxury hotels, gourmet shops, boutiques, French hand laundries, and special cleaners that ornament the new urban landscape illustrates this trend. Furthermore, there is a continuing need for low-wage industrial services, even in such sectors as finance and specialized services. A second development that has reached significant proportions is what I call the downgrading of the manufacturing sector, a process in which the share of unionized shops declines and wages deteriorate while sweatshops and industrial homework proliferate. This process includes the downgrading of jobs within existing industries and the job supply patterns of some of the new industries, notably electronics assembly. It is worth noting that the growth of a downgraded manufacturing sector has been strongest in cities such as New York and London.

The expansion of low-wage jobs as a function of *growth* trends implies a reorganization of the capital–labor relation. To see this, it is important to distinguish the characteristics of jobs from their sectoral location, since highly dynamic, technologically advanced growth sectors may well contain low-wage dead-end jobs. Furthermore, the distinction between sectoral characteristics and sectoral growth patterns is crucial: backward sectors, such as downgraded manufacturing or low-wage service occupations, can be part of major growth trends in a highly developed economy. It is often assumed that backward sectors express decline trends. Similarly, there is a tendency to assume that advanced sectors, such as finance, have mostly good, white-collar jobs. In fact, they contain a good number of low-paying jobs, from cleaner to stock clerk.

These, then, are the major themes and implications of my analysis.

Finally, I must sketch the reasons why producer services and finance have grown so rapidly since the 1970s and why they are so highly concentrated in cities such as New York, London, and Tokyo. The familiar explanation is that the decade of the 1980s was but a part of a larger economic trend, the shift to services. And the simple explanation of their high concentration in major cities is that this is because of the need for face-to-face communication in the services community. While correct, these cliches are incomplete.

We need to understand first how modern technology has not ended nineteenth-century forms of work; rather, technology has shifted a number of activities that were once part of manufacturing into the domain of services. The transfer of skills from workers to machines once epitomized by the assembly line has a present-day version in the transfer of a variety of activities from the shop floor into computers, with their attendant technical and professional personnel. Also, functional specialization within early factories finds a contemporary counterpart in today's pronounced fragmentation of the work process spatially and organizationally. This has been called the "global assembly line," the production and assembly of goods from factories and depots throughout the world, wherever labor costs and economies of scale make an international division of labor cost-effective. It is, however, this very "global assembly line" that creates the need for increased centralization and complexity of management, control, and planning. The development of the modern corporation and its massive participation in world markets and foreign countries has made planning, internal administration, product development, and research increasingly important and complex. Diversification of product lines, mergers, and transnationalization of economic activities all require highly specialized skills in top-level management (Chandler, 1977). These have also "increased the dependence of the corporation on producer services, which in turn has fostered growth and development of higher levels of expertise among producer service firms" (Stanback and Noyelle, 1982: 15). What were once support resources for major corporations have become crucial inputs in corporate decision-making. A firm with a multiplicity of geographically dispersed manufacturing plants contributes to the development of new types of planning in production and distribution surrounding the firm.

The growth of international banks and the more recent diversification of the financial industry have also expanded the demand for highly specialized service inputs. In the 1960s and 1970s, there was considerable geographic dispersal in the banking industry, with many regional centers and offshore locations mostly involved in fairly traditional banking. The diversification and internationalization of finance over the last decade resulted in a strong trend toward concentrating the "management" of the global industry and the production of financial innovations in a more limited number of major locations. This dynamic is not unlike that of multi-site manufacturing or service firms.

Major trends toward the development of multi-site manufacturing, service, and banking have created an expanded demand for a wide range of specialized service activities to manage and control global networks of factories, service outlets, and branch offices. While to some extent these activities can be carried out in house, a large share of them cannot. High levels of specialization, the possibility of externalizing the production of some of these services, and the growing demand by large and small firms and by governments are all conditions that have both resulted from and made possible the development of a market for freestanding service firms that produce components for what I refer to as global control capability.

The growth of advanced services for firms, here referred to as producer services, along with their particular characteristics of production, helps to explain the centralization of management and servicing functions that has fueled the economic boom of the early and mid-1980s in New York, London, and Tokyo. The face-to-face explanation needs to be refined in several ways. Advanced services are mostly producer services; unlike other types of services, they are not dependent on proximity to the consumers served. Rather, such specialized firms benefit from and need to locate close to other firms who produce key inputs or whose proximity makes possible joint production of certain service offerings. The accounting firm can service its clients at a distance but the nature of its service depends on proximity to other specialists, from lawyers to programmers. Major corporate transactions today typically require simultaneous participation of several specialized firms providing legal, accounting, financial, public relations, management consulting, and other such services. Moreover, concentration arises out of the needs and expectations of the high-income workers employed in these firms. They are attracted to the amenities and lifestyles that large urban centers can offer and are likely to live in central areas rather than in suburbs.

The importance of this concentration of economic activity in New York, London, and Tokyo is heightened by the fact that advanced services and finance were the fastest-growing sectors in the economies of their countries in the 1980s. It is a common mistake to attribute high growth to the service sector as a whole. In fact, other major services, such as public and consumer services, have leveled off since the middle or late 1960s in the United States and since the 1970s in the United Kingdom and Japan. In other words, the concentration of advanced services and finance in major urban centers represents a disproportionate share of the nation-wide growth in employment and GNP in all these countries.

The combination of high levels of speculation and a multiplicity of small firms as core elements of the financial and producer services complex raises a question about the durability of this model of growth. At what point do the larger banks assume once again a more central role in the financial industry? And at what point do competition and the advantages of scale lead to mergers and acquisitions of small firms? Finally, and perhaps most important, at what point do the sources of profits generated by this form of economic growth become exhausted?

During the 1980s, major economic growth trends have produced spatial and social arrangements considerably divergent from the configuration that characterized the preceding decades. The economic sectors, localities and occupations that account for a large share of economic growth in 1990 differ from those central to the immediate post-World War II period. Most commonly, this process has been interpreted as the decline of old and the emergence of new industries, typically seen as two somewhat unconnected events necessary for the renewal of all economy. I shall challenge this disconnecting view, which means asserting that new growth rests, to a significant extent, on deep structural processes of decline. The question of the long-term durability of the global city that I have just posed turns on not seeing decline and growth as distinct. The "high-flying" 1980s might emerge as a passing phenomenon, even as manufacturing of the old sort continues to decline.

This systemic connection, I will argue, plays itself out in several economic arenas. I propose to examine this through several working hypotheses. They are the following: first, the geographic dispersal of manufacturing, which contributed to the decline of old industrial centers, created a demand for expanded central management and planning and the necessary specialized services, key components of growth in global cities. The move of large corporations into consumer services and the growing complexity of governmental activity further fed the demand for specialized services and expanded central management and planning, though they did not necessarily feed the decline of certain localities, as in the case of the dispersal of manufacturing. Second, the growth of the financial industry, and especially of key sectors of that industry, benefited from policies and conditions often harmful to other industrial sectors, notably manufacturing. The overall effect again was to feed growth of specialized services located in major cities and to undermine the economic base of other types of localities. Third, the conditions and patterns subsumed under the first two working hypotheses suggest a transformation in the economic relationships among global cities, the nation-states where they are located, and the world economy. Prior to the current phase, there was high correspondence between major growth sectors and overall national growth. Today we see increased asymmetry. The conditions promoting growth in global cities contain as significant components the decline of other areas of the United States, the United Kingdom, and Japan and the accumulation of government debt and corporate debt. Fourth, the new conditions of growth have contributed to elements of a new class alignment in global cities. The occupational structure of major growth industries characterized by the locational concentration of major growth sectors in global cities in combination with the polarized occupational structure of these sectors has created and contributed to growth of a high-income stratum and a low-income stratum of workers. It has done so directly through the organization of work and occupational structure of major growth sectors. And it has done so indirectly through the jobs needed to service the new high-income workers, both at work and at home, as well as the needs of the expanded low-wage work force.

References

Bell, Daniel. 1973. *The Coming of Post-Industrial Society: A Venture in Social Forecasting.* New York: Basic Books.

Chandler, Alfred. 1977. *The Visible Hand: The Manager in American Business.* Cambridge, Mass.: Harvard University Press.

Friedmann, John. 1986. "The World City Hypothesis." *Development and Change* 17: 69–84.

Stanback, Thomas M., Jr, and Thierry J. Noyelle. 1982. *Cities in Transition: Changing Job Structures in Atlanta, Denver, Buffalo, Phoenix, Columbus (Ohio), Nashville, Charlotte.* Totowa, NJ: Allanheld, Osmun.

Weber, A. 1909. *Theory of the Location of Industries.* Chicago: University of Chicago Press.

4

The Informational Mode of Development and the Restructuring of Capitalism

Manuel Castells

Introduction: Modes of Production, Modes of Development, and Social Structure

Technological change can only be understood in the context of the social structure within which it takes place. Yet such an understanding requires something more than a historically specific description of a given society. We must be able to locate technology in the level and process of the social structure underlying the dynamics of any society. On the basis of a theoretical characterization of this kind we may then go on to investigate the actual manifestations of the interaction between technology and the other elements of social structure in a process that shapes society and, therefore, space. To proceed along these lines it is necessary to introduce some theoretical propositions and to advance a few hypotheses that attempt to place the analysis of technological change and economic restructuring, as presented in this chapter, within the framework of a broader social theory that informs the overall investigation.

Reprinted by permission from Manuel Castells, 1989, *The Informational City*.

The analytical focus here is on the emergence of a new mode of development, which I will call the "informational mode," in historical interaction with the process of restructuring of the capitalist mode of production. Therefore, definitions are needed of the concepts of mode of production, mode of development, and restructuring. Such definitions, if they are to be theoretical and not simply taxonomic, require succinct presentation of the broader social theory that lends analytical meaning to such concepts as tools of understanding social structures and social change. For the purposes of this chapter, the presentation of the overall theoretical framework must be reduced to the few elements indispensable for communicating my hypothesis that the interaction between modes of production and modes of development is at the source of the generation of new social and spatial forms and processes.

This theoretical perspective postulates that societies are organized around human processes structured by historically determined relationships of production, experience and power.[1] Production is the action of humankind on matter to appropriate and transform it for its benefit by obtaining a product, consuming part of it (in an unevenly distributed manner), and accumulating the surplus for investment in accordance with socially determined goals. Experience is the action of human subjects on themselves within the various dimensions of their biological and cultural entity in the endless search for fulfillment of their needs and desires. Power is that relationship between human subjects which, on the basis of production and experience, imposes the will of some subjects upon others by the potential or actual use of violence.

Production is organized in class relationships that define the process by which the non-producers appropriate the surplus from the producers. Experience is structured around gender/sexual relationships, historically organized around the family, and characterized hitherto by the domination of men over women. Sexuality, in the broad, psychoanalytic sense, and family relationships, structure personality and frame symbolic interaction.

Power is founded upon the state, since the institutionalized monopoly of violence in the state apparatus ensures the domination of power holders over their subjects. The symbolic communication between subjects on the basis of production, experience, and power, crystallizes throughout history on specific territories and thus generates cultures.

All these instances of society interact with one another in framing social phenomena; however, given the particular research interest of this work in the relationship between technological change and economic restructuring, the effort of theoretical definition will here be focused on the structure and logic of the production process.

Production has been defined above as the purposive action of humankind to appropriate and transform matter, thus obtaining a product. It is a complex process because each one of its elements is itself made up of relationships between other elements. Humankind, as a collective actor, is differentiated in the production process between labor and the organizers of production; labor is internally differentiated and stratified according to the role of the producers in the production process. Matter includes nature, human-modified nature, and human-produced matter,[2] the labors of history forcing us to move away from the classic distinction between humankind and nature which has been largely superseded by the reconstruction of our environment through millennia of human action.

The relationship between labor and matter in the process of work is also complex: it includes the use of means of production to act upon matter, on the basis of energy and knowledge. Technology refers to the type of relationship established between labor and matter in the production process through the intermediation of a given set of means of production enacted by energy and knowledge.[3]

The product is itself divided into two main categories, according to its utilization in the overall process of production and reproduction: reproduction and surplus. Reproduction includes three sub-categories: reproduction of labor, reproduction of social institutions (ultimately enforcing relationships of production), and reproduction of means of production and their technological support basis. The surplus is the share of the product that exceeds the historically determined needs for the reproduction of the elements of the production process. It is divided again into two major categories, according to its destination: consumption and investment. Consumption is stratified according to societal rules. Investment is geared toward the quantitative and qualitative expansion of the production process according to the objectives determined by the controllers of the surplus.

Social structures interact with production processes by determining the rules for the appropriation and distribution of the surplus. These rules constitute modes of production, and these modes define social classes on the basis of social relationships of production. The structural principle by which the surplus is appropriated, thus designating the structural beneficiary of such appropriation, namely the dominant class, characterizes a mode of production. In contemporary societies there are two fundamental modes of production: capitalism and statism. Under capitalism, the separation between producers and their means of production, the commodification of labor, and the private ownership of the means of production on the basis of control of commodified surplus (capital), determine the basic principle of appropriation and distribution of surplus by the capitalist class, not necessarily for its exclusive benefit, but for the processes of investment and consumption decided by that class in the specific context of each unit of production under its control. Under statism, the control of the surplus is external to the economic sphere: it lies in the hands of the power-holders in the state, that is, in the apparatus benefiting from the institutional monopoly of violence. In both cases there is expropriation of the producers from their control over the surplus, although criteria for the distribution of consumption and allocation of investment vary according to the respective structural principles of each mode of production. Capitalism is oriented toward profit-maximizing, that is, toward increasing the amount and proportion of surplus appropriated on the basis of the control over means of production. Statism is oriented toward power-maximizing, that is, toward increasing the military and ideological capacity of the political apparatus for imposing its goals on a greater number of subjects and at deeper levels of their consciousness.

Modes of production do not appear as a result of historical necessity. They are the result of historical processes in which a rising social class becomes dominant by politically, and often militarily, defeating its historical adversaries, building social alliances and obtaining support to construct its hegemony. By hegemony I understand, in the Gramscian tradition, the historical ability of a given class to legitimate its claim to establish political institutions and cultural values able to mobilize the majority of the society, while fulfilling its specific interests as the new dominant class.

The social relationships of production, and thus the mode of production, determine the appropriation and distribution of the surplus. A separate, yet fundamental question is the *level* of such surplus, determined by the productivity of a particular process of production, that is, by the ratio of the value of each unit of output to the value of each unit of input. Productivity levels are themselves dependent on the relationship between labor and matter as a function of the use of means of production by the application of energy and knowledge. This process is characterized by technical relationships of production, defining a *mode of development*. Thus, modes of development are the technological arrangements through which labor acts upon matter to generate the product, ultimately determining the level of surplus. Each mode of development is defined by the element that is fundamental in determining the productivity of the production process. In the agrarian mode of development, increases in the surplus result from quantitative increases in labor and means of production, including land. In the industrial mode of development, the source of increasing surplus lies in the introduction of new energy sources and in the quality of the use of such energy. In the informational mode of development, the emergence of which is hypothesized here, the source of productivity lies in the quality of knowledge, the other intermediary element in the relationship between labor and the means of production. It should be understood that knowledge intervenes in all modes of development, since the process of production is always based on some level of knowledge. This is in fact what technology is all about, since technology is "the use of scientific knowledge to specify ways of doing things in a reproducible manner."[4] However, what is specific to the informational mode of development is that here knowledge intervenes upon knowledge itself in order to generate higher productivity. In other words, while in the preindustrial modes of development knowledge is used to organize the mobilization of greater quantities of labor and means of production, and in the industrial mode of development knowledge is called upon to provide new sources of energy and to reorganize production accordingly, in the informational mode of development knowledge mobilizes the generation of new knowledge as the key source of productivity through its impact on the other elements of the production process and on their relationships. Each mode of development has also a structurally determined goal, or performance principle, around which technological processes are organized: industrialism is oriented toward economic growth, that is, toward maximizing output; informationalism is oriented toward technological development, that is, toward the accumulation of knowledge. While higher levels of knowledge will result in higher levels of output, it is the pursuit and accumulation of knowledge itself that determines the technological function under informationalism.

Social relationships of production, defining modes of production, and technical relationships of production (or productive forces), defining modes of development, do not overlap, although they do interact in contemporary societies. In this sense, it is misleading to pretend that the informational mode of development (or postindustrial society) replaces capitalism, since, as Alain Touraine, Radovan Richta, and Daniel Bell indicated years ago,[5] these are different analytical planes, one referring to the principle of social organization, the other to the technological infrastructure of society. However, there are between the two structural processes complex and significant interactions which constitute a fundamental element in the dynamics of our societies.

Societies are made up of a complex web of historically specific relationships that combine modes of production, modes of development, experience, power, and cultures. Under capitalism, because of its historical reliance on the economic sphere as the source of power and legitimacy, the mode of production tends to organize society around its logic, without ever being able to exhaust the sources of social reproduction and social change within the dynamics of capital and labor. However, given the structural preponderance of capitalist social relationships in the class structure, and the influence they exercise on culture and politics, any major transformation in the processes by which capital reproduces itself and expands its interests affects the entire social organization. Modes of production – and capitalism is no exception – evolve with the process of historical change. In some instances, this leads to their abrupt supersession; more often, they transform themselves by responding to social conflicts, economic crises, and political challenges, through a reorganization that includes, as a fundamental element, the utilization of new technical relationships of production that may encompass the intro-duction of a new mode of development. By *restructuring* is understood the process by which modes of production transform their organizational means to achieve their *unchanged* structural principles of performance. Restructuring processes can be social and technological, as well as cultural and political, but they are all geared toward the fulfillment of the princi-ples embodied in the basic structure of the mode of production. In the case of capitalism, private capital's drive to maximize profit is the engine of growth, investment, and consumption.

Modes of development evolve according to their own logic; they do not respond mechanically to the demands of modes of production or of other instances of society. However, since technical relationships are histori-cally subordinated to social relationships of production, experience, and power, they tend to be molded in their structure and orientation by restructuring processes. On the other hand, they do have a specific logic that dominant social interests ignore only at the risk of spoiling their tech-nological potential – as, for example, a narrow orientation toward secretive, applied military technology can frustrate scientific advance-ment. Modes of development emerge from the interaction between scientific and technological discovery and the organizational integration of such discoveries in the processes of production and management. Since these processes are dependent upon the overall social organization, and particularly upon the dynamics of the mode of production, there is indeed a close interaction between modes of development and modes of production. This interaction occurs in different forms according to the pace of historical change. There is a continuous, gradual adaptation of new technologies to the evolving social relationships of production; there are also periods of major historical change, either in technology or in social organization. When historical circumstances create a convergence between social change and technological change, we witness the rise of a new technological paradigm, heralding a new mode of development. This, I contend, is what has brought the rise of the informational mode of development in the last quarter of the twentieth century.

The New Technological Revolution and the Informational Mode of Development

The New Technological Paradigm

During the two decades from the late 1960s to the late 1980s a series of scientific and technological innovations have converged to constitute a new technological paradigm.[6] The scientific and technological core of this paradigm lies in microelectronics, building on the sequential discoveries of the transistor (1947), the integrated circuit (1957), the planar process

(1959), and the microprocessor (1971).[7] Computers, spurred on by exponential increases in power and dramatic decreases in cost per unit of memory, were able to revolutionize information processing, in both hardware and software. Telecommunications became the key vector for the diffusion and full utilization of the new technologies by enabling connections between processing units, to form information systems. Applications of these microelectronics-based information systems to work processes in factories and offices created the basis for CAD/CAM (computer aided design/computer aided manufacturing) and Flexible Integrated Manufacturing, as well as for advanced office automation paving the way for the general application of flexible integrated production and management systems. Around this nucleus of information technologies, a number of other fundamental innovations took place, particularly in new materials (ceramics, alloys, optical fiber), and more recently, in superconductors, in laser, and in renewable energy sources. In a parallel process, which benefited from the enhanced capacity to store and analyze information, genetic engineering extended the technological revolution to the realm of living matter. This laid the foundations for biotechnology, itself an information technology with its scientific basis in the ability to decode and reprogram the information embodied in living organisms.[8]

Although the scientific foundations of these discoveries had already come into existence, over timescales varying from field to field, the relatively simultaneous emergence of these various technologies, and the synergy created by their interaction, contributed to their rapid diffusion and application, and this in turn expanded the potential of each technology and induced a broader and faster development of the new technological paradigm.[9] A key factor in this synergistic process relates to the specific nature of this process of innovation: because it is based on enhanced ability to store, retrieve, and analyze information, every single discovery, as well as every application, can be related to developments in other fields and in other applications, by continuous interactions through the common medium of information systems, and communicating by means of the common language of science, in spite of the persistence of specialization in different scientific fields.

Social, economic, and institutional factors have, as I will argue, been decisive in the coming together of these different social innovations under the form of a new technological paradigm.[10] However, the specificity of the new technologies plays a major role in the structure and evolution of this paradigm, and imposes the materiality of their internal logic on the articulation between the process of innovation and the process of social organization. The new technological paradigm is characterized by two fundamental features.[11] First, the core new technologies are *focused on information processing*. This is the primary distinguishing feature of the emerging technological paradigm. To be sure, information and knowledge have been crucial elements in all technological revolutions, since technology ultimately boils down to the ability to perform new operations, or to perform established practices better, on the basis of the application of new knowledge. However, what differentiates the current process of technological change is that *its raw material itself is information, and so is its outcome*. What an integrated circuit does is to speed up the processing of information while increasing the complexity and the accuracy of the process. What computers do is to organize the sets of instructions required for the handling of information, and, increasingly, for the generation of new information, on the basis of the combination and interaction of stored information. What telecommunications does is to transmit information, making possible flows of information exchange and treatment of information, regardless of distance, at lower cost and with shorter transmission times. What genetic engineering does is to decipher and, eventually, program the code of the living matter, dramatically expanding the realm of controllable information processing.

The output of the new technologies is also information. Their embodiment in goods and services, in decisions, in procedures, is the result of the application of their informational output, not the output itself. In this sense, the new technologies differ from former technological revolutions, and justify calling the new paradigm the "informational technological paradigm," in spite of the fact that some of the fundamental technologies involved in it (for example, superconductivity) are not information technologies. But the paradigm itself exists and articulates a convergent set of scientific discoveries by focusing on information processing and by using the newly found informational capacity to enable articulation and communication throughout the whole spectrum of technological innovations. Furthermore, with the progress of the new technological revolution, the machines themselves take second place to the creative synergy made possible by their use as sources of productivity. This trend is often referred to in the literature as the growing importance of software over hardware, a theme stimulated by the promise of research in such fields as artificial intelligence. However, this is still an open debate in scientific terms. Better design of integrated circuits, ever larger-scale integration, enhanced telecommunications capability, and the use of new material in the manufacturing of information-processing devices are in the medium-term perspective probably more important than artificial intelligence as a basis for information-handling and information-generation capacity. The fundamental trend overall seems to depend not so much on the somewhat obsolete idea of the growing dominance of software over hardware, as on the ability of new information technologies to generate new information, thus emphasizing the specific nature of their output *vis-à-vis* former technological paradigms.

The second major characteristic of the new technologies is in fact common to all major technological revolutions.[12] The main effects of their innovations are on *processes* rather than on *products*.[13] There are, of course, major innovations in products, and the surge of new products is a fundamental factor in spurring new economic growth. However, the deepest impact of innovation is associated with the transformation of processes.[14] This was also the case with the two industrial revolutions associated with technical paradigms organized respectively around the steam engine and around electricity.[15] In both cases, energy was the pivotal element which, by gradually penetrating all processes of production, distribution, transportation, and management, revolutionized the entire economy and the whole society, not so much because of the new goods and services being produced and distributed, but because of the new ways of performing the processes of production and distribution, on the basis of a new source of energy that could be decentralized and distributed in a flexible manner. The new energy-based industrial and organizational processes gave birth to goods and services, hence products, that could not even have been imagined before the diffusion of energy-processing devices. But it was the revolution in energy, with its influence on all kinds of processes, that created the opportunity for the surge in new products. Process comands products, although functional, economic, and social feedback effects are crucial to an understanding of the historical process.

Similarly, in the current informational revolution, what new information technologies are about in the first place is process. A chip has value only as a means of improving the performance of a machine for an end-use function. A computer is a tool for information handling, whose usefulness for the organization or individual using it depends on the purpose of the information-processing activity. A genetically modified cell will take on its actual significance in its interaction with the whole body. While all social and biological activities are in fact processes, some elements of these processes crystallize in material forms that constitute goods and services, the usual content of economic products. Technological revolutions are made up of innovations whose products are in fact processes.

These two major characteristics of the informational–technological paradigm[16] have fundamental effects on its impact on society. (Society itself, as stated above, frames and influences technological innovation in a dialectical relationship of which, at this point, we are only examining one factor, namely, the influence of new technologies on social organization.)

A fundamental consequence is derived from the essential process-orientation of technological innovation. Because processes, unlike products, enter into all spheres of human activity, their transformation by such technologies, focusing on omnipresent flows of information, leads to modification in the material basis of the entire social organization. Thus, new information technologies are transforming the way we produce, consume, manage, live, and die; not by themselves, certainly, but as powerful mediators of the broader set of factors that determines human behavior and social organization.

The fact that new technologies are focused on information processing has far-reaching consequences for the relationship between the sphere of socio-cultural symbols and the productive basis of society. Information is based upon culture, and information processing is, in fact, symbol manipulation on the basis of knowledge; that is, codified information verified by science and/or social experience. Thus, the predominant role of new information technologies in the process of innovation is to establish ever more intimate relationships among the culture of society, scientific knowledge, and the development of productive forces. If information processing becomes the key component of the new productive forces, the symbolic capacity of society itself, collectively as well as individually, is tightly linked to its developmental process. In other words, the structurally determined capacity of labor to process information and generate knowledge is, more than ever, the material source of productivity, and therefore of economic growth and social well-being. Yet this symbolic capacity of labor is not an individual attribute. Labor has to be formed, educated, trained, and retrained, in flexible manipulation of symbols, determining its ability constantly to reprogram itself. In addition, productive organizations, social institutions, and the overall structure of society, including its ideology, will be key elements in fostering or stalling the new information-based productive forces. The more a society facilitates the exchange of information flows, and the decentralized generation and distribution of information, the greater will be its collective symbolic capacity. It is this capacity which underlies the enhancement and diffusion of information technologies, and thus the development of productive forces.

In this sense, the new informational technological paradigm emphasizes the historical importance of the Marxian proposition on the close interaction between productive forces and social systems.[17] Perhaps it is only in the current historical period, because of the close connection between information and culture through the human mind, and thus between productivity and social organization, that such inspired anticipation bears its full meaning. However, if this perspective is to be intellectually fruitful it must be purified both from any ideological assumption of historical directionality and from any value judgment. The development of productive forces by the liberation of information flows does not require that capitalism be superseded. In fact, state-planned societies have proved more resistant to the new technological revolution than market-based economies, in contradiction of Marx's prophecy that socialism possessed a superior ability to develop productive forces. Equally unfounded is the opposite ideological position which states that market forces are innately superior in steering development in information technologies. Japan's leadership in the field has been built on strong systematic state intervention in support of national companies, to raise their technological level in pursuit of the national goal of establishing Japan as a world power on non-military grounds.

The key mechanism for the development of productive forces in the new informational technological paradigm seems to be the ability of a given social organization to educate and motivate its labor force while at the same time setting up an institutional framework that maximizes information flows and connects them to the developmental tasks. The social and political means of achieving such goals vary historically, as do the societal outcomes of the development processes. However, not all these processes are undetermined, and relationships can certainly be found between social structures, techno-economic development, and institutional goals. Nevertheless, the present purpose is more limited and more focused. It is sufficient here to pinpoint the fact that because the new productive forces are information based, their development is more closely related than ever to the characteristics of symbolic production and manipulation in every society, actually fulfilling the hypothesis proposed by Marx on the relationship between social structure and techno-economic development.

From the characteristics of the process-orientation of information-based technology, there derives a third fundamental effect of the new technological paradigm on social organization: namely, increased *flexibility* of organizations in production, consumption, and management. Flexibility, in fact, emerges as a key characteristic of the new system taking shape;[18] yet it takes place within a context of large-scale production, consumption, and management, generally associated with large organizations and/or extended organizational networks. What happens is that new technologies build on the organizational capacity resulting from the industrial form of production and consumption, particularly during its mature stage (generally associated with what has been labeled in the literature as "Fordism," a very misleading term);[19] but they contribute both to transforming this system and enhancing that organizational capacity by preserving the economies of scale and the depth of organizational power, while overcoming rigidity and facilitating constant adaptation to a rapidly changing context. In this way, the historical oppositions between craft production and large-scale manufacture, between mass consumption and customized markets, between powerful bureaucracies and innovative enterprises, are dialectically superseded by the new technological medium, which ushers in an era of adaptive organizations in direct relationship with their social environments.[20] By increasing the flexibility of all processes, new information technologies contribute to minimizing the distance between economy and society.

The organizational transition from industrialism to informationalism

The new technological paradigm has fundamental social consequences linked to the specific logic of its basic characteristics. Yet, the new technologies are themselves articulated into a broader system of production and organization, whose ultimate roots are social, but to whose development new technologies powerfully contribute.[21] It is this complex, interacting system of technology and organizational processes, underlying economic growth and social change, that we call a *mode of development.* It is not the product of new technologies, nor are the new technologies a mechanical response to the demands of the new organizational system. It is the convergence between the two processes that changes the technical relationships of production, giving rise to a new mode of development. The previous section presented in summary form the relatively autonomous evolution of technological innovation which has led to the emergence of the informational technological paradigm. This section will examine, even more succinctly, the main organizational and structural trends that characterize the transition from the industrial to the informational mode of development.

The main process in this transition is not the shift from goods to services but, as two main theorists of the "postindustrial society"[22] proposed many years ago, Alain Touraine in 1969 and Daniel Bell in 1973, the emergence of information processing as the core, fundamental activity conditioning the effectiveness and productivity of all processes of production, distribution, consumption, and management. The new centrality of information processing results from evolution in all the fundamental spheres of the industrial mode of development, under the influence of economic and social factors and structured largely by the mode of production. Specifically, the secular trend toward the increasing role of information results from a series of developments in the spheres of production, of consumption, and of state intervention.

In the sphere of *production*, two major factors have fostered information-processing activities within the industrial mode of development. The first is the emergence of the large corporation as the predominant organizational form of production and management.[23] An economy based on large-scale production and centralized management generated the growing number of information flows that were needed for efficient articulation of the system. The second resides within the production process itself (considering producton in the broad sense, that is including production of both goods and services), and is the shift of the productivity sources from capital and labor to "other factors" (often associated with science, technology, and management), as shown by the series of econometric analyses in the tradition best represented by Robert Solow.[24] The hard core of these information-processing activities is composed of knowledge, which structures and provides adequate meaning to the mass of information required to manage organizations and to increase productivity.

In the sphere of *consumption*, two parallel processes have emphasized the role of information. On the one hand, the constitution of mass markets, and the increasing distance between buyers and sellers, have created the need for specific marketing and effective distribution by firms, thus triggering a flurry of information-gathering systems and information-distributing flows, to establish the connection between the two ends of the market.[25] On the other hand, under the pressure of new social demands, often expressed in social movements, a growing share of the consumption process has been taken over by collective consumption, that is, goods and services directly or indirectly produced and/or managed by the state,[26] as a right rather than as a commodity, giving rise to the welfare state. The formation of the welfare state has produced a gigantic system of information flows affecting most people and most activities, spurring the growth of bureaucracies, the formation of service delivery agencies, and consequently the creation of millions of jobs in information handling.[27]

In the sphere of *state intervention*, the past half-century has seen a huge expansion of government regulation of economic and social activities that has generated a whole new administration, entirely made up of information flows and information-based decision processes.[28] Although variations in the mode of production lead to a bureaucratic cycle, with upswings and downturns in the trend toward regulation, state intervention is in more subtle ways a structural feature of the new mode of development, in a process that Alain Touraine has characterized as "la société programmée."[29] This is the process by which the state sets up a framework within which large-scale organizations, both private and public, define strategic goals, which may be geared toward international economic competitiveness or military supremacy, that permeate the entire realm of social activities without necessarily institutionalizing or formalizing the strategic guidance of these activities. To be able to steer a complex society without suffocating it, the modern state relies on a system of "neo-corporatist" pacts, in Philippe Schmitter's terms,[30] which mobilize and control society through a series of incentives and disincentives made up of storage of information, emission of signals, and management of instructions. The state of the informational mode of development, be it under capitalism or under statism, exercises more intervention than ever, but it does so by controlling and manipulating the network of information flows that penetrate all activities. It does not follow that society is doomed to the Orwellian vision, since the intervention of the state will be informed by the political values emerging from the dynamics of the civil society, and thus its enhanced power could be used to counteract the built-in bureaucratic tendencies of state apparatuses.[31] As Nicos Poulantzas wrote in 1978: "This statism does not refer to the univocal reinforcement of the State, but it is rather the effect of one tendency, whose two poles develop unevenly, toward the simultaneous reinforcing–weakening of the state."[32] The attempt by the state to override the contradiction between its increasing role and its decreasing legitimacy by diffusing its power through immaterial information flows greatly contributes to the dramatic explosion of information-processing activities and organizations. This is because the state sets up a series of information systems that control activities and citizens' lives through the codes and rules determined by those systems.

These structural trends, emerging and converging in a society largely dominated by the industrial mode of development, pave the way for the transformation of that mode, as information processing, with its core in knowledge generation, detracts from the importance of energy in material production, as well as from the importance of goods-producing in the overall social fabric. However, this transformation of the mode of development could not be accomplished without the surge of innovation in information technologies which, by creating the material basis from which information processing can expand its role, contributes to the change both in the structure of the production process and in the organization of society. It is in this sense that I hypothesize the formation of a new, informational mode of development: on the basis of the convergence through interaction of information technologies and information-processing activities into an articulated techno-organizational system.

The interaction between technological innovation and organizational change in the constitution of the informational mode of development

The convergence between the revolution in information technology and the predominant role of information-processing activities in production, consumption, and state regulation, leads to the rise of the new, informational mode of development. This process triggers a series of new structural contradictions which highlight the relative autonomy of technological change in the process of social transformation. In fact, the diffusion of new technologies under the new mode of development calls into question the very processes and organizational forms that were at the basis of the demand for information technologies. This is because these organizational forms were born within the industrial mode of development, under the influence of the capitalist mode of production, and generally reflect the old state of technology. As the new technologies, and the realm of the possibilities they offer, expand, those same organizational forms that were responsible for the demand for new technologies are being rendered obsolete by their development. For instance, the large corporation was critical in fostering the demand for computers. But as microcomputers increase in power and become able to constitute information systems in harness with advanced telecommunications, it is no longer the large, vertical conglomerate but the network which is the most flexible, efficient form of management.

In another crucial development, the old form of the welfare state loses relevance. Previously its operation had called for the expansion of information-processing activities: but as information itself becomes a productive force, so the social characteristics of labor reproduction (and thus of collective consumption: education, health, housing, etc.) become key elements in the development of productive forces, embodied in the cultural capacity of labor to process information. Thus, the old, redistributive welfare state becomes obsolete, not so much because it is too expensive (this is the capitalist critique, not the informational challenge), as because it has to be restructured to connect its redistributional goals with its new role as a source of productivity by means of the investment in human capital.

A third manifestation of the process of institutional change set in motion by the new technologies concerns the role of the state. The expansion of state regulatory intervention underlay the explosion of government-led information activities, enhancing its dominant role, within the limits of its legitimacy. However, rapid innovation in information technologies has created the facility for two-way information flows, making it possible for civil society to control the state on democratic priciples, without paralyzing its effectiveness as a public interest agency. In this situation, the persistence of bureaucratic aloofness, once deprived of its former technical justification, emphasizes authoritarian tendencies within the state, delegitimizes its power, and prompts calls for institutional reform toward more flexible and more responsive government agencies.

The organizational transformation of the mode of development, then, leads to the expansion of information technologies, whose effect triggers pressure for further organizational change. The informational mode of development is not a rigid structure, but a constant process of change based on the interaction between technology and organization. Yet the logic of this process of change does not depend primarily on the interaction between these two planes, for modes of development are conditioned in their historical evolution by the dynamics of specific societies, themselves largely conditioned by the contradictions and transformations of the modes of production that characterize them. More specifically, the evolution of the informational mode of development, with its changing interaction between technology and organizational structures, depends, in our societies, on the restructuring of the capitalist mode of production that has taken place in the past decade. The transition between modes of development is not independent of the historical context in which it takes place; it relies heavily on the social matrix initially framing the transition, as well as on the social conflicts and interests that shape the transformation of that matrix. Therefore, the newly-emerging forms of the informational mode of development, including its spatial forms, will not be determined by the structural requirements of new technologies seeking to fulfil their developmental potential, but will emerge from the interaction between its technological and organizational components, and the historically determined process of the restructuring of capitalism.

The Restructuring of Capitalism in the 1980s

When social systems experience a structural crisis, as a result of historical events acting on their specific contradictions, they are compelled either to change their goals, or to change their means in order to overcome the crisis. When the system changes its goals (or structural principles of performance), actually becoming a different system, there is a process of social transformation. When the system changes the institutionalized means by which it aims to achieve its systemic goals, there is a process of social restructuring. Each restructuring process leads to a new manifestation of the system, with specific institutional rules which induce historically specific sets of contradictions and conflicts, developing into new crises that potentially trigger new restructuring processes. This sequence goes on until the social equation underlying both structures and processes makes possible historical change to replace the old system by a new one.

The transformation of the capitalist mode of production on a global scale follows, in general terms, this social logic. The Great Depression of the 1930s, followed by the dislocation of World War II, triggered a restructuring process that led to the emergence of a new form of capitalism very different from the laissez-faire model of the pre-Depression era.[33] This new capitalist model, often characterized by the misleading term "Keynesianism,"[34] relied on three major structural modifications:[35]

1 A social pact between capital and labor which, in exchange for the stability of capitalist social relationships of production and the adaptation of the labor process to the requirements of productivity, recognized the rights of organized labor, assured steadily rising wages for the unionized labor force, and extended the realm of entitlements to social benefits, creating an ever-expanding welfare state.
2 Regulation and intervention by the state in the economic sphere: key initiatives in the accumulation process, stimulation of demand through public expenditures, and absorption of surplus labor by increasing public employment.

3 Control of the international economic order by intervention in the sphere of circulation via a set of new international institutions, organized around the International Monetary Fund and under the hegemony of the United States, with the imposition of the dollar (and to some extent the pound) as the standard international currency. The ordering of world economic processes included the control by the center of the supply and prices of key raw materials and energy sources, most of these being produced by a still largely colonized Third World.

This state-regulated capitalism assured unprecedented economic growth, gains in productivity, and prosperity in the core countries for about a quarter of a century. In retrospect, history will probably consider these years as the golden age of western capitalism.

As I have shown elsewhere,[36] these same structural elements that accounted for the dynamism of this model were the very factors that led to its crisis in the 1970s, under the stress of its contradictions, expressed through rampant inflation that disrupted the circulation process, and under the pressure of social movements and labor struggles whose successful social and wage demands lowered the rate of profit. The oil shocks of 1974 and 1979 were precipitant events which, acting on structurally determined inflation, drove the circulation of capital out of control, prompting the need for austerity policies and fiscal restraint, and thus undermining the economic basis for state intervention. Although in strictly economic terms the increase in oil prices was not the cause of the structural crisis, its impact was crucial in calling into question the post-World War II model of capitalism, because of the pervasive effects of energy cost and supply in an economic system relying on an industrial mode of development based upon energy.

The crisis of the system in the 1970s revealed the declining effectiveness of the mechanisms established in the 1930s and 1940s in ensuring the fulfillment of the basic goals of the capitalist economy.[37] Labor was steadily increasing its share of the product. Social movements outside the workplace were imposing growing constraints on the ability of capital and bureaucracies to organize production and society free from social control. The state entered a fiscal crisis brought on by the contradiction between growing expenditures (determined by social demands) and comparatively decreasing revenues (limited by the need to preserve corporate profits).[38] The international order was disrupted by the surge of Third World nationalism (simultaneously opposed, supported, and manipulated by the strategies of the superpowers), and by the entry into the international economy of new competitive actors. The structural difficulty of making hard choices led companies to pass costs on into prices, the state to finance its intervention through debt and money supply, and the international economy to prosper through financial speculation and irresponsible lending in the global markets. After a series of unsuccessful stop-and-go policies, the second oil shock of 1979 revealed the depth of the crisis and necessitated a restructuring process that was undertaken simultaneously by both governments and firms, while international institutions such as the IMF imposed the new economic discipline throughout the world economy.

A new model of socioeconomic organization had to be established which would be able to achieve the basic aims of a capitalist system, namely: to enhance the rate of profit for private capital, the engine of investment, and thus of growth; to find new markets, both through deepening the existing ones and by incorporating new regions of the world into an integrated capitalist economy; to control the circulation process, curbing structural inflation; and to assure the social reproduction and the economic regulation of the system through mechanisms that would not contradict those established to achieve the preceding goals of higher profit rates, expanding demand, and inflation control.

On the basis of these premises, a new model of capitalism emerged which, with national variations and diverse fortunes, actually character-izes most of the international system in the late 1980s. Reducing the new model to its essentials, we can summarize it in three major features which simultaneously address the four goals stated above as the funda-mental requirements for the restructuring of capitalism to operate successfully.

(1)   *The appropriation by capital of a significantly higher share of surplus from the production process.* This is a reversal of the historical power relationship between capital and labor, and a negation of the social pact achieved in the 1930s and 1940s. This fundamental goal is achieved by combining increases in productivity and increases in exploitation, by means of a fundamental restructuring of the work process and of the labor market which includes the following aspects:

(a)   Higher productivity derived from technological innovation, combined with the uneven distribution of the productivity gains in favor of capital.

(b)   Lower wages, reduced social benefits, and less protective working conditions.

(c)   Decentralization of production to regions or countries characterized by lower wages and more relaxed regulation of business activities.

(d)   Dramatic expansion of the informal economy, at both the core and the periphery of the system. By the informal economy is meant income-generating activities that are unregulated by the institutional system, in a context where similar activities are regulated. Much of the develop-ment of the informal economy has to do with the dismantling in practice of many provisions of the welfare state, for example, avoiding the payment of social benefits and contravening the legislation protecting workers.[39]

(e)   A restructuring of labor markets to take in growing proportions of women, ethnic minorities, and immigrants, namely, those social groups which, because of institutionalized discrimination and social stigma, are most vulnerable in society and thus in the marketplace.[40] However, it is important to observe that such vulnerability is socially determined. Should the social context change, this supposedly docile labor would not be incorporated into the new labor markets. For example, while immigration has boomed during the restructuring process in the US, it has been practically halted in western Europe. Although part of the difference has to lie in the ability of the US to create millions of new unskilled jobs, a substantial factor is the unionization and rising consciousness of immigrant workers in Europe during the 1970s, to the point where, in countries such as Switzerland and Germany, they have become the militant vanguard among factory workers.[41] It makes little sense for European management to continue to import labor which, despite its social vulnerability, could turn into a focus for militancy while not being responsive to the same mechanisms of integration that are operative with respect to native workers.

(f)   The weakening of trade unions – a fundamental, explicit goal of the restructuring process in most countries, and in fact, probably the most important single factor in achieving the overall objective of restoring the rate of profit at a level acceptable to business. By and large this objective has been achieved. Organized labor in most capitalist countries, with the exception of Scandinavia, is at the lowest point of its power and influence in the last thirty years, and its situation is still deteriorating rapidly. Some of the reasons for this decline are structural: for example, the fading away of traditional manufacturing, where the strength of the unions was concentrated, and the parallel expansion of a weakly unionized service economy. Other factors have to do directly with the transformation of labor markets, as noted under (e) above: women, often because of the sexism of the labor unions, are less unionized; many immigrants do not feel that the unions represent them; the informal economy detracts from the socializing effects of the workplace. However, organized labor has also been weakened as a result of targeted policies by both governments and firms, engaging in a deliberate effort at achieving what is perceived as a historical objective that would dramatically increase the freedom of capital to steer the economy and society.[42] Thus, Reagan's tough handling of the 1981 air traffic controllers' strike in the US, ending up with the deregistration of their union (PATCO), and the placement of the names of all the strikers in a blacklist to ban them from future Federal government employment, sent out a powerful signal that was well heard by business. Similarly, Thatcher's merciless repression of the coal miners' strike in the UK ushered in a new era of management–labor relations that put the British Trade's Union Congress on the defensive. The historical reversal of the capital–labor power relationship, encapsulated in the gradual decline of the trade union movement, is the cornerstone of the restructuring of capitalism in the 1980s.

(2)   *A substantial change in the pattern of state intervention, with the emphasis shifted from political legitimation and social redistribution to political domination and capital*

accumulation.[43] Although the "Keynesian" model regulation of capitalist growth was also a key objective, the means by which such regulation was exercised included widespread expansion of the welfare state, as well as both direct and indirect creation of public-sector jobs, stimulating demand and contributing to the reproduction of labor power. The new forms of state intervention are much more directly focused on capital accumulation, and give priority to domination over legitimation in the relationship between state and society, in response to the emergency situation in which the system found itself in the 1970s. However, in contradiction of the ideological self-representation of the restructuring process by its main protagonists, what we are witnessing is not the withdrawal of the state from the economic scene, but the emergence of a new form of intervention, whereby new means and new areas are penetrated by the state, while others are deregulated and transferred to the market. This simultaneous engagement and disengagement of the state in the economy and society is evident in several mechanisms that express the new form of state support of capitalism:

(a)   Deregulation of many activities, including relaxation of social and environmental controls in the work process.

(b)   Shrinkage of, and privatization of productive activities in, the public sector.

(c)   Regressive tax reform, favoring corporations and upper-income groups.

(d)   State support for high-technology R&D and leading industrial sectors which form the basis of the new informational economy. This support usually takes the dual form of financing infrastructure and research, and favorable fiscal policies.

(e)   Accordance of priority status to defense and defense-related industries, combining, in pursuit of the objectives of the new state, the reinforcement of military power and the stimulation of a high-technology dominated defense sector. Following an old formula of Herbert Marcuse, I will call this trend the rise of the "warfare state." Defense spending and the development of new defense industries is also a fundamental way of creating new markets to compensate for retrenchment in other public-sector expenditures, as well as for the loss of demand resulting from the lowering of wages in the production process.

(f)   Shrinkage of the welfare state, with variations within and between countries according to the relative power of affected groups.

(g)   Fiscal austerity, with the goal of a balanced budget, and tight monetary policy. These are key policies for the new model of capitalism, as the fundamental means of controlling inflation. However, while fiscal conservatism is an integral component of the new capitalism, recent historical experience shows the possibility of huge budget deficits resulting from the contradictions consequent in the implementation of the model in a given country, in particular in the US.

(3)   *The third major mechanism of the restructuring of capitalism is the accelerated internationalization of all economic processes, to increase profitability and to open up markets through the expansion of the system.*

The capitalist economy has been, since its beginnings, a world economy, as Braudel and Wallerstein have reminded us.[44] However, what is new is the increasing interpenetration of all economic processes at the international level with the system working as a unit, worldwide in real time. This is a process that has grown steadily since the 1950s and has accelerated rapidly in the 1970s and 1980s as an essential element of the restructuring process. It embraces capital movements, labor migration, the process of production itself, the interpenetration of markets, and the use of nation states as elements of support in an international competition that will ultimately determine the economic fate of all nations.

The internationalization of capitalism enhances profitability at several levels:

(a)   It allows capital to take advantage of the most favorable conditions for investment and production anywhere in the world. Sometimes this translates into low wages and lack of government regulation. In other instances, penetration of key markets or access to technology are more important considerations for the firm. But the fact remains that the increasing homogenization of the economic structure across nations allows for a variable geometry of production and distribution that maximizes advantages in terms of opportunity costs.

(b)   By allowing round-the-clock capital investment opportunities worldwide, internationalization dramatically increases the rate of turnover of capital, thus enhancing profit levels for a given profit rate, although at the cost of increasing instability built into the system.

(c)   The internationalization process also opens up new markets, and connects segments of markets across borders, increasingly differentiating societies vertically while homogenizing markets horizontally. This expansion of demand through new markets is absolutely crucial in a model that relies on the reduction of wages in the core countries, since the loss in potential demand has to be made up by the incorporation of whichever new markets may exist anywhere in the world. This is particularly important in the transitional period of restructuring, when wages have to be kept at the lowest possible level to increase profits and attract investment, while keeping demand high enough to justify new investment.

The process of internationalization offers dynamic expansion possibilities that could substantially benefit the capitalist system. But it can also pose fundamental problems to individual units of that system, be they firms or countries, which are faced with new, tougher competition from the new actors which are incorporated into the system and quickly learn the ruthlessness of the game. This has been the case for the US, which has lost market share, in both its domestic market and the international economy, to Japan and the newly-industrialized countries. Given the interdependence of economic processes and national policies, the internationalization process prepares the ground for future major crises: on the one hand, any significant downturn has immediate repercussions worldwide, and is thus amplified; on the other hand, competition constantly provokes the threat of protectionism which could wreck the very basis of the system. A system in which the interests of the totality are not necessarily the interests of each competitive unit in every moment in time could become increasingly disruptive. When "the creative destruction" process[45] takes place at the international level, the intermixing of national interests with competitive strategies becomes explosive.

The overpowering of labor by capital, the shift of the state toward the domination–accumulation functions of its intervention in economy and society, and the internationalization of the capitalist system to form a worldwide interdependent unit working in real time are the three fundamental dimensions of the restructuring process that has given birth to a new model of capitalism, as distinct from the "Keynesian" model of the 1945–75 era as that one was from "laisser-faire" capitalism.[46]

These three processes are present in most countries' recent economic policies, but their relative importance may vary considerably according to each country's history, institutions, social dynamics, and place in the world economy. Thus, the UK has emphasized the overpowering of labor as the rallying cry of the Thatcher government; the US has made the emergence of a new "warfare state," based upon high-technology development, the centerpiece of its economic recovery; Japan has saved itself much of the pain of the restructuring process by riding the crest of the internationalization wave. However, since the capitalist system is a world system at the level of the mode of production (although certainly not at the level of societies), the different dimensions of the restructuring process are interconnected across the various regions of the international economy.

Also, the actual practice of restructuring is full of contradictions. Not only social, but economic as well. For instance, in the case of the Reagan Administration in the US the dramatic defense build-up, combined with a regressive tax reform and the political inability to dismantle Social Security, led to the biggest budget deficit in American history, under one of the most ideologically committed Administrations to fiscal conservatism. The budget deficit was financed to a large extent by foreign capital, attracted by high interest rates, driving up the dollar's exchange rate. Together with declining competitiveness of American manufacturing, this evolution resulted in catastrophic trade deficits that weakened the American economy. The twin mega-deficits have spoiled to a large extent the benefits of restructuring for American capitalism and will, most likely, lead to austerity policies in the 1989–91 period that could trigger a world recession. While our purpose here goes far beyond economic forecasting we want to emphasize that the process of restructuring is by no means exempt of contradictions. While fiscal austerity was a must of the new model, and as such was formulated by its supply-side defenders, it could not actually be implemented because the political support for the boldest extremes of restructuring could not be marshalled. The artificial implementation of the model (on the basis of debt-financed military expenditures, a policy we have labeled "perverted Keynesianism")[47] could lead to its demise or to its sharpening through reinforced austerity policies, ushering in a new crisis.

However, in spite of these contradictory trends, a new model of capitalism has emerged that could outlast the forthcoming crises. One of the reasons for its likely durability, we hypothesize, is that it has encompassed in its expansion the informational mode of development that was bursting into life in a process of historical simultaneity. It is the interaction and the articulation between the informational mode of development and the restructuring of capitalism that creates the framework shaping the dynamics of our society and our space.

The Articulation between the Informational Mode of Development and the Restructuring of Capitalism: Reshaping the Techno-Economic Paradigm

The historical coincidence of the restructuring of capitalism and the rise of the informational mode of development has created a structural convergence resulting in the formation of a specific techno-economic paradigm at the very roots of our social dynamics. Because political and organizational decision-makers are always primarily concerned to perpetuate the interests they represent, and therefore concerned with the process of restructuring, it is under the dominance of that process that the merger has taken place. However, the two components of the paradigm are distinguishable only analytically, because while informationalism has now been decisively shaped by the restructuring process, restructuring could never have been accomplished, even in a contradictory manner, without the unleashing of the technological and organizational potential of informationalism.

Given the complexity of the articulation process, I will differentiate between the two dimensions that compose the informational mode of development: the *technological* and the *organizational*. Both have been fundamental in giving rise to a new form of capitalism which, in turn, has stimulated and supported the technological revolution and has adopted new organizational forms.

New *information technologies* have been decisive in the implementation of the three fundamental processes of capitalist restructuring.

(1) *Increasing the rate of profit* by various means:

(a) Enhancing productivity by the introduction of microelectronics-based machines that transform the production process.

(b) Making possible the decentralization of production, and the spatial separation of different units of the firm, while reintegrating production and management at the level of the firm by using telecommunications and flexible manufacturing systems.

(c) Enabling management to automate those processes employing labor with a sufficiently high cost level and a sufficiently low skill level to make automation both profitable and feasible. These jobs happened to be those concentrated in the large-scale factories that had become the strongholds of labor unions, and better remunerated labor, during the industrial era.

(d) Positioning capital in a powerful position *vis-à-vis* labor. Automation, flexible manufacturing, and new transportation technologies provide management with a variety of options that considerably weaken the bargaining position of the unions. Should the unions insist on preserving or improving their levels of wages and benefits, the company can automate or move elsewhere, or both, without losing its connections with the market or with the network of production. Thus, either by using automation to substitute for labor, or by extracting concessions by wielding the threat to automate or relocate, capital uses new technologies to free itself from the constraints of organized labor.

(2) New technologies are also a powerful instrument in weighting the accumulation and domination functions of state intervention. This occurs on two main levels:

(a) On the one hand, rapid technological change makes obsolete the entire existing weapons system, creating the basis for the expansion of the "warfare state" in a political environment characterized by states striving for military supremacy and therefore engaging in a technological arms race that can only be supported by the resources of the state.

(b) On the other hand, the strategic role played by high technology in economic development draws the state to concentrate on providing the required infrastructure, downplaying its role in redistributional policies.

(3) The process of *internationalization of the economy* could never take place without the dramatic breakthroughs in information technologies. Advances in telecommunications, flexible manufacturing that allows simultaneously for standardization and customization, and new transportation technologies emerging from the use of computers and new materials, have created the material infrastructure for the world economy, as the construction of the railway system provided the basis for the formation of national markets in the nineteenth century. In addition, the economic effects of new technologies are also crucial in the formation of an international economy. Their effects on process condition the international competitiveness of countries and firms. Their effects on new products create new markets in which the harshest competitive battles are fought, with new economic actors trying to short-circuit the sequence of development

by leapfrogging into state-of-the-art high-technology markets through dramatic efforts of national development. The new technological division of labor is one of the fundamental lines of cleavage in the emerging international economic order.

The *organizational* components of the informational mode of development are also fundamental features in the restructuring process. Three major organizational characteristics of informationalism may be distinguished, each of them affecting the three dimensions of the restructuring process.

(1)   There is a growing *concentration of knowledge-generation and decision-making processes in high-level organizations* in which both information and the capacity of processing it are concentrated. The informational world is made up of a very hierarchical functional structure in which increasingly secluded centers take to its extreme the historical division between intellectual and manual labor. Given the strategic role of knowledge and information control in productivity and profitability, these core centers of corporate organizations are the only truly indispensable components of the system, with most other work, and thus most other workers, being potential candidates for automation from the strictly functional point of view. How far this tendency toward widespread automation is actually taken in practice is a different matter, depending on the dynamics of labor markets and social organization.

   This concentration of information power in selected segments of the corporate structure greatly favors the chances of the restructuring process in the three dimensions presented:

   (a)   Productive labor can be reduced to its essential component, thus downgrading the objective bargaining power of the large mass of functionally dispensable labor.
   (b)   The rise of the technocracy within the state displaces the traditional integrative functions of the politically determined bureaucracy, establishing a tight linkage between the high levels of the state and the corporate world through the intermediary of the scientific establishment. The rise of the meritocracy, using the notion advanced by Daniel Bell, establishes new principles of legitimacy in the state, further removing it from the political controls and constituencies represented by the diversity of social interests.
   (c)   As technology transfer becomes the key to competition in the international economy, that process is controlled by knowledge holders in the centers of the dominant scientific and corporate organizations. It follows that the effective accomplishment of the internationalization process requires access to those knowledge centers, ruling out the adoption of an isolationist stance, which would only lead to the technological obsolescence of those economies and firms holding it.

(2)   The second major organizational characteristic of informationalism concerns the *flexibility* of the system and of the relationships among its units, since flexibility is both a requirement of and a possibility offered by new information

technologies.[48] Flexibility acts powerfully as a facilitator of the restructuring process in the following ways:

(a)   It changes capital–labor relationships, transforming a potentially permanent and protected worker status into a flexible arrangement generally
adapted to the momentary convenience of management. Thus,
temporary workers, part-time jobs, homework, flexitime schedules,
indefinite positions in the corporate structure, changing assignments,
varying wages and benefits according to performance, etc., are all
creative expedients of management that, while they increase tremendously the flexibility and thus the productivity of the firm, undermine
the collective status of labor *vis-à-vis* capital.

(b)   In the restructuring of the state, organizational flexibility contributes to
the formation of public–private partnerships and to the blurring of
the distinction between the public and private spheres. Segments of the
welfare state are being shifted to the private sector, corporations are
being brought into the formulation of public policies, and a selective
interpenetration of state and capital is diminishing the autonomy of the
state, along the lines of the "recapitalization" of the state, characteristic
of the restructuring process.[49]

(c)   Flexibility is also a necessary condition for the formation of the new
world economy, since it is the only organizational form that allows
constant adaptation of firms to the changing conditions of the world
market.[50]

(3)   A third fundamental organizational characteristic of informationalism is the shift from *centralized* large corporations to *decentralized* networks made up of a plurality of sizes and forms of organizational units.[51] Although networking increases flexibility, it is actually a different characteristic, since there are forms of flexibility that do not require networks. These networks, which could not exist on such a large scale without the medium provided by new information tech-nologies, are the emerging organizational form of our world, and have played a fundamental role in ensuring the restructuring process:

(a)   They are the prevalent form of the informal economy, as well as of the
sub-contracting practices that have disorganized and reorganized the
labor process, enhancing capital's profitability.[52]

(b)   They have provided the model for the constitution of the new warfare
state, on the basis of the interaction between different specialized
government agencies, the defence industry, high-technology firms, and
the scientific establishment.

(c)   They are the organizational form used by major multinational corporations that have established variable strategic alliances to compete in the
international economy.[53] Unlike the tendency of the industrial mode of
development toward oligopolistic concentration, in the informational
era large corporations set up specific alliances for given products,
processes, and markets: these alliances vary according to time and space,
and result in a variable geometry of corporate strategies that follow the

logic of the multiple networks where they are engaged rather than the monolithic hierarchy of empire conglomerates.

Networks, on the basis of new transformation technologies, provide the organizational basis for the transformation of socially and spatially based relationships of production into flows of information and power that articulate the new flexible system of production and management. The restructuring of capitalism has used the adaptive potential of organizational networking to find breathing room for its "creative–destructive" energy, hitherto constrained by the social and political bonds inflicted upon it by a society reluctant to be but a commodity. The libertarian spirit of capitalism finally found itself at home at the last frontier where organizational networks and information flows dissolve locales and supersede societies. Informationalism and capitalism have historically merged in a process of techno-economic restructuring whose social consequences will last far beyond the social events and political circumstances that triggered the decisions leading to its development in the 1980s.

Notes

1   The social theory underlying this analysis cannot be fully presented in the context of this chapter, which addresses a specific research topic. However, it is intellectually important to relate this study to the overall theoretical framework that informs it. The elaboration of this theory has built upon several classical traditions: Marx for the analysis of class relationships; Freud and Reich for the understanding of personality on the basis of sexual and family relationships; Weber for the analysis of the state. A number of contemporary social scientists have been crucial to my understanding of links and developments not covered in the classical writings: Nicos Poulantzas, for the recasting of the theory of social classes and the state; Alain Touraine for his analysis on postindustrialism; Nancy Chodorow for the intellectual connection between feminist theory and the psychoanalytical tradition; Agnes Heller, for the understanding of the historical creation of social needs; and Michel Foucault and Richard Sennett for the connection between power and culture. In making explicitly known my theoretical sources, I hope to help place this brief summary of my underlying theoretical framework in the ongoing intellectual debates in social sciences.

2   Under the term "human-modified matter" I would include what could be called at the risk of paradox, "immaterial matter," that is, the set of symbols and communication codes that are generated by the human mind and which, while they are intangible, are a fundamental part of matter, since they are indeed a material force. One way to understand the informational mode of development, that I will not explore at present, could be the shift from physical matter to mental matter in the process of expansion of nature.

3   The definition is from Harvey Brooks, cited in Daniel Bell, *The Coming of Post-industrial Society* (New York, Basic Books, 1973) p. 29 of the 1976 edition.

4   Ibid.

5   Alain Touraine, *La Société post-industrielle* (Paris, Denoel, 1969); Radovan Richta, *La Civilisation au carrefour* (Paris, Anthropos, 1969); Bell, *Post-industrial Society.*

6   For a summary, informed presentation of the rise and implications of information technology see, for instance, Tom Forester, *High Tech Society: The Story of the Information Technology Revolution* (Oxford, Blackwell, 1987); also Bruce R. Guile (ed.), *Information Technologies and Social Transformation* (Washington DC, National Academy Press, 1985).

7   See E. Braun and S. MacDonald, *Revolution in Miniature* (Cambridge, Cambridge University Press, 1982).

8   See Edward J. Sylvester and Lynn C. Klotz, *The Gene Age: Genetic Engineering and the Next Industrial Revolution* (New York, Scribner, 1983).

9   See John S. Mayo, "The Evolution of Information Technologies," in Guile, *Information Technologies,* pp. 7–33.

10   Nathan Rosenberg, "The Impact of Historical Innovation: A Historical View," in Ralph Landau and Nathan Rosenberg (eds), *The Positive Sum Strategy: Harnessing Technology for Economic Growth* (Washington DC, National Academy Press, 1986).

11   See Melvin Kranzberg, "The Information Age: Evolution or Revolution," in Guile, *Information Technologies,* pp. 35–55.

12   See Melvin Kranzberg and Carroll W. Pursell, Jr (eds), *Technology in Western Civilization* (New York, Oxford University Press, 1967), 2 vols.

13   I. Mackintosh, *Sunrise Europe: The Dynamics of Information Technology* (Oxford, Blackwell, 1986).

14   Nathan Rosenberg, *Perspectives on Technology* (Cambridge, Cambridge University Press, 1976).

15   See Eugene S. Ferguson, "The Steam Engine before 1830," John R. Brae, "Energy Conversion," and Harold I. Sharlin, "Applications of Electricity," in Kranzberg and Pursell, *Technology in Western Civilization.*

16   For the notion of "technical paradigm" see the analysis in Carlota Perez, "Structural Change and the Assimilation of New Technologies in the Economic and Social Systems," *Futures,* 15 (1983), pp. 357–75.

17   Marx developed his most far-reaching analysis of the social implications of technology in the *Grundrisse.*

18   See Robert Boyer and Benjamin Coriat, *Technical Flexibility and Macro Stabilisation,* paper presented at the Venice Conference on Innovation Diffusion, 17–21 March 1986 (Paris, CEPREMAP, 1986).

19   For an analysis of "Fordism" see Robert Boyer, *Technical Change and the Theory of Regulation* (Paris, CEPREMAP, 1987).

20   Michael Piore and Charles Sabel, *The Second Industrial Divide* (New York, Basic Books, 1984).

21   See the fundamental work on the whole series of issues discussed in this chapter, Peter Hall and Paschal Preston, *The Carrier Wave: New Information Technology and the Geography of Innovation, 1846–2003* (London, Unwin Hyman, 1988).

22   For a discussion of postindustrialism, see Manuel Castells, *The Economic Crisis and American Society* (Oxford, Blackwell, 1980), pp. 164–78.

23   Alfred D. Chandler, *The Visible Hand* (Cambridge, Cambridge University Press, 1977).

24 Robert Solow, "Technical Changes and the Aggregate Production Function," in *Review of Economics and Statistics*, August 1957. For a summary of the debate on the sources of productivity, see Richard R. Nelson, "Research on Productivity Growth and Productivity Differences: Dead Ends and New Departures," in *Journal of Economic Literature*, XIX (September 1981), pp. 1029–64.

25 I have relied for this analysis on Nicole Woolsey-Biggart, "Direct Sales and Flexible Market Strategies," forthcoming.

26 Manuel Castells, "Collective Consumption and Urban Contradictions in Advanced Capitalism," in Leo Lindberg et al. (eds), *Stress and Contradiction in Modern Capitalism* (Lexington, Mass., Heath, 1974).

27 Morris Janowitz, *Social Control of the Welfare State* (Chicago, University of Chicago Press, 1976).

28 Michel Aglietta, *Une Théorie de la régulation économique: le cas des Etats-Unis* (Paris, Calmann-Levy, 1976).

29 Alain Touraine, *La Voix et Le Regard* (Paris, Seuil, 1978).

30 Philippe Schmitter, *Interest Conflict and Political Change in Brazil* (Stanford, Stanford University Press, 1981).

31 Gordon Clark and Michael Dear, *State Apparatus* (Boston, Allen & Unwin, 1984).

32 Nicos Poulantzas, *L'Etat, le pouvoir, le socialisme* (Paris, Presses Universitaires de France, 1978), p. 226 (my translation).

33 See James O'Connor, *Accumulation Crisis* (Oxford, Blackwell, 1984).

34 Post-Depression capitalism did not actually follow the policies proposed by Keynes: the state acted on supply as much as on demand. It would be more appropriate to refer to this form of capitalism as state-regulated capitalism.

35 See Michel Aglietta, *Régulation et crises du capitalisme* (Paris, Calmann-Levy, 1976).

36 For the analysis of the causes of the economic crisis of the 1970s and of the potential way out of it through the restructuring process, see Castells, *The Economic Crisis and American Society*.

37 Samuel Bowles et al., *Beyond the Wasteland* (New York, Doubleday, 1983).

38 See James O'Connor's classic, *The Fiscal Crisis of the State* (New York, St. Martin's, 1973).

39 See Manuel Castells and Alejandro Portes, "World Underneath: The Origins, Dynamics and Consequences of the Informal Economy," in Alejandro Portes, Manuel Castells, and Lauren Benton (eds), *The Informal Economy* (Baltimore, Johns Hopkins University Press, 1989).

40 Michael Reich, *Discrimination in Labor Markets* (Princeton, Princeton University Press, 1982).

41 Manuel Castells, "Immigrant Workers and Class Struggle in Western Europe," *Politics and Society*, 2 (1975).

42 Joel Krieger, *Reagan, Thatcher and the Politics of Decline* (New York, Oxford University Press, 1986).

43 I rely here on an analysis of the state, adapted from Nicos Poulantzas' work, that sees the state's relatively autonomous actions taking place within a dialectical process of ensuring domination and accumulation on the one hand, while trying to maintain legitimation and redistribution on the other. For an attempt at using these concepts in empirical research,

see   Manuel Castells and Francis Godard, *Monopolville* (Paris, Mouton, 1974).

44   Fernand Braudel, *Capitalisme et civilisation matérielle* (Paris, Armand Colin, 1979); Immanuel Wallerstein, *The Modern World System* (New York, Academic Press, 1974).

45   By the "creative destruction" of capitalism I refer, of course, to the notion proposed by Schumpeter in his *Business Cycles*.

46   Robert Boyer (ed.), *Capitalismes fin de siècle* (Paris, Presses Universitaires de France, 1986).

47   See our analysis of "Reaganomics" in Martin Carnoy and Manuel Castells, "After the Crisis?," in *World Policy Journal*, May 1984.

48   On the role of flexibility see Boyer and Coriat, *Technical Flexibility*.

49   The notion of the "recapitalization" of the state has been proposed by S. M. Miller.

50   For an analysis of flexibility in enhancing competitiveness in the international economy, see Manuel Castells, "Small Business in the World Economy: The Hong Kong Model of Economic Development", Berkeley Roundtable on the International Economy (Berkeley, University of California, forthcoming).

51   On the analysis of networks see Piore and Sabel, *The Second Industrial Divide;* and Woolsey-Biggart, "Direct Sales."

52   For evidence on the fundamental role of networks in the informal economy, see Portes, Castells, and Benton, *The Informal Economy*.

53   See Peter Schulze, "Shifts in the World Economy and the Restructuring of Economic Sectors: Increasing Competition and Strategic Alliances in Information Technologies" (Berkeley, University of California, Institute of International Studies, 1987).

5

The Economics of Postwar Regional Disparity

Ann R. Markusen

In the postwar period, American regions have again been host to major political disagreement. These antagonisms have arisen from unique sectoral specializations within the capitalist economy, from disparate pressures exerted on regional economies in the process of international integration, and from dramatically skewed military spending patterns. This chapter reviews the major contemporary forces operating on regional economies.

In this chapter, three forces shaping contemporary regional economic differentiation and change are charted: (1) the growing specializations of individual regions in the new international division of labor, (2) the profit cycle behavior of individual sectors, and (3) the growing militarization of production in the United States. Each has contributed to the unique set of issues and adjustments confronted by north versus south, east versus west, and interior versus perimeter. The final section treats the interactions among all three. The net result has been the growing disparity in north–south growth rates, an exacerbation of east–west sectoral distinctiveness, and a growing cleavage between coastal regions and the interior in both rate and composition of economic development. These set the stage for renewed regional hostilities in the 1970s and 1980s.

Reprinted by permission from Ann Markusen, 1987, *Regions*.

The New International Division of Labor

The growing integration of the international economy has dramatically affected existing domestic economies.[1] Restless geographical expansion has been a hallmark of capitalist development for the past century and a half. However, the pace of change does seem to have accelerated, creating adjustment problems on a massive scale. In addition, irreversible institutional alterations are channeling economic energies in novel directions. The underlying dynamic is the incessant search on the part of owners and managers of capital to find new markets, cheaper labor and raw materials, and more congenial public sector attitudes. Business strategies may concentrate on reshaping an existing built environment or labor force, as for instance downtown urban renewal has in the postwar period. Or, more significant for regionalism, they may take on an explicitly spatial dimension, where production activities are shifted from one region to another to secure higher levels of profitability and to discipline labor and political coalitions in the regions of origin.[2]

Several features of evolving capitalist economic structure are particularly central to an interpretation of regional politics in the postwar period: accelerated market penetration, the transformation of labor market characteristics, the rise of international oligopolistic firms with spatially segregated functions, and the state as a major planner and distributor. Together these forces have undermined the status of the United States as the preeminent industrial economy. Internally they have left their mark most dramatically in growing sectoral differentiation and in severe north–south and coastal–interior growth differentials.

Accelerated international market penetration

First, there has been a qualitative leap in the degree of market interpenetration in the postwar period. Aggressive international marketing was first pursued by corporations from advanced capitalist countries – Coca-Cola is perhaps the best known example – and was a complement to the search for raw materials (furs, precious metals, and agricultural produce). By the postwar period, more than two centuries of imperialism had irreversibly destroyed the older forms of subsistence economy prevailing in most Third World countries and had imposed upon them a wage labor, commodity exchange economy. Textiles, shoes, toys, and apparel began to be produced in these countries and imported into industrialized countries.

By the mid-1960s, consumer goods imports were joined by durables like autos and producer goods like steel. Heightened competition also came about through expanded trade and new investments by leading multinationals in each other's territory. By the mid-1970s, the growing competitiveness of both these types of imports resulted in an acceleration in their successful penetration of new markets. Steel imports into the United States, for instance, rose from about 5 percent of the domestic tonnage consumption in 1960 to about 22 percent by 1980 and 26 percent by 1985. Overall, by early 1986, manufactured imports had reached 21 percent of the domestic market.

This massive interpenetration of national economies owes much to improved techniques of communication and transportation. The net effect of telecommunications innovations and of new commodity-moving machines such as the super-tanker and the cargo airplane has been to lower the cost of negotiating exchanges across space. Where transport costs were once prohibitive, the Japanese can now import coal from the American west and iron ore from Australia, make steel in Japan, and reship it back to the West Coast of the United States, where it has so successfully undersold its domestic competitors that virtually all integrated steel capacity is in danger of final shutdown. Furthermore, rapid and cheap communications technology permits very rapid servicing of these American markets by plants in Japan without large inventories.

The 1970s acceleration of market interpenetration is also a product of the extraordinary destruction and subsequent wholesale rebuilding of industrial capacity in the losing nations after the war. Investment is always a relatively lumpy process, where new rounds of construction of the most modern plants put a newcomer country or region at the lead of an industry for a decade or more. The full impact of the extaordinary reinvestment in Japan and Germany following the war tended to bunch up in the late 1960s and 1970s, when their relatively new and "best practice" plants (in steel, chemicals, autos, and consumer electronics) far outdistanced the serviceable but outdated American capacity, which dates back as far as the early decades of the century (in the case of steel) or to the interwar period (autos).

In response to heightened competition, corporate leaders in most industrialized countries have found a means of overcoming their domestic cost disadvantages by directly locating plants in newly industrializing nations or by selling them the technology they need to build their own. The largest, most modern steel mill in the world was constructed in South Korea; the Japanese steel corporations have been willing advisors and suppliers of the technology. Increasingly, US corporations are producing major components for their domestically assembled autos overseas – particularly high-value-to-bulk items such as engines and transmissions. Where corporations in advanced capitalist countries once maintained their competitiveness by constantly harnessing the most superior technologies, enabling them to pay workers relatively higher wages because productivity was so much higher, this route is no longer a viable one. Technologies themselves have become commodities and are now available in very short order to any would-be producer in any global location. In addition, institutional changes in the nature of corporations and financial institutions (addressed below) have made money capital much easier to shift around spatially.

The major spatial consequences of this market interpenetration are (1) the dramatic sectoral recomposition of the US economy and (2) growing regional disparities in growth rates. Manufacturing sectors which had been major supporters as well as domestic suppliers shrank under the inundation of imports, first in consumer goods and more recently in capital goods. Business, finance, and transportation services, on the other hand, boomed. Spatially, this dramatic new specialization in the US trade role meant the displacement of large segments of manufacturing in the Northeast, and later, Midwest, while the new world cities of New York, Los Angeles, Miami, and Chicago (international agricultural trade) trans- formed their central city economies. Meanwhile import pressure accelerated internal migration of capital from the older, unionized manu- facturing centers, including parts of California as well as the "rust belt," to the underdeveloped, nonunionized south.[3]

Qualitative changes in the international labor force

Increasingly, then, the high level of market interpenetration, with its consequences in the diminished ability of any one nation to police its own economy, is a product of the elimination of barriers to commodity, capital, and technology movements across national boundaries. These changes have taken place without a concomitant removal of barriers to labor movement across the same boundaries. As a consequence, the differen- tial development of the labor force among nations becomes the major distinguishing characteristic of the new international division of labor. The nature of the labor force – its skills, its culture, its degree of internal homogeneity, its own class institutions – in any one country is of course a product of a long period of cultural evolution. In the twentieth century, the nature of the labor force in both industrialized and Third World countries has changed dramatically both as a result of the maturation of class conflict between capital and labor, and as a product of the role which the state has taken on in arbitrating this conflict in paving the way for capital internationally.

While capital and corporations have become increasingly inter- national, even to the point of losing their national identities, the labor force in most nations remains highly local in character. At best, in advanced capitalist countries, it may have a national organizational and political presence. But to date, it has no international unity or presence to speak of. Two parallel transformations have occurred over the course of the last century in the industrialized and Third World countries of the capitalist sphere and each is central to the character of contemporary regional labor differentiation.

In the industrialized countries with capitalist modes of production, important segments of the working class have managed to surmount ethnic differences, corporate and state violence (Carnegie's Pinkertons or the state militia, for instance), intraclass distinctions (such as occupational differences), cultural proscriptions (religious virtues such as meekness), and prior threats of corporate mobility to build strong working-class economic and political institutions. In Europe, these not only encompass workplace organizations which are joined into national industrial unions (although with competing political ties) but include national political parties which are significant contenders for State power. In the United States, where this latter phenomenon of a national labor party is absent, trade unions have a major role within many basic industries and do form a respectable caucus within the Democratic party. In many industrial regions within these countries, the role of unions in social life and community politics is even stronger.

As a result of continual struggle over the past century or more for gains both in and out of the workplace, these working-class organizations have achieved substantial gains. Among them we might list the forty-hour work week, a living wage, child labor laws, the legal right to organize, time-and-a-half for overtime, seniority rights, pensions, unemployment compensation, the right to bargain, the right to strike, social welfare programs, social security, a national commitment to full employment, occupational health and safety, automatic cost-of-living adjustments, and a clean and safe environment. Each of these represents a fetter of some sort on the organization of production and thus an additional charge on the cost of doing business, which cuts into corporate profitability.

It is logical that capitalists and their organizations, both corporate and political, would choose to oppose these innovations and that they would seek to avoid them in whatever manner possible. As long as barriers to international trade and production kept individual economies isolated, labor was relatively "scarce" and capital had few alternatives. Indeed, as Hobsbawm has argued, the relative scarcity of labor explains much of the inducement to substitute highly productive machinery for men in nineteenth-century American agriculture. It also kept wages relatively high for a large portion of skilled laborers, resulting in a tremendously strong internal market for manufactured commodities that helped propel US industrial development. Yet once new reservoirs of cheaper labor opened up, and despite the extraordinary depressive effects on the home economy, corporations have been eager to escape a well-developed set of working-class institutions for more acquiescent sites elsewhere.

The creation of these new sources of labor through the transformation of work and subsistence in Third World countries is the accompanying process which permits successful relocation of production abroad. The traditional rural subsistence economies of many Third World countries have been irrevocably altered by the introduction of capitalist agriculture. Tremendous consolidation of landholdings and dispossession of native groups has often accompanied this centuries-long pattern of supplanting cultivation for use with cash crop exports. In addition, large productivity increases in some forms of agriculture make small-scale commercial agriculture unviable, so that even in cases where an indigenous population maintains ownership of the land, modest levels of trade that provide a little cash income dry up. Both land ownership patterns and productivity changes have converted a large portion of rural subsistence farmers into wage laborers in agriculture. Since the structure of the agricultural sector does not absorb enough of the displaced subsistence workers, many become members of a migratory wage labor force drawn to cities where job possibilities exist in industry and the informal economy.

This newly-formed labor pool is not attractive to industrial employers, however, unless it lacks the organizational strength, wage demands, working conditions, and social services that prevail in advanced capitalist countries. In developing countries, the more youthful labor force is relatively less skilled and acculturated to capitalist workplace behavior. While there are instances of labor organizing in Third World countries, in most cases the absence of a long-term stable urban community, the repressive attitudes of government, and the wariness of multinational corporations about any effort to assert working-class rights all contribute to a pacific labor front. As a result, wages are in some cases one-tenth of what they are in industrialized countries, and there are few work stoppages, few demands for a safe and healthful working environment, and no well-developed employer-supported unemployment compensation systems. It seems probable that workers' rights to organize and to a decent wage will indeed be pressed in the future in these countries. But for the present, great discrepancies between the cultures and standards of living of workers in the two spheres are major inducements to relocate production abroad.

Ironically, and despite the formidable border barriers erected by industrialized countries, this same discrepancy serves as a tremendous incentive to Third World workers to migrate to the United States.[4] Particularly in regions like the Southwest and Florida, they have been relatively successful in avoiding immigration restrictions, often with the collaboration of agribusinesses who are eager to use them in seasonal, low-paid field work. In these states, they increasingly form a low-skilled labor pool, which in turn has lured apparel producers and other light assembly operations to these regions. Due to fear of deportation, these workers are often difficult to organize and do not demand the same rights as resident workers. And so, to a certain extent, the international division of labor seeps home, even without the legitimacy and resources available to the movers of capital. In sum, then, the quantitative expansion of the international labor force available to capitalist firms and its qualitative transformation toward a more highly skilled but less organizationally developed pool quickened the international migration of capital toward southern locations. This shift was complemented by the considerable immigration of workers from poorer nations into southern and coastal regions, where they broadened the labor pool and involuntarily constituted a damper on wage rates and unionization efforts.

Qualitative changes in corporate form and behavior

Several evolving features of twentieth-century business structure have important implications for regional differentiation and change. These are: (1) the dominance of oligopolies in major commodity lines since the turn of the century; (2) the increasing tendency within the corporation to institutionally separate its planning, management, and production activities; (3) the emergence of the conglomerate as the major new form of corporate structure; and (4) the increasingly multinational nature of operations. In some cases these have merely accelerated existing tendencies toward spatial decentralization. In other cases they have had distinct retarding or reorienting effects. Each deserves separate consideration.

The arrival, beginning in the late nineteenth century, of the oligopoly as a common form of producer collusion to control the market ushered in quite distinctive forms of corporate behavior. Oligopolies, such as US Steel and its few sizeable competitors, the Duke Tobacco Trust, or the pure monopoly Aluminum Company of America (ALCOA), could engineer the stabilization of price levels which had previously formed the major element in market competition. Their attention could then be turned to managing the market through market research, sales efforts, product rather than price competition (as in the frequent style changes in consumer commodities), the exercise of political power, and efforts to discipline workers internally.

The invidious competition among the few giants in many of these industries and their mutual need for mutual monitoring of each other's actions resulted in a tendency for these firms to overcentralize production in the locations where the oligopoly was first formed (Pittsburgh in steel, Detroit in autos, Milwaukee in brewing, and Akron in rubber). Concomitantly, newly-developing areas which might otherwise have sprouted their own indigenous firms were retarded in their receipt of new capacity, often (as was the case with west coast steel) through direct buy-outs of local firms by the dominant corporations and their decisions continually to expand capacity in the core regions. In some cases, including steel and autos, this spatial imbalance was reinforced by the popularity of the "basing point" system for colluding on prices – an automatic price leadership system where all steelmakers would quote the "Pittsburgh Plus" price of delivered steel regardless of their own location or cost of production.[5]

At the same time, the prominence of a paricular oligopoly within a region, while providing more direct jobs locally than would a competitive structure, will tend to squeeze out entrepreneurs in unrelated sectors whose entry might have helped to diversify the region. The dominant sectors – again, steel and autos are an outstanding example – have first pick of the labor force, create the regional social structure for white collar employees, control internally a large portion of regional capital, and have extraordinary sway with local politicians. All of these features make the particular regional economy quite vulnerable to a downturn or the permanent demise of the oligopolistic sector around which their economies have been structured.

The increasing size and concentration of corporate operations has also produced a qualitative change in the nature of production activities at any one site. It used to be that the corporate headquarters, research and development labs, planning and sales divisions, division management, and actual production all were sited on the same large lot. As multidivisional corporations emerged, these began to be located in separate buildings although often within the same urban area. But beginning in the interwar period and accelerating since World War II, these various functions, each of which has quite different land, labor, and transportation requirements, have increasingly been spatially segregated.[6] Nowadays, a headquarters may be located in New York (where it may have moved from more provincial origins), its R&D labs may be in Chapel Hill, North Carolina; its divisional management in regional centers like Des Moines, Iowa and Denver, Colorado; and its actual production facilities in small towns like Cloquet, Minnesota and Cedar City, Utah.

As a result, the labor force across these locations is becoming increasingly segregated. There are significant differences in the composition of streams of labor migration from and toward each type of city (professional and technical workers to Silicon Valley and Boston, for example, and lower-skilled production workers to the outskirts of Phoenix). In addition, most sites now have spatial competitors rendering them much more vulnerable to punitive closings actions by the absentee management. Headquarters cities like New York, San Francisco, Los Angeles, and a few others might be exceptions, but in a similar manner, they may now be forced to compete with each other to fill newly-built downtown office space with trade and management-related business services.

The evolution of the conglomerate as the dominant form of large corporation has also contributed to an accleration in the patterns of regional differentiation and change. The conglomerate, which combines disparate types of commodity production under one organizational roof, permits a super layer of management to treat each of its product lines as an element in a larger "portfolio." Acting as its own internal banker, broker, and capital market, it can shift profits from one operation to another or decide to close lower-return operations in order to diversify into yet other lines, often by merger rather than in-house expansion. Bluestone and Harrison (1982) offer convincing evidence that the conglomerate form hastens the dispersal of production activities to lower-cost sites and tends to encourage the "milking" of relatively efficient but older plants to provide short-run returns without reinvesting in plant, equipment, and maintenance.

In addition to diversifying across sectors, the major corporations are also increasingly operating across national boundaries. This gives them greater flexibility in trading off among differently composed ensembles of productive environments. Multinational capabilities are embodied in nonproduction headquarters personnel whose job it is to research the international production and market possibilities, make connections with foreign suppliers, brokers, and governments, and plan global output and exchange. The transnational character of leading corporations leads to an exacerbation in the segregation of management, control, and production functions discussed above and accelerates the rate at which capital can be redeployed across national boundaries. In some cases, through joint ventures, the national character of corporations is itself disappearing, with dramatic implications for the role of national governments.

All three of the forces analyzed so far – international integration, labor force transformations, and alterations in corporate structure, have contributed to internal realignments in US economic structure. The resulting regional differentials are paradoxical, for it would seem that each force ought to contribute to increasing homogenization across territory. Yet the opposite is occurring – the net result has been greater spatial separation of production versus circulation functions, heightened sectoral differentiation, and increasingly divergent growth trajectories. Capital's ability to take advantage of land-based and labor-based differentials leads to greater growth disparities in eras of rapid territorial expansion.

Changes in the role of the State

It is often alleged that national governments are more involved in the economy today than they have been in the past. This growing role is perhaps overstated – consider the role of nation-states in the mercantilist eighteenth century and the American land disposal and infrastructure programs (especially railroads) in the nineteenth century. However, the nature of central government intervention has indeed changed over time and certain of its present features are important, though often unintended, contributors to regional change.[7]

Domestically, the federal government has been a major contributor to regional differentiation through the enormous defense budget. This phenomenon is explored at greater length in the next section. The interstate freeway system, initiated in 1956 and still under construction, has been a second major contributor to regional differentiation. Its network of highways has dramatically shifted low-cost locations from central city to suburban areas and from the manufacturing belt to outlying areas. The energy programs of the federal government in the 1970s, which rapidly stepped up the pace of exploration, construction and production from Alaska through the Black Mesa in Arizona, is a third major contributor.

Federal government actions with less explicitly regional orientations have also contributed to the changing economic structures of regions. The national tax code, for instance, particularly the nature of the investment tax credit and the allowances for accelerated depreciation, have consistently favored new plants over older ones, and new investment over maintenance as a survival strategy.[8] Similarly, housing policies granting tax breaks for new construction have played a similar role. On another front, the failure of the federal government to assume responsibility for uniform welfare standards across the country and for the guarantee of worker's rights to organize in all states have both exacerbated the inter-state movement of jobs and capital.

A final and perhaps unintended federal government factor in internal spatial restructuring has been the increased mobility permitted students and retired people from the federal education and social security programs. When students and older people were largely supported by their families, their residence was much more closely tied to the latter's. A significant portion of the internal migration of recent years, both inter-regional and from urban to more rural areas within regions, has consisted of people in these life stages.

Not only has the role of the State contributed to a growing internal division of work and residence and to diverging rates of regional growth, but it has been a major player in the international sphere, helping to create the extraordinarily favorable conditions for the international migration of capital. Aggressive marketing (often tied to aid) of US commodities like agricultural surpluses, with their depressing effects on Third World countries' abilities to develop their own agricultural sectors, led to the latter's efforts to build "import-substituting" sectors and later, manufacturing export sectors, to help adverse balance of payments from debt, agriculture, and capital imports. International agencies like the World Bank, largely under the control of the US government, were central in selecting the countries and sectors to be favored with large loans for industrialization. Support for repressive regimes has helped to create the docile and disenfranchised labor pools that multinational corporations find so attractive in the contemporary period. Thus, State posture has augmented the uneven regional development created by private-sector internationalization.

Profit Cycles and Sectoral Differentiation

The new international division of labor has indeed placed generic stresses on regions with differential degrees of capitalistic maturation. However, differences in contemporary regional experience cannot be laid solely to these economy-wide phenomena. Cities like Detroit, Pittsburgh, Cleveland, Chicago, and St Louis have had highly varied fortunes recently despite their common membership in a larger manufacturing belt with well-developed working-class organizations and a local state commitment to a decent social wage. What distinguishes them from each other are the relatively unique sectoral configurations of their local economies. Regions and cities manifesting strong regional consciousness or severe planning problems often owe their politics and predicament to one or more sectors which dominate the local economy.

It can be argued that individual sectors (aluminum, autos, brewing, chemicals, and so on) display quite distinct forms of competition and corporate strategy at any given time.[9] Most sectors do appear to pass through a life cycle across which the conditions governing profitability are quite different in sequential periods. Production and marketing decisions, including where to locate plants and jobs, vary in a relatively predictable manner as the source of profit changes. In a formulation I call the profit cycle, four stages can be identified: an innovative stage of superprofits, a competitive stage of "normal" profits, an oligopolistic stage of monopolistic profits, and an obsolescent stage of profit squeeze.

1. Innovation, superprofits, and agglomeration

When a new industry is "born," as for instance the steel industry in the 1870s or the electronics industry in the 1960s, it generally enjoys an initial era of extraordinary growth and high returns.[10] These superprofits, defined as the difference of revenues over cost per unit, arise from the special use value that the new commodity has in contrast to existing methods or products.[11] In the short run, potential competitors will have a difficult time entering the new market, for lack of expertise, delays in organizational formation, and the discouraging presence of patents. Superprofits will not necessarily make original entrepreneurs rich, since they will immediately be plowed back into new capital expenditures and experimentation to expand the business and to maintain market leadership.

In an innovative era, the firms forming a new sector will tend to cluster around one or a few nodes. These sites may be close to existing pools of professional–technical labor and corporate headquarters, or they may be in quite accidental locations (an inventor's or founder's residence).[12] Wherever this initial site, the rapid growth of the industry in its youth will tend to reinforce the importance of these sites as agglomerative centers.[13] New firms are frequently formed from employees' spinning off older firms. Competitive efforts will focus on product design, on prototype construction and testing, and on organization building, all activities which rely heavily upon a skilled labor pool, skewed toward the professional–technical categories. The young firms will tend to recruit labor from outside the region and to attract subcontracting firms and suppliers around them. Any inclination to disperse production to cheaper peripheral sites will be tempered by the need to be near the center of ongoing innovative activity and to have ready access to new information about the evolving market. Shoemaking in the Boston area is an early example of this type of innovative agglomeration; autos in Detroit, rubber in Akron, steel in Pittsburgh, farm machinery in Chicago, brewing in Milwaukee, flour milling in Minneapolis, oil in Houston, cereals in Battle Creek, and electronics in Santa Clara Valley are others.

2. Standardization, normal profits, and dispersion

As firms successfully perfect the product and set in place a standard process for large-scale production, much of the strategic need to be near the centers of origin disappears. Organizational attention turns toward market penetration and away from the innovative process itself. The superprofits of the previous period disappear under heightened competition from new entrants, increasing the volume of sales to capture economies of scale and spread organizational overhead thus becomes the major source of expanded profits.[14] At the same time, firms in this stage require fewer experimental and innovative personnel and have less interest in remaining close to competitors.

In this stage, corporations will find it more attractive to migrate to or site new plants at least-cost locations and near developing markets. Textile plants have migrated to the American South and offshore in the past fifty years because labor costs at these sites are so much lower; Coca-Cola bottling plants have been located in every major metropolitan area. In some cases, higher costs at the initial location – because of labor organizations and pressures on locally scarce resources like land and air quality – will help push production out. In general, then, industries in this stage will tend to disperse from original sites under the discipline of normal competition.[15]

3. Market power, monopoly profits, and uneven development

Yet a third era characterizes those industries that develop a substantial degree of concentration of market power in the hands of a few firms. The spatial tendencies associated with such power depend upon whether or not oligopoly appears early in a sector's life cycle or later, once standardization has taken place. In the former case, the emergence of market power will tend to retard decentralization and reinforce initial agglomerative tendencies. However, unlike the product-testing and market-exploration activities that hold innovative industries to their youthful centers, it is the market-policing activities of oligopolies, discussed in the previous section, that encourage their continued commitment to centralized operations. Thus while agglomeration can be viewed as economically rational in innovative sectors, in mature but monopolistic sectors it is an aberration from the interregional patterns of production which would otherwise develop in the absence of market power.

On the other hand, if oligopolistic power emerges late in a sector's development, as appears to be the case in brewing, for instance, after it has become relatively dispersed, then it may have the effect of accelerating a spatial reordering which will selectively close some regional plants while consolidating and enlarging the position of others. Those plants closed will be the older, high-cost plants, often where labor is unionized, while the new clusters of ultra-modern plants will tend to be arrayed on the outskirts of major metropolitan areas drawn by both markets and a relatively unorganized labor force. This tendency may also occur in industries with a long history of oligopoly where profit margins are being eroded by substitutes from other sectors or heightened competition from new levels of import penetration.[16] In this case, the adverse consequences for original centers will be severe because, having been overbuilt and underdiversified as discussed above, they will be particularly vulnerable to shutdowns. Oligopolies will have the size and resources to clear out very rapidly, as the steel industry has done in Pittsburgh, Youngstown, and Buffalo.

4. Market decline, profit squeeze, and plant closings

A final era is characterized by shrinkage of output and the decline of profit rates to a less-than-average level. Most commodities in capitalist society face ultimate extinction as substitutes emerge to replace them – a function of the relentless search for new profit arenas that is endemic to capitalist systems. Take for example copper. Most major US mines have shut down in recent years, in part due to depletion and import penetration, but in large part due to the substitution of fiber optics in communications uses, of polyvinylchloride in sewer and water pipes, and aluminum in radiators. If such substitutes are not pioneered internally, the industry producing the older commodity will find its market demand dropping and its profit rate falling. It will respond by trying to rationalize – closing down older capacity, and if entrepreneurial, modernizing existing operations and diversifying into new product lines.

Generally, the net effect of this behavior is the systematic elimination of capacity in the older regions, with maintenance or at least fewer closings in regions of more recent entry. As a result, the industry will appear to be shifting spatially, even reconcentrating its capacity at the more youthful sites. Take the textile and shoe industries, for example. Once almost entirely a New England phenomenon, newer plants were dispersed to lower cost locations in the southeastern Piedmont and the Kentucky–Tennessee interior throughout the first half of the twentieth century. Once heightened competition from imports pressed domestic producers, the older New England plants were eliminated so that both of these sectors now seem to have reconcentrated in a small number of southeastern states.[17]

These four types of profitability experience, generally found sequentially,[18] and their behavioral counterparts are quite helpful for distinguishing among regional growth dilemmas at any one point in time. It helps explain why, even in an era of rapid market interpenetration and huge wage gaps across countries, some regions of the United States are still hosting job growth. Indeed, this profit cycle model enables us to distinguish between two very different forms of regional growth. A large increase in employment registered in a region may mean either the birth of a new sector or the dispersion or relocation of a more established sector from some other region.

The local consequences of these two types of sectoral growth are dramatically different. In the former, we might expect the generation of a highly skilled labor force and associated agglomerative activity, which can set off a major long growth spurt.[19] In the latter case, long-term growth prospects may be an illusion, as the relocation is due solely to the response of corporations to the relative underdevelopment of the regional economy.[20] As this new presence helps create a local labor market, pushes up wages, and encourages unionization, these very benefits may choke off any further growth. The same cost-cutting insistence that encouraged the original relocation may lead to a further round of relocations to offshore sites, rendering the promise of sustained regional development even more ephemeral.

These distinctions between stage status of incoming sectors have dramatic consequences for development potential. If the new activities are in the superprofit stage, they introduce the inmigration of technical and professional labor, dramatic expansion in local business services, pressures on housing, transportation infrastructure, and air quality – in other words they bring robust job growth rates with disruptive land use and public sector consequences. If the incoming sector is a mature, profit-squeezed activity fleeing high tax and wage levels and lured by financial and other incentives, it will bring to its new host problems similar to those of the region it left – heightened capital–labor conflict and the threat of closure or overseas relocation – as well as pressures on local carrying capacity. Thus, the Deep South's efforts to attract post-normal-profit stage corporations will result in a very different developmental path for the region than will the Southwest's defense and the electronics-induced growth.

In addition to aggregate employment levels, the spatial behavior of sectors at different points of the product cycle affects both the occupational composition and structures of the business community within regions. Firms in the initial, superprofit stage will tend to have relatively high proportions of professional–technical workers. As the productions workforce grows subsequently, a dual workforce emerges in the region.[21] Corporations in the last two stages will tend also to have a bifurcated class structure – managerial and production – but it is more likely to be spatially segregated inter- or intraregionally. The growth of employment, therefore, will result in very different occupational structures locally depending on which stage of the profit cycle – agglomeration or re-location – is involved. Class conflicts on the regional level will be a direct function of class structure and sectoral dynamics.

Entrepreneurial and unionization structures at the local or regional level will also be affected by sectoral type and dynamic. Regions with dominant sectors in the early stages of development will tend to have a large and robust entrepreneurial class composed of managers and propri-etors of small firms. An example is the nineteenth-century agricultural Midwest, the basis of the birth of Republicanism. Regions of origin with dominant sectors in the oligopolistic normal-profit-plus stage will produce a resident regional capitalist class that has a discouraging effect on other entrepreneurial aspirants. Unionization will be advanced in these regions, with patent consequences for regional politics. Regions hosting new dispersals or relocations from existing corporations in other regions will experience an absentee capitalist class, quite distinct from local small business persons in the tertiary sector. Unionization will not typically be extensive in these locations, although efforts to organize workers will sooner or later develop.

In summary, then, the determinants of profitability for sectors at different developmental stages will create differential locational impulses. Superprofit sectors will agglomerate, creating pressures for new infra-structure and amenities required for their professional stratum employees. Profit-squeezed sectors will disperse in search of lower production costs and more efficient market penetration. Oligopolistic market structures will retard dispersion, if they appear early in the profit cycle, but are capable of accelerating it in periods of retrenchment. Three distinct regional experiences are linked to the profit cycle's rhythm: regions losing profit-squeezed sectors, regions gaining the same, and regions hosting youthful, superprofitable sectors. Each is associated with specific political tendencies.

The Militarization of the Economy

A major difference in postwar urbanization patterns between the United States and its European industrialized partners is the degree to which population has migrated internally and shaken up the hierarchy of major cities and regions. A major cause of this remarkable recomposition is the growing role that the military plays as a consumer of manufacturing output. As weaponry has changed over the past two centuries from manual and mechanical to electronic, the location of arms production and deployment has also changed. In the postwar era, for strategic, bureaucratic, and cultural reasons, the industries serving the US Department of Defense have located at suburban sites in the nation's "defense perimeter." Here, they have created relatively homogeneous, politically conservative, suburban communities favoring white male professional and technical workers. They have pointedly shunned the industrial heartland.

Military-led innovation

World War II was won with American technology. During the war, the US government began shifting massive resources into many technological areas which paid off militarily – proximity fuses, penicillin, nuclear weaponry, autopilots, crypt-analytical machinery, and advances in radar. By the war's end, warfare had emerged into the electronics era. Subsequently, the goal of strategic defense became the creation of ships and planes that would move faster, maneuver better, and be unde-tectable and deadly. Indeed, this is the basis of the postwar high-tech revolution, a notion that has had its military connection obscured.

These preoccupations led to increasingly greater government domi-nation of the inventive and innovative process in the United States. Up to World War II, the federal government accounted for only about 15 percent of research and development funding. By the 1960s, this share, the bulk of it in military matters, had increased to above 60 per-cent and has not declined since (Markusen, 1986d).[22] Unlike the lumpy process of private-sector innovation, which tends to be cosmetic in boom times and more revolutionary in troughs, military-led innova-tion has been more or less continual. It is a natural counterpart of the

Cold War, the goal being continually to render obsolete the opposition's weaponry.

These innovations have had spin-offs which have dramatically affected
nonmilitary sectors, particularly by automating production. The commercial counterpart of "removing the soldier from the hazards of duty" has
been the removal of workers from the process of production. By
constantly revolutionizing the means of production, this military-
initiated stream of innovations has mitigated the tendency towards
overproduction. Yet it has created new contradictions. One is the
accelerated displacement of workers in traditional manufacturing.
Another is the enlarged burden on the State sector, manifest in huge
budget deficits that represent the cost of this role of increasing
militarization.

This militarization of innovation has produced a new trend in the
location of military-related hardware production. Increasingly, the bulk
of the expenditure goes towards electronic and related devices, new
synthetic materials, and sophisticated and custom-made communications
systems designed for aircraft or submarines. The type of labor required is
largely professional and technical, heavily skewed toward the engineering occupations. Generally speaking, this stratum of the workforce prefers
to live in relatively urbanized settings with a high level of amenities. The
salaries that contractors are willing to pay under cost-plus arrangements
permit the realization of these goals. Both the corporation and its
employees find sites close to good research universities and/or government labs and testing facilities an added attraction. As a result, the major
portion of defense-related production has taken place in suburban areas
attached to preexisting standard metropolitan statistical areas (SMSAs) or
medium-sized towns. Indeed, military-related communities appear to
have pioneered much of the suburban "California lifestyle" so widely
imitated throughout the country.

The defense perimeter versus the industrial heartland

The preference for major research presence and nice living quarters for
their professional–technical workforce does not satisfactorily explain why
military-related production has shifted so decisively away from the industrial heartland. That the shift has occurred is fairly well established
empirically. Prime contracts, which in 1951 were skewed toward the
northeastern and north central states, had shifted by 1976 toward the
southern and western states, by both aggregate and per capita measures.
This bias continued into the 1980s. If subcontracting patterns are added
in, the picture does not change much. Input–output studies in the 1960s
and 1970s showed that nondefense priorities would have shifted
economic activity back toward the manufacturing belt, at the expense of
California and Texas in particular.[23]

In the 1980s, the shift accelerated with the Reagan military build-up. Hardware purchases by the Department of Defense (DOD) are now so high-tech intensive that the demand for the Midwest's industrial output, even the capital goods so concentrated in that region, is minimal. The Department of Defense alone accounts for a large share of output in the high-tech sectors of radio and TV communications equipment (63 percent), aircraft (46 percent), missiles (80 percent), engineering instruments (34 percent), and electronic components (20 percent). Computers and related electronics sectors are the largest gainers under the Reagan build-up. Department of Defense-originated demand for computers was estimated to increase 141 percent from 1982 to 1987.[24]

In contrast, the sectors in which the industrial belt specializes – steel (79 percent), fabricated matals (79 percent), machine tools (79 percent), and metal stampings (9 percent) – sell very small shares of their output to DOD-related contractors. Even with a large increase under the Reagan build-up, none will sell as much as 10 percent to the military sector by 1987. Meanwhile military priorities are cutting deeply into orders that might otherwise come from nondefense priorities – social spending, infrastructure improvement, industrial rehabilitation. Nor is there research money available for badly needed innovation in industries like steel.

The new high-tech industries that dominate the current defense hardware budget have by and large not grown in the industrial belt, stretching from New York through Detroit, Milwaukee, St Louis, and Baltimore. The newer sunbelt SMSAs garnered the greatest shares of high-tech job growth in the 1970s. While Chicago was the nation's number 2 high-tech center in 1977, principally because of its prominence in the machine tools industry, it fell far below a number of newer SMSAs in absolute job gains. Indeed, half of the top ten in 1977 failed to rank in the top ten in terms of absolute job growth, not to mention percentage growth rates. All but one of these were in the industrial belt (Chicago, Detroit, Philadelphia, and Newark).[25]

The major defense-related high-tech job growth since the early 1970s has taken place on the "defense perimeter," an area stretching from the Boston area south through Connecticut, Long Island to Newport News, Huntsville (Alabama) and Melbourne (Florida) across the gulf states to Dallas and Houston, and encompassing much of the Intermountain West as well as the Pacific Coast. Metropolitan areas like Anaheim (next to Los Angeles), Worcester (next to Boston), Dallas, Houston, and Lakeland (Florida) were among the top ten job gainers.

Regionally, the Pacific region tops the list for military expenditures per capita (table 5.1). The only other regions which show a greater than national average share are the mountain states, New England, and the South Atlantic region, in that order. Among the beneficiaries of military outlays, New England and the Pacific States rank extraordinarily high in procurement outlays, while the Mountain and South Atlantic states receive a disproportionate share in the form of military base personnel and pay. However, the South Atlantic region is the single largest recipient, share-wise, of research and development expenditures. Remarkably, none of the four interior regions, the "centrals," came within 90 percent of the national average of military receipts (Stein, 1985).

Table 5.1   Relative regional per capita military receipts, 1983

Region	Total Receipts ($ bills)	Procurement ratio[a]	Personnel ratio[a]	Research ratio[a]	Total ratio
New England	18.21	2.06	0.74	1.57	1.44
Mid-Atlantic	24.18	0.83	0.44	0.61	0.64
East North Central	18.02	0.45	0.44	0.14	0.43
West North Central	15.03	1.07	0.60	0.91	0.85
South Atlantic	53.38	0.97	1.67	2.27	1.35
East South Central	10.05	0.53	0.84	0.41	0.66
West South Central	23.39	0.81	1.08	0.21	0.89
Mountain	18.40	0.96	2.08	1.14	1.47
Pacific	56.69	1.85	1.44	1.75	1.66

[a] The ratios represent the regions' per capita receipts divided by the national per capita expenditure for 1983.
Source: Jay Stein, "US Defense Spending: Implications for Economic Development Planning," Working Paper, Georgia Institute of Technology, City Planning Program, 1985, table 3.

When measured a different way, by shares of manufacturing shipments directed toward the military, the same rankings occur. Certain states within the regions account for the bulk of military shipments, even when normalized for different size production complexes. In the West, California, Arizona and Utah all rank within the top five defense shipment location quotients, meaning that their manufacturing sectors are heavily dependent upon the military (table 5.2). Oregon and Idaho, on the other hand, have almost no military-related manufacturing. Similarly, the South Atlantic, Florida, Maryland, and Virginia are the big winners, while the Carolinas and West Virginia rank near the bottom.

Table 5.2   Highest and lowest ranking states in military
shipments, 1983

Rank	Top states	Military shipments location quotient	Rank	Bottom states	Military shipments location quotient
1	California	2.62	50	Arkansas	0.001
2	Connecticut	2.49	49	West Virginia	0.02
3	Missouri	2.49	48	Idaho	0.06
4	Arizona	2.30	47	North Carolina	0.07
5	Utah	2.10	46	South Carolina	0.08
6	Maryland	1.97	45	Kentucky	0.10
7	New Hampshire	1.88	44	Nebraska	0.12
8	Kansas	1.85	43	Alabama	0.26
9	Massachusetts	1.71	42	Montana	0.27
10	Vermont	1.66	41	Wisconsin	0.28
11	Virginia	1.55	40	Tennessee	0.30
12	Rhode Island	1.35	39	Oregon	0.33
13	Florida	1.25	38	Iowa	0.33
14	Colorado	1.23	37	Delaware	0.43
15	Texas	1.17	36	Michigan	0.45

Source: Breandan O hUallachain, "Some Implications of Recent Growth in
the American Military-Industrial Complex," Working Paper, Northwestern
University, Department of Geography, 1986, table 1, p. 4. Data are from
the Department of Commerce's *Current Industry Reports* and were weighted
by 1982 employment levels to reflect the lag between production and final
delivery.

The state figures for manufacturing shipments bear out the defense
perimeter argument. With the exception of Missouri and Kansas, no
other noncoastal state between the Appalachians and the Rockies ranks
in the top fifteen. Symmetrically, the bottom fifteen states are predominantly interior states, and include some of the more significant
manufacturers like Wisconsin and Michigan. The magnitudes of the
differences are quite striking. While California ships out military material at a rate in excess of 150 percent of the national average, for
manufacturing, states like West Virginia and Arkansas are more than 90
percent below that average. This disparity has intensified under the
Reagan build-up. From 1977 to 1983, the states of Massachusetts, Texas,
and California, all large to begin with, increased their shares of defense
purchases at the expense of most other states (O hUallachain, 1986).

Why defense-related manufacturing is where it is

In the literature on high-tech location, a skilled labor force and amenities are often cited as the dominant locational factors (Rees and Stafford, 1983; Joint Economic Committee, 1982). However, it is apparent that skilled labor is highly mobile, especially in these industries. The Department of Defense permits its contractors to earn a profit on the cost of relocating engineers. Many first-rate engineering schools exist in the Midwest, and anecdotal evidence suggests that currently as many as half of California's new hires come from these midwestern universities. In a large-scale regression analysis of all 277 US metropolitan areas, we found that research and development funds at area universities were *not* an important influence on high-tech growth.[26] This must be because many industrial belt states have superior engineering schools yet are not gaining the high-tech spinoffs.

Furthermore, amenities variables were only modestly important in explaining high-tech location in the 1970s. More consistently important were per capita defense expenditures and percent black (negatively related). While climate was significant in the model, there are stunning anomalies here – both Minneapolis and Boston are lodged in the frost-belt. These findings suggest that factors other than skilled labor, engineering schools, and amenities are driving the distribution of defense dollars, which was not highly correlated with any of the other twelve characteristics.

Why defense-related manufacturing has located far from the pre-existing industrial centers of the country is a complicated matter. The present pattern is the product of five decades of location decisions, and the dominant locational factors do change over time. Three factors that loom larger than labour and amenities are strategic choices by the military itself, the geopolitics of congressional operation and Pentagon constituency-building, and the cultural proclivities of military-related managers in a liberal democratic society.

Clearly, strategic decisions made by the military have shaped the longer-term spatial patterning of high-tech and defense spending. Among these are sitings of military bases, many made before the era in question. Base locations were often the determining element in early aircraft assembly relocation, since military airfields and pilots would provide accessible (and often free) testing facilities to manufacturers. Some of the relocation to the Sunbelt, especially of aircraft assembly during the 1930s, can be explained by this proximity.

But even more significant was the opening up of the Pacific Front in World War II. During the brief war years, a tremendous number of civilian and military personnel were transferred to the West Coast, and an industrial complex that included shipyards, steel mills, machining factories, and electronics was underwritten by the federal government.

This immense wartime physical plant persisted after the war and drew around it a new and distinctive aerospace and communications complex.

In contrast, the postwar industrialists of the manufacturing belt, whose factories had also been converted to wartime production, dismantled their operations and reconverted them into consumer and capital goods production, to feed the immense pent-up wartime demand. Only those areas of the country without a diversified industrial base became permanent military-industrial complexes. The outstanding examples are Los Angeles, where 44 percent of all employment in the Los Angeles–Long Beach area was derived from defense and space activity, and New England, whose older textile and shoemaking activities were destroyed during the 1950s (Harrison, 1984).

Geopolitical power is also an important determinant. During much of the postwar period, presidents hailed from the defense perimeter. Johnson, in particular, is often cited as a major political force behind the space program's location in and around the Gulf States. During the postwar era, military appropriations committees were dominated by southern conservative Democratic leadership, with the result that military bases and contracts often were skewed toward their districts. While prime contracts in recent years have been too concentrated to correlate with congressional status, some evidence remains that informal relationships between the Pentagon, its contractors, and politicians reinforce the Sunbelt-oriented pattern (Rundquist, 1983; Adams, 1981). More recently, political scrutiny appears to have encouraged the Pentagon to engage in geographical constituency building, in which it carefully scrutinizes the regional distribution of contracts and lobbies congresspersons for support in return.

A third factor, and one that appears to be growing in importance, is the apparent repugnance of both the Pentagon and military contractors for the cosmopolitan, liberal democratic culture that characterizes the older manufacturing belt. The institutionalization of capital–labor conflict in the collective bargaining process, the commitment on the part of state and local governments to high levels of social spending, and the political machines that dominate most cities embody cultural traits antithetical to the military model of labor and command. Military contractors are frequently vehement opponents of organized labor, even those whose unions date from World War II, when they were largely imposed by the government in return for industrial peace.

The Pentagon has gone out of its way to aid and encourage contractors to move away from unions, to engage in union busting, and to automate their production processes to rid themselves of blue collar labor (Markusen, 1985c). They fear organized labor not because of wage issues but because of the threat of work stoppages, a severe problem for performance-oriented contractors. Former military officers now turned corporate managers may prefer the military model of loyalty, hierarchy, lack of employment mobility, and absence of adversial relationships in the newly constructed defense communities.

In summary, then, defense expenditures and even more powerfully, defense-led innovation have fueled the shift of capital goods production toward the defense perimeter and away from the industrial heartland. They have had a major role in determining the siting of new, superprofit sectors like electronics, when they agglomerate around these initial regions. The sheer size of these government-engendered sectors and the unique geopolitical and strategic forces which shaped their regional distribution explain in large part why the United States has had such massive postwar internal redistribution of productive capacity, unlike any other major industrialized nation.

Interrelationships among Sectoral Dynamics, Institutional Change, and Military-led Innovation

It is useful to illustrate the interconnections between the forces just surveyed using two instances. First of all, a strong relationship appears to exist between innovation in individual sectors, the periodicity of long waves, and increasingly, military-led technological change. Several scholars have observed that the initiation of new sectors and the demise of older ones seem to bunch up in the troughs of long waves.[27] During times of prosperity corporations are preoccupied with retaining market share, with product differentiation, with streamlining production processes, and pseudo-innovation. Only during times of economywide stagnation are corporate resources directed toward basic innovation. This suggests that ensembles of new sectors may emerge in tandem, not continuously over time, and that whole new eras may be characterized by a set of such fundamental innovations. The regional implication is that during the trough of a long wave, as many believe we are currently experiencing, differences in the age and type of sector may be much more significant in explaining the divergence in regional economic fortunes than would be the case in more stable periods. If the state, via the military budget, is playing an increasingly powerful role in this process, then its locational preferences will exacerbate uneven regional outcomes.

A second example is the interaction between the existence of market power in a sector and the changing role of the state. Hypothetically, any large industry with relatively few corporate competitors will have greater clout in political arenas, although this of course is mediated by such factors as the degree of regional spread, which suggests the number of congressional votes that can be easily influenced. Small-scale competitive industries, such as agriculture, can substitute trade association strength for lack of existing organizational leadership, although this example is perhaps an exception.

An outstanding illustration of the way in which an oligopolistic industry has been able to bend government policy to its ends is the energy industry, dominated by large oil and electric corporations. Although the federal government initiated a huge program to make the United States energy self-sufficient, it shunned small-scale, decentralized, renewable energy resources like solar power for expensive corporate owned, built, and operated programs such as nuclear energy and synthetic fuels, preserving throughout the dominance of the energy corporations and their monopolistic profit margins. Similarly, the Pentagon appears to support a structure of several large firms in each of its major weapons markets to the detriment of smaller would-be competitors.

Notes

1   This discussion draws upon Frobel et al. (1980), Sassen-Koob (1982), Noyelle (1983), Hansen (1979), Bluestone and Harrison (1982), Friedmann (1986), and Friedmann and Wolfe (1982).
2   Both Harvey (1982) and Bluestone and Harrison (1982) suggest that capital is increasingly enjoying this "spatial" strategy as a part of its new attack on labor gains in the postwar period in advanced industrial countries.
3   Evidence on the magnitude of north–south investment differentials is contained in Browne (1980).
4   A substantial portion of this immigrant workforce has been aggressively recruited, both historically and currently. See Piore (1979) for an account of this strategy.
5   This argument and that of the next few paragraphs are developed at much greater length in my companion volume, *Profit Cycles, Oligopoly and Regional Development* (1985c). A similar argument can be found in Chinitz (1960) and for steel in Stocking (1954).
6   First hypothesized by Hymer (1972), this analysis has been expanded upon by Cohen (1977) and Noyelle (1983). Noyelle and Stanback (1983) have tried to allocate metropolitan areas into categories based upon which type of corporate activity is most prevalent in each.
7   Wolfe (1977) has constructed a typology of changes in forms of state promotion of private capital. O'Connor (1973) offers the best Marxist-based conceptual approach to evaluating budgetary components of the federal governments. Castells (1980) and Mollenkopf (1981) both analyze changing public sector impacts on growth of cities.
8   See Luger's (1981) documentation of this bias. A general overview of the distributional pattern of federal aid and outlays can be found in Markusen, Saxenian, and Weiss (1981b).
9   The following material is a brief summary of my argument in a companion volume, *Profit Cycles, Oligopoly and Regional Development*, chs 3–6. The debt to

both Marxist and Schumpeterian traditions should be clear and is discussed at length in Markusen 1986b.

10   A new industry or sector (to avoid tedium I use these terms interchangeably) can be distinguished from new products or processes in existing industries by the tendency for wholly new firms to be formed around the new innovation.

11   The phrase "superprofits" was coined by Mandel (1975).

12   Taylor (1975) argues that most firms originate in the founder's home town, although Feller (1974) argues that there is no necessary relationship between inventive activity and subsequent location.

13   On the relationships between innovation and agglomeration, see Thompson (1969), Pred (1976), and Friedmann (1973).

14   Similar observations are made in the product cycle literature, originating with Kuznets (1930) and Burns (1934) and reviewed by Vernon (1966) and Hirsch (1967).

15   The normalcy of agglomeration followed by dispersion was first hypothesized by Hoover (1948). See Persky (1978) and Hansen (1980) for a debate over the extent to which postwar north–south differentials can be attributed to product life cycle–spatial filtering processes. Bergman and Goldstein (1983) show that noncyclical structural change has been a prominent feature in U.S. metropolitan shifts in the 1970s.

16   Postwar additions of new auto-assembly plants and breweries have both followed the Hotelling-type pattern of clustering around new regional nodes. Hotelling (1929) hypothesized that industries with a strong market orientation and limited numbers of competitors would tend to cluster around a central place whereas unlimited numbers of competitors would disperse throughout the market area.

17   See the separate accounts of the textile and shoe industries in chapters 9 and 10 of Markusen (1985c). See also Harrison (1984).

18   Some sectors may skip the competitive era altogether and this may be increasingly common. Some may become oligopolistic even after profit squeeze has set in. In a study of fifteen 4-digit manufacturing sectors, I found only one – wineries – that did not pass through clear sequential stages and that case was unique because of Prohibition.

19   The interrelationship of high-tech sectors and a professional–technical labor force is acknowledged in the literature, but no consensus exists as to whether or not one follows the other spatially. See Oakey, Thwaites, and Nash (1980), and Ewers and Wettmann (1980).

20   Several researchers have documented that branch plants, particularly in maturer sectors, are less apt to spawn other new businesses and more apt to close down than nonbranch plants. See Thompson (1969), Thwaites (1978), Johnson and Cathcart (1979), Erickson and Leinbach (1979), Hansen (1979), and Erickson (1980). Bluestone and Harrison (1980) reported that textile plants were closing in the South at a faster rate than in the North, although their entry into the former region is more recent.

21   See Saxenian (1980) for empirical documentation of this phenomenon in Silicon Valley.

22   The material in this section is treated at much greater length in Markusen (1985a, 1985b, 1986a, and 1986c).

23   McBreen (1977), Mazza and Wilkinson (1980), Anderson (1983), Karaska
     (1967), Rees and Stafford (1982) Malecki (1984), Leontieff et al. (1965),
     Bezdek (1975).
24   Figures are from Henry (1983). They do not include the defense portions
     of NASA, Department of Energy and other non-Pentagon military
     programs.
25   See Markusen, Hall, and Glasmeier (1986).
26   See Markusen, Hall, and Glasmeier (1986).
27   See in particular, Mensch (1970); Abernathy (1978); Hall (1981); Freeman,
     Clark and Soete (1982); and Rostow (1977).

References

Abernathy, William J. 1978. *The Productivity Dilemma: Roadblock to Innovation in the
     Automobile Industry*. Baltimore: Johns Hopkins University Press.
Adams, Gordon. 1981. *The Iron Triangle: The Politics of Defense Contracting*. New
     York: Council on Economic Priorities.
Anderson, James. 1983. *Bankrupting American Cities: The Tax Burden and
     Expenditures of the Pentagon by Metropolitan Area*. Lansing, Mich.:
     Employment Research Associates.
Bergman, Edward, and Harvey Goldstein. 1983. "Dynamics and Structural
     Change in Metropolitan Economies." *American Planning Association Journal*
     (Summer): 263–79.
Bezdek, Roger. 1975. "The 1980 Impact – Regional and Occupational – of
     Compensated Shifts in Defense Spending." *Journal of Regional Science* 15, no.
     2: 183–98.
Bluestone, Barry, and Bennett Harrison. 1980. *Capital and Communities: The Causes
     and Consequences of Private Disinvestment*. Washington D.C.: Progressive
     Alliance.
——. 1982. *The Deindustrialization of America*. New York: Basic Books.
Browne, Lynn. 1980. "Regional Investment Patterns." *New England Economic
     Review*, July/August: 5–23.
Burns, Arthur F. 1934. *Production Trends in the United States*. New York: Bureau of
     Economic Research.
Castells, Manuel. 1980. *Multinational Capital, National States, and Local Communities*.
     University of California, Institute of Urban and Regional Development,
     Working Paper no. 334. Berkeley.
Chinitz, Benjamin. 1960. "Contrasts in Agglomeration: New York and
     Pittsburgh." *American Economic Association, Papers and Proceedings*, 50:
     279–89.
Cohen, Robert. 1977. "Multinational Corporations, International Finance, and
     the Sunbelt." In *The Rise of the Sunbelt Cities*, edited by David Perry and Alfred
     Watkins, 211–26. Beverley Hills: Sage Publications.
Erickson, Rodney. 1980. "Corporate Organization and Manufacturing Branch
     Plant Closures in Non-Metropolitan Areas." *Regional Studies* 14, no.6:
     491–501.
Erickson, Rodney, and Thomas Leinbach. 1979. "Characteristics of Branch Plants

Attracted to Nonmetropolitan Areas." in *Nonmetropolitan Industrialization*, edited by Richard Lonsdale and H. L. Seyler, 57–78. New York: Halsted Press.

Ewers, H. J., and R. W. Wettmann. 1980. "Innovation-Oriented Regional Policy." *Regional Studies* 14, no. 3: 161–79.

Feller, Irwin. 1974. "The Diffusion and Location of Technological Change in the American Cotton-Textile Industry, 1890–1970." *Technology and Culture* 15, no. 4: 569–93.

Freeman, Christopher, John Clark, and Luc Soete. 1982. *Unemployment and Technical Innovation*. London: Frances Pinter.

Friedmann, John. 1973. *Urbanization, Planning and National Development*. Beverly Hills: Sage.

——— . 1986. "The World City Hypothesis." *Development and Change* 17, no. 1: 69–84.

Friedmann, John, and Goetz Wolfe. 1982. "World City Formation: An Agenda for Research and Action." *International Journal of Urban and Regional Research* 6, no. 3: 309–44.

Frobel, Folker, Jurgen Heinrichs, and Otto Kreye. 1980. *The New International Division of Labor*. Translated by Pete Burgess. Cambridge: Cambridge University Press.

Hall, Stuart. 1981. "The Great Moving Right Show." *Socialist Review* 11, no. 1: 113–37.

Hansen, Niles. 1979. "The New International Division of Labor and Manufacturing Decentralization in the United States." *Review of Regional Studies* 9, no. 1: 1–11.

——— . 1980. "Dualism, Capital–Labor Ratios and the Regions of the U.S.: A Comment." *Journal of Regional Science* 20, no. 3: 401–3.

Harrison, Bennett. 1984. "Regional Restructuring and 'Good Business Climate': The Economic Transformation of New England Since World War II." In *Sunbelt/Snowbelt: Urban Development and Regional Restructuring*, edited by Larry Sawers and William K. Tabb. New York: Oxford University Press.

Harrison, Bennett, and Barry Bluestone. 1981. *The Incidence and Regulation of Plant Shutdowns*. Joint Center for Urban Studies of MIT and Harvard University Working Paper. Cambridge, Mass.

Harvey, David. 1982. *The Limits to Capital*. Oxford: Basil Blackwell.

Henry, David. 1983. "Defense Spending: A Growth Market for Industry." *U.S. Industrial Outlook 1983*, xxxix–xlvii.

Hirsch, Seev. 1967. *Location of Industry and International Competitiveness*. London: Oxford University Press.

Hobsbawm, Eric. 1964. "Introduction." Karl Marx, *Precapitalist Economic Formations*, translated by Jack Cohen. London: Lawrence & Wishart.

——— . 1972. "Some Reflections on Nationalism." In *Imagination and Precision in Social Sciences: Essays in Memory of Peter Nettles*. 385–406. London: Faber & Faber.

——— . 1975. *The Age of Capital: 1848–1875*. London: Weidenfeld & Nicolson.

——— . 1977. "Some Reflections on 'The Breakup of Britain.'" *New Left Review* no. 105 (September–October): 3–23.

Hoover, Edgar. 1948. *The Location of Economic Activity*. New York: McGraw-Hill.

Hotelling, Harold. 1929. "Stability in Competition." *Economic Journal* 39, no. 1: 41–57.

Hymer, Stephen H. 1974. "The Multinational Corporation and the Law of Uneven Development." In *Economic and World Order*, edited by J. W. Bhagwati, 113–40. New York: Macmillan.

Joint Economic Committee. 1982. *Location of High Technology Firms and Regional Economic Development*. Washington D.C.: Government Printing Office.

Johnson, P. S., and D. G. Cathcart. 1979. "New Manufacturing Firms and Regional Development: Some Evidence from the Northern Region." *Regional Studies* 13: 269–80.

Karaska, Gerald J. 1967. *Variation of Input–Output Coefficients for Philadelphia Manufacturing*. Philadelphia: Regional Science Institute.

Kuznets, Simon. 1930. *Secular Movements in Production and Prices*. Boston: Houghton-Mifflin.

Leontieff, Wassily, Alison Morgan, Karen Polenske, David Simpson, and Edward Tower. 1965. "The Economic Impact – Industrial and Regional – of an Arms Cut." *Review of Economics and Statistics* 47, no. 3: 217–41.

Luger, Michael. 1981. *Regional Employment Effects of Federal Business Tax Incentives*. Ph.D. diss., University of California, Berkeley.

Malecki, Edward. 1984. "Military Spending and the U.S. Defense Industry: Regional Patterns of Military Contracts and Subcontracts." *Environment and Planning C: Government and Policy*, 2: 31–44.

Mandel, Ernest. 1975. *Late Capitalism*. (Originally published in French, 1972.) London: New Left Books.

Markusen, Ann. 1985a. "Defense Spending: A Successful Industrial Policy?" In *The Politics of Industrial Policy*, edited by Sharon Zukin. New York: Praeger Publishers.

——. 1985b. "Military Spending and Urban Development in California." *The Berkeley Planning Journal* 3, no. 1.

——. 1985c. *Profit Cycles, Oligopoly and Regional Development*. Cambridge, Mass.: MIT Press.

——. 1986a. "Defense Spending and the Geography of High Tech Industries." In *Technology, Regions and Policy*, edited by John Rees, 94–119. New York: Praeger Publishers.

——. 1986b. "Empirical Research in the Marxist and Schumpeterian Traditions: Reflections on Explaining Spatial Change." In *Marx, Schumpeter, Keynes: A Centenary Celebration of Dissent*, edited by Susan Helburn and David Bramhall. New York: M. E. Sharpe.

——. 1986c. "The Military Remapping of the United States." *The Built Environment* 11, no. 3: 171–80.

——. 1986d. "Military Spending and the US Economy." *World Policy Journal* 3, no. 3: 495–516.

Markusen, Ann, Peter Hall, and Amy Glasmeier. 1986. *High Tech America: The What, How, Where and Why of the Sunrise Industries*. London: Allen & Unwin.

Markusen, Ann, Annalee Saxenian, and Marc Weiss. 1981a. "Who Benefits from Intergovernmental Transfers?" In *Cities Under Stress: The Fiscal Crises of Urban America*, edited by Robert Burchell and David Listoken. New Brunswick, N.J.: Rutgers University Center for Urban Policy Research.

———. 1981b. "Who Benefits from Intergovernmental Transfers?" *Publius* 2, no. 1 (Winter): 5–13.

Mazza, Jacqueline, and Dale Wilkinson. 1980. *The Unprotected Flank: Regional and Strategic Imbalances in Defense Spending Patterns.* Washington D.C.: Northeast-Midwest Institute.

McBreen, Maureen. 1977. "Regional Trends in Federal Defense Expenditures: 1950–1976." Report to the US Senate Committee on Appropriations Ninety-fifth Congress. In *Selected Essays on Patterns of Regional Change,* October: 511–41, Washington D.C.: Government Printing Office.

Mensch, Gerhard. 1970. *Stalemate in Technology: Innovations Overcome the Depression.* Cambridge, Mass.: Ballinger.

Mollenkopf, John. 1981. "Paths Toward the Post-Industrial Service City: The Northeast and the Southwest." In *Cities Under Stress: The Fiscal Crises of Urban America,* edited by Robert Burchell and David Listoken. New Brunswick, N.J.: Rutgers University, Center for Urban Policy Research.

Noyelle, Thierry. 1983. "The Implications of Industry Restructuring in the United States." In *Regional Analysis and the New International Division of Labor,* edited by Frank Moulaert and Patricia Wilson Salinas. Boston: Kluwer-Nijhoff.

Noyelle, Thierry, and Thomas Stanback, Jr. 1983. *Economic Transformation of American Cities.* Totowa, N.J.: Rowman & Allanheld.

Oakey, R. P., A. T. Thwaites, and P. A. Nash. 1980. "The Regional Distribution of Innovative Manufacturing Establishments in Britain." *Regional Studies* 14: 235–53.

O' Connor, James. 1973. *The Fiscal Crisis of the State.* New York: St. Martin's Press.

O hUallachain, Breandan. 1986. *Some Regional Implications of Recent Growth in the American Military-Industrial Complex.* Northwestern University, Department of Geography, Working Paper. Evanston, Ill.

Persky, Joseph. 1978. "Dualism, Capital–Labor Ratios and the Regions of the U.S." *Journal of Regional Science* 18, no. 3: 373–81.

Piore, Michael. 1979. *Birds of Passage: Migrant Labor and Industrial Societies.* Cambridge: Cambridge University Press.

Pred, Allan R. 1976. "The Interurban Transmission of Growth in Advanced Economies: Empirical Findings vs. Regional-Planning Assumptions." *Regional Studies* 10: 151–71.

Rees, John, and Howard Stafford. 1983. *A Review of Regional Growth and Industrial Location Theory: Toward Understanding the Development of High-Technology Complexes in the United States.* Washington D.C.: Office of Technology Assessment.

Rostow, Walt. 1977. "Regional Change in the Fifth Kondratieff Upswing." In *The Rise of the Sunbelt Cities,* edited by David Perry and Alfred Watkins, 83–103. Beverly Hills: Sage Publications.

Rundquist, Barry. 1983. "Politics' Benefits and Public Policy: Interpretation of Recent U.S. Studies." *Environment and Planning C: Government and Policy* 1: 401–12.

Sassen-Koob, Saskia. 1982. "Recomposition and Peripheralization at the Core." *Contemporary Marxism* no. 5 (Summer): 88–100.

Saxenian, Annalee. 1980. *Silicon Chips and Spatial Structure: The Semiconductor Industry and Urbanization in Santa Clara County, California.* Master's thesis,

Department of City and Regional Planning, University of California at Berkeley.

Stein, Jay. 1985. *US Defense Spending: Implications for Economic Development Planning*. Georgia Institute of Technology, City Planning Program Working Paper. Atlanta.

Stocking, George. 1954. *Basing-Point Pricing and Regional Development*. Chapel Hill: University of North Carolina Press.

Taylor, M. J. 1975. "Organizational Growth, Spatial Interaction and Locational Decision-Making." *Regional Studies* 9: 313–23.

Thompson, Wilbur. 1969. "The Economic Base of Urban Problems." In *Contemporary Economic Issues*, edited by Neil Chamberlain, 1–47. Homewood, Ill.: Richard Irwin.

Thwaites, A. T. 1978. "Technological Change, Mobile Plants and Regional Development." *Regional Studies* 12: 445–61.

Vernon, Raymond. 1966. "International Investment and International Trade in the Product Cycle." *Quarterly Journal of Economics*, 80, no. 2: 190–207.

Wolfe, Alan. 1977. *The Limits of Legitimacy: Political Contradictions of Contemporary Capitalism*. New York: Free Press.

6

Reading the Map: A Theory of Military–Industrial Places

Ann R. Markusen, Peter Hall,

Scott Campbell, and

Sabina Deitrick

Why did a dramatic regional shift in US military production occur? To track the development of the gunbelt and its constituent parts, we invite you on an odyssey through geographical space and historical time. As a guide for this journey, we need a road map. Geographers, like other travelers, use ordinary maps to find which highway to drive. But they also use an array of more specialized material that allows them to antici- pate and interpret the landscape before them. Geologic and topographic maps tell them that the going may get rough and the stopping places may be few; population-density maps will confirm the facts. To understand

Reprinted by permission from Ann Markusen, Peter Hall, Scott Campbell and Sabina Deitrick, 1991, *The Rise of the Gunbelt: The Military Remapping of Industrial America.*

the gunbelt as it unfolds before us, we shall use a similar kind of composite map.

The map must convey some rather esoteric information. By using only the obvious sources, we run the risk of drawing the wrong inferences – like poor Inspector Lestrade, before Sherlock Holmes arrived on the scene and put him right. Climate maps show that Los Angeles enjoys plenty of sun; therefore, pilots found it easy to fly, and airplane manufacturers located around their needs. The map of education shows that universities cluster in New England; therefore, science begat advanced technology there. Both these conclusions contain a small grain of truth and a huge accretion of untruth. Other parts of America have sun, but attracted no early aircraft industry; snow-flecked Buffalo and rain-soaked Seattle did. Other parts of the country have good universities, yet few developed schools of aeronautical engineering and even fewer generated an advanced avionics industry. And some that did begat no aircraft industry.

So old-fashioned geographical location theory, the kind that still shows up in some textbooks, will not get us far. The truth, as usual, is more complex. Like Holmes, we must start our investigation in more obscure places.

The right place proves to be at the stratospheric level: the United States' mission, the vision the president and Pentagon top brass share about the nation's global role. As this vison has changed – from isolationism to global conflict to cold war – so has the basic philosophy of the right strategic response. The defence of the coasts was replaced by strategic bombing, then by intercontinental missilery, and finally by Star Wars. From that overarching imperative derive certain interlocking structures of defense production: the roles and powers of the different armed services; the demands of each service for military procurement; and, finally, the evolution of the military–industrial complex, a feature of the post-world war era that is unique in strategic history.

This maze of structural features affords space to a set of diverse actors – ranging from generals to university presidents, civic boosters to congressmen, heroic entrepreneurs to bureaucratic managers – each with individual preferences and perspectives. Then, coming right down to the ground, there are the places, each with its attributes – sometimes present and evident, sometimes latent and awaiting exploitation by local boosters – that present themselves to the locational actors as they traverse the landscape in search of possible production sites. Together they shape the historical growth trajectories of new military–industrial centers, which – quite unlike the machines they turn out – follow no simple parabolic course; instead, they exhibit multistage paths, with many slippages and even catastrophes en route.

Of course, this way of approaching the gunbelt suggests that it, in turn, plays no causal role in encouraging interservice rivalries or in shaping military appropriations or strategic policy. That is highly unlikely.

Strategic Missions, Service Roles

During this century, the United States' strategic role has gone through at least six main phases: dominant isolationism almost to the eve of World War II; active involvement in global conflict, followed by a brief period of disarmament; a long period of cold war marked by America's assumption of a global strategic role; a time of doubts and reversals broken by intense local conflict in Vietnam; the dismantling of some defense systems during the 1970s; and the development of the Strategic Defense Initiative in the 1980s.[1]

Prehistory, 1918–1941: Isolationism and the fight for the Air Force

In the prehistory of the gunbelt, the period between the two world wars, the United States was still committed to its historic doctrine of isolationism, albeit inconsistently. The armed forces were seen as having purely defensive roles as guardians of America's coasts. This reinforced the conservatism of the two established service arms, the Army and the Navy, and made them resistant to the arguments of the fledgling airmen for an air force with an independent attack capacity. Major General William "Billy" Mitchell, assistant chief of the Army Air Service, argued that in future wars airplanes would attack far behind enemy lines, destroying the enemy's industrial capacity and sapping the morale of the civilian population. But Mitchell's strident campaign led to his court-martial in 1925 and resignation in 1926.[2]

In that year came a small concession: Congress accepted the 1925 report of the independent Morrow Board and created the semi-independent Air Corps headed by an Army major general; it was planned to have an eventual complement of 1,650 officers, 15,000 men, and 1,800 aircraft by 1932. But the funds were never forthcoming, and the goal was never achieved.[3] Another inquiry, carried out by the Baker Board of 1934, led to yet another compromise: the establishment in 1935 of an independent air force general headquarters, which resulted in perversely divided responsibilities – air strike capacity, on one side, supply and training, on the other. Not until June 1941 did an Army regulation create the Army Air Forces under a chief who was also Deputy Chief of Staff for Air; not until March 1942 did the AAF gain virtually complete autonomy under a single chief, General H. H. "Hap" Arnold.[4]

Until 1938, even Arnold was committed to the limited doctrine of defense of the shores. So, throughout the interwar period, the infant aircraft manufacturers, still dominated by founder engineer-entrepreneurs and by former wartime flyers, struggled to survive, often solely on small military infusions. To defend their position and argue their

case before Congress and the Army, the airplane makers formed a manufacturers' association, but at first it enjoyed little success. A boom came
in the late 1920s, with expansion of the commercial airline business;
during 1927 to 1929, there was a fevered series of takeovers and mergers.
With the Depression came collapse. Dependent both on a depressed
commercial sector and on savagely reduced congressional Air Corps
appropriations, many firms faced bankruptcy.[5]

Looming war in Europe brought only limited relief, although orders
from future belligerents were helpful. As late as 1937 and 1938, obsessed
by the notion of the Air Corps's subordinate defensive role, Army chiefs
refused to concede the case for the B-17 bomber, and the Navy strongly
opposed it. At the start of 1936, the Army Air Corps had a mere 1,100
planes, 300 of which were front-line combat aircraft; the Navy, 800. Well
might Billy Mitchell rail, in 1935:

> We have subsidized an aircraft monopoly which is arming our potential
> enemies because we refuse to buy enough of its products to keep it going . . .
> When war comes we will have to take what the manufacturer happens to
> have on the market. We will spend billions of dollars until we have some-
> thing workable. And we will encourage the growth of the most dangerous
> monopoly in the world.[6]

So as late as 1939, deprived of a mass market, the industry was innocent
of mass-production techniques: "One typical aircraft manufacturer, and
a highly efficient one too, turned out only two or three units a day in
comparison with Detroit's production of two or three automobiles per
minute."[7] And until the 1938 buildup, the industry was regarded as financially shaky.[8]

In September 1938, President Roosevelt reversed policy: he announced
a program to build 10,000 planes, more than the Air Corps had requested.
Arnold later wrote that this was the most important event in his career,
and in the history of the service.[9] The beneficiaries were the pioneer
airframe firms that had survived the Depression – Lockheed, Douglas,
North American, Grumman, Curtiss-Wright, and Boeing – and the areas
where these firms clustered: Los Angeles, Seattle, Buffalo, Long Island,
and New England.

Global conflict, 1941–1945

Thus the threat of war, followed by real war, gave the airmen what they
had so long wanted: autonomy and a strategic offensive role. World War
II showed that the airmen had been right: indeed, one nation could inflict
huge damage on another nation's productive capacity and will to fight.
Bombing extended the battle past the front lines and deep into enemy
territory, destroying factories, transportation lines, cities, and civilians

with frightening efficiency and rapidity.[10] The atomic bomb and its progeny, the hydrogen bomb, were the ultimate steps in the evolution of air warfare.

The major instruments of military power consequently became the bombers that could wreak such havoc. With strategic warfare's eclipse of the Army's machine guns, artillery, and tanks, and the Navy's battleships and submarines, the role of these services paled in comparison with that of the new Air Force, which emerged during World War II to play the leading role in cold war technology. And the Strategic Air Command was elevated from junior to senior military partner.

In parallel, the aircraft manufacturers played a heroic role, developing within a few years from a cottage industry to mass production. FDR's 1940 goal, 50,000 planes a year, was 100 times the output of the industry in the late 1930s; yet it was reached by 1942, and doubled by 1944.[11] North American, the most spectacular case, expanded from 6,000 employees in one plant in the summer of 1940 to 92,000 in five plants by 1943. Between January 1939 and September 1945, it produced over 42,000 planes, 10 percent more than its rival Convair and 14 percent of American World War II production.[12] Lockheed produced over 19,000 planes and expanded from 2,500 workers in late 1938 to 60,000 by early 1945, when it was the biggest American aircraft company. Douglas made 10,000 military versions of its famous DC-3.[13]

The message was not lost. Air power now dominated, and a new service emerged to manage it. In December 1945, President Truman was calling for a Department of National Defense, in which the Air Force would have full parity. The National Security Act of 1947 finally established the post of Secretary of Defense, a national military establishment in the Pentagon, and separate departments of the Army, Navy, and Air Force.[14]

At war's end, the war machine was brought to a shuddering halt. The services were demobilized. Plants were closed and mothballed. Many military producers, above all the aircraft manufacturers, struggled to survive. The American leadership and the American people shared a notion that life would return to normal – that is, to minimal military involvement in world affairs. The wartime alliance, and the resulting victory, gave rise to hopes of an epoch of global peace.

The cold war, 1948–1980

The uneasy peace lasted a scant three years. With the onset of the cold war, the Berlin blockade and airlift of 1948, and the Truman Doctrine of 1949, the United States was back on the world stage for good. Then came the Korean War and the report of Soviet parity in atom-bomb production. In 1953, the United States exploded a "dry" H-bomb, capable of being carried as a lightweight warhead.[15] The result, in January 1954, was the "doctrine of massive retaliation," backed by an armory of sophisticated new weapons with unparalleled destructive force.[16] Then, in 1957, came the Soviet *Sputnik* and the race into space. Together, these events brought about the aerospace revolution.

The essential feature of the mid-century military–political landscape was the cold war – a type of strife radically unlike any other in history. Weapons for the first time were designed not to be used; they were sought for their preemptive value. Each combatant had to continually improve its arsenal, so as to deter the other from using its arms. Fewer and fewer units of each successive weapon were made, but each was much more technically sophisticated than the last. A process of institutionalized innovation was set in motion. The new form of warfare, atmospheric rather than ground or sea, radically altered both the conduct of war-making and the production complex that fashioned the weapons and support equipment.[17]

Now, another ideological fight broke out – this time, within the newly independent Air Force. An older generation of wartime "flying generals," committed to the doctrine of strategic bombing, lacked enthusiasm for becoming "silent silo-sitters."[18] They were challenged by a group of Young Turks who were committed to space warfare through guided missiles: a war without soldiers. Triggered by a technological breakthrough – the lightweight H-bomb – these space warriors achieved a major shift in strategic planning: from the mid-1950s, Air Force strategy was based on a combination of intercontinental missiles, highly sophisticated fighters and reconnaissance planes, and a radar shield backed by defensive cruise missiles.

In turn, this brought a shift in procurement: within a few years, the call was no longer for conventional aircraft, but for craft – whether manned or unmanned – stuffed with complex electronic guidance and sensing equipment. The Atlas intercontinental ballistic missile (ICBM) received top-priority status from the Air Force in May 1954 and top national status in the summer of 1955.[19] In November 1955, an intermediate range missile received joint top priority. The IRBM, the Thor, was launched in 1957; the Atlas ICBM, a year later.[20] The industry faced a sudden challenge of reorientation as it labored to create completely new products requiring new components, skills, and a commitment to scientific research and development. The military–industrial complex was born, and it was not a child of the heartland.

With the arrival of President Kennedy in the White House and Ford Motors' Robert McNamara at the Pentagon, a new era began. Although the nation's broad military objectives remained the same, the means radically altered. Planning, programming, and budgeting promised to produce a new, rational, highly economic system of procurement.[21] Before the promise could be realized, however, the escalating Vietnam War upset everyone's assumptions; here again was hot war, but of a new kind, requiring that the Army learn the enemy's guerrilla tactics. The end of that war was followed by the defense contraction of the mid to late 1970s. But as we have seen, these events had little effect on where military production took place.

The 1980s peacetime buildup

President Reagan's bold defense initiatives marked a partial return to the 1950s, with a boom in spending on major new weapons systems, an emphasis on aerospace, and growing expenditure on R&D, particularly in the fields of advanced radar devices, surveillance, communications systems, and information processing. New firms offering systems engineering and technical assistance (SETA) came to the fore, many of them spin-offs from aerospace companies under conflict-of-interest rules. They tended to concentrate in new centers like Washington, D.C., the military command-and-control headquarters; Colorado Springs, the nerve center for strategic defense and test bed for SDI; Huntsville, Alabama, and Titusville–Melbourne, Florida, both dedicated to military space activity; and, of course, aerospace industry headquarters in southern California.

Service Traditions and Service Rivalries

Central to the rise of the gunbelt was the victory of the Air Force's strategy for outsourcing to private firms over the Army's preferred strategy of in-house design and development. Ever since the earliest days of the republic, the Army had been wedded to the arsenal system, by which research, prototype development, and sometimes even production of weapons were conducted in government-owned and -run plants. The navy yard system, which dates back to the original Washington Navy Yard of 1790, was based on the same practice. For the young airmen of the 1920s, who tried the system at Wright Field in Dayton, it was an anachronism that did not work. But neither did the alternative of going to established automobile manufacturers, which had proved an expensive fiasco during World War I. This convinced Arnold and his fellow officers that the only way to get planes built was to go to their equally young and struggling colleagues in the infant aircraft industry. During the lean years of the 1920s and 1930s, the airmen did their best to supply the industry with small-scale orders. In 1938, when mass production became the order of the day, they logically went back to their industry colleagues.

   In the aerospace revolution of the 1950s, the same tension between the Army and the Air Force reappeared. General Bernard Schriever, chief architect of the ICBM program, was fully committed to the Air Force doctrine of "going to industry and having industry develop and produce for us." Air Force's competitors were Wernher von Braun and his former German colleagues, brought to America at war's end to work at the

Army's Redstone Arsenal at Huntsville, Alabama. They preferred to develop their missiles in-house, contracting out to the Army's old friend, the auto industry, for fabrication. In this battle, the Air Force won. By eschewing any in-house capacity, the Air Force commanded a big, well-heeled constituency of scientists, organized labor, and industry. Its impeccable free-enterprise viewpoint removed most of the stigma from the surge in public spending that the arms revolution entailed.

Later, in 1960, von Braun had his moment of triumph when his team became a critical nucleus of the new National Aeronautics and Space Administration (NASA). From then on, there were effectively two major sources of R&D and of procurement in the closely related missile and space fields: one, defense-based, under the control of the Air Force; the other, space-related, under the control of an ex-Army team in an ex-Army arsenal. But, final irony, the Army group found that it could not produce such complex equipment single-handily; it had to go to the same contractors the Air Force used. Private-sector, for-profit contracting had won out over the old in-house arsenal system.

The Military–Industrial Complex

The military–industrial complex has certain goals and characteristics that make it quite unlike any business cluster that has ever existed in the world, let alone the capitalist production system. Over the postwar period, its mandate had been the cold war imperative to keep in the technical lead. With less manpower and more highly developed science than the Soviet Union, the United States chose to fight the cold war by continually creating new and more terrible weapons that would deter. As a result the R&D component of the defense effort has risen dramatically over the postwar period, accelerating in the Star Wars era.[22] With this heavy commitment to publicly financed research and development has come an expansion in the ranks of the electrical and aeronautical engineers, nuclear physicists, mathematicians, systems analyists, and computer programmers required to design, develop, test, and evaluate high-tech weaponry. Airplanes that will flip over faster, fly a few hundred feet above the ground, and be less easily detected; radar that will more rapidly and accurately sense and identify the advance of an aggressive bomber or missiles; computers that can cope with a great mass and diversity of data piped in from satellites, radars, ships, and aircraft sensors – all of these must be designed and developed by highly skilled professionals and technicians.[23]

This process of defense-led innovation, which often produces economy-altering spin-offs, is different from all previous innovation in capitalist history. Whatever their different theoretical perspectives, economic historians have regarded innovation as an individual or a corporate entrepreneurial act whose risk and financing are assumed by the innovator in the hope of superprofitable returns.[24] But once the state steps in and sponsors nonstop research and innovation for narrow military ends, the nature of innovation changes. In the United States, where the national government now underwrites 70 percent of all R&D – almost three-quarters of which is military-related – innovation has become institutionalized, accelerated, and less sensitive to business cycles (although quite vulnerable to political cycles). The military–industrial complex is a new form of continual industrial innovation, even if its market spin-offs may be minimal.

A second feature of the military–industrial complex is its preoccupation with automated warfare. In addition to the aircraft and missile "frames," or "bodies," the "payload" they carry has become more significant and more sophisticated. Pilots and remote operators have come to rely increasingly on radar, guidance systems, communications equipment, and cybernetics to tell them where to fly, where to aim, what to dodge, and how to make decisions under conditions of uncertainty and rapid change. Strategic warfare has moved from bombers to missiles, becoming ever more capital- and technology-intensive. Electronic components, for instance, account for a larger share of value-added in each successive generation of weapons systems. By the 1960s, electronics composed 13 to 20 percent of an airplane's value, and 50 percent of that of a missile.[25]

The aerospace giants and their communications and electronics suppliers broke ranks with industrial leaders of the mechanical era. Indeed, they are almost entirely a new breed. Firms like Hughes, McDonnell-Douglas, Rockwell, Grumman, General Dynamics, United Technologies, TRW, Litton, and Lear-Siegler were not major players before World War II. They not only are preoccupied with defense work, but have two other unusual features: a high degree of concentrated market power and extraordinary dependence on one buyer, the federal government.

Concentration among military contractors has been a feature, and a worry, since the very beginning of the aerospace industry. In early years, scale economies seemingly favored concentration, although some analysts believe that the government wanted few competitors, in part to ensure secrecy in bomber development. In 1930, forty-one aircraft models were manufactured by eighteen companies; by 1935, the number fell to twenty-six models by twelve companies. Thereafter, as aircraft-development financing by government ballooned from 45 percent to 67 percent in 1939 and 92 percent during World War II, the number of big contract winners declined precipitously, and companies divided into predominantly commercial and military camps.[26]

This concentration has been maintained throughout the postwar period, despite decades of government commitment to small business set-asides. By the mid-1980s, the top 100 companies accounted for 70 percent of total defense business, the top 20 for nearly 50 percent, and the top 5 for 20 percent (table 6.1). At the level of individual weapons systems or parts, firms generally compete with only one or two others for an initial contract and, after winning it, exercise a virtual monopoly. Concentration has also evolved in supplier sectors. Most large aerospace firms have developed long-term relationships with one or a few highly reliable and responsive firms for each component. Many subcontractors have survived by occupying market niches and monopolizing the production of certain specialized parts.[27]

Table 6.1.   Top twenty prime contracting firms, 1958 and 1984

Rank	1958		1984	
------	Company	*Value (millions of dollars)*	Company	*Value (millions of dollars)*
	1958		*1984*	
	Company	*Value (millions of dollars)*	Company	*Value (millions of dollars)*
1	Boeing	2,131.0	McDonnell-Douglas	7,684.2
2	General Dynamics	1,383.2	Rockwell–North American	6,219.3
3	General Electric	783.4	General Dynamics	5,951.5
4	Lockheed Aircraft	755.1	Lockheed Corp.	4,967.5
5	United Aircraft	661.1	Boeing	4,563.8
6	AT&T	659.8	General Electric	4,514.5
7	North American	647.7	Hughes Medical	3,230.5
8	Douglas Aircaft	513.4	United Technologies	3,206.8
9	Hughes Aircraft	472.6	Raytheon	3,093.0
10	Martin Co.	400.2	Litton	2,440.7
11	Sperry-Rand	370.1	Grumman Corp.	2,419.0
12	Chance-Vought	360.4	Martin-Marietta	2,260.7
13	McDonnell	352.0	Westinghouse	1,943.5
14	IBM	316.5	LTV Corp.	1,655.3
15	RCA	288.3	Sperry Corp.	1,615.2
16	Northrop Aircraft	283.5	IBM	1,571.6
17	General Motors	280.9	Honeywell	1,354.4
18	Westinghouse	269.3	FMC Corp.	1,156.8
19	Republic Aviation	264.7	ITT Corp.	1,139.7
20	Chrysler Corp.	58.6	Ford Motor Co.	1,124.1
Cumulative share				
	Top 20 Companies	52.6%		46.5%

Source: *Aviation Week and Space Technology.*

The aerospace industry and its suppliers, the communications-equipment and electronics/instrumentation industries, are heavily dependent on defense spending. According to the Department of Commerce's input–output model, the more traditional weapons industries – tanks, ammunition, ordnance, and shipbuilding – are highly defense-dependent; but so are missiles, aircraft, and communications.[28] Furthermore, individual firms and their divisions tend to serve just one master, either commercial markets or the military.[29]

This unusual fact of government-as-monopsonistic-buyer makes the aerospace marketplace different from other manufacturing concerns. To confound the picture even further, the government does not behave the way a textbook private monopsonist would. The latter strives to maximize profits by squeezing the seller; the former is obsessed by a search for technical perfection. In contrast to practice in commercial factories, where a certain percentage of output is expected to be faulty, the Pentagon is concerned primarily with precision and performance on the part of the aircraft: because of the obvious dangers of combat flying, safety and quality have always been high priorities. As one contractor told us, "You face demands for time, performance, and cost. You can have two, but not three. When selling to the Pentagon, it's the time and performance that matters, and cost goes out the window."[30]

As a result of these peculiar market features, workers in defense firms operate in a paradoxical environment: although the new cold warfare is extremely capital-intensive, the equipment that delivers it is made by very labor-intensive methods. Aircraft and missiles do not lend themselves to the assembly-line techniques so fashionable in the twentieth-century consumer-goods industries. Rather, they depend on a tremendous amount of teamwork, as well as highly specialized individual contributions to handle specific production problems. Cold warfare paraphernalia is produced in small batches, often to unique design specifications and with experimentation embedded in the construction itself. Often, too, defense-plant work is highly sensitive and classified, because the product is valuable only as long as the other side cannot replicate it.

Thus as early as 1947, 46 percent of Lockheed's costs consisted of labor inputs, compared with 34 percent in materials.[31] Parts production – whether in engines, fueling systems, or communications equipment – was also highly labor-intensive. Over time, this labor component has grown more and more sophisticated, and the share of high-tech labor – scientists, engineers, technicians – in strategic weaponry has risen as the share of materials and semi- and unskilled labor declined.

A New Locational Logic

All these features have generated a locational calculus that is quite different from the traditional one in the economic-geography textbooks. First, the new weapons systems created the possibility of new production complexes far from traditional centers. The technologies and production processes for aircraft are quite different from those for metals, autos, and other consumer goods.[32] Certain aspects of airframes, in particular, favored locations with a climate and topography that differed from that of the industrial heartland.[33] In addition, the peculiarities of military production – the need for secrecy and small-batch production, the emphasis on teamwork and experimental fabrication, the attitudes consonant with a career in designing ever-more-destructive weaponry – favored new centers outside the traditional heartland.

Second, the continual pressure to innovate has engendered and reinforced a tendency toward agglomeration and clustering on the part of the aerospace industry and its suppliers. In this, they are no different from other innovative industries, with their proclivity to concentrate in a few geographical arenas.[34] What distinguishes cold war military-production complexes from their commercial counterparts, however, is the continual nature of the innovative process. In these industries, products never reach the point of mass production. Manufacturers thus avoid the pressure to disperse to lower-cost production sites. Instead, the conditions of a youthful, innovative industry are perpetuated by Pentagon demand and dollars. Industries get stuck in the superprofit stage; with only a few conspicuous exceptions, they stay in the centers where they first emerged.[35]

These features are accentuated and complicated by other characteristics of the military–industrial complex. The presence of few competitors reinforces the tendency toward agglomeration by encouraging firms to cluster.[36] Only with proximity can competitors watch one another's moves carefully, manage the market, and maintain market shares. Specialized services that enhance this oligopolistic structure cement the cluster, as do the requirements for frequent communication between monopolistic parts suppliers and their big final-assembly clients.

And because of the unique fact of government as monopsonistic buyer, clustering tends to encompass close proximity not only among competitors and suppliers, but also between buyer and sellers. With only one buyer, however complex, it pays to be nearby, with hired eyes and ears to the ground to detect future requirements, gather information, and market a continual supply of new military products. The aerospace industry thus becomes a "camp follower," setting up at least some of its operations in tandem with the military purchasing agents, planners, and funds appropriators in certain locales where this special client–seller relationship is present. This is especially true of certain types of operation, such as SETA, C^3I (command, control, communications, and intelligence), software, and systems engineers. The Pentagon and service agencies are located far from the major centers of commercial activity in the United States, raising the possibility that the preferences of the monopsonistic buyer powerfully helps determine which sites become new military production centers.

This geographically dispersed pattern of military–industrial production is reinforced by another feature of the Pentagon as buyer. Since cost is not a primary issue, the conventional pressure to minimize charges – for labor, transportation, and so on – is by and large absent. Instead, a premium is placed on being sited where the company can maximize its quality, reliability, and promptness in production – high cost or no.

Labor provides a good example. Highly skilled labor consumes a very large and ongoing share of the military procurement dollar, yet the location of such labor may not be at all crucial to the creation of a military–industrial center. This is because the government not only allows contractors to charge it for the costs of recruiting and moving skilled labor interregionally, but actually permits them to include these expenses in their cost base. Since contractors add their profit to this base, they have an actual incentive to move skilled labor around. One might even argue that the government has been running a massive for-profit population-resettlement program in the postwar period.

The new trend toward joint ventures also helps to anchor military-oriented producers in their new locations. The increasing sophistication of cold war weaponry has progressively emphasized the design stage and rendered it so complicated that no single firm is capable of turning out a new weapons system on its own. In the 1980s, just as the military services themselves were forced into greater cooperation and joint commands, the big aerospace contractors had to assemble teams to design, bid on, and eventually construct new weapons systems. This reinforces existing locations and favors proximity among cooperating firms. Often, since firms are based in disparate gunbelt sites, projects must be overseen by branch offices set up in selected central locations.

But the continual innovation inherent in cold war contracting has a contrary, destabilizing effect. The evolution of highly sophisticated computers with enormous computational capabilities may require ever larger contingents of private-sector contractors to write software and integrate systems located at the point where the military uses the equipment. And the new joint commands in the 1980s, made imperative by the incredible mobility and efficiency of modern weaponry, may accelerate the clustering of contractors that provide defense-planning services and C³I around Washington, D.C., the central command-and-control headquarters of the nation's military effort.

In our tour through the gunbelt, then, we can suppose that military-production complexes develop in three stages. First, new centers emerge, a function of the peculiarities of the strategic mission of the cold war. Second, these centers have extraordinary agglomerative growth trajectories, because of the prolongation of innovation stages by the cold war and because of the unique feature of government-as-buyer. And third, as innovation alters the technology of warfare, new weapons and strategies themselves favor yet newer centers of activity, tailored to the requirements of the times. Older centers may compete, but existing business cultures often make this difficult. Together, these facets of the military–industrial complex heighten the tendency to cluster and draw the clusters toward locations favored by the military – locations likely to be found outside the traditional industrial heartland. And these features give a special role to the preferences and prejudices of individual actors: founders, managers, top military brass, promoters, boosters, and others.

Founders, Generals, Congressmen, and Boosters

Because of the unique market structure of military provisioning, both private- and public-sector actors can powerfully influence the selection of sites. On the supply side, the firm's behavior is well captured by the notion of profit-maximizing; but on the demand side, the picture is much more complex, encompassing bureaucratic "satisficing," strategic concerns, and electioneering goals. "Satisficing" means that Pentagon and military staff may prefer to maximize the size of their bureaus or the perks of their jobs, rather than modernize the defense services delivered to the nation.

Our story of the development of the military–industrial complex features two key groups of supply-side actors. First, there are the entrepreneurs or founding fathers (this story has no founding mothers) who set up the offices, plants, and facilities that ultimately grew to be major aerospace firms. Successful innovators require a nurturing environment, one that favors the fragile and risky initiative on which they embark.[37] Such an environment can be a hometown, the founder's actual birthplace or the seat of the university or firm for which he was working when he branched out on his own. It can also be a locale far from his home base, a place to which he flees because his local environment quashes his ambitions and refuses him the resources to succeed. Founders may be drawn to new locations by a number of factors: a lucrative defense contract, an irresistible offer from local boosters, or a sense that a new locale is the perfect place to live and work. Differential costs of production are generally unimportant in this first critical step, so personal preferences and/or serendipity may play an important role.

The second group of actors are the managers of established firms and branches. Their room for personal preference is much smaller. As technologies mature – in standard aircraft or electronics parts, for instance – defense managers feel the same pressure as their commercial counterparts: to lower costs by building plants in outlying locations or closer to end markets, profiting from proximity to the monopsonistic buyer. This is more likely to occur in lines of defense output where competition is intense; less so, where a firm has few rivals. In monopolistic situations, a manager may try to pass on the higher costs of a satisficing location in his contract. Or, if unable to, he may chose to trade off excess profits for the privilege of living and working in a favored place. Amenities, either cosmopolitan or environmental, may thus enter into the locational calculus. And in cases where a firm's status is judged by its letterhead, the mere "image" of being in Sunnyvale, Costa Mesa, or Chula Vista may shape a managerial location decision.

On the demand side of this military-equipment market lies the complicated institution of the state. Here, no single individual plays a dominant role, yet several sets of actors are alert to locational issues and employ their influence to shape the evolution of military-production geography. These actors include the generals and colonels responsible for the military planning and strategy, the president (the military commander-in-chief) and his advisers who are responsible for foreign policy and budget formation, and the members of Congress who review and vote on military appropriations.

Military leaders are concerned primarily with strategic goals and therefore with the safety and efficiency of the "defense industrial base." Their notion of efficiency, however, may not be confined to issues of dollars and cents. For instance, Pentagon strategists may want defense facilities to be located in relatively remote interior areas where they will be less vulnerable to enemy attack. They may prefer to maintain duplicate and redundant facilities to ensure a source of supply. They may favor the siting of certain production and service activities close to their operational commands or procurement offices, to maximize interaction and cut down on delivery or installation time.[38] Such requirements may be written into contracts, even when firms are reluctant to comply. The costs of the consequent locational inefficiencies are absorbed by the service in question and covered in the contract.

The military may also use contracting power to create industrial communities that are more amenable to the defense presence. In the United States, ulike many other industrialized nations, the military top brass have never been accorded very high status in the cosmopolitan capitalist culture that emerged in the late nineteenth century.[39] Military leaders may thus favor the development of production facilities in communities that hold the military in relatively high regard. Forced to be very mobile throughout their professional lives, and scheduled for retirement at an early age, they may favor certain sites as potential retirement communities and may commit resources to these areas to enhance their attractiveness. San Diego, San Antonio, Los Angeles, and Colorado Springs, each with large concentrations of retired military, may have been favored in this way. Least attractive in this regard are large, established metropolitan centers dominated by a liberal social and business elite.

The location of private-sector defense activity may also be affected by military preferences. Remote places with residential communities of like-minded people may be favored over established industrial centers by military procurers, and by military personnel who have crossed over into private-sector management. The local politics and hardball labor practices that typify the industrial heartland – including collective bargaining, responsiveness to financial incentives, and job-hopping – are inimical to the military mode, with its rigid internal structure, narrowly restricted labor mobility, and emphasis on loyalty to the organization.[40] The search for commercial and community cultures congenial to military–industrial activity may draw contract dollars far from the Rustbelt.

Finally, rivalries among the service branches, and even within them, may emerge as powerful locational forces. During the 1950s, the struggle between the Air Force and the Army, with their very different visions of how strategic missiles ought to be made, was associated with a competition between Los Angeles and Huntsville for a major increment to the local defense economy. Many such controversies dot the history of strategic warfare. In some cases, the locational question is inconsequential in the larger conflict over weapons capabilities, service missions, and product management.[41] But in others, the fact that a certain military official is simply head of base x, y, or z, and that his personal prestige and chances of advancement will be greatly enhanced if he gets a certain new weapons system assigned to his territory, results in his lobbying hard for it, even if his location is not the strategically optimal one. National security policy-making is imperfect, so the literature tells us, allowing nonrational elements to come into play.

This most often happens at military middle-management level. Illogical factors may be embedded in the plans that colonels give their commanding officers for approval or in the requests that field commanders pass on to Washington. The top brass themselves may be indifferent to locational choices, although it is quite possible that generals will express preferences for certain key sites. Sometimes, the regional affinities of the topmost people will dictate the location of a military-related production complex. This has certainly been demonstrated in the case of the Houston Space Center, started when Lyndon B. Johnson was vice president.

Congress is a different matter. Indeed, much of the 1980s literature on the geography of defense outlays vilifies Congress as the agency most responsible for the skewed pattern.[42] The argument is that Congress treats the defense budget like a pork barrel, with every member scrambling for a chunk of contract dollars. Senators and representatives with the most clout – those chairing military-appropriations committees and those with the most seniority – can divert military dollars their constituents' way. Members of Congress have an incentive to maximize both votes and political campaign contributions, and thus can be expected to lobby hard for military contracts for their jurisdictions.

Overall, such a theory would suggest broad dispersion of defense contracts across the states, rather than concentration. Yet, while a few singular cases of the exercise of political muscle can be cited, empirical studies show a remarkable lack of general evidence.[43] A pork-barrelling model is difficult to defend, given the extraordinary concentration of prime contracts. Congress can only approve or deny expenditures and is generally not involved in initiating a weapons system. The potential bidders are identified far ahead of time, and it is the pre-existing location of defense factories and offices that explains the vast bulk of contemporary defense expenditures. Congress can be mobilized only very late in this process, making it more difficult to block an entire weapons system or to demand that a new plant be built in a virgin location. Although legislators from the industrial northeast dominated Congress well into the 1970s, this region continually lost ground in defense production.

Congressional logrolling does reinforce the tendency of military production to cluster in centers that are not preoccupied with civilian production. Representatives of military-dependent districts may win support for bills favorable to defense firms by agreeing to vote in favor of other constituencies' priorities – agricultural states' farm bills, say, or the Midwest's auto and steel tariffs.[44] And since productive capacity tends to grow through expansions rather than new plants, existing centers would seem to have an edge over potential locations. Members of Congress may be more effective in responding to an existing constituency by blocking plant or base closings, than in selecting a new military-production site on the basis of the area's potential.

Congressional influence, then, is limited. Despite the fact that individual legislators loudly protest plant closings, complain about discrimination in funding, and demand that contracts be let locally, most of this is done principally to get the legislator's name into the local paper. Military managers have no incentive to maintain a high profile, nor would it be considered appropriate or ethical for them to do so, but in our view military managers figure much more prominently than legislators as creators of the gunbelt.

Local civic boosters constitute the last set of actors that engages in efforts to build military-production centers. This group may be motivated by a desire to expand the area's tax base, enhance real-estate values, and create jobs for local residents. Historically, the strenuous rival efforts of such groups often left their marks on the geography of military production. In the early decades of the twentieth century, San Diego, Los Angeles, and San Francisco competed fiercely to be the home of the Navy's pricipal West Coast naval base.[45] In the 1960s, Colorado Springs successfully competed for the title of space command center.

Local boosters – who include city officials, real-estate developers, locally tied business interests (newspapers, banks, sports teams), and even universities[46] – may offer defense firms and the military the same incentives that they offer other enterprises: land, infrastructure, financing for industrial plants and related housing construction, and tax breaks. But perhaps most important, they can offer military decision-makers the promise of enthusiastic acceptance by the local community and the city's elite, as well as the kind of business culture and environment that is so important to these groups.[47] Such guarantees loomed large in the success of many gunbelt centers.

Military Places Rated

We now need to focus on the actual places on the American road map that compete for defense projects. Of course, "places" do not compete; their business elites do. Some fail; some succeed. To determine which characteristics seem to make for success, we will look at each area the way an economic developer would.[48] If you wanted to be a military–industrial town, how would you rate?[49]

Many factors – topography, climate, entrepreneurship, labor, government labs, universities, military bases, and local cultural and business climates – have been hypothesized to affect military–industrial location, especially the more glamorous, high-tech end. Many observers have stressed sun, clear skies, and flat terrain as ideal, simplifying construction of aircraft and missiles – important for small start-up companies[50] – and making it easier to test prototypes. Coastal sites provide access to international markets, very important in the pioneer days.[51] But, as mentioned above, for every case that seems to prove the rule, there are several that disprove it: Boeing did well in Seattle; Grumman, on Long Island; Honeywell, in Minneapolis. Climate was at best an eccentric and intermittent determinant.

Human capital

Entrepreneurs cannot easily be treated as indigenous or fixed regional factors, since they are quintessentially mobile. Nevertheless, sometimes the location of a military-production plant may be explained by the simple fact that a founder started it in his hometown (Boeing in Seattle) or a place in which he settled and that he came to love (Douglas or Kindelberger in Los Angeles). Entrepreneurs, of course, can also be seen as products of their environments – and so it is helpful to know something of the cultural and industrial milieu where they spent their formative years.[52]

Skilled labor is quite another matter. Most of the literature on high-tech location stresses specialized pools of labor as a necessity.[53] But, as already argued, labor cannot be considered an exogenous, fixed locational factor, because so much of it has been highly mobile and so much of this mobility has been underwritten by government.[54] Since new military-production complexes have emerged far from traditional centers, it is evident that massive population resettlement occurred during the hot wars of the 1940s and 1950s, and continued throughout the cold war period.

Occasionally, already extant labor pools can be dipped into. Indeed, military bases themselves serve as sources of labor. Soldiers are recruited more or less ubiquitously from all over the United States, but the bases at which they live and work are concentrated in the sunbelt. Mustered-out or retired military personnel composed the single largest group of interregional migrants in the years from 1969 to 1976.[55] They knew the labor market around their bases far better than that of their hometowns, a fact that encouraged many to stay in the vicinity. As we shall see, firms are attracted to these areas by the presence of people who have an institutional knowledge of weapons systems, the procurement process, and/or the services themselves, specialized training in operating certain weapons, and expertise in maintaining these weapons.

Universities may also be important regional suppliers of labor. Firms might locate near first-rate engineering schools, such as Caltech or MIT, to have "first dibs" on graduates. Employees seeking to advance professionally enroll in night classes and special "executive" programs for returning and working students; this, in turn, may make locating near a good universtiy more attractive to employers.[56] Consulting by university professors for private firms, and the less frequent instance in which a professor sets up a contracting firm, are other ways in which universities may act as conduits of human capital for a nascent military–industrial complex. Universities, indeed, play a central role in the interregional redistribution of engineering and scientific talent. First, they admit students from all over the nation, with the better schools attracting high proportions of out-of-state entrants. Then, although many of these students are subsequently redispersed nationally through their university's placement office, many chose to stay in the school's environs. This has been particularly true of the Boston area.

A great deal of the literature on high-tech industry has stressed the importance of amenities in the ability of firms to attract and hold professional and technical labor. The hypothesis suggests that professional and technical workers have a strong position in their labor markets, effectively pulling firms to the places where they want to live. But there is disagreement about just what those amenities might be. While some scientists may be infatuated with the opera, others may prefer the wide-open spaces, the seashore, or mountains to climb. Then, too, other studies dissent, noting that engineers and scientists have shown an extraordinary proclivity to follow the best job, wherever it is.

The availability of blue-collar labor was traditionally a major concern for aerospace companies. In the early decades, firms needed to be near a medium-size city; during the war years, government agencies and funds helped facilitate the recruitment of thousands of workers from labor-surplus areas to labor-deficit ones, even as they tried to decentralize manufacturing capacity toward areas of high unemployment. In certain places, the competition for blue-collar labor has been intense. Some authors suggest that there has been substantial labor-hoarding by aircraft-engine firms in New England and – to a lesser extent – by the airframe industry in the southwest.[57]

But the "quality" of blue-collar labor matters, too: many defense contractors have shown an unusual antipathy toward unions and heavily unionized cities and regions, not principally because of wage demands, but for fear of work stoppages and resistance to changing work rules in an industry where timely delivery is critical and military models of labor relations prevail.[58] Like the military itself, these firms see themselves as having a mission to perform: they want their product to be "the best," and they need a dedicated , team-work-oriented, pliant work force. Places without a well-developed industrial capitalist culture may thus fare better as potential military–industrial centers than Chicago, Detroit, Cleveland, or Philadelphia. Some may object that New England, a region with adversarial labor relations, disproves this theory, but New England suffered twenty years of deindustrialization before its military-based resurgence, decimating union ranks, and has benefited from its strong educational system. And Los Angeles, once a virulently anti-union town, had to accept unions as part of the national wartime accords – organizing permitted but no strikes allowed.

Blue-collar labor, though, may not be the locational force it once was. With weaponry more and more dependent on innovation, the need increasingly is for very high-level engineering and technical expertise – the kind that comes from university Ph.D. programs rather than from trade schools. Today, a typical defense worker is more likely to be an engineer than a machinist, a software writer than a riveter, a skilled technician than an assembly-line worker, a physicist experimenting with gallium arsenide semiconductors rather than a metal bender. And, importantly, a member of a professional organization rather than a member of a union.

As with geophysical features, there are many examples where human capital has played a role, but also many where it has not. Many military bases have drawn no appreciable military–industrial activity, while some successful defense cities, like Boston, have few bases from which to recruit. Some centers, such as Boston and San Jose, have benefited from the presence of a major technical university, while other regions with first-rate engineering schools continue to export most of their graduates. Many engineers swear by Seattle, Rockford, and even frigid Minneapolis; and winters are long in New England, too. Remote cities like Colorado Springs seem to have no trouble drawing highly-educated workers, despite the absence of cosmopolitan cultural offerings. High rates of unionization do not seem to have harmed the military–industrial cores of Boston and Los Angeles. In sum, no single element appears to be a necessary prerequisite to the initiation of a military–industrial center. These labor features seem so clearly crucial and yet so endogenous, evolving simultaneously with the military production centers themselves.

Idea mills: Government, university, and corporate labs

Another locational factor might be the presence of an "idea mill": a place where military-oriented innovation is institutionalized as an ongoing activity. Wellsprings such as government R&D labs, university labs, and corporate labs might be expected both to generate new entrepreneurs and to attract outside entrepreneurs, who would seek proximity to and contact with the idea-makers.

The federal government runs and funds a number of major research laboratories around the country, including several elite national labs (Livermore, Los Alamos) that do purely weapons-related work. They are much more spatially decentralized than are either university or corporate labs.[59] We might expect, then, that military ideas centers would draw along in their wake new forms of related for-profit activity. In fact, as we shall see, few have.

Universities might operate in the same fashion: their labs might generate ideas that local entrepreneurs could pick up on. Certainly, this is the theory behind the recently fashionable university research park.[60] And universities may also be contractors themselves. Military RDT&E contracts to educational institutions amounted to $850 million by the early 1980s. Several well-known concentrations of high-technology industry, with strong defense components – Boston's Route 128, California's Silicon Valley, and England's Cambridge Science Park – have been linked to major research universities.[61]

Corporate laboratories, too, could devote some of their overhead to military-oriented activities. In general, they are highly concentrated in the traditional industrial heartland, near big corporate headquarters cities like New York and Chicago, and key industrial enclaves for particular industries, like Detroit. But this strategy would most likely depend on the prospects for these firms in their existing markets. We might expect more experimentation in regions with a structurally declining economic base, especially in eras of major recession or depression.

Nonetheless, "idea mills" may prove very questionable locational factors. Federal R&D centers tend to be heavily committed to secrecy and may offer their employees such favorable civil service perks that no local spin-off activity is generated. Well-paid and with job security for life, employees are less inclined to risk the rigors of the marketplace. Existing weapons labs show this clearly. Universities may generate the ideas essential to military innovation, but their host communities may not exploit the fact – as witness the top Midwest engineering schools. Conversely, many places without top-ranked research universities – including Colorado Springs, central Florida, Washington, D.C., and Huntsville, Alabama[62] – have been sites of high-tech military-oriented activities.

Defense markets

Traditional location theory stressed the importance of overcoming the "friction of distance": industries would locate at sites that minimized the costs of assembling production inputs and reaching the market, all else being equal. But for modern defense industries, these assumptions do not work very well. In defense production, material supplies account for a small and shrinking share of total costs, and they are generally high in value relative to transport costs. Likewise, the cost of transporting the product to market does not matter much. Some assembled products, like ships, submarines, and aircraft, literally transport themselves to market, obviating transportation costs altogether.[63] Other products are designed for "mobilization," making the physical link to markets largely irrelevant. Military products that are stockpiled and stored for some future mobilization are placed in armories and receptacles – missile silos are a good example – whose locations are dispersed, classified, or frequently changed.

True, there are important exceptions. Overseas destinations may have mattered in the critical period of the 1930s, favoring coastal production sites. Military facilities might be needed for design and testing, or service and maintenance contracts may tie firms to a particular site. In one sense, the Department of Defense and Congress form the market, because they construct the budget and appropriate the money. If firms need timely or inside information, or if their client needs them close by to execute information-intensive C^3I contracts, we might expect them to set up shop around Washington, D.C. Conversely, contractors that want an inside track on the next innovative challenge may decide to establish storefronts or larger research-and-development branch offices close to leading-edge commands. Yet, all this said, city fathers of many towns have vigorously pursued military-related activity without success.

The important point here is that with the shift from large-volume, shooting-war production to small-volume, technology-intensive, proto-typical design and testing, cost in the traditional sense no longer matters; what matters is getting or failing to get information. In this sense, defense industries are more like informational service industries than traditional manufacturing. The archetype is the SETA operations, which proliferated wildly during the 1980s and locate close to the contracting agencies, both at military bases and in central facilities in Los Angeles, Colorado Springs, and Washington, D.C.

It is going to be difficult to judge the relative effect of these conflicting factors – geophysical traits, human capital, idea mills, government presence – or to rank military-production enclaves according to them. We might try distinguishing between active factors – key elements that trigger the military-production-center building process – and passive factors that help maintain a center in place. The problem is that these elements may change over time as the technologies of warfare change and as the missions and fortunes of the services wax and wane. Thus we come full circle, back to the structural and behavioral forces that led to the construction of military-production complexes in places far from the old industrial heartland.[64]

How Military-Production Centers are Built

How, exactly, do these new centers develop? Revolutionary breakthroughs in war technology, sudden shifts in foreign policy, and dramatic institutional changes within the military–industrial complex create ratchet effects that propel certain places to the fore. But something must be there to begin with: a critical element, like the grain of sand around which the oyster's pearl grows – a founding father who sets up a military-oriented plant, a pre-existing industrial firm that decides to risk entering military-oriented production,[65] a local university or research lab with an interest in a particular military mission, or a strategic imperative that compels the government to start a new base or a new factory. In the twisted skein of cause-and-effect over time, distinguishing the initial cause may prove difficult, particularly if there are subsequent key events that might also explain a production center's success or failure.[66]

Once a site is selected for a military-oriented plant, agglomeration economies set in motion a dynamic process of local economy-building.[67] A specialized labor pool, a set of specialized business-service firms, and competitive spin-off firms begin to proliferate. New enterprises may be attracted by the resulting agglomeration of talent and ideas. "Progressive internalization" reinforces the process, as import-substituting activities supply specialized goods and services – as in Los Angeles in the 1930s and 1940s, where the airframe industry attracted machining, communications, electronics, software, and service industries, none of which had existed there before.[68] This tendency to agglomerate is very deep-set for defense-based industries: they will continue to cluster long beyond the point where economic rationality would suggest decentralization. Service procurement agencies may even be attracted by the resulting concentration of specialized firms. Thus, over time, entire metropolitan areas may come to depend substantially on military enterprise.

This is a multistage process, full of dynamic changes, discontinuities, and contingencies, unpredictable and sometimes random, and thus difficult to handle within the covential static framework of neoclassical economics. It is analogous to a golf game, with the host cities as players of various sizes, strengths, smarts, and physical endowments. Each tees off with a certain strategy in mind; subsequent strokes are heavily shaped by the outcome of that first shot. Meanwhile, the weather may change, a crucial club may break, a competitor may make a brilliant move, their eye or their judgment may take a sudden turn. It is impossible to predict the final outcome or the best path to follow.

Five Models of the Military–Industrial City

We can distinguish at least five such paths to the development of a military–industrial city.

Model A: The seedbed transformed

An existing agglomeration of firms, services, and skilled labor pools may act as a "seedbed of innovation" for new defense-oriented activity.[69] Established centers with their corporate R&D labs, good universities, diversified business services, and extensive skilled-labor markets harness these resources to new tasks. An existing commercially oriented firm – in, say, instruments (Honeywell in Minneapolis) or radio (Raytheon in Massachusetts) or precision machining (Pratt & Whitney in Connecticut) – reorientates itself toward an emerging military mission and market. Successful entry on the ground floor leads to dependable, lucrative contracts for development as well as production. In turn, suppliers and/or competing rivals emerge around these key firms. This stimulates yet another round of skilled-labor-pool formation and local business services. A major obstacle to be overcome may be the hold that more established industries have on resources and, more subtly, on local attitudes.

Model B: The upstart military–industrial city

A second, almost diametrically opposed model is one in which a single individual or small group starts up a military-oriented firm, sometimes with military support, at a site far from existing industrial centers. Founders, for reasons explored above, may prefer remote locations. Their Pentagon patrons, comfortable with frontier locations, may give them the initial contracts necessary for survival. The forces of agglomeration are thus set in motion, as in Los Angeles in the 1920s and 1930s.

Such a new center faces a formidable task. It must gather the multifarious resources that are readily available in existing seedbeds: a pool of engineers, scientists, and technicians; a technical-university system; and a crop of supporters in Congress. On the plus side, an upstart military developer has no encumbrances in the form of competing traditional industries and fixed business cultures.

Model C: The booster-incubated military–industrial complex

A third model centers on the formation of an extraordinary local coalition, including members of Congress, to recruit military facilities and defense contractors. Since at key times the military–industrial complex shows a proclivity to relocate production plants or develop new bases, a town may be able to garner a share by vigorously promoting itself as an ideal site. Many such local efforts are mounted, but only a handful succeed. A favorable outcome usually hinges on an area's having something special: a local resource, a piece of land, surplus capital, or a unique environmental setting.

Once a locale attracts a military facility, it must develop agglomeration economies like those of established places. This may be difficult, since service bases and branch plants are often quite isolated, self-contained, and narrowly specialized. Thus the complex may have to be built in steps, through a grueling process of recruiting and wheedling in federal arenas. A military base, for instance, might provide the personnel to attract a few high-tech branch plants. Or it may draw around it special defense-service contractors. Or its military function may be upgraded. These, in turn, may further enhance the area's attractiveness as a defense research-and-production center, convincing other large firms to enter and encouraging local start-ups and spin-offs.

Model D: The military–educational complex

Universities whose faculty and administrators face strong incentives to solicit outside research support may agressively pursue military-funded research. Over time, some of these projects may evolve into off-campus research institutes or independent firms. Their military connections may allow, or even encourage, them to move from R&D into production. Agglomeration economies set in, and the area becomes a specialized military-production center, maintaining the university–industry link that affords it a steady supply of new ideas and talent. Stanford and Silicon Valley, MIT and Route 128, are the classic cases. Less well known is Caltech's role in engendering the Los Angeles aerospace complex.

Model E: The installation-based military–industrial complex

Key military facilities – aircraft-testing grounds, defense nerve centers, deployment centers for missiles and space craft – may be positioned without local boosterism and may set off a growth dynamic, attracting production and/or service facilities. The military installation may generate a labor pool – short-term technicians and mechanics, intermediate-term engineers, and twenty-year retiring officers – who in turn may attract yet other firms. Such a center will most easily achieve the cultural characteristics that are favorable to an ongoing defense presence. In another version of this trajectory, the Pentagon may dictate the location of a defense plant for strategic reasons, and this may set off a process like that of the upstart-city model.

Model F: The defense-services complex

A special variant of Model E is Model F, the defense-services city. The obvious example is Washington, D.C. The "installation" in this case is the core set of gorvernment institutions concerned with the military–industrial complex: the Pentagon, the White House, and the Congress. They constitute the command-and-control headquarters of the military–industrial complex, much in the same way that New York, London, and Tokyo operate as command-and-control headquarters for private financial and industrial capital in their respective countries. Just as for commercially oriented corporations, transportation and communication improvements have caused the major military-oriented firms to fragment their functions, with production far from the Washington center but large branch offices in nearby D.C. suburbs.[70] Such a defense-services city builds on these interconnections between government and private suppliers, developing a very specialized profile, with little or no manufacturing.

These models each posit a different initiating source and thus a different set of challenges and evolutionary steps. The end result for each defense-based city is a special kind of production complex, a function of its particular mission and of the period in which its greatest growth was engendered. Some cities may contain elements of more than one model.

Clearly, many aspiring cities fall by the wayside. Each model demands that a number of successive steps be taken. Simply attracting a plant or military base will not by itself ensure an agglomerative dynamic. Some military–industrial cities may remain one-plant towns. Others may fail altogether: San Antonio and Atlanta are examples.

Notes

1   A lively debate concerns the formation of military and foreign policies and the extent to which each is influenced by economic interests. See the thoughtful reviews in Lovering, 1987.

2   Greer, 1955: 17–20; B. Davis, 1967: 173–76; Weigley, 1973: 230, 234, 236–37; Kelsey, 1982: 47; Douhet, 1983: 126; Shiner, 1983: 19–21; Sherry, 1987: 23–24, 36–7. After a Far East tour in 1923 and 1924, Mitchell astonishingly forecast that Japan would launch a surprise attack at Pearl Harbor.

3   McClendon, 1952: 127–32; Goldberg, 1957: 36–37; Kelsey, 1982: 32; Shiner, 1983: 25, 31; Ravenstein, 1986: 5.

4   McClendon, 1952: 175, 190–91, 215–24; Goldberg, 1957: 39–41, 95–96; Higham, 1972: 72; Hurley, 1975: 133–34; Shiner, 1983: 94.

5   Kelsey, 1982: 35, 43.

6   Glines, 1980: 143.

7   Holley, 1964: 26.

8   Ibid.: 38.

9   Greer, 1955: 110, 118; Goldberg, 1957: 43; Copp, 1980: 455; Sherry, 1987: 79–80.

10   Tobias et al., 1982: 50.

11   Kelsey, 1982: 15–16, 20–22.

12   Schoneberger, 1984: 55–56.

13   Anderson, 1983: 26, 28, 31; Schoneberger, 1984: 30–32, 50–51.

14   McClendon, 1952: 252–54; MacCloskey, 1968: 142.

15   U.S. Congress, House, 1959: 11; Futrell, 1974: 242–44; Bright, 1978: 41–42.

16   Tokaty, 1964: 280–82; Weigley, 1973: 400–3; Futrell, 1974: 213.

17   For an elaboration on this theme, see Markusen, 1990a, 1991.

18   York, 1970: 53; Futrell, 1974: 239, 256.

19   Schwiebert, 1965: 22, 69–72, 80, 217; Armacost, 1969: 58; Futrell, 1974: 244–45; von Braun and Ordway, 1975: 132–33; Hall, 1988: passim.

20   U.S. Congress, House, 1959: 23–25; Peck and Scherer, 1962: 230; Schwiebert, 1965: 113–14; Armacost, 1969: 59–60, 71, 86–87; von Braun and Ordway, 1975: 128, 131; Heims, 1980: 273; Bilstein, 1984: 209.

21   Hitch, 1965: passim.

22   Stekler, 1965: 18–22; Markusen, (1986e) shows how military R&D has risen from a small share of national R&D in the 1930s to about 50 percent in the mid-1980s. For a stunning comparison of modern rates of military innovation compared with historical rates, see Tobias et al., 1982, chap.1.

23   Markusen, Hall, and Glasmeier (1986: 18–19) show that missiles are the most high-tech of all industries, as measured by the share of engineers, scientists, and technicians in their occupational structure – 41 percent compared with 22 percent in communications equipment, 19 percent in aircraft, and 13 percent in electronics. See also the studies of defense dependency of various occupations in Rutzick, 1970; Dempsey and Schmude, 1971; Oliver, 1971; DeGrasse, 1983; Reppy, 1985; U.S. Congress, Office of Technology Assessment, 1985; Hartung et al., 1985; Henry and Oliver, 1987.

24   Examples of each tradition are Schumpeter, 1939, 1961; Mandel, 1973, 1980; Rosenberg, 1972. Both Schumpeter and Kondratieff (1935, 1984)

suggested the link between troughs in long waves and the bunching up of new innovations. The modern scholars of innovation, like Rosenberg, and Nelson, Peck, and Kalacheck (1967) tend to see it as technology-driven, where technology is an exogenous force; Schumpeter began with this view, but altered it later in life (Phillips, 1971: 4–6).

25   Stekler, 1965: 18–21.

26   See Cunningham, 1951: 25–26; Phillips, 1971: 119; Steckler, 1965: 3–6.

27   Gansler, 1980: 36–45, 128–44; Adams, 1981: 33–41; Baldwin, 1967: 62–78, Marfels, 1978; Bluestone, Jordan, and Sullivan, 1981: 55. There is some debate about the extent to which Defense Department patronage has also prevented even greater monopolization in the industry (Phillips, 1971: 1–3).

28   For a number of reasons, these estimates are unduly low. They include only Department of Defense expenditures, not foreign military sales, the Department of Energy's nuclear warheads, or NASA's space defense activities. See the discussion in Markusen, 1986b: 109–11. Regrettably, these figures also exclude service industries, some of which, like computer software, have large defense components. We use the term "industry" in the broader sense, including service activities.

29   Gansler (1982: 39–41) shows the sensitivity of military orientation to political cycles. In 1958, at the end of the initial cold war decade, the top twenty-five contractors had 40 percent of their business in defense. By 1975, this had fallen to 10 percent, but most of this apparent diversification was achieved through acquisitions. The defense division of these companies, and certainly individual plants within them, remained almost exclusively defense-dependent.

30   An excellent, although somewhat dated, literature exists in the industrial organizational tradition on the structure of defense markets. See Peck and Scherer, 1962; Baldwin, 1967; Gansler, 1980; Adams and Adams, 1982.

31   Cunningham, 1951: 17. He also noted that by the late 1930s, 90 percent of aircraft labor was either skilled or semiskilled, although this share declined somewhat during the heavy production runs of World War II (p. 21).

32   This was less the case with mechanical and electrical machinery. Some segments of the precision-machining industry and radio industries were able to make the transition into aircraft engines and radar.

33   Cunningham (1951: 29–31) argues that the infant airframe industry gravitated toward the clear, predictable weather of the southwest, which permitted more flying days and more frequent testing, lowered the risk of missing delivery dates, and minimized heating and storage costs for space-extensive assembly. Topography, too, he claims, favored coastal plains like those on Long Island, around Lake Erie, and in the Los Angeles Basin. In the final section of this chapter, we argue that these factors may have been overstated in the literature and offer evidence of cases where aircraft manufacture endured, despite climatic and topographical disadvantages.

34   For a review of the literature on the tendency of innovative industries to cluster in initial superprofit stages, see Markusen, 1985b.

35   For this reason, we suspect that some scholars' efforts to proclaim the industrial era over and to celebrate the advent of flexible specialization and innovative industrial districts miss underlying causal relationships.

Interestingly, the better scholars in this field are often generalizing from their observations in their own regional economies, which are among the most military-dependent in the nation: Scott, 1982, 1983a, 1983b, 1984a, 1984b, 1985, 1986a, 1986b, 1986c, 1987; Scott and Angel, 1987; Scott and Storper (1986b) in the Orange County/Los Angeles area; Piore and Sabel (1984) in New England. The aerospace industry, as of 1964, consumed 38 percent of the nation's R&D funds, most of it from government coffers and most of it concentrated in New England and southern California (Bluestone, Jordan, and Sullivan, 1981: 159).

36   This argument about oligopolistic clustering is reviewed at length in Markusen, 1985b.

37   Starting with Pirenne's (1914: 259) reflections on how existing capitalists are displaced by "new men, bold, entrepreneurial, who allow themselves audaciously to be driven by the wind," continuing through Schumpeter's (1939) "new men," and reaching to modern analysts like Andersson (1985a, 1985b) and Andersson and Strömquist (1988), a lively literature exists in entrepreneurship, including its locational attributes. For an overview of the literature on founding fathers, see chapters 4–7 of Markusen et al. (1991).

38   In such instances, a prior question is why military facilities and procurement offices are located where they are. This we have not been able to explore thoroughly, although in our case studies we do inquire into the origins of certain key military installations when they become important lures for private-sector activity.

39   On the military's response to this status problem, see Janowitz, 1960. On the military profession generally, see also Huntington, 1957.

40   For an exposition of these differences, see Fallows, 1981: 107–14. Japanese labor relations are much closer to the military model.

41   The arsenal vs contractor debate, documented earlier, reaches back to efforts by both the Army and the Navy to build their own aircraft in factories in Dayton and Philadelphia, respectively. It also, as we will show, has a contemporary counterpart in the current struggle over who will build booster rockets for space missions.

42   See for instance, J. Anderson, 1983; Mazza and Wilkinson, 1980.

43   For a review and comparison of a raft of studies by political scientists on this question, see Rundquist, 1983.

44   It is important to note that some districts heavily favored by defense spending are represented in Congress by men and women who are staunch doves. In the mid-1980s, for instance, George Brown in southern California and Ron Dellums and Barbara Boxer in northern California all strongly supported significant defense cut-backs. See the extended discussion in Markusen, 1990b.

45   Lotchin (1984) describes this competition and suggests, among other things, that the unity of San Diego-area local governments, compared with the internal squabbling among the Bay Area cities of Oakland, Vallejo, and San Francisco, helped swing the base toward that southernmost port.

46   A number of urban historians have documented the prominent role of boosters in the West. See Abbott, 1981; Glabb and Brown, 1976; Boorstin,

1965; Reps, 1979; McWilliams, 1946. For a conceptual model of locally tied interests, see Markusen, 1987b, chap. 7.

47   We have not included here others whose actions may heighten or damage a place's chances of becoming a military-production center, specifically labor unions, peace groups, and professional and technical employees of defense firms. We do cite instances in the chapters that follow, particularly negative ones. But we are not convinced that any of these groups are important enough as decision-makers to have had a significant impact on the generalized pattern of military production that has evolved across the nation. Business culture has been increasingly viewed as an important determinant of location, particularly in the siting of new innovative activity. See Stowsky, 1989.

48   Scott and Angel (1987) argue, "The seeds of many of these growth sectors seem to have been planted at particular locations in what amounts to a set of highly contingent circumstances . . . The main analytical issue here, however, is not so much how these centers came to be precisely where they are, but how they subsequently grew quite systematically as a function of their own internal dynamic . . ." (p. 878). They then proceed to examine new regional high-tech complexes in and of themselves, without comparative reference to other candidate regions. We try here to reinsert this comparative sensitivity, because it is particularly important in fashioning policy recommendations.

49   In early orientation to commercial industrial location, this body of theory assumed perfectly competitive markets and a fixed panoply of differentially endowed regions. It then derived the profit-maximizing locations of individual firms and sectors (Weber, 1929), the optimal pattern of land uses (von Thünen, 1966), and a set of central places with functional hierarchies for the total urban system (Christaller, 1966; Lösch, 1954). It is possible to relax many of the constraining assumptions of the original formulations to encompass, for instance, imperfect competition, knowledge as an input, and even simultaneous movements of labor and capital, to modernize the theory.

50   Cunningham, 1951: 25, 29-30; Stekler, 1965: 2–4. Before the early 1930s, airframe companies paid for their own construction facilities. By 1934, 45 percent of new capacity was financed by government advances and payments under contracts. This rose to 67 percent in 1939 and 92 percent during World War II. Aircraft-engine makers, on the other hand, had substantial government patronage from a much earlier date.

51   Cunningham, 1951: 20; Stekler, 1965: 2.

52   See, for instance, the account of why Detroit was a logical center for auto production, and thus why Henry Ford and others might have succeeded there where their New England counterparts failed (Markusen, 1985b: 168–69). See also Koestler's account (1975: 121–24) of how Gutenberg invented the printing press by combining three disparate technologies – wood-block engraving, raised letters, and the wine press – all practiced in his wine-growing region of Mainz.

53   See, for instance, Rees and Stafford, 1983; Joint Economic Committee, 1982.

54   Sometimes this has been a wholesale process. In 1948, when Chance Voight

moved from San Diego to Dallas, at the government's urging, the Pentagon paid to move 1,500 families (Cunningham, 1951: 23).

55   Long (1976); Bluestone, Jordan, and Sullivan (1981) found that 12 percent of the new hires of New England aircraft firms came from the military in the period from 1964 to 1967. Some states deliberately foster this presence. Florida's Department of Education has a computer program listing the skills and availability of 13,000 military retirees in the state for the use of company recruiters ("Florida's Business Climate Attracting New Industry," *Aviation Week and Space Technology*, February 21, 1983: 63).

56   Markusen, Hall, and Glasmeier (1986) found that the incidence of educational options – the number of postsecondary educational programs in a metropolitan area – was significantly and positively related to high-tech growth and distribution in the 1970s.

57   Bluestone, Jordan, and Sullivan, 1981: 140–48.

58   Cunningham, 1951: 22–23; Bluestone, Jordan, and Sullivan, 1981: 107, 153. In the postwar period, a number of important moves appear to have been made to escape unions, including Pratt & Whitney's move to Maine, General Electric's moves to Vermont and Kentucky, and Litton's construction of its Pascagoula, Mississippi, shipyards. Many aircraft and related companies reluctantly permitted unionization during World War II, as part of the deal for a no-strike pledge, but have chafed under them ever since. However, Markusen, Hall, and Glasmeier (1986: 155) found no significant inverse relationship between rates of unionization and metropolitan high-tech activity. Indeed, they found a positive relationship between the two in explaining high-tech job and plant distribution in 1977.

59   Malecki, 1981a.

60   For a review of research parks in the United States, see Goldstein and Luger, 1988.

61   Dorfman, 1982, 1983; Saxenian, 1985a, 1985b; Segal Quince Wicksteed, 1985.

62   In a national study of university research-and-development spending across all 277 metropolitan areas, we found a negative relationship between such spending and high-tech location and growth. (Markusen, Hall, and Glasmeier, 1986: chap. 9.)

63   Others, like shuttles or communications satellites, may require costly strapping on 747s to deliver them to Cape Canaveral.

64   Several scholars, building on an established tradition in regional science and in the industrial restructuring literature, have recently worked on the ideas of "production complexes" (Scott, 1982, 1983a, 1985, 1986b, 1986c); industrial enclaves (Markusen, 1988); and industrial districts (Piore and Sabel, 1984). These extend pioneering studies of new industrial places by Perloff et al. (1960) and Duncan and Lieberson (1970).

65   Some, notably Scott and Angel (Scott, 1986a; Scott and Angel, 1987), have argued that the question of proximate causation is neither important nor interesting. They reject the notion of a privileged "independent variable" that anchors the entire locational process (Scott, 1984: 25) and concentrate instead on the dynamic process in which conditions of growth are reproduced. While their contributions to the explication of the clustering process are significant, we think that their indifference to proximate causes leads

them in some cases to misinterpret and overstate the endogeneity of development. In their analysis of Orange County, for instance, they miss the crucial connection between new "innovative" defense subcontractors and SETA firms, whose location and apparent "disintegration" have explanatory roots in the military–industrial complex and cold war dynamics described above. When Scott (1986a) characterized Orange County as "a major growth center in the classical sense of the term . . . characterized by a core of dynamic propulsive (high technology) industries around which a penumbra of dependent input suppliers has grown up" (p. 21), he credits the Orange County complex with a degree of autonomy that is belied by its Pentagon client and its origins in and ongoing ties with the Los Angeles aerospace industry.

66   Scott (1984a: 25) makes this point well; yet this argument easily leads to the artificial detachment of a local or regional inquiry form the larger structural forces that gave it its start. This is the central dilemma in modern regional geography, articulated powerfully by Massey and her collegues in their original papers on industrial restructuring as a derivative of capitalist dynamics (Massey and Meegan, 1978) and their more recent emphatic claim that "geography matters!" (Massey, 1984; Massey and Allen, 1984).

67   See Perroux, 1961: 152, 168. Many contemporary scholars have combined the older mechanics of agglomeration with an emphasis on innovation. See, for instance, the creative milieu (Aydalot, 1986b, 1988; Aydalot and Keeble, 1988b), creative drift (Jacobs, 1984: 230), the creative city (Andersson, 1985a, 1985b; Andersson and Strömquist, 1988), and creative economic regions (Johansson, 1987; Johansson and Westin, 1987).

68   See Vance, 1970: 103-52; Jacobs, 1984: 141–48, 230.

69   The seedbed function has been developed by Thompson (1965, 1975), Hägerstrand (1967), Pred (1977), and others pondering the stability of the hierarchy of cities. See the lengthier discussion of this literature in Chapter 4 of this book.

70   For the original work on spatially differentiated activities within a single corporate entity, see Hymer, 1973.

References

Abbott, Carl. 1981. *Boosters and Businessmen: Popular Economic Thought and Urban Growth in the Antebellum Middle West.* Westport, Conn.: Greenwood Press.

Adams, Gordon. 1981. *The Iron Triangle: The Politics of Defense Contracting.* New York: Council on Economic Priorities.

Adams, Walter, and William James Adams. 1982. "The Military–Industrial Complex: A Market Structure Analysis." *Papers and Proceedings* (American Economic Association) 62: 279–87.

Anderson, Roy A. 1983. *A Look at Lockheed.* New York: Newcomen Society in North America.

Andersson, Åke E. 1985a. "Creativity and Regional Development." *Papers of the Regional Science Association* 56: 5–20.

Andersson, Åke E. 1985b. *Kreativitet: StorStadens Framtid.* Stockholm: Prisma.

Andersson, Åke E., and Ulf Strömquist. 1988. *K—Samhällets Framtid.* Stockholm: Prisma.

Armacost, Michael H. 1969. *The Politics of Weapons Innovation: The Thor–Jupiter Controversy.* New York: Columbia University Press.

Aydalot, Philippe. 1986b. "Trajectoires technologiques et milieux innovateurs." In *Milieux innovateurs en Europe*, ed. Philippe Aydalot. Paris: GREMI (privately printed).

Aydalot, Philippe. 1988. "Technological Trajectories and Regional Innovation in Europe." In *High Technology Industry and Innovative Environments: The European Experience*, ed. Philippe Aydalot and David Keeble. London: Routledge and Kegan Paul.

Aydalot, Philippe, and David Keeble. 1988b. "High Technology Industry and Innovative Environments in Europe: An Overview." In *High Technology Industry and Innovative Environments: The European Experience*, ed. Philippe Aydalot and David Keeble. London: Routledge and Kegan Paul.

Baldwin, William L. 1967. *The Structure of the Defense Market, 1955–1964.* Durham, N.C.: Duke University Press.

Bilstein, Roger E. 1984. *Flight in America, 1900–1983: From Wrights to the Astronauts.* Baltimore: Johns Hopkins University Press.

Bluestone, Barry, Peter Jordan, and Mark Sullivan. 1981. *Aircraft Industry Dynamics: An Analysis of Competition, Capital, and Labor.* Boston: Auburn House.

Boorstin, Daniel J. 1965. *The Americans. Vol. 2: The National Experience.* New York: Random House.

Bright, Charles D. 1978. *The Jet Makers: The Aerospace Industry from 1945 to 1972.* Lawrence: Regents Press of Kansas.

Christaller, Walter. [1933] 1966. *Central Places in Southern Germany.* Translated by C. W. Baskin. Englewood Cliffs, N.J.: Prentice-Hall.

Copp, Dewitt S. 1980. *A Few Great Captains: The Men and Events that Shaped the Development of U.S. Air Power.* Garden City, N.Y.: Doubleday.

Cunningham, William G. 1951. *The Aircraft Industry: A Study in Industrial Location.* Los Angeles: Morrison.

Davis, Burke. 1967. *The Billy Mitchell Affair.* New York: Random House.

DeGrasse, Robert, Jr. 1983. *Military Expansion, Economic Decline: The Impact of Military Spending on U.S. Economic Performance.* New York: Sharpe.

Dempsey, Richard, and Douglas Schmude. 1971. "Occupational Impact of Defense Expenditures." *Monthly Labor Review* (December): 12–15.

Dorfman, Nancy S. 1982. *Massachusetts' High Technology Boom in Perspective: An Investigation of Its Dimensions, Causes, and of the Role of New Firms.* Cambridge, Mass.: MIT, Center for Policy Alternatives.

Dorfman, Nancy S. 1983. "Route 128: The Development of a Regional High-Technology Economy." *Research Policy* 12: 299–316.

Douhet, Giulio. 1983. *The Command of the Air.* USAF Warrior Studies. Translated by D. Ferrari. Washington, D.C.: United States Air Force, Office of Air Force History.

Fallows, James. 1981. *National Defense.* New York: Random House.

Futrell, Robert F. 1974. *Ideas, Concepts, Doctrine: A History of Basic Thinking in the United States Air Force, 1907–1964.* Maxwell, Ala.: Air Force University. Reprint. New York: Arno press, 1980.

Gansler, Jacques S. 1980. *The Defense Industry.* Cambridge, Mass.: MIT Press.

Glabb, Charles N., and A. Theodore Brown. 1976. *A History of Urban America*. 2nd ed. New York: Macmillan.

Glines, Carroll G. 1980. *The Compact History of the United States Air Force*. 2nd rev. ed. New York: Arno Press.

Goldberg, Alfred, ed. 1957. *A History of the United States Air Force 1907–1957*. Princeton, N.J.: Van Nostrand.

Goldstein, Harvey, and Michael Juger. 1988. "Science/Technology Parks and Regional Economic Development." Paper presented at the European Community PR Joint Sessions, Bologna, Italy.

Greer, Thomas H. 1955. *The Development of Air Doctrine in the Army Air Arm, 1917–1941*. Maxwell, Ala.: Air Force University, Research Studies Institute. Reprint. Washington, D.C.: United States Air Force, Office of Air Force History, 1985.

Hägerstrand, Torsten. 1967. *Innovation Diffusion as a Spatial Process*. Chicago: University of Chicago Press.

Hall, Peter. 1988. "The Creation of the American Aerospace Complex, 1955–65: A Study in Industrial Inertia." In *Defense Expenditure and Regional Development*, ed. Michael Breheny. London: Mansell.

Hartung, William et al. 1985. *The Strategic Defense Initiative: Costs, Contractors, and Consequences*. New York: Council on Economic Priorities.

Heims, Steve J. 1980. *John von Neumann and Norbert Wiener: From Mathematics to the Technologies of Life and Death*. Cambridge, Mass.: MIT Press

Henry, David, and Richard Oliver. 1987. "The Defense Buildup, 1977–85: Effects on Production and Employment." *Monthly Labor Review* (August): 3–11.

Higham, Robin. 1972. *Air Power: A Concise History*. New York: St. Martin's Press.

Hitch, Charles J. 1965. *Decision-Making for Defense*. Berkeley: University of California Press.

Holley, Irving B. 1964. *Buying Aircraft: Matériel Procurement for the Army Air Forces*. Washington D.C.: Department of the Army, Office of the Chief of Military History.

Huntington, Samuel P. 1957. *The Soldier and the State: The Theory and Politics of Civil/Military Relations*. Cambridge, Mass.: Belknap Press.

Hurley, Alfred F. 1975. *Billy Mitchell: Crusader for Air Power*. Bloomington: Indiana University Press.

Hymer, Stephen. 1973. "The Multinational Corporation and the Law of Uneven Development." In *Economic and World Order*, ed. J. W. Baghwati. New York: Macmillan.

Janowitz, Morris. 1960. *The Professional Soldier: A Social and Political Portrait*. New York: Free Press.

Johansson, Börje. 1987. "Information Technology and the Viability of Spatial Networks." *Papers of the Regional Science Association* 61: 51–64.

Johansson, Börje, and Lars Westin. 1987. "Technical Change, Location, and Trade." *Papers of the Regional Science Association* 62: 13–25.

Joint Economic Committee. 1982. *Location of High Technology Firms and Regional Economic Development*. Washington, D.C.: Government Printing Office.

Kelsey, Benjamin S. 1982. *The Dragon's Teeth: The Creation of United States Air Power for World War II*. Washington D.C.: Smithsonian Institute.

Koestler, Arthur. 1975. *The Act of Creation*. London: Picador.

Kondratieff, Nikolai D. 1935. "The Long Waves in Economic Life." *Review of Economic Statistics* 17: 105–15.

Kondratieff, Nikolai D. 1984. *The Long Wave Cycle.* New York: Richardson and Snyder.

Long, John F. 1976. "Interstate Migration of the Armed Forces." Paper presented at the annual meeting of the Southern Sociological Society, Miami (April).

Lösch, August. [1944] 1954. *The Economics of Location.* Translated by W. H. Woglom. New Haven, Conn.: Yale University Press.

Lotchin, Roger W., ed. 1984. *The Martial Metropolis: US Cities in War and Peace.* New York: Praeger.

Lovering, John. 1987. "Militarism, Capitalism, and the Nation-State: Toward a Realist Synthesis." *Environment and Planning D: Society and Space* 5: 283–302.

MacClosky, Monro. 1968. *From Gasbags to Spaceships: The Story of the US Air Force.* New York: Richards Rosen.

Malecki, Edward J. 1981a. "Government-funded R&D: Some Regional Economic Implications." *Professional Geographer* 33: 72–82.

Mandel, Ernest. 1973. *Late Capitalism.* Atlantic Highlands, N.J.: Humanities Press.

Mandel, Ernest. 1980. *Long Waves of Capitalist Development.* Cambridge: Cambridge University Press.

Markusen, Ann R. 1985b. *Profit Cycles, Oligopoly, and Regional Development.* Cambridge, Mass.: MIT Press.

Markusen, Ann R. 1986b. "Defense Spending and the Geography of High Tech Industries." In *Technology Regions and Policy,* ed. John Rees. New York: Praeger.

Markusen, Ann R. 1986e. "The Military Remapping of the United States." *Built Environment* 11: 171–80.

Markusen, Ann R. 1987b. *Regions: The Economics and Politics of Territory.* Totowa, N.J.: Rowman and Littlefield.

Markusen, Ann R. 1988. "Industrial Restructuring and Regional Politics." In *Spatial Variations: Community, Politics and Industry in the Postwar United States,* ed. Robert Beauregard. Newbury Park, Calif.: Sage.

Markusen, Ann R. 1990a. "The Economic, Industrial and Regional Consequences of Defense-led Innovation." In *Technology, Innovation, and Society,* ed. Åke Andersson.

Markusen, Ann R. 1990b. "Government as Market: Industrial Location in the U.S. Defense Industry." In *Industrial Location and Public Policy,* ed. Henry Herzog and Allan Schlottman. Knoxville: University of Tennessee Press.

Markusen, Ann R. 1991. *The Cold War Economy.* New York: Basic Books.

Markusen, Ann R., Peter Hall, and Amy Glasmeier. 1986. *High Tech America: The What, How, Where, and Why of the Sunrise Industries.* Boston: Allen & Unwin.

Markusen, Ann R., Peter Hall, Scott Campbell, and Sabina Deitrick. 1991. *The Rise of the Gunbelt: The Military Remapping of Industrial America.* New York: Oxford University Press.

Massey, Doreen. 1984. *Spatial Divisions of Labor: Social Structures and the Geography of Production.* New York: Methuen.

Massey, Doreen, and John Allen, eds. 1984. *Geography Matters: A Reader.* Cambridge: Cambridge University Press.

Massey, Doreen, and Richard Meegan. 1978. "Industrial Restructuring Versus the Cities." *Urban Studies* 15: 273–88.

Mazza, Jacqueline, and Dale E. Wilkinson. 1980. *The Unprotected Flank: Regional and Strategic Imbalances in Defense Spending Patterns*. Washington D.C.: Northeast-Midwest Institute.

McClendon, R. Earl. 1952. *The Question of Autonomy for the United States Air Arm, 1907–1945*. Maxwell, Ala. Air Force University, Research Studies Institute, Documents Research Division.

McWilliams, Carey. 1946. *Southern California Country: An Island on the Land*. New York: Duell, Sloan & Pearce.

Nelson, Richard R., Merton J. Peck, and Edward D. Kalachek. 1967. *Technology, Economic Growth and Public Policy*. Washington, D.C.: Brookings Institution.

Oliver, Richard P. 1971. "Employment Effects of Reduced Defense Spending." *Monthly Labor Review* (December): 3–11.

Peck. Merton J., and Frederick W. Scherer. 1962. *The Weapons Acquisition Process*. Boston: Harvard University, Graduate School of Business Administration.

Perloff, Harvey, Edgar Dunn Jr, Eric Lampard, and Richard Muth. 1960. *Regions, Resources and Economic Growth*. Baltimore: Johns Hopkins University Press.

Perroux, François. 1961. *L'Economie du XX siècle*. Paris: Presses Universitaires de France.

Phillips, Almarin. 1971. *Technology and Market Structure: A Study of the Aircraft Industry*. Lexington, Mass.: Lexington Books.

Piore, Michael J., and Charles F. Sabel. 1984. *The Second Industrial Divide: Possibilities for Prosperity*. New York: Basic Books.

Pirenne, Henri. 1914. "Les Périodes de l'histoire sociale du capitalisme." *Bulletin de l'Académie Royale de Belgique* 5: 258–99.

Pred, Allan. 1977. *City-Systems in Advanced Economies: Past Growth, Present Processes, and Future Development Options*. London: Hutchinson.

Ravenstein, Charles A. 1986. *The Organization and Lineage of the United States Air Force*. Washington D.C.: United States Air Force, Office of Air Force History.

Rees, John, and Howard A. Stafford. 1983. *A Review of Regional Growth and Industrial Location Theory: Toward Understanding the Development of High Technology Complexes in the United States*. Washington, D.C.: Office of Technology Assessment.

Reppy, Judith. 1985. "Military R&D and the Civilian Economy." *Bulletin of the Atomic Scientists* 41: 3–7.

Reps, John William. 1979. *Cities of the American West: A History of Frontier Urban Planning*. Princeton, N.J.: Princeton University Press.

Rosenberg, Nathan. 1972. *Technology and American Economic Growth*. New York: Harper & Row.

Rundquist, Barry. 1983. "Politics' Benefits and Public Policy: Interpretation of Recent U.S. Studies." *Environment and Planning C: Government and Policy* 1: 401–12.

Saxenian, AnnaLee. 1985a. "The Genesis of Silicon Valley." In *Silicon Landscapes*, ed. Peter Hall and Ann R. Markusen. Boston: Allen & Unwin.

Saxenian, AnnaLee. 1985b "Innovative Manufacturing Industries: Spatial Incidence in the United States." In *High Technology, Space, and Society*, ed. Manuel Castells, Urban Affairs Annual Reviews, no. 28. Beverly Hills, Calif.: Sage.

Schoneberger, William A. 1984. *California Wings: A History of Aviation in the Golden State*. Woodland Hills, Calif.: Windsor.

Schumpeter, Joseph A. 1939. *Business Cycles*. New York: McGraw-Hill.

Schumpeter, Joseph A. [1911] 1961. *The Theory of Economic Development.* Cambridge, Mass.: Harvard University Press.

Schwiebert, Ernest G., ed. 1965. *A History of the U.S. Air Force Ballistic Missiles*. New York: Praeger.

Scott, Allen J. 1982. "Locational Patterns and Dynamics of Industrial Activity in the Modern Metropolis." *Urban Studies* 19: 114–42.

Scott, Allen J. 1983a. "Industrial Organization and the Logic of Intra-Metropolitan Location: I. Theoretical Considerations." *Economic Geography* 59: 233–50.

Scott, Allen J. 1983b. "Industrial Organization and the Logic of Intra-Metropolitan Location: II. A Case Study of the Printed Circuits Industry in the Greater Los Angeles Region." *Economic Geography* 59: 343–67.

Scott, Allen J. 1984a. "Industrial Organization and the Logic of Intra-Metropolitan Location: III. A Case Study of the Women's Dress Industry in the Greater Los Angeles Region." *Economic Geography* 60: 3–27.

Scott, Allen J. 1984b. "Territorial Reproduction and Transformation in a Local Labor Market: The Animated Film Workers of Los Angeles." *Environment and Planning D: Society and Space* 2: 277–307.

Scott, Allen J. 1985. "Industrialization and Urbanization: A Geographical Agenda." *Annals of the Association of American Geographers* 76: 25–37.

Scott, Allen J. 1986a. "High Technology Industry and Territorial Development: The Rise of the Orange County Complex, 1955–1984." *Urban Geography* 7: 3–45.

Scott, Allen J. 1986b. "Industrial Organization and Location: Division of Labor, the Firm, and Spatial Process." *Economic Geography* 62: 215–231.

Scott, Allen J. 1986c. "Location Processes, Urbanization, and Territorial Development: An Exploratory Essay." *Environment and Planning A* 17: 479–501.

Scott, Allen J. 1987. "The Semiconductor Industry in Southeast Asia: Organization, Location, and the International Division of Labor." *Regional Studies* 21: 143–60.

Scott, Allen J., and David P. Angel. 1987. "The U.S. Semiconductor Industry: A Locational Analysis." *Environment and Planning A* 19: 875–912.

Scott, Allen J., and Michael Storper. 1986b. "Industrial Change and Territorial Organization: A Summing Up." In *Production, Work, Territory: The Geographical Anatomy of Industrial Capitalism*, ed. Allen J. Scott and Michael Storper. Boston: Allen and Unwin.

Segal Quince Wicksteed. 1988. *Universities, Enterprise and Local Economic Development: An Exploration of Links, Based on Experience from Studies in Britain and Elsewhere*. A Report to the Manpower Services Commission. London: HMSO.

Sherry, Michael S. 1987. *The Rise of American Air Power: The Creation of Armageddon*. New Haven, Conn.: Yale University Press.

Shiner, John F. 1983. *Foulois and the U.S. Army Air Corps, 1931–1935*. Washington, D.C.: United States Air Force, Office of Air Force History.

Stekler, Herman O. 1965. *The Structure and Performance of the Aerospace Industry*. Berkeley: University of California Press.

Stowsky, Jay. 1989. "Regional Histories and the Cycle of Industrial Innovation: A Review of Some Recent Literature." *Berkeley Planning Journal* 4: 114–24.

Thompson, Wilbur. 1965. *A Preface to Urban Economics*. Baltimore: Johns Hopkins University Press.

Thompson, Wilbur. 1975. "Internal and External Factors in Urban Economies." In *Regional Development and Planning: A Reader*, ed. John Friedmann and William Alonso. Cambridge, Mass.: MIT Press.

Tobias, Sheila, Peter Goredinoff, Stefan Leader, and Shelah Leader. 1982. *What Kind of Guns Are They Buying for Your Butter?* New York: Morrow.

U.S. Congress. House of Representatives. 1959. *Organization and Management of Missile Programs: Hearings Before a Subcommittee of the Committee on Government Operations*. 86th Cong. 1st sess. Washington, D.C.: Government Printing Office.

U.S. Congress. Office of Technology Assessment. 1985. *Demographic Trends and the Scientific and Engineering Work Force: A Technical Memorandum*. Washington, D.C.: Office of Technology Assessment.

Vance, James E. 1970. *The Merchant's World: The Geography of Wholesaling*. Englewood Cliffs, N.J.: Prentice-Hall.

von Braun, Wernher, and Frederick I. Ordway. 1975. *History of Rocketry and Space Travel*. 3rd ed. New York: Crowell.

von Thünen, Johann H. [1826] 1966. *von Thünen's Isolated State*. Edited by P. Hall, translated by C. M. Wartenberg. Oxford: Pergamon Press.

Weber, Alfred. [1909] 1929. *Alfred Weber's Theory of the Location of Industries*. Translated by C. J. Friedrich. Chicago: University of Chicago Press.

Weigley, Russell F. 1973. *The American Way of War: A History of United States Military Strategy and Policy*. New York: Macmillan.

York, Herbert F. 1970. *Race to Oblivion: A Participant's View of the Arms Race*. New York: Simon and Schuster.

7

The Changing World Economy and Urban Restructuring

Susan S. Fainstein

Restructuring and Locality

There are two ways of analyzing cities, neither incorrect. The first, or global, approach scrutinizes the international system of cities (and its national and regional subsystems). While noting particularities, this mode of explanation attributes them to the niche or specific node that a city occupies within the overall network. Scholars using this perspective predict uneven development and consequent territorial difference; from their vantage point, which particular places win or lose matters less than that there inevitably will be winners and losers.[1] In contrast, the second approach, which works from the inside out, examines the forces creating the particularities of a specific place – its economic base, its social divisions, its constellation of political interests, and the actions of participants. Within the first framework, differences among cities are manifestations of the varying components that comprise the whole. The second traces urban diversity to internal forces and the tactics used by local actors.

The same city can thus be regarded both as part of a totality and as a

Reprinted by permission from Susan S. Fainstein, 1990, "The Changing World Economy and Urban Restructuring," in Dennis Judd and Michael Parkinson (eds), *Leadership and Urban Regeneration*.

unique outcome of its particular history. To offer an example that illustrates the point: it is possible to tell the story of Houston using either
analytic framework. Using a world system approach, we see Houston as
building its prosperity on its unique function as the center of the US oil
industry and the headquarters of firms dominating world petroleum
exploration and marketing. The economic decline that it suffered during
the eighties resulted from global economic factors including plummeting
oil prices and overvaluation of the dollar, which heavily damaged the
ability of Texas manufacturing firms to export. Moreover, its role as a
regional financial center weakened as a consequence of bank failures
caused by over-extension during the preceding boom period, particularly
lavish financing of real estate development, which itself was premised on
ever-increasing affluence. From this perspective Houston's rise and
decline can be traced to its place in controlling, financing, and marketing
one of the most important commodities in international trade, and one
that has been particularly affected by world political and economic
currents.[2]

Most important, this approach provides insight into the general
relationship between macroeconomic forces and urban outcomes. This
argument is as follows: changing modes of corporate finance and control,
causing and produced by the geographic decentralization of production,
globalization of financial and product markets, and internationalization
of the giant corporations, increase the vulnerability of places to disruptions in the markets of commodities on which they are dependent for
their economic well-being. Moreover, the instability of foreign exchange
levels increases their exposure to uncontrollable outside forces, regardless of their efficiency of production, since it causes the world-market
price of their output to vary independently of their production costs.

The inside-out approach to explaining urban restructuring, on the
other hand, allows us to identify the dynamic factors driving Houston's
adaptation to changing circumstances. Applying this analytic mode, we
explain the city's past status by relating its development as the capital of
the petroleum industry to its entrepreneurial culture and favorable business climate. We identify the industry leaders who founded enterprises
in Houston and trace the city's expansion to federal subsidies attracted by
well-connected politicians (Feagin, 1988, chap. 6). One reason for the
sharpness of Houston's recent decline and the extremity of its effects on
its poorest residents is the past reluctance of the public sector to intervene
in the economy and to provide social welfare. At least part of the explanation for Houston's present turn-around lies in an increased willingness
to plan and manage growth.

We can similarly assess the decline of many other old commercial and
industrial cities and the regeneration of some. Probably no city in the
advanced capitalist world has been unaffected by the reorganization of
the global economy of the past two decades. For those places especially

dependent on dying manufacturing and port industries, local leadership has been one element that could improve their competitive position, although always within the serious constraints posed by historic economic base, regional location, and national policy.

To understand the process by which improvement has occurred, we must identify the changes in economic functions resulting from shifts in the world and national economy and examine the activities of groups and leaders within particular cities that affected their new roles. Thus, Pittsburgh and Sheffield similarly suffered form the world's increase in steel capacity, reduced demand for metals products, and heightened international competition. Both have had local leadership that sought to restructure their economies so as to develop new economic functions and indeed have seen economic revivals. A similar transformation has occurred in the old port cities of Baltimore and Hamburg: after long periods of decline, enterprising municipal administrations identified new opportunities and managed to attract outside investment to their locales. In the case of Baltimore these were primarily tourist oriented, while Hamburg followed the high-tech route.

This chapter briefly recapitulates the now extremely familiar story of economic restructuring and urban transformation. It then examines the varying interpretations of urban trajectories and potential according to the two vantage points sketched above. It will summarize the right and left ideological responses to economic restructuring; and finally it will set forth the types of policies available to progressive local regimes and oppositional movements, concluding with a discussion of the relationship between the politics of locality, economic forces, and national governments.

Economic Change and Urban Restructuring

We remember now only with difficulty the immediate post-World War II period, when industrialization seemingly offered the key to economic prosperity. Cities with large, diverse manufacturing bases promised secure growth and stable employment; the Soviet Union set its goal as outpacing the West through the development of heavy industry; and the task in front of war-ravaged Europe was the reconstruction of its manufacturing capacity. Now, in a world awash in commodities, peripheral locations have become the most advantageous sites for manufacturing. The future of older cities appears to depend on capturing the financial, informational, and managerial functions that determine the world's capital flows, although some areas can alternatively rely on tourism, scientific or medical services, and high-technology manufacturing to maintain a competitive edge. Overall, in the advanced capitalist world, massive employment losses in manufacturing sectors have been balanced or mitigated by gains in services and wholesale and retail trade; many places, however, have never fully recovered from the rapid loss of manufacturing jobs and are still characterized by high unemployment rates and continued outflow of population.

One of the main lessons of the past two decades is that the economic composition of places seems to have become less and less permanent (see Harvey, 1989). While restructuring of manufacturing industry may have passed its peak, a similar rationalization of tertiary industries has possibly just begun. During the 1980s many cities have shown signs of regeneration, evidenced in new office towers, gentrified inner-city neighborhoods, and job creation. However, the internationalization of economic competition, which was one of the principal causes of manufacturing decline, also threatens this new vitality. While globalization has enhanced the importance of financing, informational, and control functions, it has also enlarged the number of competitors in the tertiary sector. Within Europe, each nation has hopes of housing the control center of the European Community after 1992 and is competing fiercely to attract headquarters and financing operations; the glut of office space that currently characterizes United States metropolitan areas may soon spread to Europe, where numerous large office projects are under construction in anticipation of European union. In the United States financial interests look warily at the expanding Japanese presence in the banking and investment industries, which threatens to make Tokyo the world's financial capital.

Within each country, even domestically owned financial and service firms have become increasingly footloose as they emulate industrial corporations by separating their routine processing functions from more complex operations and decentralizing them to low-cost areas. Furthermore, prosperity based on the advanced-service and financial sectors remains hostage to the health of financial markets. The shock of October 1987 continues to reverberate through diminished employment in financial sector firms and reduced consumption in cities dependent on that industry.

Even successful regeneration, therefore, demonstrates signs of instability and social fragmentation. While financial centers benefit from merger and acquisition activities, other cities find that consolidation of the new conglomerates results in the closing down of formerly profitable establishments now redundant or too encumbered with debt to remain viable. Efforts to spur central business district development and the "realistic" dismissal of manufacturing as the future basis for growth have displaced residents and small firms and left blue-collar workers stranded.

Along with deindustrialization has come the decline of a homogeneous, relatively well-paid working class and the growth in size of income strata at both extremes of the spectrum (Harrison and Bluestone, 1988, chap. 5). The outmigration or closing of factories and obsolete shipping facilities has produced desolate landscapes of unused structures in once central locations. Changes in social groupings have resulted in homelessness and the decay of formerly stable working-class residential districts, on the one hand; on the other, they have heightened the demand for converted, well-located structures and luxury new construction. Combined with demographic changes due to dropping birth rates, growing numbers of single-member and female-headed households as well as high-income, two-earner couples, and large-scale immigration, these factors have heightened the fragmentation of urban space (see Mingione, 1991). Moreover, cities with low unemployment rates and new investment still face fiscal problems that severely restrict governmental efforts on behalf of low-income residents and limit necessary investment in the physical infrastructure required for future growth.

Social scientists generally agree that the trickle-down effects of new development in "successfully" restructured cities have excluded a large proportion of the population and may even have worsened their situation (Parkinson and Judd, 1988; Squires, 1989). For the many locales that remain trapped in the trajectory of industrial decline and high unemployment, circumstances are obviously worse. To formulate a political stance that effectively addresses the economic distress of old cities requires identifying points of indeterminacy as global forces operate on particular places. Only after such an analysis do local policies stand a chance of stimulating growth; it, however, offers no guarantee and in some cases may prove extremely discouraging to local action.

The Global Perspective

Localities are forever in the position of adjusting to forces beyond their control. The oil crises of the 1970s, the rise of manufacturing economies of the Far East, the management failures of Western oligopolistic industries, the rationalization of firms through decentralization of their various components into least-cost locations, global sourcing, and modern telecommunications have all had profound effects on urban economic structures. While technology is not the cause of increased capital mobility, the loosening of natural and technical constraints on location has allowed firms to further exploit socially created locational advantages (Fainstein and Fainstein, 1988). Most important of these advantages is the group of attributes often called the business climate. Also significant is proximity to markets, which matters far more to most businesses than closeness to raw materials or natural features like rivers.[3] Proximity to markets, however, may only require location close to an airport rather than placement within an actual agglomeration.

For many medium-size cities the weakening in importance of their natural advantages has meant the termination of their *raison d'être*. For example, although port facilities continue to be important generators of economic growth, their existence depends less on the quality of the available water berths than on the pricing of dock labor and the presence of modern container-handling operations. The enhanced capacity of a few ports to handle greatly increased amounts of tonnage along with the ease of transferring containerized loads to trucks and trains reduces the need for numerous ports dotting a single shoreline (Hoyle, 1988). While for London and New York the decline of the port was within the context of diverse other economic functions, for Liverpool or Baltimore port-related activities defined their specialized niche in the system of cities. Consequently, they were particularly vulnerable to technological transformation, and they lacked economic leaders capable of developing other functions since they had few sectors independent of the port. A similar problem exists for the steel-fabricating areas of northern France or the American Midwest.

Such cities then are systemically disadvantaged. The lack of vital private business outside the declining sectors leaves only the public sector to offer a potential engine for stimulating new growth. For the public sector to do so means finding a new niche that the locality can occupy.[4] It is in this possibility of identifying a new niche that indeterminacy exists within the global framework of analysis, and it is here that the two approaches to urban analysis complement each other (see Riley and Shurmer-Smith, 1988).

Urban growth coalitions, however, find themselves in a prisoner's dilemma in that their success in finding a new area of specialization depends on leadership groups elsewhere not initiating the same strategy. Festive retailing may work for the first cities that revitalize their waterfronts using this formula, but impulse-buying tourists can support only so many stores selling brass ships' furnishings and Irish shawls. Research parks have spurred development in Cambridge, England, and Charlotte, North Carolina, but they are predestined to languish in most places. Just as in the market economy as a whole, latecomers to an industrial sector will not see the profits of the innovators, so cities that are imitators are unlikely to flourish. Hence, while a city's economic leadership has leeway in choosing new niches, it does so within the framework of a system of competing cities, putting the public's investment at risk.

The Local Autonomy Perspective

Viewing from the inside, we can see each city as having a potential for regeneration that is dependent on the actions of its constituent groups. There are three major dimensions on which cities vary according to the character of state intervention aimed at economic regeneration: (1) extent of governmental entrepreneurship, (2) amount of planning, and

(3) level of priority to those in greatest need. Which growth strategy is followed within a city and the city's commitment to targeting low-income groups are consequences of political struggle and are largely independent of external forces (Smith, 1988) – although, as indicated above, whether the growth strategy works is less open.[5]

Entrepreneurship

Whereas city governments once restricted their activities to building infrastructure and providing services, virtually all now take an active role in promoting economic growth. Eisinger (1988) contends that, within the US, city and state governments have moved from an initial, naive "supply-side" strategy for stimulating private investment to "demand-side" policies:

> *What guides the entrepreneurial state is attention to the demand side of the economic growth equation. Underlying the actions of the entrepreneurial state is the assumption that growth comes form exploiting new or expanding markets. The state role is to identify, evaluate, anticipate, and even help to develop and create these markets for private producers to exploit, aided if necessary by government as subsidizer or coinvestor. The policies of the entrepreneurial state are geared to these functions. They include the generation of venture capital for selected new and growing businesses, the encouragement of high-technology research and product development to respond to emerging markets, and the promotion of export goods produced by local businesses to capitalize upon new sources of demand.* (Eisinger, 1988, p. 9)

This terminology is confusing since the term "demand side" usually refers to a policy that subsidizes consumers rather than investors. By *demand side* Eisinger simply means a more entrepreneurial or active policy that identifies market opportunities rather than indiscriminately subsidizing all investors. His general point, however, is that subnational governments in the United States increasingly seek to encourage specialized development where their economic policymakers have identified a strategic advantage. He considers that this entrepreneurship represents a new and important role for the subnational state, although he considers the resultant programs of "modest dimensions and uncertain impact" (Eisinger, 1988, p. 34).[6]

Planning

Cities also vary according to the amount of planning they do, both within countries and from country to country. The United States and Great Britain differ considerably from Canada and continental Europe in the extent to which growth is channeled through the planning process. The construction of La Défense in Paris as a corporate center, for example, and the current development of that city's southeast sector as a financial district result from a very strong governmental role in guiding development (Savitch, 1988, chap. 5). In contrast, almost all US cities allow office developers broad limits within which to choose their sites. British restrictions on office locations have been greatly relaxed, allowing simultaneous competing projects. According to the head of the London Regional Planning Office, "boroughs that had formerly tried to stop office development will do so no longer." Or, in the words of the chief planner of one of London's boroughs, "even developers would like more planning."[7]

Growth regulation for environmental protection, the preservation of low-income housing, or the maintenance of manufacturing sites is frequently criticized. Critics assert that such planning is, depending on whether it is in growing or declining areas, either exclusionary or a luxury that deteriorating communities cannot afford (Sternlieb, 1986). Without planning, however, urban landscapes become the product of impersonal market forces, dominated by the interests of capital (Foglesong, 1986). Not only does the absence of planning prevent the general public from being able to affect urban outcomes, but it also denies real-estate interests a regulatory body to insure against overdevelopment. Consequently we see the oversupply of office space that now threatens the future stability of regenerating cities.

Economic growth at the bottom

Within the capitalist countries that have undergone restructuring, urban regeneration has largely taken place under elite leadership, although some exceptions like the "third Italy" exist. As might be expected from a top-down phenomenon, participating economic elites have been the primary direct beneficiaries of the growth of new industries and the rehabilitation of housing in old industrial settings. Relatively few city governments have devoted themselves consistently to using municipal instruments to direct the dividends of growth toward improving the economic situation of low-income people.

During the period when public housing construction flourished in Europe, municipalities led in providing the social wage. Recent policies of privatization and fiscal conservatism, however, indicate a major withdrawal by local governments from social welfare provision, although a few progressive governments in the United States (Clavel, 1986), some of the "red" municipalities of Italy and France, and local administrations in the north European welfare states continue to offer housing and services to low-income residents (Pickvance and Preteceille, 1990). In the United Kingdom withdrawal of the local state from its former redistributional role has been sharpest; Margaret Thatcher's "enterprise state" remains committed to encouraging private-sector activity without the imposition of either planning or linkage policies (Martin, 1986).

While municipalities have become more active and autonomous in their pursuit of growth policies, in the United States and United Kingdom national economic and political forces have restricted their freedom of action when they have tried to improve conditions at the bottom of the social hierarchy. U.S. firms, reacting to the high costs of doing business in cities with substantial welfare and social service budgets, fled to more hospitable locales, effectively punishing those municipalities substituting public benefits for private wages. Simultaneously, the federal government sharply reduced its subsidies for urban social programs. In Britain central government terminated the metropolitan governments, which it regarded as undercutting its policies, and severely limited the financing powers of local government, effectively preventing it from taxing its constituents to pay for higher levels of service. Thus, increases in municipal capacity in one arena have been balanced off by restrictions in another.

Ideological Interpretations

Neither the systemic nor the localistic perspective on urban restructuring is necessarily connected with a particular ideological interpretation. Rather, ideology is associated with identification of the heroes and villains of the piece. The right attributes economic decline to overpaid and unproductive workers, governmental welfarism, insufficient incentives to entrepreneurship, and political intrusion into the market. While, according to this view, much of the fault lay outside municipal boundaries in national unionism and the welfare state, it also had specifically local roots:

> Current legislation to reduce local government autonomy is only the latest episode [for the Thatcherites] in a recurrent problem [with local political consciousness]. Those political processes leading to "municipal Marxism" in Sheffield or Lambeth can be replaced by "neutral" equations and civil service procedures in Marsham Street [where the Department of the Environment is located]; the Docklands Action Group can be shunted aside and "sensible" development, free of the inefficiencies of local politics, can be undertaken by the Docklands Development Corporation. (Duncan and Goodwin, 1982, p. 94)

The right's prescription for regeneration therefore requires shifting the role of government from inhibitor of growth to provider of incentives. Its ideological triumphs have been enhanced by the recent introduction of market processes to the eastern socialist economies and the explicit admissions of economic failure by the Eastern Bloc leadership. Whatever the weakenesses of the logic of free markets as the basis for renewal, the right can point to the failures of communism and, in the United States and Great Britain, the economic stagnation that occurred under Democratic and Labour governments. The strength of mixed economies in northern Europe is usually underestimated or ignored in these arguments.

For leftists, urban restructuring has been produced by the greed of corporate capitalists rather than as a necessary response to the heavy hand of the state. Its outcome has been increased wealth for investors, particularly financial and real-estate speculators, and impoverishment of a growing proportion of the population. The stimulus for the process was an initial crisis of profitability caused by international competitive pressure resulting from unmanaged international trade and overproduction. Capital responded by heightening the rate of exploitation of labor. A combination of tactics was used to achieve this end, including union busting, automation, relocation of production sites, and reduction of social welfare programs that competed with the private wage (Harrison and Bluestone, 1988). At the local level capitalists worked through urban growth coalitions to establish environments favorable to cost-cutting through reduced expenditures on labor, taxes, and physical plant. Nationally and internationally they sought the locales promising the greatest return on investment, whipsawing one against the other.

According to this analysis, the effort to alleviate the situation in which most people are seeing increased insecurity and declining living conditions requires far more than a strategy for growth. Rather, it necessitates finding a formula that will limit capitalist hegemony within both the workplace and the community. No benign assumption can be sustained that, once economic growth is reestablished in a city, wage increases and a growing public fisc will follow. For instance, the recent Boeing Aircraft strike in Seattle, Washington, illustrates the way in which business seeks to exclude labor from the gains of growth. Boeing, which is the largest US exporter and which currently has a huge backlog of orders, was offering a pay raise of only 10 percent over three years, based on the grounds of needing to compete internationally. Its union contended that when the firm was having hard times, it had accepted give-backs; now that the company was enormously profitable, the question was entirely one of the division between wages and profits, not of the need to sacrifice in order to promote competitiveness (Uchitelle, 1989c).

The fiscal effects of economic growth are similarly contested. For example, New York City business leaders, after a decade of economic growth, were pressing for across-the-board tax reductions despite dramatically growing service needs. And, in the face of serious budgetary shortfall, New York State was embarking on the third phase of a multi-year tax-reduction program, which had originally been enacted on the basis of mistaken estimates of revenue expansion. Again, the justification is competitiveness. A report sponsored by the top executives of New York City's leading firms declared:

> *The increase in competitive pressures in the financial services industry has made firms more cost conscious than ever before. While cost control has always been important in choosing locations for back offices and data centers, front offices are also increasingly concerned about operating costs . . . New York City and State impose the highest tax burden in the nation. Reducing this burden is the most important step that the city and state can take to reduce the cost of doing business in New York City, and thereby retain and promote financial services job growth in New York City.* (New York City Partnership, 1989, p. 23)

The triumph of progressive regimes is as important as a successful growth strategy to the well-being of citizens of declining cities. Indeed, economic stagnation may well be preferable to development if the latter is based on ruthless tax and cost reductions. The policies of progressive regimes involve public and/or worker participation in economic decision-making, emphasis on indigenous business development, linkage policies, housing subsidies, and a stress on neighborhood over downtown development. For cities to escape from total determination by outside forces, local entrepreneurship, planning, and distributive policies are a necessary condition. The character of the local regime determines whether, and how, these functions are carried out. But, in the old Marxist phrase, "not under conditions of their own making."

Growth and Equity

The flaw of the leftist analysis, with which this chapter is otherwise generally sympathetic, is that it does not offer a formula for growth. So far, the left has not discovered an effective method for stimulating substantial investment in declining areas that differs significantly from the business subsidy approach of the right.

There are four conceivable sources of risk capital for economic regeneration: the private, for-profit sector; the state; employee savings and benefit funds; and the nonprofit sector. To attract private capital to territories not regarded as inherently profitable by capitalist managers, state officials feel compelled to offer incentives with all the likely negative consequences outlined above. State participation in quasi-governmental corporations has saved failing industries and is more amenable to public control of the outcomes than is state subsidy of purely private entities. (AMTRAK, the US passenger railroad corporation which connects a number of old US central cities and whose revival has spun off an important employment and retailing multiplier, is a good example of revitalization through the use of this kind of instrument.) Such corporations, though, when they are profitable and capitalized on a large scale, tend to behave little differently from private firms (Rueschemeyer and Evans, 1985, pp. 57–59) and, when not restricted locationally, will also seek least-cost locations. In contrast, firms run directly by the state will be less profit-oriented and, theoretically at least, susceptible to democratic control. They tend, however, to avoid risks, invest insufficiently, and avoid cost reduction measures.

Employee-owned firms offer the greatest potential for maintaining efficient operations without abandoning geographic locations that have been the site of private disinvestment. Employee takeovers, however, obviously can occur only when a firm is already in existence and must usually confront heavy debt encumbrance. Economic development corporations and economic cooperatives of various sorts have opened new enterprises and prospered in different places ranging from Chicago to Mondragon to Emilio-Romagna (Piore and Sabel, 1984). Except in Italy, however, their total contribution to economic development is tiny, and few locales possess established traditions of this sort of enterprise.

A workable, large-scale strategy based on local economic development corporations or cooperatives needs the formation of new kinds of credit institutions. Eisinger (1988, chap. 10) lists a number of innovative development banking institutions that now exist in the United States to provide loans to small businesses. Although the amount of capital so far expended is very small, Eisinger anticipates long-term cumulative benefits. As presently constituted, however, these loan funds simply do what private banking institutions do at a higher level of risk. Such funds, if constituted on more progressive principles, would issue loans containing assurances that successful firms could not be bought out, then moved or folded up. Alternatively, they could include recapture provisions such that profits from a buy-out would revert to the community.

The left needs to devise its own version of the public–private partnership. This means a reorientation away from manufacturing toward the service sector, recognition of the importance of management and entrepreneurship, and a coming-to-terms with the multinational corporation. The reality that giant multinational corporations dominate economic transactions means that the left must find ways of tapping into their economic power rather than dismissing them on moral grounds. Public–private partnerships under these conditions are inevitable; what needs to be done is ensure that the public component is more controlling and shares more in the proceeds.[8]

Romanticization of the Italian machine shop cooperatively run by worthy artisans will not suffice as a model for development of old inner cities. Public sponsorship of consulting, computer, high-tech, restaurant franchise, nursing home, home health care, and similar enterprises could generate a stable, small business sector to occupy inner-city sites. If such

businesses are to thrive, they will involve internal hierarchies with sufficient returns to managers as to induce competent, experienced
individuals to assume these roles. They will also have to allow managers
discretion in rewarding worker performance. Social equalization, if it is
to occur, would come through redistribution within the tax and welfare
system rather than the firm. In other words, the left will have to accept
serious inequalities in the rewards to labor if it is to stimulate growth.

The task for progressive movements within declining cities is to formulate a strategy that is as creative and less destructive than the *modus
operandi* of typical urban growth coalitions. Social democrats need to do
what is necessary to foster incentives and reward entrepreneurship.
Without a program for growth, except in cities like Santa Monica or
Toronto that have to fend off private capital, the left has little chance of
achieving political power. Criticisms of the depredations caused by unregulated capital or prescriptions for cooperative industry are insufficient.
Most people will accept growing inequality in preference to stagnation or
absolute decline in the standard of living.

To speak, however, of the tasks for progressive local forces without
noting their national context is to dodge a central issue. Cities are limited
in their autonomy not only by general economic forces but also by the
national political system of which they form a part. Ideological, institutional, and fiscal factors constrain their ability to operate in political
isolation from the rest of the nation. Within the United States and the
United Kingdom, where conservative forces dominate nationally, local
regimes with a different agenda must swim against the ideological
current. The trickle-down model dominates the definition of economic
improvement in these countries, causing other methods to be automati-
cally suspect. Progressive local forces have difficulty maintaining a broad
base of support when the national propaganda attack pictures them as
loony or unrealistic. In the continental European states, where planning
and social welfare maintain much greater national legitimacy, national
regimes are less inclined to glorify the unshackled free market and, therefore, they give localities greater capabilities for managing development.

The extent of local entrepreneurship also depends on the amount of
institutional decentralization existing within a nation's urban system. In
the United States the federal system and the widespread acceptance of
"home rule" have both heightened interurban competition and given
cities considerable leeway to determine their own policies (Fainstein and
Fainstein, 1989). In contrast, Britain's increasingly centralized system has
blocked radical local councils from pursuing their own development and
expenditure policies (Lawless, 1987). France, previously the most
centralized of European nations, has gone through a period of decentralization that has made possible more active local efforts to foster growth.

Finally, the availability of funds to local governments and the terms
under which they can use them significantly affects their capabilities.

Subnational governments in the United States can tap into national financial resources through issuing tax-free industrial revenue bonds, but they have no similar source of funds for job-training and placement programs. There have been sharp reductions in direct federal support of local development and welfare programs, but localities may use their own tax revenues as they please. In contrast, in the United Kingdom, local councils, which have also seen major cutbacks in national subventions, are largely prevented from making up for the shortfall locally.

In conclusion, then, we have seen an upsurge in public-sector entrepreneurship and considerable variation in the extent to which local governments have sought to spread the benefits of growth to the whole population. We can propose programs that will increase the public benefits of growth even while encouraging private sector participation in regeneration activities. Without a broad national movement to support such programs, however, we must expect that local initiatives will be blocked by higher levels of government and by footloose capital that will play one locality against another. Entrepreneurship by urban progressive coalitions thus requires that they aim not only at stimulating local investment but also at building a national movement for growth with equity.

Notes

1   There are two variants of the systemic perspective. The first, exemplified by Noyelle and Stanback's (1984) study of the changing American urban hierarchy, emphasizes impersonal economic forces (increasing size of markets; changes in transport and technology; increased importance of public and nonprofit sector activities; corporate concentration) that produce economic growth and decline in particular locations. The second, most strongly presented in the work of David Harvey (1985), stresses the role of the capital-controlling class in maximizing profits through use of the "spatial fix." For Harvey, uneven development is not an unintended consequence of investment processes; rather capitalists create and use it so as to lower production costs, protect themselves from regulation, increase profitability, and produce speculative gains.

2   This kind of analysis is susceptible to the criticism that it assumes any phenomenon fulfills a necessary function and that any existing institution or activity had to be. One need not, however, engage in a totally deterministic argument to accept that certain social practices do serve the ends of dominant groups and that these practices can be institutionalized so that concerted, conscious activity is not required to perpetuate them. Because some system requirements are fulfilled does not mean that all are, and when they are, the outcome is not an automatic response to need, but can ultimately be traced back to human agency. Moreover, practices may also exist that are dysfunctional for achieving the aims of dominant social interests, and systems produce contradictions as well as functionalities.

3   A pair of articles in The New York Times (Uchitelle, 1989a, 1989b) chronicled

the globalization of the Stanley Tool Company, an old New England manufacturer of screwdrivers, tape measures, and other common tools. Even though it made a seemingly low-tech, standard product, Stanley needed to be close to its foreign markets:

> The . . . [tape measure's] popularity at home raises the possibility that Stanley could increase production in New Britain [Connecticut], which turns out 200,000 tape rulers a day for the American market, and simply export the rest from here. But this approach violates principals held by Mr. Ayers [the chief executive officer] and other advocates of global manufacturing.
>
> One is that factories should be close to the customers they serve – to get inside tariff barriers, to give the impression that they are local companies, to reduce delivery time, and to "capture" manufacturing techniques not readily available back home.
>
> Another is that big factories are inefficient. The maximum for Mr. Ayers, and for many others intent on globalizing, is 500 employees, the number at the tape factory here [in France].
>
> Finally, Mr. Ayers does not like to have, as he puts it, all his eggs in one basket. "With one plant, if there is a strike or shutdown you're out of business," he said. "With several, you can switch production to another country or back and forth among countries." (Uchitelle, 1989a, p. 10)

4   The problem is more acute in America than European cities, because the jurisdictional fragmentation of US metropolitan areas means that even if new functions arise in an area (e.g., Greater Cleveland or Greater Saint Louis), they may be located outside the boundary of the central city and spin off few benefits for its residents.

5   Peterson (1981) argues that growth and redistribution are necessarily antagonistic at the urban level and that the general consensus in favor of growth therefore precludes local redistributional activity, or at any rate should do so. The literature disputing his argument is by now vast, particularly concerning whether growth strategies really are supported by a consensus on values (Fainstein and Fainstein, 1988; Sanders and Stone, 1987).

6   The active agency in promoting growth within metropolitan areas in both the United States and Europe is often an intermediate level of government (states or regional authorities).

7   Quotations are from interviews carried out by the author in 1989.

8   Robert Beauregard (1989) discusses the importance of the state playing a role in requiring preferential hiring agreements for residents when it participates in development. His analysis is restricted to construction hiring, but the principle can be extended to operating firms. Another example of the public capture of benefits from major private investment is the Battery Park City project in New York. Since a public authority maintains ownership of the land, it receives an escalating rental based on profits from the structures constructed. More than $1 billion of this revenue is currently

designated for low-income housing construction. This is far greater than the amounts typically allocated under linkage programs.

References

Beauregard, R. A. (1989). Local politics and the employment relation: Construction jobs in Philadelphia. In R. A. Beauregard (ed.). *Economic restructuring and political response* (pp. 149–180). Newbury Park, CA.: Sage.

Clavel, P. (1986). *The progressive city.* New Brunswick, NJ: Rutgers University Press.

Duncan, S.S., and Goodwin, M. (1982, January). The local state: Functionalism, autonomy and class relations in Cockburn and Saunders. *Political Geography Quarterly, 1,* 77–96.

Eisinger, P. K. (1988). *The rise of the entrepreneurial state.* Madison: University of Wisconsin Press.

Fainstein, S. S., and Fainstein, N. (1989, September). The ambivalent state: Economic development policy in the U.S. federal system under the Reagan administration. *Urban Affairs Quarterly, 20,* 41–62.

Fainstein, S. S., and Fainstein, N. (1988). Technology, the new international division of labor, and location: Continuities and disjunctures. In R. A. Beauregard (ed.). *Economic restructuring and political response* (pp. 17–40). Newbury Park, CA: Sage.

Feagin, J. R. (1988). *Free enterprise city.* New Brunswick, NJ: Rutgers University Press.

Foglesong, R. E. (1986). *Planning the capitalist city.* Princeton: Princeton University Press.

Harrison, B., and Bluestone, B. (1988). *The great U-turn.* New York: Basic Books.

Harvey, D. (1989). *The condition of postmodernism.* Oxford: Basil Blackwell.

Harvey, D. (1985). *The urbanization of capital.* Baltimore: Johns Hopkins University Press.

Hoyle, B. (1988). Development dynamics at the port–city interface. In B. S. Hoyle, D. A. Pinder, and M. S. Husain. *Revitalising the waterfront* (pp. 3–19). London: Belhaven Press.

Lawless, P. (1987). Urban development. In M. Parkinson (ed.). *Reshaping local government* (pp. 122-137). New Brunswick, NJ: Transaction Books.

Martin, R. (1986). Thatcherism and Britain's industrial landscape. In R. Martin and B. Rowthorn. *The geography of de-industrialisation* (pp. 238–290). London: Macmillan.

Mingione, E. (1991). *Fragmented societies.* Oxford: Basil Blackwell.

New York City Partnership, Financial Services Task Force. (1989). *Meeting the challenge: Maintaining and enhancing New York City as the world financial capital.* New York: New York City Partnership.

Noyelle, T. J. and Stanback, T. M., Jr. (1983). *The economic transformation of American cities.* Totowa, NJ: Rowman and Allanheld.

Parkinson, M., and Judd, D. (1988). Urban revitalisation in America and the U.K. – the politics of uneven development. In M. Parkinson, B. Foley, and D. Judd. *Regenerating the cities* (pp. 1–8). Manchester, UK: Manchester University Press.

Peterson, P. (1981). *City limits.* Chicago: University of Chicago Press.

Pickvance, C., and Preteceille, E. (1990). *State and locality: A comparative perspective on state restructuring.* London: Frances Pinter.

Piore, M. J., and Sabel, C. F. (1984). *The second industrial divide.* New York: Basic Books.

Rueschemeyer, D., and Evans, P. B. (1985). The state and economic transformation: Toward an analysis of the conditions underlying effective intervention. In P. B. Evans, D. Rueschemeyer, and T. Skocpol. *Bringing the state back in* (pp. 44–77). Cambridge: Cambridge University Press.

Riley, R., and Shurmer-Smith, L. (1988). Global imperatives, local forces and waterfront redevelopment. In B. S. Hoyle, D. A. Pinder, and M. S. Husain. *Revitalising the waterfront* (pp. 38-51). London: Belhaven Press.

Sanders, H. T., and Stone, C. N. (1987, June). Developmental politics reconsidered. *Urban Affairs Quarterley, 22,* 521–539.

Savitch, H. V. (1988). *Post-industrial cities.* Princeton: Princeton University Press.

Smith, M. P. (1988). *City, state, and market.* Oxford: Basil Blackwell.

Squires, G. D. (ed.). (1989). *Unequal partnerships.* New Brunswick, NJ: Rutgers University Press.

Sternlieb, G. (1986). *Patterns of development.* New Brunswick, NJ: Rutgers University Center for Urban Policy Research.

Uchitelle, L. (1989a, July 23). The Stanley Works goes global. *The New York Times,* sec. 3.

Uchitelle, L. (1989b, July 24). Only the bosses are American. *The New York Times,* p. D1.

Uchitelle, L. (1989c, October 12). Boeing's fight over bonuses. *The New York Times.*

Part II

Race and Urban Poverty

Introduction to Part II

American cities differ from European ones in their relation to their suburban periphery. Whereas the European urban center has remained a desirable place to live, its American counterpart has suffered from depopulation and impoverishment. Individual preferences for a suburban life style constitute one factor causing the discrepancy between the center and its outskirts within the United States; another is the economic advantages that accrue to ownership of a single-family house. In almost every US metropolitan area, however, race has been an additional, powerful causal element in determining spatial patterns. "White flight," and more recently an outmigration of middle-class African-Americans, has resulted in the increasing ghettoization and relative poverty of the central city. The readings in Part II examine aspects of the relationship between ghettoization processes and the relationship between racially homogeneous areas and the life chances of the people residing within them.

William Julius Wilson's extremely influential book, *The Truly Disadvantaged*, stimulated an extraordinary research effort to investigate the extent, causes, and consequences of ghettoization. His argument is that conditions of discrimination in the first half of the century had resulted in highly segregated neighborhoods. The relaxation of measures that had forced upwardly mobile elements of the black community to stay within undesirable neighborhoods led to their rapid outmigration. The consequence was homogeneously poor neighborhoods singularly lacking in role models and employment opportunities. These in turn bred dysfunctional forms of behavior that inhibited residents from taking advantage of whatever economic opportunities did exist. In the absence of supportive family structures and employment skills, the occupants of ghetto neighborhoods constitute an underclass isolated from the labor market. Wilson argues that affirmative action policies comprise an insufficient approach to alleviating the situation of the ghetto poor. Instead he calls for a comprehensive program of economic and social reform that will address the structural disadvantages that underlie severe economic deprivation.

Norman Fainstein contends that Wilson's thesis resulted in a focus on the characteristics of the underclass that distracted researchers from examining the situation of working- and middle-class blacks. He documents the continuing economic disadvantage of employed African-Americans and relates it to the overall socio-economic structure. In examining the question of the relative importance of class versus race in shaping the situation of African-Americans, he maintains that racial discrimination continues to exact a toll even among those who have seemingly escaped its worst ravages.

One unexamined implication of Wilson's thesis is that those middle-class African-Americans who have managed to leave the inner city are living in an intergrated suburbia where race does not constitute a barrier to economic opportunity. Dennis Keating's research, however, shows that racial segregation persists in suburban areas. The selection from Keating's book, *The Suburban Racial Dilemma*, examines the potential to achieve racial diversity in suburbia. He emphasizes the role of fair housing organizations in working toward that goal and also the instability of inte-grated communities where they have been achieved.

8

The Truly Disadvantaged: The Hidden Agenda

William Julius Wilson

The inner city is less pleasant and more dangerous than it was prior to 1960. Despite a high rate of poverty in inner-city areas during the first half of this century, rates of joblessness, out-of-wedlock births, single families, welfare dependency, and serious crime were significantly lower than they are today and did not begin to rise rapidly until after the mid-1960s, with extraordinary increases during the 1970s. The questions of why social problems in the inner city sharply increased when they did and in the way they did, and why existing policy programs assumed to be relevant to such problems are either inappropriate or insufficient, were addressed in the preceding chapters. In this chapter I should like, by way of summary and conclusion, to outline some of the central substantive and theoretical arguments presented in this study on the ghetto under-class and social change in the inner city and to draw out in sharper relief the basic policy implications of my analysis.

Reprinted by permission from William Julius Wilson, 1987, *The Truly Disadvantaged.*

The Ghetto Underclass and Social Dislocations

Why have the social conditions of the ghetto underclass deteriorated so rapidly in recent years? Racial discrimination is the most frequently invoked explanation, and it is undeniable that discrimination continues to aggravate the social and economic problems of poor blacks. But is discrimination really greater today than it was in 1948, when black unemployment was less than half what it is now, and when the gap between black and white jobless rates was narrower?

As for the poor black family, it apparently began to fall apart not before but after the mid-twentieth century. Until publication in 1976 of Herbert Gutman's *The Black Family in Slavery and Freedom*, most scholars had believed otherwise. Stimulated by the acrimonious debate over the Moynihan report, Gutman produced data demonstrating that the black family was not significantly disrupted during slavery or even during the early years of the first migration to the urban North, beginning after the turn of the century. The problems of the modern black family, he implied, were associated with modern forces.

Those who cite discrimination as the root cause of poverty often fail to make a distinction between the effects of *historic* discrimination (i.e., discrimination prior to the mid-twentieth century) and the effects of *contemporary* discrimination. Thus they find it hard to explain why the economic position of the black underclass started to worsen soon after Congress enacted, and the White House began to enforce, the most sweeping civil rights legislation since Reconstruction.

The point to be emphasized is that historic discrimination is more important than contemporary discrimination in understanding the plight of the ghetto underclass – that in any event there is more to the story than discrimination (of whichever kind). Historic discrimination certainly helped create an impoverished urban black community in the first place. In his recent *A Piece of the Pie: Black and White Immigrants since 1880* (1980), Stanley Lieberson shows how, in many areas of life, including the labor market, black newcomers from the rural South were far more severely discriminated against in northern cities than were the new white immigrants from southern, central, and eastern Europe. Skin color was part of the problem but it was not all of it.

The disadvantage of skin color – the fact that the dominant whites preferred whites over nonwhites – is one that blacks shared with the Japanese, Chinese, and others. Yet the experience of the Asians, who also experienced harsh discriminatory treatment in the communities where they were concentrated, but who went on to prosper in their adopted land, suggests that skin color per se was not an insuperable obstacle. Indeed, Lieberson argues that the greater success enjoyed by Asians may well be explained largely by the different context of their contact with whites. Because changes in immigration policy cut off Asian migration to America in the late nineteenth century, the Japanese and Chinese population did not reach large numbers and therefore did not pose as great a threat as did blacks.

Furthermore, the discontinuation of large-scale immigration from Japan and China enabled those Chinese and Japanese already in the United States to solidify networks of ethnic contacts and to occupy particular occupational niches in small, relatively stable communities. For blacks, the situation was different. The 1970 census recorded 22,580,000 blacks in the United States but only 435,000 Chinese and 591,000 Japanese.

If different population sizes accounted for a good deal of the difference in the economic success of blacks and Asians, they also helped determine the dissimilar rates of progress of urban blacks and the new European arrivals. European immigration was curtailed during the 1920s, but black migration to the urban North continued through the 1960s. With each passing decade there were many more blacks who were recent migrants to the North, whereas the immigrant component of the new Europeans dropped off over time. Eventually, other whites muffled their dislike of the Poles and Italians and Jews and directed their antagonism against blacks.

In addition to the problem of historic discrimination, the black migration to New York, Philadelphia, Chicago, and other northern cities – the continued replenishment of black populations there by poor newcomers – predictably skewed the age profile of the urban black community and kept it relatively young. The number of central-city black youths aged sixteen to nineteen increased by almost 75 percent from 1960 to 1969. Young black adults (aged twenty to twenty-four) increased in number by two-thirds during the same period, three times the increase for young white adults. In the nation's inner cities in 1977, the median age for whites was 30.3, for blacks 23.9. The importance of this jump in the number of young minorities in the ghetto, many of them lacking one or more parents, cannot be overemphasized.

Age correlates with many things. For example, the higher the median age of a group, the higher its income; the lower the median age, the higher the unemployment rate and the higher the crime rate (more than half of those arrested in 1980 for violent and property crimes in American cities were under twenty-one). The younger a woman is, the more likely she is to bear a child out of wedlock, head up a new household, and depend on welfare. In short, part of what had gone awry in the ghetto was due to the sheer increase in the number of black youth.

The population explosion among minority youth occurred at a time when changes in the economy were beginning to pose serious problems for unskilled workers. Urban minorities have been particularly vulnerable to the structural economic changes of the past two decades: the shift from goods-producing to service-producing industries, the increasing polarization of the labor market into low-wage and high-wage sectors, innovations in technology, and the relocation of manufacturing industries out of the central cities.

Most unemployed blacks in the United States reside within the central cities. Their situation, already more difficult than that of any other major ethnic group in the country, continues to worsen. Not only are there more blacks without jobs every year; men, especially young males, are dropping out of the labor force in record proportions. Also, more and more black youth, including many who are no longer in school, are obtaining no job experience at all.

However, the growing problem of joblessness in the inner city both exacerbates and is in turn partly created by the changing social composition of inner-city neighborhoods. These areas have undergone a profound social transformation in the last several years, as reflected not only in their increasing rates of social dislocation but also in the changing class structure of ghetto neighborhoods. In the 1940s, 1950s, and even the 1960s, lower-class, working-class, and middle-class black urban families all resided more or less in the same ghetto areas, albeit on different streets. Although black middle-class professionals today tend to be employed in mainstream occupations outside the black community and neither live nor frequently interact with ghetto residents, the black middle-class professionals of the 1940s and 1950s (doctors, lawyers, teachers, social workers, etc.) resided in the higher-income areas of the inner city and serviced the ghetto community. The exodus of black middle-class professionals from the inner city has been increasingly accompanied by a movement of stable working-class blacks to higher-income neighborhoods in other parts of the city and to the suburbs. Confined by restrictive covenants to communities also inhabited by the urban black lower classes, the black working and middle classes in earlier years provided stability to inner-city neighborhoods and perpetuated and reinforced societal norms and values. In short, their very presence enhanced the social organization of ghetto communities. If strong norms and sanctions against aberrant behavior, a sense of community, and positive neighborhood identification are the essential features of social organization in urban areas, inner-city neighborhoods today suffer from a severe lack of social organization.

Unlike in previous years, today's ghetto residents represent almost exclusively the most disadvantaged segments of the urban black community – including those families that have experienced long-term spells of poverty and/or welfare dependency, individuals who lack training and skills and have either experienced periods of persistent unemployment or have dropped out of the labor force altogether, and individuals who are frequently involved in street criminal activity. The term *ghetto under-class* refers to this heterogeneous group of families and individuals who inhabit the cores of the nation's central cities. The term suggests that a fundamental social transformation has taken place in ghetto neighborhoods, and the groups represented by this term are collectively different from and much more socially isolated than those that lived in these communities in earlier years.

The significance of changes embodied in the social transformation of the inner city is perhaps best captured by the concepts *concentration effects* and *social buffer*. The former refers to the constraints and opportunities associated with living in a neighborhood in which the population is overwhelmingly socially disadvantaged – constraints and opportunities that include the kinds of ecological niches that the residents of these communities occupy in terms of access to jobs, availability of marriageable partners, and exposure to conventional role models. The letter refers to the presence of a sufficient number of working- and middle-class professional families to absorb the shock or cushion the effect of uneven economic growth and periodic recessions on inner-city neighborhoods. The basic thesis is not that ghetto culture went unchecked following the removal of higher-income families in the inner city, but that the removal of these families made it more difficult to sustain the basic institutions in the inner city (including churches, stores, schools, recreational facilities, etc.) in the face of prolonged joblessness. And as the basic institutions declined, the social organization of inner-city neighborhoods (defined here to include a sense of community, positive neighborhood identification, and explicit norms and sanctions against aberrant behavior) likewise declined. Indeed, the social organization of any neighborhood depends in large measure on the viability of social institutions in that neighborhood. It is true that the presence of stable working- and middle-class families in the ghetto provides mainstream role models that reinforce mainstream values pertaining to employment, education, and family structure. But, in the final analysis, a far more important effect is the institutional stability that these families are able to provide in their neighborhoods because of their greater economic and educational resources, especially during periods of an economic downturn – periods in which joblessness in poor urban areas tends to substantially increase.

In underlining joblessness as an important aspect of inner-city social transformations, we are reminded that in the 1960s scholars readily attributed poor black family deterioration to problems of employment. Nonetheless, in the last several years, in the face of the overwhelming attention given to welfare as the major source of black family breakup, concerns about the importance of joblessness have diminished, despite the existence of evidence strongly suggesting the need for renewed scholarly and public policy attention to the relationship between the disintegration of poor black families and black male labor-market experiences.

Although changing social and cultural trends have often been said to explain some of the dynamic shifts in the structure of the family, they appear to have more relevance for changes in family structure among whites. And contrary to popular opinion, there is little evidence to support the argument that welfare is the primary cause of family– out-of-wedlock births, breakups, and female-headed households. Welfare does seem to have a modest effect on separation and divorce, particularly for white women, but recent evidence indicates that its total effect on the proportion of all female householders is small.

By contrast, the evidence for the influence of joblessness on family structure is much more conclusive. Research has demonstrated, for example, a connection between an encouraging economic situation and the early marriage of young people. In this connection, black women are more likely to delay marriage and less likely to remarry. Although black and white teenagers expect to become parents at about the same ages, black teenagers expect to marry at later ages. The black delay in marriage and the lower rate of remarriage, each associated with high percentages of out-of-wedlock births and female-headed households, can be directly tied to the employment status of black males. Indeed, black women, especially young black women, are confronting a shrinking pool of "marriageable" (that is economically stable) men.

White women are not experiencing this problem. Our "male marriageable pool index" shows that the number of employed white men per one hundred white women in different age categories has either remained roughly the same or has only slightly increased in the last two decades. There is little reason, therefore, to assume a connection between the recent growth of female-headed white families and patterns of white male employment. That the pool of "marriageable" white men has not decreased over the years is perhaps reflected in the earlier age of first marriage and the higher rate of remarriage among white women. It is therefore reasonable to hypothesize that the rise in rates of separation and divorce among whites is due mainly to the increased economic independence of white women and related social and cultural factors embodied in the feminist movement.

The argument that the decline in the incidence of intact marriages among blacks is associated with the declining economic status of black men is further supported by an analysis of regional data on female headship and the "male marriageable pool." Whereas changes in the ratios of employed men to women among whites have been minimal for all regions of the country regardless of age from 1960 to 1980, the ratios among blacks have declined significantly in all regions except the West, with the greatest declines in the northeastern and north-central regions of the country. On the basis of these trends, it would be expected that the growth in numbers of black female-headed households would occur most rapidly in the northern regions, followed by the South and the West.

Regional data on the "male marriageable pool index" support this conclusion, except for the larger-than-expected increase in black female-headed families in the West – a function of patterns of selective black migration to the West.

The sharp decline in the black "male marriageable pool" in the northeastern and north-central regions is related to recent changes in the basic economic organization in American society. In the two northern regions, the shift in economic activity from goods production to services has been associated with changes in the location of production, including an interregional movement of industry from the North to the South and West and, more important, a movement of certain industries out of the older central cities where blacks are concentrated. Moreover, the shrinkage of the male marriageable pool for ages sixteen to twenty-four in the South from 1960 to 1980 is related to the mechanization of agriculture, which lowered substantially the demand for low-skilled agricultural labor, especially during the 1960s. For all these reasons, it is often necessary to go beyond the specific issue of current racial discrimination to understand factors that contribute directly to poor black joblessness and indirectly to related social problems such as family instability in the inner city. But this point has not been readily grasped by policymakers and civil rights leaders.

The Limits of Race-specific Public Policy

In the early 1960s there was no comprehensive civil rights bill and Jim Crow segregation was still widespread in parts of the nation, particularly in the Deep South. With the passage of the 1964 Civil Rights Bill there was considerable optimism that racial progress would ensue and that the principle of equality of individual rights (namely, that candidates for positions stratified in terms of prestige, power, or other social criteria ought to be judged solely on individual merit and therefore should not be discriminated against on the basis of racial origin) would be upheld.

Programs based solely on this principle are inadequate, however, to deal with the complex problems of race in America because they are not designed to address the substantive inequality that exists at the time discrimination is eliminated. In other words, long periods of racial oppression can result in a system of inequality that may persist for indefinite periods of time even after racial barriers are removed. This is because the most disadvantaged members of racial minority groups, who suffer the cumulative effects of both race and class subjugation (including those effects passed on from generation to generation), are disproportionately represented among the segment of the general population that has been denied the resources to compete effectively in a free and open market.

On the other hand, the competitive resources developed by the *advantage minority members* – resources that flow directly from the family stability, schooling, income, and peer groups that their parents have been able to provide – result in their benefiting disproportionately from policies that promote the rights of minority individuals by removing artificial barriers to valued positions.

Nevertheless, since 1970, government policy has tended to focus on formal programs designed and created both to prevent discrimination and to ensure that minorities are sufficiently represented in certain positions. This has resulted in a shift from the simple formal investigation and adjudication of complains of racial discrimination to government-mandated affirmative action programs to increase minority representation in public programs, employment, and education.

However, if minority members from the most advantaged families profit disproportionately from policies based on the principle of equality of individual opportunity, they also reap disproportionate benefits from policies of affirmative action based solely on their group membership. This is because advantaged minority members are likely to be disproportionately represented among those of their racial group most qualified for valued positions, such as college admissions, higher paying jobs, and promotions. Thus, if policies of preferential treatment for such positions are developed in terms of racial group membership rather than the real disadvantages suffered by individuals, then these policies will further improve the opportunities of the advantaged without necessarily addressing the problems of the truly disadvantaged such as the ghetto underclass.[1] The problems of the truly disadvantaged may require *nonracial* solutions such as full employment, balanced economic growth, and manpower training and education (tied to – not isolated from – these two economic conditions).

By 1980 this argument was not widely recognized or truly appreciated. Therefore, because the government not only adopted and implemented antibias legislation to promote minority individual rights, but also mandated and enforced affirmative action and related programs to enhance minority group rights, many thoughtful American citizens, including supporters of civil rights, were puzzled by recent social developments in black communities. Despite the passage of civil rights legislation and the creation of affirmative action programs, they sensed that conditions were deteriorating instead of improving for a significant segment of the black American population. This perception had emerged because of the continuous flow of pessimistic reports concerning the sharp rise in black joblessness, the precipitous drop in the black–white family income ratio, the steady increase in the percentage of blacks on the welfare rolls, and the extraordinary growth in the number of female-headed families. This perception was strengthened by the almost uniform cry among black leaders that not only had conditions worsened, but that white Americans had forsaken the cause of blacks as well.

Meanwhile, the liberal architects of the War on Poverty became puzzled when Great Society programs failed to reduce poverty in America and when they could find few satisfactory explanations for the sharp rise in inner-city social dislocations during the 1970s. However, just as advocates for minority rights have been slow to comprehend that many of the current problems of race, particularly those that plague the minority poor, derived from the broader processes of societal organization and therefore may have no direct or indirect connection with race, so too have the architects of the War on Poverty failed to emphasize the relationship between poverty and the broader processes of American economic organization. Accordingly, given the most comprehensive civil rights and antipoverty programs in America's history, the liberals of the civil rights movement and the Great Society became demoralized when inner-city poverty proved to be more intractable than they realized and when they could not satisfactorily explain such events as the unprecedented rise in inner-city joblessness and the remarkable growth in the number of female-headed households. This demoralization cleared the path for conservative analysts to fundamentally shift the focus away from changing the environments of the minority poor to changing their values and behavior.

However, and to repeat, many of the problems of the ghetto underclass are related to the broader problems of societal organization, including economic organization. For example, as pointed out earlier, regional differences in changes in the "male marriageable pool index" signify the importance of industrial shifts in the Northeast and Midwest. Related research clearly demonstrated the declining labor-market opportunities in the older central cities. Indeed, blacks tend to be concentrated in areas where the number and characteristics of jobs have been most significantly altered by shifts in the location of production activity and from manufacturing to services. Since an overwhelming majority of inner-city blacks lacks the qualifications for the high-skilled segment of the service sector such as information processing, finance, and real estate, they tend to be concentrated in the low-skilled segment, which features unstable employment, restricted opportunities, and low wages.

The Hidden Agenda: From Group-specific to Universal Programs of Reform

It is not enough simply to recognize the need to relate many of the woes of truly disadvantaged blacks to the problems of societal organization; it is also important to describe the problems of the ghetto underclass candidly and openly so that they can be fully explained and appropriate policy programs can be devised. It has been problematic, therefore, that liberal journalists, social scientists, policymakers, and civil rights leaders were reluctant throughout the decade of the 1970s to discuss inner-city social pathologies. Often, analysts of such issues as violent crime or teenage pregnancy deliberately make no references to race at all, unless perhaps to emphasize the deleterious consequences of racial discrimination or the institutionalized inequality of American society. Some scholars, in an effort to avoid the appearance of "blaming the victim" or to protect their work from charges of racism, simply ignore patterns of behavior that might be construed as stigmatizing to particular racial minorities.

Such neglect is relatively recent. During the mid-1960s, social scientists such as Kenneth B. Clark, Daniel Patrick Moynihan, and Lee Rainwater forthrightly examined the cumulative effects of racial isolation and class subordination on inner-city blacks. They vividly described aspects of ghetto life that, as Rainwater observed, are usually not discussed in polite conversations. All of these studies attempted to show the connection between the economic and social environment into which many blacks are born and the creation of patterns of behavior that, in Clark's words, frequently amounted to "self-perpetuating pathology."

Why have scholars tended to shy away from this line of research? One reason has to do with the vitriolic attack by many blacks and liberals against Moynihan upon publication of his report in 1965 – denunciations that generally focused on the author's unflattering depiction of the black family in the urban ghetto rather than on the proposed remedies or his historical analysis of the black family's social plight. The harsh reception accorded *The Negro Family* undoubtedly dissuaded many social scientists from following in Moynihan's footsteps.

The "black solidarity" movement was also emerging during the latter half of the 1960s. A new emphasis by young black scholars and intellectuals on the positive aspects of the black experience tended to crowd out older concerns. Indeed, certain forms of ghetto behavior labeled pathological in the studies of Clark and colleagues were redefined by some during the early 1970s as "functional" because, it was argued, blacks were displaying the ability to survive and in some cases flourish in an economically depressed environment. The ghetto family was described as resilient and capable of adapting creatively to an oppressive, racist society. And the candid, but liberal writings on the inner city in the 1960s were generally denounced. In the end, the promising efforts of the early 1960s – to distinguish the socioeconomic characteristics of different groups within the black community, and to identify the structural problems of the United States economy that affected minorities – were cut short by calls for "reparations" or for "black control of institutions serving the black community."

If this ideologically tinged criticism discouraged research by liberal scholars on the poor black family and the ghetto community, conservative thinkers were not so inhibited. From the early 1970s through the first half of the 1980s, their writings on the culture of poverty and the deleterious effects of Great Society liberal welfare policies on ghetto underclass behavior dominated the public policy debate on alleviating inner-city social dislocations.

The Great Society programs represented the country's most ambitious attempt to implement the principle of equality of life chances. However, the extent to which these programs helped the truly disadvantaged is difficult to assess when one considers the simultaneous impact of the economic downturn from 1968 to the early 1980s. Indeed, it has been argued that many people slipped into poverty because of the economic downturn and were lifted out by the broadening of welfare benefits. Moreover, the increase in unemployment that accompanied the economic downturn and the lack of growth of real wages in the 1970s, although they had risen steadily from 1950 to about 1970, have had a pronounced effect on low-income groups (especially black males).

The above analysis has certain distinct public policy implications for attacking the problems of inner-city joblessness and the related problems of poor female-headed families, welfare dependency, crime, and so forth. Comprehensive economic policies aimed at the general population but that would also enhance employment opportunities among the truly disadvantaged – both men and women – are needed. The research presented in this study suggests that improving the job prospects of men will strengthen low-income black families. Moreover, underclass absent fathers with more stable employment are in a better position to contribute financial support for their families. Furthermore, since the majority of female householders are in the labor force, improved job prospects would very likely draw in others.[2]

I have in mind the creation of a macroeconomic policy designed to promote both economic growth and a tight labor market.[3] The latter affects the supply-and-demand ratio and wages tend to rise. It would be necessary, however, to combine this policy with fiscal and monetary policies to stimulate noninflationary growth and thereby move away from the policy of controlling inflation by allowing unemployment to rise. Furthermore, it would be important to develop policy to increase the competitiveness of American goods on the international market by, among other things, reducing the budget deficit to enhance the value of the American dollar.

In addition, measures such as on-the-job training and apprenticeships to elevate the skill levels of the truly disadvantaged are needed. I will soon discuss in another context why such problems have to be part of a more universal package of reform. For now, let me simply say that improved manpower policies are needed in the short run to help lift the truly disadvantaged from the lowest rungs of the job market. In other words, it would be necessary to devise a national labor-market strategy to increase "the adaptability of the labor force to changing employment opportunities." In this connection, instead of focusing on remedial programs in the public sector for the poor and the unemployed, emphasis would be placed on relating these programs more closely to opportunities in the private sector to facilitate the movement of recipients (including relocation assistance) into more secure jobs. Of course there would be a need to create public transitional programs for those who have difficulty finding immediate employment in the private sector, but such programs would aim toward eventually getting individuals into the private sector economy. Although public employment programs continue to draw popular support, as Weir, Orloff, and Skocpol point out, "they must be designed and administered in close conjunction with a nationally oriented labor market strategy" to avoid both becoming "enmeshed in congressionally reinforced local political patronage" and being attacked as costly, inefficient, or "corrupt."[4]

Since national opinion polls consistently reveal strong public support for efforts to enhance work in America, political support for a program of economic reform (macroeconomic employment policies and labor-market strategies including training efforts) could be considerably stronger than many people presently assume.[5] However, in order to draw sustained public support for such a program, it is necessary that training or retraining, transitional employment benefits, and relocation assistance be available to all members of society who choose to use them, not just to poor minorities.

It would be ideal if problems of the ghetto underclass could be adequately addressed by the combination of macroeconomic policy, labor-market strategies, and manpower training programs. However, in the foreseeable future employment alone will not necessarily lift a family out of poverty.[6] Many families would still require income support and/or social services such as child care. A program of welfare reform is needed, therefore, to address the current problems of public assistance, including lack of provisions for poor two-parent families, inadequate levels of support, inequities between different states, and work disincentives. A national AFDC benefit standard adjusted yearly for inflation is the most minimal required change. We might also give serious consideration to programs such as the Child Support Assurance Program developed by Irwin Garfinkel and colleagues at the Institute for Research on Poverty at the University of Wisconsin, Madison.[7] This program, currently in operation as a demonstration project in the state of Wisconsin, provides a guaranteed minimum benefit per child to single-parent families regardless of the income of the custodial parent. The state collects from the absent parent through wage withholding a sum of money at a fixed rate and then makes regular payments to the custodial parent. If the absent parent is jobless or if his or her payment from withholdings is less than the minimum, the state makes up the difference. Since all absent parents regardless of income are required to participate in this program, it is far less stigmatizing than, say, public assistance. Moreover, preliminary evidence from Wisconsin suggests that this program carries little or no additional cost to the state.

Many western European countries have programs of family or child allowances to support families. These programs provide families with an annual benefit per child regardless of the family's income, and regardless of whether the parents are living together or whether either or both are employed. Unlike public assistance, therefore, a family allowance program carries no social stigma and has no built-in work disincentives. In this connection, Daniel Patrick Moynihan has recently observed that a form of family allowance is already available to American families with the standard deduction and Earned Income Tax Credit, although the latter can only be obtained by low-income families. Even though both have been significantly eroded by inflation, they could represent the basis for a more comprehensive family allowance program that approximates the European model.

Neither the Child Support Assurance Program under demonstration in Wisconsin nor the European family allowances program is means tested; that is, they are not targeted at a particular income group and therefore do not suffer the degree of stigmatization that plagues public assistance programs such as AFDC. More important, such universal programs would tend to draw more political support from the general public because the programs would be available not only to the poor but to the working- and middle-class segments as well. And such programs would not be readily associated with specific minority groups. Nonetheless, truly disadvantaged groups would reap disproportionate benefits from such programs because of the groups' limited alternative economic resources. For example, low-income single mothers could combine work with adequate guaranteed child support and/or child allowance benefits and therefore escape poverty and avoid public assistance.

Finally, the question of child care has to be addressed in any program designed to improve the employment prospects of women and men. Because of the growing participation of women in the labor market, adequate child care has been a topic receiving increasing attention in public policy discussions. For the overwhelmingly female-headed ghetto underclass families, access to quality child care becomes a critical issue if steps are taken to move single mothers into education and training programs and/or full- or part-time employment. However, I am not recommending government-operated child care centers. Rather it would be better to avoid additional federal bureaucracy by seeking alternative and decentralized forms of child care such as expanding the child care tax credit, including three- and four-year-olds in preschool enrollment, and providing child care subsidies to the working-poor parents.

If the truly disadvantaged reaped disproportionate benefits from a child support enforcement program, child allowance program, and child care strategy, they would also benefit disproportionately from a program of balanced economic growth and tight labor-market policies because of their greater vulnerability to swings in the business cycle and changes in economic organization, including the relocation of plants and the use of labor-saving technology. It would be shortsighted to conclude, therefore, that universal programs (i.e., programs not targeted at any particular group) are not designed to help address in a fundamental way some of the problems of the truly disadvantaged, such as the ghetto underclass.

By emphasizing universal programs as an effective way to address problems in the inner city created by historic racial subjugation, I am recommending a fundamental shift from the traditional race-specific approach of addressing such problems. It is true that problems of joblessness and related woes such as poverty, teenage pregnancies, out-of-wedlock births, female-headed families, and welfare dependency are, for reasons of historic racial oppression, disproportionately concentrated in the black community. And it is important to recognize the racial differences in rates of social dislocation so as not to obscure problems currently gripping the ghetto underclass. However, as discussed above, race-specific policies are often not designed to address fundamental problems of the truly disadvantaged. Moreover, as also discussed above, both race-specific and targeted programs based on the principle of equality of life chances (often identified with a minority constituency) have difficulty sustaining widespread public support.

Does this mean that targeted programs of any kind would necessarily be excluded from a package highlighting universal programs of reform? On the contrary, as long as a racial division of labor exists and racial minorities are disproportionately concentrated in low-paying positions, antidiscrimination and affirmative action programs will be needed even though they tend to benefit the more advantaged minority members. Moreover, as long as certain groups lack the training, skills, and education to compete effectively on the job market or move into newly created jobs, manpower training and education programs targeted at these groups will also be needed, even under a tight-labor-market situation. For example, a program of adult education and training may be necessary for some ghetto underclass males before they can either become oriented to or move into an expanded labor market. Finally, as long as some poor families are unable to work because of physical or other disabilities, public assistance would be needed even if the government adopted a program of welfare reform that included child support enforcement and family allowance provisions.

For all these reasons, a comprehensive program of economic and social reform (highlighting macroeconomic policies to promote balanced economic growth and create a tight labor-market situation, a nationally oriented labor-market strategy, a child support assurance program, a child care strategy, and a family allowances program) would have to include targeted programs, both means tested and race-specific. However, the latter would be considered an offshoot of and indeed secondary to the universal programs. The important goal is to construct an economic-social reform program in such a way that the universal programs are seen as the dominant and most visible aspects by the general public. As the universal programs draw support from a wider population, the targeted programs included in the comprehensive reform package would be indirectly supported and protected. Accordingly, *the hidden agenda for liberal policymakers is to improve the life chances of truly disadvantaged groups such as the ghetto underclass by emphasizing programs to which the more advantaged groups of all races and class backgrounds can positively relate.*

I am reminded of Bayard Rustin's plea during the early 1960s that blacks ought to recognize the importance of fundamental economic reform (including a system of national economic planning along with new education, manpower, and public works programs to help reach full employment) and the need for a broad-based political coalition to achieve it. And since an effective coalition will in part depend upon how the issues are defined, it is imperative that the political message underline the need for economic and social reforms that benefit all groups in the United States, not just poor minorities. Politicians and civil rights organizations, as two important examples, ought to shift or expand their definition of America's racial problems and broaden the scope of suggested policy programs to address them. They should, of course, continue to fight for an end to racial discrimination. But they must also recognize that poor minorities are profoundly affected by problems in America that go beyond racial considerations. Furthermore, civil rights groups should also recognize that the problems of societal organization in America often create situations that enhance racial antagonisms between the different racial groups in central cities that are struggling to maintain their quality of life, and that these groups, although they appear to be fundamental adversaries, are potential allies in a reform coalition because of their problematic economic situations.

The difficulties that a progressive reform coalition would confront should not be underestimated. It is much easier to produce major economic and social reform in countries such as Sweden, Norway, Austria, the Netherlands, and West Germany than in the Untied States. What characterizes this group of countries, as demonstrated in the important research of Harold Wilensky,[8] is the interaction of solidly organized, generally centralized, interest groups – particularly professional, labor, and employer associations with a centralized or quasi-centralized government either compelled by law or obliged by informal agreement to take the recommendations of the interest group into account or to rely on their counsel. This arrangement produces a consensus-making organization working generally within a public framework to bargain and produce policies on present-day political economy issues such as full employment, economic growth, unemployment, wages, prices, taxes, balance of payments, and social policy (including various forms of welfare, education, health, and housing policies).

In all of these countries, called "corporatist democracies" by Wilensky, social policy is integrated with economic policy. This produces a situation whereby, in periods of rising aspirations and slow economic growth, labor – concerned with wages, working conditions, and social security – is compelled to be attentive to the rate of productivity, the level of inflation, and the requirements of investments, and employers – concerned with profits, productivity, and investments – are compelled to be attentive to issues of social policy.[9]

The corporatist democracies, which are in a position to develop new consensus on social and economic policies in the face of declining economies because channels for bargaining and influence are firmly in place, stand in sharp contrast to the decentralized and fragmented political economies of the United States, Canada, and the United Kingdom. In these latter countries – none of which is a highly progressive welfare state – the proliferation of interest groups is not restrained by the requisites of national trade-offs and bargaining, which therefore allows parochial single issues to move to the forefront and thereby exacerbates the advanced condition of political immobilism. Reflecting the rise of single-issue groups has been the steady deterioration of political organizations and the decline of traditional allegiance to parties among voters. Moreover, there has been a sharp increase in the influence of the mass media, particularly the electronic media, in politics and culture. These trends, typical of all Western democracies, are much more salient in countries such as the United States, Canada, and the United Kingdom because their decentralized and fragmented political economies magnify the void created by the decline of political parties – a void that media and strident, single-issue groups rush headlong to fill.[10]

I raise these issues to underline some of the problems that a political coalition dedicated to developing and implementing a progressive policy agenda will have to confront. It seems imperative that, in addition to outlining a universal program of reform including policies that could effectively address inner-city social dislocations, attention be given to the matter of erecting a national bargaining structure to achieve sufficient consensus on the program of reform.

It is also important to recognize that just as we can learn from knowledge about the efficacy of alternative bargaining structures, we can also benefit from knowledge of alternative approaches to welfare and employment policies. Here we fortunately have the research of Alfred J. Kahn and Sheila Kamerman, which has convincingly demonstrated that countries that rely the least on public assistance, such as Sweden, West

Germany, and France, provide alternative income transfers (family allowances, housing allowances, child support, unemployment assistance), stress the use of transfers to augment both earnings and transfer income, provide both child care services and day-care programs, and emphasize labor-market policies to enhance high employment. These countries, therefore, "provide incentives to work, supplement the use of social assistance generally because, even when used, it is increasingly only one component, at most, of a more elaborate benefit package." By contrast, the United States relies more heavily than all the other countries (Sweden, West Germany, France, Canada, Austria, the United Kingdom, and Israel) on public assistance to aid poorer families. "The result is that these families are much worse off than they are in any of the other countries."[11]

In other words, problems such as poverty, joblessness, and long-term welfare dependency in the United States have not been addressed with the kinds of innovative approaches found in many western European democracies. "The European experience," argue Kamerman and Kahn, "suggests the need for a strategy that includes income transfers, child care services, and employment policies as central elements." The cornerstone of social policy in these countries is employment and labor-market policies. "Unless it is possible for adults to manage their work and family lives without undue strain on themselves and their children," argue Kamerman and Kahn, "society will suffer a significant loss in productivity, and an even more significant loss in the quantity and quality of future generations." [12]

The social policy that I have recommended above also would have employment and labor-market policies as its fundamental foundation. For in the final analysis neither family allowance and child support assurance programs, nor means-tested public assistance and manpower training and education programs can be sustained at adequate levels if the country is plagued with prolonged periods of economic stagnation and joblessness.

A Universal Reform Package and the Social Isolation of the Inner City

The program of economic and social reform outlined above will help address the problems of social dislocation plaguing the ghetto underclass. I make no claims that such programs will lead to a revitalization of neighborhoods in the inner city, reduce the social isolation, and thereby recapture the degree of social organization that characterized these neighborhoods in earlier years. However, in the long run these programs will lift the ghetto underclass from the throes of long-term poverty and welfare dependency and provide them with the economic and educational resources that would expand the limited choices they now have with respect to living arrangements. At the present time many residents of isolated inner-city neighborhoods have no other option but to remain in those neighborhoods. As their economic and educational resources improve they will very likely follow the path worn by many other former ghetto residents and move to safer or more desirable neighborhoods.

It seems to me that the most realistic approach to the problems of concentrated inner-city poverty is to provide ghetto underclass families and individuals with the resources that promote social mobility. Social mobility leads to geographic mobility. Geographic mobility would of course be enhanced if efforts to improve the economic and educational resources of inner-city residents were accompanied by legal steps to eliminate (1) the "practice at all levels of government" to "routinely locate housing for low-income people in the poorest neighborhoods of a community where their neighbors will be other low-income people usually of the same race"; and (2) the manipulation of zoning laws and discriminatory land use controls or site selection practices that either prevent the "construction of housing affordable to low-income families" or prevent low-income families "from securing residence in communities that provide the services they desire."[13]

This discussion raises a question about the ultimate effectiveness of the so-called self-help programs to revitalize the inner city, programs pushed by conservative and even some liberal black spokespersons. In many inner-city neighborhoods, problems such as joblessness are so overwhelming and require such a massive effort to restabilize institutions and create a social and economic milieu necessary to sustain such institutions (e.g., the reintegration of the neighborhood with working- and middle-class blacks and black professionals) that it is surprising that advocates of black self-help have received so such serious attention from the media and policy makers.[14]

Of course some advocates of self-help subscribe to the thesis that problems in the inner city are ultimately the product of ghetto-specific culture and that it is the cultural values and norms in the inner city that must be addressed as part of a comprehensive self-help program.[15] However, cultural values emerge from specific circumstances and life chances and reflect an individual's position in the class structure. They therefore do not ultimately determine behavior. If ghetto underclass minorities have limited aspirations, a hedonistic orientation toward life, or lack of plans for the future, such outlooks ultimately are the result of restricted opportunities and feelings of resignation originating from bitter personal experiences and a bleak future. Thus the inner-city social dislocations emphasized in this study (joblessness, crime, teenage pregnancies, out-of-wedlock births, female-headed families, and welfare dependency) should be analyzed not as cultural aberrations but as symptoms of racial-class inequality.[16] It follows, therefore, that changes in the economic and social situations of the ghetto underclass will lead to changes in cultural norms and behavior patterns. The social policy program outlined above is based on this idea.

Before I take a final look, by way of summary and conclusion, at the important features of this program, I ought briefly to discuss an alternative public agenda that could, if not challenged, dominate the public policy discussion of underclass poverty in the next several years.

A Critical Look at an Alternative Agenda: New-Style Workfare

In a recent book on the social obligations of citizenship, Lawrence Mead contends that "the challenge to welfare statesmanship is not so much to change the extent of benefits as to couple them with serious work and other obligations that would encourage functioning and thus promote the integration of recipients." He argues that the programs of the Great Society failed to overcome poverty and, in effect, increased dependency because the "behavioral problems of the poor" were ignored. Welfare clients received new services and benefits but were not told "with any authority that they ought to behave differently." Mead attributes a good deal of the welfare dependency to a sociological logic ascribing the responsibilities for the difficulties experienced by the disadvantaged entirely to the social environment, a logic that still "blocks government from expecting or obligating the poor to behave differently than they do."[17]

Mead believes that there is a disinclination among the underclass to either accept or retain many available low-wage jobs. The problem of nonwhite unemployment, he contends, is not a lack of jobs, but a high turnover rate. Mead contends that because this kind of joblessness is not affected by changes in the overall economy, it would be difficult to blame the environment. While not dismissing the role discrimination may play in the low-wage sector, Mead argues that it is more likely that the poor are impatient with the working conditions and pay of menial jobs and repeatedly quit in hopes of finding better employment. At the present time, "for most jobseekers in most areas, jobs of at least a rudimentary kind are generally available." For Mead it is not that the poor do not want to work, but rather that they will work only under the condition that others remove the barriers that make the world of work difficult. "Since much of the burden consists precisely in acquiring skills, finding jobs, arranging child care, and so forth," states Mead, "the effect is to drain work obligation of much of its meaning."[18]

In sum, Mead believes that the programs of the Great Society have exacerbated the situation of the underclass by not obligating the recipients of social welfare programs to behave according to mainstream norms – completing school, working, obeying the law, and so forth. Since virtually nothing was demanded in return for benefits, the underclass remain socially isolated and could not be accepted as equals.

If any of the social policies recommended by conservative analysts are to become serious candidates for adoption as national public policy, they will more likely be based on the kind of argument advanced by Mead in favor of mandatory workfare. The laissez-faire social philosophy represented by Charles Murray is not only too extreme to be seriously considered by most policymakers, but the premise upon which it is based is vulnerable to the kind of criticism raised in chapters 1 and 4, namely, that the greatest rise in black joblessness and female-headed families occurred during the very period (1972–80) when the real value of AFDC plus food stamps plummeted because states did not peg benefit levels to inflation.

Mead's arguments, on the other hand, are much more subtle. If his and similar arguments in support of mandatory workfare are not adopted wholesale as national policy, aspects of his theoretical rationale on the social obligations of citizenship could, as we shall see, help shape a policy agenda involving obligational state programs.

Nonetheless, whereas Mead speculates that jobs are generally available in most areas and therefore one must turn to behavioral explanations for the high jobless rate among the underclass, my research shows: (1) that substantial job losses have occurred in the very industries in which urban minorities are heavily concentrated and substantial employment gains have occurred in the higher-education-requisite industries that have relatively few minority workers; (2) that this mismatch is most severe in the Northeast and Midwest (regions that also have had the sharpest increases in black joblessness and female-headed families); and (3) that the current growth in entry-level jobs, particularly in the service establishments, is occurring almost exclusively outside the central cities where poor minorities are concentrated. It is obvious that these findings and the general observations about the adverse effects of the recent recessions on poor urban minorities raise serious questions not only about Mead's assumptions regarding poor minorities, work experience, and jobs, but also about the appropriateness of his policy recommendations.[19]

In raising questions about Mead's emphasis on social values as an explanation of poor minority joblessness, I am not suggesting that negative attitudes toward menial work should be totally dismissed as a contributing factor. The growing social isolation, and the concentration of poverty in the inner city, that have made ghetto communities increasingly vulnerable to fluctuations in the economy, undoubtedly influence attitudes, values, and aspirations. The issue is whether attitudes toward menial employment account in large measure for the sharp rise in inner-city joblessness and related forms of social dislocation since the formation of the Great Society programs. Despite Mead's eloquent arguments the empirical support for his thesis is incredibly weak.[20] It is therefore difficult for me to embrace a theory that sidesteps the complex issues and consequences of changes in American economic organization with the argument that one can address the problems of the ghetto underclass by simply emphasizing the social obligation of citizenship. Nonetheless, there are clear signs that a number of policymakers are now moving in this direction, even liberal policymakers who, while considering the problems of poor minorities from the narrow visions of race relations and the War on Poverty, have become disillusioned with Great Society-type programs. The emphasis is not necessarily on mandatory workfare, however. Rather the emphasis is on what Richard Nathan has called "new-style workfare," which represents a synthesis of liberal and conservative approaches to obligational state programs.[21] Let me briefly elaborate.

In the 1970s the term *workfare* was narrowly used to capture the idea that welfare recipients should be required to work, even to do make-work if necessary, in exchange for receiving benefits. This idea was generally rejected by liberals and those in the welfare establishment. And no workfare program, even Governor Ronald Reagan's 1971 program, really got off the ground. However, by 1981 President Ronald Reagan was able to get congressional approval to include a provision in the 1981 budget allowing states to experiment with new employment approaches to welfare reform. These approaches represent the "new-style workfare." More specifically, whereas workfare in the 1970s was narrowly construed as "working off" one's welfare grant, the new-style workfare "takes the form of obligational state programs that involve an array of employment and training services and activities – job search, job training, education programs, and also community work experience."[22]

According to Nathan, "we make our greatest progress on social reform in the United States when liberals and conservatives find common ground. New-style workfare embodies both the caring commitment of liberals and the themes identified with conservative writers like Charles Murray, George Gider, and Lawrence Mead." On the one hand, liberals can relate to new-style workfare because it creates short-term entry-level positions very similar to the "CETA public service jobs we thought we had abolished in 1981"; it provides a convenient "political rationale and support for increased funding for education and training programs"; and it targets these programs at the most disadvantaged, thereby correcting the problem of "creaming" that is associated with other employment and training programs. On the other hand, conservatives can relate to new-style workfare because "it involves a strong commitment to reducing welfare dependency on the premise that dependency is bad for people, that it undermines their motivation to self-support and isolates and stigmatizes welfare recipients in a way that over a long period feeds into and accentuates the underclass mind set and condition."[23]

The combining of liberal and conservative approaches does not, of course, change the fact that the new-style workfare programs hardly represent a fundamental shift from the traditional approaches to poverty in America. Once again the focus is exclusively on individual character-istics – whether they are construed in terms of lack of training, skills, or education, or whether they are seen in terms of lack of motivation or other subjective traits. And once again the consequences of certain economic arrangements on disadvantaged populations in the United States are not considered in the formulation and implementation of social policy. Although new-style workfare is better than having no strategy at all to enhance employment experiences, it should be emphasized that the effectiveness of such programs ultimately depends upon the availability of jobs in a given area. Perhaps Robert D. Reischauer put it best when he stated that: "As long as the unemployment rate remains high in many regions of the country, members of the underclass are going to have a very difficult time competing successfully for the jobs that are available. No amount of remedial education, training, wage subsidy, or other embellishment will make them more attractive to prospective employers than experienced unemployed workers."[24] As Reischauer also appropri-ately emphasizes, with a weak economy "even if the workfare program seems to be placing its clients successfully, these participants may simply be taking jobs away from others who are nearly as disadvantaged. A game of musical underclass will ensue as one group is temporarily helped, while another is pushed down into the underclass."[25]

If new-style workfare will indeed represent a major policy thrust in the immediate future, I see little prospect for substantially alleviating in-equality among poor minorities if such a workfare program is not part of a more comprehensive program of economic and social reform that recognizes the dynamic interplay between societal organization and the behavior and life chances of individuals and groups – a program, in other words, that is designed to both enhance human capital traits of poor minorities and open up the opportunity structure in the broader society and economy to facilitate social mobility. The combination of economic and social welfare policies discussed in the previous section represents, from my point of view, such a program.

Conclusion

In this chapter I have argued that the problems of the ghetto underclass can be most meaningfully addressed by a comprehensive program that combines employment policies with social welfare policies and that features universal as opposed to race- or group-specific strategies. On the one hand, this program highlights macroeconomic policy to generate a tight labor market and economic growth; fiscal and monetary policy not only to stimulate noninflationary growth, but also to increase the competitiveness of American goods on both the domestic and international markets; and a national labor-market strategy to make the labor force more adaptable to changing economic opportunities. On the other hand, this program highlights a child support assurance program, a family allowance program, and a child-care strategy.

I emphasized that although this program also would include targeted strategies – both means tested and race-specific – they would be considered secondary to the universal program so that the latter are seen as the most visible and dominant aspects in the eyes of the general public. To the extent that the universal programs draw support from a wider population, the less visible targeted programs would be indirectly supported and protected. To repeat, the hidden agenda for liberal policymakers is to enhance the chances in life for the ghetto underclass by emphasizing programs to which the more advantaged groups of all class and racial backgrounds can positively relate.

Before such programs can be seriously considered, however, cost has to be addressed. The cost of programs to expand social and economic opportunity will be great, but it must be weighed against the economic and social costs of a do-nothing policy. As Levitan and Johnson have pointed out, "the most recent recession cost the nation an estimated $300 billion in lost income and production, and direct outlays for unemployment compensation totaled $30 billion in a single year. A policy that ignores the losses associated with slack labor markets and forced idleness inevitably will underinvest in the nation's labor force and future economic growth." Furthermore, the problem of annual budget deficits of around $200 billion dollars (driven mainly by the peacetime military buildup and the Reagan administration's tax cuts), and the need for restoring the federal tax base and adopting a more balanced set of budget priorities have to be tackled if we are to achieve significant progress on expanding opportunities.[26]

In the final analysis, the pursuit of economic and social reform ultimately involves the question of political strategy. As the history of social provision so clearly demonstrates, universalistic political alliances, cemented by policies that provide benefits directly to wide segments of the population, are needed to work successfully for major reform.[27] The recognition among minority leaders and liberal policymakers of the need to expand the War on Poverty and race relations visions to confront the growing problems of inner-city social dislocations will provide, I believe, an important first step toward creating such an alliance.

Notes

1   James Fishkin covers much of this ground very convincingly. See his *Justice, Equal Opportunity and the Family* (New Haven, Conn.: Yale University Press, 1983).

2   Kathryn M. Neckerman, Robert Aponte, and William Julius Wilson, "Family Structure, Black Unemployment, and American Social Policy," in *The Politics of Social Policy in the United States*, ed. Margaret Weir, Ann Shola Orloff, and Theda Skocpol (Princeton, N.J.: Princeton University Press, 1988).

3   The essential features of such a policy are discussed in William J. Wilson, *The Truly Disadvantaged* (Chicago: University of Chicago Press, 1987), chap. 5, "The Case for a Universal Program."

4   Margaret Weir, Ann Shola Orloff, and Theda Skocpol, "The Future of Sociology Policy in the United States: Political Constraints and Possibilities," in Weir, Orloff, and Skocpol, *Politics of Social Policy in the United States.*

5   Theda Skocpol, "Brother Can You Spare a Job?: Work and Welfare in the United States," paper presented at the Annual Meeting of the American Sociological Association, Washington, D.C., August 27, 1985.

6   Part of the discussion on welfare reform in the next several pages is based on Neckerman, Aponte, and Wilson, "Family Structure, Black Unemployment, and American Social Policy."

7   Irwin Garfinkel and Sara S. McLanahan, *Single Mothers and Their Children: A New American Dilemma* (Washington, D.C.: Urban Institute Press, 1986).

8   Harold L. Wilensky, "Evaluating Research and Politics: Political Legitimacy and Consensus as Missing Variables in the Assessment of Social Policy," in *Evaluating the Welfare State: Social and Political Perspectives*, ed. E. Spiro and E. Yuchtman-Yarr (New York: Academic Press, 1983). I am indebted to Wilensky for the following discussion on corporatist democracies.

9   Ibid.

10   Ibid.

11   Sheila S. Kamerman and Alfred J. Kahn, "Income Transfers, Work and the Economic Well-being of Families with Children," *International Social Security Review* 3 (1982): 376.

12   Sheila S. Kamerman and Alfred Kahn, "Europe's Innovative Family Policies," *Transatlantic Perspectives*, March 1980, p. 12.

13   William L. Taylor, "*Brown*, Equal Protection, and the Isolation of the Poor," *Yale Law Journal* 95 (July 1986): 1729–30.

14   I have in mind the numerous editorials and op-ed columns on self-help in widely read newspapers such as the *Washington Post, New York Times, Wall Street Journal*, and *Chicago Tribune*; articles in national magazines such as *The New Republic* and *Atlantic Monthly*; and the testimony that self-help advocates, particularly black conservative supporters of self-help, have given before the U.S. Congress.

15   The most sophisticated and articulate black spokesperson of this thesis is Harvard University professor Glenn Loury. See, e.g., Glen Loury, "The Need for Moral Leadership in the Black Community," *New Perspectives* 16 (Summer 1984): 14–19.

16   Stephen Steinberg makes a compelling case for this argument in his

stimulating book *The Ethnic Myth: Race, Ethnicity and Class in America* (New York: Atheneum, 1981).

17   Lawrence M. Mead, *Beyond Entitlement: The Social Obligations of Citizenship* (New York: Free Press, 1986), pp. 4, 61.

18   Ibid., pp. 73, 80.

19   See, for example, Michael Sosin's excellent review of *Beyond Entitlement* in *Social Service Review* 61 (March 1987): 156–59.

20   Wilson, *The Truly Disadvantaged*, chaps 2 and 4.

21   R. Nathan, "The Underclass – Will It Always Be with Us?" Paper presented at a symposium on the Underclass, New School for Social Research, New York, N.Y., November 14, 1986.

22   Ibid., p. 18.

23   Ibid., pp. 19–21. Although Lawrence Mead is highly critical of new-style workfare (because it reinforces the sociological view of the disadvantaged by assuming that before the recipients can work, the program has to find the client a job, arrange for child care, solve the client's help problems, and so on), his elaborate theory of the social obligation of citizenship is being adopted by policymakers to buttress the more conservative side of the new workfare programs.

24   Robert D. Reischauer, "America's Underclass: Four Unanswered Questions," paper presented at The City Club, Portland, Oreg., January 30, 1986.

25   Robert D. Reischauer, "Policy Responses to the Underclass Problem," paper presented at a symposium at the New School for Social Research, November 14, 1986.

26   S. A. Levitan and C. M. Johnson, *Beyond the Safety Net: Reviving the Promising of Opportunity in America* (Cambridge, Mass.: Ballinger Publishing Co., 1984), pp. 169–70.

27   Skocpol, "Brother Can You Spare a Job?"

9

Race, Class, and Segregation: Discourses about African Americans

Norman Fainstein

It is common in the social sciences for research topics, evidence, interpretations and intellectual conflict to be organized within a dominant discourse. Examples that come readily to mind include modernization, community power structure and pluralism. Like great hippopotamuses, these linguistic animals take up much space and eat up resources within academic disciplines, the media and government. Of course, there are usually other intellectual animals lurking around these giants, not merely raising dissenting voices, but even trying to speak other languages. Dominant discourses become dominant in the first place, however, because they reflect and reinforce an array of interests – cultural, political, economic – generally, though not solely, those of the rich and powerful. So it is not easy for other voices to be heard, much less to redefine the reigning way of talking about things. Yet ways of speaking do change when the moment is right. Perhaps we are at that point now with regard to the discourse about class and race in America, where the *under-*

Reprinted by permission from Norman Fainstein, 1993, "Race, Class, and Segregation: Discourses about African Americans," *International Journal of Urban and Regional Research* 17 (Fall).

class has been the reigning hippopotamus. This paper constitutes a modest effort to sum up some of the dissident voices and dissonant evidence with regard to the topic of the social-economic situation of African Americans,[1] and perhaps thereby to break free of our obsessive use of underclass discourse to frame our discussions.

The Underclass Narrative

In sociological research on African Americans, the present dominant discourse was established in the latter part of the 1970s. At that time, two strands of thought were woven together. One may be attributed to William Julius Wilson, who displaced Charles Hamilton and his black power paradigm and emerged as arguably the leading African American social scientist with the publication of *The Declining Significance of Race* (Wilson, 1978). In that influential book, Wilson looked back over the first three-quarters of the century and saw a sharp decline in racism in the United States, with blacks being treated more and more like whites, that is, stratified and differentiated by class. Black society was, he argued, increasingly bifurcated, with the 'black poor falling further and further behind middle- and upper-income blacks'. These 'talented and educated blacks' were experiencing rapid upward mobility, 'opportunities that [were] at least comparable to whites with equivalent qualifications' (Wilson, 1978: 151–2).

The second strand of thought predated Wilson, though it was developed by him in a series of publications culminating in *The Truly Disadvantaged* (1987). Low-income, typically black, inner city neighbourhoods were being described in the media as increasingly wild, inhabited by a socially deviant, dependent and lawless population – 'The American underclass', as it was called on the cover of *Time* magazine (1977). Ten years later, nothing had changed for the better:

> *Today's ghetto neighborhoods are populated almost exclusively by the most disadvantaged segments of the black urban community, that heterogeneous grouping of families and individuals who are out of the mainstream of the American occupational system. Included in this group are individuals who lack training and skills and either experience long-term unemployment or are not members of the labor force, individuals who are engaged in street crime and other forms of aberrant behavior, and families that experience long-term spells of poverty and/or welfare dependency. These are the populations to which I refer when I speak of the* underclass. *I use this term to depict a reality not captured in the more standard designation* lower class. (Wilson, 1987: 7–8)

In combination, the ideas of the declining significance of race and the growing pathology and danger posed by people who were, it seemed, under or outside of the 'normal' class structure established the dominant discourse of the underclass, the study of which has become a veritable industry, nearly monopolizing foundation and government resources committed to research on poverty, constituting the subject of numerous conferences and, of course, generating a considerable literature.[2] A real sign that the underclass discourse is indeed dominant may be found in the fact that it subsumes debate over class, race and poverty. The underclass hippopotamus takes up nearly the whole political spectrum in the social sciences, as radical, liberal and conservative analysts each impart their particular spin to its interpretation, differing in their emphases on economic versus cultural factors, in their attachment of culpability to members of the underclass, and especially in whether they blame prior liberal government policies or extant conservative ones for the growth and bad behaviour of the underclass.

Whatever their political and theoretical perspective, participants in the discourse of the underclass share a deep narrative. Like other deep narratives[3] – the collapse of socialism is a ubiquitous story these days – that of the underclass is both explicit and implicit, saying much in its omissions. Its logic is relatively transparent, constructed along four lines. *First, underclass terminology offers a way of speaking about race in a language of class that implicitly rejects the importance of race.* While the term in theory should be deployed universally against all those who fit its behavioural conditions – like its ancient relative 'the undeserving poor', and its modern cognate 'the culture of poverty' – in practice it is reserved for African Americans. That is why Wilson (1991), responding to criticism, could ask in his 1990 presidential address to the American Sociological Association that 'ghetto poor' replace 'underclass' in the language of the social sciences. 'Ghetto' we all understand here to be a contraction of 'black ghetto', or simply a euphemism for black. Yet race itself is not theorized in any kind of direct manner, possibly because of the obvious implication that the black poor may share certain structural, political or cultural attributes that differentiate them from others with low income – in other words, that race continues to matter.

Second, research on the underclass tends to study the attributes or behaviours of a category of the population that is nominally separated from other groups and from processes that affect larger populations. This, instead of beginning with labour and housing markets which establish the life chances for all black persons, underclass research quickly focuses on blacks who are poor, unemployed and concentrated in 'ghetto' neighbourhoods.[4] Such a theoretical or methodological approach allows the researcher to avoid highly politicized questions about wage structure, the condition of the millions of poor blacks and others who are fully employed at poverty wages, or about the ways in which public finance and services affect the life chances of low-income populations. To understand the high incidence of out-of-wedlock births among poor black women, for example, it makes more intellectual sense to study marriage and the family across the class and ethnic spectrum than to focus on the cluster of attributes that define the behaviour of the ghetto poor. The latter approach does however, garner much better funding, since it addresses 'one of the most important domestic problems of the last quarter of the twentieth century' (Wilson, 1991: 1).

The explanation of the situation of the underclass encompasses a variety of elements, the precise mix depending to some extent on the politics of the researcher.[5] But common to all approaches is *the third component of the underclass narrative: recognition of the increasing concentration and isolation of the ghetto poor, which, according to the plot, has resulted in significant part, and ironically, from the success of working- and middle-class blacks in escaping the ghetto*. These non-underclass African Americans used to live in the ghetto, in a (vaguely specified) past when all blacks faced racial discrimination. At that time, the narrative asserts, working- and middle-class blacks provided the poor with role models, connections to the labour market, and economically heterogeneous institutions like the church; they generally policed and stabilized the potentially unruly who finally came to comprise an underclass.

> *In the 1940s, 1950s, and as late as the 1960s such [black] communities featured a vertical integration of different segments of the urban black population. Lower-class, working-class, and middle-class black families all lived more or less in the same communities (albeit in different neighborhoods), sent their children to the same schools, availed themselves of the same recreational facilities, and shopped in the same stores . . . Accompanying the black middle-class exodus has been a growing movement of stable working-class blacks from ghetto neighborhoods to higher income neighborhoods in other parts of the city and to the suburbs. In the early years, the black middle and working classes were confined by restrictive covenants to communities also inhabited by the lower class; their very presence provided stability to inner city neighborhoods and reinforced and perpetuated mainstream patterns of norms and behavior.* (Wilson, 1987: 7)[6]

By an unstated logic, therefore, the underclass not only results from the increasing bifurcation of black society, but reaffirms by its existence the reality of black success. It would not be too much to say, in fact, that the narrative of the underclass tells whites that working- and middle-class blacks, including, of course, black professionals, are *not* the underclass, that the appropriate lens with which to examine the economic situation of African Americans is class, not race.[7]

Thus, we arrive at *the final element of the underclass narrative, namely, that it does not need to tell the story of African Americans who are in the 'stable' working and middle class*. These blacks, perhaps two-thirds or more of the black population, are assumed to have benefited from increasing educational attainment and better employment, using these advantages to move out of the ghetto (the term no longer being used, we must remember, for all segregated black districts, but limited to impoverished black neighbourhoods inhabited by the underclass). Where they have moved to is not an object of discussion, but is assumed to be nice city neighbourhoods or the suburbs. Justifying this lacunae in the research agenda is an even deeper premise that racial residential segregation must have decreased substantially or that, at worst, better-off blacks live in all-black neighbourhoods far away from impoverished blacks, receiving advantages of spatial economic segregation similar to their white counterparts. Rarely are these assertions tested with evidence by the active voices of the underclass discourse.

An Other-narrative: The Story of Working- and Middle-class Blacks

Three recent books (Jencks, 1992; Orfield and Ashkinaze, 1991; and Hacker, 1992), written by prominent and definitely mainstream social scientists, have challenged in different ways the dominant narrative of the underclass.[8] Christopher Jencks (1992) directs most of his attention to the intersection of race and poverty. He undermines assumptions that the 'underclass' is a single social type by showing that its various dimensions are but weakly correlated, and that the underclass has not on the whole expanded during the last two decades.

Gary Orfield and Carole Ashkinaze[9] (1991) take on a broader subject by examining the situation of black households in Atlanta and its suburbs. That city has often been held aloft as a model of economic growth, enlightened government and black progress – social, economic, political. Orfield and Ashkinaze show instead that a black mayor and regional economic development have been unable to overcome local racism and conservative national policies: black progress in Atlanta has been greatly exaggerated. In particular, they find that non-poor African Americans were kept segregated during the 1980s in city neighbourhoods and suburbs sharply inferior in housing quality, government services and schools to those of whites of similar social class. The other-narrative of Atlanta leads Orfield and Ashkinaze (1991: 15) to take on underclass mythology:

[William Julius] Wilson's work strongly deemphasizes the racial problems faced by middle-class blacks and sees isolation primarily as a problem of the inner-city 'underclass' population. This study finds the vast majority of blacks in metropolitan Atlanta in segregated neighbourhoods and schools, reflecting, in part, a very large pattern of segregated suburbanization. It

reports evidence of continuing racial discrimination in housing and in mort-
gage lending. In a society where the maintenance of middle class status is
strongly dependent upon the provision of college education for the next gener-
ation, it shows sharp declines in college access. We estimate that racial
barriers directly affect and harm a much larger portion of the black popu-
lation than is suggested in Wilson's work.

In a widely reviewed work, Andrew Hacker (1992) examines an extensive body of evidence from every sphere of life to show that the United
States remains *Two nations* – the title of his book drawn from Disraeli and
the subtitle, 'Black and white, separate, hostile, and unequal', from the
1968 Report of the National Advisory Commission on Civil Disorders,
which warned of this possible negative trajectory for America. Hacker has
importantly added the word 'hostile' to the Commission's prediction, for
he discovers that not only have material differences remained large
between the races across the class spectrum, but political-cultural cleavages appear to have widened as well.

Together these books might finally shove the underclass hippopotamus
sufficiently aside to make room for a fresh discussion of class and race,
especially one that incorporates the considerable scholarship of the last
five or so years, which emphasizes the continuing significance of race and
may even suggest the declining significance of class in explaining the situation of African Americans.[10] An other-narrative of race can be pieced
together from this literature and reinforced by recent census data. In
outlining its elements, I will not dwell on its critique of the underclass
narrative, since it seems most important to discuss that part of African-
American society about which the underclass narrative has been silent or
rather misleading.

Growing economic inequality

The other-narrative of race begins by telling the story of our economy
over the last 20 years, a history of slow growth and increasing inequality, with the richest Americans reaping nearly all of the wealth created in
the Reagan fantasy.[11] Median household income, controlled for inflation,
was $29,108 in 1973 – the peak year of the postwar American boom –
and $29,943 in 1990, virtually unchanged.[12] But this income was re-
distributed upward, as the percentage of households receiving more than
$50,000 increased, with the sharpest gain among those in the $100,000
and above category – from 2.3 to 4.3 percent of all households.
Conversely, middle-income households with annual incomes of
$25–50,000 declined from 37.1 percent of all households to 33.3 percent.

Many other measures show the same pattern of a declining middle and
expanding top of the income distribution, especially the very top. For
example, the richest 5 percent of American families received 25.7 percent

of total *after-tax* income in 1992, compared with 18.5 percent in 1977 (and the richest 1 percent, 13.4 percent of after-tax income in 1992 as against 7.3 percent in 1977); however, the share of the middle quintile declined from 16.3 percent to 14.9 percent in these same years.[13] Wage patterns followed a similar course (Harrison and Gorham, 1992). Such an aggregate social economy creates a pattern of zero-sum games among racial groups – improvement can only be at someone else's expense. Everyone tries to protect his or her own position.

In this kind of a situation, African Americans, who were disadvantaged at the start, could not be expected to make much economic progress along the way (Swinton, 1991). So it is unremarkable that black median household income increased by less than $1000 dollars between 1973 and 1990, with the typical black household remaining at only 59–60 percent of the income of a typical white household (table 9.1). The black middle class (incomes of $25–50,000) *contracted* slightly during the period.[14] And while upper-middle-class and elite black households grew in these 17 years, they still comprised but 12 percent of all black households compared with 26 percent of white households. By contrast, the percentage of blacks in poverty has *not* increased since 1973; in fact, it contracted by more than 1.5 percent, though of course it remains very high, at more than two-fifths of all black households. These data explain why our counter to the underclass story should begin by describing the economic situation of all African Americans. That situation reflects the continued

Table 9.1   Race and income structure, 1973–90: distribution of households among income classes (1990 $, CPI-U-X1)

	Poverty ≤14,999	Marginal 15–24,999	Middle 25-49,999	Upper Mid. 50–99,999	Elite ≥100,000	MEDIAN
Black distribution						
1973	43.8	21.8	27.3	6.8	0.4	$17,957
1985	44.0	20.3	25.5	9.5	0.8	$18,000
1990	42.4	19.1	26.6	10.8	1.1	$18,676
White distribution						
1973	23.3	17.6	38.3	18.4	2.5	$30,507
1985	23.6	18.1	34.5	20.3	3.6	$30,255
1990	22.0	17.7	34.1	21.5	4.7	$31,231

Note: The ratio of black to white median incomes was .59 in 1973 and 1985, and .60 in 1990. The median income of all US households was $29,108 in 1973, $28,688 in 1985 and $29,943 in 1990.
Source: US Bureau of the Census (1991), table B-10.

racial disadvantage experienced across the entire black class structure, rather than just the impoverishment of lower-class blacks.

Conservative public policy

The other-narrative continues by examining the impact of government policies – again, not as they are directed particularly at the black poor, much less the so-called underclass, but as they affect blacks at every economic level. The relative lack of economic progress of the great majority of non-poor African Americans is what must be explained. Put most briefly, governments throughout the federal system have been influenced by the conservative tide since the late 1970s, with the national government directing the redeployment of public policies in ways that have badly harmed African Americans. Federal aid to individuals above the poverty line contracted sharply, both in direct transfers like grants for college attendance, and in indirect transfers which passed through sub-national governments, for instance for public schools and job training. Washington virtually eliminated long-extant housing programmes for low- and moderate-income groups, from which blacks benefited dispro-portionately. And the withdrawal of federal aid to cities helped precipitate the tax revolts which compounded the decline in services to African Americans. Working- and middle-class blacks who had gained much in the 1960s and early 1970s saw their mobility routes blocked, as government employment grew only slowly or contracted in the older cities where they are concentrated. John Jacob (1991: 1), president of the politi-cally centrist National Urban League, summed up what had happened:

A strategic goal of the Reagan administration was to limit government's ability to undertake social and economic programs by choking off available resources through tax cuts and higher military spending. The success of that strategy was seen in the virtual abandonment of important job training, health, and housing programs and crippling cuts in other domestic programs. But it was most obvious in the recurring refrain that responded to virtually all proposals for government programs that would . . . create opportunities in the 1980s – 'we can't afford to do it.'

Moreover, the conservative regimes in Washington reversed the policies of the Civil Rights Commission, the Department of Justice and the Equal Employment Opportunity Commission, packed the Supreme Court, and in numerous other ways effectively ended federal actions to reduce racial discrimination in employment, education, housing and public services. Playing their part in the story, actors in all sectors of our society – whether realtors, school superintendents, employers, fire-fighters' unions or suburban government officials – took their cues from Washington and reduced their commitment to racial integration, however low had been its previous level. Blacks for their part, too, stopped pushing for integration, with a small but vocal minority preaching black separatism, a message that many whites took to heart. Separatism between the races expanded in political–cultural space, even as it failed to contract geographically.[15]

Persistent residential segregation

The geographical separation of the races continues through processes that involve the segmentation of housing markets, active racial discrimination by realtors and banks (Galster, 1987) and the use of governmental boundaries as racial barricades.[16] Far from the pleasant but undocumented picture of working- and middle-class dispersal from the ghetto assumed in the underclass narrative, the students of residential segregation describe a very different scene as of 1980, the latest year for which national data are available, and more recent evidence gives little reason to believe there has been much improvement since then.[17] In fact, except for metropolitan areas with very small black populations, racial segregation remained virtually constant in the 1970s (Massey and Gross, 1991). The small increase in the suburbanization of African Americans was largely in jurisdictions contiguous to urban black neighbourhoods, and signified neither a substantial increase in the deconcentration of blacks[18] (relative to white decentralization) nor much improvement in the likelihood that even middle-class blacks would be living in racially integrated neighbourhoods (Massey and Denton, 1988; Galster, 1991). Douglas Massey (1990: 354), perhaps America's leading contemporary expert on racial segregation, reminds us that

> two decades after the passage of the Fair Housing Act, levels of black segregation remain exceedingly high in large urban areas . . . This high level of segregation cannot be explained by blacks' objective socioeconomic characteristics, their housing preferences, or their limited knowledge of white housing markets. Rather, it is linked empirically to the persistence of discrimination in housing markets and to continuing antiblack prejudice.[19]

The underclass narrative emphasizes the departure of higher-income black households from impoverished 'ghettos'.[20] We know that most of these households will none the less continue to live in all-black neighbourhoods, whether in the central cities or in suburbs. The question by our other-narrative is one of degree: how much income segregation is there among blacks compared with other social groups, and how much has it changed. In the only study of its kind, Massey and Eggers (1990: table 2) examined 60 metropolitan areas in 1980. Using the index of dissimilarity (see note to table 9.7, below), they compared levels of *economic* segregation among whites, blacks, hispanics and Asians. They found that blacks showed moderate levels of segregation (.342), higher than whites (.254), but lower than hispanics (.479) and Asians (.565). *Segregation by income among blacks is, in fact, less than half the level of segregation by race among persons with similar incomes* (table 9.7, below).[21] While economic segregation among blacks increased in the 1970s, the changes were quite small (.029) and may largely reflect increasing inequality within the black income distribution. 'Because of persisting segregation, middle- and upper-class blacks are less able to separate themselves from the poor than the privileged of other groups, and recent increases in black interclass segregation probably represent a movement toward parity with other groups' (Massey and Eggers, 1990: 1186).[22]

Before wrapping up all the strands of our other-narrative, I would like to examine some recent evidence about the economic situation of middle-class blacks and, more generally, about the extent to which racial differences are narrowed by keeping social class constant. If race really has declined in significance, we should be seeing a great deal of progress among middle-class blacks relative to middle-class whites.

Class Differences and Life Chances

The data in table 9.2 allow us to compare black and white earnings among college graduates (those with passports into the middle class), high school graduates and the entire population for three age cohorts in 1990. Let us first consider the case of males. We see that among the youngest workers, higher education improves the earnings ratio between black and white men (from 74.5 percent among all men to 83.3 percent among college grads). For older male workers, however, education has little effect. In fact, the wage ratio of black to white male high school graduates among 45 to 54-year-olds is actually better than among college graduates of the same age. One possible explanation for these cohort differences is that racial discrimination is declining for highly educated young blacks, compared to older blacks. But if we look at the actual dollar amounts in the table, another conclusion is much more likely. Young workers enter jobs with a relatively small wage spread. As male workers age and move up the job hierarchy, the variance in salaries increases substantially. White male college graduates move farther up the income scale with age than do black college graduates. For example, the median income of prime age white college graduates (45 to 54 years old) exceeds that of young white workers by more than $18,000, while the comparable difference among blacks is less than $12,000. There is little reason from this evidence to think that college education is closing the racial gap in earnings.

For women, the picture is quite different. Table 9.2 presents women's income as a percentage of white male earnings. We find that racial

Table 9.2   Income of cohorts with similar education, YRFT workers: median annual earnings and percentage of white male earnings, 1990

Males	25–34 yrs		35–44 yrs		45–54 yrs	
College grads						
Black	26,787	(83.3)	35,931	(80.9)	38,560	(76.6)
White	32,130		44,125		50,325	
HS grads						
Black	17,197	(74.8)	21,778	(79.3)	26,426	(84.5)
White	22,985		27,472		31,255	
All						
Black	19,200	(74.5)	26,023	(79.5)	25,965	(73.4)
White	25,767		32,750		35,364	
Females	**25–34 yrs**		**35–44 yrs**		**45–54 yrs**	
College grads						
Black	25,714	(80.0)	28,978	(65.2)	33,378	(66.3)
White	26,787	(83.4)	30,939	(69.6)	31,209	(62.0)
HS grads						
Black	14,132	(61.5)	18,033	(65.6)	18,954	(60.6)
White	16,481	(71.7)	18,733	(68.1)	18,460	(59.1)
All						
Black	17,121	(66.4)	20,875	(63.7)	19,699	(55.7)
White	19,974	(77.5)	21,833	(66.6)	21,113	(59.7)

Note: 'YRFT' (year-round full-time) are persons employed every week in the specified year on a full-time basis; 'HS grads' are persons who graduated high school but have never attended college; 'College grads' are persons who have completed at least four years of college.

Source: US Bureau of the Census (1991), table 29, and author's calculations.

differences in earnings among women are quite small, whether we look at all women, or at college and high school grads separately. While college education increases earnings, the wage spread of all women is relatively narrow, and the median wages of women in every category but the youngest college graduates remains in the range of 60–65 percent of comparable white males. This happens because there is almost no wage hierarchy for women. For example, the spread between young and prime age white women college graduates is less than $5,000, compared with more than $18,000 among men. In sum, then, black women do quite as well as white women of similar education, sometimes even better, and education increases the earnings of all women, but women as a gender receive significantly lower wages than men. Because black households are much more dependent on women's earnings than are white households, the depressed level of women's earnings, even among prime age college graduates, contributes to the economic disadvantage of blacks across the class structure.

Did racial differences in earnings within the middle class decline during the last decade? Tables 9.3 and 9.4 provide several indicators that address the question respectively for male and female college graduates. The results are mixed, leaning toward the negative. The median earnings of black male college graduates improved versus that of whites, as did that of full-time year-round workers (table 9.3a, 9.3b), but among women there was either no improvement or actual decline (table 9.4b, 9.4a). The percentage of both black men and black women who occupied high-wage jobs decreased substantially – though the absence of comparable white figures means that we do not know if the racial gap widened or narrowed (tables 9.3c, 9.4c).

Finally, blacks in the cohort of young, college-educated workers slipped further behind whites during the decade. The real salaries of all young male college graduates declined in the 1980s (table 9.3d), but those of black males declined more than those of white males; young college-educated black men, who had mean earnings of 80.6 percent of those of similar whites in 1980, dropped to 73.6 percent in 1990.[23] Given the pattern we saw in table 9.2 of increasing racial differences as workers age, these data portend quite negatively for black male college graduates, and suggest that intraclass racial differences may grow larger in coming years.

An even wider gap developed among young female college graduates during the 1980s (table 9.4d). Whereas black female mean earnings were 122.2 percent of the white figure in 1980, they were only 91.2 percent of the white level in 1990 – another sign of growing racial differences within the middle class. Overall, then, the evidence in tables 9.2, 9.3 and 9.4 hardly supports the notion that race is declining in significance as a determinant of the economic situation of blacks, even among the best educated.

At a time when the penalty for not graduating from college is increasing for all workers, blacks are falling further behind whites. Table 9.5 presents college enrolment and graduation rates normalized for cohort size. The performance on both indicators of young blacks has deteriorated steadily since 1976 compared with that of whites. For example, the ratio of the black male college graduation rate to the white male rate declined from 41 percent to 35 percent. Much attention has been

Table 9.3   Incomes of male college graduates in the 1980s (expressed in constant (1990) dollars)

	Black	White	B/W (%)
(a)			
Median earnings			
persons 25 yrs and older			
1982	25,904	36,916	70.2
1990	30,282	37,996	79.7
(b)			
Median earnings YRFT workers			
25 yrs and older			
1982	29,482	41,813	70.5
1990	32,145	41,661	77.2
(c)			
Persons earning $40,000			
or more on an annualized			
basis (%)			
1979	23.4	NA	
1987	19.5	NA	
(d)			
Mean annual earnings			
persons aged 25–34			
1980	27,744	34,408	80.6
1990	25,241	34,272	73.6

Note: All dollar amounts are converted using the CPI-U-X1 cost of living index. (b) Year-round, full-time workers. (c) Annualized wages are calculated by extrapolating actual earnings to a YRFT equivalent. Since not all workers were employed YRFT, this figure overestimates the percentage with high earnings. The deflator used here is the poverty line, with high earnings defined as 3 or more times the annual income for a family of 4 at the prevailing poverty line. (d) The use of mean earnings slightly increases the dollar amounts compared with medians. The 1980 figures are drawn from the decennial census, which uses a methodology different from the 1990 Current Population Surveys, and are not strictly comparable to CPS estimates. The census methodology relies on self-reporting and tends to underestimate income by a few percentage points compared to the CPS, which uses trained interviewers following a detailed protocol.

Source: (a) and (b) US Bureau of the Census (1983: table 47) and (1991: table 29); (c) Harrison and Gorham (1992: 66); (d) 1990 as in (a); 1980 from Farley and Allen (1980: table 11.4). CPI-U-X1 from US Bureau of the Census (1991: table B-1).

Table 9.4   Incomes of female college graduates in the 1980s (expressed in constant (1990) dollars)

	Black	White	B/W (%)
(a)			
Median earnings			
persons 25 yrs and older			
1982	21,012	18,169	115.6
1990	25,874	23,598	109.6
(b)			
Median earnings YRFT workers			
25 yrs and older			
1982	23,619	26,833	88.0
1990	25,874	29,109	88.9
(c)			
Persons earning $40,000			
or more on an annualized			
basis (%)			
1979	12.4	NA	
1987	7.6	NA	
(d)			
Mean annual earnings			
persons aged 25–34			
1980	21,436	17,480	122.6
1990	21,850	23,962	91.2

Note: All dollar amounts are converted using the CPI-U-X1 cost of living index. (b) Year-round, full-time workers. (c) Annualized wages are calculated by extrapolating actual earnings to a YRFT equivalent. Since not all workers were employed YRFT, this figure overestimates the percentage with high earnings. The deflator used here is the poverty line, with high earning defined as 3 or more times the annual income for a family of 4 at the prevailing poverty line. (d) The use of mean earnings slightly increases the dollar amounts compared with medians. The 1980 figures are drawn from the decennial census, which uses a methodology different from the 1990 Current Population Surveys, and are not strictly comparable to CPS estimates. The census methodology relies on self-reporting and tends to underestimate income by a few percentage points compared to the CPS, which uses trained interviewers following a detailed protocol.

Source: (a) and (b) US Bureau of Census (1983: table 47) and (1991: table 29); (c) Harrison and Gorham (1992: 66); (d) 1990 as in (a); 1980 from Farley and Allen (1980: table 11.4). CPI-U-X1 from US Bureau of the Census (1991: table B-1).

Table 9.5   College completion rates for persons 18–24 years

| | Enrolled in college (%) | | | Graduated college (%) | | |
	Black	White	B/W	Black	White	B/W
Men						
1976	22.0	28.8	76.4	1.6	3.9	41.0
1981	18.8	27.7	67.9	1.4	3.4	41.0
1985	20.1	29.3	68.6	1.3	3.6	36.1
1989	19.6	31.5	62.2	1.4	4.0	35.0
Women						
1976	23.0	25.6	89.8	1.8	3.1	58.1
1981	20.7	25.8	80.2	1.8	3.2	56.3
1985	19.5	28.2	69.1	1.7	3.7	45.9
1989	23.5	32.2	73.0	1.9	4.3	44.2

Note: 'College graduation rate' is calculated by dividing the number of bachelor's degrees conferred by the number of 18 to 24-year-olds in that year. This measure therefore controls approximately for cohort size. The ratio B/W (expressed as a percentage) indicates the relative probability of a black person in the black cohort receiving a bachelor's degree versus a white person in the white cohort. Thus, in 1976 the chances of the average black male aged 18–24 graduating college was 41.0 percent of that of the average white male; by 1989, it was 35.0 percent.

Source: American Council on Education (1992: tables 2, 10), and author's calculations.

devoted to the high proportion of black college graduates who are female (about 57 percent of the cohort in 1989), yet the fact remains that black females found themselves well below white females in both college attendance and graduation rates in 1976, and the gap has steadily and substantially widened. Whereas the female black/white graduation ratio stood at 58.1 percent in 1976, it had declined to 44.2 percent by 1989. The import of the data in table 9.5 for both genders is, then, that the black middle class is likely to contract in coming years, at least to the extent that the human capital stock of the next generation remains on its current downward trajectory.

Nor can blacks depend much on actual capital to improve their economic situation or to at least guarantee intergenerational reproduction of prior gains. The median wealth of African American households

Table 9.6   Wealth versus income for African Americans and whites: median net worth by average household monthly income, 1988

	Black Median $	Black (% hhds)	White Median $	White (% hhds)	B$/W$(%)
Income quintile ($ range)					
Lowest (0–939)	0	(37.4)	8,839	(17.7)	0.0
Second (940–1699)	2,408	(22.5)	26,299	(19.7)	9.2
Third (1700–2568)	8,461	(17.9)	32,802	(20.4)	25.8
Fourth (2569–3883)	20,215	(14.1)	50,372	(20.8)	40.1
Highest (3884+)	47,160	(8.1)	119,057	(21.4)	39.6
All	4,169	(100.0)	43,279	(100.0)	9.6

Note: Net worth includes houses, furnishings, automobiles, real property, stocks, bonds, savings accounts, accounts and all other forms (current) of wealth except vested interest in pension funds less all mortgages, debts and liabilities.

Source: US Bureau of the Census (1990).

was less than 10 percent of that of white households in 1988 (Table 9.6). While the gulf narrowed with increasing income, among middle-income blacks, household net worth was only about one-quarter that of whites with similar incomes, and even among households with the greatest monthly income (the top 8.1 percent of black households), the wealth ratio between the races was only 39.6 percent.[24] From this we conclude that even black households with relatively high incomes are asset-poor. Measured by wealth, in fact, the black middle class is minute and the working class would be classified as poor, were it white.

A significant reason for this racial capital disadvantage undoubtedly stems from the depressed value of black housing at every income level, since throughout most of the USA income distribution equity in home ownership is the principal source of household wealth. The devalorization of houses owned by blacks itself results from the racism and

Table 9.7   Segregation of African Americans from whites: index of racial residential segregation (D) in Standard Metropolitan Areas (SMAs) with largest black populations, 1980

| | *Index of segregation from white persons* | |
	Regardless of income or education of white persons	*White persons with same income or education*
Black persons		
Family income		
Under $10,000	.79	.76
$15–19,999	.76	.75
$25–34,999	.77	.76
$50,000 or more	.79	.79
Education		
9–11 years	.83	.77
High school graduate	.78	.76
Some college	.75	.74
College graduate	.72	.71

Note: Both columns exhibit values of the index of dissimilarity (D), a measure of residential segregation. It measures the number of black households that would have to change census tracts within a metropolitan area in order to be distributed in the same manner as the comparative white population. D ranges between zero and 1.000. (In this table, D is rounded off to 100ths and ranges between zero and 1.00.) For the distribution of D, 0–.300 is considered low, .300–.600 moderate, and .600–1.000 high. Thus, all values of D in this table are in the high range.

The columns are drawn from two somewhat different but overlapping samples. The first comprises the 10 metropolitan areas with the largest black populations in 1980. Here D shows how many black persons with a particular characteristic of family income or personal education would have to be redistributed to match the distribution of all whites among census tracts in each SMA. The final number is a weighted average of D for all 10 SMAs. The second column uses the same methodology for the 16 SMAs with the largest black populations. But here D measures the redistribution of black persons required to match the distribution of white persons with the *same* characteristic. For example, the number .71 in the lower right-hand corner of the table means that 71 percent of college-educated black persons would need to change census tract in order to match the distribution of college-educated white persons.

Sources: (First column) Denton and Massey (1988: table 1); (second column) Farley and Allen (1980: table 5.10).

Table 9.8   African-American and white class capacity for spatial isolation: probability of residential contact (P*) between high-status persons and low-status persons by race, city of Philadelphia, 1980

| | Low-status persons, all races | | |
	High-school dropout	Family on welfare	Female-headed family
High-status persons			
White collar			
Black	.406	.227	.214
White	.336	.081	.074
Ratio: B/W	1.2	2.8	2.9
Some college or more			
Black	.393	.221	.210
White	.289	.080	.080
Ratio: B/W	1.4	2.8	2.6
Middle-class income			
Black	.398	.216	.206
White	.336	.076	.068
Ratio: B/W	1.2	2.8	3.0

Note: The cells indicate the probability (P*) of a random person in the high-status group having residential contact with a person in the low-status category. Residential contact is defined as living in the same census tract. In effect, then, P* is the percentage of persons in the low-status category living in the census tract of an average person in the high-status group. For example, the first cell value of .406 means that the average black person with a white-collar occupation lives in a census tract where .406 persons of any race are high-school dropouts. The ratio B/W measures the relative likelihood of a black person versus a white person within the high-status group encountering a person of any race with a specific low-status attribute. For example, white-collar black persons are 1.2 times more likely than white-collar white persons to have residential contact with a high-school dropout of any race.

Source: Massey *et al.* (1987: table 6).

segmentation in housing markets, and the persistence of interracial segregation at every class level. In table 9.7 we look at evidence of black–white segregation using both income and education as indicators of social class. The first column shows the degree of segregation of blacks at specified income or education levels from whites in any income or education. For example, the index number is .79 for blacks with income of $50,000 or more in 1980. This means the 79 percent of these black persons would have had to move from their census tracts in order to match the distribution of whites as a whole within their metropolitan area. It is apparent from the data that blacks at every class are equally isolated from white society. In the second column, we look at segregation with class controlled for both blacks and whites, in other words, at the level of interracial segregation of blacks and whites with the same incomes or educations. Again, race overwhelms class. Middle-class blacks, working-class blacks and poor blacks are equally segregated from their white class counterparts. Clearly, better class standing does little to buy African Americans a racially integrated environment.[25]

Nor does it allow black households to distance themselves from lower-class cultural influences to the same extent as whites. Table 9.8 presents evidence from a study of Philadelphia, a city with black neighbourhoods at every class level. Using three different indicators of social class, the table shows that middle-class whites are much less likely than middle-class blacks to encounter people with so-called underclass attributes in their neighbourhoods. Equally important, the study examines in great detail other measures of the quality of life in neighbourhoods occupied by working- and middle-class blacks versus those occupied by whites of similar class. It finds that class simply does not buy blacks the environment that it buys whites in a society where class stratification is expressed spatially:

> *High status blacks, like whites, seek to convert past socioeconomic attainments into improved residential circumstances. However, very few blacks are successful in achieving these locational outcomes. The vast majority live in segregated neighborhoods where blacks have long been, or are rapidly becoming, the majority, areas characterized by high crime, poor schools, economic dependency, unstable families, dilapidated housing, and poor health. All evidence indicates that blacks are no different than whites in trying to escape such an environment, when they are able. They are just less able.* (Massey et al., 1987: 52)

The authors suggest the consequences of the relative social heterogeneity of middle-income black neighbourhoods for reducing the ability of the black middle class to reproduce itself through cultural capital transmission:

Table 9.9 Effect of family background on educational performance

(a)	SAT Score 1984			SAT Score 1990		
	Black	*White*	*Diff.*	*Black*	*White*	*Diff.*
Family income (1990 dollars)						
10–20,000	646	863	217	704	879	175
30–40,000	724	908	174	751	908	157
50–60,000	773	948	175	790	947	157
70,000+	832	981	149	854	998	144
Median	715	932	217	737	933	196

(b)   *Effect of parental education on children's educational attainment*

	Decade when child was 15 years of age			
	1940–49	*1950–59*	*1960–69*	*1970–82*
Regression of child's schooling on father's (mother's) schooling				
Blacks	.331	.260	.214	.199
Whites	.326	.315	.324	.315

Note: (a) SAT (Scholastic Aptitude Test) scores are the sum of the verbal and mathematical scores. The sum ranges between 400 and 1600. In each case, this table employs median scores. The table combines two data sources with different presentations of income ranges, so there might be minor variations from actual scores. None the less, the basic picture would remain unchanged. (b) Father's education is used as the independent variable unless only mother was present when child was 15. The regression coefficients predict additional years of school of child for an increase of one year in parental education. For example, one year more parental education on average resulted in .331 years of greater education among black children who were 15 in 1940–9. The overall data set encompasses respondents over the age of 25 interviewed between 1972 and 1989.

Source: (a) *Chronicle of Higher Education,* 16 January 1985; Hacker (1992: 143); (b) Jencks (1992: table 5.8).

Because of residential segregation, middle class blacks must send their children to public schools with children far below their own class standing, children with more limited cognitive, linguistic, and social skills. Given the strong effect of peer influences and environment on aspirations, motivation, and achievement, it is hardly surprising that so many young black people, even those from middle class families, fail to achieve high test scores or educational distinction.[26] (Massey et al., 1987: 54)

There is much evidence that class background simply does not translate into educational performance for blacks to the same extent as it does for whites.[27] Table 9.9 illustrates these findings. The upper panel arrays SAT scores by family income. Even if critics of the Scholastic Aptitude Tests are right when they claim that these tests are culturally biased and largely reflect middle-class white language and knowledge, the SAT can at least be interpreted as a measure of cultural capital among students who aspire to college educations and good incomes. The results are only slightly encouraging. On the positive side, black SAT scores improved between 1984 and 1990, reducing the interracial gap from 217 to 196 points. And in both years, black–white differences were reduced with increasing family income. None the less, these differences remain so large that in 1984 and in 1990, black students from families with upper-middle-class incomes of better than $70,000 did worse on the SAT than white students from families in or near poverty, with incomes between $10,000 and $20,000. Clearly, some combination of lower cultural capital among the parents of black children, inferior schooling and perhaps reduced motivation, must be at work to explain such large and persistent differences in an important national measure of cultural and linguistic convergence (or divergence).

The lower panel presents evidence of the power of family background in predicting children's educational attainment. This is another indicator of the transmission of class advantage among blacks compared to whites. Table 9.9 shows that the regression coefficient for whites has remained relatively constant since the Second World War. For blacks, however, the coefficient has declined steadily, beginning at a level higher than that for whites and reaching a point more than one-third below the white coefficient for children who were 15 years old between 1970 and 1982. For whatever reasons – possibly including differences in family composition – the educational attainment of black parents has been less and less a predictor of the educational attainment of black children. This is another sign of a declining significance of class as a differentiating factor within the black population.[28]

A last piece of evidence along the same lines may be found in out-of-wedlock childbirth (table 9.10). Among the least educated whites, more than 65 percent were married when their child was born in 1986. That figure rises to well over 90 percent in the white middle class (those with

Table 9.10   Percentage of mothers unmarried when baby
was born

| | Education of mother | | | |
	Less than high school	HS graduate	Some college	College graduate
1969				
Black	41.9	28.0	21.5	6.6
White	7.9	4.1	4.1	1.2
B/W	5.3	6.8	5.2	5.5
1986				
Black	79.4	61.9	45.5	20.8
White	34.8	13.9	7.2	2.2
B/W	2.3	4.5	6.3	9.5

Source: Jencks (1992: table 5.15).

some college or college graduates). Among whites, the class background of the mother is thus a very strong predictor of normative behaviour. The same is much less true of black mothers. The illegitimacy rate was 45.5 percent in 1986 among black mothers who attended college and 20.8 percent among college graduates. Whereas in 1969 the black/white illegitimacy ratio remained constant across class categories, by 1986 it increased steadily with ascending class. Thus, while among the least educated mothers of both races the ratio was 2.3:1, among college graduates it was 9.5:1. Here we have a final, and telling, example of the declining significance of class in controlling, much less eliminating, racial differences.

Boyz 'n the Hood

The well-publicized story of the decade may be the presence in many of our cities of a disorderly, impoverished black population, but alongside that story must be placed the narrative of the working-poor and of the better-off African American population, who have neither moved up economically nor become more integrated into white society. Indeed, in this other-narrative, the two subplots must be related. On the one hand, the continuing isolation of non-poor blacks from white America is undoubtedly encouraging their greater alienation, a growing disillusion with the possibility of escaping race and racism, and the continued de-legitimization of American social and political institutions – a consciousness widely shared within the black community. On the other hand, the presence of impoverished black households, the drug culture, criminal behaviour, all those elements of the 'underclass', may well be exacerbating the difficulties of working- and middle-class blacks in maintaining their economic gains and seeing their children move up socially, or at least not sink into poverty and/or criminality.

Many of us have seen the film *Boyz 'n the Hood*.[29] It presents this same other-narrative, albeit in a more graphic and much more entertaining manner. The plot is well known. Hard-working black people, some with professional careers, occupy a reasonably attractive LA black neighbourhood. Within that same neighbourhood live lower-income blacks. The streets and schools where adolescents spend their lives are a constant source of exposure to temptations and dangers, which lead to economic failure at best, and death at worst. Some of the sons and daughters of working- and middle-class black families escape this environment unharmed (though none are benefited by it); many others succumb. This is not the underclass narrative. It is the other-narrative of a racially segregated and segmented society where class means one thing for whites and another for blacks, where for African Americans, class (in the white sense) is not nearly as important as race, and may actually be declining in significance.

Notes

1   I will use the terms 'African Americans' and 'blacks' interchangeably.
2   For example, conferences devoted to the subject culminated in a special issue of the *Annals* (Wilson, 1989) on 'The ghetto underclass' and in *The Urban Underclass* (Jencks and Peterson, 1991). Since the mid-1980s the influential Social Science Research Council has sponsored a research committee on the underclass. Many foundations have provided Wilson and others with very substantial funding.

An incisive review of the literature may be found in Marks (1991).
3   The term 'myth', in the sense made famous by Roland Barthes, could equally well be utilized.
4   Wacquant and Wilson (1989) further add to the linguistic confusion by defining ghettos as places inhabited largely by the underclass, while one of the characteristics of poor people that places them in the underclass is their concentration in ghettos – a line of reasoning that is uncomfortably tautological. Wilson and other underclass researchers have by this linguistic sleight of hand deprived themselves of any commonly understood term which might describe the places into which non-underclass blacks are segregated. If these are no longer ghettos, just what are they?

I should note that despite his co-authorship with Wilson of the aforementioned article, Wacquant (forthcoming) rejects the concept of 'underclass'. Instead he recognizes the term to be an ideological construct that functions to demonize the poor and mystify the role of state policy in determining the condition of inner-city neighbourhoods. None the less, he is quite adamant about reserving the term 'ghetto' just for the areas with extreme levels of misery, crime and social disorganization (undergoing what he calls de-civilization).

'A ghetto', according to Wacquant, 'is not simply a segregated neighbourhood but a specific set of spatially-articulated mechanisms of racial closure. To put it differently: all segregated (even racially segregated) areas are not [*ipso facto*] ghettos. What to call the segregated neighborhoods founded by the new black (petty) [*sic*] bourgeoisie outside the historic Black Belt is difficult but it's certainly not a ghetto in the sociological, communal sense' (personal correspondence, 6 October 1992).

In my view, Wacquant is mistaken. A ghetto *is* 'simply' a segregated neighbourhood, to the extent that segregation is societally imposed and based on race, ethnicity or religion. In fact, black ghettos in the USA most certainly are produced by exactly the 'spatially articulated mechanisms of racial closure' that Wacquant specifies. Like the Jewish ghettos of Venice and eastern Europe, black ghettos encompass a range of class groupings, housing quality and lifestyles. That is just the point – everyone who is black is compelled to live within a racially defined district, regardless of their other attributes. Of course, all blacks do not live under the same conditions in the ghetto; rather, they occupy different quarters with varying economic characteristics. Why not identify these places, for example, as 'poor', 'working-class', 'middle-class' and 'mixed-income' *neighbourhoods* in the ghetto under discussion? (See n.6 for discussion of the term 'communal' in Wacquant's definition.)

5   Conservatives like Lawrence Mead (1989) placed much of the blame on social welfare programmes which undermine the work ethic among low-income blacks. Social democrats like Wilson usually rely on the work of John Kasarda (1985; 1989), who has popularized the notion that there is a mismatch between the skills of central city residents and the demands of employers in 'knowledge-intensive' service industries. Elsewhere (Fainstein, 1986) I have provided a lengthy critique of mismatch theory as an adequate economic analysis of the labour-market situation of African Americans.

6   The literature is replete with such assertions, always presented in global terms, and rarely supported by evidence. For example, in a well-known study of Philadelphia in the 1980s, Elijah Anderson (1990: 58–9) refers frequently to the time 'in the past [when] blacks of various social classes lived side by side', when 'successful people' were 'effective, meaningful role models, lending the community a certain moral integrity'. He cites as support Drake and Cayton (1945), who never set foot in Philadelphia and, as noted previously, took a much less sanguine view of the Chicago ghetto. He also cites, again without specifics, Kenneth Clark's *Dark Ghetto* (1964: 81). Yet Clark said of Harlem in the 1950s and early 1960s: 'The dark ghetto is institutionalized pathology.' Much of his book was, in fact, devoted to excoriating Harlem's leaders and institutions.

The extent of 'community' in a ghetto as a whole, or in its neighbourhoods, must be determined empirically. In general, however, one should be careful about supposing that there was ever a period when the ghetto was internally integrated, when its institutions effected social control over all, when social anomie did not accompany extreme poverty. Thus, Drake and Cayton (1945: ch. 18) in their study of the Chicago black ghetto during its supposedly most 'communal' days – the 1930s – find a world divided by class, religious commitment and varying degrees of criminality. Their description of the worst, lower-class neighbourhoods sounds remarkably contemporary (see ch. 21).

7   The narrative here reinforces its first element through an entirely circular process of reasoning. The correct lens is one of class, but class as applied to the underclass somehow elides into being a racial category, since it is really only the *black* underclass that gets discussed.

8   A radical attack against the prevailing discourse may be found in Raymond Franklin's (1991) recent book, which will probably be viewed as falling beyond the boundaries of 'responsible' social science. Although I do not discuss it here, Michael Katz's *The Undeserving Poor* (1989) should be reread along with the new books by Jencks, Orfield and Ashkinaze, and Hacker.

9   Gary Orfield's co-author, Carole Ashkinaze, is a journalist who has won a Pulitzer Prize for investigative reporting.

10 Aside from the work on residential segregation which I will discuss below, see, for example, Landry (1987), Collins (1989), Fainstein and Fainstein (1989), Jaynes and Williams (1989), Feagin (1991), Swinton (1991), Waldinger and Bailey (1991) and Galster and Hill (1992).

11 Other interrelated changes were also involved, of course, including economic restructuring, decentralization of production, shifts in the occupational structure, and growth in female employment. There is a vast literature on these subjects which I cannot address here.

12 These data are in constant (1990) dollars and are drawn from US Bureau of the Census (1991): table B-10.

13 These data are based on a Congressional Budget Office simulation model using actual data through 1989 and projecting to 1992. Comparisons that reflect actual data, e.g. 1977 versus 1988, are virtually identical (US House of Representatives, Committee on Ways and Means, 1991: appendix J, table 23).

14 Table 9.1 also shows that the proportion of white households in the middle-income category declined by more than 4 percent. Thus, the contraction of the middle class was not particularly a black phenomenon.

15 For an excellent review of policies, politics and political culture, see Edsall and Edsall (1991). Hacker (1992) also documents the differing and increasingly disparate mentalities of blacks and whites. Judd (1991) discusses the historical and continuing role of the national government in promoting racial segregation.

16 On the role of governmental units in metropolitan areas, see Weiher (1991) and Stearns and Logan (1986).

17 See Orfield and Ashkinaze (1991) and the first analysis of 1990 census data from New York City, discussed below.

18 Galster (1991: 624) examines three indicators of suburbanization of blacks in 40 metropolitan areas, comparing 1970 and 1980. Using simply the percentage of blacks living in suburbs, he finds an increase of 4.2 percent in black suburbanization, from 20.2 to 24.4. When he controls for the change in the percentage of whites living in suburbs by employing the ratio

between the races, the improvement in black suburbanization is only 2.3 percent, from 33.8 to 36.1 (in other words, in both years blacks were about one-third as likely as whites to be suburbanized). Galster then constructs a measure of decentralization which ignores nominal jurisdictional boundaries, reflecting only distance from the metropolitan core. This measure actually shows a minute increase in racial segregation during the 1970s: compared to the decentralization of the white population in the 1970s, the black population did not improve its position, remaining just as concentrated in the central rings of metropolitan areas.

19   Massey (1990). Massey here includes numerous references which I have omitted, but see, for example, Denton and Massey (1988), Farley and Allen (1987), Massey and Denton (1988).

20   An interesting case in point is provided by Wacquant and Wilson (1989), who contrast the differences between life in extremely poor black neighbourhoods ('ghettos') and merely low-income ones in Chicago in 1980. The authors criticize conservatives who fail to recognize the 'unprecedented concentration of the most socially excluded and economically marginal members of the dominated economic and racial group', i.e. African Americans. To that end, they demonstrate that social pathology is concentrated in the poorest black neighbourhoods (with a poverty rate of 40 percent or more) and that black neighbourhoods with somewhat lower poverty rates (20–30 percent) are not nearly so bad, being much more economically heterogeneous. In these ('non-ghetto') neighbourhoods, working-class (55 percent) and even middle-class blacks (11 percent) live in proximity to the welfare poor, the long-term unemployed, in short, to households that have been characterized as belonging to the underclass. Instead of asking what this means for 'stable' black households and for the dynamics of race and class, Wilson and Wacquant use their evidence to demonstrate that many blacks who live in low-income neighbourhoods do not have the attributes of the underclass. What they are doing there, and what happens to their children (do they disproportionately fall into the underclass?) is not the subject of analysis. (In other respects, the article deviates from the usual underclass interpretation. Perhaps its ambiguous approach reflects an effort to reconcile the quite divergent approaches of its two authors.)

21   Initial evidence from a study of 5700 block groups (units smaller than census tracts) in New York City indicates that the pattern has persisted in the 1980s (Roberts, 1992). Andrew Beveridge, analysing the 1990 census, finds that segregation by race is much greater than by income within and between racial groups, and that the level of racial segregation (even when income is controlled) remained at the same level in 1990 as in 1980 (with an index of dissimilarity above .80) (Roberts, 1992).

22   The main thrust of this article was not to study the situation of higher-income blacks, but to test Wilson's thesis that increasing spatial separation between the poor and higher-income blacks contributed to the growth of the underclass. Based on a regression of poverty concentration against various measures of segregation, Massey and Eggers (1990: 1183) reject the underclass narrative:

> *In short, the class-based arguments put forth by Wilson and others to explain levels and trends in the concentration of poverty are seriously incomplete without reference to patterns and levels of racial and ethnic segregation. Our results suggest that unusually high and rising concentrations of poverty among blacks outside the West and Hispanics in the Northeast cannot be attributed to the flight of middle-class minorities from ghetto or barrio neighborhoods. Rather, they reflect the bifurcation of black and Hispanic income distribution during a period of unusual economic stress and the consequent rise of poverty within a highly segregated residential environment.*

23 Note that tables 9.3d and 9.4d present *mean* earnings, while table 9.2 uses *median* earnings, which are, of course, much less affected by high-end earners.

24 Upper-income blacks (i.e. those with incomes that would place them within the top 20 per cent of the national household income distribution) actually saw their relative position slip from four years earlier, when it had stood at 45 percent of white net worth for households in the same income category.

25 As noted earlier, preliminary evidence from the 1990 census (Roberts, 1992) shows that racial segregation remained unchanged during the decade of the 1980s, whether or not social class is controlled.

26 I should note that in spite of the common sense of this idea, and the fact that everyone in America tries to isolate themselves from economic or racially undesirable neighbours, social scientists have had a difficult time demonstrating that neighbourhood effects actually 'matter'. As I read it, the recent lengthy review of the literature by Jencks and Mayer (1990) proves to be largely inconclusive. None the less, I continue to throw in my lot with logic and actual behaviour, noting that few social scientists are personally willing to take the chance of raising their children in even a working-class neighbourhood, not to mention an impoverished one.

27 Hacker (1992) and Jencks (1992) both offer lengthy reviews and thoughtful discussions.

28 Further evidence reinforces the point. In 1985 the Educational Testing Service examined a sample of American young adults (aged 21–25) to determine their level of functional literacy (Jaynes and Williams, 1989: 353–4). The tests measured reading comprehension, ability to use documents like grocery store coupons and street maps, and practical quantitative reasoning. The results showed strong racial differences. For example, about 90 percent of whites could find a location on a street map compared with 56 percent of blacks. Sixty-five percent of whites could use a map and follow directions to a particular location, compared with 20 percent of blacks. Practical tests associated with everyday life produced similar results on the other measures.

Moreover, controlling for income had relatively little effect on reducing these racial differences. Thus, without any controls, black–white differences averaged between 51 and 60 points on the various measures (the standard deviation was about 50 points). When class background and education attainment were factored out, racial differences were reduced only by about ten points, to between 41 and 50 points. In other words, among young

adults of similar social class, black performance in functional literacy
remained nearly a standard deviation below that of whites.

29   In standard English: 'Boys in the neighbourhood'.

References

American Council on Education (1992) *Minorities in Higher Education 1991, tenth
   annual status report*. American Council on Education, Washington DC.

Anderson, E. (1990) *Streetwise*. University of Chicago Press, Chicago.

Clark, K. (1964) *Dark Ghetto*. Harper and Row, New York.

Collins, S. M. (1989) The marginalization of black executives. *Social Problems* 36,
   4, 317–31.

Denton, N. A. and D. S. Massey (1988) Residential segregation of blacks, hispanics, and Asians by socioeconomic status and generation. *Social Science
   Quarterly* 69, 797–817.

Drake, St C. and H. R. Cayton (1945) *Black Metropolis*. Harcourt, Brace, New York.

Edsall, T. B. and Edsall, M. D. (1991) *Chain Reactions*. W. W. Norton, New York.

Fainstein, N. (1986) The underclass/mismatch hypothesis as an explanation for
   black economic deprivation. *Politics and Society* 15, 403–51.

Fainstein, S. and N. Fainstein (1989) The racial dimension in urban political
   economy. *Urban Affairs Quarterly* 25.2, 187–99.

Farley, R. and W. Allen (1987) *The Color Line and the Quality of Life in America*.
   Russell Sage Foundation, New York.

Feagin, J. R. (1991) The continuing significance of race. *American Sociological
   Review* 56, 101–16.

Franklin, R. (1991) *Shadows of Race and Class*. University of Minnesota Press,
   Minneapolis.

Galster, G. (1987) The ecology of racial discrimination in housing. *Urban Affairs
   Quarterly* 23.1, 84–107.

—— (1991) Black suburbanization: has it changed the relative location of races?
   Urban Affairs Quarterly 26.4, 621–8.

—— and E. Hill (eds) (1992) *The Metropolis in Black and White: Place, power and
   polarization*. Rutgers University Center for Urban Policy Research, New
   Brunswick, NJ.

Hacker, A. (1992) *Two Nations: Black and white, separate, hostile, unequal*. Scribners,
   New York.

Harrison, B. and L. Gorham (1992) What happened to African American wages
   in the 1980s? In Galster and Hill (1992).

Hughes, M. A. (1987) Moving up and moving out: confusing ends and means
   about ghetto dispersal. *Urban Studies* 24, 503–17.

Jacob, J. (1991) Black America 1990: an overview. In *The State of Black America*,
   National Urban League, New York.

Jaynes, G. D. and R. M. Williams Jr (eds) (1989) *A Common Destiny: Blacks and
   American society*. National Academy Press, New York.

Jencks, C. (1992) *Rethinking Social Policy: Race, poverty, and the underclass*. Harvard
   University Press, Cambridge, MA.

—— and S. E. Mayer (1990) The social consequences of growing up in a poor
   neighborhood. In National Research Council, *Inner-city Poverty in the United
   States*, National Research Council, Washington DC.

—— and P. E. Peterson (eds) (1991) *The Urban Underclass*. Brookings Institution, Washington DC.

Judd, D. R. (1991) Segregation forever? *The Nation* (9 December), 740–4.

Kasarda, J. (1985) Urban change and minority opportunities. In P. Peterson (ed.), *The New Urban Reality*, Brookings Institution, Washington DC.

—— (1989) Urban industrial transformation and the underclass. In Wilson (1989).

Katz, M. B. (1989) *The Undeserving Poor*. Pantheon, New York.

Landry, B. (1987) *The New Black Middle Class*. University of California Press, Berkeley.

Marks, C. (1991) The urban underclass. *Annual Review of Sociology* 17, 445–66.

Massey, D. S. (1990) American apartheid: segregation and the making of the underclass. *American Journal of Sociology* 96.2, 329–57.

——, G. A. Condran and N. A. Denton (1987) The effect of residential segregation on black social and economic well-being. *Social Forces* 66.1, 29–56.

—— and N. A. Denton (1988) Suburbanization and segregation in US metropolitan areas. *American Journal of Sociology* 94.1, 592–626.

—— and M. L. Eggers (1990) The ecology of inequality: minorities and the concentration of poverty, 1970–1980. *American Journal of Sociology* 95.5, 1153–88.

—— and A. B. Gross (1991) Explaining trends in racial segregation, 1970–1980. *Urban Affairs Quarterly* 27.1, 13–35.

Mead, L. (1989) The logic of workfare: the underclass and work policy. In Wilson (1989).

Orfield, G. and C. Ashkinaze (1991) *The Closing Door: Conservative policy and black opportunity*. University of Chicago, Chicago.

Roberts, S. (1992) Shifts in 80's failed to ease segregation. *New York Times*, 15 July, B1.

Stearns, L. B. and J. R. Logan (1986) The racial structuring of the housing market and segregation in suburban areas. *Social Forces* 65.1, 28–42.

Swinton, D. H. (1991) The economic status of African Americans: *permanent poverty and inequality*. In National Urban League, *The State of Black America, 1991*, National Urban League, New York.

Time Magazine (1977) The American underclass: destitute and desperate in the land of plenty. 29 August, 14–27.

US Bureau of the Census (1983) *Current Population Reports*. Series P-60, no. 142.

—— (1990) *Household Wealth and Asset Ownership: 1988. Current Population Reports*. Series P-70, no. 22.

—— (1991) *Current Population Reports*. Series P-60, no. 174.

US House of Representatives, Committee on Ways and Means (1991) *Overview of Entitlement Programs, 1991 green book*. US Government Printing Office, Washington DC.

Wacquant, L. Décivilisation et diabolisation: la mutation du ghetto noir américain. In T. Bishop and C. Faure (eds). *L'Amérique des français*, Editions François Bourin, Paris.

—— and W. J. Wilson (1989) The cost of racial and class exclusion in the inner city. In Wilson (1989).

Waldinger, R. and T. Bailey (1991) The continuing significance of race. *Politics and Society* 19.3, 291–323.

Weiher, G. (1991) *The Fractured Metropolis: Political fragmentation and metropolitan segregation*. SUNY Press, Albany, NY.

Wilson, W. J. (1978) *The Declining Significance of Race*. University of Chicago Press, Chicago.

—— (1987) *The Truly Disadvantaged*. University of Chicago Press, Chicago.

—— (1989) The ghetto underclass: social science perspectives. Edited volume, *Annals*, vol. 501 (January).

—— (1991) Studying inner-city social dislocations: the challenge of public agenda research. *American Sociological Review* 56, 1–14.

10

Toward Greater Racial Diversity in the Suburbs

W. Dennis Keating

The struggle for racially diverse suburbs in metropolitan Cleveland has been waged for three decades. If this were to be considered a war, some battles have been won, many have been lost, the trends have not been encouraging, and the outcome remains unknown. Although Cleveland was considered the second most racially isolated metropolis in the United States in 1990, it has also been the site of some of the most innovative and persistent pro-integrative efforts in the United States. Important lessons have been learned that can contribute to greater progress in the future in the struggle for a more tolerant and racially mixed society.

The Cleveland experience also parallels that of the fair housing movement in other metropolitan areas such as Chicago and Detroit. A fair housing movement persists in the United States, despite the indifference or even hostility of national administrations over most of the past twenty-five years. Although occasional legislative victories have been won, such as the 1968 federal Fair Housing Act, the Home Mortgage Disclosure Act in 1975 and the Community Reinvestment Act in 1977 regulating lenders, and the 1988 strengthening of federal fair housing law, the battle has mostly been waged at the municipal and metropolitan level, as well as in the courts. What has been attempted and accomplished during this period?

Reprinted by permission from W. Dennis Keating, *The Suburban Racial Dilemma: Housing and Neighborhoods.*

Fair Housing Policies and Programs in Metropolitan Cleveland

Several different approaches have been tried in metropolitan Cleveland over the past three decades. One approach has been on a person-to-person level, within the context of neighborhood organizing in a city undergoing racial transition. The Shaker Heights neighborhoods of Ludlow, Lomond, and Moreland pioneered this approach through community associations formed in the late 1950s and early 1960s. In Cleveland Heights in the 1960s, white residents were organized by the Heights Citizens for Human Rights and the Heights Area Project of the Jewish Community Federation. Organizers sought to allay the fears of white residents and to persuade them of the benefits of racially integrated neighborhoods and public schools. The Heights Community Congress continued this organizing in Cleveland Heights in the 1970s, focusing on block clubs and neighborhood organizations. Such organizing efforts have succeeded in preventing blockbusting and white flight and have contributed to the development of citywide, pro-integrative, multiracial policies and programs that resulted in long-term racial diversity in many of the neighborhoods of these two suburbs. This diversity has gained these two suburbs their reputation as vigorous proponents of racial diversity.

This type of organizing has been tried elsewhere in Cleveland suburbs but often has failed to stem the tide of resegregation (e.g., East Cleveland and Warrensville Heights in the 1960s and 1970s and Bedford Heights in the 1980s). Pro-integrative community organizations in suburbs such as Euclid (Euclid Community Concerns, organized in 1981) and South Euclid (Hillcrest Neighbors, organized in 1983) have survived but to date have had only minimal impact in influencing their municipal governments to adopt affirmative, pro-integrative policies. One likely reason for the difficulties experienced by these groups in trying to convert white residents to such policies is that many of these residents had previously fled ethnic neighborhoods in Cleveland that were undergoing racial transition. Many residents particularly elderly residents now in retirement, may fear experiencing yet another racial transition.

Another form of person-to-person advocacy has been the use of pro-integrative mortgage incentives to persuade white and black homebuyers to consider neighborhoods where their race is under-represented. Beginning in Shaker Heights in the 1950s and continuing into the 1990s in Cleveland Heights, Shaker Heights, University Heights, and the Hillcrest suburbs, fair housing organizations, both municipal and regional (e.g., the East Suburban Council for Open Communities and the Cuyahoga Plan), have tried to convince individuals to make this very important, personal decision, sometimes making these residents pioneers in the fair housing movement. This approach has been successful, but, because fewer than a thousand homebuyers have received these mortgage incentives over a quarter-century, it has made only a marginal impact on Cleveland's suburban racial patterns (Keating, 1992). A study of the Lomond neighborhood of Shaker Heights did indicate that the use of pro-integrative mortgage incentives after the 1985 creation of the Fund for the Future of Shaker Heights did have a positive impact on racial diversity and contributed to stable housing values (Cromwell, 1990).

A second approach to integration has been the effort to change municipal housing policies to embrace affirmative, pro-integrative policies and programs. Certainly, the cities of Cleveland Heights and Shaker Heights have been the leaders and most successful in their efforts. Their policies have been a combination of regulatory ordinances (e.g., banning "for sale" signs, monitoring the conduct of real estate firms, and strictly enforcing housing codes); incentives (e.g., pro-integrative mortgage incentives and housing rehabilitation loans); and civic promotion (e.g., creation of municipal housing offices and support for fair housing groups). These kinds of policies came too late in East Cleveland to prevent resegregation. Court imposition of fair housing policies in Parma (underway since the early 1980s) has so far had only marginal impact in changing that city's racial composition. The majority of suburbs in Cuyahoga County have taken no affirmative actions, mostly limiting their "action" to the mere adoption of a fair housing resolution (Cuyahoga Plan, 1989).

A third approach has been to promote affirmative fair housing policies at metropolitan and subregional levels. Efforts at the former level have been represented by Operation Equality, Plan of Action for Tomorrow's Housing (PATH), and the Cuyahoga Plan. Operation Equality (1966–1973) pioneered in promoting black migration to Cleveland's suburbs, supported by Fair Housing, Inc., the interracial real estate brokerage firm established in 1963 to serve pro-integrative suburban moves by homebuyers. After passage of the federal fair housing legislation in 1968, Operation Equality was the most visible vehicle for the enforcement of the antidiscrimination legislation in Cuyahoga County. However, its role was superseded by the Cuyahoga Plan after the latter's creation in 1974.

Like its counterparts in other metropolitan areas, the Cuyahoga Plan has over its life mainly been a vehicle for the investigation of racial discrimination and the documentation of patterns of racial segregation and isolation in housing and neighborhoods throughout its metropolitan area. While it has enjoyed fairly consistent support from several cities, Cuyahoga County, and philanthropic foundations, it has not converted a majority of the county's suburbs to support of its efforts or initiation of their own programs. The Cuyahoga Plan, from its beginnings in the mid-1970s to its most recent crisis in 1992, has never been able fully to resolve the tension between the freedom of choice approach (i.e., mere enforcement of antidiscrimination laws) and the affirmative, pro-integrative approach, featuring race-conscious policies.

PATH, during its brief life (1967–74), was notably unsuccessful in its efforts to lobby for and litigate dispersion of federally subsidized public housing throughout Cuyahoga County's suburbs. The effort to promote a countywide fair-share plan for low-income housing, at least partially successful in a few metropolitan areas (e.g., Dayton, Minneapolis, and Washington, D.C.) in the 1970s, met heavy resistance from suburban officials, which PATH could not overcome.

A subregional approach to promotion of affirmative fair housing policies has been to form organizations to try to attract blacks to the Hillcrest suburbs (six cities) on Cleveland's east side, in part to relieve the pressure on pro-integrative suburbs such as Cleveland Heights and Shaker Heights. This approach was pioneered by Suburban Citizens for Open Housing in the late 1960s, in tandem with Operation Equality and Fair Housing, Inc. However, all three of these organizations disappeared in the early 1970s, having made only a minor impact.

In 1984 this approach was renewed, supported by the cities of Cleveland Heights, Shaker Heights, and University Heights and their school boards. The East Suburban Council for Open Communities (ESCOC), working with cooperative realty firms and landlords, using advertising and an escort service, and providing pro-integrative mortgage incentives to black homebuyers, did make progress, although the number of its clients who chose to live in Hillcrest was relatively small. Its efforts to enlist the support, overt or unofficial, of the six municipalities in the Hillcrest area were unsuccessful. When it dissolved in 1990 over differences concerning its future direction, its efforts seemingly ended. However, with the continuation of its housing service, now administered by the Cuyahoga Plan, hope remains that it can continue to attract at least small numbers of blacks to the Hillcrest communities and contribute to greater racial diversity in an area where such efforts are now more than two decades old.

Open Door West, active only since 1990, has adopted a much less visible approach to facilitating greater racial diversity in the west side of the city of Cleveland and the western suburbs of Cuyahoga County. It has not yet made a noticeable impact in changing suburban housing patterns.

A fourth approach to integration in the Cleveland metropolitan area has been litigation. This has taken different forms.

First, individuals (e.g., landlords and homesellers) and organizations (e.g, realty firms) have been sued for alleged violations of applicable fair housing law. These lawsuits have certainly created a better public understanding of fair housing law, but the approach does not seem to have deterred altogether those determined to discriminate. Second, key real estate industry agencies (e.g., HGM–Hilltop Realty) have been sued (e.g, by the Heights Community Congress and the city of Cleveland Heights) for alleged systematic violations of fair housing law. These two types of litigation have influenced the real estate industry to accept greater education of real estate brokers and agents about fair housing law.

Third, suburban municipalities have been sued for alleged exclusionary practices, that is, practices designed to exclude the poor, including racial minorities. In the case of East Cleveland, the U.S. Supreme Court struck down a strict interpretation of the city's housing code that arbitrarily excluded certain blood relatives from living with other family members (*Moore v. East Cleveland*, 431 U.S. 494 [1977]). In contrast, PATH's attempt to force suburban municipalities to provide public housing and to have the federal requirement for cooperation agreements between suburbs and the Cuyahoga Metropolitan Housing Authority (CMHA) invalidated was rejected by the federal courts. Likewise, in a challenge to a mandatory referendum requirement, affecting subsidized housing, that had been enacted by the Lake County suburb of Eastlake, the U.S. Supreme Court upheld this democratic version of land use planning in the absence of proof that it had an intended or disparate exclusionary racial impact. Mandatory referenda regulating land use and development were subsequently widely adopted by Cuyahoga County suburbs.

Fourth, one suburb, Parma, was sued by the U.S. Department of Justice and found guilty of a long-standing pattern of fair housing violations. The tangible results of a remedial court order to promote greater racial diversity remain minimal after more than a decade. The city's black population is still below 1 percent. Despite similar patterns of racial segregation (or non diversity) in many other predominantly white suburbs, no other suburb in Cuyahoga County has been similarly sued.

Barring the advent of a much different national administration, one determined to attack suburban residential segregation in the courts as violative of federal fair housing law, it is most unlikely that the courts can be a vehicle for systematically addressing suburban integration problems. Without the involvement of the federal government, it is very unlikely that fair housing advocacy groups will be able to afford to engage in such costly and time-consuming litigation. The Parma litigation took seven years from the filing of the lawsuit by the U.S. Justice Department to the trial, and a decision and an appeal lasted another two years. A county-wide fair housing organization such as the Cuyahoga Plan, which has been heavily dependent on suburban governments for financial support, is not in a position to engage in litigation against those same suburban municipalities. The history of fair housing litigation suggests that the role of the courts will continue to be that of a mostly passive forum where individual complaints of racial discrimination in housing can be heard, if administrative attempts to resolve them fail.

Three Decades of Racial Transition in Metropolitan Cleveland: Progress or Not?

The post-World War II racial patterns of metropolitan Cleveland have been in transition for more than three decades. Based on indexes of dissimilarity derived from decennial census data, the ranking of the Cleveland metropolitan area as one of the most racially isolated or segregated in the United States, second only to Chicago in 1990, would seem to indicate that little or no progress has been made with regard to race relations in housing. Sporadic but regular racial incidents and confrontations, mostly occurring in the city of Cleveland, have underscored the continued racial tension in the metropolis.

Black suburbanization has continued to increase, as it has elsewhere in the United States, but resegregation has occurred, most notably in the suburbs of East Cleveland and Warrensville Heights and also in neighborhoods of cities such as Euclid, Maple Heights, and South Euclid. But for the efforts of the many fair housing organizations that have struggled to eliminate racial discrimination and to promote greater racial diversity, there undoubtedly would be even less racial diversity in 1992 than does exist.

Due to the efforts of the fair housing organizations and changing social attitudes, the white population of metropolitan Cleveland and its suburbs has shown an increasing awareness of the problem of racial discrimination in housing, has supported enforcement of fair housing legislation, has indicated an increasing tolerance for racially mixed neighborhoods, and has shown very little preference for all-white neighborhoods. However, these attitudinal changes have not been translated into changed residential patterns. Whites have not, by and large, sought out racially diverse neighborhoods.

The exceptions have been those few suburbs, such as Cleveland Heights and Shaker Heights and their counterparts in suburban Chicago, Oak Park and Park Forest, that have adopted pro-integrative housing policies and implemented them over a long period. The experience of these Cleveland and Chicago suburbs has demonstrated that there are significant numbers of whites interested in living in racially diverse communities. The participation and leadership of interfaith clergy and churches; neighborhood-based community organizing; and the support of municipal government, the public schools, and philanthropic foundations have all been critical to these suburbs' success. Their experience gives support to the possibility of promoting and sustaining racially integrated living patterns on a much broader scale throughout the Chicago and Cleveland metropolitan regions. The continuation of white demand in now predominantly black neighborhoods in Cleveland Heights, Shaker Heights, Oak Park, and Park Forest has shown that the "tipping point" phenomenon is not inevitable (Galster, 1990a). To achieve sustained racial diversity, however, much different public policies, particularly as implemented by predominantly white suburban municipalities, will be required.

In the suburbs of metropolitan Cleveland, responses to the experience of racial transition have been mixed. Among those suburbs experiencing a noticeable growth of black population, some have supported the activities of the Cuyahoga Plan and designated their own staff to deal with race-related issues (e.g., Euclid). Others have not gone this far and have rejected overtures to join or support ESCOC's activities (e.g., South Euclid). Those suburbs with a negligible black population have mostly done nothing, with few exceptions (e.g., Lakewood). If the pattern of the past three decades continues, more of Cleveland's inner-ring, older suburbs will experience the black suburbanization that has already occurred in cities such as Euclid, South Euclid, Bedford Heights, Garfield Heights, and Maple Heights (all of which are on the east side). If they adopt pro-integrative policies, it is conceivable that they may successfully promote long-term, stable racial diversity in their communities. But if they choose not to act unless problems arise, it is entirely likely that some of their neighborhoods will resegregate, as many whites leave when the black population rises above what they consider to be acceptable levels.

The 1991 Citizens League Research Institute survey indicated that if nonwhite (e.g., black) in-migration numbered "only a few," then only a small percentage of whites would merely consider moving out. This reflects the willingness of most whites to have black neighbors (Schuman and Bobo, 1988). If black in-migration were to grow, then the rate of possible white flight would increase (table 10.1). A similar pattern emerged when whites were asked if they would actually move out in the face of black in-migration (table 10.2).

If whites perceive that white demand for housing is rapidly declining or disappearing, increasing numbers indicated that they would either consider moving or would actually move out.

This response pattern seems to confirm the tipping point theory, although it also demonstrates that total resegregation is not inevitable.

Table 10.1   Whites considering out-migration with black in-migration, Cleveland, 1991

Black In-Migration	White Out-Migration (%)
Only a few	15
About one-quarter	20
About one-half	38
Most	54

Source: CLRI, 1991: 53, graph V–3.

Table 10.2   Whites planning out-migration with black in-migration, Cleveland, 1991

Black In-Migration	White Out-Migration (%)
Only a few	7
About one-quarter	14
About one-half	35
Most	49

Source: CLRI, 1991: 54, graph V–4.

An orderly transition to a racially mixed neighborhood does not inexorably lead to resegregation. Rather, long-term, stable racial diversity is possible, particularly if affirmative, pro-integrative policies are in effect. Contrary to W. A. V. Clark's (1991) conclusion, long-term, stable racial diversity is possible, difficult as this has been. Beyond prejudicial white attitudes, what must change is behavior in the housing market.

What can be done in metropolitan Cleveland and other, similar metropolitan areas to encourage greater racial diversity while preventing resegregation?

A Metropolitan Perspective, Metropolitan Strategies

The Cleveland experience shows that "gradualism," that is, the piecemeal migration of blacks to suburbs and subsequent inaction by suburbs, is not leading to greater racial diversity. Instead, blacks will likely gravitate to those suburbs and suburban neighborhoods with the highest proportional black populations, where they will feel most "comfortable," and whites will continue to gravitate to predominantly white suburbs and white suburban neighborhoods. The exception, as shown in the 1987 study of suburban Cleveland homebuyers (Keating, Pammer, and Smith, 1987), consists of those white and black homebuyers and renters who wish to live in a racially diverse community and who are aware of the affirmative, pro-integrative policies of such suburbs as Cleveland Heights and Shaker Heights. However, while this provides these suburbs with a special market, it does not broaden the number of pro-integrative suburbs and, insofar as blacks are attracted to these magnet, racially diverse suburbs, could actually threaten the racial diversity that these suburbs have worked so long to maintain.

If most suburban municipalities will not adopt pro-integrative, affirmative policies voluntarily, then only two options exist: these policies can be mandated by higher levels of government (regional, state, and federal) or incentives can be provided to those suburbs willing to cooperate. The former policy is more likely to have the greater impact but is politically less feasible. The latter policy may have a greater possibility of acceptance but is likely to have much less impact, either because most suburbs will decline to participate or because recipients of pro-integrative incentives may still gravitate toward the few pro-integrative magnet suburbs that exist, as long as their housing is affordable to them.

Governmental mandates for pro-integrative, affirmative housing policies and programs

A federal mandate could conceivably make the most impact. As George Galster (1990b) has suggested, federal aid to state and local governments could require the creation and implementation of affirmative fair housing plans by jurisdictions receiving federal aid, whether by entitlement or discretion. An example would have been requiring this in the Comprehensive Housing Assistance Strategy, which is a prerequisite for use of HUD funding under the 1990 housing act. However, reflecting the conservative nature of contemporary national politics, this requirement was not made or even discussed in Congress. In the face of White House opposition to affirmative action, which the Bush administration chose to characterize as racial quotas, the Democratically controlled Congress had difficulty in overriding a presidential veto of civil rights legislation. Internally, the Democrats themselves are divided on the politically volatile issue of making federal aid contingent on the institution of affirmative, pro-integrative programs. Federal social policy mandates also fly in the face of the continuing strong trends to deconcentrate federal regulatory control and to institute additional block grant funding without too many strings attached.

Finally, with the continued existence of huge federal budget deficits, absent a peace dividend devoted to domestic social spending, there is little new federal funding available to all states and localities to which such a mandate could be tied. The most likely general funding would be for infrastructure improvements, education, and environmental and anti-crime programs. Politically, it would be very difficult to attach fair housing mandates to federal support to state and local governments for these purposes. Tying fair housing requirements to federal lower-income housing assistance is not likely to work because most suburbs do not seek such aid, even if available, because they do not want below-market housing in the community.

Although federal mandates can require local funding for implementation, it is most unlikely that a Congress increasingly influenced by suburban representatives would mandate fair housing opposed by their suburban constituents (even with federal subsidies provided to help achieve compliance). The fair-share housing plans supported by the federal government in the 1970s were not mandated by Congress. Given the drastic reductions in newly constructed, federally subsidized housing since the election of Ronald Reagan in 1980 and the suburban resistance to regional fair-share housing plans, it is not likely that such a policy could be revived and receive the support of the federal government. Politically, it is unclear that the representatives of central cities, which are increasingly composed of a majority of minority residents, would even support such a federal policy if it were proposed. Thus what is left is the uncontroversial funding by HUD of fair housing organizations to assist in the enforcement of antidiscrimination legislation. In the 1992 federal budget, HUD's funding of its Fair Housing Initiatives Program amounted to only a few million dollars.

If federal mandates are not likely options, then another possibility is state-mandated fair housing policy. No state has yet adopted such a policy. One state, New Jersey, has mandated regional fair-share housing, but only because of state supreme court rulings based on an interpretation of New Jersey's constitution as guaranteeing a right to housing. Implemention of the *Mt. Laurel* decision, ongoing since the initial decision in 1975, could change exclusionary racial patterns. However, the impetus for the case was primarily economic, rather than racial, discrimination. The ability of suburbs since 1985 to "sell" part of their fair-share obligation to central cities, where the poorer minority population is concentrated, will undoubtedly reduce the pro-integrative impact of the future implementation of the order (Seton Hall University Colloquium, 1991). Other states, such as California, Massachusetts, and Oregon, that have legislatively required that local land use plans allow for broad housing opportunities for all income groups have not linked this policy to affirmative municipal action to promote greater racial diversity in housing.

While states are involved in the enforcement of anti-housing discrimination laws, in tandem with federal and local government, this has not led to greater racial diversity. One of the few hopeful signs has been the designation of a percentage of first-time homebuyer mortgage subsidies by the Ohio Housing Finance Agency for pro-integrative moves. If this policy were incorporated into all state – as well as federal and municipal – home purchase programs, then the states could take the lead in promoting greater racial diversity. This would require considerable political pressure on state housing finance agencies by fair housing advocates, as occurred in Ohio in the 1980s (Thomas, 1991: 944–48; Bromley, 1992). The alternative would be court-mandated state programs to promote greater residential racial integration, such as occurred in Wisconsin and greater Milwaukee in the late 1980s (Thomas, 1991: 948–50). However, there is little prospect that either political or legal pressure will persuade or force states to take the lead in promoting greater racial diversity, especially in the suburbs of metropolitan areas. In proposing state legislation requiring a set-aside for racial minorities of at least 25 percent of the units in any new housing development of five or more units, M. F. Potter (1990) conceded that adoption of such legislation was not politically feasible.

The final possibility for government-mandated, pro-integrative, affirmative housing policy lies at the metropolitan level. Regional fair-share housing plans, which could include affirmative pro-integrative policies, could be mandated by a metropolitan government, if one exists, or agreed upon voluntarily, as happened in a few metropolitan areas such as Dayton in the 1970s through councils of governments (COGS). As Glaster argues, it is critical that all, or at least most, of the local governments in a region comply; otherwise, progress toward greater racial integration will be piecemeal (Galster, 1990b: 149). Unfortunately, regional government does not exist in most of the United States, and there is little prospect of any change in this regard. Single-purpose metropolitan agencies with jurisdiction over housing also do not exist, with the exception of a few public housing authorities such as Cleveland's Cuyahoga Metropolitan Housing Authority (CMHA). However, as the history of CMHA and the short-lived efforts of PATH demonstrate, most suburbs will not cooperate with a regional public housing authority, leaving most public housing concentrated in the central city. In the case of CMHA, its central-city public housing is racially segregated for the most part.

The alternative is a consensual agreement among cooperating municipalities in a metropolitan region operating through a COG. If a consensus like that achieved in Dayton, Ohio, in 1970 could be voluntarily attained, then the mandate problem could be avoided. But the dilemma is that there is little indication of any interest in such a policy by most predominantly white suburbs. The fact that most of Cuyahoga County's predominantly white suburbs have not financially supported the activities of the Cuyahoga Plan since its creation in 1974 is an indication of this prevailing attitude. This disheartening pattern is even more discouraging because the Cuyahoga Plan primarily confined its activities to assisting in enforcement of antidiscrimination laws and has not taken the lead in promoting pro-integrative policies. And even if some form of a consensus could be reached by some municipalities in a region, COGS have no power to enforce such a policy. COGS have been weakened since the Reagan administration began to reduce federal mandates and eliminated much of federal support for regional planning (Ross, Levine, and Stedman, 1991:296).

Incentives for pro-integrative, affirmative housing policies

The alternative to a mandatory policy approach is to provide financial incentives to promote racial integration in housing, "carrots" instead of "sticks." Anthony Downs (1973: 161–62) proposed providing financial assistance to cooperating suburbs, lower-income central-city residents willing to move to the suburbs, and housing developers who build subsidized housing in the suburbs. Ronald Silverman (1977) proposed similar policies and also advocated providing cash awards to residents of "receiving" suburban neighborhoods to prevent their moving out and resegregation occurring. He admitted the offensive appearance of subsidizing tolerance (Silverman, 1977: 488–91) but advocated this approach, at least on an experimental basis.

A weaker version of this notion is to guarantee property owners in racially transitional neighborhoods that their property values will remain stable, a policy adopted by Oak Park, Illinois, which has an "equity assurance" program available to concerned homeowners (Goodwin, 1979). When a similar program was enacted for white neighborhoods in Chicago, black mayor Eugene Sawyer vetoed the ordinance. Subsequently, the Illinois State Legislature adopted similar legislation applicable to Chicago (Goel, 1990: 379).

Elements of the incentives approach have been tried with some success. The court-ordered remedies in the *Gautreaux* (Chicago) and *Mt. Laurel* (New Jersey) cases have led to the suburban entry of a few thousand lower-income minority residents through federal, state, and local housing subsidies. The use of pro-integrative mortgages in Ohio (beginning in metropolitan Cleveland), Milwaukee, Philadelphia and Washington, D.C., has proven successful in persuading or reinforcing the decision of voluntarily participating homebuyers to choose homes in racially mixed neighborhoods.

With the massive reduction of federal subsidy programs for new housing under the Reagan and Bush administrations, there is little prospect in the near future for even debating the efficacy of the Downs and Silverman recommendations. They assumed the availability of large-scale federal housing subsidy programs that would be applicable to the suburbs, such as briefly existed during the period from 1969 to 1972, before Richard Nixon's moratorium on federal housing subsidy programs in January 1973. The 1990 revival of federal funding authority for new below-market housing programs is modest, and metropolitan dispersion of this housing was not a goal of its proponents.

There is virtually no chance, given federal fiscal problems, of federal funding being made available to reward suburban communities that are willing to participate in pro-integrative housing programs. The same is true for fiscally strapped states, which were cutting back on social welfare programs in 1992 to eliminate growing budget deficits.

Whether such race-conscious governmental policies would be politically feasible, even if funding could be made available, is highly debatable. There has been opposition, mostly from black real estate interests, to Ohio's pro-integrative mortgage program, resulting in the creation of a separate minority homebuyers program, which has no geographical restrictions as to where participants purchase. There was also some conservative opposition to the idea of race-based incentives. In a conservative political climate in which affirmative action policies have been under threat of elimination and attacked as unjustifiable racial quotas, the question of winning public support for pro-integrative policies is a most difficult political issue.

The 1991 survey of suburban Cuyahoga County residents indicated that a majority (54 percent overall, including 49 percent of whites) supported a policy of providing pro-integrative mortgage incentives to voluntarily participating homebuyers, and only a fairly small minority (20 percent) opposed this type of program (Keating, 1992). White support was much higher in the suburbs of Cleveland Heights and Shaker Heights than in predominantly white suburbs, especially the western suburbs. A 1992 survey of the opinions of greater Clevelanders showed less support for this approach. When asked whether "housing incentives (for example, lower mortgage rates) should be offered to homebuyers who move into neighborhoods which are mostly of a different race," only 43 percent either agreed or strongly agreed. While a majority of blacks (60 percent) and Hispanics (50 percent) agreed with this policy, only 35 percent of whites were supportive. Only 38 percent of suburbanites interviewed were supportive.

In contrast, just over one-half (52 percent) of all interviewed (city and suburban residents) agreed that "there should be government programs to help integrate neighborhoods." However, only 43 percent of whites were supportive, compared to 78 percent of blacks. Just under one-half (46 percent) of suburbanites were supportive (CLRI, 1991). This indicates that there is not yet majority white and suburban support for affirmative governmental policies, including pro-integrative mortgage incentives, to promote racially integrated neighborhoods.

Whether broad political consensus for a much more visible program of pro-integrative mortgage incentives, with greatly increased public funding, could gain support and whether this support would continue if most predominantly white suburbs were targeted is unknown. Polls indicate that white tolerance for greater racial diversity, especially if a minority presence is relatively small, has increased since the dawning of the civil rights era, despite the backlash that has occurred since the 1970s.

Legally, the 1992 refusal by an increasingly conservative U.S. Supreme Court to review the decision upholding the validity of the voluntary race-conscious policies that were challenged in *South Suburban Housing Center* indicates that pro-integrative housing programs can avoid the fatal claim that they are the type of illegal racial quotas found to have violated the equal protection clause and fair housing law in *Starrett City* (Simon, 1991; Thomas, 1991).

The Viability of a Metropolitan Strategy

What is the answer to the dilemma that a metropolitan pro-integrative housing strategy is imperative but a viable metropolitan strategy dependent on public approval and funding seems to be highly unlikely? The answer must be a quasi-governmental strategy. Short of court-ordered regional or state mandates, the remaining alternative is to develop the type of metropolitan strategy represented by ESCOC. While ESCOC affected only six of fifty-eight Cuyahoga County suburbs, it could be applied to virtually all of Cleveland's suburbs. Of course to make any impact there would have to be much more funding than has been available to date to ESCOC and its successor agency to provide pro-integrative mortgage incentives. Unless there are pro-integrative suburban municipalities such as Cleveland Heights, Shaker Heights, and University Heights (and, preferably, their school boards) in existence that are willing to provide support, or unless urban counties can be persuaded to provide financial assistance, funding must be obtained from private sources (e.g., philanthropic foundations) and, if feasible, from state housing finance agencies.

If extended to entire metropolitan areas and sustained over long periods of time (and assuming that participants are satisfied and supportive and that there is little active opposition from their neighbors and the municipalities to which they move), this approach represents the best available hope for affecting residential patterns in all of metropolitan America, rather than only a few isolated suburbs. Providing financial incentives for pro-integrative action can affect the behavior as well as the attitudes of whites, not only those participating directly but also their friends and neighbors, giving greater hope for gradually reducing the segregative racial patterns that so characterize the suburbs of metropolitan America.

This modest proposal presumes that there is still a sizable constituency, both white and black, that supports the dreams and ideals of Martin Luther King, Jr., and the civil rights movement, which espoused the goal of a racially integrated society. The Kerner Commission warned that, unless drastic changes occurred, that goal would not be reached and the United States would become even more racially segregated and separated by spatial and political borders. In addition to race, it suggested that Americans would continue to be divided by class, as reflected in income. African Americans on the average still earn far less than whites. To the extent that the black middle class continues to suburbanize, they remain more acceptable to whites, particularly their social peers (according to education, occupation, income and value of their home). However, not all middle-class black suburbanites necessarily adhere any longer to the integrationist ideal, as is illustrated by the attitudes of many black residents in Prince Georges County, Maryland (Dent, 1992). The much more difficult problem is to persuade suburbanites, especially whites, to accept as neighbors those of a lower social status. Economic, as opposed to racial, diversity is perhaps even more difficult to envision in most American suburbs. Therefore, the goals of the fair housing movement are best pursued primarily through the promotion of greater racial diversity among homeowners living in neighborhoods that otherwise are mostly homogeneous.

The goal of racial diversity in housing and neighborhoods can be achieved. But it must be remembered that there is no end to this struggle. With the mobility of Americans and the resultant turnover of houses, their owner-occupants, and residential neighborhoods, there must be a constant educational process reminding suburbanites of the benefits of living in a racially diverse society. Suburban governments must actively support pro-integrative, affirmative housing policies. There must be continuing liaison with the real estate industry and enforcement of antidiscrimination legislation. Those suburbs profiled in this book that have kept alive the goal of racial integration over a long period, despite controversy and setbacks, demonstrate that it is not an idle hope or impossible dream. In all of the case studies of suburbs and fair housing organizations profiled herein, it is a handful of fair housing advocates, many of them clergy or affiliated with religious organizations, who have kept the often flickering flame of interracial community alive. Whether they represent a movement of the past or prologue to the future remains an unanswered question.

References

Bromley, C. H. 1992. "The Politics of Race Reform of the Single Family Mortgage Revenue Bond Program in the State of Ohio 1983–1988." Paper presented at the annual meeting of the Urban Affairs Association, Cleveland.

Citizens League Research Institute (CLRI). 1991. *Race Relations in Greater Cleveland: A Report on the Attitudes, Opinions, and Experiences of Greater Clevelanders.* Cleveland: CLRI.

Clark, W. A. V. 1991. "Residential Preferences and Neighborhood Racial Segregation: A Test of the Schelling Segregation Model." *Demography* 28: 1–19.

Cromwell, A. 1990. *Prointegrative Subsidies and Their Effect on Housing Markets: Do Race-based Loans Work?* Cleveland: Federal Reserve Bank (Working Paper No. 9018).

——. 1989. *Municipal Approaches to Fair Housing in Greater Cleveland.* Cleveland: Cuyahoga Plan.

Dent, D. J. 1992. "The New Black Suburbs." *New York Times Magazine,* 14 June, Sec. 6, p. 18.

Downs, A. 1973. *Opening Up the Suburbs: An Urban Strategy for America.* New Haven: Yale University Press.

Galster, G. C. 1990a. "Racial Discrimination in Housing Markets in the 1980s: A Review of the Audit Evidence." *Journal of Planning Education and Research* 9: 165–75.

——. 1990b. "Federal Fair Housing Policy: The Great Misapprehension." In D. DiPasquale and L. C. Keyes, eds, *Building Foundations: Housing and Federal Policy.* Philadelphia: University of Pennsylvania Press.

Goel, A. J. 1990. 'Maintaining Integration against Minority Interests: An Anti-Subjugation Theory for Equality in Housing." *Urban Lawyer* 22: 369–416.

Goodwin, C. 1979. *The Oak Park Strategy: Community Control of Social Change.* Chicago: University of Chicago Press.

Keating, W. D. 1992. *An Evaluation of Pro-Integrative Mortgage Incentives in Suburban Cuyahoga County.* Cleveland: Maxine Goodman Levin College of Urban Affairs, Cleveland State University.

Keating, W. D., W. J. Pammer, Jr, and L. S. Smith. 1987. *A Comparative Study of Three Models of Racial Integration in Suburban Cleveland.* Cleveland: Maxine Goodman Levin College of Urban Affairs, Cleveland State University.

Potter, M. F. 1990. "Racial Diversity in Residential Communities: Societal Housing Patterns and a Proposal for a 'Racial Inclusionary Ordinance.' " *Southern California Law Review* 63: 1151–1235.

Ross, H. R., M. A. Levine, and M. S. Stedman, Jr. 1991. *Urban Politics: Power in Metropolitan America.* 4th ed. Itasca, Ill. Peacock.

Schuman, H., and L. Bobo. 1988. "Survey-based Experiments on White Racial Attitudes toward Residential Integration." *American Journal of Sociology* 94: 273–99.

Seton Hall University Center for Social Justice Affordable Housing Colloquium. 1991. "*Mount Laurel* and the Fair Housing Act: Success or Failure?" *Fordham Urban Law Journal* 19: 59–86.

Silverman, R. H. 1977. "Subsidizing Tolerance for Open Communities." *Wisconsin Law Review*: 375–401.

Simon, T. W. 1991. "Double Reverse Discrimination in Housing: Contextualizing the *Starrett City* Case." *Buffalo Law Review* 39: 803–53.

Thomas, S. A. 1991. "Efforts to Integrate Housing: The Legality of Mortgage-Incentive Programs." *New York University Law Review* 66: 940–78.

Part III

The Politics of Redevelopment, Public–Private Partnerships, and Gentrification

Introduction to Part III

The dominant development trend in both the United States and the United Kingdom has been towards decentralization of employment and population. Nevertheless, considerable investment has gone into central business districts, and there has been a detectable migration of well-to-do people into formerly working-class inner-city residential districts. These movements have resulted from the interaction of governmental policy and the private market. They have been widely criticized for channeling their benefits narrowly to developers, downtown businesses, and upper middle-class gentrifiers at the expense of the working class and the poor.

The principal vehicle for inner-city redevelopment has become the public–private partnership. In his discussion of this supposedly new phenomenon of government–business cooperation, Squires contends that it has existed throughout American history. He roots it in an ideology of privatism, which he criticizes for insulating policy-makers from accountability and for inflicting serious costs on vulnerable groups. He concludes by proposing alternative paths for central-city redevelopment.

Whereas Squires stresses the role of ideology in shaping redevelopment policy, Logan and Molotch scrutinize the economic interests that constitute the "growth machine." Like Squires they identify its deep historical roots. They show the role played by political rather than purely impersonal market forces in effecting urban growth. Finally, they reveal the factors that make the political objectives of this coalition so potent and subject these objectives to a broad critique.

Neil Smith's examination of gentrification – the displacement of lower-by upper-income people in urban neighborhoods – likewise points to ideological elements in shaping developmental patterns. He shows how the ideology of the frontier connects with the profitability of developing previously devalued urban land. Like many of the authors in this volume he links the flows of investment into and out of the city to the larger processes of global economic restructuring.

11

Partnership and the Pursuit of the Private City

Gregory D. Squires

> ... Two hundred and sixty-eight years of laissez-faire economics had left
> the city in a hell of a mess.
>
> *Joseph S. Clark, Jr.,*
> *Mayor of Philadelphia 1952–1956*
> *(Warner, 1987, p. xi)*

Public–private partnerships have become the rallying cry for economic development professionals throughout the United States (Davis, 1986; Porter, 1989). As federal revenues for economic development, social service, and other urban programs diminish such partnerships are increasingly looked to as the key for urban revitalization (G. Peterson and Lewis, 1986). These partnerships take many forms. Formal organizations of executives from leading businesses have been established that work directly with public officials. In some cases public officials as well as representatives from various community organizations are also members. Some partnerships have persisted for decades working on an array of issues while others are ad hoc arrangements that focus on a particular time-limited project. Direct subsidies from public agencies to private firms

Reprinted by permission from Gregory D. Squires, 1991, "Partnership and the Pursuit of the Private City," in Mark Goettdiener and Chris Pickvance (eds), *Urban Life in Transition*.

have been described as public–private partnerships. If economic development has emerged as a major function of local government, public–private partnerships are increasingly viewed as the critical tool.

The concept of partnership is widely perceived to be an innovative approach that is timely in an age of austerity. In fact, "public–private partnership" is little more than a new label for a long-standing relationship between the public and private sectors. Growth has been the constant, central objective of that relationship, though in recent years subsidization of dramatic economic restructuring has become a complementary concern. While that relationship has evolved throughout U.S. history, it has long been shaped by an ideology of privatism that has dominated urban redevelopment from colonial America through the so-called postindustrial era (Barnekov, Boyle, and Rich, 1989; Krumholz, 1984; Levine, 1989; Warner, 1987). The central tenet of privatism is the belief in the supremacy of the private sector and market forces in nurturing development, with the public sector as a junior partner whose principal obligation is to facilitate private capital accumulation. Individual material acquisitiveness is explicitly avowed, but that selfishness is justified by the public benefits that are assumed to flow from the dynamics of such relations.

One need look no further than the roadways, canals, and railroads of the eighteenth and nineteenth centuries to see early concrete manifestations of large-scale public subsidization of private economic activity and the hierarchical relationship between the public and private sectors (Krumholz, 1984; Langton, 1983). These relationships crystallized in the urban renewal days of the 1950s and 1960s and the widely celebrated partnerships of the 1980s. Structural changes in the political economy of cities, regions, and nations altered the configuration of specific public–private partnerships, but not the fundamental relationship between the public and private sectors. These structural changes have, however, influenced the spatial development of cities and exacerbated the social problems of urban America.

The continuity reflected by public–private partnerships, despite some new formulations in recent years, is revealed by the persistence in the corporate sector's efforts to utilize government to protect private wealth, and primarily on its terms. Demands on the state to subsidize a painful restructuring process have placed added strains on public–private relations. The glue that holds these efforts together, despite these tensions, is the commitment to privatism.

Focusing on the postwar years, this chapter examines the ideology of privatism, its influence on the evolution of public–private partnerships, and their combined effects on the structural, spatial, and social development of cities in the United States, and the lives of people residing in the nation's urban neighborhoods. Perhaps the most striking feature of the evolution of American cities, to be explored in the following pages, is the uneven nature of urban development. To many, such uneven development simply reflects the "creative destruction" that Schumpeter (1942) asserted was essential for further economic progress in a capitalist economy. To others, however, the unevenness generated by unrestrained market-based private capital accumulation constitutes the core of the nation's urban problems. After reviewing the theoretical debates over privatism, various contours of uneven development and the role of partnerships in particular and privatism generally in nurturing such inequalities are examined. Industrial restructuring and uneven spatial development of urban America, along with the many social costs associated with such development, are delineated, with a particular focus on the changing dynamics of racial inequality. Drawing from data pertaining to national trends in urban development as well as developments within specific cities, the mutually reinforcing effects of race and class are explored. This chapter concludes with a discussion of recent challenges to the ideology of privatism. City dwellers, many community organizations, and a significant number of public officials have begun to develop specific policy alternatives, including more inclusive partnerships, in hopes of achieving something better than the "mess of laissez-faire."

Privatism

The American tradition of privatism was firmly established by the time of the Revolution in the 1700s. According to this tradition individual and community happiness are to be achieved through the search for personal wealth. Individual loyalties are to the family first, and the primary obligation of political authorities is to "keep the peace among individual money-makers" (Warner, 1987, p. 4). Always implicit, and frequently explicit, from colonial days to the present has been the primacy of private action and actors.

Consistent with free market, neoclassical economic theory generally, theory and policy in economic development and urban redevelopment circles have focused on private investors and markets as the appropriate dominating forces. Private economic actors are credited with being the most productive, innovative, and effective. Presumably neutral and impersonal market signals are deemed the most efficient and therefore appropriate measures for determining the allocation of economic resources. Given Adam Smith's invisible hand, the greatest good for the greatest numbers is achieved by nurturing the pursuit of private wealth.

Public policy, from this perspective, should serve private interests. Government has an important role, but one that should focus on the facilitation of private capital accumulation via the free market. (Privatism should not be confused with privatization. The former refers to a broader ideological view of the world generally and relationships between the public and private sectors in particular. The latter constitutes a specific policy of transferring ownership of particular industries or services from government agencies to private entrepreneurs.) While urban policy must acknowledge the well-known problems of big cities, it can do so best by encouraging private economic growth. A critical assumption is that the city constitutes a unitary interest and all citizens benefit from policies that enhance aggregate private economic growth (P. Peterson, 1981). Explicit distributive or allocational choices are to be avoided whenever possible, with the market determining where resources are to be directed. Public policy should augment but not supplant market forces (Barnekov et al., 1989; Levine, 1989).

The ideology of privatism has been tested in recent years by regional shifts in investment and globalization of the economy in general that have devastated entire communities (Bluestone and Harrison, 1982; Eisinger, 1988). Advocates of privatism attribute such developments primarily to technological innovation and growing international competition. They claim the appropriate response is to accommodate changes in the national and international economy. Given that redevelopment is presumed to be principally a technical rather than political process, cities must work more closely with private industry to facilitate such restructuring in order to establish more effectively their comparative advantages and market themselves in an increasingly competitive economic climate. Such part-nerships, it is assumed, will bring society's best and brightest resources (which reside in the private sector) to bear on its most severe public problems.

Where such efforts cannot succeed cities must adjust, which in some cases means to downsize, just like their counterparts in the private sector. So-called pro-people rather than pro-place policies are offered to help individuals accommodate such changes. These adjustments may well mean moving from one city and region to another. Policies that might intervene in private investment decision making or challenge market forces for the betterment of existing communities are explicitly rejected (Kasarda, 1988; McKenzie, 1979; President's Commission for a National Agenda for the Eighties, 1980).

Concretely, the policies of privatism consist of financial incentives to private economic actors that are intended to reduce factor costs of produc-tion and encourage private capital accumulation, thus stimulating investment, ultimately serving both private and public interests. The search for new manufacturing sites, retooling of obsolete facilities, and restructuring from manufacturing to services have all been facilitated by such subsidization. During the postwar years cities have been dramati-cally affected by the focus on downtown development that has generally taken the form of office towers, luxury hotels, convention centers, recre-ational facilities, and other paeans to the postindustrial society. Real estate investment itself is frequently viewed as part of the antidote to deindustrialization. All of this is justified, however, by the assumption that a revitalized economy generally and a reinvigorated downtown in particular will lead to regeneration throughout the city. As more jobs are created and space is more intensively utilized, more money is earned and spent by local residents, new property and income tax dollars bolster local treasuries, and new wealth trickles down throughout the metropolitan area. Among the specific policy tools are tax abatements, low-interest loans, land cost writedowns, tax increment finance districts (TIFS), enterprise zones, urban development action grants (UDAGs), industrial revenue bonds (IRBs), redevelopment authorities, eminent domain, and other public–private activities through which private investment is publicly subsidized. The object of such incentives, again, is the enhancement of aggregate private economic growth by which it is assumed the public needs of the city can be most effectively and efficiently met.

Privatism has been a powerful ideological force in all areas of American life. That it has dominated urban policy should come as no surprise. But the pursuit of the private city has had its costs. And the advocates of privatism have had their critics.

Responses to Privatism

The most fundamental intellectual and political challenges to privatism are directed to its central assumptions regarding the neutrality and impersonality of the market. Rather than viewing the market as a mechanism through which random decisions made by many individual willing buyers and sellers yields the most efficient production and distribution of resources for cities and society generally, it is argued that the market is an arena of conflict. Logan and Molotch (1987) observe that markets themselves are cultural artefacts bound up with human interests. Markets are structured by, and reflect differences in, wealth and power. They reinforce prevailing unequal social relations and dominant values, including a commitment to privatism. Markets are not simply neutral arbiters maximizing efficiency in production and distribution. They are social institutions firmly embedded in the broader culture of American society.

A related critique of privatism is the argument that a city does not constitute a unitary interest that can best be advanced through aggregate private economic growth, but rather a series of unequal and conflictual interests, some of which are advanced through a political process. As Stone (1987) has argued, local economic development policy represents the conscious decisions made by individuals with highly unequal power in a community in efforts by competing groups to further their own interests. Assumptions of a unitary interest or the benevolence of market-based allocation mystifies important decisions made at the local level that clearly favor some interests at the expense of others.

Development, therefore, is not a technical problem but rather a political process. As Stone concludes, "urban politics still matters" (1987, p. 4).

While economic development and urban redevelopment are political matters, one consequence of the pursuit of the private city has been a reduction in the public debate over development policy and the account-ability of public officials and other actors for the consequences of their activities. Quasi-public redevelopment authorities have provided selected private investors with responsibilities traditionally vested in the public sector. Hidden incentives have been provided through such off-budget subsidies as industrial revenue bonds and bailouts for large but failing firms. Eminent domain rights have been granted to and exercised for private interests where public interests are most vaguely identified (Barnekov et al., 1989). The beneficaries of these policies include real estate developers, commercial business interests, manufacturers, and others who view the city primarily in terms of the exchange value of its land at the expense of the majority for whom the city offers important use values as a place to live, work, and play (Logan and Molotch, 1987). But it is not just the immediate beneficiaries who share this view of local governance. As Gottdiener concluded, "The reduction of the urban vision to instrumental capital growth, it seems, gains hegemony everywhere" (Gottdiener, 1986, p. 287).

Declining accountability may be a factor contributing to a more concrete challenge to privatism. Simply put, it has not worked. That is, the array of subsidies and related supply-side incentives have not created the anticipated number of jobs or jobs for the intended recipients, tax revenues have not been stabilized as initially expected, and the urban renaissance remains, at best, a hope for the future (Barnekov et al., 1989; Center for Community Change, 1989; Levine, 1987). While not always ineffective, such incentives are not primary determinants of private investment decisions. And they often embody unintended costs resulting in minus-sum situations as public subsidies outrun subsequent public benefits (Eisinger, 1988, pp. 200–224). One reason for the disappointing results is that with the proliferation of incentives, the competitive advan-tage provided by any particular set of subsidies is quickly lost when other communities match them. The number of state location incentive programs alone increased from 840 in 1966 to 1,633 in 1985 (Eisinger, 1988, p. 19). Indeed, many states and municipalities feel obligated to offer additional incentives of acknowledged questionable value simply to keep up with their neighbors and provide symbolic assurance that they offer a good business climate. As Detroit Mayor Coleman Young observed:

> *Those are the rules and I'm going by the goddamn rules. This suicidal outthrust competition among the states has got to stop but until it does, I mean to compete. It's too bad we have a system where dog eats dog and the devil takes the hindmost. But I'm tired of taking the hindmost.* (Greider, 1978)

Ironically, one of the costs is the reduced ability of local municipalities to provide the public services that are far more critical in assuring a favorable climate for the operation of successful businesses. Tax dollars that are utilized as subsidies for private development are dollars that are not available for vital public services. In Detroit, for example, the quality of public education has declined precipitously in recent years, undercutting the ability of that city's youth to compete for jobs and the city's ability to attract employers (Thomas, 1989).

Another factor contributing to the disappointing results strikes at the heart of the ideology of privatism. As Bluestone and Harrison (1982) concluded in discussing such approaches to reindustrialization, "all share a studied unwillingness to question the extent to which conventional private ownership of industry and the more-or-less unbridled pursuit of private profit might be the causes of the problem" (1982, p. 230).

If privatism has not generated the anticipated positive outcomes, economic restructuring associated with privatism has generated a host of social costs that are either ignored or accepted by its proponents as an inevitable price to be paid for progress. Job loss and declining family income resulting from a plant closing are just the most obvious direct costs. There are also "multiplier effects." Economic stress within the family often leads to family conflicts, including physical abuse, frequently culminating in divorce. Increasing physical and medical health problems, including growing suicide rates, have been clearly connected to sudden job loss. The economic stability of entire communities and essential public services have been crippled (Bluestone and Harrison, 1982). Even the winners of the competition have suffered severe social costs. Sudden growth has generated unmanageable traffic congestion and skyrocketing housing costs often forcing families out of their homes and business to pay higher salaries for competent employees (Dreier, Schwartz and Greiner, 1988). Gentrification moves many poor people around but does little to reduce poverty. Even in Houston, the "free enterprise city," sudden private economic growth has generated serious problems in sewage and garbage disposal, flooding, air and water pollution, congestion, and related problems (Feagin, 1988). Perhaps the most destructive aspect of this "creative" process is the uneven nature of the spatial development of cities and the growing inequality associated with race and class (Bluestone and Harrison, 1988). Privatism and the economic restructuring that it has nurtured have created costs that are quite real, but not inevitable. As the critics of privatism note, they reflect political conflicts and political decisions (discussed in the following section), not natural outcomes of ultimately beneficial market forces.

The pursuit of the private city appears to have produced many ironies. Given the array of incentives, those firms intending to expand or relocate anyway often shop around for the best deal they can get. Consequently, local programs designed to leverage private investment are turned on their head. That is, the private firms leverage public funds for their own development purposes; and they can punish local governments that are not forthcoming with generous subsidies. A logical consequence of these developments is that private economic growth has become its own justification. As William E. Connolly observed:

> at every turn barriers to growth become occasions to tighten social control, to build new hedges around citizen rights, to insulate bureaucracies from popular pressures while opening them to corporate influence, to rationalize work processes, to impose austerity on vulnerable constituencies, to delay programs for environmental safety, to legitimize military adventures abroad. Growth, previously seen as the means to realization of the good life, has become a system imperative to which elements of the good life are sacrificed. (1983, pp. 23–24)

But perhaps these outcomes are not ironic. In fact, they may well be the intended results. As Barnekov et al. concluded in evaluating privatism in the 1980s, "The overriding purpose of the 'new privatism' was not the regeneration of cities but rather the adaptation of the urban landscape to the spatial requirements of a post-industrial economy" (1989, p. 12). That adaptation has been the central objective of public–private partnerships in the "postindustrial" age of urban America.

The postwar debate over privatism, like debates over redevelopment in general, have taken place within the context of dramatic structural changes in the political economy of American cities. The spatial development of urban America has clearly been influenced by these changes. In turn, the structural and spatial developments of cities have given rise to a host of social problems with which policymakers continue to wrestle. These struggles have included efforts to challenge the ideology and politics of privatism; challenges that have met with some success, including capturing the mayor's office in a few major cities. These efforts are discussed in the concluding section. The following section examines the evolving dynamics of privatism and partnerships for urban America during the postwar years, developments that have prepared the ground for challenges to privatism in recent years.

Structural, Spatial, and Social Development

Urban renewal and the prosperous postwar years

The United States emerged from World War II as a growing and internationally dominant economic power. Given its privileged structural position at that time, the end of ideology was declared and optimism for future growth and prosperity was widespread (Bell, 1960).

Yet blighted conditions within the nation's central cities posed problems for residents trapped in poverty and for local businesses threatened by conditions within and immediately surrounding the downtown business center. Recognizing the "higher uses" (i.e., more profitable for developers and related businesses) for which such land could be utilized, a policy of urban renewal evolved that brought together local business and government entities in working partnerships with the support of the federal government. At the same time, federal housing policy and highway construction stimulated homeownership and opened up the suburbs, while reinforcing the racial exclusivity of neighborhoods.

As Mollenkopf (1983) has observed, urban renewal and related federal programs reflected a political coalition of disparate groups. Local entrepreneurial Democratic politicians, along with their counterparts at the federal level, created large-scale downtown construction projects that benefited key local contractors and unions, machine politicians and reformers, and white ethnic groups along with at least some racial minorities. These emerging political alliances were clearly, though not always explicitly, committed to economic growth (particularly downtown) with the private sector as the primary engine for, and beneficiary of, that development (Mollenkopf, 1983).

Although urban renewal was launched and initially justified as an effort to improve the housing conditions of low-income urban residents, it quickly became a massive public subsidy for private business development, particularly downtown commercial real estate interests (Barnekov et al., 1989, pp. 39–48; Hays, 1985, pp. 173–191). Shopping malls, office buildings, and convention centers rather than housing became the focus of urban renewal programs. Following the lead of the Allegheny Conference on Community Development formed in Pittsburgh in 1943, coalitions of local business leaders were organized in most large cities to encourage public subsidization of downtown development. Examples include the Greater Milwaukee Committee, Central Atlanta Progress, Inc., Greater Philadelphia Movement, Cleveland Development Foundation, Detroit Renaissance, the Vault (Boston), the Blyth-Zellerback Committee (San Francisco), Greater Baltimore Committee, and Chicago Central Area Committee. Using their powers of eminent domain, city officials generally would assemble land parcels and provide land cost writedowns for private developers. In the process local business associations frequently operated as private governments as they designed and implemented plans that had dramatic public consequences but did so with little public accountability.

If such developments were justified rhetorically as meeting important public needs, indeed urban renewal took sides. Not all sides were represented in the planning process and the impact of urban renewal reflected such unequal participation (Friedman, 1968). Some people were forcefully relocated so that others could benefit. According to one estimate, by

1967 urban renewal had destroyed 404,000 housing units, most of which had been occupied by low-income tenants, while just 41,580 replacement units for low- and moderate-income families were built (Friedland, 1983, p. 85). As Chester Hartman concluded, "the aggregate benefits are private benefits that accrue to a small, select segment of the city's elite 'public,' while the costs fall on those least able to bear them" (Hartman, 1974, p. 183).

At the same time that the public sector was subsidizing downtown commercial development, it was also subsidizing homeownership and highway construction programs to stimulate suburban development. Through Federal Housing Administration (FHA), Veterans Administration (VA) and related federally subsidized and insured mortgage programs launched around the war years, long-term mortgages requiring relatively low down payments made home ownership possible for many families who previously could not afford to buy. With the federal insurance, lenders were far more willing to make such loans (Hays, 1985; Jackson, 1985). (An equally if not more compelling factor leading to the creation of these programs was the financial assistance they provided to real estate agents, contractors, financial institutions, and other housing related industries [Hays, 1985]). Since half the FHA and VA loans made during the 1950s and 1960s financed suburban housing, the federal government began, perhaps unwittingly, to subsidize the exodus from central cities to suburban rings that characterized metropolitan development during these decades (Hays, 1985, p. 215). The Interstate Highway Act of 1956, launching construction of the nation's high-speed roadway system, further subsidized and encouraged that exodus.

A significant feature of these developments was the racial exclusivity that was solidified in part because the federal government encouraged it. Through the 1940s the FHA's underwriting manuals warned of "inharmonious racial or nationality groups" and maintained that "if a neighborhood is to retain stability, it is necessary that properties shall continue to be occupied by the same social and racial classes" (Jackson, 1985, p. 208). If redlining practices originated within the nation's financial institutions, the federal government sanctioned and reinforced such discriminatory practices at a critical time in the history of suburban development. The official stance of the federal government has changed in subsequent decades, but the patterns established by these policies have proven to be difficult to alter.

During the prosperous postwar years of the 1950s and 1960s urban redevelopment strategies were shaped by public–private partnerships. But the private partner dominated as the public sector's role consisted principally of "preparing the ground for capital." Spatially, the focus was on downtown and the suburbs. Socially, the dominant feature was the creation and reinforcement of racially discriminatory dual housing markets and homogeneous urban and suburban communities. The basic patterns have persisted in subsequent years when the national economy was not so favorable.

Partnerships in an age of decline

The celebrated partnerships of the 1980s reflect an emerging effort to undermine the public sector, particularly the social safety net it has provided, and to reaffirm the "privileged position of business" (Lindblom, 1977) in the face of declining profitability brought on by globalization of the U.S. economy and its declining position in that changing marketplace. Government has a role, but again it is a subordinate one. As Bluestone and Harrison (1988) recently argued:

> Leaders may call these deals "public–private partnerships" and attempt to fold them under the ideological umbrella of laissez-faire. But they must be seen for what they really are: the re-allocation of public resources to fit a new agenda. That agenda is no longer redistribution, or even economic growth as conventionally defined. Rather, that agenda entails nothing less than the restructuring of the relations of production and the balance of power in the American economy. In pursuit of these dubious goals, the public sector continues to play a crucial role. (pp. 107–108)

Global domination by the U.S. economy peaked roughly 25 years following the conclusion of World War II. After more than two decades of substantial economic growth subsequent to the war, international competition, particularly from Japan and West Germany but also from several Third World countries, began to challenge the U.S. position as productivity and profitability at home began to decline (Bluestone and Harrison, 1988; Bowles, Gordon, and Weisskopf, 1983; Reich, 1983). As both a cause and effect of the general decline beginning in the late 1960s and early 1970 the U.S. economy experienced significant shifts out of manufacturing and into service industries. Between 1970 and 1987 the U.S. economy lost 1.9 million manufacturing jobs and gained 13.9 million in the service sector (Mishel and Simon, 1988 p. 25). Perhaps even more important than the overall trajectory of decline has been the response to these developments on the part of corporate America and its partners in government. Such economic and political restructuring provided the context that has shaped the spatial development of cities and, in turn, the quality of life in urban America.

Between 1960 and 1980 the U.S. share of the world's economic output declined from 35 percent to 22 percent (Reich, 1987, p. 44). As profitability began to decline, U.S. corporations responded with an array of tactics aimed at generating short-term profits at the expense of long-term productivity (Hayes and Abernathy, 1980).

Rather than directing investment into manufacturing plants and equipment or research and development to improve the productivity of U.S. industry, corporate America pursued what Robert B. Reich labeled "paper entrepreneurialism" (Reich, 1983, pp. 140–172). That is, capital was expended on mergers and acquisitions, speculative real estate ventures, and other investments in which "some money will change hands, and no new wealth will be created" (Reich, 1983, p. 157). Rather than strategic planning for long-term productivity growth, the pursuit of short-term gain has been the objective.

Reducing labor costs has constituted a second component of an overall strategy aimed at short-term profitability. A number of tactics have been utilized to reduce the wage bill including decentralizing and globalizing production, expanding part-time work at the expense of full-time positions, contracting out work from union to non-union shops, aggressively fighting union organizing campaigns, implementing two-tiered wage scales, and outright demands for wage concessions. Rather than viewing human capital as a resource in which to invest to secure productivity in the long run, labor has increasingly been viewed as a cost of production to be minimized in the interests of short-term profitability (Bluestone and Harrison, 1988).

If production has been conceded by corporate America, control has not. Administration and a range of professional services have been consolidated and have grown considerably in recent years. If steel, automobile, and electronics production has shifted overseas, legal and accounting – along with other financial and related services – have expanded. Other service industries that have also grown include health care, state and local government, and personal services. Such developments lead some observers to dismiss the significance of a decline in manufacturing and celebrate the emergence of a postindustrial society (Becker, 1986; Bell, 1973). Yet at least half of those jobs in service industries are dependent on manufacturing production, though not necessarily production within the United States. Service and manufacturing are clearly linked; one cannot supplant the other. The health of both manufacturing and services depend on their mutual development. A service economy, without a manufacturing base to service, is proving to be a prescription for overall economic decline within those communities losing their industrial base (Cohen and Zysman, 1987).

True to the spirit of privatism, government has nurtured these developments through various forms of assistance to the private sector. Federal tax laws encourage investment in new facilities, particularly overseas, rather than reinvestment in older but still usable equipment, thus exacerbating the velocity of capital mobility (Bluestone and Harrison, 1982). State and local governments have offered their own inducements to encourage the pirating of employers in all industries ranging from heavy manufacturing to religious organizations (Eisinger, 1988; Goodman, 1979). Further inducements have been offered to the private sector through reductions in various regulatory functions of government. Civil rights, labor law, occupational health and safety rules, and environmental protection were enforced less aggressively in the 1980s than had been the case in the immediately preceding decades (Chambers, 1987; Taylor, 1989). If the expansion of such financial incentives and reductions in regulatory activity were initially justified in terms of the public benefits that would accrue from a revitalized private sector, in recent years unbridled competition and minimal government have become their own justification and not simply means to some other end (Bender, 1983; Connolly, 1983; Smith and Judd, 1984).

The impact of these structural developments is clearly visible on the spatial development of American cities. Accommodating these national and international trends, local partnerships have nurtured downtown development to service the growing service economy. If steel is no longer produced in Pittsburgh, the Golden Triangle has risen as the city's major employers now include financial, educational, and health care institutions (Sbragia, 1989). If auto workers have lost jobs by the thousands in Detroit, the Renaissance Center, a major medical center, and the Joe Louis Sports Arena have been built downtown (Darden, Hill, Thomas and Thomas, 1987). Most major breweries have left Milwaukee, but the Grand Avenue Shopping Mall, several office buildings for legal, financial, and insurance companies, a new Performing Arts Center, and the Bradley Center housing the professional basketball Milwaukee Bucks are growing up in the central business district (Norman, 1989). With the US economy deindustrializing and corporations consolidating administrative functions, downtown development to accommodate these changes is booming. These initiatives are more ambitious than urban renewal efforts that focused on rescuing downtown real estate, but many of the actors are the same and the fundamental relationships between the public and private entities prevail. In city after city such developments are initiated by the private side of local partnerships, usually with substantial public economic development assistance in the forms of UDAGs, IRBs, and other subsidies.

As cities increasingly become centers of administration, they experience an influx of relatively high-paid professional workers, the majority of whom are suburban residents (Levine, 1989, p. 26). Despite some pockets of gentrification, most of the increasing demand for housing for such workers has been in the suburbs. Retail and commercial businesses have expanded into the suburbs to service that growing population. To the extent that metropolitan areas have experienced an expansion of existing manufacturing facilities or have attracted new facilities, this growth has also disproportionately gone to the suburbs (Squires, Bennett, McCourt and Nyden, 1987; White, Reynolds, McMahon, and Paetsch, 1989). Extending a trend that goes back before the war years, suburban communities have continued to grow.

The city of Chicago, often labeled the prototypical American industrial city, is also illustrative of the postindustrial trends. Between 1979 and 1987 downtown investment exceeded $6 billion as parking lots and skid row hotels have been replaced with office towers, up-scale restaurants and shops, and luxury housing (Schmidt, 1987). Yet overall during the postwar decades, manufacturing employment in the city has been cut in half while it tripled in the suburban ring. Total employment in the city of Chicago in the 1970s dropped by 14 percent while it increased by almost 45 percent in the suburbs (Squires et al., 1987). Continuation of downtown and suburban growth coupled with decline of urban communities in between led *Chicago Tribune* columnist Clarence Page to describe his city as having a "dumbbell economy" (personal communication, March 19, 1987).

Throughout urban America, the rise of service industry jobs has fueled downtown and suburban development while the loss of manufacturing jobs has devastated blue-collar urban communities. Such uneven development is not simply the logical or natural outcome of impersonal market forces. The "supply-side" revolution at the federal level with the concomitant paper entrepreneurialism in private industry, the array of subsidies offered by state and local governments, and other forms of public intervention into the workings of the economy and the spatial development of cities, reveal the centrality of politics. As Mollenkopf concluded in reference to the postindustrial transformation of the largest central cities in the United States, "while its origins may be found in economic forces, federal urban development programs and the local progrowth coalitions which implemented them have magnified and channeled those economic forces" (Mollenkopf, 1983, p. 19). Uneven development therefore reflects conscious decisions made in both the public and private sectors in accordance with the logic of privatism, to further certain interests at the expense of others. Ideology has remained very much alive. Consequently, serious social costs have been paid.

Many of the social costs of both sudden economic decline and dramatic growth have been fully documented. As indicated above they include a range of economic and social strains for families, mental and physical health difficulties for current and former employees, fiscal crises for cities, and a range of environmental and community development problems. Among the more intangible yet clearly most consequential costs have been a reduction in the income of the average family and increasing inequality among wage earners and their families. Uneven economic and spatial development of cities has yielded unequal access to income and wealth for city residents.

For approximately 30 years after World War II family income increased and the degree of income inequality remained fairly constant. These trends turned around in the mid 1970s. Between 1977 and 1988 the vast majority of Americans experienced a decline in the buying power of their family incomes. Families in the lower 80 percent of the income distribution (four out of five families) were able to purchase fewer goods with their incomes by the end of the 1980s than they were able to do just 10 years earlier. The most severely affected were those in the bottom 10th who experienced a drop of 14.8 percent. Only those in the top 10th experienced a significant increase that, for them, was 16.5 percent. (Families in the 9th decile experienced a 1.0 percent increase.) Most of this increase went to families in the upper 1 percent who enjoyed a gain of 49.8 percent. While GNP grew during these years and the purchasing power of the average family income increased by 2.2 percent, the top 20 percent received all of the net increase and more, reflecting the increasing inequality. Consequently, when adjusted for inflation, the lower 80 percent experienced a net decrease in the purchasing power of their family incomes (Gottdiener, 1990; Levy, 1987; Mishel and Simon, 1988, p. 6).

This growing inequality in the nation's income distribution reflects two basic trends. First is the shift from relatively high-paid manufacturing positions to lower paid service jobs. While service sector jobs include some highly paid professional positions, the vast majority of service jobs are low-paid, unskilled jobs. To illustrate, the Bureau of Labor Statistics projects an increase of approximately 250,000 computer systems analysts between 1986 and 2000 but more than 2.5 million jobs for waiters, waitresses, chambermaids and doormen, clerks, and custodians. There have also been income declines within industrial sectors reflecting the second trend, noted above, which is increasingly successful efforts by U.S. corporations to reduce the wage bill (Bluestone and Harrison, 1988).

Perhaps more problematic has been the growing racial gap. Racial disparities did decline in the first two decades following the war. Between 1947 and 1971 median black family income rose gradually from 51 percent to 61 percent of the white median. It fluctuated for a few years, reaching 61 percent again in 1975 but dropping consistently to 56 percent in 1987 (U.S. Bureau of the Census, 1976, 1980 [Table H7], 1989). For black men between the ages of 25 and 64 the gap improved between 1960 and 1980 from 49 percent to 64 percent, but dropped to 62 percent by 1987 (Jaynes and Williams, 1989, p. 28). Within cities, and in particular big cities, the racial gaps have grown larger. Between 1968 and 1986 black median family income in metropolitan areas dropped from 63.7 percent to 57.4 percent of the white median. And in metropolitan areas with more than one million people, the ratio within the central city dropped from 69.7 percent to 59.0 percent (Squires, 1991).

Racial disparities in family wealth are even more dramatic. The median wealth of black households is 9 percent of the white household median. At each level of income and educational attainment, blacks control far fewer assets then do whites. Among those with monthly incomes below $900, black net worth is 1 percent that of whites with similar incomes.

Education helps but does not close the gap. Among college educated householders 35 years of age or less with incomes of more than $48,000 annually, black net worth is 93 percent that of whites (Jaynes and Williams, 1989, pp. 276, 292).

Not only are blacks and whites separated economically, but racial segregation in the nation's housing markets persists. During the 1970s the degree of racial isolation in the nation's major cities remained virtually unchanged according to several statistical measures, leading two University of Chicago sociologists to identify 10 cities as "hypersegregated" (Massey and Denton, 1987, 1989). The degree of segregation differs little if at all by income for racial minorities. Among the consequences are unequal access to areas where jobs are being created and inequitable distribution of public services including education for minorities, and heightened racial tensions and conflicts for all city residents (Orfield, 1988).

Not surprisingly, it is predominantly black neighborhoods that have been most adversely affected by the uneven development of U.S. cities. For example, in Chicago between 1963 and 1977 the city experienced a 29 percent job loss but predominantly black communities lost 45 percent of all jobs. The increasing incidence of crime, drug abuse, teenage pregnancy, school dropout rates, and other indicators of so-called underclass behavior are clearly linked to the deindustrialization and disinvestment of city neighborhoods outside the central business district (Harris and Wilkins, 1988; Wilson, 1987).

Uneven structural and spatial development of cities adversely affects racial minorities. But racial inequalities in U.S. cities are not simply artefacts of those structural and spatial developments. Racism has its own dynamic. Blacks who have earned all the trappings of middle-class life in terms of a professional occupation, four-bedroom house, and designer clothes are still routinely subject to demeaning behavior that takes such forms as name calling on the streets by anonymous passers-by, discourteous service in restaurants and stores, and harassment on the part of police, all simply because of their race (Feagin, undated). Racially-motivated violence in Bensenhurst and Howard Beach, Sambo parties and other racially derogatory behavior on several college campuses, and letter bombings of civil rights lawyers and judges confirm the continuity of vicious racism. The dynamics of class and race remain very difficult to disentangle, but the effects of both are all too real in urban America.

Alternatives to the Pursuit of the Private City

Privatism and the policies that flow logically from that ideology have benefited those shaping redevelopment policy, including members of most public–private partnerships. But these policies have not stimulated redevelopment of cities generally. Structural, spatial, and social imbalances remain and are reinforced by the dynamics of privatism. To address the well-known social problems of urban America successfully, policies must be responsive to the structural and spatial forces impinging on cities. At least fragmented challenges to privatism have emerged in local redevelopment struggles in recent years. Alternative conceptions of development, the nature of city life, and human relations in general have been articulated and have had some impact on redevelopment efforts.

In several cities community groups have organized, and in some cases captured the mayor's office, in efforts to pursue more balanced redevelopment policies (Clavel, 1986). Explicitly viewing the city in terms of its use value rather than as a profit center for the local growth machine, initiatives have been launched to democratize the redevelopment process and to assure more equitable outcomes of redevelopment policy. Among the specific ingredients of this somewhat inchoate challenge to privatism are programs to retain and attract diverse industries including manufacturing, targeting of initiatives to those neighborhoods and population groups most in need, human capital development, and other public investments in the infrastructure of cities. A critical dimension of many of these programs is a conscious effort to bring neighborhood groups and residents, long victimized by uneven development, into the planning and implementation process as integral parts of urban partnerships.

When Harold Washington was elected mayor of Chicago in 1983, he launched a redevelopment plan that incorporated several of these components. The planning actually began during the campaign when people from various racial groups, economic classes, and geographic areas were brought together to identify goals and policies to achieve them under a Washington administration. Shortly after the election Washington released *Chicago Works Together: Chicago Development Plan 1984*, which reflected that involvement. Explicitly advocating a strategic approach to pursuing development with equity, the plan articulated five major goals: increased job opportunities for Chicagoans; balanced growth; neighborhood development via partnerships and coordinated investment; enhanced public participation in decision making; and pursuit of a regional, state, and national legislative agenda (*Chicago Works Together*, 1984, p. 1). As development initiatives proceeded under Washington, strategic plans were implemented that involved industrial and geographic sector-specific approaches to retain manufacturing and regenerate older neighborhoods, affirmative action plans to bring more minorities and women into city government as employees and as city contractors, provision of business incentives that were conditioned on locational choices and other public needs, and a planning process that involved community groups, public officials, and private industry.

Specific tactics included funding the Midwest Center for Labor

Research to create an early warning system for the purposes of identifying potential plant closings and where feasible, interventions that would forestall the closing. Linked development programs were negotiated with specific developers to spread the benefits of downtown development. Planned manufacturing district legislation was enacted to control conversion of industrial zones to commercial and residential purposes, thus retaining some manufacturing jobs that would otherwise be lost. As the widely publicized "Council Wars" attested, Washington encountered strong resistance to many of his proposals (Bennett, 1988). The efforts of his administration demonstrated, however, that uneven urban development was not simply the outcome of natural or neutral market forces. Politics, including the decisions of public officials, mattered and those decisions under Washington were responsive to both public need and market signals (Giloth and Betancur, 1988; Mier, 1989; Mier, Moe, and Sherr, 1986).

In 1983 Boston also held a significant mayoral election. At the height of the Massachusetts miracle the city's economy was prospering and Raymond L. Flynn was elected with a mandate to "share the prosperity." Several policies have been implemented in order to do so.

Boston's strong real estate market in the early 1980s led to a shortage of low- and middle-income housing. Flynn played a central role in the implementation of a linkage program that took effect one month before he was elected. Under the linkage program a fee was levied on downtown development projects to assist construction of housing for the city's low- and middle-income residents. Shortly after taking office, the Flynn administration negotiated inclusionary zoning agreements with individual housing developers to provide below-market rate units in their housing developments or to pay an "in lieu of" fee into the linkage fund. To further alleviate the housing shortage, in 1983 the Boston Housing Partnership was formed to assist community development corporations in rehabilitating and managing housing units in their neighborhoods. The partnership's board includes executives from leading banks, utility companies, and insurance firms; city and state housing officials; and directors of local community development corporations.

Boston also established a residents job policy under which developers and employers are required to target city residents, minorities, and women for construction jobs and in the permanent jobs created by these developments. These commitments hold for publicly subsidized developments and, in an agreement reached by the mayor's office, the Greater Boston Real Estate Board, the Buildings Trade Council, and leaders of the city's minority community, for private developments as well.

The Boston Compact represents another creative partnership in that city. Under this program the public schools agreed to make commitments to improve the schools' performance in return for the business community's agreement to give hiring preferences to their graduates. Schools have designed programs to encourage students to stay in school, develop their academic abilities, and learn job readiness skills. Several local employers, including members of the Vault, have agreed to provide jobs paying more than the minimum wage and financial assistance for college tuition to students who succeed in the public schools.

As in Chicago, the Flynn administration in Boston has consciously pursued balanced development and efforts to bring previously disenfranchised groups into the development process. The specific focus has been on housing and jobs, but the broader objective has been to share the benefits of development generally throughout the city (Dreier, 1989).

The Community Reinvestment Act (CRA) passed by Congress in 1977 has led to partnerships for urban reinvestment in cities across the nation. The CRA requires federally regulated banks and savings and loans to assess and be responsive to the credit needs of their service areas. Failure to do so can result in lenders being denied charters, new branches, or other corporate changes they intend to make. Neighborhood groups can challenge lenders' applications for such business operations with federal regulators, thus providing lenders with incentives to meet their CRA obligations (Potomac Institute, 1980). Subsequently, community groups and lenders have negotiated CRA agreements in more than 125 cities totaling approximately $6 billion in neighborhood reinvestment (Bradford, 1989). Examples include a $100-million loan pool created by 46 California banks to finance low-income housing, a $200-million commitment by Chase Manhatten Bank of New York for a community development fund, and a $245-million agreement negotiated by Chicago housing and neighborhood groups with several Chicago area lenders for various housing and business development projects (Guskind, 1989).

A unique lending partnership was created in Milwaukee in 1989. In response to the 1989 study finding Milwaukee to have the nation's highest racial disparity in mortgage loan rejection rates, the city's Democratic Mayor and Republican Governor created a committee to find ways to increase lending in the city's minority community. The Fair Lending Action Committee (FLAC) (1989) included lenders, lending regulators, real estate agents, community organizers, civil rights leaders, a city alderman, and others. An ambitious set of recommendations was unanimously agreed to in its report *Equal Access to Mortgage Lending: The Milwaukee Plan.* The key recommendation in the report was that area lenders would direct 13 percent of all residential, commercial real estate, and business loans to racial minorities by 1991. (After much debate the 13 percent figure was agreed to because that was the current minority representation in the population of the four-county Milwaukee metropolitan area.) Several low-interest loan programs were proposed to be financed and administered by lenders, city officials, and neighborhood groups. Fair housing training programs were recommended for all segments of the housing industry including lenders, real estate agents, insurers, and appraisers. The lending community was advised to provide $75,000 to support housing counseling centers that assist first-time home buyers. The city, county, and state were called upon to consider a linked deposit program to assure that public funds would go to those lenders responsive to the credit needs of the entire community. Specific recommendations were made to increase minority employment in the housing industry. And a permanent FLAC was called for to monitor progress in implementing the report's recommendations. The report concluded:

> There is a racial gap in mortgage lending in the Milwaukee metropolitan area. Implementation of these recommendations will be a major step in eliminating that gap. The Fair Lending Action Committee constitutes a partnership that is committed to the realization of fair lending and the availability of adequate mortgage loans and finance capital for all segments of the Milwaukee community. Building on the relationships that have been established among lenders, public officials, and community groups, neighborhood revitalization throughout the city and prosperity throughout the entire metropolitan area can and will be achieved. (Fair Lending Action Committee, 1989: 14)

At the press conference releasing the report, Governor Tommy G. Thompson "eloquently" stated, "Neither I nor the Mayor are the kind of guys who commission reports only to see them collect dust." The lenders indicated their own institutions and the local trade associations would support the report and implement its recommendations. Representatives of community groups, whose own reports have gathered much dust on bureaucrats' book cases, nodded approvingly in an expression of most cautious optimism.

Release of the report concluded what had been several months of contentious debates. The unanimous support for the report expressed by committee members at the conclusion did not negate the differences of opinion that prevailed or the fact that compromises were made in the interest of a show of unity. Yet the very existence of this wide-ranging report offers some additional hope for revitalization in Milwaukee. What remains to be seen is the extent of implementation.

These diverse initiatives are illustrative of experiments being launched in small towns and large cities in all regions of the United States. While they constitute an array of programs addressing a variety of problems, there are important underlying commonalities. They are responsive to the structural and spatial underpinnings of critical urban social problems. They are premised on a commitment to growth with equity; the notion that economic productivity and social justice can be mutually reinforcing. And the objective is to make cities more liveable, not just more profitable. A more progressive city is certainly not inevitable, but these efforts are vivid reminders that the major impediments have as much to do with politics as markets.

Beyond Laissez-Faire?

The trajectory of future redevelopment activity is blurred. The ideology of privatism is being challenged. Experiments with more progressive policies have occurred. But no linear path in the overall direction of public–private partnerships in particular or urban redevelopment in general has emerged. Harold Washington was soon followed by a Daley in Chicago. Boston's economy in the early 1990s does not look as promising as it did in the early 1980s and the demand for more incentives to the business community is getting louder in the wake of the Massachusetts miracle (personal communication, Peter Dreier of the Boston Redevelopment Authority, January 6, 1990). Milwaukee's mayor frequently expresses concern about the local business climate as civil rights groups challenge him to respond to the city's racial problems. Redevelopment remains a highly contentious political matter.

The grip of privatism has waned since the height of the Reagan years. HUD abuses, the savings and loan bailout, insider trading scandals, and other manifestations of the excesses of the pursuit of personal wealth serve as reminders of the importance of a public sector role beyond subsidization of private capital accumulation. Experiments in strategic planning to achieve balanced growth in Chicago, to share the prosperity in Boston, and to expand memberships in partnerships in Milwaukee and elsewhere demonstrate the capacity to conceive a different image of the city and the ability to implement programs in hopes of realizing that image. Yet as Warner concluded, "The quality which above all else characterizes our urban inheritance is privatism" (1987, p. 202). For better or for worse, that remains the bedrock on which future plans will be built.

References

Barnekov, T., Boyle, R., and Rich, D. (1989). *Privatism and Urban Policy in Britain and the United States.* New York: Oxford University Press.

Bennett, L. (1988). Harold Washington's Chicago: Placing a progressive city administration in context. *Social Policy, 19*(2), 22–28.

Becker, G. (1986, January 27). The prophets of doom have a dismal record. *Business Week,* p. 22.

Bell, D. (1960). *The End of Ideology.* New York: Free Press.

Bell, D. (1973). *The Coming of Post-industrial Society: A venture of social forecasting.* New York: Basic Books.

Bender, T. (1983). The end of the city? *Democracy, 3* (Winter), 8–20.

Bluestone, B., and Harrison, B. (1982). *The Deindustrialization Of America: Plant closings, community abandonment, and the dismantling of basic industry.* New York: Basic Books.

Bluestone, B., and Harrison, B. (1988). *The Great U-turn: Corporate restructuring and the polarizing of America.* New York: Basic Books.

Bowles, S., Gordon, D. M., and Weisskopf, T. E. (1983). *Beyond the Waste Land: A democratic alternative to economic decline.* Garden City, NY: Anchor Press/Doubleday.

Bradford, C. (1989). Reinvestment: The quiet revolution. *The Neighborhood Works, 12*(4), 1, 22–26.

Center for Community Change. (1989). *Bright Promises, Questionable Results: An examination of how well three government subsidy programs created jobs.* Washington, DC: Center for Community Change.

Chambers, J. L. (1987). The law and black Americans: Retreat from civil rights. In J. Dewart (ed.), *The State of Black America 1987* (pp. 18–30). New York: National Urban League.

Chicago Works Together: Chicago development plan 1984. (1984). City of Chicago.

Clavel, P. (1986). *The Progressive City: Planning and participation, 1969–1884.* New Brunswick, NJ: Rutgers University Press.

Cohen, S. S., and Zysman, J. (1987). *Manufacturing Matters: The myth of the post-industrial economy.* New York: Basic Books.

Connolly, W. E. (1983). Progress, growth, and pessimism in America. *Democracy, 3*(Fall): 22–31.

Darden, J., Hill, R. C., Thomas, J., and Thomas, R. (1987). *Detroit: Race and uneven development.* Philadelphia: Temple University Press.

Davis, P. (1986). *Public-private Partnerships: Improving urban life.* New York: Academy of Political Science.

Dreier, P. (1989). Economic growth and economic justice in Boston: Populist housing and jobs policies. In G. D. Squires (ed.), *Unequal Partnerships: The political economy of urban redevelopment in postwar America* (pp. 35–58). New Brunswick, NJ: Rutgers University Press.

Dreier, P., Schwartz, D. C., and Greiner, A. (1988). What every business can do about housing. *Harvard Business Review, 66*(5), 52–61.

Eisinger, P. K. (1988). *The Rise of the Entrepreneurial State: State and local economic development policy in the United States.* Madison: University of Wisconsin Press.

Fair Lending Action Committee. (1989). *Equal Access to Mortgage Lending: The Milwaukee plan.* Report to Mayor John Norquist and Governor Tommy G. Thompson (October).

Feagin, J. R. (1988). *Free Enterprise City: Houston in political and economic perspective.* New Brunswick, NJ: Rutgers University Press.

Feagin, J. R. (undated). The continuing significance of race: The black middle class in public places. Unpublished manuscript.

Friedland, R. (1983). *Power and Crisis in the City: Corporations, unions and urban policy.* New York: Schocken.

Friedman, L. M. (1968). *Government and Slum Housing: A century of frustration.* Chicago: Rand McNally.

Giloth, R. and Betancur, J. (1988). Where downtown meets neighborhood: Industrial displacement in Chicago, 1978–1987. *Journal of the American Planning Association, 54*(3), 279–290.

Goodman, R. (1979). *The Last Entrepreneurs: America's regional wars for jobs and dollars.* Boston: South End Press.

Gottdiener, M. (1986). Retrospect and prospect in urban crisis theory. In M. Gottdiener (ed.), *Cities in Stress: A new look at the urban crisis* (pp. 277–291). Beverly Hills, CA: Sage.

Gottdiener, M. (1990). Crisis theory and state-financed capital: The new conjuncture in the USA. *International Journal of Urban and Regional Research, 14*(3), 383–404.

Greider, W. (1978). Detroit's streetwise mayor plays key role in city's turnaround. *Cleveland Plain Dealer* (July 3), cited in T. Swanstrom. (1985). *The Crisis of Growth Politics: Cleveland, Kucinich, and the challenge of urban populism.* Philadelphia: Temple University Press.

Guskind, R. (1989). Thin red line. *National Journal, 21*(43), 2639–2643.

Harris, F., and Wilkins, R. W. (eds). (1988). *Quiet Riots: Race and poverty in the United States.* New York: Pantheon.

Hartman, C. (1974). *Yerba Buena: Land grab and community resistance in San Francisco.* San Francisco: Glide.

Hayes, R. H., and Abernathy, W. J. (1980, July/August). Managing our way to economic decline. *Harvard Business Review, 58,* 67–77.

Hays, R. A. (1985). *The Federal Government & Urban Housing: Ideology and change in public policy.* Albany: SUNY Press.

Jackson, K. T. (1985). *Crabgrass Frontier: The suburbanization of the United States.* New York: Oxford University Press.

Jaynes, G. D., and Williams, R. M. (eds). (1989). *A Common Destiny: Blacks and American society.* Washington, DC: National Academy Press.

Kasarda, J. (1988). Economic restructuring and America's urban dilemma. In M. Dogan and J. Kasarda (eds), *The Metropolis Era: Vol. 1. A world of giant cities* (pp. 56–84). Newbury Park: Sage.

Krumholz, N. (1984). Recovery of cities: An alternate view. In P. R. Porter and D. Sweet (eds), *Rebuilding America's Cities: Roads to recovery* (pp. 173–192). New Brunswick, NJ: Center for Urban Policy Research.

Langton, S. (1983). Public-private partnerships: Hope or hoax? *National Civic Review, 72* (May), 256–261.

Levine, M. V. (1987). Downtown redevelopment as an urban growth strategy: A critical appraisal of the Baltimore Renaissance. *Journal of Urban Affairs, 9*(2), 103–123.

Levine, M. V. (1989). The politics of partnership: Urban redevelopment since 1945. In G. D. Squires (ed), *Unequal Partnerships: The political economy of urban redevelopment in postwar America* (pp. 12–34). New Brunswick, NJ: Rutgers University Press.

Levy, F. (1987). *Dollars and Dreams: The changing American income distribution.* New York: Russell Sage.

Lindblom, C. E. (1977). *Politics and Markets: The world's political-economic systems.* New York: Basic Books.

Logan, J. R., and Molotch, H. L. (1987). *Urban Fortunes: The political economy of place.* Berkeley: University of California Press.

Massey, D. S., and Denton, N. A. (1987). Trends in the residential segregation of blacks, Hispanics, and Asians. *American Sociological Review, 52*(6), 802–825.

Massey, D. S., and Denton, N. A. (1989). Hypersegregation in U.S. metropolitan areas: Black and Hispanic segregation along five dimensions. *Demography, 26*(3), 373–391.

McKenzie, R. (1979). *Restrictions on Business Mobility: A study in political rhetoric and economic reality.* Washington, DC: American Enterprise Institute.

Mier, R. (1989). Neighborhood and region: An experiential basis for understanding. *Economic Development Quarterly, 3*(2), 169–174.

Mier, R., Moe, K. J., and Sherr, I. (1986). Strategic planning and the pursuit of reform, economic development, and equity. *Journal of the American Planning Association, 52*(3), 299–309.

Mishel, L., and Simon, J. (1988). *The State of Working America.* Washington, DC: Economic Policy Institute.

Mollenkopf, J. H. (1983). *The Contested City.* Princeton, NJ: Princeton University Press.

Norman, J. (1989). Congenial Milwaukee: A segregated city. In G. D. Squires (ed.), *Unequal Partnerships: The Political economy of urban redevelopment in postwar America* (pp. 178–201). New Brunswick, NJ: Rutgers University Press.

Orfield, G. (1988). Separate societies: Have the Kerner warnings come true? In F. R. Harris and W. Wilkins (eds), *Quiet Riots: Race and poverty in the United States* (pp. 100–122). New York: Pantheon.

Peterson, G. and Lewis, C. (ed.). (1986). *Reagan and the Cities.* Washington, DC: The Urban Institute.

Peterson, P. E. (1981). *City Limits.* Chicago: University of Chicago Press.

Porter, D. R. (1989). Balancing the interests in public/private partnerships. *Urban Land, 48*(5), 36–37.

Potomac Institute. (1980). *Lender's guide to fair mortgage policies.* Washington, DC: Author.

President's Commission for a National Agenda for the Eighties. (1980). *A National Agenda for the Eighties.* Washington, DC: Government Printing Office.

Reich, R. B. (1983). *The Next American Frontier.* New York: Times Books.

Reich, R. B. (1987). *Tales of a New America.* New York: Times Books.

Sbragia, A. (1989). The Pittsburgh model of economic development: Partnership, responsiveness, and indifference. In G.D. Squires (ed.), *Unequal Partnerships: The political economy of urban redevelopment in postwar America* (pp. 103–120). New Brunswick, NJ: Rutgers University Press.

Schmidt, W. (1987, October 11). U.S. downtowns: No longer downtrodden. *The New York Times.*

Schumpeter, J. (1942). *Capitalism, Socialism and Democracy.* New York: Harper & Row.

Smith, M. P., and Judd, D. R. (1984). American cities: The production of ideology. In M. P. Smith and D. R. Judd (eds), *Cities in Transformation: Class, capital, and the state* (pp. 177–196). Beverly Hills, CA: Sage.

Squires, G. D. (1991). Deindustrialization, economic democracy, and equal opportunity: The changing context of race relations in urban America. *Comparative Urban and Community Research, 3,* 188–215.

Squires, G. D., Bennett, L., McCourt, K., and Nyden, P. (1987). *Chicago: Race, class, and the response to urban decline.* Philadelphia: Temple University Press.

Stone, C. N. (1987). The study of the politics of urban development. In C. N. Stone and H. T. Sanders (eds), *The Politics of Urban Development* (pp. 3–22). Lawrence: University of Kansas Press.

Taylor, W. L. (1989). Special report: Supreme Court decisions do grave damage to equal employment opportunity law. *Civil Rights Monitor*, 4(2), 1–28.

Thomas, J. M. (1989). Detroit: The centrifugal city. In G. D. Squires (ed.), *Unequal Partnerships: The political economy of urban redevelopment in postwar America* (pp. 142–160). New Brunswick, NJ: Rutgers University Press.

U.S. Bureau of the Census. (1976). *The Statistical History of the United States: From colonial times to the present.* New York: Basic Books.

U.S. Bureau of the Census. (1980). *Structural Equipment and Household Characteristics of Housing Units.* Washington, DC: Government Printing Office.

U.S. Bureau of the Census. (1989). *Statistical Abstract of the United States: 1989.* Washington, DC: Government Printing Office.

Warner, S. B. Jr (1987). *The Private City: Philadelphia in three periods of its growth.* Philadelphia: University of Pennsylvania Press.

White, S. B., Reynolds, P. D., McMahon, W., and Paetsch, J. (1989). *City and Suburban Impacts of Industrial Change in Milwaukee, 1978–87.* Milwaukee: University of Wisconsin-Milwaukee, The Urban Research Center.

Wilson, W. J. (1987). *The Truly Disadvantaged: The inner city, the underclass, and public policy.* Chicago: University of Chicago Press.

12

The City as a Growth Machine

John R. Logan
and Harvey L. Molotch

Traditional urban research has had little relevance to the day-to-day activities of the place-based elites whose priorities affect patterns of land use, public budgets, and urban social life. It has not even been apparent from much of the scholarship of urban social science that place is a market commodity that can produce wealth and power for its owners, and that this might explain why certain people take a keen interest in the ordering of urban life.

Research on local elites has been preoccupied with the question "Who governs?" (or "Who rules?"). Are the politically active citizens of a city split into diverse and competing interest groups, or are they members of a coordinated oligarchy? Empirical evidence of visible cleavage, such as disputes on a public issue, has been accepted as evidence of pluralistic competition (Banfield, 1961; Dahl, 1961). Signs of cohesion, such as common membership in voluntary and policy groups, have been used to support the alternative view (see Domhoff, 1970).

We believe that the question of who governs or rules has to be asked in conjunction with the equally central question "For what?" With rare exceptions (see Smith and Keller, 1983), one issue consistently generates consensus among local elite groups and separates them from people who

Reprinted by permission from John Logan and Harvey Molotch, 1987, *Urban Fortunes*.

use the city principally as a place to live and work: the issue of growth. For those who count, the city is a growth machine, one that can increase aggregate rents and trap related wealth for those in the right position to benefit. The desire for growth creates consensus among a wide range of elite groups, no matter how split they might be on other issues. Thus the disagreement on some or even most public issues does not necessarily indicate any fundamental disunity, nor do changes in the number or variety of actors on the scene (what Clark [1968] calls "decentralization") affect the basic matter. It does not even matter that elites often fail to achieve their growth goal; with virtually all places in the same game, some elites will inevitably lose no matter how great their effort (Lyon et al., 1981; Krannich and Humphrey, 1983).

Although they may differ on which particular strategy will best succeed, elites use their growth consensus to eliminate any alternative vision of the purpose of local government or the meaning of community. The issues that reach public agendas (and are therefore available for pluralists' investigations) do so precisely because they are matters on which elites have, in effect, agreed to disagree (Molotch and Lester, 1974, 1975; see Schattschneider, 1960). Only under rather extraordinary circumstances is this consensus endangered.

For all the pluralism Banfield (1961) uncovered in Chicago, he found no disagreement with the idea that growth was good. Indeed, much of the dissension he did find, for example, on where to put the new convention center, was part of a dispute over how growth should be internally distributed. In his studies of cities on both sides of the southern U.S. border, D'Antonio found that when community "knowledgeables" were "asked to name the most pressing problems facing their respective cities," they cited finding sufficient water for both farming and urban growth (Form and D'Antonio, 1970:439). Whitt (1982) found that in formulating positions on California transportation policies, elites carefully coordinated not only the positions they would take but also the amount of money each would give toward winning relevant initiative campaigns. Thus on growth infrastructure, the elites were united.

Similarly, it was on the primacy of such growth and development issues that Hunter found Atlanta's elites to be most unified, both at the time of his first classic study and during its replication twenty years later (Hunter, 1953, 1980). Hunter (1953:214) reports, "They could speak of nothing else" (cited in Domhoff, 1983:169). In his historical profiles of Dallas and Fort Worth, Melosi (1983:175) concludes that "political power in Dallas and Fort Worth has typically been concentrated in the hands of those people most willing and able to sustain growth and expansion." Finally, even the ecologically oriented scholars with a different perspective, Berry and Kasarda (1977:371), have remarked, "If in the past urbanization has been governed by any conscious public objectives at all, these have been, on the one hand, to encourage growth, apparently for its own sake, and on the other hand, to provide public works and public welfare programs to support piecemeal, spontaneous development impelled primarily by private initiative." And even Hawley (1950:429) briefly departs from his tight ecological schema to remark that "competition is observable . . . in the struggle for transportation and communication advantages and superior services of all kinds; it also appears in efforts to accelerate rates of population growth."

All of this competition, in addition to its critical influence on what goes on *within* cities, also influences the distribution of populations throughout cities and regions, determining which ones grow and which do not. The incessant lobbying, manipulating, and cajoling can deliver the critical resources from which great cities are made. Although virtually all places are subject to the pervasive rule of growth boosters, places with more active and creative elites may have an edge over other areas. In a comparative study of forty-eight communities, Lyon et al. (1981) indeed found that cities with reputedly more powerful elites tended to have stronger growth rates. This may mean that active elites stimulate growth, or it may mean that strong growth emboldens elites to actively maintain their advantage. Although we suspect that both perspectives are valid, we stress that the activism of entrepreneurs is, and always has been, a critical force in shaping the urban system, including the rise and fall of given places.

Growth Machines in U.S. History

The role of the growth machine as a driving force in U.S. urban development has long been a factor in U.S. history, and is nowhere more clearly documented than in the histories of eighteenth- and nineteenth-century American cities. Indeed, although historians have chronicled many types of mass opposition to capitalist organization (for example, labor unions and the Wobblie movement), there is precious little evidence of resistance to the dynamics of value-free city building characteristic of the American past. In looking back we thus have not only the benefit of hindsight but also the advantage of dealing with a time in which "the interfusing of public and private prosperity" (Boorstin, 1965:116) was proudly proclaimed by town boosters and their contemporary chroniclers. The creators of towns and the builders of cities strained to use all the resources at their disposal, including crude political clout, to make great fortunes out of place. The "lively competitive spirit" of the western regions was, in Boorstin's view (1965:123), more "a competition among communities" than among individuals. Sometimes, the "communities" were merely subdivided parcels with town names on them, what Wade (1959) has called "paper villages," on whose behalf governmental actions could nonetheless be taken.[1] The competition among them was primarily among growth elites.

These communities competed to attract federal land offices, colleges and academies, or installations such as arsenals and prisons as a means of stimulating development. These projects were, for many places, "the only factor that permitted them to outdistance less favored rivals with equivalent natural or geographic endowments" (Scheiber, 1973:136). The other important arena of competition was also dependent on government decision making and funding: the development of a transportation infrastructure that would give a locality better access to raw materials and markets. First came the myriad efforts to attract state and federal funds to link towns to waterways through canals. Then came efforts to subsidize and direct the paths of railroads (Glaab, 1962). Town leaders used their governmental authority to determine routes and subsidies, motivated by their private interest in rents.

The people who engaged in this city building have often been celebrated for their inspired vision and "absolute faith." One historian characterizes them as "ambitious, flamboyant, and imaginative" (Fuller, 1976:41). But more important than their personalities, these urban founders were in the business of manipulating place for its exchange values. Their occupations most often were real estate or banking (Belcher, 1947). Even those who initially practiced law, medicine, or pharmacy were rentiers in the making. These professional roles became sidelines: "Physicians became merchants, clergymen became bankers, lawyers became manufacturers" (Boorstin, 1965:123). Especially when fortunes could be made from growth, the elite division of labor was overwhelmed and "specialized skills . . . had a new unimportance" (Boorstin, 1965:123). Speaking of the early settlers' acquisition of speculative lands through the preemption regulations of the 1862 Homestead Act, Leslie Decker remarks that "the early comers to any town – from lawyers to doctors to merchants, to just plain town developers – usually diversified in this fashion" (quoted in Wolf, 1981:52; see also Swierenga, 1966).

The city-building activities of these growth entrepreneurs in frontier towns became the springboard for the much celebrated taming of the American wilderness. As Wade (1959) has argued, the upstart western cities functioned as market, finance, and administrative outposts that made rural pioneering possible. This conquering of the West, accomplished through the machinations of "the urban frontier," was critically bound up with a coordinated effort to gain rents. In order for town leaders to achieve their goals, there was "ingenious employment of the instruments of political and economic leverage at [their] disposal" to build the cities and regions in which they had made investments (Scheiber, 1973:136).

Perhaps the most spectacular case of urban ingenuity was the Chicago of William Ogden. When Ogden came to Chicago in 1835, its population was under four thousand. He succeeded in becoming its mayor, its great railway developer, and the owner of much of its best real estate. As the organizer and first president of the Union Pacific (among other railroads) and in combination with his other business and civic roles, he was able to make Chicago (as a "public duty") the crossroads of America, and hence the dominant metropolis of the Midwest. Chicago became a crossroads not only because it was "central" (other places were also in the "middle") but because a small group of people (led by Ogden) had the power to literally have the roads cross in the spot they chose. Ogden candidly reminisced about one of the real estate deals this made possible: "I purchased for $8,000, what 8 years thereafter, sold for 3 millions of dollars" (Boorstin, 1965:117). The Ogden story, Boorstin says (p. 118), "was re-enacted a thousand times all over America."

This tendency to use land and government activity to make money was not invented in nineteenth-century America, nor did it end then. The development of the American Midwest was only one particularly noticed (and celebrated) moment in the total process. One of the more fascinating instances, farther to the West and later in history, was the rapid development of Los Angeles, an anomaly to many because it had none of the "natural" features that are thought to support urban growth: no centrality, no harbor, no transportation crossroads, not even a water supply. Indeed, the rise of Los Angeles as the preeminent city of the West, eclipsing its rivals San Diego and San Francisco, can only be explained as a remarkable victory of human cunning over the so-called limits of nature. Much of the development of western cities hinged on access to a railroad; the termination of the first continental railroad at San Francisco, therefore, secured that city's early lead over other western towns. The railroad was thus crucial to the fortunes of the barons with extensive real estate and commercial interests in San Francisco – Stanford, Crocker, Huntington, and Hopkins. These men feared the coming of a second cross-country railroad (the southern route), for its urban terminus might threaten the San Francisco investments. San Diego, with its natural port, could become a rival to San Francisco, but Los Angeles, which had no comparable advantage, would remain forever in its shadow. Hence, the San Francisco elites used their economic and political power to keep San Diego from becoming the terminus of the southern route. As Fogelson (1967:51, 55) remarks, "San Diego's supreme asset, the bay, was actually its fatal liability," whereas the disadvantage of Los Angeles – "its inadequate and unprotected port – was its saving grace." Of course, Los Angeles won in the end, but here again the wiles of boosters were crucial: the Los Angeles interests managed to secure millions in federal funds to construct a port – today the world's largest artificial harbor – as well as federal backing to gain water (Clark, 1983:273, 274).

The same dynamic accounts for the other great harbor in the Southwest. Houston beat out Galveston as the major port of Texas (ranked third in the country in 1979) only when Congressman Tom Ball of Houston successfully won, at the beginning of this century, a

million-dollar federal appropriation to construct a canal linking land-
locked Houston to the Gulf of Mexico (Kaplan, 1983:196). That was the
crucial event that, capitalizing on Galveston's susceptibility to hurricanes,
put Houston permanently in the lead.

In more recent times, the mammoth federal interstate highway system,
hammered out by "a horde of special interests representing towns and
cities" (Judd, 1983:173), has similarly made and unmade urban fortunes.
To use one clear case, Colorado's leaders made Denver a highway crossroads by convincing President Eisenhower in 1956 to add three hundred
miles to the system to link Denver to Salt Lake City by an expensive
mountain route. A presidential stroke of the pen removed the prospects
of Cheyenne, Wyoming, of replacing Denver as a major western transportation center (Judd, 1983:173). In a case reminiscent of the
nineteenth-century canal era, the Tennessee–Tombigbee Waterway
opened in 1985, dramatically altering the shipping distances to the Gulf
of Mexico for many inland cities. The largest project ever built by the U.S.
Corps of Engineers, the $2 billion project was questioned as a boon-
doggle in Baltimore, which will lose port business because of it (Maguire,
1985), but praised in Decatur, Alabama, and Knoxville, Tennessee, which
expect to profit from it. The opening of the canal cut by four-fifths the
distance from Chattanooga, Tennessee, to the Gulf, but did almost
nothing for places like Minneapolis and Pittsburgh, which were previously about the same nautical distance from the Gulf as Chattanooga.

Despite the general hometown hoopla of boosters who have won infrastructural victories, not everyone gains when the structural speculators
of a city defeat their competition. It is too easy, and misleading, to say
that "the public benefits . . . because it got the railroads" (Grodinsky, as
cited in Klein, 1970:294).[2] Given the stakes, the rentier elites would obviously become engulfed by the "booster spirit." But despite the long-held
supposition of an American "antiurban bias" (White and White, 1962),
researchers have made little effort to question the linkage between public
betterment and growth, even when they could see that specific social
groups were being hurt. Zunz reports that in industrializing Detroit, city
authorities extended utility service into uninhabited areas to help development rather than into existing residential zones, whose working-class
residents went without service even as they bore the costs (through taxes)
of the new installations. There was a "bias in favor of speculators and
against the working class" (Zunz, 1982:116). Even the great urban
reformers, such as Detroit's Mayor Hazen Pingree, while working to
change this "standard practice" for financing growth (Zunz, 1983:118),
were doing so in order to increase the overall efficiencies of urban services
and hence "engineer growth better" (Zunz, 1982:111). "Real estate
specialists and builders were more involved in the city-building process,"
Zunz (1982:162) says, "than anybody else." Reviewing urbanization from
1850 to 1930, Lewis Mumford observed: "That a city had any other

purpose than to attract trade, to increase land values, and to grow is something, if it uneasily entered the mind of an occasional Whitman, never exercised any hold on the minds of our countrymen" (quoted in Mollenkopf, 1983:14).

This is the consensus that must be examined, particularly in light of recent urban development. Let us turn now to a description of the ingenious modern incarnations of the growth machines and to an analysis of how they function, a task made more difficult for modern times because the crucial participants seldom speak so openly as did Mr Ogden.

The Modern-day Good Business Climate

The jockeying for canals, railroads, and arsenals of the previous century has given way in this one to more complex and subtle efforts to manipulate space and redistribute rents. The fusing of public duty and private gain has become much less acceptable (both in public opinion and in the criminal courts); the replacing of frontiers by complex cities has given important roles to mass media, urban professionals, and skilled political entrepreneurs. The growth machine is less personalized, with fewer local heroes, and has become instead a multifaceted matrix of important social institutions pressing along complementary lines.

With a transportation and communication grid already in place, modern cities typically seek growth in basic economic functions, particularly job intensive ones. Economic growth sets in motion the migration of labor and a demand for ancillary production services, housing, retailing, and wholesaling ("multiplier effects"). Contemporary places differ in the type of economic base they strive to build (for example, manufacturing, research and development, information processing, or tourism). But any one of the rainbows leads to the same pot of gold: more intense land use and thus higher rent collections, with associated professional fees and locally based profits.

Cities are in a position to affect the "factors of production" that are widely believed to channel the capital investments that drive local growth (Hawley, 1950; Summers et al., 1976). They can, for example, lower access costs of raw materials and markets through the creation of shipping ports and airfields (either by using local subsidies or by facilitating state and federal support). Localities can decrease corporate overhead costs through sympathetic policies on pollution abatement, employee health standards, and taxes, Labor costs can be indirectly lowered by pushing welfare recipients into low-paying jobs and through the use of police to constrain union organizing. Moral laws can be changed; for example, drinking alcohol can be legalized (as in Ann Arbor, Mich., and Evanston, Ill.) or gambling can be promoted (as in Atlantic City, N.J.) to build tourism and convention business. Increased utility costs caused by new development can be borne, as they usually are (see, for an example, Ann Arbor, Michigan, Planning Department, 1972), by the public at large rather than by those responsible for the "excess" demand they generate. Federally financed programs can be harnessed to provide cheap water supplies; state agencies can be manipulated to subsidize insurance rates; local political units can forgive business property taxes. Government installations of various sorts (universities, military bases) can be used to leverage additional development by guaranteeing the presence of skilled labor, retailing customers, or proximate markets for subcontractors. For some analytical purposes, it doesn't even matter that a number of these factors have little bearing on corporate locational decisions (some certainly do; others are debated); just the *possibility* that they might matter invigorates local growth activism (Swanstrom, 1985) and dominates policy agendas.

Following the lead of St. Petersburg, Florida, the first city to hire a press agent (in 1918) to boost growth (Mormino, 1983: 150), virtually all major urban areas now use experts to attract outside investment. One city, Dixon, Illinois, has gone so far as to systematically contact former residents who might be in a position to help (as many as twenty thousand people) and offer them a finder's fee of up to $10,000, for directing corporate investment toward their old home town (*San Francisco Chronicle*, May 10, 1984). More pervasively, each city tries to create a "good business climate." The ingredients are well known in city-building circles and have even been codified and turned into "official" lists for each regional area. The much-used Fantus rankings of business climates are based on factors like taxation, labor legislation, unemployment compensation, scale of government, and public indebtedness (Fantus ranks Texas as number one and New York as number forty-eight). In 1975, the Industrial Development Research Council, made up of corporate executives responsible for site selection decisions, conducted a survey of its members. In that survey, states were rated more simply as "cooperative," "indifferent," or "antigrowth"; the results closely paralleled the Fantus rankings of the same year (Weinstein and Firestine, 1978:134–44).

Any issue of a major business magazine is replete with advertisements from localities of all types (including whole countries) striving to portray themselves in a manner attractive to business. Consider these claims culled from one issue of *Business Week* (February 12, 1979):

> *New York City is open for business. No other city in America offers more financial incentives to expand or relocate . . .*

The state of Louisiana advertises

> *Nature made it perfect. We made it profitable.*

On another page we find the claim that "Northern Ireland works" and has a work force with "positive attitudes toward company loyalty, productivity and labor relations." Georgia asserts, "Government should strive to improve business conditions, not hinder them." Atlanta headlines that as "A City Without Limits" it "has ways of getting people like you out of town" and then details its transportation advantages to business. Some places describe attributes that would enhance the life style of executives and professional employees (not a dimension of Fantus rankings); thus a number of cities push an image of artistic refinement. No advertisements in this issue (or in any other, we suspect) show city workers living in nice homes or influencing their working conditions.

While a good opera or ballet company may subtly enhance the growth potential of some cities, other cultural ingredients are crucial for a good business climate. There should be no violent class or ethnic conflict (Agger, Goldrich, and Swanson, 1964:649; Johnson, 1983:250–51). Rubin (1972:123) reports that racial confrontation over school busing was sometimes seen as a threat to urban economic development. Racial violence in South Africa is finally leading to the disinvestment that reformers could not bring about through moral suasion. In the good business climate, the work force should be sufficiently quiescent and healthy to be productive; this was the rationale originally behind many programs in work place relations and public health. Labor must, in other words, be "reproduced," but only under conditions that least interfere with local growth trajectories.

Perhaps most important of all, local publics should favor growth and support the ideology of value-free development. This public attitude reassures investors that the concrete enticements of a locality will be upheld by future politicians. The challenge is to connect civic pride to the growth goal, tying the presumed economic and social benefits of growth in general (Wolfe, 1981) to growth in the local area. Probably only partly aware of this, elites generate and sustain the place patriotism of the masses. According to Boorstin, the competition among cities "helped create the booster spirit" as much as the booster spirit helped create the cities (1965:123). In the nineteenth-century cities, the great rivalries over canal and railway installations were the political spectacles of the day, with attention devoted to their public, not private, benefits. With the drama of the new railway technology, ordinary people were swept into the competition among places, rooting for their own town to become the new "crossroads" or at least a way station. "The debates over transportation," writes Scheiber (1973:143), "heightened urban community consciousness and sharpened local pride in many western towns."

The celebration of local growth continues to be a theme in the culture of localities. Schoolchildren are taught to view local history as a series of breakthroughs in the expansion of the economic base of their city and region, celebrating its numerical leadership in one sort of production or another; more generally, increases in population tend to be equated with local progress. Civic organizations sponsor essay contests on the topic of local greatness. They encourage public celebrations and spectacles in which the locality name can be proudly advanced for the benefit of both locals and outsiders. They subsidize soapbox derbies, parade floats, and beauty contests to "spread around" the locality's name in the media and at distant competitive sites.

One case can illustrate the link between growth goals and cultural institutions. In the Los Angeles area, St Patrick's Day parades are held at four different locales, because the city's Irish leaders can't agree on the venue for a joint celebration. The source of the difficulty (and much acrimony) is that these parades march down the main business streets in each locale, thereby making them a symbol of the life of the city. Business groups associated with each of the strips want to claim the parade as exclusively their own, leading to charges by still a fifth parade organization that the other groups are only out to "make money" (McGarry, 1985:II:1). The countercharge, vehemently denied, was that the leader of the challenging business street was not even Irish. Thus even an ethnic celebration can receive its special form from the machinations of growth interests and the competitions among them.

The growth machine avidly supports whatever cultural institutions can play a role in building locality. Always ready to oppose cultural and political developments contrary to their interests (for example, black nationalism and communal cults), rentiers and their associates encourage activities that will connect feelings of community ("we feelings" [McKenzie, 1922]) to the goal of local growth. The overall ideological thrust is to deemphasize the connection between growth and exchange values and to reinforce the link between growth goals and better lives for the majority. We do not mean to suggest that the only source of civic pride is the desire to collect rents; certainly the cultural pride of tribal groups predates growth machines. Nevertheless, the growth machine coalition mobilizes these cultural motivations, legitimizes them, and channels them into activities that are consistent with growth goals.

The Organization of the Growth Coalition

The people who use their time and money to participate in local affairs are the ones who – in vast disproportion to their representation in the population – have the most to gain or lose in land-use decisions. Local business people are the major participants in urban politics (Walton, 1970), particularly business people in property investing, development, and real estate financing (Spaulding, 1951; Mumford, 1961). Peterson (1981:132), who applauds growth boosterism, acknowledges that "such policies are often promulgated through a highly centralized decision-making process involving prestigious businessmen and professionals. Conflict within the city tends to be minimal, decision-making processes tend to be closed." Elected officials, says Stone (1984:292), find themselves confronted by "a business community that is well-organized, amply supplied with a number of deployable resources, and inclined to act on behalf of tangible and ambitious plans that are mutually beneficial to its own members."

Business people's continuous interaction with public officials (including supporting them through substantial campaign contributions) gives them *systemic* power (Alford and Friedland, 1975; Stone, 1981, 1982). Once organized, they stay organized. They are "mobilized interests" (Fainstein, Fainstein, and Armistead, 1983:214). Rentiers need local government in their daily money-making routines, especially when structural speculations are involved. They are assisted by lawyers, syndicators, and property brokers (Bouma, 1962), who prosper as long as they can win decisions favoring their clients. Finally, there are monopolistic business enterprises (such as the local newspaper) whose futures are tied to the growth of the metropolis as a whole, although they are not directly involved in land use. When the local market is saturated with their product, they have few ways to increase profits, beyond expansion of their surrounding area. As in the proverbial Springdale, site of the classic Vidich and Bensman (1960:216) ethnography of a generation ago, there is a strong tendency in most cities for "the professionals (doctors, teachers, dentists, etc.), the industrial workers, the shack people and the lower middle-class groups [to be] for all intents and purposes disenfranchised except in terms of temporary issues."

Because so much of the growth mobilization effort involves government, local growth elites play a major role in electing local politicians, "watchdogging" their activities, and scrutinizing administrative detail. Whether in generating infrastructural resources, keeping peace on the home front, or using the city mayor as an "ambassador to industry" (Wyner, 1967), local government is primarily concerned with increasing growth. Again, it is not the only function of local government, but it is the key one.

In contrast to our position, urban social scientists have often ignored the politics of growth in their work, even when debates over growth infrastructures were the topic of their analyses (see Banfield, 1961; Dahl, 1961). Williams and Adrian (1963) at least treat growth as an important part of the local political process, but give it no priority over other government issues. There are a number of reasons why growth politics is consistently undervalued. The clue can be found in Edelman's (1964) distinction between two kinds of politics.

The first is the "symbolic" politics of public morality and most of the other "big issues" featured in the headlines and editorials of the daily press: school prayer, wars on crime, standing up to communism, and child pornography, for example. News coverage of these issues may have little to do with any underlying reality, much less a reality in which significant local actors have major stakes. Fishman (1978) shows, for example, that reports of a major crime wave against the elderly in New York City appeared just at a time when most crimes against the elderly were actually on the decline. The public "crime wave" was created by police officials who, in responding to reporters' interest in the topic, provided "juicy" instances that would make good copy. The "crime wave" was sustained by politicians eager to denouce the perpetrators, and these politicians' pronouncements became the basis for still more coverage and expressions of authoritative police concern. Once this symbiotic "dance" (Molotch, 1980) is in motion, the story takes on a life of its own, and fills the pages and airwaves of news media. Such symbolic crusades provide the "easy news" (Gordon, Heath, and leBailly, 1979) needed by reporters pressed for time, just as these crusades satisfy the "news needs" (Molotch and Lester, 1974) of politicians happy to stay away from issues that might offend growth machine interests. The resulting hubbubs often mislead the general public as well as the academic investigator about what the real stuff of community cleavage and political process might be. To the degree that rentier elites keep growth issues on a symbolic level (for example, urban "greatness"), they prevail as the "second face of power" (Bachrach and Baratz, 1962), the face that determines the public agenda (McCombs and Shaw, 1972).

Edelman's second kind of politics, which does not provide easy news, involves the government actions that affect the distribution of important goods and services. Much less visible to publics, often relegated to back rooms or negotiations within insulated authorities and agencies (Caro, 1974: Friedland, Piven, and Alford, 1978), this is the politics that determines who, in material terms, gets what, where, and how (cf. Lasswell, 1936). The media tend to cover it as the dull round of meetings of water and sewer districts, bridge authorities, and industrial development bonding agencies. The media attitude serves to keep interesting issues away from the public and blunt widespread interest in local politics generally. As Vidich and Bensman (1960:217) remark about Springdale, "business control rests upon a dull but unanimous political facade," at least on certain key issues.

Although there are certainly elite organizational mechanisms to inhibit them (Domhoff, 1971, 1983; Whitt, 1982), cleavages within the growth machine can nevertheless develop, and internal disagreements sometimes break into the open. But even then, because of the hegemony of the growth machine, *its* disagreements are allowable and do not challenge the belief in growth itself. Unacceptable are public attacks on the pursuit of exchange values over citizens' search for use value. An internal quarrel over where a convention center is to be built, Banfield (1961) shows us, becomes the public issue for Chicago; but Banfield didn't notice that there was no question about whether there should be a convention center at all.

When elites come to see, for example, that inadequate public services are repelling capital investment, they can put the issue of raising taxes on the public agenda. Trillin (1976:154) reports on Rockford, Illinois, a city whose school system was bankrupted by an antitax ideology. Initially, local elites opposed taxes as part of their efforts to lure industry through a low tax rate. As a result, taxes, and therefore tax money for schools, declined. Eventually, the growth coalition saw the educational decline, not the tax rate, as the greatest danger to the "economic vitality of the community." But ironically, elites are not able to change overnight the ideologies they have put in place over decades, even when it is in their best interests to do so.[3] Unfortunately, neither can the potential *opponents* of growth. As the example of Rockford shows, even such issues as public school spending can become subject to the growth maximization needs of locality. The appropriate level of a social service often depends, not on an abstract model of efficiency or on "public demand" (cf. Tiebout, 1956), but on whether the cost of that service fits the local growth strategy (past and present).

By now it should be clear how political structures are mobilized to intensify land uses for private gain of many sorts. Let us look more closely, therefore, at the various local actors, besides those directly involved in generating rents, who participate in the growth machine.

Politicians

The growth machine will sustain only certain persons as politicians. The campaign contributions and public celebrations that build political careers do not ordinarily come about because of a person's desire to save or destroy the environment, to repress or liberate the blacks or other disadvantaged groups, to eliminate civil liberties or enhance them. Given their legislative power, politicians may end up doing any of these things. But the underlying politics that gives rise to such opportunities is a person's participation in the growth consensus. That is why we so often see politicians springing into action to attract new capital and to sustain old investments. Even the pluralist scholar Robert Dahl observed in his New Haven study that if an employer seriously threatened to leave the community, "political leaders are likely to make frantic attempts to make the local situation more attractive" (quoted in Swanstrom, 1981:50).

Certainly, politicians differ in a number of ways. Like Mayor Ogden of Chicago, some are trying to create vast fortunes for themselves as they go about their civic duties on behalf of the growth machine. Robert Folson, the mayor of Dallas, has direct interests in over fifty local businesses, many of which have stakes in local growth outcomes. When the annexation of an adjacent town came up for a vote, he had to abstain because he owned 20 percent of it (Fullinwider, 1980). Another Texan, former governor John Connally, has among his holdings more than $50 million in Austin-area real estate, property slated to become its county's largest residential and commercial development ("Austin Boom," *Santa Barbara News Press*, June 24, 1984, p. B-8). According to Robert Caro (1974), Commissioner Robert Moses was able to overcome opposition to his vast highway and bridge building in the New York City area in part because the region's politicians were themselves buying up land adjacent to parkway exits, setting themselves up for huge rent gains. Most of Hawaii's major Democrat politicians, after winning election on a reform platform in 1954, directly profited as developers, lawyers, contractors, and investors through the zoning and related land-use decisions they and their colleagues were to make over the next thirty years of intensive growth and speculation (Daws and Cooper, 1984). Machine politics never insulated candidates from the development process; builders, railroaders, and other growth activists have long played crucial roles in boss politics, both in immigrant wards (Bell, 1961) and in WASP suburbs (Fogelson, 1967:207). All this is, as George Washington Plunkitt said in 1905, "honest graft" as opposed to "dishonest graft" (quoted in Swanstrom, 1985:25).[4]

Although a little grease always helps a wheel to turn, a system can run well with no graft at all – unless using campaign contributions to influence elections is considered graft. Virtually all politicians are dependent on private campaign financing (Alexander, 1972, 1980, 1983; Boyarsky and Gillam, 1982; Smith, 1984), and it is the real estate entrepreneurs – particularly the large-scale structural speculators – who are particularly active in supporting candidates. The result is that candidates of both parties, of whatever ideological stripe, have to garner the favor of such persons, and this puts them squarely into the hands of growth machine coalitions. Thus many officeholders use their authority, not to enrich themselves, but to benefit the "whole community" – that is, to increase aggregate rents. Again, this does not preclude politicians' direct participation in property dealing on occasion and it certainly does not preclude giving a special hand to particular place entrepreneurs with whom a politician has a special relationship.

Elected officials also vary in their perception of how their authority can best be used to maximize growth. After his thorough study of the Cleveland growth machine, Swanstrom (1985) concluded that there are two types of growth strategists: the "conservative" and the "liberal." The former, paramount during the city's age of steel, favor unbridled exploitation of the city and its labor force, generally following the "free economy" political model. Programs of overt government intervention, for purposes of planning, public education, or employee welfare, are all highly suspect. The liberal growth machine strategy, in contrast,

acknowledges that longer-term growth can be facilitated by overt government planning and by programs that pacify, co-opt, and placate
oppositions. This is a more modern form of growth ideology. Some
politicians, depending on place and time, tend to favor the hard-line
"unfettered capitalism" (Wolfe, 1981); others prefer the liberal version,
analogous to what is called, in a broader context, "pragmatic state capitalism" (Wolfe, 1981; see also Weinstein, 1968). These positions became
more obvious in many regions when urban renewal and other federal
programs began penetrating cities in the postwar period. Especially in
conservative areas such as Texas (Melosi, 1983:185), elites long debated
among themselves whether or not the newfangled growth schemes
would do more harm than good.

On the symbolic issues, politicians may also differ, on both the content
of their positions and the degree to which they actually care about the
issues. Some are no doubt sincere in pushing their "causes"; others may
cynically manipulate them to obscure the distributional consequences of
their own actions in other matters. Sometimes the results are positive, for
example, when Oklahoma City and Dallas leaders made deliberate efforts
to prevent racist elements from scaring off development with "another
Little Rock." Liberal growth machine goals may thus help reform reactionary social patterns (Bernard, 1983:225; Melosi, 1983:188). But
despite these variations, there appears to be a "tilt" to the whole system,
regardless of time and place. Growth coalition activists and campaign
contributors are not a culturally, racially, or economically diverse cross
section of the urban population. They tend to give a reactionary texture
to local government, in which the cultural crusades, like the material
ones, are chosen for their acceptability to the rentier groups. Politicians
adept in both spheres (material and symbolic) are the most valued, and
most likely to have successful careers. A skilled politician delivers growth
while giving a good circus.

The symbolic political skills are particularly crucial when unforeseen
circumstances create use value crises, which can potentially stymie a
locality's basic growth strategy. The 1978 Love Canal toxic waste emergency at Niagara Falls, New York, reveals how local officials use their
positions to reassure the citizens and mold local agendas to handle disruptive "emotional" issues. In her detailed enthnographic account, Levine
(1982:59) reports that "the city's chief executives, led by the mayor, minimized the Love Canal problem in all public statements for two years no
matter how much personal sympathy they felt for the affected people
whose health was threatened by the poisons leaking into their homes"
(see also Fowlkes and Miller, 1985). Lester (1971) reports a similar stance
taken by the Utah civic leadership in response to the escape of nerve gas
from the U.S. military's Dugway Proving Grounds in 1969 (see also
Hirsch, 1969). The conduct of politicians in the face of accidents like the
leakage of poison into schoolyards and homes in Niagara Falls or the

sheep deaths in Utah reveal this "backup" function of local leaders (Molotch and Lester, 1974, 1975).

Still another critical use of local politicians is their ability to influence higher-level political actors in their growth distribution decisions. Although capital has direct links to national politicians (particularly in the executive office and Senate, see Domhoff [1967, 1970, 1983]), rentier groups are most parochial in their ties, although they may have contact with congressional representatives. Hence, rentiers need local politicians to lobby national officials. The national politicians, in turn, are responsive because they depend on local political operators (including party figures) for their own power base. The local politicians symbiotically need their national counterparts to generate the goods that keep them viable at home.

The goods that benefit the local leaders and growth interests are not trivial. The development of the Midwest was, as the historical anecdotes make clear, dependent on national decisions affecting canal and railroad lines. The Southwest and most of California could be developed only with federal subsidies and capital investments in water projects. The profound significance of government capital spending can be grasped by considering one statistic: direct government outlays (at all levels) in 1983 accounted for nearly 27 percent of all construction in the United States (Mollenkopf, 1983:43). The figure was even higher, of course, during World War II, when federal construction expenditures laid the basis for much of the infrastructural and defense spending that was to follow.

Local media

One local business takes a broad responsibility for general growth machine goals – the metropolitan newspaper. Most newspapers (small, suburban papers are occasionally an exception) profit primarily from increasing their circulation and therefore have a direct interest in growth.[5] As the metropolis expands, the newspaper can sell a larger number of ad lines (at higher per line cost), on the basis of a rising circulation base; TV and radio stations are in a similar situation. In explaining why his newspaper had supported the urbanization of orchards that used to cover what is now the city of San Jose, the publisher of the *San Jose Mercury News* said, "Trees do not read newspapers" (Downie, 1974:112, as cited in Domhoff, 1983:168). Just as newspaper boosterism was important in building the frontier towns (Dagenais, 1967), so today "the hallmark of media content has been peerless boosterism: congratulate growth rather than calculate consequences; compliment development rather than criticize its impact" (Burd, 1977:129; see also Devereux, 1976; Freidel, 1963). The media "must present a favorable image to outsiders" (Cox and Morgan, 1973:136),[6] and only "sparingly use their issue-raising capacities" (Peterson, 1981:124).

Amercian cities tend to be one-newspaper (or one-newspaper company) towns. The newspaper's assets in physical plant, in "good will," and in advertising clients are, for the most part, immobile. The local newspaper thus tends to occupy a unique position: like many other local businesses, it has an interest in growth, but unlike most others, its critical interest is not in the specific spatial pattern of that growth. The paper may occasionally help forge a specific strategy of growth, but ordinarily it makes little difference to a newspaper whether the additional population comes to reside on the north side or the south side, or whether the new business comes through a new convention center or a new olive factory. The newspaper has no ax to grind except the one that holds the community elite together: growth.

This disinterest in the specific form of growth, but avid commitment to development generally, enables the newspaper to achieve a statesman-like position in the community. It is often deferred to as a neutral party by the special interests. In his pioneering study of the creation of zoning laws in New York City in the 1920s, Makielski (1966:149) remarks, "While the newspapers in the city are large landholders, the role of the press was not quite like that of any of the other nongovernmental actors. The press was in part one of the referees of the rules of the game, especially the informal rules, calling attention to what it considered violations." The publisher or editor is often the arbiter of internal growth machine bickering, restraining the short-term profiteers in the interest of more stable, long-term, and properly planned growth.

The publishing families are often ensconced as the most important city builders within the town or city; this is the appropriate designation for such prominent families as Otis and Chandler of the *Los Angeles Times* (see Clark, 1983:271; Halberstam, 1979); Pulliam of the *Arizona Republic* and *Phoenix Sun* (see Luckingham, 1983:318); and Gaylord of the *Daily Oklahoman* (see Bernard, 1983:216). Sometimes these publishers are directly active in politics, "kingmaking" behind the scenes by screening candidates for political office, lobbying for federal contracts and grants, and striving to build growth infrastructure in their region (Fainstein, Fainstein, and Armistead, 1983:217; Judd, 1983:178). In the booming Contra Costa County suburbs of the San Francisco Bay Area, the president of the countrywide organization of builders, real estate investors, and property financiers was the owner of the regional paper. In his home county, as well as in the jurisdictions of his eleven other suburban papers, owner Dean Lesher ("Citizen Lesher") acts as "a cheerleader for development" who simply kills stories damaging to growth interests and reassigns unsympathetic reporters to less controversial beats (Steidtmann, 1985). The local newspaper editor was one of the three "bosses" in Springdale's "invisible government" (Vidich and Bensman, 1960:217). Sometimes, the publisher is among the largest urban landholders and openly fights for benefits tied to growth in land: the owners of the *Los Angeles Times* fought for the water that developed their vast properties for both urban and agricultural uses. The editorial stance is usually reformist, invoking the common good (and technical planning expertise) as the rationale for the land-use decisions the owners favor. This sustains the legitimacy of the paper itself among all literate sectors of society and helps mask the distributive effects of many growth developments.

The media attempt to attain their goals not only through news articles and editorials but also through informal talks between owners and editors and the local leaders. Because newspaper interests are tied to growth, media executives are sympathetic to business leaders' complaints that a particular journalistic investigation or angle may be bad for the local business climate, and should it nevertheless become necessary, direct threats of advertising cancellation can modify journalistic coverage (Bernard, 1983:220). This does not mean that newspapers (or advertisers) control the politics of a city or region, but that the media have a special influence simply because they are committed to growth per se, and can play an invaluable role in coordinating strategy and selling growth to the public.

This institutional legitimacy is especially useful in crises. In the controversy surrounding the army's accidental release of nerve gas at the Dugway Proving Grounds, Lester found that the Utah media were far more sympathetic to the military's explanations than were media outside Utah (Lester, 1971). The economic utility of the Dugway Proving Grounds (and related government facilities) was valued by the local establishment. Similarly, insiders report that publicizing toxic waste problems at Love Canal was hindered by an "unwritten law" in the newsroom that "a reporter did not attack or otherwise fluster the Hooker [Chemical Company] executives" (Brown, 1979, citied in Levine, 1982:190).

As these examples indicate, a newspaper's essential role is not to protect a given firm or industry (an issue more likely to arise in a small city than a large one) but to bolster and maintain the predisposition for general growth. Although newspaper editorialists may express concern for "the ecology," this does not prevent them from supporting growth-inducing investments for their regions. The *New York Times* likes office towers and additional industrial installations in the city even more than it loves "the environment." Even when historically significant districts are threatened, the *Times* editorializes in favor of intensification. Thus the *Times* recently admonished opponents to "get out of the way" of the Times Square renewal, which would replace landmark structures (including its own former headquarters at 1 Times Square) with huge office structures (*New York Times*, May 24, 1984, p. 18). Similarly, the *Los Angeles Times* editorializes against narrow-minded profiteering that increases pollution or aesthetic blight – in other cities. The newspaper featured criticism, for example, of the Times Square renewal plan (Kaplan, 1984:1), but had enthusiastically supported development of the environmentally devastating supersonic transport (SST) for the jobs it would presumably lure to Southern California. In an unexpected regional parallel, the *Los Angeles Times* fired celebrated architectural critic John Pastier for his incessant criticisms of Los Angeles's downtown renewal projects (Clark, 1983:298), and the *New York Times* dismissed Pulitzer Prize winner Sydney Schanberg as a columnist apparently because he "opposed civic projects supported by some of New York's most powerful interests, particularly those in the real estate industry" (Rosenstiel, 1985:21).

Although newspapers may openly support "good planning principles" of a certain sort, the acceptable form of "good planning" does not often extend to limiting growth or authentic conservation in a newspaper's home ground. "Good planning principles" can easily represent the opposite goals.

Utilities

Leaders of "independent" public or quasi-public agencies, such as utilities, may play a role similar to that of the newspaper publisher: tied to a single locale, they become growth "statesmen" rather than advocates for a certain type of growth or intralocal distribution of growth.

For example, a water-supplying agency (whether public or private) can expand only by acquiring more users. This causes utilities to penetrate deep into the hinterlands, inefficiently extending lines to areas that are extremely costly to service (Gaffney, 1961; Walker and Williams, 1982). The same growth goals exist within central cities. Brooklyn Gas was an avid supporter of the movement of young professionals into abandoned areas of Brooklyn, New York, in the 1970s, and even went so far as to help finance housing rehabilitation and sponsor a traveling slide show and open houses displaying the pleasant life styles in the area. All utilities seem bent on acquiring more customers to pay off past investments, and on proving they have the good growth prospects that lenders use as a criterion for financing additional investments. Overall efficiencies are often sacrificed as a result.

Transportation officials, whether of public or private organizations, have a special interest in growth: they tend to favor growth along their specific transit routes. But transportation doesn't just serve growth, it creates it. From the beginning, the laying-out of mass transit lines was a method of stimulating development; indeed, the land speculators and the executives of the transportation firms were often the same people. In part because of the salience of land development, "public service was largely incidental to the operation of the street railways" (Wilcox, quoted in Yago, 1984:44). Henry Huntington's Pacific Electric, the primary commuting system of Los Angeles, "was built not to provide transportation but to sell real estate" (Clark, 1983:272; see also Binford, 1985; Fogelson, 1967; Yago, 1984). And because the goal of profitable transportation did not guide the design and routing of the system, it was destined to lose money, leaving Los Angeles without a viable transit system in the end (Fogelson, 1967).

Transit bureaucrats today, although not typically in the land business, function as active development boosters; only in that way can more riders be found to support their systems and help pay off the sometimes enormous debts incurred to construct or expand the systems. On the national level, major airlines develop a strong growth interest in the development of their "hub" city and the network it serves. Eastern Airlines must have growth in Miami, Northwest Airlines needs development in Minneapolis, and American Airlines rises or falls with the fortunes of Dallas-Fort Worth.

Auxiliary Players

Although they may have less of a stake in the growth process than the actors described above, certain institutions play an auxiliary role in promoting and maintaining growth. Key among these auxiliary players are the cultural institutions in an area: museums, theaters, universities, symphonies, and professional sports teams. An increase in the local population may help sustain these institutions by increasing the number of clients and support groups. More important, perhaps, is that such institutions often need the favor of those who are at the heart of local growth machines – the rentiers, media owners, and politicians, who can make or break their institutional goals. And indeed, cultural institutions do have something to offer in return.

Universities

The construction and expansion of university campuses can stimulate development in otherwise rural landscapes; the land for the University of California at Los Angeles (UCLA) was originally donated for a state normal school in 1881 "in order to increase the value of the surrounding real estate" (Clark, 1983:286). Other educational institutions, particularly the University of California campuses at Irvine and Santa Barbara, had similar origins, as did the State University of New York at Stony Brook and the University of Texas at San Antonio (Johnson, 1983). Building a university campus can be the first step in rejuvenating a deteriorated inner-city area; this was the case with the Chicago branch of the University of Illinois (Banfield, 1961), the expansions of Yale University in New Haven (Dahl, 1961; Domhoff, 1978), and the University of Chicago (Rossi and Dentler, 1961). The use of universities and colleges as a stimulus to growth is often made explicit by both the institution involved and the local civic boosters.

The symbiotic relationship between universities and local development intensified in the 1980s. Drawing on the precedent of Silicon Valley (with Stanford University as its intellectual center) and Route 128, the high-tech highway, in the Boston area (with MIT as its intellectual center), many localities have come to view universities as an infrastructure for cutting edge industrial growth. Universities, in turn, have been quick to exploit this opportunity to strengthen their local constituency. A clear illustration is the Microelectronics and Computer Technology Corporation (MCTC), a newly created private firm with the mission of keeping the United States ahead of Japan in the microelectronics field. Jointly funded by twelve of the most important American firms in advanced technology, the new company had to build, at its founding, a $100 million installation. Austin, Texas, won the project, but only after the local and state governments agreed to a list of concessions, including subsidized land, mortgage assistance for employees, and a score of faculty chairs and other positions at the University of Texas for personnel relevant to the company mission (Rivera, 1983a).

The Austin victory reverberated especially through California, the location of the runner-up site. A consensus emerged, bolstered by an MCTC official's explicit statement, that faltering support for California higher education had made Texas the preferred choice. The view that a decline in the quality of higher education could drive away business may have been important in the fiscally conservative governor's decision to substantially increase allocations to the University of California in the following year. Budget increases for the less research-oriented state college system were at a much lower level; the community college system received a decrease in real dollar funding. The second and third groups of institutions play a less important role in growth machine strategies. As the president of the University of Texas said after his institution's victory, "The battle for national leadership among states is being fought on the campuses of the great research universities of the nation" (King, 1985:12).

Museums, theaters, expositions

Art and the physical structures that house artworks also play a role in growth strategies. In New York City, the art capital of the country, the arts generate about $1.3 billion in annual economic activity, a sum larger than that contributed by either advertising or computer services (Pittas, 1984). In Los Angeles, another major art center, urban redevelopment funds are paying for the new Museum of Contemporary Art, explicitly conceived as a means of enhancing commercial success for adjacent downtown residential, hotel, and office construction. Major art centers are also being used as development leverage in downtown Miami, Tampa (Mormino, 1983:152), and Dallas. The new Dallas Museum of Art will be the central focus of "the largest downtown development ever undertaken in the United States" (Tomkins, 1983:92). Whatever it may do to advance the cause of artists in Texas, the museum will do much for nearby rents. According to a Dallas newspaper report, "The feeling persists that the arts have been appropriated here primarily to sell massive real estate development" (quoted in Tomkins, 1983:97).

Other sorts of museums can be used for the same purpose. Three Silicon Valley cities are locked in a battle to make themselves the site for a $90 million Technology Museum that "is expected to draw one million visitors a year, boost hotel occupancy and attract new business" (Sahagun and Jalon, 1984:1). Two of the competing cities (Mountain View and San Jose), in promising millions in subsidies, would use the museum as a focal point for major commercial developments. In a not dissimilar, though perhaps less highbrow effort, the city of Flint, Michigan ("the unemployment capital of America") invested city money in a Six Flags Auto World Theme Park that displayed cars (old and new) and used the auto as a motif for its other attractions. The facility was situated so as to boost the city's crumbling downtown; unhappily, gate receipts were poor and the park was closed, and the $70 million public–private investment was lost (Risen, 1984).

Theaters are also being used as a development tool. Believing that the preservation of the legitimate theater will help maintain the "vitality" of Midtown Manhatten, city officials are considering a plan to allow theater owners to sell the "development rights" of their properties, which the dense zoning in the theater district would otherwise permit. The buyer of these rights would then be allowed bonus, or greater, densities on other nearby sites, thereby protecting the theaters' existence while not blocking the general densification of the area (*New York Times*, September 19, 1983, p. 1). In many parts of the country, various individuals and groups are encouraging (and often subsidizing) the construction and rehabilitation of theaters and concert halls as growth instruments. Downtown churches are looking to the heavens for financial returns, arranging to sell air rights over their imposing edifices to developers of nearby parcels.

These programs allow cultural institutions, in effect, to collect rents they otherwise could gain only by tearing down their structures. The arrangement heads off any conflict between developers and those oriented to the use values that theaters and historic buildings might provide and helps to maintain these "city treasures" that help sustain the economic base. But aggregate levels of development are not curtailed.

Still another kind of cultural institution involved in the growth apparatus is the blue-ribbon committee that puts together local spectaculars, like annual festivals and parades, or a one-shot World's Fair or Olympics competition. These are among the common efforts by Chambers of Commerce and Visitors Bureaus to lure tourists and stimulate development. There are industrial expositions, music festivals, and all manner of regional annual attractions. Such events are considered ways of meeting short-term goals of generating revenue, as well as ways of meeting long-term goals of attracting outside businesses. They show off the locality to outsiders who could generate additional investments in the future. Los Angeles business leaders, for example, "created the Rose Parade to draw national attention to Southern California's balmy weather by staging an outdoor event with fresh flowers in the middle of winter" (Clark, 1983:271).

The short-term results of big events can mean billions of dollars injected into the local economy, although costs to ordinary citizens (in the form of traffic congestion, higher prices, and drains on public services) are notoriously understated (Clayton, 1984; Shlay and Gilroth, 1984). To help gain the necessary public subsidies for such events, the promoters insist that "the community" will benefit, and they inflate revenue expectations in order to make trickle-down benefits at least seem plausible (Hayes, 1984). The 1983 Knoxville World's Fair, one of the few World's Fairs to actually produce a profit on its own books, nevertheless left its host city with $57 million in debts (Schmidt, 1984), a debt large enough to require an 8 percent increase in property taxes in order to pay it off. The 1984 New Orleans World's Fair showed a $100 million loss (Hill, 1984). Other spectaculars, like the Los Angeles Olympics, do come out ahead, but even so, certain costs (like neighborhood disruption) are simply not counted.

Clearly, a broad range of cultural institutions, not often thought of in terms of land development, participate closely as auxiliary players in the growth process for many reasons. Some participate because their own organizational goals depend on local growth, others because they find it diplomatic to support the local rentier patrons, others because their own properties become a valuable resource, and still others because their boards of directors are closely tied to local elites. Whatever the reasons, the growth machine cuts a wide institutional swath.

Professional Sports

Professional sports teams are a clear asset to localities for the strong image they present and tourist traffic they attract (Eitzen and Sage, 1978:184). Baseball, the American pastime, had its beginning in amusement parks; many of the team owners were real estate speculators who used the team to attract visitors to the subdivisions they offered for sale. Fans would ride to the park on trolley lines that the team owner also owned (Roderick, 1984). In more recent years, baseball and football stadia and hockey and basketball arenas have been used by local *governments* to provide a focus for urban renewal projects in Pittsburgh, Hartford, Minneapolis, and other cities (Roderick, 1984). New Orleans used the development of the Superdome "to set the stage for a tourist-based growth strategy for the future development of downtown" (Smith and Keller, 1983:134). The facility ended up costing $165 million (instead of the projected $35 million), and has had large annual operating losses – all absorbed by the state government.

St. Petersburg, Florida, seems to be following the example of New Orleans. The Florida city has agreed to invest $59.6 million in a new stadium *in the hope* that it will lure a major league franchise to a city that woefully lacks the demographic profile necessary to support major league sports. So far the project has required displacement of four hundred families (primarily black) and saddled the city with a huge debt. A city official insists it will be worth it because

> *When you consider what it would mean in new business for hotels, jobs, pride, tourism – then it's a real good deal. We believe for every dollar spent inside a stadium, seven are spent outside.* (Roderick, 1984:24).

In an even more dubious effort, the city of Albany, New York, gained popular support (and some state funding) for a $40 million multipurpose downtown civic center on the grounds that it *might* attract a hockey team to the city (D'Ambrosio, 1985). Like the New Orleans project, this plan puts sports boosters behind a project that will help local business with its other events (such as conventions), regardless of its success in attracting a professional team.

Local teams are an industry in themselves. Atlanta's professional sports organizations have been estimated to be worth over $60 million annually to the local economy (Rice, 1983:38). But a local team does much more than the direct expenditures imply: it helps a city's visibility, putting it "on the map" as a "big league city," making it more noticeable to all, including those making investment decisions. It is one of "the visible badges of urban maturity" (Rice, 1983:38). Within the city, sports teams have an important ideological use, helping instill civic pride in business through jingoistic logic. Whether the setting is soccer in Brazil (Lever, 1983) or baseball in Baltimore, millions of people are mobilized to pull for the home turf. Sports that lend themselves to boosting a locality are the useful ones. Growth activists are less enthusiastic about sports that honor individual accomplishment and are less easily tied to a locality or team name (for example, tennis, track, or swimming). Only when such sports connect with rent enhancement, for example, when they are part of an Olympic competition held on home ground, do they receive major support.

The mobilization of the audience is accomplished through a number of mechanisms. Money to construct stadia or to attract or retain the home team is raised through public bond issues. About 70 percent of current facilities were built with this tool, often under conditions of large cost overruns (Eitzen, 1978). Enthusiastic corporate sponsorship of radio and TV broadcasts greatly expands public participation (and by linking products with local heroes this form of sponsorship avoids any danger of involving the corporate image with controversial topics). Finally, the news media provide avid coverage, giving sports a separate section of the newspaper and a substantial block of broadcast time during the period designated for the news (including the mention of the city name on national news). No other single news topic receives such consistent and extensive coverage in the United States.

The coverage is, of course, always supportive of sports itself and the home team in particular. There is no pretense of objectivity. It is all part of the ideological ground for other civic goals, including the successful competition of cities for growth-inducing projects. Professional teams serve many latent social functions (Brower, 1972); sustaining the growth ideology is clearly one of them.

Organized labor

Although they are sometimes in conflict with capitalists on other issues, labor union leaders are enthusiastic partners in growth machines, with little careful consideration of the long-term consequences for the rank and file. Union leadership subscribes to value-free development because it will "bring jobs," particularly to the building trades, whose spokespersons are especially vocal in their support of development. Less likely to be openly discussed is the concern that growth may bring more union members and enhance the power and authority of local union officials.[7]

Union executives are available for ceremonial celebrations of growth (ribbon cuttings, announcements of government contracts, urban redevelopment ground breakings). Entrepreneurs frequently enlist union support when value-free development is under challenge; when growth control was threatened in the city of San Diego in 1975, three thousand labor union members paraded through downtown, protesting land-use regulations they claimed were responsible for local unemployment (Corso, 1983: 339). Labor leaders are especially useful when the growth machine needs someone to claim that development opponents are "elitist" or "selfish." Thus, in a characteristic report on a growth control referendum in the city of Riverside, California, Neiman and Loveridge (1981:764–65) found that the progrowth coalition "repeated, time and again, that most of organized labor in the area opposed Measure B, firms wishing to locate in Riverside were being frightened away . . . and thousands of voters would lose their jobs if Measure B passed." Although this technique apparently worked in Riverside at the polls and in San Diego in the streets, it is doubtful that the majority of the rank and file share the disposition of their leaders on these issues. Nevertheless, the entrepreneurs' influence over the public statements and ceremonial roles of union leaders, regardless of what their members think, helps the rentiers in achieving their aggressive growth policies.

The co-optation of labor leadership is again evident in its role in national urban policy. Labor essentially is a dependable support of growth – anywhere, anytime. Although its traditional constituency is centered in the declining areas of the country, the unions' national hierarchy supports policies little more specific than those that provide "aid to the cities." The active campaign by the United Auto Workers (UAW) for increased investment in Detroit and other sections of the country's "automotive realm" (Hill, 1984) is an exception. Although unions may be especially concerned with the future of the declining areas, they have not tried to develop an effective strategy for directing investment toward these places, at the expense of other places. Labor cannot serve the needs of its most vulnerable and best organized geographical constituency because it won't inhibit investment at any given place. The inability of labor to influence the distribution of development within the United States (much less across world regions) makes organized labor helpless in influencing the political economy of places. Labor becomes little more than one more instrument to be used by elites in competing growth machines.

Self-employed professionals and small retailers

Retailers and professionals ordinarily have no clear interest in the generation of aggregate rents. The stake of these groups in growth depends on their particular situation, including the possibility that growth may displace a clientele upon which they are dependent. Any potential opposition from these groups is, however, blunted by a number of factors, two of which are especially important. Retailers need customers and this often leads them to equate aggregate growth in a locality with an increase in sales and profits for themselves. They also have social ties with local rentier groups, whose avid growth orientation may have a strong influence.

By contrast, larger but locally based retailing chains with substantial local market shares have a direct interest in local growth. They can grow more cheaply by expanding in their own market area (where media and other overhead costs can be spread among existing stores) than by penetrating distant regions. But a larger population base also draws new competitors, since retailing is more competitive than most other businesses. In particular, on reaching a certain size, markets become more attractive to higher-volume, national retailers, such as McDonald's or chain department stores and the malls that house them. Large operations are especially drawn to fast-growing areas in which an early decision to locate can preempt other national competitors. Department stores and chain restaurants displace an enormous number of smaller entrepreneurs (Friedland and Gardner, 1983). Despite these prospects, small retailers are often supporters of local growth machines, even when it means bringing in directly competitive operations. In this instance, ideology seems to prevail over concrete interests and the given record.

Well-paid professionals such as doctors and lawyers sometimes invest their own high salaries in property syndicates (often unprofitable ones) that are put together for them by brokers and financial advisers. This gives the professionals the direct stake in growth outcomes that we ordinarily associate with place entrepreneurs. As social peers of the rentiers, and as vague supporters of value-free production generally, these professionals are often sympathetic to growth. They seem less supportive than business groups, but more supportive than lower-paid professionals or members of the working class (Albrecht, Bultena, and Hoiberg, forthcoming). A critical issue for the affluent professionals is whether their own use of places – to live, shop, and earn money – is compatible with growth. Professionals can avoid the dilemma by investing at a distance from their own homes. As we will see in the next two chapters, professionals not tied to the growth machine make particularly effective citizen opponents of the growth coalition.

Corporate capitalists

Most capitalists, like others whose primary attachment to place is for use values, have little direct interest in land-use intensification in a specific locality. They are in business to gain profits, not rents. Particularly when local corporate leaders are division heads of multilocational firms, there is little reason for direct involvement (see Schulze, 1961). In his report on Houston's historical development, Kaplan quotes a local observer who remarks that the "pro-growth faction" consists of people "whose very good livelihoods depend on a local government that will continue to make the 'right' policy decisions." "Surprisingly," Kaplan comments (1983:204), "the oil and gas industry remains aloof from local Houston politics, preferring to concentrate on the national and international policies crucial to its interests." This disinterest of the large industrials is not a surprise to us.

Nevertheless, corporate actors do have an interest in sustaining the growth machine ideology (as opposed to the actual growth of the area surrounding their plant). This ideology helps make them respected people in their area. Their social worth is often defined in terms of "size of payroll," and their payroll in turn helps them get land-use and budget policies consistent with corporate needs. As long as the rentiers dominate locality, capitalists and their managers need not play a direct role. They may choose to do so anyway, particularly when they are natives of the locale (not branch plant functionaries) with ties to rentier groups (Friedland and Palmer, 1984; Galaskiewicz, 1979a, 1979b). But the absence of corporate officials in local politics (especially branch plant managers), repeatedly observed by various investigators (see Banfield and Wilson, 1963; Dahl, 1961; Schulze, 1961), is not a sign of their lack of power. It can instead be evidence that the local agenda is so pervasively shaped by their interests that they have no need to participate. Like good managers generally, they work through others, leaving their relative invisibility as a sign of their effectiveness. Only when there is a special opportunity, as in modern-day company towns, or when ordinary hegemonic mechanisms fail, do we find corporate functionaries again active in urban politics.

The Effects of Growth

By claiming that more intensive development benefits virtually all groups in a locality, growth machine activists need pay no attention to the distinction between use and exchange values that pervades our analysis. They assert that growth strengthens the local tax base, creates jobs, provides resources to solve existing social problems, meets the housing needs caused by natural population growth, and allows the market to serve public tastes in housing, neighborhoods, and commercial development. Similarly, Paul Peterson speaks of development goals as inherently uncontroversial and "consensual" because they are aligned with the "collective good" (1981:147), "with the interests of the community as a whole" (1981:143). Speaking in characteristically sanguine terms even about urban renewal (widely known by then for its detrimental effects on cities), Peterson says in his celebrated book: "Downtown business benefits, but so do laborers desiring higher wages, homeowners hoping house values will rise, the unemployed seeking new jobs, and politicians aiming for reelection" (1981:147).

Some of these claims, for some times and places, are true. The costs and benefits of growth depend on local circumstance. Declining cities experience problems that might be eased by replacement investments. Even in growing cities, the costs of growth can conceivably be limited by appropriate planning and control techniques. Nevertheless, for many places and times, growth is at best a mixed blessing and the growth machine's claims are merely legitimating ideology, not accurate descriptions of reality. Residents of declining cities, as well as people living in more dynamic areas, are often deceived by the extravagant claims that growth solves problems. These claims demand a realistic evaluation.

Fiscal health

Systematic comparative analyses of government costs as a function of city size and growth have found that cost is positively related to both size of place and rate of growth, at least for middle-size cities (see Appelbaum et al., 1976; Follett, 1976). Of course, the *conditions* of growth are important. The overall fiscal state of a city depends on the kind of growth involved (industrial versus residential, and the subtypes of each) and the existing capacities of the local infrastructure. In general, most studies (see Stuart and Teska, 1971) conclude that housing development represents a net fiscal loss because of the service costs that residents require, although housing for the rich is more lucrative than housing for the poor. Industrial and commercial growth, on the other hand, tends to produce net benefits for the tax base, but only if the costs of servicing additions to the local labor force are omitted from the calculations. If local government provides special tax incentives or other sorts of subsidies to attract new industries, the fiscal costs of development will obviously be higher.

Growth can also at times save a local government money. A primary factor in this possibility is the existence of "unused capacities." If a town has a declining birth rate and thus a school district with empty classrooms, officials may try to attract additional families to increase the efficient use of the physical plant and thereby reduce the per capita costs. If a city is paying off a bonded debt on a sewer plant that could serve double its present demand, officials may seek additional users in order to spread the costs to a larger number and thus decrease the burden for current residents.

Under other conditions, however, even small increases in demand can have enormous fiscal costs if the increases entail major new public expenditures. In many cases infrastructures must be built "all at once"; these are "lumpy" costs. Additional water supplies can sometimes be gained only by constructing a vast aqueduct system that can transport 100,000 acre feet annually as easily as a single acre foot. The costs of such utility investments are usually shared equally by all users; the "new people" don't have to pay more because of the extraordinary costs their presence creates. The developer of a "leap frog" housing tract (one that jumps beyond existing urban development) doesn't pay more than previous entrepreneurs to run utilities a greater distance, despite the higher costs entailed by the location. This pricing system, in which each user pays the same amount regardless of when or how the user joined the client group, tends to mask the cost of additional growth (or the irrationalities of its distribution). These costs can be especially high because the cheap sources of water, power, and highway rights of way are the first ones tapped; expansion thus tends to be increasingly expensive.

Costs to existing residents can be particularly high if the anticipated growth does not materialize. In what Worster (1982:514) calls the "infrastructural trap," localities that place bets on future growth by investing in large-scale capacities then must move heaven and earth to make sure they get that growth. Whether through deceitful plot or inadvertent blunder, the results can be a vicious cycle of crisis-oriented growth addiction as various infrastructures collapse from overuse and are replaced by still larger facilities, which then can only be paid for with additional growth that again creates another crisis of overuse.

All of this resembles the infrastructure crises of much earlier efforts at growth inducement in the nineteenth century. Scheiber (1973) reports absurd redundancies in the canal-building spree of the state of Ohio as each politically powerful land group demanded a linkage to the great waterways. The scenario was repeated with turnpikes and railroads, leading to absurd overcapacity and the "intolerable indebtedness" that led to bond defaults by several states (Goodrich, 1950). Costs of construction were considerably increased through corrupt management, and the viability of the completed projects was eroded by duplication and irrational routings. The result was "bitter disillusionment" (Scheiber, 1973:138) when prosperous towns did not materialize where expected (almost everywhere) and the costs of overbuilt infrastructures remained as a continuous drain on public budgets.

It is less likely today that a single project could bring about such a fiscal disaster, although the nuclear power bankruptcy in 1983 of the major utility in the state of Washington is one case in point, just as similar nuclear power problems threaten other ratepayers elsewhere. In most instances, growth spending corrodes subtly, slowly eroding fiscal integrity as the service costs of new developments outweigh the revenues they generate. Some localities have demanded "hard looks" at the precise cumulative costs, and have come up with striking results. A 1970 study for the city of Palo Alto, California, found that it would be cheaper for that city to purchase its privately owned undeveloped foothills at full value, rather than allow the land to be developed and enter the tax rolls (Livingston and Blayney, 1971). Again, a study of Santa Barbara, California, demonstrated that service expenditures for virtually any population growth would require raising property taxes and utility rates, with no compensatory public service benefits for local residents (Appelbaum et al., 1976). Similar conclusions on the costs of growth have resulted from studies of Boulder, Colorado (citied in Finkler, 1972), and Ann Arbor, Michigan (Ann Arbor, Michigan, Planning Department, 1972). In their review of case studies of the effects of industrial growth in small towns, Summers and Branch (1984) report that increments to the local tax base were in most cases outweighed by added service burdens, except when industrial development was not subsidized by local government and new employees lived in other communities.

The kinds of cities that have undertaken these studies, primarily university towns, are by no means typical U.S. places; in the declining cities of the frostbelt, the results might well be different. And cities can, in reality, manipulate the fiscal consequences of growth to benefit them. Here we want to stress that growth cannot, just because it "adds to the tax base," be assumed beneficial to a city's fiscal well-being. Only a careful analysis of the details can yield accurate conclusions about a specific place at a given time. We suspect that the promised benefits of growth would be found, more often than not, to have been greatly exaggerated by the local growth activists, who, while portraying themselves as the prudent guardians of the public purse, often lead their cities into terrible fiscal troubles.

Employment

A key ideological prop for the growth machine, especially in appealing to the working class, is the assertion that local growth "makes jobs." This claim is aggressively promulgated by developers, bankers, and Chamber of Commerce officials – people whose politics otherwise reveal little concern for problems of the working class. The emphasis on jobs becomes a part of the statesmanlike talk of media editorialists. Needless to say, the benefits in profits and rents are seldom brought up in public.

The reality is that local growth does not make jobs: it only distributes them. In any given year the United States will see the construction of a certain number of new factories, office units, and highways – regardless of where they are put. Similarly, a given number of automobiles, missiles, and lampshades will be made in this country, regardless of where they are manufactured. The number of jobs in this society, whether in the building trades or in any other economic sector, will therefore be determined by rates of return on investments, national trade policy, federal decisions affecting the money supply, and other factors unrelated to local decision making. Except for introducing draconian measures that would replicate Third World labor conditions in U.S. cities (not as remote a possibility as we might think), a locality can only compete with other localities for its share of newly created U.S. jobs. Aggregate employment is unaffected by the outcome of this competition among localities to "make" jobs. The bulk of studies that search, either through cross-sectional or longitudinal analysis, for relations between size or growth of places and unemployment rates fail to show significant relationships (Applebaum et al., 1976; Follett, 1976; Garrison, 1971; Greenberg, n.d; Hadden and Borgatta, 1965:108; Samuelson, 1942; Sierra Club of San Diego, 1973; Summers et al., 1976; Summers and Branch, 1984; but see Eberts, 1979).

Despite the pain and difficulty often associated with interurban migrations, there is enough worker mobility, at least within national boundaries, to fill jobs at geographically distant points, including even the wilds of Alaska. When jobs develop in a fast-growing area, workers from other areas are attracted to fill the developing vacancies, thus preserving the same unemployment rate as before the growth surge. Indeed, especially in cases of rapid, "boom town" growth, enthusiastic media coverage can prompt large numbers of workers to migrate, much in excess of immediate job openings. A large surplus of workers results when the boom comes to its inevitable end, often with many of the infrastructural

costs still to be paid (Markusen, 1978). The human strain of migration –
people forced to leave their relatives and neighborhood behind – may
prove to have been for nothing. Unemployment rates in the state of
Alaska, a boom region for many years, exceeded the national average
from 1972 to 1982 every year except one. In 1978, even before oil prices
began their precipitous fall, the national unemployment rate was 6.1
percent and the Alaska rate was 11.2 percent.

Similarly, just as "new jobs" may not change the aggregate *rate* of
unemployment (either locally or nationally), they may also have little
effect on unemployed *individuals* in a given place. For example, cities that
are able to reverse chronic economic decline and stagnation, as Atlantic
City has done through its recent gambling boom, often provide new jobs
primarily for suburbanites and other "outsiders," rather than for the
indigenous working class in whose name the transformation was justified (Sternlieb and Hughes, 1983a; see also Greenberg, n.d.; Summers et
al., 1976). Summers and Branch (1984) draw the same conclusion in
their review of the effects of growth on small towns, reporting that typically less than 10 percent of new industrial jobs are filled by persons who
were previously unemployed (of whatever residential origin). Evidently,
the new jobs are taken by people who already have jobs, many of whom
are migrants.[8] Summers observes that "newcomers intervene between
the jobs and the local residents, especially the disadvantaged," because
they possess "more education, better skills, or the 'right' racial heritage"
(as quoted in Bluestone and Harrison, 1982:90).

It is still possible that certain patterns of growth may stimulate employment without attracting migrants. New jobs that bring underemployed
women or youths into the work force may have this effect. It is also true
that certain categories of workers can be especially penalized if local labor
markets fail to expand, for example, those immobilized by ill health,
family commitments, or other factors that limit mobility. But overall,
even though local growth may sometimes have beneficial effects on
specific individuals and subgroups, both the weight of empirical evidence
and the logic of the process indicate that net benefits do not follow as a
matter of course. Indeed, our conclusions reinforce what has been called
the "unanimous" agreement among economists that "the only jurisdiction that should be concerned with the effects of its policies on the level
of employment is the Federal government. Small jurisdictions do not
have the power to effect significant changes in the level of unemployment" (Levy and Arnold, 1972:95).

The real problem is that the United States is a society of constant
joblessness, with unemployment rates conservatively estimated by the
Department of Commerce at 4 to 11 percent of the work force defined as
ordinarily active. A game of musical chairs is being played at all times,
with workers circulating around the country, hoping to land in an empty
position when the music stops. Redistributing the stock of jobs among

places may move the chairs around, but it does not alter the number of chairs available to the players.

Job and income mobility

Related to the issue of unemployment is the question of occupational mobility in general. It seems obvious that only in the largest places is it possible to attain the highest incomes in the lucrative occupations; for individuals with such ambitions, large may be the only option. Other than moving (the more efficient mechanism), growth of place is the only answer. In general, studies that have compared wage rates among places have found that urban areas with more people have higher wages rates, although the differences between places are small (Alonso, 1973; Appelbaum, 1978; Fuchs, 1967; Hoch, 1972).

More relevant in the present context than the issue of how size affects wages is the issue of how income is influenced by urban *growth*. In his study of matched "self-contained" cities, Appelbaum (1978) found that there was indeed a positive relation between family income and rate of urban growth (see Eberts [1979] for similar results using Northeast counties). But the size and growth effects together had a small *net* effect: controlling for other variables, size and growth explained about 8 percent of the variance in income among places. More crucially, we don't learn in these studies whether growth tends to merely attract higher-wage workers from other areas (which then "decline" in median income as a result), or growth itself benefits indigenous populations.

Also complicating the interpretation of the growth-related income difference is evidence that larger places (and in particular fast-growing ones) have higher living costs, which offset the higher wages. The degree to which this occurs is a matter of debate (Appelbaum, 1978; Hoch, 1972; Shefer, 1970). Although most evidence suggests that *size* has little effect on living costs, *growth* has a much greater effect. This is especially true for housing costs; the effects of growth on prices are especially strong for both single-family houses and apartments (Appelbaum, 1978:36–37; Appelbaum and Gilderbloom, 1983). Because so many detrimental effects of growth on costs are not reflected in these studies of household income – for example, the effects of pollution on health care and building maintenance expenses – we must conclude that growth does not benefit a family in terms of net income or quality of life.

An alternative way of investigating the connection between growth and the personal income of local populations is through case studies of how growth has affected the wages of specific social and occupational groups in given places. Greenberg (n.d.) carried out such a study with a special focus on low-wage groups and, in particular, poor blacks in southern counties of three sub-regions that were experiencing different patterns of development. Although all the areas in her study experienced rates of growth exceeding the national growth rate between 1960 and 1980, the economic basis of that growth was different in each place and had distinct consequences for specific labor groups. There were three different patterns: (1) growth in service industry in an area of declining low-wage manufacturing; (2) invasion of manufacturing jobs into an agricultural zone; and (3) major expansion of government jobs in an area with a mixed economy.

In the first case, found in Durham, North Carolina, the transition from a manufacturing to a service economy meant "that blacks simply exchanged low wage jobs in low growth sectors of the economy for low wage jobs in high growth sectors" (Greenberg, n.d.:23). In the second pattern, found in the area outside Durham, in which manufacturing invaded a former agricultural zone, Greenberg found that incoming industrialization did not bring higher living standards: "The transition from agriculture to low wage manufacturing has done little to improve the relative economic position of blacks in most types of nonagricultural employment. Whites also earn substantially less than their counterparts in the adjacent urban counties" (Greenberg, n.d.:24). In Greenberg's third growth pattern, there were substantial gains for blacks and, presumably, the poor in general. In Wake County, the growth in employment was based heavily on expansion by the government. The number of blacks in high-level jobs increased and their wage gains outpaced the national average for blacks during this period. Although Greenberg attributes these gains for blacks to the increased "diversity" of the economy that government employment provided, we might put equal stress on the civil service and affirmative action requirements of government hiring and promotion (see Baron and Bielby, 1980).

Whatever the specific reasons for the differences among places, Greenberg's findings indicate that "growth *per se* is no panacea for urban poverty" (Greenberg, n.d.: 26). Instead, the issue is the *kind* of growth that is involved, and the degree (ordinarily, limited) to which local residents are given an advantage over migrants in the competition for jobs. Otherwise, local growth may be only a matter of making the local rich even richer, or, alternatively, of moving those already privileged in their jobs from one part of the country to another part of the country. To stay with our metaphor of musical chairs, the number of *comfortable* chairs and the basis for allocating them does not change; only their *location* is altered. As Summers and Branch conclude on the basis of their own growth studies, "Industrial location has a small or even negative effect on the local public sector and on economically disadvantaged citizens" (1984:153; see also Garrison, 1971). This is hardly consistent with the myth of opportunity promoted by supporters of the growth machine.

Eliminating social problems

The idea that an increase in numbers and density leads to severe social pathology has been, at long last, thoroughly discredited (see, for example, Fischer, Baldasarre, and Ofshe, 1975). We do believe, however, that size and rate of growth have a role in creating and exacerbating urban problems such as segregation and inequality.

The great population explosions that marked America's industrial cities earlier in this century cannot be said to have increased levels of either equality or class and racial integration. Instead, greater numbers seem to have increased spatial and social segregation between rich and poor, black and white (Lieberson, 1980; Zunz, 1982). In a more contemporary context, Sternlieb and Hughes (1983a) have studied the social effects of the growth of gambling in Atlantic City, New Jersey – the revitalization of a service sector industry. Sternlieb and Hughes report that the consequences have been extremely negative for existing residents. The growth boom has set up "walled off universes" of casino-generated wealth, with the old people and poor finding their former "dismal comforts being swept away," without the compensation of better jobs.[9] The original residents are not participating in the new economy, except at the bottom (as is consistent with Greenberg's findings, discussed above), and the overall effect of the gambling boom on the community is to exacerbate visible cleavages between the rich and the poor (see also Markusen, 1978).

More generally, growth may not be the cause of problems, but increases in scale make it more difficult to deal with those that do exist. Racial integration is more difficult when members of a minority are concentrated in large ghettos within a vast, and often politically divided, region. It becomes harder to accomplish school integration without busing pupils over long distances and across jurisdictional lines. Busing generates controversy and high costs to public budgets as well as taking up children's time. In small places, racially and economically diverse social groups can more easily end up in the same schools, as well as the same shopping, recreation, and work settings. Whether through fortuitous movements of people or through managed intervention programs, small places can be more easily integrated, racially and economically. Under current jurisdictional and ecological patterns, growth tends to intensify the separation and disparities among social groups and communities.

Growth is likely to increase inequality within places through its effects on the distribution of rents. Increases in urban scale mean larger numbers of bidders for the same critically located land parcels (for example, the central business district or the site for a freeway intersection), inflating land prices relative to wages and other wealth sources. Although growth expands the center zone (as well as stimulating other pockets in the area) the critical locations remain unique. Hence we see the familiar pattern of an intense use of critical spots (for example, Wall street or Rodeo Drive) with a sharp drop in rent levels just outside their boundaries. Growth disproportionately increases the value of strategic parcels, generating monopoly effects for their owners. Thus, in terms of rental wealth, urban growth is likely to increase inequality.

There is some empirical evidence showing greater income disparities within larger and faster-growing places, whether from monopoly rent effects or another factor (Haworth, Long, and Rasmussen, 1978; but see Walker, 1978). Other studies, however, find little or no impact of size or growth rates on wealth distribution (Alonso, 1973; Appelbaum, 1978; Betz, 1972). Our own conclusion is that growth mainly hurts those in its direct path whose primary tie to place is for its residential use value. When tracing the effect of growth, we must look at how particular groups, at a given time and place, are affected by development.

Environment

Growth has obvious negative consequences for the physical environment; growth affects the quality of air and water, and the ease of getting around in a town or city. Growth obliterates open spaces and damages the aesthetic features of a natural terrain. It decreases ecological variety with a consequent threat to the larger ecosystem.

Though sometimes viewed as trivial concerns of an idle middle class ("rich housewives," according to the stereotype), these blows to the physical environment most heavily affect the less well to do. A high-quality physical environment constitutes a free public good for those who have access to it (Harvey, 1973). Those who are unable to buy amenities in the market lose most from the unavailability of such resources. More concretely, since the poor are most likely to live and work in close proximity to pollution sources, the poor are more affected by growth-induced environmental decay than are the rich.

Perhaps nowhere are the effects of environmental decline more dramatically displayed than in those places with the most rapid growth experiences. Feagin (1983a), for example, has compiled a list of Houston's problems that have accompanied that city's emergence as "capital of the sunbelt." These include crises in sewage disposal, toxic dumps, water supplies, and transportation. In addition to the visible increases in pollution and congestion, past environmental sins will entail vast cleanup costs – what Worster (1982:514) calls "ecological backlash." By 1983, Houston was second only to New York City in per capita bonding liability. Environmental decline, here as elsewhere, can exacerbate fiscal problems and inequality of life chances among rich and poor.

Accommodating natural increase

Growth activists incessantly raise the problem of providing "homes and jobs for our children." To avoid the forced exile of their youth, towns and cities might reasonably have as a goal the maintenance of economic expansion sufficient to provide jobs and housing for new generations. These expansions would be modest in scale, given the low rates of birth that are characteristic of U.S. urban populations. The difficulty is "reserving" the right openings for the right youths, a goal that is unrealistic given the nature of the hiring queue and the constitutional limitations on restraint of trade. Virtually no local growth policy could effectively guarantee local jobs for local people. Many of the young prefer, of course, to leave their home town anyway, and this in itself probably eliminates the problem of having to create large numbers of jobs to accommodate local youth.

Satisfying public taste

The current pattern of urbanization is not necessarily a response to people's wishes. As Sundquist has remarked,

> The notion commonly expressed that Americans have "voted with their feet" in favor of the great cities is, on the basis of every available sampling, so much nonsense . . . What is called "freedom of choice" is, in sum, freedom of employer choice or, more precisely, freedom of choice for that segment of the corporate world that operates mobile enterprises. The real question, then, is whether freedom of corporate choice should be automatically honored by government policy at the expense of freedom of individual choice where those conflict. (1975:258)

Most evidence suggests that people prefer living in small places or rural areas (Appelbaum et al., 1974:4.2–4.6; Finkler, 1972:2, 23; Hoch, 1972:280; Mazie and Rowlings, 1973; Parke and Westoff, 1972). Although only 8 percent of Americans in 1977, for example, lived in small towns and farm areas, 48 percent gave such places as their residential preference (Fischer, 1984:20). The larger the metropolis, the greater the proportion of people (in both the central city and suburbs) who express a desire to move away (Gallup, 1979:85). If people's responses to surveys are any indication, a substantial portion of the migration to the great metropolitan areas of the postwar decades was more in spite of tastes than because of them.

Growth Trade-offs

Although there is clear evidence on some of the effects of growth, urban size is fundamentally a political or value issue in which one person's criteria are lined up against another's (see Duncan, 1957). It may, for example, be necessary to sacrifice clean air to build a population base large enough to support a major opera company. If one loves music enough, the price may be worth paying. But in reality, differential material interests influence the trade-offs. If one happens to be on the winning side of the rent intensification process (or in the opera business), the pleasures of cleaner air or lower taxes will be easier to forgo.

Besides the variations between individuals and groups, the actual price to be paid for growth and the willingness to pay it will vary somewhat. Having an opera house is probably more important to the Viennese than to the residents of Carmel, California, and in the same way the preferred trade-offs in population size will vary. On more prosaic grounds, certain places may need additional population to absorb the costs of existing road and sewer systems, however misguided the initial commitment to build them. People in some small towns may want a population increase in order to make rudimentary specialization possible in their public school system. In other instances, a past history of outmigration may have left behind a surplus of unused capacities, which would easily accommodate additional growth and provide public benefits of various sorts.

These variations notwithstanding, the evidence on fiscal health and economic or social problems indicates clearly that the assumptions of value-free development are false. In many cases, probably in most, additional local growth under current arrangements is a transfer of wealth and life chances from the general public to the rentier groups and their associates. Use values of a majority are sacrificed for the exchange gains of the few. To question the wisdom of growth for any specific locality is to threaten a benefit transfer and the interests of those who gain from it.

Notes

1   The same phenomenon is found today in Chicago suburbs formed principally to benefit from state fiscal codes.

2   We were struck by the naive wording used by one historian in commenting upon the life of an urban booster-lawyer: "*despite* [our emphasis] his extensive business career, Brice delved deeply into politics as well. His devotion to the State [Ohio] and its economic interests won him wide popularity there" (Klein, 1970:110).

3   Trillin remarks that rejection of high taxes by the citizens of Rockford is "consistent with what the business and industrial leadership of Rockford has traditionally preached. For years, the industrialists were considered to be in complete control of the sort of local government industrialists traditionally favor – a conservative, relatively clean administration committed

to the proposition that the highest principle of government is the lowest property tax rate" (Trillin, 1976:150).

4   Local planning officials also sometimes get in on some of the corruption; they may make real estate investments of their own. Los Angeles Planning Director Calvin Hamilton was pressured to resign after twenty years on the job in part because of revelations that he accepted free rent from developers for a side business and had other conflicts of interest (Clifford, 1985d).

5   Although many suburban newspapers encourage growth, especially of tax-generating businesses, the papers of exclusive suburban towns may instead try to guard the existing land-use patterns and social base of their circulation area. Rudel (1989:104) describes just this sort of situation in Westport, Connecticut. There are a number of reasons for this occasional deviation from the rule we are proposing. When trying to attract advertising dollars, newspapers prefer a small, rich readership to a larger but poorer one. Maintaining exclusivity is itself occasionally a growth strategy for smaller communities. Opposition to growth in these cases is consistent with the desires of local elites.

6   Cox and Morgan's study of British local newspapers indicates that the booster role of the press is not unique to the United States.

7   Unions oppose growth projects that bring nonunion shops; the UAW did not welcome Japanese-owned auto plants that would exclude the union.

8   Further, new industrial investment in one city often eliminates jobs at another city, with no net gain.

9   "Atlantic City Hurt by Gambling, Study Finds," *Los Angeles Times*, November 2, 1983, sec. I. p. 11.

References

Agger, Robert, Daniel Goldrich, and Bert E. Swanson. 1964. *The Rulers and the Ruled: Political Power and Impotence in American Communities.* New York: Wiley.

Albrecht, Don, Gordon Bultena, and Eric O. Hoiberg. Forthcoming. "Constituency of the Antigrowth Movement: A Comparison of the Growth Orientations of Urban Status Groups." *Urban Affairs Quarterly.*

Alexander, Herbert E. 1972. *Money in Politics.* Washington, D.C.: Public Affairs Press.

Alexander, Herbert. 1980. *Financing Politics: Money, Elections and Political Reform.* 2nd ed. Washington, D.C.: Congressional Quarterly Press.

Alexander, Herbert. 1983. *Financing the 1980 Election.* Lexington, Mass.: D. C. Heath.

Alford, Robert, and Roger Friedland. 1975. "Political Participation and Public Policy." *Annual Review of Sociology* 1:429–79.

Alonso, William. 1973. "Urban Zero Population Growth." *Daedalus* 102(4):191–206

Ann Arbor, Michigan, Planning Department. 1972. *The Ann Arbor Growth Study.* Ann Arbor, Mich.: City Planning Department.

Appelbaum, Richard P. 1977. "The Future Is Made, Not Predicted – Technocratic Planners vs. Public Interests." *Society* 14(4):45–53.

Appelbaum, Richard P., and John Gilderbloom. 1983. "Housing Supply and Regulation: A Study of the Rental Housing Market." *Journal of Applied Behavioral Science* 19(1):1–18.

Applebaum, Richard P., Jennifer Bigelow, Henry Kramer, Harvey Molotch, and Paul Relis. 1976. *The Effects of Urban Growth.* New York: Praeger.

Applebaum, Richard P. 1978. *Size, Growth and U.S. Cities.* New York: Praeger

Applebaum, Richard P., Jennifer Bigelow, Henry Kramer, Harvey Molotch, and Paul Relis. 1974. *Santa Barbara: The Impacts of Growth.* Santa Barbara, Cal.: Office of the City Clerk.

Bachrach, Peter, and Morton Baratz. 1962. "The Two Faces of Power." *American Polictical Science Review* 56:947–952.

Banfield, Edward C. 1961. *Political Influence.* New York: Macmillan.

Banfield, Edward C., and James Q. Wilson. 1963. *City Politics.* Cambridge, Mass.: Harvard University Press.

Baron, James N., and William T. Bielby. 1984. "The Organization of Work in a Segmented Economy." *American Sociological Review* 49(4):454–473.

Belcher, Wyatt W. 1947. *The Economic Rivalry between St. Louis and Chicago, 1850–1880.* New York: Columbia University Press.

Bell, Daniel. 1961. "Crime as an American Way of Life." Pp. 127–150 in Daniel Bell, *The End of Ideology: On the Exhaustion of Political Ideas in the Fifties.* New York: Collier Books.

Bernard, Richard M. 1983. "Oklahoma City: Booming Schooner." Pp. 213–234 in Richard M. Bernard and Bradley R. Rice (eds.), *Sunbelt Cities: Politics and Growth since World War II.* Austin: University of Texas Press.

Berry, Brian J. L., and John Kasarda. 1977. *Contemporary Urban Ecology.* New York: Macmillan.

Betz, D. Michael. 1972. "The City as a System Generating Income Inequality." *Social Forces* 51(2):192–198.

Binford, Henry C. 1985. *The First Suburbs: Residential Communities on the Boston Periphery 1815–1860.* Chicago: University of Chicago Press.

Boorstin, Daniel. 1965. *The Americans: The National Experience.* New York: Random House.

Bouma, Donald. 1962. "Analysis of the Social Power Position of a Real Estate Board." *Social Problems* 10(Fall):121–132.

Boyarsky, Bill, and Jerry Gillam. 1982. "Hard Times Don't Stem Flow of Campaign Gifts." *Los Angeles Times,* April 4, sec. I, pp. 1,3,22,23.

Brower, John. 1972. *The Black Side of Football.* Ph.D. dissertation, Department of Sociology, University of California, Santa Barbara.

Burd, Gene. 1977. "The Selling of the Sunbelt: Civic Boosterism in the Media." Pp. 129–150 in David Perry and Alfred Watkins (eds.), *The Rise of the Sunbelt Cities.* Beverly Hills, Calif.: Sage.

Caro, Robert A. 1974. *The Power Broker: Robert Moses and the Fall of New York.* New York: Knopf.

Clark, David L. 1983. "Improbable Los Angeles." Pp. 268–308 in Richard M. Bernard and Bradley R. Rice (eds.), *Sunbelt Cities: Politics and Growth since World War II.* Austin: University of Texas Press.

Clark, Terry. 1968. "Community Structure, Decision-Making, Budget Expenditures, and Urban Renewal in Fifty-one American Cities." *American Sociological Review* 33(August):576–593.

Clayton, Janet. 1984. "South-Central L.A. Fears Olympics to Disrupt Lives." *Los Angeles Times,* February 5, sec. II, p. 1.

Clifford, Frank. 1985d. "Ouster of City Planner Sought." *Los Angeles Times,* July 15, Sec. I, pp. 1, 13.

Corso, Anthony. 1983. "San Diego: The Anti-City." Pp. 328–344 in Richard M. Bernard and Bradley R. Rice (eds.), *Sunbelt Cities: Politics and Growth since World War II.* Austin: University of Texas Press.

Cox, Harvey, and David Morgan. 1973. *City Politics and the Press: Journalists and the Governing of Merseyside.* Cambridge: Cambridge University Press.

Dagenais, Julie. 1967. "Newspaper Language as an Active Agent in the Building of a Frontier Town." *American Speech* 42(2):114–121.

Dahl, Robert Alan. 1961. *Who Governs?* New Haven: Yale University Press.

D'Ambrosio, Mary. 1985. "Coyne Slates Talks on Hockey Franchise." *Albany Times Union,* February 14, sec. B, p. 1.

Daws, Gavan, and George Cooper. 1984. *Land and Power in Hawaii: The Democratic Years.* Honolulu: Benchmark Press.

Devereux, Sean. 1976. "Boosters in the Newsroom: The Jacksonville Case." *Columbia Journalism Review* 14:38–47.

Domhoff, G. William. 1967. *Who Rules America?* Englewood Cliffs, N.J.: Prentice-Hall.

Domhoff, G. William. 1970. *The Higher Circles: The Governing Class in America.* New York: Random House.

Domhoff, G. William. 1971. *The Higher Circles: The Governing Class in America.* New York: Random House.

Domhoff, G. William. 1978. *Who Really Rules: New Haven Community Power Re-Examined.* Santa Monica, Calif.: Goodyear.

Domhoff, G. William. 1983. *Who Rules America Now? A View for the 80's.* Englewood Cliffs, N.J.: Prentice-Hall.

Duncan, Otis Dudley. 1957. "Optimum Size of Cities." Pp. 759–773 in Paul K. Hatt and Albert J. Reiss, Jr. (eds), *Readings in Urban Sociology,* 2nd ed. Glencoe, Ill.: Free Press.

Eberts, Paul R. 1979. "Growth and the Quality of Life: Some Logical and Methodological Issues." Pp. 159–184 in Gene F. Summers and Arne Selvik (eds.), *Nonmetropolitan Industrial Growth and Community Change.* Lexington, Mass.: Lexington Books.

Edelman, Murray. 1964. *The Symbolic Uses of Politics.* Urbana: University of Illinois Press.

Eitzen, D. Stanley, and George H. Sage. 1978. *Sociology of American Sport.* Dubuque, Iowa: William C. Brown.

Fainstein, Susan, Norman Fainstein, and P. Jefferson Armistead. 1983. "San Francisco: Urban Transformation and the Local State." Pp. 202–244 in Susan Fainstein (ed.), *Restructuring the City.* New York: Longman.

Feagin, Joe R. 1983a. "The Capital of the Sunbelt: Houston's Growth and the Oil Industry." Unpublished manuscript, Department of Sociology, University of Texas, Austin.

Finkler, Earl. 1972. "No-Growth as a Planning Alternative." Planning Advisory Report No. 283. Chicago: Amercian Society of Planning Officials.

Fischer, Claude S. 1982. *To Dwell among Friends.* Chicago: University of Chicago Press.

Fischer, Claude S. 1984. *The Urban Experience*. San Diego: Harcourt Brace Jovanovich.

Fischer, Claude S., Mark Baldasarre, and R. J. Ofshe. 1975. "Crowding Studies and Urban Life – A Critical Review." *Journal of the American Institute of Planners* 41(6):406–418.

Fishman, Mark. 1978. "Crime Waves as Ideology." *Social Problems* 25(5):532–543.

Fogelson, Robert M. 1967. *The Fragmented Metropolis: Los Angeles, 1850–1930*. Cambridge, Mass.: Harvard University Press.

Follett, Ross. 1976. "Social Consequences of Urban Size and Growth: An Analysis of U.S. Urban Areas." Ph.D. dissertation, Department of Sociology, University of California, Santa Barbara.

Form, William H., and William V. D'Antonio. 1970. "Integration and Cleavage among Community Influentials in Two Border Cities." Pp. 431–442 in Michael Aiken and Paul E. Mott (eds.), *The Structure of Community Power*. New York: Random House.

Fowlkes, Martha R., and Patricia Miller. 1985. "Toward a Sociology of Unnatural Disaster." Paper presented at the 80th annual meeting of the American Sociological Association, Washington, D.C., August 31.

Freidel, Frank. 1963. "Boosters, Intellectuals and the American City." Pp. 115–120 in Oscar Handlin and John Burchard (eds.), *The Historian and the City*. Cambridge, Mass.: MIT Press.

Friedland, Roger, and Carole Gardner. 1983. "Department Store Socialism." Testimony before the City of Santa Barbara Redevelopment Agency. Photocopy.

Friedland, Roger, and Donald Palmer. 1984. "Park Place and Main Street: Business and the Urban Power Structure." Pp. 393–416 in Ralph Turner (ed.), *Annual Review of Sociology*, vol. 10. Beverly Hills, Cal.: Sage.

Friedland, Roger, Frances Piven, and Robert Alford. 1978. "Political Conflict, Urban Structure, and the Fiscal Crisis." Pp. 175–225 in Douglas Ashford (ed.), *Comparing Urban Policies*. Beverly Hills, Calif.: Sage.

Fuchs, Victor. 1967. "Differentials in Hourly Earnings by Region and City Size, 1959." Paper 101. New York: National Bureau of Economic Research.

Fuller, Justin. 1976. "Boomtowns and Blast Furnaces: Town Promotion in Alabama, 1885–1893." *Alabama Review* 29(January):37–48.

Fullinwider, John. 1980. "Dallas: The City with No Limits?" *In These Times* 5(6):12–13.

Gaffney, M. Mason. 1961. "Land and Rent in Welfare Economics." Pp. 141–167 in *Land Economics Research* (papers presented at a symposium on land economics research, Lincoln, Nebraska, June 16–23). Washington, D.C.: Resources for the Future. Distributed by Johns Hopkins University Press, Baltimore.

Galaskiewicz, Joseph. 1979a. *Exchange Networks and Community Politics*. Beverly Hills, Calif.: Sage.

Galaskiewicz, Joseph. 1979b. "The Structure of Community Organizational Networks." *Social Forces* 57(4):1346–1364.

Gallup, George H. (ed.). 1979. *The Gallup Poll: Public Opinion, 1978*. Wilmington, Del.: Scholarly Resources.

Garrison, Charles B. 1971. "New Industry in Small Towns: The Impact on Local Government." *National Tax Journal* 21(4):493–500.

Glaab, Charles N. 1962. *Kansas City and the Railroads*. Madison: State Historical Society of Wisconsin.

Goodrich, Carter. 1950. "The Revulsion against Internal Improvements." *Journal of Economic History* 10:145–151.

Gordon, Margaret T., Linda Heath, and Robert leBailly. 1979. "Some Costs of Easy News: Crime Reports and Fear." Paper presented at the annual meeting of the American Psychological Association, New York.

Greenberg, Stephanie. n.d. "Rapid Growth in a Southern Area: Consequences for Social Inequality." Unpublished manuscript, Denver Research Institute, University of Denver, Denver, Colorado.

Hadden, Jeffrey K., and Edgar Borgatta. 1965. *American Cities: Their Social Characteristics*. Chicago: Rand McNally.

Halberstam, David. 1979. *The Powers That Be*. New York: Knopf.

Harvey, David. 1973. *Social Justice and the City*. Baltimore: Johns Hopkins University Press.

Hawley, Amos. 1950. *Human Ecology: A Theory of Community Structure*. New York: Ronald Press.

Haworth, Charles T., James E. Long, and David W. Rasmussen. 1978. "Income Distribution, City Size, and Urban Growth." *Urban Studies* 15(1):1–7.

Hayes, Thomas C. 1984. "Shortfall Likely in Olympic Income." *New York Times*. May 9. p. 5.

Hill, Richard Child. 1984. "Economic Crisis and Political Response in the Motor City." Pp. 313–338 in Larry Sawers and William K. Tabb (eds.). *Sunbelt/Snowbelt: Urban Development and Regional Restructuring*. New York: Oxford University Press.

Hirsch, Seymour. 1969. "On Uncovering the Great Nerve Gas Coverup." *Ramparts* 3(July):12–18.

Hoch, Irving. 1972. "Urban Scale and Environmental Quality." Pp. 231–286 in U.S. Commission on Population Growth and the American Future, Ronald G. Ridker (ed.), *Population, Resources, and the Environment*, vol. 3 of Commission Research Reports. Washington, D.C.: Government Printing Office.

Hunter, Floyd. 1953. *Community Power Structure: A Study of Decision Makers*. Chapel Hill: University of North Carolina Press.

Hunter, Floyd. 1980. *Community Power Succession*. Chapel Hill: University of North Carolina Press.

Johnson, David R. 1983. "San Antonio: The Vicissitudes of Boosterism." Pp. 235–254 in Richard M. Bernard and Bradley R. Rice (eds.), *Sunbelt Cities: Politics and Growth since World War II*. Austin: University of Texas Press.

Judd, Dennis. 1983. "From Cowtown ot Sunbelt City." Pp. 167–201 in Susan Fainstein (ed.), *Restructuring the City*. New York: Longman.

Kaplan, Barry J. 1984. "Houston: The Golden Buckle of the Sunbelt." Pp. 196–212 in Richard M. Bernard and Bradley R. Rice (eds.), *Sunbelt Cities: Politics and Growth since World War II*. Austin: University of Texas Press.

King, Wayne. 1985. "U. of Texas Facing Cuts in Its Budget." *New York Times*, March 17, p. 12.

Klein, Maury. 1970. *The Great Richmond Terminal: A Study of Businessmen and Business Strategy*. Charlottesville: Univeristy Press of Virginia.

Krannich, Richard S., and Craig R. Humphrey. 1983. "Local Mobilization and

Community Growth: Toward an Assessment of the 'Growth Machine' Hypothesis." *Rural Sociology* 48(1):60–81.

Lasswell, Harold. 1936. *Politics: Who Gets What, When, How.* New York: McGraw-Hill.

Lester, Marilyn. 1971. "Toward a Sociology of Public Events." Master's thesis, Department of Sociology, University of California, Santa Barbara.

Lever, Janet. 1983. *Soccer in Brazil: Sports' Contribution to Social Integration.* Chicago: University of Chicago Press.

Levine, Adeline Gordon. 1982. *Love Canal: Science, Politics and People.* Lexington, Mass.: D. C. Heath.

Levy, Steven, and Robert K. Arnold. 1972. "An Evaluation of Four Growth Alternatives in the City of Milpitas, 1972–1977." Technical Memorandum Report. Palo Alto, Calif.: Institute of Regional and Urban Studies.

Lieberson, Stanley. 1980. *A Piece of the Pie: Blacks and White Immigrants since 1800.* Berkeley and Los Angeles: University of California Press.

Livingston, Laurence, and John A. Blayney. 1971. "Foothill Environmental Design Study: Open Space vs. Development." Final report to the City of Palo Alto. San Francisco: Livingston and Blayney.

Luckingham, Bradford. 1983. "Phoenix: The Desert Metropolis." Pp. 309–327 in Richard M. Bernard and Bradley R. Rice (eds.), *Sunbelt Cities: Politics and Growth since World War II.* Austin: University of Texas Press.

Lyon, Larry, Lawrence G. Felice, M. Ray Perryman, and E. Stephen Parker. 1981. "Community Power and Population Increase: An Empirical Test of the Growth Machine Model." *American Journal of Sociology* 86(6):1387–1400.

McCombs, Maxwell E., and Donald Shaw. 1972. "The Agenda Setting Function of Mass Media." *Public Opinion Quarterly* 36:176–187.

McGarry, T. W. 1985. "Irish Will March to Four Different Drummers." *Los Angeles Times*, March 14, sec. II, pp. 1, 3.

McKenzie, R. D. 1922. "The Neighborhood: A Study of Local Life in the City of Columbus Ohio – Conclusion." *American Journal of Sociology* 27:780–799.

Maguire, Miles. 1985. "Boondoggle or Marvel: Tenn-Tom Waterway Locks Open." *Baltimore Sun*, January 13, sec. D, p. 1.

Makielski, Stanislaw J. 1966. *The Politics of Zoning: The New York Experience.* New York: Columbia University Press.

Markusen, Ann. 1978. "Class, Rent and Sectoral Conflict: Uneven Development in Western U.S. Boomtowns." *Review of Radical Political Economics* 10(3):117–129.

Mazie, Sara Mills, and Steve Rowlings. 1973. "Public Attitude toward Population Distribution Issues." Pp. 603–615 in Sara Mills Mazie (ed.), *Population Distribution and Policy.* Washington, D.C.: Commission on Population Growth and the American Future.

Melosi, Martin. 1983. "Dallas-Fort Worth: Marketing the Metroplex." Pp. 162–195 in Richard M. Bernard and Bradley R. Rice (eds.), *Sunbelt Cities: Politics and Growth since World War II.* Austin: University of Texas Press.

Mollenkopf, John. 1983. *The Contested City.* Princeton, N.J.: Princeton University Press.

Molotch, Harvey. 1980. "Media and Movements." Pp. 71–93 in Mayer Zald and John McCarthy (eds.), *The Dynamics of Social Movements.* Cambridge, Mass.: Winthrop.

Molotch, Harvey, and Marilyn Lester. 1974. "News as Purposive Behavior: On the Strategic Use of Routine Events, Accidents, and Scandals." *American Sociological Review* 39(1):101–113.

Molotch, Harvey, and Marilyn Lester. 1975. "Accidental News: The Great Oil Spill as Local Occurrence and National Event." *American Journal of Sociology* 81(2):235–260.

Mormino, Gary R. 1983. "Tampa: From Hell Hole to the Good Life." Pp. 138–161 in Richard M. Bernard and Bradley R. Rice (eds.), *Sunbelt Cities: Politics and Growth since World War II.* Austin: University of Texas Press.

Mumford, Lewis. 1961. *The City in History.* New York: Harcourt.

Neiman, Max, and Ronald O. Loveridge. 1981. "Environmentalism and Local Growth Control: A Probe into the Class Bias Thesis." *Environment and Behavior* 13(6):759–772.

New York Times. 1984a. "Some Affluent Jersey Towns Bow to Court and Accept Low-Income Homes." *New York Times*, February 29, sec. A, p. 1, sec. B, p. 5.

New York Times. 1984b. "California's Split on the Unitary Tax." *New York Times,* September 18, sec. D, p. 4.

New York Times. 1984c. "Census Report Shows Rise in Foreign-Born Americans." *New York Times,* October 21, sec. A, p. 60.

New York Times. 1984d. "Plan for Nuclear Dump Divides Dakota Town." *New York Times,* November 4, sec. A, p. 76.

Parke, Robert, Jr., and Charles Westoff (eds.). 1972. *Aspects of Population Growth Policy* (report of the U.S. Commission on Population Growth and the American Future, vol. 6). Washington, D.C.: Commission on Population Growth and the American Future.

Peterson, Paul E. 1981. *City Limits.* Chicago: University of Chicago Press.

Pittas, Michael. 1984. "The Arts Edge: Revitalizing Economic Life in California's Cities." Speech presented at a conference sponsored by the California Economic Development Commission Local Government Advisory Committee, Santa Barbara, July 15.

Rice, Bradley R. 1983. "If Dixie Were Atlanta." Pp. 31–57 in Richard M. Bernard and Bradley R. Rice (eds.), *Sunbelt Cities: Politics and Growth since World War II.* Austin: University of Texas Press.

Risen, James. 1984. "Auto World Theme Park to Close." *Los Angeles Times,* June 12, sec. IV, p. 1.

Rivera, Nancy. 1983a. "High Tech Firm Picks Austin over San Diego." *Los Angeles Times,* May 18, sec. IV, pp. 1, 2.

Roderick, Kevin. 1984. "Cities Play Hardball to Lure Teams." *Los Angeles Times,* June 30, sec. I, pp. 1, 24.

Rosenstiel, Thomas B. 1985. " 'Killing Fields' Writer Loses N.Y. Times Column, to Be Reassigned." *Los Angeles Times,* August 21, sec. I, p. 21.

Rossi, Peter, and Robert Dentler. 1961. *The Politics of Urban Renewal.* New York: Free Press.

Rubin, Lillian B. 1972. *Busing and Backlash: White against White in an Urban School District.* Berkeley and Los Angeles: University of California Press.

Rudel, Thomas K. 1989. *Situations and Strategies in American Land-Use Planning.* New York: Cambridge University Press.

Sahagun, Louis, and Allan Jalon. 1984. "Cities Battle to House Technology Museum." *Los Angeles Times,* Novermber 29, sec. IV, pp. 1, 4.

Samuelson, Paul. 1942. "The Business Cycle and Urban Development." Pp. 6–17 in Guy Greer (ed.), *The Problems of Cities and Towns.* Cambridge, Mass.: Harvard University Press.

San Francisco Chronicle. 1984. "Reagan's Hometown Offers Bounty to Lure More Business to the Area." *San Franscisco Chronicle,* May 10, p. 4.

Santa Barbara News Press. 1984. "Lowering the Boom." *Santa Barbara News Press,* June 21, sec. E, p. 12.

Schattschneider, Elmer Eric. 1960. *The Semisovereign People.* New York: Holt, Rinehart and Winston.

Scheiber, Harry N. 1973. "Urban Rivalry and Internal Improvements in the Old Northwest, 1820–1860." Pp. 135–46 in Alexander B. Callow, Jr. (ed.), *American Urban History,* 2nd edn. New York: Oxford University Press.

Schmidt, William E. 1984. "Suburbs' Growth Pinches Atlanta." *New York Times,* April 24, sec. A, p. 14.

Schulze, Robert O. 1961. "The Bifurcation of Power in a Satellite City." Pp. 19–80 in Morris Janowitz (ed.), *Community Political Systems.* Glencoe, Ill.: Free Press.

Shefer, Daniel. 1970. "Comparable Living Costs and Urban Size: A Statistical Analysis." *Journal of the American Institute of Planners* 36(November):417–421.

Shlay, Anne B., and Robert P. Gilroth. 1984. "Gambling on World's Fairs: Who Plays and Who Pays." *Neighborhood Works* 7(August):11–15.

Sierra Club of San Diego. 1973. "Economy, Ecology, and Rapid Population Growth." San Diego: Sierra Club.

Smith, Michael Peter, and Marlene Keller. 1983. "Managed Growth and the Politics of Uneven Development in New Orleans." Pp. 126–166 in Susan Fainstein (ed.), *Restructuring the City.* New York: Longman.

Smith, Reginald. 1984. "Willie Brown's Big Income Revealed in State Report." *San Francisco Chronicle,* March 7, p. 12.

Spaulding, Charles. 1951. "Occupational Affiliations of Councilmen in Small Cities." *Sociology and Social Research* 35(3): 194–200.

Steidtmann, Nancy. 1985. "Citizen Lesher: Newspaper Publisher." *Bay Area Business Magazine* IV(October 3):14–18.

Sternlieb, George, and James W. Hughes. 1983a. *The Atlantic City Gamble.* Piscataway, N.J.: Center for Urban Policy Research.

Stone, Clarence N. 1981. "Community Power Structure – A Further Look." *Urban Affairs Quarterly* 16(4):505–515.

Stone, Clarence N. 1982. "Social Stratification, Non-Decision-Making and the Study of Community Power." *American Politics Quarterly* 10(3):275–302.

Stone, Clarence N. 1984. "City Politics and Economic Development: Political Economy Perspectives." *Journal of Politics* 46 (1): 286–99.

Stuart, Darwin, and Robert Teska. 1971. *Who Pays for What: Cost Revenue Analysis of Suburban Land Use Alternatives.* Washington, D.C.: Urban Land Institute.

Summers, Gene F., and Kristi Branch. 1984. "Economic Development and Community Social Change." *Annual Review of Sociology* 10: 141–166.

Summers, Gene F., et al. 1976. *Industrial Invasion of Nonmetropolitan America: A Quarter Century of Experience.* New York: Praeger.

Sundquist, James. 1975. *Dispersing Population: What America Can Learn from Europe.* Washington, D.C.: Brookings Institute.

Swanstrom, Todd. 1981. "The Crisis of Growth Politics: Cleveland, Kucinich, and the Challenge of Urban Populism." Ph.D. dissertation, Princeton University.

Swanstrom, Todd. 1985. *The Crisis of Growth Politics: Cleveland, Kucinich, and the Challenge of Urban Populism.* Philadelphia: Temple University Press.

Swierenga, Robert P. 1966. "Land Speculator 'Profits' Reconsidered: Central Iowa as a Test Case." *Journal of Economic History* 26(1):1–28.

Tiebout, Charles M. 1956. "A Pure Theory of Local Expenditures." *Journal of Political Economy* 64(October):416–424.

Tomkins, Calvin. 1983. "The Art World: Dallas." *New Yorker* 59(17): 92–97.

Trillin, Calvin. 1976. "U.S. Journal: Rockford, Illinois – Schools without Money." *New Yorker* 52(38):146–154.

Vidich, Arthur J., and Joseph Bensman. 1960. *Small Town in Mass Society: Class, Power and Religion in a Rural Community.* Garden City, N.Y.: Doubleday.

Wade, Richard C. 1959. *The Urban Frontier: The Rise of Western Cities, 1790–1830.* Cambridge, Mass.: Harvard University Press.

Walker, Richard A. 1978. "Two Sources of Uneven Development under Advanced Capitalism – Spatial Differentiation and Capital Mobility." *Review of Radical Political Economics* 10(3):28–38.

Walker, Richard A., and Matthew J. Williams. 1982. "Water from Power: Water Supply and Regional growth in the Santa Clara Valley." *Economic Geography* 58(2):95–119.

Walton, John. 1970. "A Systematic Survey of Community Power Research." Pp. 443–464 in Michael Aiken and Paul Mott (eds.), *The Structure of Community Power.* New York: Random House.

Weinstein, Bernard L., and Rober E. Firestine. 1978. *Regional Growth and Decline in the United States.* New York: Praeger.

Weinstein, James. 1968. *The Corporate Ideal in the Liberal State, 1900–1918.* Boston: Beacon Press.

White, Morton, and Lucia White. 1962. *The Intellectual versus the City.* Cambridge, Mass.: Harvard University Press.

Whitt, J. Allen. 1982. *Urban Elites and Mass Transportation: The Dialectics of Power.* Princeton, N.J.: Princeton University Press.

Williams, Oliver, and C. R. Adrian. 1963. *Four Cities: A Study of Comparative Policy Making.* Philadelphia: Temple University Press.

Wolf, Peter. 1981. *Land in America: Its Value, Use and Control.* New York: Pantheon.

Wolfe, Alan. 1981. *America's Impasse: The Rise and Fall of the Politics of Growth.* New York: Pantheon.

Worster, Donald. 1982. "Hydraulic Society in California: An Ecological Interpretation." *Agricultural History* 56(July):503–515.

Wyner, Allen. 1967. "Governor-Salesman." *National Civic Review* 61 (February):81–86.

Yago, Glenn. 1984. *The Decline of Transit: Urban Transportation in German and U.S. Cities, 1900–1970.* New York: Cambridge University Press.

Yago, Glenn, Hyman Korman, Sen-Yuan Wu, and Michael Schwartz. 1984. "Investment and Disinvestment in New York, 1960–1980." *Annals of the American Academy of Political and Social Science* 475(September):28–38.

Zunz, Olivier. 1982. *The Changing Face of Inequality: Urbanization, Industrial Development, and Immigrants in Detroit, 1880–1920.* Chicago: University of Chicago Press.

13

Gentrification, the Frontier, and the Restructuring of Urban Space

Neil Smith

In his seminal essay on "The significance of the frontier in American history," written in 1893, Frederick Jackson Turner (1958 edn) wrote:

> American development has exhibited not merely advance along a single line, but a return to primitive conditions on a continually advancing frontier line, and a new development for that area. American social development has been continually beginning over again on the frontier . . . In this advance the frontier is the outer edge of the wave – the meeting point between savagery and civilization . . . The wilderness has been interpenetrated by lines of civilization growing ever more numerous.

For Turner, the expansion of the frontier and the rolling back of wilderness and savagery were an attempt to make livable space out of an unruly and uncooperative nature. This involved not simply a process of spatial expansion and the progressive taming of the physical world. The develop-

Reprinted by permission from Neil Smith, 1986, "Gentrification, the Frontier, and the Restructuring of Urban Space," in Neil Smith and Peter Williams (eds), *Gentrification of the City*.

ment of the frontier certainly accomplished these things, but for Turner it was also the central experience which defined the uniqueness of the American national character. With each expansion of the outer edge by robust pioneers, not only were new lands added to the American estate but new blood was added to the veins of the American democratic ideal. Each new wave westward, in the conquest of nature, sent shock waves back east in the democratization of human nature.

During the twentieth century the imagery of wilderness and frontier has been applied less to the plains, mountains and forests of the West, and more to the cities of the whole country, but especially of the East. As part of the experience of suburbanization, the twentieth-century American city came to be seen by the white middle class as an urban wilderness; it was, and for many still is, the habitat of disease and crime, danger and disorder (Warner, 1972). Indeed these were the central fears expressed throughout the 1950s and 1960s by urban theorists who focused on urban "blight" and "decline," "social malaise" in the inner city, the "pathology" of urban life; in short, the "unheavenly city" (Banfield, 1968). The city becomes a wilderness, or worse a jungle (Long, 1971; Sternlieb, 1971; see also Castells, 1976a). More vividly than in the news media or social science theory, this is the recurrent theme in a whole genre of "urban jungle" Hollywood productions, from *West Side Story* and *King Kong* to *The Warriors*.

Anti-urbanism has been a dominant theory in American culture. In a pattern analogous to the original experience of wilderness, the last 20 years have seen a shift from fear to romanticism and a progression of urban imagery from wilderness to frontier. Cotton Mather and the Puritans of seventeenth-century New England feared the forest as an impenetrable evil, a dangerous wilderness, but with the continual taming of the forest and its transformation at the hands of human labor, the softer imagery of Turner's frontier was an obvious successor to Mather's forest of evil. There is an optimism and an expectation of expansion associated with "frontier"; wilderness gives way to frontier when the conquest is well under way. Thus in the twentieth-century American city, the imagery of urban wilderness has been replaced by the imagery of urban frontier. This transformation can be traced to the origins of urban renewal (see especially Abrams, 1965), but has become intensified in the last two decades, as the rehabilitation of single-family homes became fashionable in the wake of urban renewal. In the language of gentrification, the appeal to frontier imagery is exact: urban pioneers, urban homesteaders and urban cowboys are the new folk heroes of the urban frontier.

Just as Turner recognized the existence of Native Americans but included them as part of his savage wilderness, contemporary urban-frontier imagery implicitly treats the present inner-city population as a natural element of their physical surroundings. Thus the term "urban pioneer" is as arrogant as the original notion of the "pioneer" in that it conveys the impression of a city that is not yet socially inhabited; like the Native Americans, the contemporary urban working class is seen as less than social, simply a part of the physical environment. Turner was explicit about this when he called the frontier "the meeting point between savagery and civilization," and although today's frontier vocabulary of gentrification is rarely as explicit, it treats the inner-city population in much the same way (Stratton, 1977).

The parallels go further. For Turner, the westward geographical progress of the frontier line is associated with the forging of the national spirit. An equally spiritual hope is expressed in the boosterism which presents gentrification as the leading edge of an American urban renaissance; in the most extreme scenario, the new urban pioneers are expected to do for the national spirit what the old ones did: to lead us into a new world where the problems of the old world are left behind. In the words of one Federal publication, gentrification's appeal to history involves the "psychological need to re-experience successes of the past because of the disappointments of recent years – Vietnam, Watergate, the energy crisis, pollution, inflation, high interest rates, and the like" (Advisory Council on Historic Preservation, 1980: 9). No one has yet seriously proposed that we view James Rouse (the American developer responsible for many of the highly visible downtown malls, plazas, markets and tourist arcades) as the John Wayne of gentrification, but the proposal would be quite in keeping with much of the contemporary imagery. In the end, and this is the important conclusion, the imagery of frontier serves to rationalize and legitimate a process of conquest, whether in the eighteenth- and nineteenth-century West or in the twentieth-century inner city. The imagery relies on several myths but also has a partial basis in reality. Some of the mythology has already been hinted at, but before proceeding to examine the realistic basis of the imagery, I want to discuss one aspect of the frontier mythology not yet touched upon: nationalism.

The process of gentrification with which we are concerned here is quintessentially international. It is taking place throughout North America and much of western Europe, as well as Australia and New Zealand, that is, in cities throughout most of the Western advanced capitalist world. Yet nowhere is the process less understood than in the United States, where the American nationalism of the frontier ideology has encouraged a provincial understanding of gentrification. The original pre-twentieth-century frontier experience was not limited to the United States, but rather exported throughout the world; likewise, although it is nowhere as rooted as in the United States, the frontier ideology does emerge elsewhere in connection with gentrification. The international influence of the earlier American frontier experience is repeated with the twentieth-century urban scene; the American imagery of gentrification is simultaneously cosmopolitan and parochial, general and local. It is general in image if often contrary in detail. For these reasons, the critique of the frontier imagery does not condemn us to repeating Turner's nationalism, and should not be seen as a nationalistic basis for a discussion of gentrification. The Australian experience of frontier, for example, was certainly different from the American, but was also responsible (along with American cultural imports) for spawning a strong frontier ideology. And the American frontier itself was as intensely real for potential immigrants in Scandinavia or Ireland as it was for actual French or British immigrants in Baltimore or Boston.

However, as with every ideology, there is a real, if partial and distorted, basis for the treatment of gentrification as a new urban frontier. In this idea of frontier we see an evocative combination of economic and spatial dimensions of development. The potency of the frontier image depends on the subtlety of exactly this combination of the economic and the spatial. In the nineteenth century, the expansion of the geographic frontier in the US and elsewhere was simultaneously an economic expansion of capital. Yet the social individualism pinned onto and incorporated into the idea of frontier is in one important respect a myth; Turner's frontier line was extended westward less by individual pioneers and homesteaders, and more by banks, railways, the state and other speculators, and these in turn passed the land on (at profit) to businesses and families (see, for example, Swierenga 1968). In this period, economic expansion was accomplished in part through absolute geographical expansion. That is, expansion of the economy involved the expansion of the geographical arena over which the economy operated.

Today the link between economic and geographical development remains, giving the frontier imagery its present currency, but the form of the link is very different. As far as its spatial basis is concerned, economic expansion takes place today not through absolute geographical expansion but through the internal differentiation of geographical space (N. Smith, 1982). Today's production of space or geographical development is therefore a sharply uneven process. Gentrification, urban renewal, and the larger, more complex, processes of urban restructuring are all part of the differentiation of geographical space at the urban scale; although they had their basis in the period of economic expansion prior to the current world economic crisis, the function of these processes today is to lay one small part of the geographical basis for a future period of expansion (Smith, 1984). And as with the original frontier, the mythology has it that gentrification is a process led by individual pioneers and homesteaders whose sweat equity, daring and vision are paving the way for those among us who are more timid. But even if we ignore urban renewal and the commercial, administrative and recreational redevelopment that is taking place, and focus purely on residential rehabilitation, it is apparent that where the "urban pioneers" venture, the banks, real-estate companies, the state or other collective economic actors have generally gone before. In this context it may be more appropriate to view the James Rouse Company not as the John Wayne but as the Wells Fargo of gentrification.

In the public media, gentrification has been presented as the pre-eminent symbol of the larger urban redevelopment that is taking place. Its symbolic importance far outweighs its real importance; it is a relatively small if highly visible part of a much larger process. The actual process of gentrification lends itself to such cultural abuse in the same way as the original frontier. Whatever the real economic, social and political forces that pave the way for gentrification, and no matter which banks and real-tors, governments and contractors are behind the process, gentrification appears at first sight, and especially in the US, to be a marvelous testa-ment to the values of individualism and the family, economic opportunity and the dignity of work (sweat equity). From appearances at least, gentri-fication can be played so as to strike some of the most resonant chords on our ideological keyboard.

As early as 1961, Jean Gottmann not only caught the reality of changing urban patterns, but also spoke in a language amenable to the emerging ideology, when he said that the "frontier of the American economy is nowadays urban and suburban rather than peripheral to the civilized areas" (Gottmann, 1961: 78). With two important provisos, which have become much more obvious in the last two decades, this insight is precise. First, the urban frontier is a frontier in the economic sense, before anything else. The social, political and cultural transforma-tions in the central city are often dramatic and are certainly important as regards our immediate experience of everyday life, but they are associ-ated with the development of an economic frontier. Second, the urban frontier is today only one of several frontiers, given that the internal differentiation of geographical space occurs at different scales. In the context of the present global economic crisis, it is clear that international capital and American capital alike confront a global "frontier" that incor-porates the so-called urban frontier. This link between different spatial scales, and the importance of urban development to national and inter-national recovery, was acutely clear in the enthusiastic language used by supporters of the urban Enterprise Zone, an idea pioneered by the Thatcher and Reagan administrations. To quote just one apologist, Stuart Butler (a British economist working for the American right-wing think tank, the Heritage Foundation):[1]

It may be argued that at least part of the problem facing many urban areas today lies in our failure to apply the mechanism explained by Turner (the continual local development and innovation of new ideas) . . . to the inner city "frontier." Cities are facing fundamental changes, and yet the measures applied to deal with these changes are enacted in the main by distant govern-ments. We have failed to appreciate that there may be opportunities in the cities themselves, and we have scrupulously avoided giving local forces the chance to seize them. Proponents of the Enterprise Zone aim to provide a climate in which the frontier process can be brought to bear within the city itself. (Butler, 1981: 3)

The circumspect observation of Gottmann and others has given way 20 years later to the unabashed adoption of the "urban frontier" as the keystone to a political and economic program of urban restructuring in the interests of capital.

The frontier line today has a quintessentially economic definition – it is the frontier of profitability – but it takes on a very acute geographical expression at different spatial scales. Ultimately, this is what the twentieth-century frontier and the so-called urban frontier of today have in common. In reality, both are associated with the accumulation and expansion of capital. But where the nineteenth-century frontier represented the consummation of *absolute geographical expansion* as the primary spatial expression of capital accumulation, gentrification and urban redevelopment represent the most advanced example of the *redifferentiation* of geographical space toward precisely the same end. It is just possible that, in order to understand the present, what is needed today is the substitution of a true geography in place of a false history.

The Restructuring of Urban Space

It is important to understand the present extent of gentrification in order to comprehend the real character and importance of the restructuring process. If by gentrification we mean, strictly, the residential rehabilitation of working-class neighborhoods, then, in the United States (where the process is probably most dramatic), it shows up clearly in data at the census tract level but not yet at the scale of the Standard Metropolitan Statistical Area (Chall, 1984; Schaffer and Smith, 1984). For a number of cities, income, rent and other indicators from the 1980 census show clear evidence of gentrification in central tracts. However, the process has not yet become significant enough to reverse or even seriously counter the established trends toward residential suburbanization. Although this is an interesting empirical pattern, alone it hardly amounts to a secular change in patterns of urban development. If, however, we eschew the narrow ideology fostered around gentrification, and see the process in relation to a number of broader if still less "visible" urban developments; if, in other words, we examine the momentum of the process, not a static empirical count, then a coherent pattern emerges of a far more significant restructuring of urban space.

Before examining the precise trends that are leading toward the restructuring process, it is important to note that the question of spatial scale is central to any relevant explanation. We can say that the restructuring of the urban-space economy is a product of the uneven development of capitalism or of the operation of a rent gap, the result of a developing service economy or of changed life-style preferences, the suburbanization of capital or the devalorization of capital invested in the urban built environment. It is, of course, a product of all of these forces, in some way, but to say so tells us very little. These processes occur at several different spatial scales, and although previous attempts at explanation have tended to fasten on one or the other trend, they may not in fact be mutually exclusive. Where authors have attempted to incorporate more than one such trend, they have generally been content to list these as factors. Yet this version of "factor analysis" is quite unambitious. The whole question of explanation hinges not upon identifying factors but upon understanding the relative importance of, and relation between, so-called "factors." In part, this is a question of scale.

But there is a second question of scale concerning levels of generality. We accept here that the restructuring of urban space is general but by no means universal. What does this mean? It means, first, that the restructuring of urban space is not, strictly speaking, a new phenomenon. The entire process of urban growth and development is a constant patterning, structuring and restructuring of urban space. What *is* new today is the degree to which this restructuring of space is an immediate and systematic component of a larger economic and social restructuring of advanced capitalist economies. A given built environment expresses specific patterns of production and reproduction, consumption and circulation, and as these patterns change, so does the geographical patterning of the built environment. The walking city, we have been told, is not the automobile city, but of greater importance, perhaps, the city of small craft manufacturing is not the metropolis of multinational capital.

The geographical restructuring of the space economy is always uneven; thus urban restructuring in one region of a national or international economy may not be matched in either quality or quantity, character or extent, by restructuring in another. This is immediately evident in the comparison of developed and underdeveloped parts of the world economy. The basic structure of most Third World cities, and the processes at work, are quite different from those in Europe, Oceania or North America. But equally, within the developed economies, there are strong regional differences. If Baltimore and Los Angeles are both experiencing a rapid transformation of their space economies, there are as many differences between them as similarities. Still other cities, such as Gary, Indiana, may be experiencing a secular decline and little restructuring (as opposed to continued destruction). In short, there is an overlay of regional and international patterns that complicate the extent urban patterns. Although they focus on the general causes and background to the contemporary restructuring of urban space, the explanations offered will be successful only to the extent that they can begin to explain the diversity of urban forms resulting from the process as well as complete exceptions to the apparent rule. This again calls not for a "factor analysis" (a list of factors) but for an integrated explanation; we have to explain not just the location but also the timing of such dramatic urban change. But perhaps the most basic distinction that will emerge is between those trends and tendencies which are predominantly responsible for the *fact* of urban restructuring and those responsible for the *form* the process takes.

The most salient processes responsible for the origins and shaping of urban restructuring can perhaps be summarized under the following headings:

(a)   suburbanization and the emergence of the rent gap;
(b)   the deindustrialization of advanced capitalist economies and the growth of white-collar employment;
(c)   the spatial centralization and simultaneous decentralization of capital;
(d)   the falling rate of profit and the cyclical movement of capital;
(e)   demographic changes and changes in consumption patterns.

In consort, these developments and processes can provide a first approximation toward an integrated explanation of the different facets of gentrification and urban restructuring.

Suburbanization and the emergence of the rent gap

The explanation of suburban development is more complex than is often thought, and a revisionist alternative to traditional, transport-based explanations is beginning to emerge (Walker, 1978, 1981). The point here is not to give a comprehensive account of suburbanization but to summarize some of the most important conclusions.

The suburbanization process represents a simultaneous centralization and decentralization of capital and of human activity in geographical space. On the national scale, suburbanization is the outward expansion of centralized urban places, and this process should be understood in the most general way as a necessary product of the spatial centralization of capital. It is the growth of towns into cities into metropolitan centers.

At the urban scale, however, from the perspective of the urban center, suburbanization is a process of decentralization. It is a product not of a basic impulse toward centralization but of the impulse toward a high rate of profit. Profit rates are location specific, and at the urban scale as such, the economic indicator that differentiates one place from another is ground rent. Many other forces were involved in the suburbanization of capital, but pivotal in the entire process was the availability of cheap land on the periphery (low ground rent). There was no natural necessity for the expansion of economic activity to take the form of suburban development; there was no technical impediment preventing the movement of modern large-scale capital to the rural backwaters, or preventing its fundamental redevelopment of the industrial city it inherited, but instead the expansion of capital led to a process of suburbanization. In part this had to do with the impetus toward centralization (see below), but given the economics of centralization, it is the ground-rent structure that determined the suburban location of economic expansion (Smith, 1984).

The outward movement of capital to develop suburban, industrial, residential, commercial, and recreational activity results in a reciprocal change in suburban and inner-city ground-rent levels. Where the price of suburban land rises with the spread of new construction, the relative price of inner-city land falls. Smaller and smaller quantities of capital are funneled into the maintenance and repair of the inner-city building stock. This results in what we have called a *rent-gap* in the inner city between the actual ground rent capitalized from the present (depressed) land use and the potential rent that could be capitalized from the "highest and best" use (or at least a "higher and better" use), given the central location. This suburbanization occurs in consort with structural changes in advanced economies. Some of the other processes we shall examine are more limited in their occurrence; what is remarkable about the rent gap is its near universality. Most cities in the advanced capitalist world have experienced this phenomenon, to a greater or lesser extent. Where it is allowed to run its course at the behest of the free market, it leads to the substantial abandonment of inner-city properties. This devalorization of capital invested in the built environment affects property of all sorts, commercial and industrial as well as residential and retail. Different levels and kinds of state involvement give the process a very different form in different economies, and abandonment (the logical end-point of the process) is most marked in the US, where state involvement has been less consistent and more sporadic.

At the most basic level, it is the movement of capital into the construction of new suburban landscapes and the consequent creation of a rent gap that create the economic *opportunity* for restructuring the central and inner cities. The devalorization of capital in the center creates the opportunity for the revalorization of this "underdeveloped" section of urban space. The actual realization of the process, and the determination of its specific form, involve the other trends listed earlier.

Deindustrialization and the growth of a white-collar economy

Associated with the devalorization of inner-city capital is the decline of certain economic sectors and land uses more than others. This is a product primarily of broader changes in the economic structure. In particular, the advanced capitalist economies (with the major exception of Japan) have experienced the onset of deindustrialization, whereas there has been a parallel if partial industrialization of certain Third World economies. Beginning in the 1960s, most industrial economies experienced a reduction in the proportion of workers in the industrial sectors (Blackaby, 1978; Harris, 1980, 1983; Bluestone and Harrison, 1982). But many urban areas began to experience the effects of deindustrialization much earlier than the last two decades. Thus the growth in manufacturing, at the national scale, since World War II was very uneven between regions. Whereas some regions, such as the West Midlands and South-East of England, or many of the southern and western states of the US, experienced a rapid growth of modern manufacturing, other regions experienced a relative disinvestment of capital in manufacturing jobs. At the urban scale the process is even more marked; most of the expanding industrial capacity of the postwar boom was not located in the inner cities, the traditional home of industry in the Chicago model of urban structure, but in suburban and peripheral locations. The result was a period of systematic disinvestment in urban industrial production, dating, in the case of some British cities, as far back as before World War I (Lenman, 1977). This was the case despite the overall growth of industrial production in the UK economy, taken as a whole, even following World War II.

The corollary to this deindustrialization is increased employment in other sectors of the economy, especially those described loosely as white-collar or service occupations. Within these broad categories, many very different types of employment are generally included, from clerical, communications and retail operatives to managerial, professional and research careers. Within this larger trend toward a growing white-collar labor force, therefore, there are very different tendencies and these have a specific spatial expression, as we shall see in the next section. By themselves, the processes of deindustrialization and white-collar growth do not at all explain the restructuring of the urban centers. Rather, these processes help to explain, first, the kinds of building stock and land use most involved in the development of the rent gap, and, second, the kinds of new land uses which can be expected where the opportunity for redevelopment is taken. Thus, although the media emphasis is on recent gentrification and the rehabilitation of working-class residences, there has also been a considerable transformation of old industrial areas of the city. This did not simply begin with the conversion of old warehouses into chic loft apartments; much more significant was the early urban renewal activity which, although certainly a process of slum clearance, was also the clearance of "obsolete" (meaning also devalorized) industrial buildings (factories, warehouses, wharves, etc.) where many of the slum dwellers had once worked.

Although the devalorization of capital and the development of the rent gap explain the possibility of reinvestment in the urban core around which gentrifying areas are developing, and the transformation in economic and employment structures suggests the kinds of activity that are likely to predominate in this reinvestment, there remains the question as to why the burgeoning white-collar employment is, at least in part, being centralized in the urban core. The existence of the rent gap is only a partial explanation; there is, after all, cheap land available elsewhere, throughout the rural periphery.

Spatial centralization and decentralization of capital

With the emergence of the capitalist mode of production, that which had hitherto been accidental disappears, is neglected, or is converted into a necessity. The accumulation of wealth had been accidental in the sense that, however much it was the goal of individuals, it was nowhere in precapitalist societies a general social rule upon which the survival of the society depended. With the emergence of capitalism, the accumulation of capital becomes a social necessity in exactly this way. Marx (1967 edn, vol. I, ch. 25) demonstrated that both a prerequisite and a product of the accumulation of capital is a certain social concentration and centralization of that capital. In short, this means that larger and larger quantities of capital are centralized under the control of a relatively small number of capitalists.

This social centralization is accomplished only through the production of specific geographical patterns, but the attendant spatial patterns are complex. At its most basic, the centralization of capital leads to a dialectic of spatial centralization and decentralization (N. Smith, 1982). If the expansion of nineteenth-century capital throughout the world is the most visible manifestation of the latter process (decentralization), the development of the urban metropolis is the most palpable product of spatial centralization. Centralization occurs at a number of spatial scales, however, besides the urban. It occurs at the level of plant size and at the level of national capitals in the world economy, and at each scale there are quite specific mechanisms that engender the process. At the urban scale, traditional theories have emphasized "agglomeration economies." The expansion of capital involves a continued division of labor, again at different scales, and thus in order to provide necessary commodities and services, a larger and larger number of separate operations have to be combined. The less the distance between these different activities, the less is the cost and time of production and transportation. Placed in the context of capital accumulation, this explanation is essentially correct concerning the original centralization of capital into urban "agglomerations."

In an interesting insight, Walker (1981: 388) notes that

> as capitalism develops, economies of agglomeration have diminished; they are a historically contingent force. But they are in part replaced by economies of (organizational) scale with the concentration of capital, so that gigantic nodes of activity still structure the urban landscape.

The central insight here is that such forces as agglomeration economies are historically contingent. Viewed from the urban centre, the suburbanization of industry represented a clear weakening of agglomeration economies, and was facilitated (not "caused") by developments in the means of transportation. Yet from the perspective of the national economy, the suburbanization of industry represented a clustering of massive and not so massive industrial facilities around established urban cores, and was thus a reaffirmation (at this scale) of the operation of agglomeration economies, however weakened. What Walker senses, though, is real; agglomeration economies operate in a different manner today, leading to clear spatial consequences. The most obvious of these involves the rapidly changing locational patterns associated with the expansion of white-collar employment.

The problem as regards white-collar employment is that a strong tendency toward centralization is matched by an equally strong if not stronger tendency toward decentralization, the movement of offices and other white-collar jobs to the suburbs. How can such apparently opposite tendencies coexist? How can suburbanization and agglomeration be coexistent? The explanation for this seeming paradox lies with a consideration of two interrelated issues. The first is the relationship between space and time *vis-à-vis* different forms of capital, and the second is the division of labor within the so-called white-collar sectors.

It is a *cliché* today to suggest that the revolution in communications technology will lead to spatial decentralization of office functions. This annihilation of space by time, as Marx had it, has indeed led to a massive suburbanization of white-collar jobs following on the heels of industrial suburbanization. With the computerization of many office functions, this trend continues. But consistent with the ideology of classlessness which first sponsored the notion of white collar, this trend is generally treated as a suburbanization of any and all types of office work from senior executives to word-processor operatives. Yet the further the trend develops, the clearer it becomes that this is not so. Thus the simultaneous centralization and decentralization of office activities represents the spatial expression of a division of labor within the so-called white-collar economy. For the most part, the office functions that are decentralized are the more routine clerical systems and operations associated with the administration, organization and management of governmental as well as corporate activities. These represent the "back offices," the "paper factories," or, more accurately, the "communication factories" for units of the broader system (Wald, 1984).

Much less usual is the suburbanization of central decision making in the form of corporate or governmental headquarters. The office boom experienced by many cities in the advanced capitalist world during the past 15 years seems to have been of this sort; it has been a continued centralization of the highest decision-making centers, along with the myriad ancillary services required by such activities: legal services, advertising, hotels and conference centers, publishers, architects, banks, financial services, and many other business services. There are exceptions to the rule, and one of the most obvious is Stamford, Connecticut, which has attracted several new corporate headquarters. Yet Stamford is in no way typical. Rather it is unique, precisely in having attracted the decentralization of ancillary administrative and professional functions central to corporate headquarters, thus resulting less in a decentralization process than in a *re*centralization of executive functions in Stamford. Whether or not this strengthens the tendency to a "multi-modal metropolis" (Muller, 1976) remains to be seen.

The question we are left with, then, is why, with the decentralization of industrial and communications factories, there continues to be a centralization of headquarter and executive decision-making centers. Traditional explanations focus on the importance of face-to-face contact. However, although the face-to-face explanation begins to identify the relevant issues, it is too unspecific. It tends to evoke a certain sentimentality for personal contact, but we can be sure that no mere sentimentality is responsible for the overbuilt skyscraper zones of contemporary central business districts. Behind the sentimentality lies a more expedient reason for personal contact, and this involves the very different standards by which time is managed in different sectors of the overall production and circulation of capital. Briefly, in the industrial factory and in the communications factory, the system itself (either the machinery or the administrative schedule) determines the basic daily, weekly and monthly rhythms of the work process. Serious change in this long-term stability comes either from external decisions or from only periodic internal disruptions such as strikes, mechanical faults, or systems failures. The temporal regularity of these production and administration systems, along with their dependence on readily available skills in the labor force and the ease of transportation and communication with ancillary activities, make suburbanization a rational decision. They have little to gain by a centralized location in the urban core, and with high ground rents they have a lot to lose.

But the temporal rhythm of the executive administration of the economy and of its different corporate units is not stable and regular in this fashion, much to the chagrin of managers and executives. At these higher levels of control, long-term strategic planning coexists with short-term response management. Changes in interest rates or stock prices, the packaging of financial deals, labor negotiations and bailouts, international transactions in the foreign exchange market or the gold market, trade agreements, the unpredictable behavior of competitors and of govern-ment bodies – all activities of this sort can demand a rapid response by corporate financial managers, and this in turn depends on having close and immediate contact with a battery of professional, administrative and other support systems, as well as with one's competitors. At this level, and in a multitude of ways, the clichéd expression that "time is money" finds its most intense realization. (On time and interest, see Harvey, 1982: 258). Less commonly voiced is the corollary that space too is money; spatial proximity reduces decision times when the decision system is suffi-ciently irregular that it cannot be reduced to a computer routine. The anarchic time regime of financial decision making in a capitalist society necessitates a certain spatial centralization. It is not just that executives *feel* more secure when packed like sardines into a skyscraper can of friends and foes. In reality they *are* more secure when rapid decisions require direct contact, information flow, and negotiation. The more the economy is prone to crisis, and thus to short-term crisis management, the more one might expect corporate headquarters to seek spatial security. Together with the expansion of this sector *per se* and the cyclical movement of capital into the built environment, this spatial response to temporal and financial irregularity helps to explain the recent office boom in urban centers. "White collar" is clearly a "chaotic concept" (Sayer, 1982) with two distinct components, each with a distinct spatial expression.

If, in the precapitalist city, it was the needs of *market exchange* which led to spatial centralization, and in the industrial capitalist city it was the agglomeration of *production* capital, in the advanced capitalist city it is the *financial* and administrative dictates which perpetuate the tendency toward centralization. This helps to explain why certain so-called white-collar activities are centralized and others are suburbanized, and why the restructuring of the urban core takes on the corporate/professional char-acter that it does.

The falling rate of profit and the cyclical movement of capital

Given, then, the spatial character of the process, how are we to explain the timing of this urban restructuring? This question hinges on the histor-ical timing of the rent gap and the spatial switch of capital back to the urban center. Far from accidental occurrences, these events are integral to the broader rhythm of capital accumulation. At the most abstract level, the rent gap results from the dialectic of spatial and temporal patterns of capital investment; more concretely it is the spatial product of the complementary processes of valorization and devalorization.

The accumulation of capital does not take place in a linear fashion but is a cyclical process consisting of boom periods and crises. The rent gap develops over a long period of economic expansion, but expansion that takes place elsewhere. Thus the valorization of capital in the construction of postwar suburbs was matched by its devalorization in the central and inner cities. But the accumulation of capital during such a boom leads to a falling rate of profit, beginning in the industrial sectors, and ultimately toward crisis (Marx, 1967 edn, vol. III). As a means of staving off crisis at least temporarily, capital is transferred out of the industrial sphere, and as Harvey (1978, 1982) has shown, there is a tendency for this capital to be switched into the built environment where profit rates remain higher and where it is possible through speculation to appropriate ground rent even though nothing is produced. Two things come together, then; toward the end of a period of expansion when the rent gap has emerged and has provided the opportunity for reinvestment, there is a simultaneous tendency for capital to seek outlets in the built environment.

The slum clearance and urban renewal schemes in many Western cities following World War II were initiated and managed by the state, and though not unconnected to the emergence of the rent gap, cannot adequately be explained simply in these economic terms. However, the function of this urban renewal was to prepare the way for the future restructuring which would emerge in the 1960s and become very visible in the 1970s. In economic terms the state absorbed the early risks associated with gentrification, as in Philadelphia's Society Hill, which was itself an urban renewal project. It also demonstrated to private capital the possibility of large-scale restructuring of the urban core, paving the way for future capital investment.

The timing of this spatial restructuring, then, is closely related to the economic restructuring that takes place during economic crises such as those the world economy has experienced since the early 1970s. A restructured economy involves a restructured built environment. But there is no gradual transition to a restructured economy; the last economic crisis was resolved only after a massive destruction of capital in World War II, representing a cataclysmic devalorization of capital and a destruction prior to a restructuring of urban space. Today, 50 years later, we are again facing the same threat.

Demographic changes and consumption patterns

The maturation of the baby-boom generation, the increased number of women taking on careers, the proliferation of one- and two-person households and the popularity of the "urban singles" life-style are commonly invoked as the real factors behind gentrification. Consistent with the frontier ideology, the process is viewed here as the outcome of individual choices. But in reality too much is claimed. We are seeing a much larger urban restructuring than is encompassed by residential rehabilitation, and it is difficult to see how such explanations could at best be more than partial. Where such explanations might just be conceivable for St. Katherine's Dock in London, they are irrelevant for understanding the London office boom and the redevelopment of the docklands. Yet these are all connected. The changes in demographic patterns and life-style preferences are not completely irrelevant, but it is vital that we understand what these developments can and cannot explain.

The importance of demographic and life-style issues seems to be chiefly in the determination of the surface *form* taken by much of the restructuring rather than explaining the fact of urban transformation. Given the movement of capital into the urban core, and the emphasis on executive, professional, administrative and managerial functions, as well as other support activities, the demographic and life-style changes can help to explain why we have proliferating quiche bars rather than Howard Johnsons, trendy clothes boutiques and gourmet food shops rather than corner stores, American Express signs rather than "cash only, no cheques." As Jager (1986) suggests, the architecture of gentrified housing is also a product of a specific class culture and set of life-styles. Thus some of the newer, less elite gentrification projects, especially those involving new construction, are beginning to replicate the worst of suburban matchbox housing, leading to a social and esthetic suburbanization of the city.

Sharon Zukin (1982a, 1982b) offers an excellent illustration of this point in her analysis of the development of loft living in SoHo and the entire Lower Manhattan area. Under the Rockefeller-inspired Lower Manhattan Plan, hatched in the 1960s, the old warehouses, wharves and working-class neighborhoods of the area were to be demolished in favor of the usual centralized, high-finance, "high-rise, high-technology modes of construction." The successful struggle against corporate redevelopment was waged in the name of "historic preservation and the arts," and, in 1971, in an extraordinary ruling, SoHo was zoned an "artists' district." However, as Zukin points out, this did not represent a victory of culture (far less "consumer preference") over capital. In fact, it represented an alternative strategy (involving different factions of capital) for the "re-capitalization" of Lower Manhattan:

> revalorization by preservation, rather than by new construction, became an "historic compromise" in the urban core . . . In Lower Manhattan the struggle to legalize loft living for artists merely anticipated, to some degree, a conjunctural response to crisis in traditional modes of real estate

development. In fact, the widening of the loft market after 1973 provided a base for capital accumulation among new, though small-scale, developers. (Zukin, 1982a: 262, 265)

Since 1973, of course, large-scale developers have become involved in the area. Where once loft co-ops were spontaneously put together among groups of prospective residents, today developers will renovate and fit a building, then put it on the market ready-made as a "co-op." And of course fewer and fewer SoHo dwellers today are artists, despite the zoning ordinance which still stands.

The point here is that even SoHo, one of the most vivid symbols of artistic expression in the landscape of gentrification, owes its existence to more basic economic forces (see also Stevens, 1982). The concentration of artists in SoHo is today more a cover for, and less a cause of, the area's popularity. This is nowhere clearer than in the exploitation of the area's artistic symbolism in aggressive real-estate advertising.

Direction and Limits of Urban Restructuring

If the restructuring that has now begun continues in its current direction, then we can expect to see significant changes in urban structure. However accurate the Chicago model of urban structure may have been, there is general agreement that it is no longer appropriate. Urban development has overtaken the model. The logical conclusion of the current restructuring, which remains today in its infancy, would be an urban center dominated by high-level executive–professional, financial, and administrative functions, middle- and upper-middle-class residences, and the hotel, restaurant, moving, retail and cultural facilities providing recreational opportunities for this population. In short we should expect the creation of a bourgeois playground, the social Manhattanization of the urban core to match the architectural Manhattanization that heralded the changing employment structure. The corollary of this is likely to be a substantial displacement of the working class to the older suburbs and the urban periphery.

This should not be taken, as it often is, as a suggestion that suburbanization is coming to an end. On the contrary, the flurry of excitement during the 1970s about so-called "non-metropolitan growth" in the US represents less a reversal of established urbanization patterns (Berry, 1976; Beale, 1977) than a continuation of metropolitan expansion well beyond the established statistical boundaries (Abu-Lughod, 1982). There is little reason to assume that suburbanization will not be more extensive than ever, should there be another period of strong economic expansion. Nor should this pattern be seen as excluding absolutely the working class from the inner urban core. Just as substantial enclaves of upper-middle-class residences remained in the largely working-class inner cities of the 1960s and 1970s, enclave working-class neighborhoods will also remain. Indeed, these would be functional in so far as the machinery and services of the bourgeois playground require a working population. The comparison – and contrast – with South Africa is instructive in this respect (Western, 1981).

The opposite alternative (that the central and inner cities would continue their absolute decline toward more widespread abandonment) could appear viable only in the United States. And indeed it *is* a possibility for some cities in the US. In so far as the restructuring of the core depends on a continued concentration and recentralization of economic control functions, it can be expected to happen strongly in national and regional centers. But the situation is less clear with smaller industrial cities, such as Gary, Indiana, where the administrative and financial functions associated with the city's industries are located elsewhere. Detroit provides an even more significant example, because the suburbanization of offices has affected not only the "back offices" but many of the headquarters themselves, and the substantial efforts at recentralization, through the Ford-inspired Renaissance Center, have not yet attracted substantial capital to downtown Detroit.

There is also little reason to doubt that the rapid devalorization of capital invested in the inner-city built environment will continue despite the beginnings of a reinvestment. In the present economic crisis, with interest rates high, it is not just new construction which is adversely affected. The same forces engender a reduction in capital invested in the maintenance and repair of existing buildings, and the consequent devalorization will lead to the outward extension of the "land value valley" of physically decayed buildings; the spatial extent over which the rent gap occurs is thus enlarged. Thus the restructuring of urban space leads to a simultaneous as well as subsequent decline and redevelopment, devalorization and revalorization.

In conclusion, we have emphasized that the restructuring of urban space is part of the larger evolution of the contemporary capitalist economy. Thus in the present context of deepening world economic crisis, our conclusions and speculations must be provisional. It is quite possible that the present economic crisis will result in very different political and economic forces, institutions and modes of control, and this could well result in very different patterns of urban growth. In particular, I have focused here on the economic background to restructuring rather than attempting to examine the political "growth coalitions" (Mollenkopf, 1978, 1983) which execute specific redevelopment plans. This was in part a choice of scale; no matter how general the process, local experiences differ greatly.

In addition, the emphasis on the logic of accumulation and its role in urban restructuring in no way presupposes a philosophical adherence to a "capital logic" approach rather than one emphasizing class struggle. As a philosophical dichotomy this is a false issue; but as an historical dialectic it is everything. The unfortunate truth is that the comparatively low levels of working-class struggle since the Cold War (with the exception of those during the late 1960s, and in much of Europe during the early 1970s) have meant that capital has had a fairly free hand in the structuring and restructuring of urban space. This does not invalidate the role of class struggle; it means that with few exceptions it was a lopsided struggle during this period, so much so that the capitalist class was generally able to wage the struggle through its economic strategies for capital investment. The investment of capital is the first weapon of struggle in the ruling-class arsenal.

An important exception to the general hegemony of capital concerns the role of European social democratic governments in providing public housing, the struggles over privatization of housing, and the rebellions in several European cities in the early 1980s over housing. These issues are not covered here and that is an important omission. What this experience suggests, however, is a further progression in our understanding of the urban frontier. The urban wilderness produced by the cyclical movement of capital and its devalorization have, from the perspective of capital, become new urban frontiers of profitability. Gentrification is a frontier on which fortunes are made. From the perspective of working-class residents and their neighborhoods, however, the urban frontier is more directly political rather than economic. Threatened with displacement as the frontier of profitability advances, the issue for them is to fight for the establishment of a political frontier behind which working-class residents can take back control of their homes: there are two sides to any frontier. The larger task is organizing to advance the political frontier, and like the frontier itself, Turneresque or urban, there are lulls and spurts in this process.

Acknowledgments

Peter Marcuse, Damaris Rose and Bob Beauregard gave me valuable comments on earlier drafts of this paper. I would also like to thank members of a seminar at Harvard University who offered comments, and members of the geography departments at Rutgers and Ohio State who further helped to refine the arguments.

Note

1   For an assessment of the Enterprise Zone experience, see Anderson (1983).

References

Abrams, C. 1965. *The City is the Frontier.* New York: Harper & Row.

Abu-Lughod, J. 1982. *The Myth of Demetropolitanization.* Paper presented at the Symposium on Social Change, University of Cincinnati.

Advisory Council on Historic Preservation 1980. *Report to the President and the Congress of the United States.* Washington, DC: Government Printing Office.

Anderson, J. 1983. Geography as ideology and the politics of crisis: the Enterprise Zones experiment. In *Redundant Spaces in Cities and Regions?*, J. Anderson and R. Hudson (eds.), 313–50. London: Academic Press.

Banfield, E. C. 1968. *The Unheavenly City: The nature and future of our urban crisis.* Boston: Little & Brown.

Beale, C. 1977. The recent shift of the United States population to non-metropolitan areas, 1970–75. *International Regional Science Review* 2 (2), 113–22.

Berry, B. J. L. 1976. The counterurbanization process: urban America since 1970. In *Urbanization and Counterurbanization*, B. Berry (ed.), 17–30. *Urban Affairs Annual Review*, vol. II. Beverly Hills: Sage Publications.

Blackaby, F. (ed.) 1978. *De-industrialization.* London: Heinemann.

Bluestone, B. and B. Harrison 1982. *The Deindustrialization of America: Plant closing, community abandonment, and the dismantling of basic industry.* New York: Basic Books.

Butler, S. 1981. *Enterprise Zones: Greenlining the inner cities.* New York: Universe Books.

Castells, M. 1976a. The wild city. *Kapitalistate* 4–5 (Summer), 2–30.

Chall, D. 1984. Neighborhood changes in New York City during the 1970s. *Quarterly Review of the Federal Reserve Bank of New York*, Winter 1983–84, 38–48.

Gottmann, J. 1961. *Megalopolis. The urbanized northeastern seaboard of the United States.* New York: Twentieth Century Fund.

Harris, N. 1980. Deindustrialization. *International Socialism* 7, 72–81.

Harris, N. 1983. *Of Bread and Guns: The world economy in crisis.* Harmondsworth: Penguin.

Harvey, D. 1978. The urban process under capitalism: a framework for analysis. *International Journal of Urban and Regional Research* 2 (1), 100–31.

Harvey, D. 1982. *The Limits to Capital.* Oxford: Basil Blackwell.

Jager, M. 1986. Class definition and the esthetics of gentrification: Victoriana in Melbourne. In *Gentrification of the City*, N. Smith and P. Williams (eds), 78–91. Boston, London and Sydney: Allen & Unwin.

Lenman, B. 1977. *An Economic History of Modern Scotland, 1660–1976.* Hamden, Conn.: Archon Books.

Long 1971. The city as reservation. *Public Interest* 25, 22–38.

Marx, K. 1967 edn. *Capital* (3 volumes). New York: International Publishers.

Mollenkopf, J. H. 1978. The postwar politics of urban development. In *Marxism and the Metropolis: New perspectives in urban political economy*, W. K. Tabb and L. Sawyers (eds), 117–52. New York: Oxford University Press.

Mollenkopf, J. H. 1983. *The Politics of Urban Development.* Princeton: Princeton University Press.

Muller, P. 1976. *The Outer City.* Resource Paper 75–2. Association of American Geographers, Washington, DC.

Sayer, A. 1982. Explanation in economic geography: abstraction versus general-
ization. *Progress in Human Geography* 6 (March), 68–88.

Schaffer, R. and N. Smith 1984. *The gentrification of Harlem*. Paper presented at the
annual conference of the American Association for the Advancement of
Science, May 27.

Smith, N. 1982. Gentrification and uneven development. *Economic Geography* 58
(2) (April), 139–155.

Smith, N. 1984. *Uneven Development*. Oxford: Basil Blackwell.

Sternlieb, G. 1971. The city as sandbox. *Public Interest* 25, 14–21.

Stevens, E. 1982. Baltimore renovates, rebuilds and revitalizes. *Art News* 81 (8),
94–7.

Stratton, J. 1977. *Pioneering in the Urban Wilderness*. New York: Urizen Books.

Swierenga, R. P. 1968. *Pioneers and Profits: Land speculation on the Iowa frontier*.
Ames, Iowa: Iowa State University Press.

Turner, F. J. 1958 edn. *The Frontier in American History*. New York: Holt, Rinehart
& Winston.

Wald, M. 1984. Back offices disperse from downtowns. *New York Times* (May 13).

Walker, R. A. 1978. The transformation of urban structure in the nineteenth
century and the beginnings of suburbanization. In *Urbanization and Conflict
in Market Societies*, K. R. Cox (ed.), 165–211. London: Methuen.

Walker, R. A. 1981. A theory of suburbanization: capitalism and the construction of urban space in the United States. In *Urbanization and Urban planning
in Capitalist Society*, M. Dear and A. J. Scott (eds), 383–429. London:
Methuen.

Warner, S. B. 1972. *The Urban Wilderness: A history of the American city*. New York:
Harper & Row.

Western, J. 1981. *Outcast Cape Town*. London: George Allen & Unwin.

Zukin, S. 1982a. Loft living as "historical compromise" in the urban core: the
New York experience. *International Journal of Urban and Regional Research* 6
(2), 256–67.

Zukin, S. 1982b. *Loft Living: culture and capital in urban change*. Baltimore: Johns
Hopkins University Press.

Part IV

The City and Contemporary Culture

Introduction to Part IV

Recent interpretations of urban development have incorporated many of the insights of cultural studies. The authors represented in Part IV, while retaining a political-economy perspective, also investigate the symbolic meanings of urban form and interactions, particularly focusing on the language in which space is depicted. They deconstruct the messages transmitted by the shining office buildings and malls, the gated communities, and the seedy barrios and ghettos of contemporary metropolitan areas. Using criteria of diversity as well as equity, they evaluate the restructured urban realm and criticize it for its inauthenticity and its failure to reflect the values of its less favored populations.

Mike Davis chronicles the role played by homeowners' associations in the increasing racial and ethnic segregation of Los Angeles. He points to the importance of the ideology of homeownership in creating this outcome, showing how the suburban dream of the single-family home led to an exclusionary environmentalism. He describes the interaction between the slow-growth and anti-tax movements and the irony of the alliance between developers, labor, and urban minority groups in opposition to suburban homeowners. Finally, he analyzes the way in which the alliances and antagonisms generated by growth politics divert attention from the issue of inner-city poverty.

Robert Beauregard looks at the words in which urban decline has been depicted in the United States. He argues that the language of decline does not simply report facts but represents a displacement of anxieties while simultaneously shaping action. He comments on the functions of this discourse for legitimating uneven development. In addition, he notes the mutability of the discussion, such that the interpretation of urban decline, while incorporating the dominant ideology of capitalism, individualism, and growth, betrays ambivalence and contradictions.

Michael Sorkin examines the symbolic meanings of the Disney theme parks, which he terms "America's stand-in for Elysium." He traces their antecedents to the World's Fair and calls London's 1851 Great Exhibition "the first great utopia of global capital." In their physical form the Disney parks recall Ebenezer Howard's model of the garden city, thereby transmuting their references to exotic locales and urban variety into a safe suburbia. Arguing that Disney has provided a model for office complexes and shopping centers throughout the world, Sorkin compares Disneyland to an airport in which the traveler "submits to an elaborate system of surveillance with the ultimate rationale of self-protection." In its orderliness and artificiality, it is the negation of the city as it really exists: "it produces a kind of aura-stripped hypercity, a city with billions of citizens (all who would consume) but no residents."

The concluding essay in this book of readings is an analysis by David Harvey of the issue of social justice and the city that takes into account the cultural insights of post-modernist thought. Harvey, a Marxist geographer, wrestles with divisions based on gender, ethnicity, race, religion, life style, and taste, as well as class. While recognizing the differences among the groups generated by these varying forces, he nevertheless argues for the possibility of coalition among disparate interests. He offers social justice as a basic ideal that would have sufficiently universalistic appeal to forge such a coalition. He rejects the post-modernist viewpoint that any effort at universalism is illegitimate. In doing so, he contends that "justice and rationality take on different meaning across space and time and persons, yet the existence of everyday meanings . . . gives the terms a political and mobilizing power . . .". He then lists six dimensions of justice. He concludes by arguing that social policy and planning must apply them both in confronting the issues of daily life and in attacking the underlying structure that he regards as the source of injustice.

14

Voices of Decline

Robert A. Beauregard

In the years just after the Second World War, the trauma of the country's large central cities could hardly be avoided. The returning veteran looking to house a new family, the automobile manufacturer considering whether and where to expand production lines, the department store executive contemplating a move to the suburbs, and the big-city mayor scrutinizing next year's budget all acted under the influence of problems increasingly associated with declining cities.

City problems were real and well known. Urban decline was widespread, its causes were said to extend rootlike throughout American society, and few were spared its consequences. No wonder the decline of cities became a topic for popular debate.

What had happened, what was happening, and what might happen to large cities were questions addressed by public commentators on almost a daily basis. An intricate national discussion ensued around the nature and condition of the country's cities; a discussion in which commentators, speaking and writing in a variety of forums and from diverse perspectives, pursued an elusive prey – the meaning of urban decline.

The central issue of that debate, then and now, has been the rapid fall from prosperity of large central cities, a drastic turn-about that seemingly began as the Second World War drew to a close. Population loss; the physical deterioration of housing, factories, and shops; the collapse of urban land values; rising city property taxes and soaring crime rates; deepening poverty and unemployment; and the growing concentration of minorities have all, at one time or another, been dominant themes. Conditions were shocking, not just because they brought hardships to households,

---

Reprinted by permission from Robert Beauregard, 1993, *Voices of Decline: The Postwar Fate of US Cities*.

investors and local governments but because they seemed to presage the demise of the large, industrial cities.

Decade after decade, the cities of the United States had grown in population. Production facilities had expanded. Employment opportunities, despite cyclical and thus temporary setbacks, had been abundant. Harland Bartholomew's comments in 1940 before the Mortgage Bankers Association of America were indicative of the expectations of experts and non-experts alike: "From 1870 to 1930 American cities experienced the most rapid growth ever before known. We came to accept growth as a matter of course."[1]

The cities had been the sites for great factories that catapulted the United States into its role as a world power able to fight a global war on two fronts and to dominate international markets. Cities had been the welcoming ports for thousands upon thousands of immigrants in search of freedom and opportunity, and had subsequently served as the cauldrons within which foreigners and natives forged an American culture. Natives, too, had migrated to the cities in search of wealth, power, and fame. For decades, the progress of the nation had been inseparable from the growth and prosperity of its cities.

In 1944, Louis Wirth, one of our most famous urban sociologists, presented a pessimistic diagnosis, one tinged with less wonderment and more resignation than Harland Bartholomew had mustered a few years earlier: ". . . the seemingly limitless growth of our cities has come to an abrupt end. This is all the more important because . . . we took it for granted that our cities would continue to grow at what now appears a fantastic rate."[2] The finality of his assessment related less to the depths to which cities had plunged – conditions would worsen – than to the sharp and shocking break with historical trends. This new phenomenon affected not only how people lived but also their image of America and themselves. One could no longer expect that past patterns of residential location, factory development, and commercial activity would continue, nor was it safe to assume that uninterrupted growth would spread evenly across the landscape.

Of course, we adapted. People found new places to establish homes, industrial and commercial investors uncovered previously hidden opportunities, and our understandings of growth and progress changed to accommodate quite different communities. Urban decline remained, and though its salience waxed and waned, its persistence could not be denied. That persistence, however, did not bring an "abrupt end" to the expansion and transformation of urban areas.

The history of the postwar United States is thus incomplete without reference to the fate of its once-mighty cities. Urban decline lurks behind every postwar story, appears in analyses of national and local economies, figures prominently in the evolution of federal, state, and municipal governments, and even surfaces as a major event in the history of the

American family. Of the many traits that distinguish postwar America from the nearly two hundred years of history that preceded it, urban decline is one of the most salient.

In fact, the significance of the postwar commentary on urban decline rests in part on the earlier fortunes and failings of these same cities. The postwar city had to compete in the public consciousness with the robust cities of the 1920s, and suffered in comparison with the great potential of the industrial cities at the turn of the century. A historical legacy had seemingly been squandered.

Nonetheless, even when cities were overflowing with new residents, factories were running at full capacity, housing construction was at its peak, and governments were investing heavily in highways, sewer systems, schools, and fire stations; these same cities were viewed by many people as sites of decay and degeneracy. From the late nineteenth century onward, growth could not dispel the perception that the large industrial cities were in decline. Objective conditions and public understandings have never been but tenuously linked and, as a result, the relentless debate about the fate of cities transcends historical events to exacerbate collective anxieties and threaten personal security.

Despite the notoriety of urban decline and despite the pervasiveness of talk about it, the discussion itself has not been closely scrutinized. It is as if the topic is so familiar that it neither deserves nor requires special attention. A public debate of such wide-ranging and long-enduring significance deserves more attention.

If we are to understand the postwar debate on urban decline, we must be sensitive to both its rhetorical qualities and its grounding in the material workings of society. Initially, my goal is to convey, in all its intricacy and inconsistencies, what was said and written about urban decline, thereby isolating this discussion from the multitude of commentaries ranging from affirmative action to foreign affairs that flow incessantly through the public consciousness. My subsequent but primary goal is to give meaning to the discourse. What has been its significance in the lives of the people who experienced, vicariously or otherwise, urban decline? What did this great American discourse about the fate of US cities mean to those who sat as its audience and acted as its subjects?[3]

The meaning of the discourse, I argue, can be found in the ways that it conveys practical advice about how we should respond to urban decline and mediates among the choices made available to us, the values we collectively espouse, and our ability to act. The discourse is about how we should live and invest, where, and with whom, and woven throughout it are reasons for making choices. The choices, however, are not obvious, and certainly not without economic and social costs. The contradictions inherent to a culturally diverse, profoundly capitalist, liberal democratic, and internationally dominant nation create a multitude of conflicting opportunities.[4] This disorderliness, in turn, also has a moral dimension:

the choices that face us are inseparable from society's inequalities and injustices. The discourse, fragmented and equivocal, thus articulates, even as it attempts to reconcile, the difficulties of resolving these dilemmas.

As a consequence, the city has become ". . . an abstract receptacle for displaced feelings about other things."[5] The city is used rhetorically to frame the precariousness of existence in a modern world, with urban decline serving as a symbolic cover for more wide-ranging fears and anxieties. In this role, urban decline discursively precedes the city's deteriorating conditions and its bleak future. The genesis of the discourse is not the entrenchment of poverty, the spreading of blight, the fiscal weakness of city governments, and the ghettoization of African-Americans, but society's deepening contradictions. To this extent, the discourse functions to site decline in the cities. It provides a spatial fix for our more generalized insecurities and complaints, thereby minimizing their evolution into a more radical critique of American society.

This interpretive reading is premised on the notion that the discourse is not simply an objective reporting of an incontestable reality but a collection of unstable and contentious interpretations. The ways in which urban decline is represented are always problematic, and although a commentator might claim privileged access to a "self-evidently solid ground of meaning," no commentator can successfully defend that exalted position.[6] All representations are indeterminant; their meanings depend not only on strategic juxtapositions with other understandings but also on shifting empirical references. Thus, we must reject a "straight" story about postwar urban decline that dismisses diverse perspectives and asserts seamless and coherent knowledge of a world external to the storyteller's craft.[7]

Shaping Attention

How do households know where to locate and whom to have as their neighbors? How do investors know where to place their factories, erect office buildings, and open retail stores? On what basis do governments decide to rebuild infrastructure, subsidize neighborhood-based housing programs, or provide fiscal relief to city governments?[8]

The decisions we make are not simply technical calculations or learned responses. Neither are they idiosyncratic. Similar decisions are made by numerous households, investors, and governments. General tendencies exist such that large-scale movements of population or capital spread across the landscape. Common perceptions are transmitted and turned into shared inclinations. How does this happen? How is it that people become comfortable, or dissatisfied, with their decisions?

The answer is "public discourse." In a variety of social settings – citizen meetings, barroom monologues, streetcorner arguments, over-the-fence conversations, dinner-table debates, academic colloquia – people come together and assess how they are living, where they should live, with whom and at what costs and benefits. Similarly, employees of business firms, nonprofit organizations, and governmental bodies participate in a variety of forums designed to help them consider what appropriate actions to take in response to changing urban conditions. In all these situations, people share preferences and intentions and develop, modify, and defend their understandings of cities.

Providing background for these encounters are numerous media presentations. On radio and television and in magazines and newspapers, commentators reflect on the state of urban America. Special reports, editorials, documentaries, and daily articles probe the depths of the city's poverty, the revival of urban retailing, and the successful struggles of neighborhood groups. Governmental officials speak out and consultant reports are summarized and evaluated. The information and impressions we glean from these presentations re-appear in our discussions with friends, neighbors, colleagues, and strangers. We verbalize our place in the world and the world of places, and by talking together form a sense of what we should do.

My interest in the discourse is as this mechanism for conveying, through its representations of urban decline, pragmatic knowledge about how and where to live and invest and, more importantly, as a discursive device for centering that knowledge in a comprehensible and legitimate story. Urban decline was and continues to be so unnerving that we have become unsure of both how we should live and how we should reconcile the inequities and injustices of prosperity and poverty with the values of equality, justice, and compassion that are ostensibly part of our national heritage. In this sense, the discourse is a ". . . [map] of [a] problematic social reality and [a matrix] for the creation of collective consciousness."[9]

Thus although I emphasize what might be termed the "performative" characteristics of the discourse, I also recognize that interpretive matrices have other ideological dimensions that figure prominently in the creation of meaning.[10] Of central importance is how our reflections on what public commentaries say fixates on whether what we hear or read is true, whether it fits our sense of what is real.[11] We ask if the discourse accurately describes an objective and external reality and clearly conveys its cause-and-effect relationships. Is the discourse credible? Does it portray truthfully the actual conditions of cities?

If the discourse is not credible, then the practical advice is likely to be ignored or viewed with great skepticism. Nevertheless, I have chosen to stress interpretation rather than explanation and the representational qualities of the discourse over its truthfulness. The public "voices" I use to present the discourse on urban decline are unlikely to make factual errors; what is most often contested, though, is the inappropriateness or unacceptability of their interpretations.[12] People decide how to respond on the basis of meanings, not on the basis of facts.

To the extent that the discourse helps us to decide how and where to live and invest, it is also about the type of society in which we wish to live. This debate, however, cannot be entered without considering the moral content of our actions; it requires us to reflect on the public good and assess the appropriateness of private actions. It pulls into our consciousness the responsibilities we share with others and the obligations that result. We are compelled to consider the virtues we deem essential to society as we simultaneously decide what makes our lives worthwhile.[13]

Essential to this moral dimension are the social obligations we have toward others, not just to our families but also to those "trapped" in inner-city ghettos, discriminated against in employment, deprived of quality education, or living in substandard housing. Compared to most, these people have fewer options from which to choose. How do we reconcile our affluence with their poverty, our safe neighborhoods with their fear, our range of choices with their constricted lives? What are we obliged to do? The discourse on urban decline is not simply pragmatic, it is also moral; it alludes to shared obligations in an unjust society.[14]

This interpretation implies a coherent and explicit discourse when quite the opposite is true. As the reader will soon discover, the discourse is disconnected, incomplete, and equivocal. Rationales for action are not tightly drawn, numerous responses appear appropriate to given conditions and specific events, and its readers and listeners encompass a vast range of resources and capabilities. As a result, the discourse exercises little predictive control over its audience. It is simply not possible to establish an explicit link between the discourse and how people react.[15]

For this reason, I will not be stating what people were being told to do at specific junctures in the discourse. To do so assumes an "ideal" reader and commentators with identical inclinations. It assumes a functionalist logic in which the discourse serves the needs of some larger entity, either society or capitalism, and ignores the unassailable actuality of a conflicted and contradictory world. One can no more identify a set of unequivocal prescriptions than one can perfectly correlate the discourse with an external reality.

The issue here is how the discourse sites in the cities the contradictions intrinsic to a heterogeneous and capitalist political economy. My specific objective is to reveal the ways in which the discourse on urban decline prescribes actions, legitimates conditions, and reconciles responsibilities in a messy world. People need to make sense of their lives in a way that allows them to live comfortably and with purpose.[16] They do so by engaging in discussions that mix understandings of objective conditions with abstract explanations, shared opinions with personal experiences, and moral evaluations with political possibilities. Unless we give meaning to our collective debate over urban decline, we will not be able to understand our postwar cities.

Foundational Urban Debates

Whether it be Boston, New Bedford, and Philadelphia during the colonial period, or Orlando, Los Angeles, and Houston in the late twentieth century, Americans have been fascinated with and perplexed by the city's contribution to the nation's identity and economic progress. The debate became even more robust when communications technology enabled commentators to speak to households across the nation, and became most heated when the industrial city – the city of smoke-bellowing factories, festering slums, and boatloads of immigrants – was at its peak.

On a broad cultural plane, and confined mainly to the twentieth century, our ruminations about the city have pivoted on its relation to "modern" society.[17] More recently, a number of scholars have argued for the demise of the modern city in the face of society's postmodern transformation. This latter concern has partially displaced, but also extended, a more specific foundational debate: the nation's supposedly anti-urban disposition. Those claiming that Americans are inherently anti-urban, however, have been challenged by others who argue instead that Americans have made a pragmatic adaptation to cities, albeit one tinged with deep ambivalence. These two foundational debates – the one on modernism and the city and the other on anti-urbanism – are central to any interpretation of urban decline and establish the context for reading its discourse.

More than a few commentators have argued that the city sits at the center of modernist sensibility.[18] The spirit of the age of science and industry, a time extending from the mid-nineteenth century to the present, was crystallized in the city by the vastness and intricacy of the built environment, the vibrancy and diversity of social life, the concentration of wealth, and the emergence of a mass culture.

The modern era severed many environmental and technological strictures that had dampened the possibilities for economic growth and physical expansion, and that had confined the population to isolated rural communities and small towns dominated by localized agricultural and commercial elites.[19] No longer did the frontier, the sea, or plantation confine economic advancement and cultured society. Opportunities for financial and artistic success became concentrated in the cities. Migrants looked to them for jobs, entrepreneurs for capital, inventors for investors. Erstwhile novelists and playwrights went to find like-minded spirits. By the twentieth century, the most successful painters, dancers, musicians, photographers, and actors followed career paths that led them to large urban centers. Fame and fortune in the modern era were to be found in the city.

The pace of economic growth, social and technological advances, and the expansion of opportunities defined only one part of the modern era. The other was the enhanced potential for subjugation and oppression, alienation, and collective destruction. The city became a metaphor for the personal estrangement and collective angst so central to the modernist sensibility.

Although the city offered numerous opportunities, it also had the potential to depersonalize by enveloping the individual in a mass society.[20] Densely packed neighborhoods, large bureaucracies, and unfathomable economic forces buffeted those without political or economic power. Wage-labor fragmented daily existence and created a pervasive dissatisfaction. Family life was made perilous by the uncertainty of the economy and the undermining of a civic morality. Technological advances, moreover, raised the potential for large-scale human catastrophes: massive fires ripping through neighborhoods, factory explosions, worldwide wars, chemical spills, and nuclear holocaust. Economic prosperity, though, made it possible for the rising middle class to attend to its individual and collective needs, even as that prosperity caused its alienation. Life might not have been any more fragile than it had been before the rise of the modern city, but its quality was certainly more pronounced as an object of concern.

Urban decline, of course, changes the terms but not the relations of the equation that juxtaposes the city with modernism. With decline, growth flees the city. Cultural affairs take on a more fragile quality, and innovation and creativity no longer mesh so well with an urban vision. Yet a projection from the decline of cities to the demise of modernism and the undermining of American prosperity and opportunity is too simplistic. Modernity itself is a paradoxical unity: "it pours us all into a maelstrom of perpetual disintegration and renewal, of struggle and contradiction, of ambiguity and anguish."[21]

Certainly some commentators did view urban decline as the end of a civilized way of life that had provided the political, financial, and intellectual foundations for modernity. As they shifted their gaze to the expanding suburbs, many observers discovered a cultural wasteland that clung parasitically to the fragile economic and social core of the cities.[22] Others celebrated the expansion of economic activity outside the older urban areas and the rapid emergence of a new consumerist culture focused on the home and the family. As always, it was easy to look at the other side of decline and remain optimistic. Suburbanization, massive new office construction and, in the 1980s, gentrification all helped to redefine urban growth and development. Of course, one could also wax romantic and focus on the "urban villages" within the declining cities, marveling at the tenacity of the human spirit.[23] In any event, the cities were not totally abandoned.

To a degree, decline represents the physical manifestations of the alienation and fragility of the modern era. The dismal conditions of the cities served as a stark reminder of the distance between economic practices and liberal aspirations. By the postwar period, the alienation of the city had become so pronounced, the ties of community so eroded, and the desirability of social and spatial mobility so ingrained that attempts to forge links between urban decline and a celebratory modernist sensibility were overwhelmed. Rather than confront its problems, the white middle class fled the city, and the country's economic and political leaders joined them in spirit if not always in fact. Urban modernity was thrown into disarray. Alienation *and* belonging were to be found in the suburbs, along with prosperous families and new industries. Modernism increasingly became associated not with the place of economic opportunity and intellectual activity – the city – but with a non-place realm of rootless individuals and non-spatial communities.

Throughout the postwar period, urban decline never drifted far from public scrutiny, but it frequently became disconnected from intellectual currents and over time had less and less impact upon the daily lives of the majority of the population. Modernists found it increasingly difficult to integrate urban decline into either the celebration of growth or the alienation of spirit characteristic of the modernist sensibility. It was better to forget the city. On a more practical level, those who could not isolate themselves spatially within the city could always, unless they were black, flee to the suburbs. Urban decline thus became nicely contained symbolically and physically, though still discussed with great passion.

A new sensibility emerged – postmodernism – to attest that such sea changes were part of the economic and cultural restructuring of capitalism.[24] The postmodern discourse of the 1980s and early 1990s, fascinated by the emergence of a postmodern architectural style and by the elusive hyperspace of late capitalism, attempted to reintegrate the city into this new material and aesthetic perspective.[25] Yet, despite the persistence of urban decline, a number of postmodernists wrote about the cities with a decided de-emphasis of the problems situated within them.

One strain of the postmodern strategy has been to focus on redevelopment.[26] A concern with the play of images and the severance of cultural from material practices led urban postmodernists to center their investigations on the affluence of the 1980s, the emergence of "young, urban professionals," and a seemingly renewed interest in "[t]he domestication of fantasy in visual consumption."[27] The postmodern city is defined in terms of its once low-income neighborhoods now gentrified by middle-class professionals; its waterfront developments that replaced dilapidated piers, fishing fleets and shipping lines with up-scale apartment complexes, festival marketplaces and marinas; office buildings with prosperous firms providing financial assistance, management advice and legal services; and retail marketplaces catering to the status-conscious consumer and the impulse buyer. These are the physical hallmarks of the postmodern city.

The emphasis is on the transition of the city from a place of industry, commerce, and ethnic neighborhoods to a place for spectacle and consumption, financial machinations, and worldwide corporate decision-making. The postmodern city is a city of advanced services arranged around banking, finance, and administrative control. Its workers are the affluent professionals who occupy gentrified neighborhoods and consume urbanity. At its apogée, the postmodern city becomes a global city, with Los Angeles, New York City, Tokyo, and London serving as models. In this context, urban decline loses visibility. It is of the past and not at all postmodern.

Yet, other voices characterize the postmodern city in quite different terms.[28] The striking affluence and new urban landscapes are recognized, but contrasted to persistent and deepening poverty, the solidification of a permanent under-class, the continued existence of slums, the rise of new immigrant neighborhoods (mostly Asian and Latin American) providing cheap labor for small-scale manufacturing firms or contributing to the expansion of an informal economy, unrelenting decline of the white population, the rigidity of fiscal problems, the emergence of a dangerous drug culture, the expansion of homelessness, and the erosion of civic commitment. The postmodern city, unlike the modern city, is cast as a city of sharp contrasts. To be postmodern is to be in the throes of deepening contradictions.

To this extent, the postmodern city articulates the modernist conflicts and contradictions that gave rise to the economic growth, cultural ferment, and new physical realms of the late twentieth century. Each advance has been built upon the oppression, suppression, exploitation, or neglect of those who lacked political influence and economic power, access to educational opportunities, and professional positions. The poor and working class began the 1980s with few assets and ended with even fewer. Rather than the alienation of modernism, the postmodern city liberated conspicuous consumption, revealed the exploitation of the under-classes, and severed individuals from ethical constraints and communal bonds. If the postmodern city is now the leading edge of civilization, taking up where the modern city has left off, then it is less a city that advances prosperity and the good life to all than one that builds affluence for a few on the exploitation of the many.

Infatuation with the postmodern city echoed, but did not revive, an earlier debate centered on the modernist city's displacement of an agrarian and pastoral society. Unlike postmodernists who generally stand in awe of the new city of conspicuous consumption, international corporate power, and self-referential architecture, commentators in the eighteenth and nineteenth centuries who witnessed the rise of the modern city were fearful.

To the extent that anti-urbanism lingers in various forms, the postwar decline of cities poses an interesting cultural and ideological problem. I know of no observer who has claimed that Americans love their cities, though certainly many Americans live within them. Americans are supposed to cling tenaciously to a deep-felt dislike of large urban places.[29]

The most important roots of anti-urbanism lie in the large commercial cities – New York, Philadelphia, Boston – of the eighteenth century that forged the links between themselves, an expanding countryside, and other nations. The anti-urban story is about the introduction in these cities of values and practices antithetical to those held and followed by people living in rural areas. The commercial world substituted cash transactions between strangers for personal relationships. Communities of whole individuals were replaced by a complex division of labor and businesses formed to facilitate trade based upon agriculture and the natural resources of the countryside. Rural values were quite the opposite: bartering, interpersonal respect, and self-sufficiency dominated. That rural farmers would subsequently feel alienated from and exploited by cities comes as no surprise, and it is only a short journey from that feeling to a broader condemnation.

This tension between the countryside and the city was exacerbated by the rise of the industrial city in the nineteenth century. The contrast between rural and urban became even more pronounced. Multitudes left the countryside for the economic and social opportunities of the big cities. In part, their migration was set in motion by the mechanization of agriculture, itself an extension of big-city values and practices. The industrial city displaced rural sensibilities and the rural pace of life by draining the countryside of its people, integrating it into the economy of the city, and championing values that appalled rural inhabitants.

Such a story, of course, if primarily about the emergence of capitalism in the United States during the eighteenth century and its subsequent entrenchment in a system of industrial production.[30] The full flowering of a capitalist political economy created a landscape of prosperity and control that privileged the city and left country dwellers overwhelmed by the reach of the industrial colossus. Not simply a clash of values, it was also a clash of interests with frontier yeomen and farmers pushed further west or enticed into a capitalist nexus that threatened their precarious existence and made them less secure.

American anti-urbanism, however, is more than the disparate powers and precarious opportunities that emerged as new economic and political practices joined large cities to the agrarian countryside. It is also about a collective image of American society that took shape during the formative years of the nation. Here the debate about values is even more pronounced.

For this story we must turn to the romantic juxtaposition of nature and society, one pure and the other corrupt, in the seventeenth and eighteenth centuries. As romanticism, the simple life of the countryside is contrasted with the artificiality of the city. Country folk are closer to nature, more in touch with basic human values, and less driven by selfish desires. Those in the city are out of step with the rhythms of rural life. They exist in a world without innocence. No longer in a state of nature, the inhabitants of cities are driven by selfish motives, distrust of others, and a severing of the ties to those basic human values that provide the foundation for a moral existence.[31]

The nature–society debate thereby extends out of the seventeenth and eighteenth centuries through the nineteenth and into the twentieth. There, it depicts city life as intrinsically immoral and the countryside as the bastion of morality. In the city, the moral strictures that governed behavior in the countryside were cast aside. Religion lost its grip and people's values atrophied. Intemperance, crime, prostitution, and other vices thrived in urban settings. Youthful rural migrants were corrupted and, as the cities spread, that corruption threatened to invade the countryside. Even city dwellers condemned the loose morals of their fellow citizens and yearned longingly for a lost pastoral ideal. Whatever the state of nature and commitment to religious values in the countryside, they had not taken hold in the cities.

Rural people were shocked by city life. Yet the equating of morality with rural and immorality with urban scarcely seems directly threatening to rural folk. Nonetheless, the immorality and deviance engendered in cities came to be viewed as dangers to democracy, despite the cities' ostensibly great contribution to modernity and civilization.

The threat that cities posed to democracy was articulated most forcefully by Thomas Jefferson. For him, democracy could only flourish where individuals lived freely and worked independently, and this could only take place in the countryside. City people were forced to work for others and thus to enter into hierarchical relations that undermined their good judgment. In turn, the city engendered and then juxtaposed inequalities, thereby making individuals susceptible to the crowd; the individual voices of free men paled against the power of mobs and their inclination toward insurrection. Probed more deeply, the threat to democracy rested on a political theory in which a land owning elite protected American democracy from the urban masses.[32]

With these arguments, one can build a case for Americans being anti-urban. Drawing upon the writings of philosophers and novelists, Morton and Lucia White in 1962 published their examination of the ". . . intellectual roots of anti-urbanism and the ambivalence toward urban life in America." *The Intellectual versus the City* offered a perspective that contained a ". . . persistent distrust of the American city."[33] Focusing on intellectual discourse from the eighteenth to the first decades of the twentieth century, their analysis placed anti-urbanism at the center of American culture. Admittedly, they included caveats that noted the difficulty of neatly summarizing American ideology, pointed to a possible gap between what intellectuals were writing and what the masses were thinking, and even exposed the equivocation of many of these intellectuals. Regardless, the broad conclusions of the book have made it the seminal statement about America's anti-urban prejudices.

Critics were quick to attack the weaknesses to which the caveats had only alluded. One line of attack focused on the relation between the rise of cities in the United States and the emergence of a civilized society. The city, it was claimed, contained the potential for leading the way to an American civilization of unprecedented technological and cultural advances.[34] It was both a challenge and a hope even if the city did not always rise to the occasion or live up to its promises. Even the Whites suggested that intellectuals condemned the city not because it was too civilized, too obverse to the values of the countryside, but rather because it was not civilized enough.[35]

Many commentators were ambivalent. Rather than being anti-urban, they vacillated between condemning the city for its weaknesses and lamenting its lack of contribution to a more civilized society. Significantly, their lament was often voiced in the context of an optimistic hope that the city was the key to prosperity and cultural advancement. The city was not being castigated and abandoned in line with a pure anti-urban ideology. Rather, it was being criticized by those who saw in it a potential for greatness that was not being achieved.

Evidence for this ambivalence can be found in the rise of industrialization.[36] Industrialization was initially a rural phenomenon; many of the early factories were built in the countryside. In Lowell, Massachusetts, for example, the factory system directly confronted agrarian society. "[T]raditional New England ideals and patterns of life . . ." entered an ". . . especially sharp and revealing confrontation with the modernizing forces of the industrial city."[37] The response to this "crisis of belief" was to search for a contrapuntal relation between the values of the city and those of the country. The issue was how to adapt behaviors and reconcile antagonistic values in such a way as to preserve what was important and good about rural communities while adapting to the imperatives of industrialization. The resulting balance of cultural forces created an urban vision unique to the nineteenth century.

This distinction between a righteous anti-urbanism and a skeptical ambivalence has its counterpart in the discourse on urban decline. In imitation of the dialectic of the urban and the pastoral, the discourse in the postwar period contrasts the decay and incapacity of cities with the growth and prosperity of suburbs. The asymmetry works to define decline and provide shape to the discourse. Postwar cities become places of crime, poverty, fiscal irresponsibility, idleness, drugs, AIDS, family breakdown, and a loss of community. The suburbs function as the opposite; deviance, immorality, and illegality are much less pronounced, while the nuclear family and a sense of community thrive. Sub-urbanites are anti-urbanites.

The discourse looks quite different, though, if one begins with urban ambivalence. To read the discourse on decline from this perspective is to confront the conflicted nature of American culture. Just as city growth established a tenuous cultural accommodation between rural and urban life, urban decline reopened those debates. The decline of cities, in an objective sense, took away the threat. Yet it also provided more fuel for popular scorn. Neither discourse – anti-urbanism, modernism and the city, or urban decline – can be fully understood absent from an appreciation of the unstable equilibrium of American values.

Contradictions and Legitimacy

The debate over whether people oppose or are basically conflicted about the city is encompassed by another debate, one that asks not just whether American values conflict but whether material relations themselves are at odds. The issue has two dimensions. One dimension concerns the objective circumstances of a society that is "precariously democratic but strongly capitalistic"; the other the ways in which we represent the ebb and flow of social relations.[38]

Obviously, whether Americans are anti-urban or ambivalent about their cities depends, to a great extent, on the way in which society is organized. For example, antagonisms between cities and the countryside in the nineteenth century were generated, in part, by the greater number of employment opportunities in the cities and the subsequent migration of rural youth. Rural areas were losing population, rural economies were being absorbed into urban networks, rural families were losing their children, and ostensibly rural values were exiled to the margins of popular acceptance. A more contemporary example is the tension between suburbs and large central cities during the 1970s when many big-city governments faced fiscal crises and looked toward suburban commuters for tax revenues or suburban state legislators for increased financial aid. Material forces that arrange economic opportunities, shift resources, and threaten prevailing patterns of political power give rise to antagonistic and ambivalent feelings about cities.

Such antagonisms are not confined to particular places. American society is replete with contradictions and tensions from which emanate a host of tenacious inequalities that serve as a constant source of political struggle and public dissent. Numerous commentators have noted the lack of consensus and the underlying fissures that give to this society its particular character. "Americans have managed to be both puritanical and hedonistic, idealistic and materialistic, peace-loving and war-mongering, isolationist and interventionist, conformist and individualistic, consensus-minded and conflict prone."[39] Nevertheless, we have tended to ignore such dualities and thus have incompletely reconciled the prevalent tensions.

Certainly tensions can be functional, but when unresolved become polarities which engender and perpetuate conflicts. One is that of collective individualism, the tension between authority and freedom, between "wanting to belong and seeking to be free . . ." Unresolved, it becomes "the ambivalent condition of life in America, the nurture of a contrapuntal civilization."[40]

Contradictory forces are not simply cultural but are joined to a multitude of conflicts that extend to the deepest and furthest reaches of society. Investors and producers compete with each other or with consumers, and the economy produces unemployment, inflation, and environmental degradation as a matter of course. Governments are nested in complex relations and hardly agree on how to solve shared problems, and with whose resources. Ethnic and religious groups clash over norms of behavior and whether behavior should be tolerated, regulated, or condemned. Households form neighborhoods of exclusion, individuals and organizations discriminate on the basis of race or sexual orientation, and elected officials engage in "dirty tricks" in order to defeat their opponents. Taken together such incongruities undermine the legitimacy of dominant institutions and mock the values of equal treatment and national consensus.

Dominating the incongruities are the conflicts and contradictions that emanate from a profoundly capitalist economy. Economic influences hardly end at factory gates or office-building lobbies. Rather, they extend throughout society, bringing with them the instabilities and contradictions which define capitalism. One does not have to cast capitalism as a hotbed of class conflict to take this position.

Joseph Schumpeter, hardly a Marxist economist, is well known for his characterization of capitalism as driven by "creative destruction."[41] Its unique trait as an economic system is its constant innovation, its fertile outpouring of new ideas, new products, and new technologies. That inventiveness, however, comes at the price of a constant stream of failures and losses. In order to create, capitalism has to destroy. As a result, those who live within a dynamic capitalist economy face a continual onslaught of discontinuities. The new quickly becomes the old, the adopted the discarded, the innovative obsolete. Daily life is constantly being disrupted. People must adapt or be shunted to the meager tributaries of a bountiful mainstream. Capitalism engenders a society that is inherently restless, with all the tensions and conflicts that such restlessness entails.

For Schumpeter, the creative destruction of capitalism is to be praised. It drives economic growth and innovation. For Karl Marx, capitalism contained fundamental contradictions whose consequences are not, either in the long run or on average, beneficial.[42] Rather, capitalism's successes are, for the most part, built upon the exploitation of the working class by those who control the means of production. The economy contains inequities whose persistence can only be overcome through a toppling of prevailing pyramids of power. At the same time, capitalism penetrates into the political sphere, as capitalists enjoy a disproportionate influence over how governments are organized and the types of activities they undertake. For these reasons, workers are in constant struggle with a capitalism that denies to them both the economic benefits it has created and influential access to political institutions.

Ample evidence of exploitation and oppression in American society exists, even if one rejects the Marxist interpretation as to their origins.[43] Throughout the twentieth century, poverty has characterized cities and rural areas alike; a great gap exists between the wealthiest families and the poorest ones. Except in times of war, unemployment has persisted, despite widespread governmental programs to eliminate it, and at no time has the economy, even with the help of government, been able to house adequately all those in need of shelter. Education is widely available, but good education for advancement to the most economically successful occupations is not universally accessible, particularly to racial minorities and those in the working and lower classes. Discrimination on the basis of race and gender continues to prevail in the face of numerous equal opportunity laws. In addition, neighborhoods with a high quality of public and private amenities are "open" only to those able to buy their way into them.[44]

Corresponding to these inequalities, the result not of individual deficiencies, but of institutional discrimination and exploitation, are a host of conflicts both latent and manifest.[45] Labor unrest has ebbed and flowed since the mid-1800s, but has never disappeared for long periods of time. Racial, ethnic, and religious confrontations are more common than unique, ranging from disputes over neighborhood boundaries, to riots in response to police brutality, and to attacks on places of worship. Public protests have been a common occurrence: anti-war rallies, marches for gay and lesbian rights, demonstrations for and against abortion, for and against equal rights for women, for and against environmental preservation, for and against nuclear power. Individual acts of violence are equally prevalent; many of which are related to poverty, unemployment, and the wretched living conditions of those cast aside by a capitalism whose interests do not extend beyond the bottom line.

One would thus be hard-pressed to admit this evidence and then cast America as a country in which values are universally shared, with widespread consensus around social goals and private wants, and made up of people living in harmony. Nevertheless, for over two hundred years with only one civil war having seriously threatened its existence, the United

States has survived as a nation, though certainly not unchanged.[46] Objective circumstances thus support an argument that America is destined to decline as a result of inherent tensions if not irresoluble contradictions. Within such a milieu, it would be astonishing to find that people were not themselves conflicted about their positions and the conditions under which they live. Antagonisms and ambivalences are rational responses to the juxtaposition of prosperity and opportunity to inequality and oppression.

The forces requiring reconciliation within the discourse on urban decline are rooted in this conflictual nature of American society. The pivotal issue is space. Under capitalism, the growth and decline of cities and regions require that individuals and investments be mobile, and that the landscape experiences incessant building up, tearing down, and renewal. Struggle over space follows as actors compete for investment opportunities and protect valued places from invasion or indifference, and as governments attempt to resolve conflicts by asserting collective values even as they provide support to favored groups. A constant movement of people, jobs, and capital characterizes development, a process that includes not only the construction of new buildings and places and the preservation of existing ones, but also the decay, destruction, and abandonment of buildings and locations no longer useful in the relentless pursuit of prosperity. The decline of cities, the emergence of suburbs, and the redevelopment of urban neighborhoods are all part of an unending uneven development of space. Growth and decline feed off each other as households, businesses, and capital switch incessantly from one place to another in search of the "good life" and political and economic rewards.[47]

In order to avoid the competition that threatens profits and to maintain appropriate levels of growth, investors are constantly looking for new markets and moving capital from one investment outlet to another. Capital pursues a spatial fix to problems of too little consumption and shrinking markets.[48] Spurred on by population growth, investors and governments expand into new locations and abandon existing ones when opportunities for investment are no longer so attractive because they are no longer so profitable. Postwar suburbanization becomes an opportunity to multiply consumption and production of housing, automobiles, land, appliances, furniture, and public schools at a time when the cities have become less desirable. Neighborhoods adjacent to central business districts become ripe for redevelopment as other investors spot opportunities for a rapid expansion of retail activities and housing values. In these and other ways, capital, often with the support of government, literally creates space.[49]

Urbanization can thus be portrayed as a constant search for new places for investment. Frontiers do not exist in an ordinary sense – lands yet to be discovered. Rather, they are places where intense development has not yet occurred (for example farmland on which massive suburban housing estates might be built) or where prior investment was followed by disinvestment (for example inner-city neighborhoods). In the latter, investors confront an investment frontier, a territory into which capital can (once again) expand. Thus, the frontier is never closed, as Frederick Turner claimed for the United States of 1890. It is always being redefined, re-created, and rediscovered. People cannot escape beyond it but must always protect themselves from becoming part of, and exploited by, a new frontier.[50]

Capitalists find it easier to exploit frontiers when people and governments are convinced that the complex and intertwined processes of investment, disinvestment and reinvestment are inevitable if not necessary. Capitalists need legitimacy. The whole process works much better when consumers and producers follow the spatial movements of investment and disinvestment, rather than resisting and obstructing "growth" with political opposition and government regulations.

From this perspective, capital would seem to be leading the way and duping consumers and governments to join the trek. In actuality, targets of investment and disinvestment are also created through the decisions of consumers, demographic trends over which investors have little control, and government initiatives designed to work sometimes in concert with and sometimes against prevailing patterns of development. Nevertheless, power lies with those who control the capital available for investment. Granted they must "read" consumer preferences and encourage other investors to join them, but urban development in the United States is, in its first instance, a process of capital investment. Intrinsic to its workings, moreover, is an ideology of development that legitimizes trends, fosters trust, and produces a modicum of acquiescence. Here is where the discourse on urban decline becomes important.[51]

An ideology that celebrates "newness" and "growth," and that portrays investors as risk-takers bringing prosperity to all and strength to the nation, legitimizes uneven spatial development.[52] By hailing restlessness as a positive virtue, and by focusing attention on the creative rather than the destructive aspects of urban development, or at least portraying them very differently – the former as desirable and the latter as unfortunate but necessary and inevitable – complex new patterns of investment and disinvestment, bearing significant costs for many groups, are justified. Urban renewal in the 1960s, with its displacement of businesses and families, becomes necessary to save the city from total decay, while federal aid to fiscally strapped urban governments in the 1970s is viewed as senseless; growth no longer characterizes these cities and their governments must shrink accordingly. Numerous other examples could be mentioned. The point is that widespread public debates concerning cities, and urban and regional development more generally, attempt to make sense of and often justify overall trends.

Legitimation, however, is fragile and seldom wholly successful; ideological reconciliation is always unstable. Disinvestment from the central cities generates significant burdens on numerous groups. Many households and businesses are directly encumbered: they are displaced, their property vandalized, or opportunities for employment or sales denied them. Minority groups find themselves in inadequate housing, locked into low-wage jobs or commuting long distances, lacking access to neighborhood amenities or public services because of shrinking government expenditures, or threatened by crime. Multitudes of city dwellers struggle to maintain a sense of community and to believe in a better future in the face of a relentless discourse that notes the decay and demise of their homes and neighborhoods. Residents of and investors in the city must reconcile their hopes with their experiences and the conditions under which they live and work with the promises of widespread opportunity in an affluent society.

Many of those who have avoided urban decline also need help in understanding how it is that their good fortunes are deserved. How do middle-class suburbanites, for example, reconcile their bounty with the problems faced by lower-class households who live in declining cities? What about the more affluent who, as urban residents, live in enclaves of stability and safety amidst areas of deep poverty, high unemployment, and homelessness? The former are insulated from urban decline. Yet, their good life is linked, sometimes directly and sometimes circuitously, but always morally, to the uneven development that creates affluent suburbs and rich inner-city neighborhoods. Urban decline is ripe with injustices, and those who have prospered and are able to avoid the ills of the cities cannot escape forever the collective responsibility they have for these conditions.

The line between an explanation of society's ills as temporary, anomalous or simply mistakes and an explanation that rationalizes them is extremely narrow. Consequently, the ideological argument that supports capitalism always hovers at the boundary between creating understanding and conveying misinformation. Here it often functions to mystify. It creates a false consciousness of how society actually works, where one is placed relative to power and privilege, and what resistance is possible. The ideology thus enables those in power, those with the privileges, to protect their positions from scrutiny and thus to deflect movements to redistribute resources and positions. To the extent that the ideology of the powerful can successfully do this, then resources do not have to be redistributed to avoid unrest and dissent, or used to squelch them if they occur.[53]

All but the smallest and most homogeneous societies, or the most totalitarian, however, are likely to have multiple ideologies competing for public attention and legitimacy. Almost by definition, a society has a dominant ideology to which most of its members subscribe, with or without a true appreciation of its mix of mystification and honesty.[54] Even the dominant ideology, at least in the United States, is contested. While most Americans might well be committed to capitalism, the more conservative often prefer a version that champions small enterprises and open markets, while the more socially liberal wish markets to be more regulated, and corporatists favor state intervention in support of oligopolies. Similar debates could be constructed for family policy, women's rights, education, electoral politics and two-party systems, and patriotism. Although an unstable consensus might exist concerning the basic values of "life, liberty, and the pursuit of happiness" and the importance of the Bill of Rights and the Constitution, those values in application become interdependent and produce contrary viewpoints that erode the purported American consensus.[55]

American society also contains ideologies in opposition to those that celebrate capitalism, individualism, and liberal democracy.[56] For over a century, a small minority of socialists have called for a non-capitalist and more democratic society, and made themselves heard in national and local forums. During the 1930s, the Communist Party was relatively active, and libertarians are more or less prominent though they remain, like all these groups, a distinct minority with little overall influence. In addition, divergent ideologies are not solely confined to the political. Various groups – the Amish, orthodox Jews, Native Americans, and numerous religious orders – maintain distinct styles of life and common values in the face of a predominant consumerist culture. Secular humanism confronts religious fundamentalism, criminal subcultures challenge law-and-order enforcement agencies, and immigrant communities negotiate their traditions and practices with those prevalent in their new nation.[57]

Despite these oppositional and alternative ideologies, one should hardly expect that a discourse channeled through the mass media is other than a variation of the dominant ideology. Access is frequently granted to people on the margins and commentators who pose subtle variations in interpretation, and critics who offer strikingly different perspectives are often allowed to voice their positions. Within a liberal democracy, tolerating dissent and presenting seemingly opposing viewpoints serve the beneficial function of reinforcing a commitment to free speech and public debate. Nonetheless, allowing critics to speak has the potential, always has the potential, to set loose critiques that reject and undermine the dominant ideology. Inclusion entails a risk.[58]

Thus, as the dominant ideology explains and gives meaning to the workings and consequences of society, it does so in a less than clear fashion. The values to embrace and the behaviors to either emulate or avoid are generally known, but enough evidence exists to suggest alternatives, depending upon actual circumstances. Thus, for example, people generally support the right of everyone to speak their beliefs, but many would suppress the Ku Klux Klan. It is not just that the dominant ideology is filled with the noise of critics; the material basis of that ideology is itself replete with conflicts and contradictions. Clarity and consistency are elusive qualities.[59]

The dominant ideology finds expression through numerous voices, carries the material contradictions of American society, and allows for alternative and oppositional criticism. It appears not as fixed and precise guidelines enabling us to understand and to act according to the interests of a liberal capitalist democracy, but as a set of deeply held abstractions whose applications and meanings are not always so easy to divine. America's dominant ideology is equally far from the double-speak of Oceania in George Orwell's *Nineteen Eighty-Four* as it is from the dogma of Stalin's Russia. One can believe and act in a variety of ways and still conform. The possibilities are numerous, though limited.

Any discourse that focuses on the nature of cities and their historical dynamics is thus likely to be replete with contradictions and tensions, and to resist unequivocal interpretation. To this extent, the discourse on urban decline favors particular responses but does not tightly constrict choice. It presents its readers with disputes about how they should live, with whom they should live, where they should shop, the best and worst places to work or play and to bring up children, and the most desirable communities in which to invest. The choices are competing and conflicting; they are the possibilities one faces in an actually existing political economy and an ever-changing culture.

Readers of the discourse are looking for direction and reassurance. They want to know what is happening to the cities and how it will affect them. What does decline mean? Should they respond? How can they respond? Not all people will relocate, change their place of work, vote against governmental aid to cities, or shift their shopping to suburban malls. Both those who act and those who remain in place will have been influenced by the discourse. The latter will come to believe that nothing should be done or, because they lack the resources to act differently, that all is well or at least reversible.

That social conditions are filled with contradictions only makes it even more important that a dominant ideology – a comprehensible, even if incomplete and ragged, explanation – is formulated to make "it possible for people to live with themselves, with their moral dilemmas, and with chronic failures to resolve the dilemmas and contradictions."[60] With choice comes moral responsibility; the decisions we make implicate us in structures of justice and injustice. Whether our actions deprive those in need, capture opportunities that others deserve more, or reduce the tenaciousness of inequalities, we cannot avoid the social responsibilities that we bear as members of moral communities. Our choices reproduce or retard a just society, but are never neutral. All action has ethical consequences.[61]

The discourse on urban decline, then, is not simply a negotiable but practical guide to how to act but also a public forum for debating moral issues. Whether as individuals or heads of households, corporate executives or elected officials, policy consultants or government bureaucrats, we are enmeshed in a matrix of unavoidable social obligations.

Those at the helms of corporations and governments, of course, have a stake in the discourse that goes beyond their own individual or familial concerns. They hold positions in which ethical considerations become even more consequential, for they make decisions that move people and capital from one place to another, change shopping behavior, introduce new life-styles, and shift political allegiances. Their actions condition the profits, access to capital, power, and cultural privilege enjoyed by economic and political elites. To the extent that powerful groups and organizations can shape the discourse to support their interests, they improve their prospects and retain their dominance.

The mechanisms for doing so are not easily manipulated. Advertisements, speeches, research studies and other commentaries on cities can be produced by a variety of commentators and made public in a variety of ways. Numerous alternatives exist to national magazines and to the radio and television programs of corporate America. Presenting dominant perspectives in the absence of dissent is nearly impossible, even though the most pervasive channels of mass communication tend toward a singular viewpoint. In addition, those with economic and political power are not in agreement. So, even if elites could control those channels, it is unlikely that they could construct an exclusive discourse, particularly in a liberal democracy.

Yet dominant ideologies are dominant for a reason; they affect people outside the dominant institutions as well. Consequently, without direct intervention or support, much of what elites wish to convey will surface. Though enmeshed in a thicket of competing and contradictory claims, at the center of the discourse of urban decline is a discussion that privileges, even if it does not explicitly condone, choices aligned imperfectly with the myriad interests of economic and political elites.

Any interpretation of the discourse, then, must recognize an American ideology that has never resolved its ambivalence about cities. That ambivalence is inseparable from, though loosely tied to, realities actually at play when commentators made their observations. In order to understand urban decline, we need to do more than respect the historical background of our deliberations. We must additionally account for the ways in which society's cultural tensions and political and economic tendencies have been filtered through an urban lens and, using the voices of commentators, have influenced how the discourse was formed, disseminated, and received.

Notes

1   Harland Bartholomew, "The American city: disintegration is taking place," *Vital Speeches of the Day*, 7 (November 1, 1940), p. 61.

2   Louis Wirth, "The cities' most serious crisis," *The American City*, 59 (November, 1944), p. 5.

3   A brief digression is called for here, one which reflects on the use of a term – discourse – that is central to my argument. A discourse is a system of meanings being continually constructed and dismantled around an equally problematic subject. While a discourse has thematic coherence, that coherence is neither stable nor closed-ended. Themes are continually being renegotiated, reintegrated, and dispersed. Thus, my use of the term has elements of Michel Foucault's usage but is not equivalent to it. His is a very different project: see *The Archaeology of Knowledge* (New York, Harper Torchbooks, 1972) and Edith Kurzweil, *The Age of Structuralism* (New York, Columbia University Press, 1980), pp. 193–226.

   Discourse as used here also reflects Clifford Geertz's approach to culture (specifically his concern with meanings and "webs of significance") and Raymond Williams' notion of structures and feeling, "meanings and values as they are actively lived and felt." To this extent, discourse involves both speaking and writing subjects as well as listeners and readers. Again, my use is similar to but does not mimic these practices. See Clifford Geertz, *The Interpretation of Cultures* (New York, Basic Books, 1973), pp. 3–30, Raymond Williams, *Marxism and Literature* (New York, Oxford University Press, 1977), pp. 128–35, and Terry Eagleton, *Literary Theory* (Minneapolis, University of Minnesota Press, 1983), p. 115.

   Regardless, the nature of a discourse is "to *constitute* the ground whereon to decide *what shall count as a fact* in the matter under consideration and to determine *what mode of comprehension* is best suited to the understanding of the facts thus constituted." On the basis of these facts, people make decisions about how to conduct their lives. See Hayden White, *Tropics of Discourse* (Baltimore, MD, Johns Hopkins University Press, 1985), p. 3.

   A more humble claim is that the discourse on urban decline is simply a "collective representation," the articulation of shared and contested meanings. See Warren Susman, "Did success spoil the United States? Dual representations in postwar America," in Larry May, ed., *Recasting America* (Chicago, University of Chicago Press, 1989), pp. 19–37.

4   Other adjectives might be used to describe the United States, for example racist, militaristic, sexist, riven with inequalities and, on the other hand, prosperous, technologically advanced, free. Each has the potential to irritate someone. The point is that the discourse confronts a multicultural society and can only be understood in its historical setting.

5   Leo Marx, "The puzzle of anti-urbanism in classic American literature," *The Pilot and the Passenger* (Oxford, Oxford University Press, 1988), p. 210.

6   Quote from Denis Donoghue, "A guide to the revolution," *New York Review of Books*, 30 (December 8, 1983), p. 45.

7   Hans Kellner has written: "To get the story crooked is to understand that the straightness of a story is a rhetorical invention . . ." See his *Language*

and *Historical Representation: Getting the Story Crooked* (Madison, WI, University of Wisconsin Press, 1989), p. xi.

8   The phrase "shaping attention" in the above heading is from Jürgen Habermas by way of John Forester. See the latter's *Planning in the Face of Power* (Berkeley, CA, University of California Press, 1989), pp. 14–24.

9   Clifford Geertz, "Ideology as a cultural system," in David E. Apter, ed., *Ideology and Discontent* (New York, The Free Press, 1964), p. 64. See also Fred Weinstein, *History and Theory after the Fall* (Chicago, University of Chicago Press, 1990), pp. 38–44.

10   My intention is not to characterize the discourse on urban decline as an ideology, but to use our understanding of ideology to provide insights into the discourse's meaning. On the distinction between ideology and discourse, see Terry Eagleton, *Ideology, An Introduction* (London, Verso, 1991), pp. 8–10. I am emphasizing what Louis Althusser called the "lived relations" of ideology.

11   This has been termed the epistemological aspect of ideology. Such an "objectivist" assessment of a portion of the discourse on urban decline is attempted by Gregory R. Weiher in his "Rumors of the demise of the urban crisis are exaggerated," *Journal of Urban Affairs*, 11 (1989), pp. 225–42.

12   Here the accusation of false consciousness comes into play; ideology as distortion. Antonio Gramsci, for example, wrote of how hegemonic ideologies blur the forms of oppression. See James Joll, *Antonio Gramsci* (New York, Viking Press, 1977), p. 130. This view is commonly associated with a Marxist critique, but also has a home in more conservative realms. Certainly it echoes loudly in Daniel Bell's assertion of an end to ideology and Frances Fukuyama's claim to an end to history. See Daniel Bell, *The End of Ideology* (New York, The Free Press, 1960) and Frances Fukuyama, *The End of History and the Last Man* (New York, The Free Press, 1992).

13   See Robert N. Bellah, et al., *Habits of the Heart* (New York, Harper & Row, 1986).

14   My premise is that societies are moral communities in which obligations and responsibilities are intrinsic components of all social relations. See, for example, Barrington Moore, Jr, *Injustice: The Social Bases of Obedience and Revolt* (White Plains, NY, M.E. Sharpe, 1976), pp. 3–48.

15   "All of this results from the fact that people are rooted in multiple social locations and are characterized by multiple identities (as workers, parents, friends, neighbors, and members of ethnic, religious, linguistic, and other groups), and it is not possible to know prospectively, and it is difficult to know retrospectively, the basis on which people will respond or have responded, as workers or parents, or as workers one time and as parents the next, and so on." See Weinstein, *History and Theory after the Fall*, p. 68.

16   See C. Wright Mills, "The big city: private troubles and public issues," in Irving Louis Horowitz, ed., *Power, Politics and People* (New York, Oxford University Press, 1967), pp. 395–402.

17   For an introduction to these issues see Lewis Mumford, *The Culture of Cities* (New York, Harcourt, Brace, 1938).

18   See William Sharpe and Leonard Wallock, eds, *Visions of the Modern City* (Baltimore, Johns Hopkins University Press, 1987) and Raymond

Williams, "Metropolitan perceptions and the emergence of modernism," *The Politics of Modernism* (London, Verso, 1989), pp. 37–48.

19   See, for example, Blake McKelvey, *The Urbanization of America, 1860–1915* (New Brunswick, NJ, Rutgers University Press, 1967) and Eric H. Monkkonen, *America Becomes Urban* (Berkeley, CA, University of California Press, 1988).

20   This, of course, is a central concern of early sociologists with their focus on the demise of community. See Thomas Bender, *Community and Social Change in America* (Baltimore, MD, Johns Hopkins University Press, 1982) and Richard Sennett, ed., *Classic Essays on the Culture of Cities* (New York, Appleton-Century-Crofts, 1969).

21   Marshall Berman, *All That Is Solid Melts into Air* (New York, Penguin, 1988), p. 15.

22   For an introduction to the history of suburbia in the United States, see Robert Fishman, *Bourgeois Utopias* (New York, Basic Books, 1987) and Kenneth T. Jackson, *Crabgrass Frontier* (New York, Oxford University Press, 1985).

23   The phrase "urban village" was made academically popular by Herbert Gans in his *The Urban Villagers* (New York, Free Press, 1962) and by Jane Jacobs in her *The Death and Life of American Cities* (New York, Vintage, 1961).

24   Discussions of postmodernism and the city can be found in Phillip Cooke, *Back to the Future* (London, Unwin Hyman, 1990); David Harvey, *The Condition of Postmodernity* (Oxford, Basil Blackwell, 1989); Edward W. Soja, *Postmodern Geographies* (London, Verso, 1989), pp. 190–248; and Sharon Zukin, *Landscapes of Power* (Berkeley, CA, University of California Press, 1991). See also Mike Davis' wonderfully rich and compelling history of Los Angeles: *City of Quartz* (London, Verso, 1990).

25   See Fredric Jameson, "Postmodernism, or the cultural logic of late capitalism," *New Left Review*, 146 (July/August, 1984), pp. 53–92 and Paul L. Knox, "The restless urban landscape," *Annals of the Association of American Geographers*, 81 (June, 1991), pp. 181–209.

26   See David Harvey, "Flexible accumulation through urbanization: reflections on 'post-modernism' in the American city," *Antipode*, 19 (December, 1987), pp. 260–86 and Edward Relph, *The Modern Urban Landscape* (Baltimore, Johns Hopkins University Press, 1987).

27   Zukin, *Landscapes of Power*, p. 221.

28   See Mike Davis, "Urban renaissance and the spirit of postmodernism," *New Left Review*, 151 (May/June, 1985), pp. 106–13; Mike Davis, "*Chinatown*, part two? The 'internationalization' of downtown Los Angeles," *New Left Review*, 164 (July/August, 1987), pp. 65–86; and Saskia Sassen, *The Global City* (Princeton, NJ, Princeton University Press, 1991).

29   See James B. Chapin, "Why Americans hate cities," *Democratic Left*, 20 (July/August, 1992), pp. 14–16 and Alfred Kazin, "Fear of the city: 1783–1983," *American Heritage*, 34 (February/March, 1983), pp. 14–23. One of the well-exercised ironic revelations in this debate is the juxtaposition of government data showing that most Americans live within cities whereas opinion polls indicate that most Americans wish to live in the suburbs or the countryside. For further consideration of this point, see

Warren Susman, "The city in American culture," *Culture as History* (New York, Pantheon, 1984), pp. 237–51.

30   Raymond Williams, *The Country and the City* (New York, Oxford University Press, 1973).

31   For a discussion of the role of nature in this discourse, see James L. Machor, *Pastoral Cities: Urban Ideals and the Symbolic Landscape of America* (Madison, WI, University of Wisconsin Press, 1987); Leo Marx, *The Machine and the Garden* (New York, Oxford University Press, 1964); Michael Paul Rogin, "Nature as politics and nature as romance in America," *"Ronald Reagan," the Movie* (Berkeley, CA, University of California Press, 1987), pp. 169–89; and Peter J. Schmidt, *Back to Nature: The Arcadia Myth in Urban America* (Baltimore, MD, Johns Hopkins University Press, 1990). On the origins of the pastoral in the foundational urban discourse, see George Shulman, "The myth of Cain: fratricide, city building, and politics," *Political Theory*, 14 (May, 1986), pp. 215–38.

32   See Thomas Bender, "The end of the city?," *Democracy*, 3 (winter, 1983), pp. 8–20 and Walter Berns, "Thinking about the city," *Commentary*, 56 (October 1973), pp. 74–7.

33   Morton White and Lucia White, *The Intellectual versus the City* (New York, New American Library, 1962). The first quote is on p. 16 – note the use of "ambivalence" – and the second on p. 221.

34   Susman, "The city in American culture."

35   White and White, *The Intellectual versus the City*, p. 227.

36   Thomas Bender, *Toward an Urban Vision* (Baltimore, MD, Johns Hopkins University Press, 1982).

37   Ibid., p. xi.

38   This strikingly apt phrase is from Forester, *Planning in the Face of Power*, p. 3.

39   Michael Kammen, *People of Paradox* (New York, Vintage, 1973), p. 290.

40   Michael Kammen, "Biformity: a frame of reference," in Michael Kammen, ed., *The Contrapuntal Civilization* (New York, Thomas Y. Cromwell, 1971), p. 29. This notion of dualities has been criticized by feminists and various postmodern theorists for shackling alternative cultural forms to a dominant male center. See Craig Owens, "The discourse of others: feminism and postmodernism," in Hal Foster, ed., *The Anti-Aesthetic* (Port Townsend, WA: Bay Press, 1983), pp. 57–88 and Denise Riley, *"Am I that Name"* (Minneapolis, MN, University of Minnesota Press, 1988). On dual representations, see also Susman, "Did success spoil the United States? Dual representations in postwar America." On the cultural commonality of dualities, see David Maybury-Lewis and Uri Almager, *The Attraction of Opposites* (Ann Arbor, MI, University of Michigan Press, 1989).

41   Joseph A. Schumpeter, *Capitalism, Socialism and Democracy* (New York, Harper & Row, 1942), pp. 81–6. For a Marxian interpretation, see Berman, *All That Is Solid*.

42   For an introduction to the contradictions of capitalism, see Jürgen Habermas, *Legitimation Crisis* (Boston, Beacon Press, 1975), pp. 33–94; David Harvey, *The Limits of Capital* (Chicago, University of Chicago Press, 1982); Geoffrey Kay, *The Economic Theory of the Working Class* (New York, St Martin's Press, 1975); Karl Marx, *Capital*, vol. 1 (New York,

International Publishers, 1967) and *Wage-Labor and Capital* (New York, International Publishers, 1967). For applications, see Ira Katznelson, *City Trenches* (Chicago, University of Chicago Press, 1981) and James O'Connor, *The Fiscal Crisis of the State* (New York, St Martin's Press, 1973).

43   Manuel Castells, *The Economic Crisis and American Society* (Princeton, NJ, Princeton University Press, 1980); Manuel Castells, "The wild city," *Kapitalistate*, 4–5 (summer, 1976), pp. 2–30; Michael Harrington, *The Twilight of Capitalism* (New York, Touchstone, 1976); Bennett Harrison and Barry Bluestone, *The Great U-Turn* (New York, Basic Books, 1988); and William Tabb and Larry Sawers, eds, *Marxism and the Metropolis* (New York, Oxford University Press, 1984, 2nd edn).

44   For an engrossing depiction of the inequalities of American society, portrayed around the controversies attendant to school desegregation in Boston in the 1970s, see J. Anthony Lukas, *Common Ground* (New York, Vintage, 1986). Also relevant are William W. Goldsmith and Edward J. Blakely, *Separate Societies* (Philadelphia, Temple University Press, 1992); Frances Fox Piven and Richard A. Cloward, *The New Class War* (New York, Pantheon, 1982); and Fred Block, Richard A. Cloward, Barbara Ehrenreich, and Frances Fox Piven, *The Mean Season: The Attack on the Welfare State* (New York, Pantheon, 1987).

45   For an introduction to such struggles, see Norman I. Fainstein and Susan S. Fainstein, *Urban Political Movements* (Englewood Cliffs, NJ, Prentice-Hall, 1974) and Frances Fox Piven and Richard A. Cloward, *Poor Peoples' Movements* (New York, Pantheon, 1977).

46   My comment is confined to internal conflicts. Moreover, it is not meant to devalue the multitude of oppositional movements and social protests that have occurred or to suppress the history of resistance carried out by Native Americans or the imperialism which extended the boundaries of the nation.

47   See John Logan and Harvey Molotch, *Urban Fortunes* (Berkeley, University of California Press, 1987); Michael Peter Smith; *City, State & Market* (New York, Basil Blackwell, 1988); Michael Peter Smith and Joe R. Feagin, eds, *The Capitalist City* (Oxford, Basil Blackwell, 1987); and Neil Smith, *Uneven Development* (Oxford, Basil Blackwell, 1984).

48   See David Harvey, "The geography of capitalist accumulation," *The Urbanization of Capital* (Baltimore, MD, Johns Hopkins University Press, 1985), pp. 32–61.

49   See Joe R. Feagin and Robert Parker, *Building American Cities* (Englewood Cliffs, NJ, Prentice-Hall, 1990) and Susan S. Fainstein, et al., *Restructuring the City* (New York, Longman, 1983).

50   The idea of "frontier" is as malleable as that of "decline." See Gerald D. Nash, "The census of 1890 and the closing of the frontier," *Pacific Northwest Quarterly*, 71 (July, 1980), pp. 98–100 and Richard Bernstein, "Unsettling the old west," *New York Times Magazine* (March 18, 1990), pp. 34, 56–7, 59. The notion of an investment frontier comes from Neil Smith. See Neil Smith, Betsy Duncan, and Laura Reid, "From disinvestment to reinvestment: tax arrears and turning points in the East Village," *Housing Studies*, 4 (1989), pp. 238–52.

51   On legitimacy, see Gordon L. Clark and Michael Dear, *State Apparatus*

(Boston, Allen & Unwin, 1984), pp. 153–174; Habermas, *Legitimation Crisis*, pp. 95–143; O'Connor, *The Fiscal Crisis of the State*; and Alan Wolfe, *The Limits of Legitimacy* (New York, The Free Press, 1977).

52   To quote Alan Wolfe, "America [just after the Second World War] embarked on a massive experiment. Politics would concern itself with the means – growth and the ends, or purpose, of social life would take care of themselves." See his *America's Impasse: The Rise and Fall of the Politics of Growth* (New York: Pantheon, 1981), p. 10.

53   Ideology is an elusive and highly contested concept. My position is that it is first and foremost a worldview that integrates cultural dispositions, current material conditions, and aspirations within a historical frame of reference. It can be self-serving, deceive, provide practical advice and make sense of the world. See Raymond Boudon, *The Analysis of Ideology* (Chicago, University of Chicago Press, 1989) and Eagleton, *Ideology*.

54   By dominant ideology, I simply mean that network of arguments, debates and discussions (i.e., discourse) that expresses the standpoint of the ruling powers as they overlap across spheres of society.

55   Leslie Berlowitz, Denis Donoghue, and Louis Menard, *America in Theory* (New York, Oxford University Press, 1988).

56   For the Marxist version of this history, see Paul Buhle, *Marxism in the USA* (London, Verso, 1987). Also useful is T. B. Bottomore, *Critics of Society* (New York, Vintage, 1969). The notion of oppositional and alternative ideologies is taken from Raymond Williams. See his *Marxism and Literature*, pp. 121–7, and *Problems in Materialism and Culture* (London, Verso, 1980), pp. 31–49.

57   Iris Marion Young discusses how we should think politically about these oppositions in her *Justice and the Politics of Difference* (Princeton, NJ, Princeton University Press, 1990).

58   See Murray Edelman, *Constructing the Political Spectacle* (Chicago, University of Chicago Press, 1988) and Michael Walzer, *The Company of Critics* (New York, Basic Books, 1988).

59   Swirling through academia in the late 1980s and early 1990s was a debate about "political correctness." The issues could basically be reduced to two: the tolerance of "unacceptable" ideas and the content of a liberal education. For various takes on this, see John Searle, "The storm over the university," *New York Review of Books*, 37 (December 16, 1990), pp. 34–42, and C. Vann Woodward, "Freedom and the universities," *New York Review of Books*, 38 (July 18, 1991), pp. 32–7.

60   Edelman, *Constructing the Political Spectacle*, p. 119. To the extent that my argument posits the importance of discourse in coordinating action and in producing normatively regulated action, it has a Habermasian flavor. See Stephen S. White, *The Recent Work of Jürgen Habermas* (Cambridge, Cambridge University Press, 1988), pp. 39–44, and Jürgen Habermas, *The Theory of Communicative Action* (Boston, Beacon Press, 1984), pp. 75–101. See also Bellah, *Habits of the Heart*, as regards Americans' search for a social philosophy.

61   On choice and social responsibility, see Isiah Berlin, "Determinism, relativism and historical judgement," in Patrick Gardiner, ed., *Theories of History* (New York, Free Press, 1959), pp. 319–29. On the issue of social

justice, see Barrington Moore, Jr. *Reflections on the Causes of Human Misery* (Boston, Beacon Press, 1973); John Rawls, *A Theory of Justice* (Cambridge, MA, Harvard University Press, 1971); and Young, *Justice and the Politics of Difference*.

15

See You in Disneyland

Michael Sorkin

As he was led manacled away after his conviction, serial killer Richard Ramirez, Los Angeles's infamous "Night Stalker," turned to the court-room audience and snarled "See you in Disneyland." America recognized the turn of phrase from the familiar TV ad that invariably follows the World Series or Super Bowl. After a montage of key plays – with "When You Wish upon a Star" swelling behind – the beaming hero of the game is caught striding off field and asked by the announcer, "What are you going to do now?"

The reply is invariable: "I'm going to Disney World."

Disney World, a theme park of theme parks, is America's stand-in for Elysium, the ultimate reward for quarterbacks and pitchers, the utopia of leisure. And it's not just America's: through those pearly gates in Orlando, Florida, lies the leading purely tourist destination on the planet, welcoming close to 100,000 people on good days, over 30 million a year, a throng that spends nearly a billion dollars each year. These staggering numbers include neither the original Disneyland in Anaheim, California, nor Tokyo Disneyland, nor Euro Disneyland, abuilding by the Marne. Thanks to Disney and like attractions, Orlando has become America's capital of tran-sience, with more hotel rooms than Chicago, Los Angeles, or New York.

But the empire of Disney transcends these physical sites; its aura is all-pervasive. Decades of films have furnished a common iconography on generations. Now there's a television channel too. And years of shrewd and massive merchandising have sold billions of Disney things – video-cassettes, comic books, pajamas, paper cups, postcards, and mouse-eared

Reprinted by permission from Michael Sorkin, 1992, "See you in Disneyland," in Michael Sorkin (ed.), *Variations on a Theme Park: The New American City and the End of Public Space*.

coin purses – which vaunt their participation in this exponentially expanding system of objects. The litter of Disneyland is underfoot in streets from New York to Shanghai. More people know Mickey than Jesus or Mao. Who doesn't live in Disney World?

The literal placemaking began with Disneyland. According to one hagiographer, the idea for the park came to Disney in 1938, on a trip to the Chicago Railroading Fair, where he was invited to don engineer's overalls and climb behind the throttle of a historic locomotive, fulfilling a childhood dream. Later, he built a miniature railroad around his own house, anticipating the rail-ringed parks to come. Another myth of the park's origins, much retold, recounts a visit by the Disney family to a conventional amusement park, and Disney's disgust at its failures of hygiene. These fantasies of transport and cleanliness culminated, one day in 1955, in Disneyland itself, the alpha point of hyperreality.

It was always to have been a utopia. Early publicity limns it:

> *Disneyland will be based upon and dedicated to the ideals, the dreams, and the hard facts that have created America. And it will be uniquely equipped to dramatize these dreams and facts and send them forth as a source of courage and inspiration to all the world.*
>
> *Disneyland will be something of a fair, an exhibition, a playground, a community center, a museum of living facts, and a showplace of beauty and magic. It will be filled with the accomplishments, the joys, the hopes of the world we live in. And it will remind us and show us how to make those wonders part of our lives.*

If this evocation is a tad fuzzy, Disneyland's immediate origins are specific. Television paid. Strapped for cash to finance spiraling construction costs, the previously TV-shy Disney cut a deal with ABC, then struggling far behind its two rivals. In return for the network's money, Disney offered his most precious commodity: the mouse. Disneyland and the Mickey Mouse Club were born as twins. The park was, as Thomas Hine has noted, "the first place ever conceived simultaneously with a TV series."

The coincidence is more than temporal. Television and Disneyland operate similarly, by means of extraction, reduction, and recombination, to create an entirely new, antigeographical space. On TV, the endlessly bizarre juxtapositions of the daily broadcast schedule continuously erode traditional strategies of coherence. The quintessential experience of television, that continuous program-hopping zap from the remote control, creates path after unique path through the infinity of televisual space. Likewise, Disneyland, with its channel-turning mingle of history and fantasy, reality and simulation, invents a way of encountering the physical world that increasingly characterizes daily life. The highly regulated, completely synthetic vision provides a simplified, sanitized experience that stands in for the more undisciplined complexities of the city.

There are more than ample precedents for such weird compendia: circuses, festivals, and fairs have long been with us. Disney is the cool P. T. Barnum – there's a simulation born every minute – and Disneyland the ultimate Big Top. Both circus and Disney entertainment are anti-carnivalesque, feasts of atomization, celebrations of the existing order of things in the guise of escape from it, Fordist fun. Disneyland, of course, also descends from the amusement park, especially that turn-of-the-century blossoming at Coney Island, inspiration to imitator parks from coast to coast. Like Disneyland, Coney Island offered itself as a kind of opposition, an Arden of leisure in symbiosis with the workaday city. Steeplechase Park, Luna Park, and Dreamland established the basic elements of this new machinery of pleasure. Their evocations of travel in time and space, lilliputianization, physics-defying rides, ecstatic relationship to new technology, efficient organizing architecture of spectacle and coercion, and aspirations to urbanism – all harbinger apotheosis at Disneyland.

The most direct ancestor, however, is the World's Fair. These spectacles evolved from the national manufacturing exhibitions that grew with the industrial revolution. Originating late in the eighteenth century, the form climaxed in the Great Exhibition of the Works of Industry of All Nations held in London in 1851 under the enormous glass roof of Joseph Paxton's Crystal Palace. William Thackeray described it in an ode written for the occasion as

> *A Palace as for a fairy prince*
> *A rare pavilion, such as man*
> *Saw never since mankind began,*
> *And built and glazed.*

This giddy positivism also shines through in the inaugural address of Prince Albert, a Mouseketeer *avant la lettre*:

Nobody who has paid any attention to the peculiar features of our present era will doubt for a moment that we are living at a period of most wonderful transition which tends rapidly to accomplish that great end, to which, indeed, all history points – the realization of the unity of mankind . . . The distances which separated the different nations and parts of the globe are rapidly vanishing before the achievements of modern invention, and we can traverse them with incredible ease; the languages of all nations are known, and their acquirement placed within the reach of everybody; thought is communicated with the rapidity, and even by the power, of lightning. On the other hand, the great principle of the division of labor, which may be called the moving power of civilization, is being extended to all branches of science,

industry, and art . . . The products of all quarters of the globe are placed at
our disposal, and we have only to choose which is the best and the cheapest
for our purposes, and the powers of production are entrusted to the stimulus
of competition and capital.[1]

The 1851 fair was the first great utopia of global capital. The Prince
Consort's evocation of a world shrunk by technology and the division of
labor is the ur-theme of the theme park, and Paxton's Crystal Palace made
this visible by canny means. First, the wealth of nations was contained
under one roof, housed in a single architectural space. And the construction itself embodied the progress of industry – assembled from a vast
number of precisely prefabricated elements, the Crystal Palace was the
great early expression of a manufactured building. Finally, the Palace
depicted paradise. Not only was it laid out like a cathedral, with nave and
transept, but it was also the largest greenhouse ever built, its interior filled
with greenery as well as goods, a climate-controlled reconciliation of
Arcadia and industry, a garden for machines.

Since efficiencies in the manufacture of glass had begun to make them
possible late in the eighteenth century, such large structures had come to
be both stand-ins for the ineffable and zoos for the menagerie of
European colonialism. In the days of the dark satanic mills, winter
gardens became hugely popular places of entertainment and assembly.
Those tropical landscapes in Berlin or Brussels helped (along with the
popular historical and geographical panoramas) to invent the idea of
simulated travel, initiating the great touristic dialectic of appearance and
reality. The decline in popularity of these environments toward the end
of the century was the result of the spread of railways, which made actual
exotic travel possible.

This dislocation is central. Whatever its other meanings, the theme
park rhapsodizes on the relationship between transportation and geography. The winter garden evokes distance, the railroad proximity. The
flicking destination board at JFK or Heathrow offers – in its graphic
anonymity – a real trip to Tangier. The winter garden – the "hothouse" –
is all artifice, about inaccessibility, about both its own simulations and the
impossibility of being present at the scene evoked: it is not recollective,
but a fantastic. At its core, the greenhouse – or Disneyland – offers a view
of alien nature, edited, a better version, a kind of sublime. Indeed, the
abiding theme of every park is nature's transformation from civilization's
antithesis to its playground.

In time, these fairs became differentiated. Soon they embraced a
variety of pavilions arranged thematically (manufacture, transport,
science, etc.), then national and entertainment pavilions, eventually
pavilions sponsored by corporations. From the first, these structures,
while impermanent, competed in architectural extravagance. And, as the
scope of the fairs grew, the ordering and connection of elements assumed

paramount importance. Reaching the scale and density of small cities, the fairs also became models, adopted visionary urbanism as an aspect of their agendas, both offering themselves as models of urban organization and providing, within their pavilions, panoramic visions of even more advanced cities to come. The crucial role played by movement systems within the enlarging fairs was not simply a product of necessity but a paradigm for physical relations in the modern city. And the fairs quickly developed "urban problems," especially in relation to their peripheries. They were conceived as exemplars, and stultifying high-mindedness was a staple. As a result, the fairs often found themselves in symbiosis with disorderly carnivals of more "popular" entertainments just beyond their boundaries, with Little Egypt doing "exotic dancing" on the Midway or strippers plying their trade on the fringes of Flushing.

The years that saw the rise of the great universal exposition also witnessed a flowering of practical utopianism. Although much of the theory originated in Europe, America became the great blank canvas for utopian experiments. Not only were new cities being built at a vast clip, communitarian citizens – Fourierites, Owenites, Shakers, Quakers, Mormons, and other affinity groups – built a breathtaking array of intentional communities. While few of these enterprises can be said to have broken much new ground in terms of the physical life of the city, they did abet an atmosphere of renovation and reform that had direct consequences for urbanism. The contrast between this positivistic, optimist vision of the perfectible future and the increasingly degraded condition of the migrant-swollen industrial city precipitated a range of proposals that took increasingly physical form.

In fact, the 1892 Fair in Chicago – aptly called the White City, for the Fair was the urban analogue of the Great White Fleet that was to convey reform in other spheres – represents a summa of one influential impulse. The City Beautiful movement was the first great model for the new city to be born in America. Its prescriptions – baroque symmetries, monumental beaux-arts architecture, abundant parks and greenery – impressed themselves on scores of cities with frequently vivifying results. The City Beautiful's fascination with sumptuousness, visible order, and parks – with the monumental, "public" aspect of the city – anticipates the physical formula of the theme park, the abstraction of good public behavior from the total life of the city. The dazzling Chicago fair showed the potential for magnificence of such concentrated architectural firepower, and virtually every city in America has a civic quarter, however slight the remnant, created under its influence.

Concurrent with the City Beautiful, the pressure of mass settlement and expanding technology created other visions of regulation, less indebted to formal ideas culled from the past. These visions appeared both in imaginary architectural schemes and in a remarkable literary outpouring: novels about happy technologized utopias, like Bellamy's *Looking Backward*, with its strikingly prescient evocation of a world at leisure. These two expressions were focused on somewhat different territories. The visionary architectural proposals – many inspired by the development of the technology of tall buildings – were prompted by the prospect of skyscraper cities and especially by the intricate movement systems that would be required to sustain them. The novels, however, tended to be fantasies about the relations of production, scenes of happy regulation set in a technologically enabled culture of convenience.

These imaginings anticipated the urbanism promulgated by modernism itself, which shows two main strains. The first is the now maligned rationalist, geometric manner – Le Corbusier its main apostle – an enormity of regimentation plopped at regular intervals across a verdant landscape. Le Corbusier's vision has become the icon of alienation, dislodged from its original status as challenge to the insalubrious dreariness of the industrial city and reincarnated as faceless urban renewal and bland 1960s downtowns. It is this version of modernist urbanism that Disneyland's architectural apologists have in mind when they propose it as a restorative.

But modernism produced another version of the city, one more central to Disney's American imaginings. The movement for garden cities, expostulated by the Englishman Ebenezer Howard in his 1902 screed *Garden Cities for Tomorrow*, stands in approximately the same relationship to Le Corbusier's Cartesian fantasies as English landscape gardening did to French in the eighteenth century. The one was a romantic ode to "wild" nature, the other an essay in submission, nature bent to the paths of order. Both, though, were versions of the pastoral, embracing the idea that the renaturalization of the "denatured" city would strip it of its dread, that the reversion to the natural would have a salutary effect on human nature itself.

The garden city is the physical paradigm that presages Disney space, the park in the theme park. Its ideology embraces a number of formal specifics. To begin with, these were to be small cities constructed, ex novo, on the exurban perimeter of existing metropolises, to function as escape valve or release from the tension and overcrowding of the old city. A picturesque plan – the stuff of the early suburbs – was as indispensable as the strict regulation of traffic. Indeed, strategies of movement became the ultimate internal rationale and formal arbiter of the garden city. These included separation of pedestrians and vehicles and a scale of distances convenient for persons on foot. Formally, the result was generally a single center and a radial plan, united by loops of circulation.

Technology and the garden city conjoined in the two great world's fairs of the 1930s: the 1933 Century of Progress Exposition in Chicago and the 1939 World's Fair in New York City. The Chicago Fair was laid out along a meandering roadway meant to evoke "an evolving incipient roadtown," a garden city. Dispersed along this route – and strongly pre-figuring the Disney solution – were a variety of pavilions celebrating scientific advance. Over it all soared the skyride: Chicago was the first fair to absolutely elevate the means of movement as its most visible sym-bol. The layout of the New York Fair evoked an earlier utopian order, the kind of geometric radiating plan characteristic of ideal communities from the Renaissance through the eighteenth century, inspiration to the garden city. However, New York also boasted two gigantic scale models of cities of the future, which between them embodied those two indis-pensable ideas of order – movement and the garden.

Both were the products of industrial designers, forerunners of Disney's imagineers. The first, "Democracity," the work of Henry Dreyfus, sat inside the famous Perisphere. Although its center was a jumbo skyscraper, the plan of the city – a constellation of sylvan towns on a green perimeter – was pure Ebenezer Howard. The second – and far more popular, perhaps because visitors rode past it in tiny cabs, Disney style – was Norman Bel Geddes's "City of 1960," designed for the General Motors Futurama. Here was the Corbusian version of modernity, a sea of skyscrapers set in green superblocks, ordered by a Cartesian grid. Of course, the rectilinear interstices swam with swift traffic, cars sailing unimpeded to the cardinal points, motion the fertilizing matrix in which the city grew.

The ideology of the garden city today has been dispersed into a wide variety of environments. Consider Opus, an office complex on the ring highway outside Minneapolis. Promotional brochures describe it as

> *an imaginative, innovative development . . . a model for a whole new gener-ation of office parks. Strategically located in southwest suburban Minneapolis, the beautifully landscaped 450-acre site is ribboned with pedestrian and bike paths, colored with flowers, shaded with trees . . . alive and inspiring. Nestled in acres of meadows, hills, and ponds, Opus is only minutes away from shopping centers, sports stadiums, the international airport, and the downtown business districts of Minneapolis and St. Paul. The site is linked to the interstate system by County Road 18 and Crosstown Highway 62.*

A look at the plan for the development elucidates the hype: Opus is the garden city with pedestrians carefully separated from vehicular traffic and picturesque circulation routes organizing lots of different sizes. Yet one thing distinguishes Opus from the garden-variety garden city. Opus is an office development, the residential component an after-thought, a few parcels set aside for outside developers to build limited amounts of housing. Given the character of the work performed in each of the office parcels ("Opus gives new meaning to the word 'work'") and the location of most services and housing off the site, there's no real reason for the elaborate pedestrian links and the careful grade separations. They do, however, "urbanize" the site, giving it a stature in theory that it lacks in use. The pedestrian system signifies benign mobility, a map of motion without movement. The real links are the highway and airport connections and, more crucially, the invisible telecommunications system that is primarily responsible for enabling the dispersed developments that now figure as the major mode of American urbanism.

The perimeter road in Atlanta, Interstate 285, is often offered as a primal scene for the proliferation of this new exurbia. It developed fast. By 1980, central Atlanta had become a symbol of the Sunbelt reborn. The city had a new profile: a classic central place diagram with a clutch of shiny skyscrapers extruding value straight up at its center. By 1985, however, the pattern had just as suddenly shifted: 4.3 million square feet of office space had been added in the center of town, but 7.6 million had been built in the oxymoronic Perimeter Center at one interstate intersection and 10.6 million had gone up in Cumberland/Galleria at another. Perimeter office space is now predominant overall.

The circulation loop that organizes the building sites within Opus recapitulates the highway loop that arrays Opus and other fringe developments around cities like Minneapolis and Atlanta. The order is centrifugal, about perimeters rather than centers, a logic of dispersion. In such spatial hierarchies, circulation always dominates. First, its requirements are literally the largest. By one standard calculation, 1300 square feet of parking space are required for every 1000 square feet of office on the urban perimeter. The physiognomy of movement orders the most primary issues of architecture, deforming it to its requirements. Like the tail-wagged dog, the workspace at the end of the movement chain seems misplaced, out of sequence, a prisoner of the prodigious life-support system necessary to sustain it in its isolation. This incessant circulation mirrors the circuit of capital – that global chain letter, faithfully accumulating – which these offices on the endless perimeter serve to accelerate. If these new developments seem schematic, it is precisely because they represent, in their primary order, an abstraction: the mobility of the capital that enables them.

The organization and scale of Disney World and the Disneylands is precisely that of the garden city. Located on the urban perimeter, they are, as phenomena, comparable to the office parks at other intersections in the highway system, if sited now for convenience of access by leisure commuters. Internally, they are also ordered according to a strict model. Radiating from a strong center – occupied by the totemic castle of fantasy

– the parks are arranged in thematic fiefs (Tomorrowland, Frontierland, etc.), which flow into one another. While the ground plane is given over to pedestrian circulation, the parks' perimeters and airspace are the terrain of elaborate transport systems: trains, monorails, and aerial gondolas.

Movement is ubiquitous and central. Disneyland and Disney World are, in the travel agent's parlance, "destinations." The implication is double, enfolding the acts of traveling and of arriving. The element of arrival is especially crucial, the idea that one is not passing through some intermediate station but has come to someplace where there is a definitive "there." In the larger discourse of travel, these places are vested with a kind of equivalence. The only relevant variable is motion. As the slogan for Busch Gardens, a rival theme park in Williamsburg, Virginia (hard by the first park, Colonial Williamsburg), proclaims – over the *Ode to Joy* – "If you want to see Europe, take a vacation in Virginia . . . It's all the fun and color of old Europe . . . but a lot closer!" (Not to mention, without pesky terrorists threatening to crimp your pleasures en route!)

Like world's fairs, both Busch Gardens and Disneyland offer intensifications of the present, the transformation of the world by an exponential increase in its commodities. World's fairs are microcosmic renditions of the "global marketplace," transnational shopping malls. At Disneyland, this monumentalized commodity fetishism is reduced to the pith of a haiku. While the nominal international "competition" at the orthodox fair centers on the "best" of national manufacture, the goods at Disneyland represent the degree zero of commodity signification. At Disney World, for example, the "national" pavilions groan with knickknacks. These are not simply emblems of participation in the enterprise of the higher, global, shopping, they are stand-ins for the act of travel itself, ersatz souvenirs. A trip to Disneyland substitutes for a trip to Norway or Japan. "Norway" and "Japan" are contracted to their minimum negotiable signifiers, Vikings and Samurai, gravlax and sushi. It isn't that one hasn't traveled – movement feeds the system, after all. It's that all travel is equivalent.

Getting there, then, is not half the fun: it's all the fun. At Disneyland one is constantly poised in a condition of becoming, always someplace that is "like" someplace else. The simulation's referent is ever elsewhere; the "authenticity" of the substitution always depends on the knowledge, however faded, of some absent genuine. Disneyland is in perpetual shadow, propelling its visitors to an unvisitable past or future, or to some (inconvenient) geography. The whole system is validated, though, by the fact that one has literally traveled, that one has, after all, chosen to go to Disneyland in lieu of any of the actual geographies represented. One has gone nowhere in spite of the equivalent ease of going somewhere. One has preferred the simulation to the reality. For millions of visitors, Disneyland is just like the world, only better.

If culture is being Disneyfied (and there's no mistaking it!) the royal road there is precisely that: going for a ride. Whatever else they subsume, the Disney zones harbor an amusement park, a compendium of rides offering both kinesis narrativized (a trip, a fantasy voyage) and that mild empirical frisson of going one-on-one with Sir Isaac, testing the laws of everyday physics. The visitor travels in order to travel. Whether experienced at 37,000 feet, on the interstate, or padding between Mike Fink's Keel Boat Ride and Captain Eo in your new Nikes, the main experience – motion – is broadened, extended right back to your front door.

Each Disney park embodies a kind of thematic of transportation. Euro-Disneyland, rising by the Marne, sits athwart a TGV line (the French bullet train – what a ride!), convenient to all Europe. Disney World exists in gravitational relationship to the airport at Orlando. Disneyland, super-annuated Shangri-la of the American fifties, is an exit on the LA freeway. In each instance, the park sits as an intensely serviced node on a modern network of global reach. The urbanism of Disneyland is precisely the urbanism of universal equivalence. In this new city, the idea of distinct places is dispersed into a sea of universal placelessness as everyplace becomes destination and any destination can be anyplace. The world of traditional urban arrangements is colonized by the penetration of a new multinational corridor, leading always to a single human subject, the monadic consumer. The ultimate consequence is likely to be the increasing irrelevance of actual movement and the substitution of the even more completely artificial reality of electronic "virtual" space. (As the Frank Zappa lyric puts its, "How can you be two places at once when you're not anywhere at all?") For the moment though, the system still spends its energies on sculpting more physical simulacra.

Consider the trip to the original Anaheim Disneyland. Conceived regionally, in the days before cheap air transport allowed its touristic reach to match its ideological grasp (who can forget poor Nikita Khrushchev's frustration at being denied a visit?), Disneyland was not simply designed for arrival by car, but was – like Los Angeles – begot by the car. One approaches Disneyland only after tooling across the vast Southern California sward of atomization, the bygone suburban utopia of universal accessibility that the automobile was supposed to guarantee.

Whatever else it represents, Disneyland is also a model of Los Angeles. Fantasyland, Frontierland, Tomorrowland – these are the historic themes of the city's own self-description, its main cultural tropes. The genius of the city, however, resides not simply in dispersal but in juxtaposition, the invention of the possibility of the Loirish Bungalow sitting chockablock with the Tudoroid. The view through the framing window of the passing car animates the townscape, cinematizing the city. This consumption of the city as spectacle, by means of mechanical movement through it, precapitulates the more global possibilities of both the multinational corridor created by air travel and the simultaneous electronic everywhere of television. Disneyland offers a space in which narrative depends on motion, and in which one is placed in a position of spectatorship of one's own spectatorship.

While the car may be LA's generator, it's also its "problem," motor of democracy and alienation both, repressor of pedestrianism and its happy random encounters. There's a school (popular along the learnedly kitsch axis of early architectural postmodernism) that exalts Disneyland as a solution to the dissipation of the public realm engendered by cars. This is achieved by relegating cars to a parking periphery, creating an auto-free zone at its center, and using efficient, technologized transport (that charismatic monorail) to mediate.

But this is only half the story. In fact, Disneyland less redeems LA than inverts it. The reason one circulates on foot in Disneyland is precisely to be able to ride. However, the central experience, by anyone's empirical calculation, is neither walking nor riding, but waiting in line. Most of a typical Disney day is thus spent in the very traffic jam one has putatively escaped, simply without benefit of car. Indeed, what's perfect, most ulti- mately viable, at Disneyland is riding. After hours of snaking through the sun with one's conscientiously well-behaved fellow citizens comes the kinetic payoff: brief, thrilling, and utterly controlled, a traffic engineer's wet dream.

There's a further inversion. Much of the riding at Disneyland – from Space Mountain to Mr Toad's Wild Ride – takes place indoors. Driving a car in Los Angeles is at once an intensely private and very public activ- ity: on the road, one is both isolated and fully visible. Disneyland surrealizes the ambiguity by making driving domestic, interior, even as it's regulated by being pared of control. Chez Mr. Toad, the line culmi- nates in a quaint Olde English manse through which one is conveyed in . . . a quaint Olde English car. One drives in exactly the only place one expects to walk in the "real" city back home.

Getting to Disney World is a more intrinsically long-distance proposition, involving a long-distance automotive schlep or passage through the global air corridor (visitors are presently divided 50/50 between road and air). Let's say the journey begins at Kennedy Airport in New York. Kennedy is organized along exactly the same ring road principles as Disneyland itself. A big vehicular loop defines a perimeter along which are arrayed the terminals of the various airlines. These buildings – most of which were designed in the late fifties or early sixties – are conceived after the fashion of the national pavilions of the world's fairs of the period, modernist shrines whose signifying tasks are engaged via abstraction rather than representation: expressions of grandeur and consequence rather than any particular evocation of regional particulars. This exaltation of the node differs from the more current paradigm – visible at the airports of Chicago, Atlanta, Dallas/Fort Worth, or Orlando – with their emphasis on the seamlessness of the intermodal transfer. Indeed, at Kennedy, this primacy of the individual terminal is purchased at the cost of considerable inconvenience to travelers transferring between airlines, and a just-begun reconstruction of the airport aims to transform it with the introduction of a "people-mover" system, a linkage-ride like the Disney monorail.

The original arrangement, however, was suited to its Eisenhowerian age, an airport structured like a suburb, America's own version of the garden city. The suburbs, of course, were predicated on the preeminence of the family, its autonomy expressed by freestanding structures on clearly delineated plots. In a time of confidence, the visibility of the economic unit was paramount on the symbolic agenda: at Kennedy, as at Disney, the corporations are surrogates for the family, everybody's big brothers. And Kennedy is likewise afflicted with the same problems of transportation as the suburbs it emulated: difficult to get to, inefficient in its internal connections, dependent on a single mode – the car. At the center of the sea of parking within the Kennedy loop – in the symbolic position occupied by Disneyland's castle, Disney World's geodesic or the 1939 World's Fair Trylon and Perisphere – stand three concrete chapels, for Catholic, Protestant, and Jewish worship. Under the reconstruction plan, they are to be replaced by a more up-to-the-minute shrine: the central node of the new airport movement system. The obliteration of the three chapels, of course, also obviates the question of an absence they so directly beg. While this religious trinity may have been sufficient for the American imperium of the late fifties and early sixties, the accelerated globalism of today does not so easily slough off religions classed simply as Other. Certainly, those chapels had to go if only to avoid the question of the missing mosque. At "Kennedy" – America's leading memorial to the great initiatory act of modern terrorism – mingling Islam and air travel would clearly be too risky.

If airports have become the locale of choice for random terror, they're also arenas for other politics. The Tokyo airport, Narita, is a perennial protest site. Located many miles from the center of Tokyo in an agricultural area typified by small landholdings, Narita's plans to build a long new runway on expropriated farm land have repeatedly fallen afoul of the local left, and numerous, often violent, demonstrations have occurred. From an American vantage point there's something at once quixotic and stirring in this rage on behalf of traditional life in a country that has become the emblem of breakneck modernization and globalized capital. But there's no mistaking the power of the runway, a spirit portal of virtually Egyptian intensity. Like an automatic teller machine, the runway is the point at which a vast, controlling, and invisible skein is made manifest. As each jumbo sets down, tarring its tread-trace in a puff of burnt rubber, the runway becomes rune-way, marker of that inescapable web.

Hartsdale airport in Atlanta is home base to Delta, the current "official" airline of Disney World. As with any fledgling nation-state, hocking its future for a pride of Boeings, an airline completes an indispensable circuit of status, a symbolic minimum apparatus of nationhood. Indeed, the world's most succinct and prospering nation, Singapore, embodies the shrunken vision to perfection. Almost no territory, an intense electronic and travel economy, a superb airline, and a bustling airport linked by modern rapid transit to a compact skyscrapered downtown, orderly to a fault, complete with hygienically retained ethnic and colonial quarters and regulated with scary draconian legality, it's a virtual Disney Nation, deftly substituting Uncle Harry for Uncle Walt. For Disney World, the relationship with Delta both opens another line of penetration into the Real World and affirms its status as perpetually offshore.

Unlike Kennedy, Hartsdale already has an automated "people-mover" transit system to link its terminal concourses. Vaunted as a panacea for urban congestion in the hardware-fixated sixties, the vision was of fleets of small, highly autonomous, "user-friendly" transit cars gliding silently on elevated tracks. People-movers were also seen as a replacement for the freeways – the previous solution – then coming to be viewed as hopelessly destructive to the urban body they were meant to heal. Although people-movers mainly proved too inefficient and expensive for city use, they were just the thing for the more specific and restricted requirements of airports, where exponential growth had stretched the distance from entry to gates to pituitary proportions.

The fantasy that undergirds the science of people-moving is regulation. It's a primal ordering: the Newtonian vision of the universe, bodies intricately meshing and revolving like ticking clockwork, divinity legible precisely in the Laws of Motion. For planners confronted by the irrationality of the city, the addition of computer-regulated, minutely responsive people-movers clearly meant bringing the global-motion net one step closer to the front door. In the space of capital, circulation is politics: its foregrounding at places like Disneyland is analogous to the barrierless vision of free trade that sparked the fairs of the nineteenth century. The driverless people-mover – its motions seemingly dictated by the invisible hand, mechanical creature of supply and demand – is symbol of this economic fantasy of perfect self-government.

On the Hartsdale people-mover, the recorded voice that signals the stops along the loop was originally female. Held to lack authority, it was changed, not to a male voice but to an electronic androgyne. This, then, is a welcome, the signal of an unspecifiable presentness of the system. Gliding to a stop, the car murmurs, "The next stop is terminal A. The color-coded maps and signs in this vehicle match the colors in the terminal." Indeed, the airport has become ("deregulation" notwithstanding) perhaps the most intensively regulated zone of common experience, a more visible version of the more discrete, concealed governings of the Disney Zones. The combined threats of narcotics and terror have given rise to unprecedented levels of policing and surveillance. Credit and passport checks, magnetic screening, irradiation of luggage, baleful agents vetting security "profiles," sniffer dogs: such are the quotidian experiences of air travel. Indeed, every year over a billion people pass through the airport security apparatus, terrified and terribly safe all at once.

The global corridor is the modern Panopticon, seething with surveillance. The genius of this system is, however, not just the drill but the invitation, the willingness of its subjects to participate. Take Williams Island, a typical upper-income enclaved community in Miami, advertised by spokesperson Sophia Loren as the "Florida Riviera." Williams offers at least a triple pitch. Its architectural centerpiece is indeed a complex of buildings meant to evoke Portofino or Saint Tropez, all tile roofs, waterside cafes, and bobbing boats. There's also an idealized movement system, consisting of footways and golf carts. In the context of the successive transformations of the garden city, the golf cart is an interesting modification. The cart's the ultimate reconciliation of machine and garden, a benign transport indigenous to leisure. And the golf course itself is a state of nature apt to the age: a vast acreage of greenery scrupulously regulated to support a network of tiny, shallow holes.

But security is the main feature. The first checkpoint at Williams Island is on the far side of a bridge from the mainland. Residents, once recognized, are admitted with a wave. Visitors undergo further scrutiny, and are directed along a succession of additional checkpoints. At buildings' edge, security becomes high-tech. Each resident of the complex has an electronic pass, like a credit card. To move through the sequence of security locks, he or she must insert the card in a slot. A central computer verifies the pass and opens the door. At the same time, a record of the cardholder's movement is printed out at the main guard post. Like the air traveler, the resident submits to an elaborate system of surveillance with the ultimate rationale of self-protection. Here, however, the surrender of privacy is a privilege. Moving through Williams Island recapitulates the larger experience of moving through the global corridor. The security checks, the certifying credit cards and passports, the disciplined, carefully segmented movements, the ersatz geography, the grafted cachet – this is Disneyville.

Arriving at Orlando airport offers the Disney-bound a hint of things to come. There's a brief people-mover ride from satellite to main terminal and a welter of advertising and Disney Reps in the main lobby. However, the cocooning shroud of automated movement stops at the main entrance. To get from the airport to Disney World, a car is required.

Indeed, the only way to arrive at Disney World is by road. This obliges a key ritual of the corridor: the modulation of the means of movement. At the entrance to Disney, the process is inverted: one passes through a customs-like toll barrier, thence to relinquish one's car to hotel, campsite, or day-tripper's parking lots and enter the system. The toll booth is also the limit of a monetary zone: within Disney World, visitors can pay either with conventional instruments or with "Disney Dollars." These – exchangeable for U.S. dollars one to one – confer absolutely no advantage, no discount, no speculative hedge. They do, however, concretize and differentiate the experience of exchange and boost the counterfeit aura of foreign-ness.

Visitors are welcomed by the mouse. Mickey – hairless, sexless, and harmless – is a summary: as Disney once put it, "Mickey is a *clean* mouse." Talk about a constructed subject – Mickey stands in the same relationship to human subjectivity as Disneyland does to urbanity. Rigorously and completely manipulated, the mouse's outward appearance is affective and cute. As a gloss on human speech, locomotion, and appearance, the mouse offers pratfalling, loopy variation. As an epistemology, Mickey sees things as we do. Mickey, like most cartoon characters, circulates in the cartoon state of nature, a place which collapses the best of Hobbes and Rousseau, a place where life's inevitable brutishness is always played for laughs, where impulses need not be censored because they are ultimately without consequences. The mechanical mouse, product of the animator's assembly line, also confirms a key switch: at Disney, nature is appearance, machine is reality.

Just as the image of the mouse on a million plastic souvenirs confers aura and legitimacy on them, so the vestiges of utopia in the Disney space certifies them as more than amusement parks. For Disneyzone – Disneyland, Disney World, and all the other Disney places – is also a state of nature, offering the fecund communism of abundance and leisure, a true technocratic postindustrial utopia. The industrial army, raised in the nineteenth century and rationalized in the twentieth, is, at Disneyzone, not dispersed but converted to a vast leisure army, sacrificing nothing in regimentation and discipline as it consumes its Taylorized fun. Disneyzone completes the circuit of world's fairism by converting the celebration of production into the production of celebration. The pivot on which this transformation turns is the essential alienation of the producer-turned-consumer, his or her dance to the routines of someone else's imagining.

The need for the efficient production of leisure activities has certainly not escaped the official strategizers of our collective future. In his 1976 *Between Two Ages*, Zbigniew Brzezinski warned his patrons of the exigencies to be faced in the coming "technotronic society." Describing the relationship between employers, labor, and the market in this new order,

Brzezinski writes that "in the emerging new society questions relating to the obsolescence of skills security, vacations, leisure, and profit-sharing dominate the relationship, and the psychic well-being of millions of relatively secure but potentially aimless lower-middle-class blue-collar workers becomes a growing problem."[2]

The relation between work and leisure is part of the conceptual problematic that kept Disney's most ambitious, most conventionalized, utopian vision, the Experimental Prototype Community of Tomorrow (Epcot) from full fruition. Epcot was prompted by a number of impulses, one of them the literal realization of a full-scale version of the kind of well-regulated one-dimensional urbanism proposed in model form at the 1939 Fair. Perhaps more strongly motivating, however, was Disney's widely reported frustration at events in Anaheim. Like so many world's fairs, Disneyland was beleaguered by an undisciplined periphery: the huge success of the park prompted developers to buy up miles of surrounding countryside, which was promptly converted to a regulationless tangle of hotels and low commerce. For Disney the frustration was double. First, at the millions lost to others who were housing his visitors. (In the first ten years, Disneyland took in $273 million, the peripherals $555 million.) And second, the disorder of it all, the sullying of his vision by a sea of sleaze.

Redress, utopia's wellspring, was thus a major motivator for Disney's next go. With guile and stealth he accumulated 28,000 acres of land near Orlando, Florida, for Disney World and its subset Epcot. As intended, the scheme was to embrace both theme park (a clone of Anaheim) and a full-blown community, initially to house his own workers, eventually to include such additional industrial and residential development as he was able to attract. Spake Disney, "Epcot will always be in a state of becoming. It will never cease to be a living blueprint of the future, where people will live a life they can't find anywhere else in the world today." Disney was able to extract extraordinary, unprecedented concessions from the government of Florida, assuring him of virtually complete sovereignty (including rights of policing, taxation, and administration, and freedom from environmental controls) over his domain.

Unfortunately, death intervened before Disney was able to materialize his dream. Its realization was left in the hands of his successors, whose view of the matter was somewhat more jaundiced. Instead of a full-blown "community," Epcot was reduced to the status of simply another theme park. Indeed, it was to become the Disney empire's most literally world's-fairian incarnation. Organized according to the familiar schema – initiatory "main street," loop of attractions – it directly reproduced the components of its predecessor fairs. Materializing the covert agenda of previous Disney Main Streets (where the ITT pavilion lurks behind the malt-shoppe facade), its main street is flanked by the pavilions of major U.S. corporations, each housing some version of a "ride" through a halcyon future. The GM pavilion with its ode to the car also offers up the Epcot theme song, the remorselessly repeated "It's a small world after all." The loop holds the pavilions of eight elected (and subsidizing) nations, an array projecting a sufficient (one from Asia, one from Latin America . . .) compendium of national diversity.

Even Epcot's symbol – a large geodesic sphere – is received. Its lineage proceeds backwards to the tacky Unisphere of the 1964 New York Fair (in which Disney participation was considerable – including an early Animatronic Abe Lincoln) and to Unisphere's own source, the mesmerizing Perisphere that accompanied the complementingly vertical Trylon to the 1939 Fair. In fact, the line extends – via the biospheres of the nineteenth century – back at least as far as the eighteenth-century French architect Boullée's proposal for a vast spherical cenotaph to Isaac Newton, its interior daubed with stars, a representation of the universe which Newton's mechanics had made so newly comprehensible. Epcot's ball is a degenerate – if still viable – totem of universality. In commercials, Mickey stands atop it, waving, an anticolossus.

It somehow seems inevitable that this puny organ of Brzezinskian "psychic well-being" should stand in for the more literal variety that Disney's fuller first vision (actual homes, actual factories) represents. The two possibilities are clearly antithetical, the one destined to annihilate the other. After all, utopia is illusory, a representation. The careful structure of entertainment and social relations (nominal egalitarianism with segmenting opportunities: meals at up- and downscale restaurants; at night you sleep with your class at hostelries ranging from modest to luxe) at Disneyland relinquishes its power to draw if it fails as an alternative to daily life.

The Disney strategy, then, inscribes utopia on the terrain of the familiar and vice versa. The economy of its representations depends on a careful calculus of degrees of difference. Like any other consumer operation, it thrives on algorithms of both the desirable and the attainable. Thus, its images never really innovate, they intensify and reduce, winnowing complexity in the name of both quick access and easy digestibility. What's being promoted is not the exceptional but rather the paranormal. Just like the real thing, only better.

In an essay on montage, the Soviet film-maker Lev Kuleshov describes a scene shot in the early 1920s with the actors Khokhlova and Obolensky:

Khokhlova is walking along Petrov Street in Moscow near the "Mostorg" store. Obolensky is walking along the embankment of the Moscow River – at a distance of about two miles away. They see each other, smile, and begin to walk toward one another. Their meeting is filmed at the Boulevard Prechistensk. This boulevard is in an entirely different section of the city. They clasp hands, with Gogol's monument as a background, and look – at the White House – for at this point, we cut in a segment from an American film, The White House in Washington. *In the next shot they are once again on the Boulevard Prechistensk. Deciding to go farther, they leave and climb up the enormous staircase of the Cathedral of Christ the Savior. We film them, edit the film, and the result is that they are seen walking up the steps of the White House. For this we used no trick, no double exposure: the effect was achieved solely by the organization of the material through its cinematic treatment. This particular scene demonstrated the incredible potency of montage, which actually appeared so powerful that it was able to alter the very essence of the material.*[3]

Kuleshov called this technique "creative geography." Like gene-splicing, the point is to create a new organism from the substance of the old. Indeed, in another famous experiment, Kuleshov used the technique to "fabricate" a new, recombinant woman, from fragments of several "other" women. The question here is whether the perpetrator is Prometheus or Frankenstein. To distinguish monstrosity from coherence, the practice of montage – and the practice of urbanism, its three-dimensional equivalent – requires a theory of juxtaposition. For the cinema, the theory is either about narrative or its interruption, about a sequence of images bound to time. Montage begs the question of the logic of this arrangement. The city is also joined in sequence. Both its construction and its politics devolve on principles of aggregation. The idealization of such principles creates utopia.

As a utopia, Disneyland's innovation lies not in its fantasy of regulation but in the elision of its place-making. Disneyland is the Holy See of creative geography, the place where the ephemeral reality of the cinema is concretized into the stuff of the city. It should come as no surprise that the most succinct manifestation to date of this crossover is the "Disney-MGM Studios" theme park, recently opened at Disney World. Here, the agenda of dislocated authenticity is carried back to its point of origin. The attraction (much indebted to its precursor Universal Studios Tour back in Los Angeles, now also in Orlando) is explicitly about movies, both the space of their realization (the "studio") and about the particular narrative spaces of particular movies.

Although the attraction is in Florida, at Disney World, and although its recreational agenda is precisely to purvey "creative geography," Disney–MGM is at pains to locate itself in a particularly referential space: Hollywood, the locus classicus of movie-making. Main Street's axial introduction is accomplished with an imaginative recasting of Hollywood Boulevard, heavy on the deco. Visitors enter through a gateway borrowed from the now-incinerated Pan-Pacific Auditorium, past a replica of the famous Crossroads of the World tower, a reincarnate Brown Derby, and a welter of familiar Los Angeles architecture, here scaled down and aggregated with an urbanity unknown at the unedited source.

At the head of this axis stands a re-created Grauman's Chinese. No longer exactly a movie palace, however, it's the queuing zone for the main event at the theme park, the Great Movie Ride, a forty-two-minute trip through scenes from well-known Disney and MGM movies, recreated by Animatronic robots. This is a fabulously compact rendition of the larger experience of Disneyfication, the suspension of the visitor in a serially realized apparatus of simulation. Like the global-corridor traveler, the visitor is propelled past a series of summary tableaux which stand in for some larger, sloughed-off, memory of reality. Of course, the Great Movie Ride goes the system one better, mechanically reproducing a mechanical reproduction.

One of the main effects of Disneyfication is the substitution of recreation for work, the production of leisure according to the routines of industry. Now, one of the products of postindustrialism is not simply the liberation of vast amounts of problematic leisure time, it's the reinvention of labor as spectacle, what Dean MacCannell has called "involuted differentiation." The positivist mythos having withered, culture turns in on itself, simply aestheticizing its internal operations, romanticizing especially those bygone. The tourist travels the world to see the wigged baker at the simulacrum of Colonial Williamsburg drawing hot-cross buns from an "authentic" brick oven or the Greek fisherman on the quay on Mykonos, mending his photogenic nets, or the Animatronic Gene Kelly "singing in the rain."

At the movie theme park this spectacle is multiplied. The "work" at Disney World is, of course, entertainment. The 26,000 employees of the place are all considered by management to be "cast-members." Transforming workers to actors presumably transforms their work into play. This plugs nicely into a familiar mode, an endless staple of the talk-show circuit: the performance of some overcompensated Hollywood sybarite talking about his or her "work" as if the activity were somehow comparable to the labors of the assembly line. It's the same grotesque operation found in the seasonal public negotiations (with frequent strikes) of overpaid sports figures which create a themed version of "old-fashioned" labor relations, rendering union–management relations ridiculous by exaggeration.

But the most important aim of this inversion is not to encourage delusional thinking by some harried cafeteria worker at Disney. It's rather to invent the empire of leisure that still differentiates Disneyworld from everyday life. Visitors to the Disney parks, polled about what they like best, cite first the cleanliness, next the friendliness of the employees. This is surely the redemption of the industrial metropolis: hygienic, staffed with unalienated workers apparently enjoying their contributions to the happy collectivity. The movie ride takes this theory of labor a logical step further. One imagines, to begin with, that the Gene Kelly automaton is working for considerably less than scale. The representation goes the "ideal" worker one better: entertaining itself – fun in the first place – has been fully automated.

Consider a further recursion. In all likelihood, as the tram rolls through the Animatronic Temple of Doom, a hundred video-cams whirringly record the "event" for later consumption at home. That tape is an astonishing artifact, unprecedented in human history. If postmodern culture can be said to be about the weaving of ever more elaborate fabrics of simulation, about successive displacements of "authentic" signifiers, then the Japanese family sitting in front of the Sony back in Nagasaki, watching their home videos of the Animatronic re-creation of the creative geography of a Hollywood "original," all recorded at a simulacrum of Hollywood in central Florida, must be said to have achieved a truly weird apotheosis of raw referentiality. Interestingly, several years ago, the inventor Nolan Bushnell proposed a further efficiency in this circuit. His notion was to place little self-propelled robots, each with a video eye, in major tourist cities – Paris, Rome, London, perhaps even Disney World. These could then be driven around by folks in Phoenix or Dubuque, giving them the experience of prowling the Champs Elysées, Regent Street, or the Via Veneto, without actually leaving home. But this is just an incremental advance, economizing only on human mobility, still premised on an old notion of the superiority of old-style "reality."

Disney's ahead of this. The Disney-MGM studio tour offers a third order of re-creation, another involuted riff on the nature of place. Part of the complex is a functioning movie studio, affording visitors the authentic frisson of a brush with living stars, an actual "production." Strolling the backlot, tourists might pass down a set for a New York City street. Although this set is constructed in the same way and with the same creatively interpolative geography as nearby "Hollywood Boulevard," the spectator's relationship to it is different. Success here depends on the apprehension of this space not primarily as a zone of leisure (as on the Great Movie Ride or the stroll down the Boulevard) but as a workplace. It's another order of tourism, like watching the muffin-bakers and glassblowers at Colonial Williamsburg, the addition of the pleasures of voyeurism to those of mere recreation.

If visitors are permitted the pleasure of circulating "backstage" at the movie studio, there's yet a further backstage that remains inaccessible. In true rational modernist fashion, the Disney parks are built on giant platforms. Underneath the attractions, a labyrinth of tunnels provides service and staff circulation for the public activities above. These areas are strictly off limits to visitors although they're often discussed in publicity as one of the keys to Disney's marvelous efficiency, and photographs – daffy shots of giant Mickey Mice padding down fluorescent-lit concrete corridors – are widely disseminated. This subterranean space inevitably conjures up other, more dystopian images, most notably the underworld in Lang's *Metropolis*, its workers trapped in carceral caverns dancing their robotic ballet like Martha Graham on Thorazine.

But – perhaps in part because a man in a mouse costume is a more genial image of dehumanization than a prole in chains – this "servant space" (in Louis Kahn's locution) has a generally happier reputation. It is, in fact, what makes Disneyland "clean." Not simply is this a venue for the efficient whisking away of the detritus of fun – the tons of Popsicle sticks and hot-dog wrappers generated daily – it divides labor into its clean, public face, and its less entertaining, less "magic" aspects. Like the tourist-popular sewers of Paris, this underworld is both alien and marvelous, "peopled" with strange denizens, inconspicuous yet indispensable, supporting the purer city of being above. It is the dream of each beleaguered city dweller: an apparatus for keeping every urban problem out of sight. In fact, though, it reverses the Langian schema. This disciplinary apparatus is not above but underground, a subterranean Panopticon, ready to spring up innumerable concealed passages to monitor and service the vast leisure army toiling at fun up above.

Such reveries of self-discipline are historic. Stuart Ewen cites a variety of sources celebrating the self-modified behavior of visitors to the White City of 1892. "Order reigned everywhere," wrote one, "no boisterousness, no unseemly merriment. It seemed as though the beauty of the place brought a gentleness, happiness, and self-respect to its visitors." Observed another, "No great multitude of people ever showed more love of order. The restraint and discipline were remarkable." And another, "Courtiers in Versailles and Fontainbleau could not have been more deferential and observant . . . the decorum of the place and occasion than these obscure and myriads of unknown laborers." Even Charlotte Brontë, visiting the Crystal Palace in 1851, opined that "the multitude . . . seems ruled and subdued by some invisible influence."[4]

Jeffrey Katzenberg, head of Disney's movie division, suggests that we "think of Disney World as a medium-sized city with a crime rate of zero." Although the claim is hyperbole (petty larceny mainly leads to expulsion from the kingdom, more serious infractions to the summoning of adjoining police forces), the perception is not: the environment is virtually self-policing. Disney World is clearly a version of a town ("Imagine a Disneyland as big as the city of San Francisco," goes a recent ad). And it's based on a particular urbanism, a crisp acceleration of trends everywhere visible but nowhere so acutely elaborated. The problems addressed by Disneyzone are quintessentially modern: crime, transportation, waste, the relationship of work and leisure, the transience of populations, the growing hegemony of the simulacrum.

But finally, Disneyzone isn't urban at all. Like the patent-medicine-plugging actor who advertises his bona fides as "I'm not a doctor but I play one on TV," Disney invokes an urbanism without producing a city. Rather, it produces a kind of aura-stripped hypercity, a city with billions of citizens (all who would consume) but no residents. Physicalized yet conceptual, it's the utopia of transience, a place where everyone is just passing through. This is its message for the city to be, a place everywhere and nowhere, assembled only through constant motion. Visitors to Disneyzone are reduced to the status of cartoon characters. (Indeed, one of the features of the studio tour is the opportunity for visitors to cinematically interpolate themselves into *Who Framed Roger Rabbit?*) This is a common failing in utopian subjectivity, the predication on a homogenized, underdimensioned citizenship. However, it's also true that there's probably no more acquiescent subject than the postindustrial tourist. And there's surely no question that a holiday-maker wants a version of life pared of its sting, that vacationing finds its fulfillment in escape. The Disney visitor seeks and delights in the relationship between what he or she finds and its obverse back home, terrain of crime, litter, and surliness.

In the Disney utopia, we all become involuntary flaneurs and flaneuses, global drifters, holding high our lamps as we look everywhere for an honest image. The search will get tougher and tougher for the fanned-out millions as the recombinant landscape crops up around the globe. One of the latest nodes appears about to be sprung at Surajkund, near New Delhi, where India's first theme park gleams in the eye of the local tourism department. "We have a whole integrated concept of a fun center," as the *New York Times* quotes S. K. Sharma, state secretary for tourism. "Like all big cities, Delhi is getting polluted. It is getting choked with people. People need amusement and clear air."[5]

Marcuse called utopia "the determinate sociohistorical negation of what exists."[6] Disneyzone – Toon Town in real stucco and metal – is a cartoon utopia, an urbanism for the electronic age. Like television, it is a machine for the continuous transformation of what exists (a panoply of images drawn from life) into what doesn't (an ever-increasing number of weird juxtapositions). It's a genetic utopia, where every product is some sort of mutant, maimed kids in Kabul brought to you on the nightly news by Metamucil, Dumbo in Japan in Florida. The only way to consume this narrative is to keep moving, keep changing channels, keep walking, get on another jet, pass through another airport, stay in another Ramada Inn. The only logic is the faint buzz of memories of something more or less similar . . . but so long ago, perhaps even yesterday.

Notes

1   "Inaugural Address of the Prince Consort Albert, May 1, 1851," quoted in Wolfgang Freibe, *Buildings of the World Exhibitions* (Leipzig: Editions Leipzig, 1985), p. 13.

2   Zbigniew Brzezinski, *Between Two Ages: America's Role in the Technotronic Era*

(New York: Viking, 1976), quoted in Collettivo Strategie, *Strategie* (Milan: Macchina Libri, 1981) included in Tony Solomonides and Les Levidow, eds., *Compulsive Technology: Computers as Culture* (London: Free Association, 1985), p. 130.

3   Lev Kuleshov, "Art of the Cinema," in Ronald Levaco, *Kuleshov on Film: Writings by Lev Kuleshov* (Berkeley: California University Press, 1974), p. 52.

4   Stewart Ewen. *All Consuming Images: The Politics of Style in Contemporary Culture* (New York: Basic Books, 1988), pp. 204–5.

5   *New York Times*, February 10, 1990.

6   Herbert Marcuse, "The End of Utopia," in *Five Lectures* (Boston: Beacon, 1970), p. 69.

16

Social Justice, Postmodernism, and the City

David Harvey

The title of this chapter is a collage of two book titles of mine written nearly 20 years apart, *Social Justice and the City* and *The Condition of Postmodernity*. I here want to consider the relations between them, in part as a way to reflect on the intellectual and political journey many have travelled these last two decades in their attempts to grapple with urban issues, but also to examine how we now might think about urban problems and how by virtue of such thinking we can better position ourselves with respect to solutions. The question of *positionality* is, I shall argue, fundamental to all debates about how to create infrastructures and urban environments for living and working in the twenty-first century.

Justice and the Postmodern Condition

I begin with a report by John Kifner in the *International Herald Tribune* (1 August 1989) concerning the hotly contested space of Tompkins Square Park in New York City – a space which has been repeatedly fought over, often violently, since the "police riot" of August 1988. The neighbourhood mix around the park was the primary focus of Kifner's

Reprinted by permission from David Harvey, 1992, "Social Justice, Postmodernism, and the City," *International Journal of Urban and Regional Research* 16.

attention. Not only were there nearly 300 homeless people, but there
were also:

*Skateboarders, basketball players, mothers with small children, radicals
looking like 1960s retreads, spikey-haired punk rockers in torn black, skin-
heads in heavy working boots looking to beat up the radicals and punks,
dreadlocked Rastafarians, heavy-metal bands, chess players, dog walkers –
all occupy their spaces in the park, along with professionals carrying their
dry-cleaned suits to the renovated "gentrified" buildings that are changing
the character of the neighbourhood.*

By night, Kifner notes, the contrasts in the park become even more
bizarre:

*The Newcomers Motorcycle Club was having its annual block party at its
clubhouse at 12th Street and Avenue B and the street was lined with chromed
Harley Davidsons with raised "ape-hanger" handlebars and beefy men and
hefty women in black leather. A block north a rock concert had spilled out
of a "squat" – an abandoned city-owned building taken over by outlaw
renovators, mostly young artists – and the street was filled with young people
whose purple hair stood straight up in spikes. At the World Club just off
Houston Street near Avenue C, black youths pulled up in the Jeep-type vehicles favored by cash-heavy teen-age crack moguls, high powered speakers
blaring. At the corner of Avenue B and Third, considered one of the worst
heroin blocks in New York, another concert was going on at an artists' space
called The Garage, set in a former gas station walled off by plastic bottles and
other found objects. The wall formed an enclosed garden looking up at
burned-out, abandoned buildings: there was an eerie resemblance to Beirut.
The crowd was white and fashionably dressed, and a police sergeant sent to
check on the noise shook his head, bemused: "It's all yuppies."*

This is, of course, the kind of scene that makes New York such a fascinating place, that makes any great city into a stimulating and exciting
maelstrom of cultural conflict and change. It is the kind of scene that
many a student of urban subcultures would revel in, even seeing in it, as
someone like Iain Chambers (1987) does, the origins of that distinctive
perspective we now call "the postmodern":

*Postmodernism, whatever form its intellectualizing might take, has been
fundamentally anticipated in the metropolitan cultures of the last twenty
years: among the electronic signifiers of cinema, television and video, in
recording studios and record players, in fashion and youth styles, in all those
sounds, images and diverse histories that are daily mixed, recycled and
"scratched" together on that giant screen that is the contemporary city.*

Armed with that insight, we could take the whole paraphernalia of postmodern argumentation and technique and try to "deconstruct" the seemingly disparate images on that giant screen which is the city. We could dissect and celebrate the fragmentation, the co-presence of multiple discourses – of music, street and body language, dress and technological accoutrements (such as the Harley Davidsons) – and, perhaps, develop sophisticated empathies with the multiple and contradictory codings with which highly differentiated social beings both present themselves to each other and to the world and live out their daily lives. We could affirm or even celebrate the bifurcations in cultural trajectory, the preservation of pre-existing and the creation of entirely new but distinctive "othernesses" within an otherwise homogenizing world.

On a good day, we could celebrate the scene within the park as a superb example of urban tolerance for difference, an exemplar of what Iris Marion Young calls "openness to unassimilated otherness". In a just and civilized society, she argues, the normative ideal of city life:

> instantiates social relations of difference without exclusion. Different groups dwell in the city alongside one another, of necessity interacting in city spaces. If city politics is to be democratic and not dominated by the point of view of one group, it must be a politics that takes account of and provides voice for the different groups that dwell together in the city without forming a community. (Young, 1990: 227)

To the degree that the freedom of city life "leads to group differentiation, to the formation of affinity groups" (ibid.: 238) of the sort which Kifner identifies in Tompkins Square, so our conception of social justice "requires not the melting away of differences, but institutions that promote reproduction of and respect for group differences without oppression" (p. 47). We must reject "the concept of universality as embodied in republican versions of Enlightenment reason" precisely because it sought to "suppress the popular and linguistic heterogeneity of the urban public" (p. 108). "In open and accessible public spaces and forums, one should expect to encounter and hear from those who are different, whose social perspectives, experience and affiliations are different." It then follows, Young argues, that a politics of inclusion "must promote the ideal of a heterogeneous public, in which persons stand forth with their differences acknowledged and respected, though perhaps not completely understood, by others" (p. 119).

In similar vein, Roberto Unger, the philosophical guru of the critical legal studies movement in the United States, might view the park as a manifestation of a new ideal of community understood as a "zone of heightened mutual vulnerability, within which people gain a chance to resolve more fully the conflict between the enabling conditions of self-assertion; between their need for attachment and for participation in group life and their fear of subjugation and depersonalization with which such engagement may threaten them" (Unger, 1987: 562). Tompkins Square seems a place where the "contrast between structure-preserving routine and structure-transforming conflict" softens in such a way as to "free sociability from its script and to make us available to one another more as the originals we know ourselves to be and less as the placeholders in a system of group contrasts". The square might even be interpreted as a site of that "microlevel of cultural-revolutionary defiance and incongruity" which periodically wells upwards into "the macrolevel of institutional innovation" (ibid.: 564). Unger is acutely aware, however, that the temptation to "treat each aspect of cultural revolution as a pretext for endless self-gratification and self-concern" can lead to a failure to "connect the revolutionary reform of institutional arrangements with the cultural-revolutionary remaking of personal relations".

So what should the urban policy-maker do in the face of these strictures? The best path is to pull out that well-thumbed copy of Jane Jacobs (1961) and insist that we should both respect and provide for "spontaneous self-diversification among urban populations" in the formulation of our policies and plans. In so doing we can avoid the critical wrath she directs at city designers, who "seem neither to recognize this force for self-diversification nor to be attracted by the esthetic problems of expressing it". Such a strategy can help us to live up to expectations of the sort which Young and Unger lay down. We should not, in short, aim to obliterate differences within the park, homogenize it according to some conception of, say, bourgeois taste or social order. We should engage, rather, with an aesthetics which embraces or stimulates that "spontaneous self-diversification" of which Jacobs speaks. Yet there is an immediate question mark over that suggestion: in what ways, for example, can homelessness be understood as spontaneous self-diversification, and does this mean that we should respond to that problem with designer-style cardboard boxes to make for more jolly and sightly shelters for the homeless? While Jane Jacobs has a point, and one which many urbanists have absorbed these last few years, there is, evidently, much more to the problem than her arguments encompass.

That difficulty is highlighted on a bad day in the park. So-called forces of law and order battle to evict the homeless, erect barriers between violently clashing factions. The park then becomes a locus of exploitation and oppression, an open wound from which bleed the five faces of oppression which Young defines as exploitation, marginalization, powerlessness, cultural imperialism and violence. The potentiality for "openness to unassimilated otherness" breaks apart and, in much the same way that the cosmopolitan and eminently civilized Beirut of the 1950s suddenly collapsed into an urban maelstrom of warring factions and violent confrontation, so we find sociality collapsing into violence (see Smith, 1989; 1992). This is not unique to New York City but is a condition of urban life in many of our large metropolitan areas – witness events in the *banlieues* of Paris and Lyons, in Brussels, in Liverpool, London and even Oxford in recent times.

In such circumstances Young's pursuit of a vision of justice that is assertive as to difference without reinforcing the forms of oppression gets torn to tatters and Unger's dreams of micro-revolutions in cultural practices which stimulate progressive rather than repressive institutional innovation became just that – dreams. The very best face that we can put upon the whole scene is to recognize that this is how class, ethnic, racial and gender struggle is, as Lefebvre (1991) would put it, being "inscribed in space". And what should the planner do? Here is how a subsequent article in the New York Times reflected on that dilemma:

> *There are neighborhood associations clamoring for the city to close the park and others just as insistent that it remain a refuge for the city's downtrodden. The local Assemblyman, Steven Sanders, yesterday called for a curfew that would effectively evict more than a hundred homeless people camped out in the park. Councilwoman Miriam Friedlander instead recommended that Social Services, like healthcare and drug treatment, be brought directly to the people living in the tent city. "We do not find the park is being used appropriately", said Deputy Mayor Barbara J. Fife, "but we recognize there are various interests". There is, they go on to say, only one thing that is a consensus, first that there isn't a consensus over what should be done, except that any new plan is likely to provoke more disturbances, more violence.*

On 8 June 1991, the question was resolved by evicting everyone from the park and closing it entirely "for rehabilitation" under a permanent guard of at least 20 police officers. The New York authorities, situated on what Davis (1990: 224) calls "the bad edge of postmodernity", militarize rather than liberate its public space. In so doing, power is deployed in support of a middle-class quest for "personal insulation, in residential work, consumption and travel environments, from 'unsavory' groups and individuals, even crowds in general". Genuinely public space is extinguished, militarized or semi-privatized. The heterogeneity of open democracy, the mixing of classes, ethnicities, religions and divergent taste cultures within a common frame of public space is lost along with the capacity to celebrate unity and community in the midst of diversity. The ultimate irony, as Davis points out, is that "as the walls have come down in Eastern Europe, they are being erected all over [our cities]".

And what should the policy-maker and planner do in the face of these conditions? Give up planning and join one of those burgeoning cultural studies programmes which revel in chaotic scenes of the Tompkins Square sort while simultaneously disengaging from any commitment to do something about them? Deploy all the critical powers of deconstruction and semiotics to seek new and engaging interpretations of graffiti which say "Die, Yuppie Scum"? Should we join revolutionary and anarchist groups and fight for the rights of the poor and the culturally marginalized to express their rights and if necessary make a home for themselves in the park? Or should we throw away that dog-eared copy of Jane Jacobs and join with the forces of law and order and help impose some authoritarian solution on the problem?

Decisions of some sort have to be made and actions taken, as about any other facet of urban infrastructure. And while we might all agree that an urban park is a good thing in principle, what are we to make of the fact that the uses turn out to be so conflictual, and that even conceptions as to what the space is for and how it is to be managed diverge radically among competing factions? To hold all the divergent politics of need and desire together within some coherent frame may be a laudable aim, but in practice far too many of the interests are mutually exclusive to allow their mutual accommodation. Even the best shaped compromise (let alone the savagely imposed authoritarian solution) favours one or other factional interest. And that provokes the biggest question of all – what is the *conception* of "the public" incorporated into the construction of public space?

To answer these questions requires some deeper understanding of the forces at work shaping conflict in the park. Kifner identified drugs and real estate – "the two most powerful forces in [New York City] today". Both of them are linked to organized crime and are major pillars of the political economy of contemporary capitalism. We cannot understand events within and around the park or strategize as to its future uses without contextualizing it against a background of the political-economic transformations now occurring in urban life. The problems of Tompkins Square Park have, in short, to be seen in terms of social processes which create homelessness, promote criminal activities of many sorts (from real estate swindles and the crack trade to street muggings), generate hierarchies of power between gentrifiers and the homeless, and facilitate the emergence of deep tensions along the major social fault-lines of class, gender, ethnicity, race and religion, lifestyle and place-bound preferences (see Smith, 1992).

Social Justice and Modernity

I now leave this very contemporary situation and its associated conundrums and turn to an older story. It turned up when I unearthed from my files a yellowing manuscript, written sometime in the early 1970s, shortly after I finished *Social Justice and the City*. I there examined the case of a proposal to put a segment of the Interstate Highway System on an east–west trajectory right through the heart of Baltimore – a proposal first set out in the early 1940s and which has still not been fully resolved. I resurrect this case here in part to show that what we would now often depict as a quintessentially modernist problem was even at that time argued about in ways which contained the seeds, if not the essence, of much of what many now view as a distinctively postmodernist form of argumentation.

My interest in the case at that time, having looked at a lot of the discussion, attended hearings and read a lot of documentation, lay initially in the highly differentiated arguments, articulated by all kinds of different groups, concerning the rights and wrongs of the whole project. There were, I found, seven kinds of arguments being put forward:

1   An *efficiency* argument which concentrated on the relief of traffic congestion and facilitating the easier flow of goods and people throughout the region as well as within the city;

2   An *economic growth* argument which looked to a projected increase (or prevention of loss) in investment and employment opportunities in the city consequent upon improvements in the transport system;

3   An *aesthetic and historical heritage* argument which objected to the way sections of the proposed highway would either destroy or diminish urban environments deemed both attractive and of historical value;

4   A *social and moral order* argument which held that prioritizing highway investment and subsidizing car owners rather than, for example, investing in housing and health care was quite wrong;

5   An *environmentalist/ecological* argument which considered the impacts of the proposed highway on air quality, noise pollution and the destruction of certain valued environments (such as a river valley park);

6   A *distributive justice* argument which dwelt mainly on the benefits to business and predominantly white middle-class suburban commuters to the detriment of low-income and predominantly African-American inner-city residents;

7   A *neighbourhood and communitarian* argument which considered the way in which close-knit but otherwise fragile and vulnerable communities might be destroyed, divided or disrupted by highway construction.

The arguments were not mutually exclusive, of course, and several of them were merged by proponents of the highway into a common thread – for example, the efficiency of the transport system would stimulate growth and reduce pollution from congestion so as to advantage otherwise disadvantaged inner-city residents. It was also possible to break up each argument into quite distinct parts – the distributive impacts on women with children would be very different from those on male workers.

We would, in these heady postmodern times, be prone to describe these separate arguments as "discourses", each with its own logic and imperatives. And we would not have to look too closely to see particular "communities of interest" which articulated a particular discourse as if it was the only one that mattered. The particularistic arguments advanced by such groups proved effective in altering the alignment of the highway but did not stop the highway as a whole. The one group which tried to forge a coalition out of these disparate elements (the *Movement Against Destruction*, otherwise known as *MAD*) and to provide an umbrella for opposition to the highway as a whole turned out to be the least effective in mobilizing people and constituencies even though it was very articulate in its arguments.

The purpose of my own particular enquiry was to see how the arguments (or discourses) for and against the highway worked and if coalitions could be built in principle between seemingly disparate and often highly antagonistic interest groups via the construction of higher order arguments (discourses) which could provide the basis for consensus. The multiplicity of views and forces has to be set against the fact that either the highway is built or it is not, although in Baltimore, with its wonderful way of doing things, we ended up with a portion of the highway that is called a boulevard (to make us understand that this six-lane two-mile segment of a monster cut through the heart of low-income and predominantly African-American West Baltimore is not what it really is) and another route on a completely different alignment, looping around the city core in such a way as to allay some of the worst political fears of influential communities.

Might there be, then, some higher-order discourse to which everyone could appeal in working out whether or not it made sense to build the highway? A dominant theme in the literature of the 1960s was that it was possible to identify some such higher-order arguments. The phrase that was most frequently used to describe it was *social rationality*. The idea of that did not seem implausible, because each of the seven seemingly distinctive arguments advanced a rational position of some sort and not infrequently appealed to some higher-order rationale to bolster its case. Those arguing on efficiency and growth grounds frequently invoked utilitarian arguments, notions of "public good" and the greatest benefit to the greatest number, while recognizing (at their best) that individual sacrifices were inevitable and that it was right and proper to offer appropriate compensation for those who would be displaced. Ecologists or communitarians likewise appealed to higher-order arguments – the former to the values inherent in nature and the latter to some higher sense of communitarian values. For all of these reasons, consideration of higher-order arguments over social rationality did not seem unreasonable.

Dahl and Lindblom's *Politics, Economics and Welfare*, published in 1953, provides a classic statement along these lines. They argue that not only is socialism dead (a conclusion that many would certainly share these days) but also that capitalism is equally dead. What they signal by this is an intellectual tradition which arose out of the experience of the vast market and capitalistic failure of the Great Depression and the second world war and which concluded that some kind of middle ground had to be found between the extremism of a pure and unfettered market economy and the communist vision of an organized and highly centralized economy. They concentrated their theory on the question of rational social action and argued that this required "processes for both rational *calculation* and effective *control*" (p. 21). Rational calculation and control, as far as they were concerned, depended upon the exercise of rational calculation through price-fixing markets, hierarchy (top-down decision-making), polyarchy (democratic control of leadership) and bargaining (negotiation), and such means should be deployed to achieve the goals of "freedom, rationality, democracy, subjective equality, security, progress, and appropriate inclusion" (p. 28). There is much that is interesting about Dahl and Lindblom's analysis and it is not too hard to imagine that after the recent highly problematic phase of market triumphalism, particularly in Britain and the United States, there will be some sort of search to resurrect the formulations they proposed. But in so doing it is also useful to remind ourselves of the intense criticism that was levelled during the 1960s and 1970s against their search for some universal prospectus on the socially rational society of the future.

Godelier, for example, in his book on *Rationality and Irrationality in Economics*, savagely attacked the socialist thinking of Oscar Lange for its teleological view of rationality and its presumption that socialism should or could ever be the ultimate achievement of the rational life. Godelier did not attack this notion from the right but from a marxist and historical materialist perspective. His point was that there are different definitions of rationality depending upon the form of social organization and that the rationality embedded in feudalism is different from that of capitalism, which should, presumably, be different again under socialism. Rationality defined from the standpoint of corporate capital is quite different from rationality defined from the standpoint of the working classes. Work of this type helped to fuel the growing radical critique of even the non-teleological and incrementalist thinking of the Dahl and Lindblom sort. This critique suggested that their definition of social rationality was connected to the perpetuation and rational management of a capitalist economic system rather than with the exploration of alternatives. To attack (or deconstruct, as we now would put it) their conception of social rationality was seen by the left at the time as a means to challenge the ideological hegemony of a dominant corporate capitalism. Feminists, those marginalized by racial characteristics, colonized peoples, ethnic and religious minorities echoed that refrain in their work, while adding their own conception of who was the enemy to be challenged and what were the dominant forms of rationality to be contested. The result was to show emphatically that there is no overwhelming and universally acceptable definition of social rationality to which we might appeal, but innumerable different rationalities depending upon social and material circumstances, group identities, and social objectives. Rationality is defined by the nature of the social group and its project rather than the project being dictated by social rationality. The deconstruction of universal claims of social rationality was one of the major achievements and continues to be one of the major legacies of the radical critique of the 1960s and 1970s.

Such a conclusion is, however, more than a little discomforting. It would suggest, to go back to the highway example, that there was no point whatsoever in searching for any higher-order arguments because such arguments simply could not have any purchase upon the political process of decision-making. And it is indeed striking that the one group that tried to build such overall arguments, *MAD*, was the group that was least successful in actually mobilizing opposition. The fragmented discourses of those who sought to change the alignment of the highway had more effect than the more unified discourse precisely because the former were grounded in the specific and particular local circumstances in which individuals found themselves. Yet the fragmented discourses could never go beyond challenging the alignment of the highway. It did indeed need a more unified discourse, of the sort which *MAD* sought to articulate, to challenge the concept of the highway in general.

This poses a direct dilemma. If we accept that fragmented discourses are the only authentic discourses and that no unified discourse is possible, then there is no way to challenge the overall qualities of a social system. To mount that more general challenge we need some kind of unified or unifying set of arguments. For this reason, I chose, in this ageing and yellowing manuscript, to take a closer look at the particular question of social justice as a basic ideal that might have more universal appeal.

Social Justice

Social justice is but one of the seven criteria I worked with and I evidently hoped that careful investigation of it might rescue the argument from the abyss of formless relativism and infinitely variable discourses and interest grouping. But here too the enquiry proved frustrating. It revealed that there are as many competing theories of social justice as there are competing ideals of social rationality. Each ideal has its flaws and strengths. Egalitarian views, for example, immediately run into the problem that "there is nothing more unequal than the equal treatment of unequals" (the modification of doctrines of equality of opportunity in the United States by requirements for affirmative action, for example, recognizes what a significant problem that is). By the time I had thoroughly reviewed positive law theories of justice, utilitarian views (the greatest good of the greatest number), social contract views historically attributed to Rousseau and powerfully revived by John Rawls in his *Theory of Justice* in the early 1970s, the various intuitionist, relative deprivation and other interpretations of justice, I found myself in a quandary as to precisely *which* theory of justice is the most just. The theories can, to some degree, be arranged in a hierarchy with respect to each other. The positive law view that justice is a matter of law can be challenged by a utilitarian view which allows us to discriminate between good and bad law on the basis of some greater good, while the social contract and natural rights views suggest that no amount of greater good for a greater number can justify the violation of certain inalienable rights. On the other hand, intuition-ist and relative deprivation theories exist in an entirely different dimension.

Yet the basic problem remained. To argue for social justice meant the deployment of some initial criteria to define which theory of social justice was appropriate or more just than another. The infinite regress of higher-order criteria immediately looms, as does, in the other direction, the relative ease of total deconstruction of the notion of justice to the point where it means nothing whatsoever, except whatever people at some particular moment decide they want it to mean. Competing discourses about justice could not be disassociated from competing discourses about positionality in society.

There seemed two ways to go with that argument. The first was to look at how concepts of justice are embedded in language, and that led me to theories of meaning of the sort which Wittgenstein advanced:

> How many kinds of sentence are there? . . . There are countless kinds: count-less different kinds of use to what we call "symbols", "words", "sentences". And this multiplicity is not something fixed, given once for all: but new types of language, new language games, as we may say, come into existence and others become obsolete and get forgotten . . . Here the term "language-game" is meant to bring into prominence the fact that the speaking of language is part of an activity, or a form of life . . . How did we learn the meaning of this word ("good" for instance)? From what sort of examples? in what language games? Then it will be easier for us to see that the word must have a family of meanings. (Wittgenstein, 1967)

From this perspective the concept of justice has to be understood in the way it is embedded in a particular language game. Each language game attaches to the particular social, experiential and perceptual world of the speaker. Justice has no universal meaning, but a whole "family" of meanings. This finding is completely consistent, of course, with anthropological studies which show that justice among, say, the Nuer, means something completely different from the capitalistic conception of justice. We are back to the point of cultural, linguistic or discourse relativism.

The second path is to admit the relativism of discourses about justice, but to insist that discourses are expressions of social power. In this case, the idea of justice has to be set against the formation of certain hegemonic discourses which derive from the power exercised by any ruling class. This is an idea which goes back to Plato, who in the *Republic* has Thrasymachus argue that:

> *Each ruling class makes laws that are in its own interest, a democracy democratic laws, a tyranny tyrannical ones and so on; and in making these laws they define as "right" for their subjects what is in the interest of themselves, the rulers, and if anyone breaks their laws he is punished as a "wrong-doer". That is what I mean when I say that "right" is the same in all states, namely the interest of the established ruling class . . .* (Plato, 1965)

Consideration of these two paths brought me to accept a position which is most clearly articulated by Engels in the following terms:

> *The stick used to measure what is right and what is not is the most abstract expression of right itself, namely justice . . . The development of right for the jurists . . . is nothing more than a striving to bring human conditions, so far as they are expressed in legal terms, ever closer to the ideal of justice, eternal justice. And always this justice is but the ideologized, glorified expression of the existing economic relations, now from their conservative and now from their revolutionary angle. The justice of the Greeks and Romans held slavery to be just; the justice of the bourgeois of 1789 demanded the abolition of feudalism on the ground it was unjust. The conception of eternal justice, therefore, varies not only with time and place, but also with the persons concerned . . . While in everyday life . . . expressions like right, wrong, justice, and sense of right are accepted without misunderstanding even with reference to social matters, they create . . . the same hopeless confusion in any scientific investigation of economic relations as would be created, for instance, in modern chemistry if the terminology of the phlogiston theory were to be retained.* (Marx and Engels, 1951: 562–4)

It is a short step from this conception of Marx's critique of Proudhon, who, Marx (1967: 88–9) claimed, took his ideal of justice "from the juridical relations that correspond to the production of commodities" and in so doing was able to present commodity production as "a form of production as everlasting as justice". The parallel with Godelier's rebuttal of Lange's (and by extension Dahl and Lindblom's) views on rationality is exact. Taking capitalistic notions of social rationality or of justice, and treating them as universal values to be deployed under socialism, would merely mean the deeper instanciation of capitalist values by way of the socialist project.

The Transition from Modernist to Postmodernist Discourses

There are two general points I wish to draw out of the argument so far. First, the critique of social rationality and of conceptions such as social justice as policy tools was something that was originated and so ruthlessly pursued by the "left" (including marxists) in the 1960s that it began to generate radical doubt throughout civil society as to the veracity of all universal claims. From this it was a short, though as I shall shortly argue, unwarranted, step to conclude, as many postmodernists now do, that all forms of metatheory are either misplaced or illegitimate. Both steps in this process were further reinforced by the emergence of the so-called "new" social movements – the peace and women's movements, the ecologists, the movements against colonization and racism – each of which came to articulate its own definitions of social justice and rationality. There then seemed to be, as Engels had argued, no philosophical, linguistic or logical way to resolve the resulting divergencies in conceptions of rationality and justice, and thereby find a way to reconcile competing claims or arbitrate between radically different discourses. The effect was to undermine the legitimacy of state policy, attack all conceptions of bureaucratic rationality and at best place social policy formulation in a quandary and at worst render it powerless except to articulate the ideological and value precepts of those in power. Some of those who participated in the revolutionary movements of the 1970s and 1980s considered that rendering transparent the power and class basis of supposedly universal claims was a necessary prelude to mass revolutionary action.

But there is a second and, I think, more subtle point to be made. If Engels is indeed right to insist that the conception of justice "varies not only with time and place, but also with the persons concerned", then it seems important to look at the ways in which a particular society produces such variation in concepts. In so doing it seems important, following writers as diverse as Wittgenstein and Marx, to look at the material basis for the production of difference, in particular at the production of those radically different experiential worlds out of which divergent language games about social rationality and social justice could arise. This entails the application of historical-geographical materialist methods and principles to understand the production of those power differentials which in turn produce different conceptions of justice and embed them in a struggle over ideological hegemony between classes, races, ethnic and political groupings as well as across the gender divide. The philosophical, linguistic and logical critique of universal propositions such as justice and of social rationality can be upheld as perfectly correct without necessarily endangering the ontological or epistemological status of a metatheory which confronts the ideological and material functionings and bases of particular discourses. Only in this way can we begin to understand why it is that concepts such as justice which appear as "hopelessly confused" when examined in abstraction can become such a powerful mobilizing force in everyday life, where, again to quote Engels, "expressions like right, wrong, justice, and sense of right are accepted without misunderstanding even with reference to social matters".

From this standpoint we can clearly see that concepts of justice and of rationality have not disappeared from our social and political world these last few years. But their definition and use has changed. The collapse of class compromise in the struggles of the late 1960s and the emergence of the socialist, communist and radical left movements, coinciding as it did with an acute crisis of overaccumulation of capital, posed a serious threat to the stability of the capitalist political-economic system. At the ideological level, the emergence of alternative definitions of both justice and rationality was part of that attack, and it was to this question that my earlier book, *Social Justice and the City*, was addressed. But the recession/depression of 1973–5 signalled not only the savage devaluation of capital stock (through the first wave of deindustrialization visited upon the weaker sectors and regions of a world capitalist economy) but the beginning of an attack upon the power or organized labour via widespread unemployment, austerity programmes, restructuring and, eventually, in some instances (such as Britain) institutional reforms.

It was under such conditions that the left penchant for attacking what was interpreted as a capitalist power basis within the welfare state (with its dominant notions of social rationality and just redistributions) connected to an emerging right-wing agenda to defang the power of welfare state capitalism, to get away from any notion whatsoever of a social contract between capital and labour and to abandon political notions of social rationality in favour of market rationality. The important point about this transition, which was phased in over a number of years, though at a quite different pace from country to country (it is only now seriously occurring in Sweden, for example), was that the state was no longer obliged to define rationality and justice, since it was presumed that the market could best do it for us. The idea that just deserts are best arrived at through market behaviours, that a just distribution is whatever the market dictates and that a just organization of social life, of urban investments and of resource allocations (including those usually referred to as environmental) is best arrived at through the market is, of course, relatively old and well-tried. It implies conceptions of justice and rationality of a certain sort, rather than their total abandonment. Indeed, the idea that the market is the best way to achieve the most just and the most rational forms of social organization has become a powerful feature of the hegemonic discourses these last 20 years in both the United States and Britain. The collapse of centrally planned economies throughout much of the world has further boosted a market triumphalism which presumes that the rough justice administered through the market in the course of this transition is not only socially just but also deeply rational. The advantage of this solution, of course, is that there is no need for explicit theoretical, political and social argument over what is or is not socially rational just because it can be presumed that, provided the market functions properly, the outcome is nearly always just and rational. Universal claims about rationality and justice have in no way diminished. They are just as frequently asserted in justification of privatization and of market action as they ever were in support of welfare state capitalism.

The dilemmas inherent in reliance on the market are well known and no one holds to it without some qualification. Problems of market breakdown, of externality effects, the provision of public goods and infrastructures, the clear need for *some* coordination of disparate investment decisions, all of these require some level of government interventionism. Margaret Thatcher may thus have abolished Greater London government, but the business community wants some kind of replacement (though preferably non-elected), because without it city services are disintegrating and London is losing its competitive edge. But there are many voices that go beyond that minimal requirement since free-market capitalism has produced widespread unemployment, radical restructurings and devaluations of capital, slow growth, environmental degradation and a whole host of financial scandals and competitive difficulties, to say nothing of the widening disparities in income distributions in many countries and the social stresses that attach thereto. It is under such conditions that the never quite stilled voice of state regulation, welfare state capitalism, of state management of industrial development, of state planning of environmental quality, land use, transportation systems and physical and social infrastructures, of state incomes and taxation policies which achieve a modicum of redistribution either in kind (via housing, health care, educational services and the like) or through income transfers, is being reasserted. The political questions of social rationality and of social justice over and above that administered through the market are being taken off the back burner and moved to the forefront of the political agenda in many of the advanced capitalist countries. It was exactly in this mode, of course, that Dahl and Lindblom came in back in 1953.

It is here that we have to face up to what Unger calls the "ideological embarrassment" of the history of politics these last hundred years: its tendency to move merely in repetitive cycles, swinging back and forth between *laissez-faire* and state interventionism without, it seems, finding any way to break out of this binary opposition to turn a spinning wheel of stasis into a spiral of human development. The breakdown of organized communism in eastern Europe and the Soviet Union here provides a major opportunity precisely because of the radical qualities of the break. Yet there are few signs of any similar penchant for ideological and institutional renovation in the advanced capitalist countries, which at best seem to be steering towards another bout of bureaucratic management of capitalism embedded in a general politics of the Dahl and Lindblom sort and at worst to be continuing down the blind ideological track which says that the market always knows best. It is precisely at this political conjuncture that we should remind ourselves of what the radical critique of universal claims of justice and rationality has been all about, without falling into the postmodernist trap of denying the validity of *any* appeal to justice or to rationality as a war cry for political mobilization (even Lyotard, that father figure of postmodern philosophy, hopes for the reassertion of some "pristine and non-consensual conception of justice" as a means to find a new kind of politics).

For my own part, I think Engels had it right. Justice and rationality take on different meanings across space and time and persons, yet the existence of everyday meanings to which people do attach importance and which to them appear unproblematic, gives the terms a political and mobilizing power than can never be neglected. Right and wrong are words that power revolutionary changes and no amount of negative deconstruction of such terms can deny that. So where, then, have the new social movements and the radical left in general got with their own conception, and how does it challenge both market and corporate welfare capitalism?

Young in her *Justice and the Politics of Difference* (1990) provides one of the best recent statements. She redefines the question of justice away from the purely redistributive mode of welfare state capitalism and focuses on what she calls the "five faces" of oppression, and I think each of them is worth thinking about as we consider the struggle to create liveable cities and workable environments for the twenty-first century.

The first face of oppression conjoins the classic notion of exploitation in the workplace with the more recent focus on exploitation of labour in the living place (primarily, of course, that of women working in the domestic sphere). The classic forms of exploitation which Marx described are still omnipresent, though there have been many mutations such that, for example, control over the length of the working day may have been offset by increasing intensity of labour or exposure to more hazardous health conditions not only in blue-collar but also in white-collar occupations. The mitigation of the worst aspects of exploitation has been, to some degree, absorbed into the logic of welfare state capitalism in part through the sheer exercise of class power and trade union muscle. Yet there are still many terrains upon which chronic exploitation can be identified and which will only be addressed to the degree that active struggle raises issues. The conditions of the unemployed, the homeless, the lack of purchasing power for basic needs and services for substantial portions of the population (immigrants, women, children) absolutely have to be addressed. All of which leads to my first proposition: *that just planning and policy practices must confront directly the problem of creating forms of social and political organization and systems of production and consumption which minimize the exploitation of labour power both in the workplace and the living place.*

The second face of oppression arises out of what Young calls *marginalization.* "Marginals", she writes, "are people the system of labour cannot or will not use." This is most typically the case with individuals marked by race, ethnicity, region, gender, immigration status, age, and the like. The consequence is that "a whole category of people is expelled from useful participation in social life and thus potentially subjected to severe material deprivation and even extermination". The characteristic response of welfare state capitalism has been either to place such marginal groups under tight surveillance or, at best, to induce a condition of dependency in which state support provides a justification to "suspend all basic rights to privacy, respect, and individual choice". The responses among the marginalized have sometimes been both violent and vociferous, in some instances turning their marginalization into a heroic stand against the state and against any form of inclusion into what has for long only ever offered them oppressive surveillance and demeaning subservience. Marginality is one of the crucial problems facing urban life in the twenty-first century and consideration of it leads to the second principle: *that just planning and policy practices must confront the phenomenon of marginalization in a non-paternalistic mode and find ways to organize and militate within the politics of marginalization in such a way as to liberate captive groups from this distinctive form of oppression.*

Powerlessness is, in certain ways, an even more widespread problem than marginality. We are here talking of the ability to express political power as well as to engage in the particular politics of self-expression which we encountered in Tompkins Square Park. The ability to be listened to with respect is strictly circumscribed within welfare state capitalism and failure on this score has played a key role in the collapse of state communism. Professional groups have advantages in this regard which place them in a different category to most others and the temptation always stands, for even the most politicized of us, to speak for others without listening to them. Political inclusion is, if anything, diminished by the decline of trade unionism, of political parties, and of traditional institutions, yet it is at the same time revived by the organization of new social movements. But the increasing scale of international dependency and interdependency makes it harder and harder to offset powerlessness in general. Like the struggle against the Baltimore expressway, the mobilization of political power among the oppressed in society is increasingly a local affair, unable to address the structural characteristics of either market or welfare state capitalism as a whole. This leads to my third proposition: *just planning and policy practices must empower rather than deprive the oppressed of access to political power and the ability to engage in self-expression.*

What Young calls *cultural imperialism* relates to the ways in which "the dominant meanings of a society render the particular perspective of one's own group invisible at the same time as they stereotype one's group and mark it out as the Other". Arguments of this sort have been most clearly articulated by feminists and black liberation theorists, but they are also implicit in liberation theology as well as in many domains of cultural theory. This is, in some respects, the most difficult form of oppression to identify clearly, yet there can surely be no doubt that there are many social groups in our societies who find or feel themselves "defined from the outside, positioned, placed, by a network of dominant meanings they experience as arising from elsewhere, from those with whom they do not identify and who do not identify with them". The alienation and social unrest to be found in many western European and North American cities (to say nothing of its re-emergence throughout much of eastern Europe) bears all the marks of a reaction to cultural imperialism, and here too, welfare state capitalism has in the past proved both unsympathetic and unmoved. From this comes a fourth proposition: *that just planning and policy practices must be particularly sensitive to issues of cultural imperialism and seek, by a variety of means, to eliminate the imperialist attitude both in the design of urban projects and modes of popular consultation.*

Fifth, there is the issue of *violence*. It is hard to consider urban futures and living environments into the twenty-first century without confronting the problem of burgeoning levels of physical violence. The fear of violence against persons and property, though often exaggerated, has a material grounding in the social conditions of market capitalism and calls for some kind of organized response. There is, furthermore, the intricate problem of the violence of organized crime and its interdigitation with capitalist enterprise and state activities. The problem at the first level is, as Davis points out in his consideration of Los Angeles, that the most characteristic response is to search for defensible urban spaces, to militarize urban space and to create living environments which are more rather than less exclusionary. The difficulty with the second level is that the equivalent of the *mafiosi* in many cities (an emergent problem in the contemporary Soviet Union, for example) has become so powerful in urban governance that it is they, rather than elected officials and state bureaucrats, who hold the true reins of power. No society can function without certain forms of social control and we have to consider what that might be in the face of a Foucauldian insistence that all forms of social control are oppressive, no matter what the level of violence to which they are addressed. Here too there are innumerable dilemmas to be solved, but we surely know enough to advance a fifth proposition: *a just planning and policy practice must seek out non-exclusionary and non-militarized forms of social control to contain the increasing levels of both personal and institutionalized violence without destroying capacities for empowerment and self-expression.*

Finally, I want to add a sixth principle to those which Young advances. This derives from the fact that all social projects are ecological projects and vice versa. While I resist the view that "nature has rights" or that nature can be "oppressed", the justice due to future generations and to other inhabitants of the globe requires intense scrutiny of all social projects for assessment of their ecological consequences. Human beings necessarily appropriate and transform the world around them in the course of making their own history, but they do not have to do so with such reckless abandon as to jeopardize the fate of peoples separated from us in either space or time. The final proposition is, then: *that just planning and policy practices will clearly recognize that the necessary ecological consequences of all social projects have impacts on future generations as well as upon distant peoples and take steps to ensure a reasonable mitigation of negative impacts.*

I do not argue that these six principles can or even should be unified, let alone turned into some convenient and formulaic composite strategy. Indeed, the six dimensions of justice here outlined are frequently in conflict with each other as far as their application to individual persons – the exploited male worker may be a cultural imperialist on matters of race and gender while the thoroughly oppressed person may be the bearer of social injustice as violence. On the other hand, I do not believe the principles can be applied in isolation from each other either. Simply to leave matters at the level of a "non-consensual" conception of justice, as someone like Lyotard (1984) would do, is not to confront some central issues of the social processes which produce such a differentiated conception of justice in the first place. This then suggests that social policy and planning has to work at two levels. The different faces of oppression have to be confronted for what they are and as they are manifest in daily life, but in the longer term and at the same time the underlying sources of the different forms of oppression in the heart of the political economy of capitalism must also be confronted, not as the fount of all evil but in terms of capitalism's revolutionary dynamic which transforms, disrupts, deconstructs and reconstructs ways of living, working, relating to each other and to the environment. From such a standpoint the issue is never about whether or not there shall be change, but what sort of change we can anticipate, plan for, and proactively shape in the years to come.

I would hope that consideration of the varieties of justice as well as of this deeper problematic might set the tone for present deliberations. By appeal to them, we might see ways to break with the political, imaginative and institutional constraints which have for too long inhibited the advanced capitalist societies in their developmental path. The critique of universal notions of justice and rationality, no matter whether embedded in the market or in state welfare capitalism, still stands. But it is both valuable and potentially liberating to look at alternative conceptions of both justice and rationality as these have emerged within the new social movements these last two decades. And while it will in the end ever be true, as Marx and Plato observed, that "between equal rights force decides", the authoritarian imposition of solutions to many of our urban ills these past few years and the inability to listen to alternative conceptions of both justice and rationality is very much a part of the problem. The conceptions I have outlined speak to many of the marginalized, the oppressed and the exploited in this time and place. For many of us, and for many of them, the formulations may well appear obvious, unproblematic and just plain common sense. And it is precisely because of such widely held conceptions that so much welfare-state paternalism and market rhetoric fails. It is, by the same token, precisely out of such conceptions that a genuinely liberatory and transformative politics can be made. "Seize the time and the place", they would say around Tompkins Square Park, and this does indeed appear an appropriate time and place to do so. If some of the walls are coming down all over eastern Europe, then surely we can set about bringing them down in our own cities as well.

Acknowledgement

I am much indebted to Neil Smith for information and ideas about the struggles over Tompkins Square Park.

References

Chambers I. (1987) Maps for the metropolis: a possible guide to the present. *Cultural Studies* 1, 1–22.

Dahl, R. and C. Lindblom (1953) *Politics, Economics and Welfare*. Harper, New York.

Davis, M. (1990) *City of Quartz: Excavating the future in Los Angeles*. Verso, London.

Godelier, M. (1972) *Rationality and Irrationality in Economics*. New Left Books, London.

Harvey, D. (1973) *Social Justice and the City*. Edward Arnold, London.

—— (1989) *The Condition of Postmodernity*. Blackwell, Oxford.

Jacobs, J. (1961) *The Death and Life of Great American Cities*. Vintage, New York.

Kifner, J. (1989) No miracles in the park: homeless New Yorkers amid drug lords and slumlords. *International Herald Tribune*, 1 August 1989, p. 6.

Lefebvre, H. (1991) *The Production of Space*. Blackwell, Oxford.

Lyotard, J. (1984) *The Postmodern Condition*. Manchester University Press, Manchester.

Marx, K. (1967) *Capital*, vol. I. International Publishers, New York.

—— and F. Engels (1951) *Selected Works*, vol. I. Progress Publishers, Moscow.

Plato (1965) *The Republic*. Penguin Books, Harmondsworth, Middlesex.

Rawls, J. (1971) *A Theory of Justice.* Harvard University Press, Cambridge, MA.

Smith, N. (1989) Tompkins Square: riots, rents and redskins. *Portable Lower East Side* 6, 1–36.

—— (1992) New city, new frontier: the Lower East Side as wild, wild west. In M. Sorkin (ed.), *Variations on a Theme Park: The new American city and the end of public space,* Noonday, New York.

Unger, R. (1987) *False Necessity: Anti-necessitarian social theory in the service of radical democracy.* Cambridge University Press, Cambridge.

Wittgenstein, L. (1967) *Philosophical Investigations.* Blackwell, Oxford.

Young, I. M. (1990) *Justice and the Politics of Difference.* Princeton University Press, Princeton, NJ.

Index